Dark Journey presents the first comprehensive account of three critical battles during New Zealand's involvement in the First World War. It brings together previous histories detailing the New Zealand Division's major Western Front battles of the First World War, *Massacre at Passchendaele* and *Spring Offensive*, with a previously unpublished account of Bapaume, the third major battle of the Somme, during which several VCs were awarded to New Zealand troops.

Glyn Harper lives in Palmerston North where he is Professor of War Studies at Massey University. He is Massey's Project Manager for the Centenary History of New Zealand and the First World War project and is writing one of the first volumes. A former teacher, Glyn joined the Australian Army in 1988 and after eight years transferred to the New Zealand Army, where he rose to the rank of lieutenant colonel. He is the author of 13 books on military history, some of which were best-sellers. Glyn has also published eight educational books for children.

Images of War: New Zealand and the First World War in photographs

The Battles of Monte Cassino: The campaign and its controversies (co-author with John Tonkin-Covell)

Letters from Gallipoli: New Zealand soldiers write home

Kippenberger: An inspired New Zealand commander

Massacre at Passchendaele: The New Zealand story

Born to Lead? Portraits of New Zealand Commanders (co-editor with Joel Hayward)

Letters from the Battlefield: New Zealand soldiers write home 1914–18

Spring Offensive: New Zealand and the Second Battle of the Somme

In the Face of the Enemy: The complete history of the Victoria Cross and New Zealand (co-author with Colin Richardson)

Best and Bravest: Kiwis awarded the Victoria Cross (co-author with Colin Richardson)

DARK JOURNEY

GLYN HARPER

HarperCollins*Publishers*

HarperCollins*Publishers*

First published in hardback in 2007
This paperback edition published in 2015
by HarperCollins*Publishers* (New Zealand) Limited
Unit D1, 63 Apollo Drive, Rosedale, Auckland 0632, New Zealand
harpercollins.co.nz

HarperCollins*Publishers*
Unit D1, 63 Apollo Drive, Rosedale, Auckland 0632, New Zealand
Level 13, 201 Elizabeth Street, Sydney NSW 2000
A 53, Sector 57, Noida, UP, India
1 London Bridge Street, London, SE1 9GF, United Kingdom
2 Bloor Street East, 20th floor, Toronto, Ontario M4W 1A8, Canada
195 Broadway, New York NY 10007, USA

ISBN 9781460750438 (paperback)
ISBN 9780730492214 (e-book)

Cover design by Matt Stanton, HarperCollins Design Studio
Cover image: New Zealand soldiers during World War I, with a wounded
dove, at Mailly-Maillet, France. Royal New Zealand Returned and Services'
Association: New Zealand official negatives, World War 1914–1918.
Ref: 1/2-013078-G. Alexander Turnbull Library, Wellington, New Zealand.
http://natlib.govt.nz/records/23220773
Text originally designed and typeset by Springfield West
Printed and bound in Australia by Griffin Press
The papers used by HarperCollins in the manufacture of this book are a
natural, recyclable product made from wood grown in sustainable plantation
forests. The fibre source and manufacturing processes meet recognised
international environmental standards, and carry certification.

If your country's worth living in, it's worth doing your bit for.
Lance Corporal Thomas Eltringham
2nd Auckland Battalion

I thought I would like to go and fight for me King and country,
not that I knew him.
William Batchelor
New Zealand Rifle Brigade

To the men and women of the New Zealand Expeditionary
Force, 1914–19, for whom honour, service and courage
were more than just words.

Contents

Foreword

Between mid-1916 and the end of the First World War in November 1918 the New Zealand Expeditionary Force served in a series of great battles on the Western Front. In *Dark Journey* Dr Glyn Harper examines the New Zealanders' part in three of these actions: the Third Battle of Ypres (Passchendaele), the Second Battle of the Somme in the spring of 1918 and, finally, the Battle of Bapaume in August 1918.

Glyn Harper brings a knowledgeable fluency to the book. For the section on Passchendaele, he uses his earlier published *Massacre at Passchendaele: The New Zealand Story* (2000), and for that part dealing with the defeat of the German offensive in 1918 *Spring Offensive: New Zealand and the Second Battle of the Somme* (2003). Moreover, by republishing this earlier work and combining it with his new study of the Battle of Bapaume, Glyn Harper gives us unparalleled insights into the highs and lows of the New Zealand Division's experiences during 1917 and 1918. From the meticulously planned and well-conducted assault on Gravenstafel Spur on 4 October 1917 and the bloody fiasco that was the attack on Bellevue Spur eight days later, through to the hard-fought victories of 1918, Glyn Harper gives a special account of the 'intensely emotional and bitter experience for those who survived' and the legacy of the New Zealand Expeditionary Force to our national consciousness.

Dark Journey is the product of a great deal of careful research. Among the sources used are official histories, unit war diaries and the letters and diaries of many men, from generals to privates. These sources are brought together expertly by Glyn Harper to produce a highly readable and coherent narrative. The first-hand accounts of the dramatic and extraordinary events which involved ordinary New Zealanders are fascinating and bring home to the reader just what an ordeal service on the Western Front was.

The pages of *Dark Journey* are full of examples of New Zealand soldiers demonstrating to the highest degree qualities such as courage, comradeship and commitment to the greater good, values that remain of paramount importance within the modern New Zealand Defence Force.

One exceptional example is Sergeant Reginald Judson VC, DCM, MM who, before enlisting in the NZEF, had been an engineer and boilermaker in Auckland. During July and August 1918 Judson displayed a combination of extreme bravery, outstanding leadership and a high level of military skill in a remarkable series of actions for which he received three gallantry decorations.

It is most appropriate that *Dark Journey* should appear in 2007, when New Zealand and the other nations involved in the terrible struggle that was the Battle of Passchendaele are commemorating its 90th anniversary, and shortly before we mark the 90th anniversary of the great battles of 1918 and finally the armistice that ended the First World War on 11 November 1918.

During its two and a half years on the Western Front, the NZEF suffered nearly 12,500 fatal casualties and thousands more were maimed, both physically and mentally. For the men and women of the NZEF, service on the Western Front was a cruel odyssey that changed them and our country for ever. Glyn Harper is to be congratulated on writing *Dark Journey*, an outstanding book, which will help ensure that the experiences and achievements of New Zealanders in the First World War are never forgotten.

J. Mateparae
Lieutenant General
Chief of Defence Force

2 August 2007

Acknowledgements

Most of the primary source material for this book has been obtained from four places. They are the National Archives, the Manuscripts and Archives section of the Alexander Turnbull Library, the Oral History Centre of the National Library of New Zealand, and the Kippenberger Military Archive and Research Library at the Army Museum in Waiouru. Once again I am deeply indebted to the staff of these research institutions for their professionalism, assistance and dedication.

Paul Lumsden produced the excellent maps from two entirely different locations: Waiouru and Nelson. I have no doubt which location Paul prefers. Anna Rogers edited part of the manuscript from her home in the 'Garden City', my old home town, while Sue Page did the same from the shores of Mount Maunganui. I am grateful to Andrew Macdonald for his assistance in providing some of the German sources used and for checking the casualty figures for Passchendaele. Christine Clement, whose emails inform me that Te Puke where she resides is the 'Kiwifruit Capital of the World', also provided invaluable assistance in calculating casualty figures.

I wish to thank the team at HarperCollins*Publishers (New Zealand) Limited* for their continuing faith in me as a historian and a writer. I am particularly grateful to Lorain Day, who commissioned this project, and Eva Chan, who tied it all together.

Finally, I wish to acknowledge the support and encouragement of my partner, Susan Lemish, who read all the first drafts, checked the footnotes and bibliography, assisted with the index and undertook a myriad of other tasks necessary to bring this book to publication. And her sanity and sense of humour remained reasonably intact throughout.

Massacre at Passchendaele

Introduction

An Untold Story

IF YOU TAKE the Zonnebeke road north of the Belgian town of Ieper (Ypres) and turn left at the major crossroads of the Passchendaele–Broodseinde road, after a kilometre you come across the Tyne Cot Cemetery. One of 174 British military cemeteries in the Ypres salient for fallen soldiers from the First World War, Tyne Cot is a special place. It is the largest British military cemetery in Europe, containing 11,956 graves, 8366 of them unnamed, and covering almost 36,000 square yards.[1] Located at this hauntingly beautiful resting place is a graceful wall: the Tyne Cot Memorial to the Missing. Fourteen feet high and some 500 feet long, this memorial wall bears the names of 35,000 men who fell in battle near here and who have no known grave. The list appears endless and is a powerful reminder of the tragic cost of war. While the missing from the Dominion armies are engraved on the Menin Gate at Ieper, the central apse of the wall is the New Zealand memorial, dedicated to New Zealand's soldiers who fell in two battles in October 1917 and whose bodies were never found. One thousand one hundred and seventy-nine names are recorded here.

Sir Philip Gibbs, a distinguished historian and a war correspondent in France from 1916 to 1918, wrote that: 'nothing that has been written is more than the pale image of the abomination of those battle-fields, and that no pen or brush has yet achieved the picture of that Armageddon in which so many of our men perished'.[2] The Armageddon to which Sir Philip Gibbs was referring was the Third Battle of Ypres, in particular the struggle for the heights of the Passchendaele Ridge in the battle's last phases. Sir Philip recognised the failure of words, no matter how powerful or how vivid, to record an event and experience that was in many ways unrecordable. Yet the historian of this particular battle must try to explain what happened and seek explanations for why things turned out as they did. The historian also aims to preserve the experiences of those caught up in this terrible battle, a battle which has came to epitomise the tragedy and suffering of all who were drawn into the Great War of 1914–18. The experiences of those who fought at Passchendaele, and other battles like it, are central to the history of the nations that took part in the war, and they should not be forgotten. Unfortunately, most New Zealanders remain ignorant of this pivotal event in their country's history, which only adds to the tragedy.

This is the story of the New Zealand attacks at Passchendaele, one of which remains New Zealand's worst military blunder and the greatest disaster of any kind to strike this small and vulnerable nation. At Passchendaele in October 1917, the New Zealand Division took part in two great attacks. The first, on 4 October 1917, was a stunning success although costly in terms of casualties. The other, on 12 October, should never have gone ahead in the conditions then prevailing, and saw more New Zealanders killed or maimed in a few short hours than has occurred on any other day since the beginning of European settlement. Though Passchendaele would eventually be claimed as a victory for the Commonwealth forces involved, no victory was more hollow.

While Passchendaele, a tragedy without equal in New Zealand history, remains unknown to most New Zealanders, the name of that disaster 'has evoked more horror and loathing than any other battle-name' in the United Kingdom, according to the British historian John Terraine.[3] Mention Passchendaele in Britain or in Canada and the reaction, usually negative, is instant. For New Zealand, though, Passchendaele is truly an untold story.

It wasn't always so. On the day of the second New Zealand attack at Passchendaele, a New Zealand Sergeant, W.K. Wilson, recorded in his diary:

> Black Friday 12 [Oct.] A day that will long be remembered by New Zealanders. Our boys and the Aussies went over at 5.30 and got practically cut to pieces . . . This is the biggest 'slap up' the NZers have had. Far worse than the Somme I believe.[4]

And at a meeting of the Imperial War Cabinet in London in June 1918, an angry New Zealand Prime Minister, William Massey, berated his British counterpart, Lloyd George:

> I was told last night by a reliable man — a man I knew years before he joined the Army — that the New Zealanders (he was one of them) were asked to do the impossible. He said they were sent to Passchendaele, to a swampy locality where it was almost impossible to walk and where they found themselves up against particularly strong wire entanglements which it was impossible for them to cut. They were, he said, simply shot down like rabbits. These are the sort of things that are going to lead to serious trouble.[5]

Yet since 1918, this battle has sadly been all but confined to the scrap heap of New Zealand history.

Passchendaele should, however, be much more than an unfamiliar name on a war memorial. In fact, one New Zealand historian has gone so far as to claim that, because of the large number of casualties with its subsequent impact on the New Zealand Division, Passchendaele 'must be considered the most important event in New Zealand military history'.[6] While not going to this extreme (similar claims have been made about Gallipoli, Crete and Cassino), it is indisputable that for New Zealand the experience of the battles at Passchendaele was an especially significant one. As has been written of Passchendaele in a recent history of the Great War:

> No British, Australian or Canadian chronicle of the war would be complete without an account of what took place there. For even more than the Somme, Passchendaele symbolises the futility of trench warfare.[7]

This is also especially true for New Zealand. Passchendaele deserves to be, and should become, as Sergeant Wilson believed it would back in October 1917, an experience 'that will long be remembered by New Zealanders'.

This section of the book aims to tell the story of this New Zealand tragedy. It does so by using, as much as possible, the words of those who took part. It will examine in some detail the two New Zealand attacks made at Passchendaele in October 1917 and explain why their outcomes were so radically different. It will then examine the impact of the disaster on New Zealand society, an impact that resonates to this day. This section will also try to offer some explanation of why the Passchendaele experience has been largely forgotten or ignored by New Zealanders. In writing this, I hope Passchendaele will remain an untold story no longer.

Chapter 1

The Military Background

NO HISTORICAL EVENT exists in isolation. Before one can fully understand what happened at Passchendaele in October 1917, it is necessary to have an overview of how the war had unfolded up to that time.

In September 1914, the British and French armies finally succeeded in halting the advancing Germans at the Battle of the Marne. Both sides then became locked in and behind their trench systems, which stretched from the Belgian coast to the Swiss border — about 350 miles. There they would remain for most of the war. The length of those trenches, some 25,000 miles, cannot be imagined today, but for the soldiers of the war they provided a stark reality, prompting one influential writer to describe them as a 'troglodyte world'.[1]

After its defeat on the Marne, Germany adopted the strategy of remaining on the defensive on the Western Front while doing all in her power on the Eastern Front to knock Russia out of the war. This presented Britain and France with a tactical dilemma which they remained unable to solve until the last year of the war. The front-line trenches of the west could not be turned from either flank; diversions elsewhere, such as the Dardanelles expedition in 1915, served only to dissipate strength; and amphibious operations, being in their infancy, were not trusted to produce the desired result. This left only the prospect of full-scale frontal assaults on the enemy entrenchments, which would, it was hoped, eventually crack open the enemy front lines and allow a return to the more mobile and open type of warfare favoured by the Allies. In an attempt to transform the Western Front from siege to open warfare, the British and French mounted a number of large set-piece battles, all of which resulted in heavy casualties but only extremely limited gains on the ground. These efforts reached their climax in 1917, which for the Allies would prove the worst year of the war. The slaughter became so bad that

1917 was described by one influential writer as a 'carnival of death'.[2]

In July 1917, prior to the start of the great offensive in Flanders, the northernmost region, the 20 miles from the coast to the town of Boesinghe, was held by the British Fourth Army and a combined French–Belgian army. The next 90 miles, from Ypres to the River Ancre, were held by the four other British (including Dominion) armies, with the French holding the southern portion of the line to the Swiss frontier. The British section of the line comprised two main sectors: the Ypres salient in Flanders and the Somme area in Picardy. In 1916, the British had made their main effort to break through the German front lines at the Somme. The results had been disastrous. The opening day of the attack had set an unenviable twentieth century record for the most men killed and wounded in a single day. In 1917, despite this being a year of almost continuous activity along the whole of the British line, the main effort would fall in the north centred around the Ypres salient in Flanders.

When deciding to launch a major offensive in Flanders in 1917, the British high command aimed for a great strategic victory — the type of victory that so far had eluded both sides. Above all, British commanders hoped that victory here would lead to the end of the war. They had good reasons for launching a large offensive in Flanders. They had not done so before (the two previous battles of Ypres having been defensive for the British), and Field Marshal Sir Douglas Haig had long harboured the desire to launch a major attack from the region. As Trevor Wilson has commented, 'no aura of past failure hung over an attack here'.[3] Field Marshal Haig and his staff hoped, by breaking through the German defences in Flanders, to secure the channel ports and the whole Belgian coastline, break out of the Ypres salient, which had imprisoned the defenders since 1914, and then strike at the Germans' extended right flank, possibly carrying the British armies into the Ruhr, Germany's industrial heartland. Any large offensive by the British armies in Flanders would also divert German forces from the French Army, now demoralised and mutinous after the costly failure of the Nivelle offensive in April 1917. The great victory now to be won was to be primarily a British Army affair; it was to be its moment of glory.

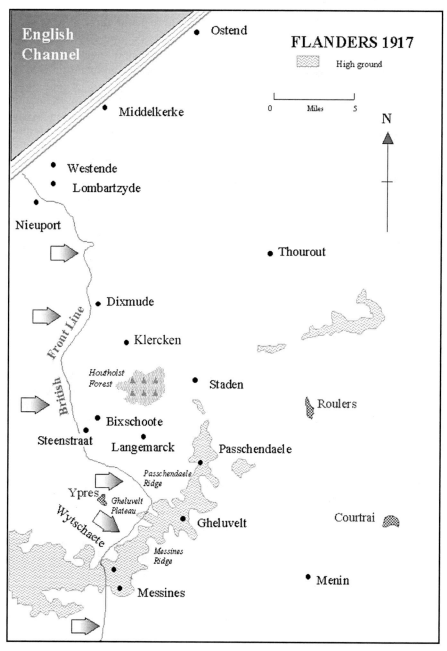

Flanders, the Ypres salient and the Passchendaele Ridge, prior to the British offensives of 1917.

Such sweeping movements of troops looked easy on paper, and Haig felt confident of success. The 'fundamental object' of the attacks made after Messines, he explained in a memorandum on 30 June, was 'the defeat of the German Army', which would only be achieved after 'very hard fighting lasting perhaps for weeks'.[4] What became evident as the great battles unfolded was that the strategic victory for which the British had planned was soon forgotten. Once all hope of this type of victory had faded after 31 July 1917, the aim of the campaign became to inflict more casualties on the Germans than their own armies were suffering, and to secure the best position from which to renew the attritional struggle in the campaigning season of 1918. Though initially aiming to achieve a decisive breakthrough, Haig all too willingly settled for more dead and wounded Germans than dead and wounded Allied soldiers.

While Haig planned for a great strategic victory, there were pressing tactical reasons for striking from Ypres. The British line in the Ypres salient was 'tactically about as bad as it could be',[5] with the British positions being overlooked from three directions — north, east and south. This meant 'no part of the Salient was safe from the enemy's guns, which searched our trenches with all the advantages of direct observation'.[6] The first stage of any great victory here had to be to eject the Germans from their present positions on the heights overlooking the town of Ypres. This would provide a tactical victory upon which an even greater victory could be launched.

To achieve this major triumph, two separate British armies were crammed into the Ypres salient. They were the Second Army, commanded by General Sir Herbert Plumer, and the Fifth Army, under General Sir Hubert Gough. All told a total of thirty-five divisions would fight in this campaign, seventeen of them in the opening thrust. With so much committed to the offensive in terms of men and firepower, Haig and his commanders felt confident of success. Yet the German commanders, especially General Ludendorff and the Bavarian Crown Prince Rupprecht, were prepared. They knew the British were planning to strike another large blow against them and felt certain it would be made somewhere in Flanders. Most divisions now being released from the Eastern Front were accordingly allocated to the Flanders region, and further reinforcements were moved to Flanders by thinning the front opposite the French Army. Ludendorff and the Crown Prince, however, did not know — and did not learn until the second week of June 1917 — that the attack would be made from the Ypres salient. The successful attack at Messines in early June, in which the New Zealand Division played a leading role, captured the vital Messines–Wytschaete portion of the ridge. After this it became impossible for the British to achieve surprise as to the location and direction of their next offensive — not that they bothered to try. On the basis of the build-up that could be readily observed by the Germans, and from their intelligence assessments, Prince Rupprecht and his Fourth Army headquarters agreed that the next British offensive must be made in the Ypres salient. As well as strengthening his front with the additional divisions now available to him, from mid June Rupprecht accelerated the construction of the concrete pillbox fortifications, thereby adding considerable depth to the Ypres frontage. As Winston Churchill commented in his history of this war:

> . . . the positions to be assaulted were immensely strong. The enemy was fully prepared. The frowning undulations of the Passchendaele–Klercken ridge had been fortified with every resource of German science and ingenuity.[7]

The British possessed several advantages in the Flanders offensive of 1917, but surprise, now considered so important it has been elevated to a principle of war, was not one of them.

The climate and terrain of the Flanders region had a major influence on the outcome of the campaign and must be examined in detail.

The Ypres salient was 14 miles long and 3 miles at its widest point. As it formed a large bulge in the front line, every part of it lay exposed to the concentrated artillery fire of the Germans on the high ground to the north. Striking from three sides, the artillery made the Salient one of the most shelled spots on earth. In this deathtrap, the British, without taking any offensive action whatsoever, suffered casualties at the rate of 7000 a week. By the end of the war the town of Ypres had been totally destroyed and became one of the enduring symbols in English literature of the destructiveness and inhumanity of the twentieth century. One New Zealand soldier reflected on marching up the line:

> A short march of three miles brought us to historic Ypres. What a pitiful sight is a beautiful city in ruins! Everywhere the streets were lined with heaps of broken masonry and bricks. Not one house had escaped the smashing shell. On the left was a twisted mass of steel rails and the battered gaunt skeleton of a large building — all that was left of the Railway yards and Station . . . Before us were the ruins of the Cloth Hall and the Cathedral. From the many pictures taken of this particular scene the sight appeared quite familiar to us. The battered tower still stood erect from amid the broken mass that once represented one of the architectural glories of the world.[8]

Something else immediately impressed itself on the senses of those moving into the Salient: the overpowering smell of death and decay. Dead men and horses were often not buried for months, so 'the stench of rotten flesh was over everything'.[9] Marching towards the front at Ypres, soldiers could smell it while still miles away.

With constant enemy shelling from three sides, so much physical destruction and the all-pervading stench of death, it is little wonder soldiers hated serving in the Ypres salient, and that some were driven mad while doing so.

Two words provide an accurate description of much of Flanders: wet and flat. The Passchendaele soil is wet, dense clay, impervious to water and permitting no natural drainage. Rain water tends to lie on the surface of the ground, forming stagnant swamps and ponds if there is no artificial drainage. Furthermore, because Flanders is close to sea level, the region has an exceptionally high water table — on average only 14 inches from the surface even in summer. This can only be controlled by a complicated series of canals and ditches, which crisscrosses the region. While Belgium is largely flat, a low ridge curls round Ypres 'like a giant pruning hook'.[10] 'Ridge' is something of a misleading term for Australians and New Zealanders — it is really only a stretch of terrain slightly higher than the surrounding land.

Passchendaele was a tiny village on the crest of the highest part of the ridge, 5 miles east of Ypres. In 1917 it was a deserted ruin. The ridge there rises some 70 yards over several miles, an almost imperceptible elevation. It is the last high ground before open country, making it a vital piece of territory to any army operating in the region.

The terrain around the Ypres salient therefore placed the British armies at a great tactical disadvantage, because all the high ground, including the Passchendaele Ridge, lay in German hands. The Germans had good observation over nearly all of the battlefield, and, equally significant, the advancing British infantry would have to battle uphill if they were ever to eject the Germans from the heights. The German positions were also relatively dry, while the British front lines were waterlogged and extremely uncomfortable.

The Germans knew the great value of the ridge, and their defences were formidable. Because the high water table mitigated against the digging of deep trench systems as they had used in the Somme, the Germans constructed hundreds of pillboxes — low, squat concrete shelters many feet thick. Each pillbox was in fact a miniature fortress that could garrison between ten and fifty men. The advantage of these 'field fortresses', as the British press called them, was that they made small targets, on average no larger than 81 square feet, so were difficult for the artillery to observe. Their design, with overhead cover as much as 6 feet thick and with elastic cushions of steel rails and air, meant they were impervious to field artillery and could only be destroyed by a direct hit from a heavy-calibre gun of at least 8 inches. The pillboxes were so well camouflaged it was often difficult to detect them from ground level until almost right on top of them. The Germans had used thousands of them to fortify the Ypres positions into six separate zones of defence. As long as a number remained intact and were able to offer protection to their neighbours, thus preventing the enemy from outflanking them, their positions remained impervious to infantry assault.

The British were also very unlucky in that the weather of 1917 could not have been worse, with heavy rain and snow, a late, brief spring and no summer to speak of. As Colonel Charles Repington recorded in his diary:

'1 April. Heavy fall of snow this morning. This winter seems endless.'[11] From July onward, rainfall was the heaviest in seventy-five years. In October, the month of the two New Zealand attacks, 4.5 inches of rain fell, compared with just over an inch in 1914 and 1915, and 2.75 inches in 1916. There were only five days in the month when it didn't rain, and it rained during both New Zealand attacks. By 1917, Flanders' drainage systems had been long destroyed by the millions of artillery shells that had fallen in the region, and the ground was a quagmire.

With all these factors — vital high ground held by the enemy and protected by such formidable defences, the going underfoot so glutinous, and Belgium's wettest and coldest winter in seventy-five years looming — it is little wonder that, after the British offensive had begun, German warlord Paul von Hindenburg recalled:

> I had a certain feeling of satisfaction when this new battle began, in spite of the extraordinary difficulties it involved for our situation on the Western Front . . . It was with a feeling of absolute longing that we waited for the beginning of the wet season. As previous experience had taught us, great stretches of the Flemish flats would then become impassable, and even in firmer places the new shell holes would fill so quickly with ground water that men seeking shelter in them would find themselves faced with the alternative, 'Shall we drown or get out of this hole?' This battle, too, must finally stick in the mud, even though English stubbornness kept it up longer than otherwise.[12]

With all these disadvantages so obvious with the benefit of hindsight, did the British armies have anything going for them? Was there anything in their favour that could have made up for such tremendous disadvantages? Surprisingly, the answer is 'Yes'.

Contrary to popular notions, Allied commanders during the Great War did learn from their costly mistakes and adjusted their tactics accordingly.[13] It had become evident from 1915 that success in land warfare now depended on the correct use of artillery. That is, artillery had to be present in large quantities and its fire carefully directed to where it could do most damage to the enemy and provide the best protection for the infantry. New artillery techniques evolved as gunners, for the first time in the war, developed the principles of scientific gunnery. The creeping barrage had been largely perfected by the end of 1916 as the Allied gunners, with better-quality shells and more of them, honed their skills to a fine edge. A creeping barrage was a wall of exploding shells that moved ahead of advancing infantry, obscuring its presence and keeping the defenders' heads down. Another development was the standing barrage, a wall of artillery fire directed in front of existing infantry positions to provide them with protection. A third, equally important development in the scientific use of artillery was counter-battery fire, using the techniques of sound ranging and flash spotting. This involved detecting enemy artillery batteries by the sound of gunfire or the muzzle flash and then directing huge concentrations of one's own artillery fire on to that location. Through a process of trial and error, both techniques were proving very successful by 1917.

Protection for the infantry usually came from the supporting field artillery, which provided creeping barrages, smashed barbed wire and other obstacles, and broke up German counterattacks. Field artillery's main weakness was a limited effective range of about 6000 yards.

To provide maximum protection, it was vitally important that the final objective to be reached by the infantry was well within the range of their supporting guns. This simple requirement, as the battle of Arras testifies, had not always been observed — the direct cause of many British failures. Two further conditions needed to be fulfilled: there had to be time to carry out the detailed planning required for each operation, and good weather to enable the infantry to advance steadily under the direct observation of the artillery. By the end of July 1917, the British armies were running short on both counts.

Infantry tactics had also been modified as a result of the slaughter on the Somme in 1916. Infantry units now advanced across no-man's-land in smaller, nonlinear columns with emphasis on the technique of fire and manoeuvre. The units retained some of their strength to mop up pockets of resistance, or as a tactical reserve to plug weak points or reinforce success. Infantry units also trained with the artillery and now appreciated that their own chances of success and survival were vitally dependent on the skill and cooperation of the artillerymen. Infantrymen knew that without effective artillery protection they could not hope to move beyond the confines of their trenches without suffering massive casualties.

The success of improved British artillery and infantry tactics forced the Germans to experiment with an elastic system of defence, whereby troops were reduced in the forward areas but now lay in considerable depth, and with reserves close at hand for counterattacks. The first line of defence was in reality an outpost zone designed to cushion the shock of the initial assault and allow reserves to deal more easily with attacking troops in a deeper Battle Zone immediately beyond the front line. These tactics soon became evident to the British, who adjusted their tactics accordingly. As Haig explained to General Plumer on 10 May:

> I called his attention to the new German system of defence. The enemy now fight not in, but for his first position. He uses considerable forces for counter-attacks. Our guns should therefore be registered beforehand to deal with these latter. Our objective is now to capture and consolidate up to the range of our guns, and at once to push on advanced guards to profit by the enemy's demoralisation after the bombardment.[14]

The Germans also began using obstacles, including wire entanglements and blockhouses of ferroconcrete (that is, pillboxes). Both of these were used in abundance at Passchendaele in 1917, and had a major influence on the outcome of the New Zealand attacks there.

Two British offensives commenced in Flanders in 1917: Messines in early June, which captured the vital Messines–Wytschaete portion of the ridge, followed, after a long, fateful gap of six weeks, by the Third Battle of Ypres, lasting from July to November. The New Zealand Division played a leading role in the outstanding success of Messines, but its involvement in Third Ypres (sometimes known just as the Battle of Passchendaele) was limited to just two battles among the eight separate offensives launched.

The eight battles of Third Ypres were:

> Pilckem Ridge (31 July–2 August)
> Langemarck (16–18 August)
> Menin Road (20–25 September)
> Polygon Wood (26 September–3 October)
> Broodseinde (4 October)
> Poelcapelle (9 October)
> First Passchendaele (12 October)
> Second Passchendaele (26 October–10 November)

While the New Zealand Division fought in only Broodseinde and First Passchendaele, a brief account of each of the preceding battles provides essential background to its involvement.

The campaign began with a mixed success. The attack of 31 July aimed to take 4000 to 5000 yards of territory in four stages to a line running from Polygon Wood through to Broodseinde and Langemarck. This was far too ambitious, as most of the Fifth Army attacks under the aggressive, impetuous, reckless cavalryman Hubert Gough proved. The preliminary bombardment began on 16 July, and for fifteen days the German positions suffered under more than 3000 British guns of all calibres, 1000 of them classified as 'heavy'. This was a ratio of one gun to every 6 yards of the front line,[15] and about 4.75 tons of high explosive ammunition to every yard of front.[16] Over four million shells together weighing more than 100,000 tons fell on the enemy positions, and in the reclaimed bog land of the Ypres salient it created a formidable obstacle for the attacking troops. The Germans' front-line positions were destroyed, but the pillboxes just beyond remained intact because rain and heavy wind made it impossible to use aerial spotting or sound ranging to detect them. The attack, made by seventeen divisions totalling more than 100,000 troops over a 15-mile front, did not reach its final objective, but Pilckem Ridge fell and the advance reached the Steenbeek stream. All told, an advance of some 3000 yards took place, but on the right (to the south), the advance reached only 1000 yards. Casualties were heavy — some 31,000. The Battle of Pilckem Ridge managed to wrest

18 square miles of ground and two defensive lines from the Germans, but did not touch the main German defensive line. No ridges were taken, and none of the vital high ground of the the Gheluvelt Plateau to the south was touched. Haig pointed out this important deficiency to Gough on 2 August and directed him to deal with it in the next attack:

> I showed him on my relief map the importance of the Broodseinde–Passchendaele Ridge, and gave it as my opinion that his main effort must be devoted to capturing that. Not until it was in his possession could he hope to advance his centre. He quite agreed.[17]

Haig also urged Gough to have patience and not to put in an infantry attack until there had been two or three days of good weather with a subsequent improvement in the state of the ground. Unfortunately, in August just over 5 inches of rain fell, almost double the monthly average. There were only three days in the whole month when it did not rain, but the operations continued as the British sought to take more ground.

In the next attack, the Battle of Langemarck, launched on 16 August, some ground was taken in the north, but nothing from the centre nor to the south. The Fifth Army's average advance was less than halfway towards the final objectives of the previous attack. There were another 15,000 casualties. Small attacks were made on 19, 22, 24, and 27 August. These served little purpose other than to wear out Gough's Fifth Army. Failures resulted from the rain and mud, the effects of which Gough tended to ignore. By the end of August, casualties had amounted to 67,000, with 10,000 killed in action.

While the British gained little ground, the August battles had a serious effect on German morale. General Ludendorff recalled later how they

> imposed a heavy strain on the western troops. In spite of all the concrete protection they seemed more or less powerless under the enormous weight of the enemy's artillery. At some points they no longer displayed the firmness which I, in common with the local commanders, had hoped for.[18]

The Fifth Army's spirit broke in these attacks, though, and of the twenty-two divisions used, fourteen had to be rebuilt. The main effort of the British now switched from the low ground to the ridges in the northeast, and to the Second Army commanded by General Herbert Charles Onslow Plumer. For the remainder of the campaign, the role allotted to Gough's shattered Fifth Army amounted to providing flank protection for the main effort made by Plumer.

For the first three weeks of September there was little activity as Plumer undertook careful preparations. One of the most competent British field commanders, he had developed a doctrine suited to conditions on the Western Front and to Flanders in particular. Reluctant to take over the main effort of the campaign, he insisted he be given the freedom of action necessary to implement the measures he felt would bring success. His conditions, characterised by one writer as 'extreme deliberation',[19] were:

— that the infantry must not be made to advance too far — 1500 yards was regarded as a prudent total if conducted in several stages
— that the artillery must support the infantry at all stages and to a depth of 2000 yards beyond the final objective
— that any attack had to be made on a wide front
— that attacks must not be rushed, but were to be well planned and allow ample time for the infantry to familiarise themselves with the terrain over which they were expected to advance.

Professor Trevor Wilson has written of the Plumer formula:

Here, then, was a true alternative to Haig's Flanders plan. Rawlinson, after Neuve Chapelle in long ago 1915, had called it 'bite and hold'. It consisted of a series of set-piece operations whose extent and frequency would depend on the range and mobility of the artillery. The objective of any infantry attack must lie within the hitting limit of the guns. Once the objective had been taken, that phase of the operation would be over. As soon as the artillery could assume new positions and register upon fresh targets, another blow would be struck.[20]

By limiting the length of any advance made, the infantry would be immune from German counterattacks, which could be easily broken by the wall of protection provided by massed artillery fire.[21] For each attack Plumer also insisted on a greater concentration of force — both artillery and infantry — in pursuit of more modest objectives than had been allocated by Gough. To ensure he could do this Plumer received artillery and men from the other British armies, and he commenced operations on 20 September with twice the fire power, against half the length of front, that had been available to Gough. He also used his artillery carefully. His Chief of Staff, General Sir Charles Harington, later recalled that at Messines, Plumer

> knew so well how much depended on the artillery plan. He viewed that from the Infantry point of view. Whilst the infantry were training in back areas or on our model . . . he was perfecting the artillery arrangements. We actually carried out artillery and machine-gun rehearsals on the enemy.[22]

One of Plumer's guiding principles was that 'His Infantry were not going to be launched at uncut wire.' At Messines, his Second Army had had to cut through 280 miles of barbed wire, and he had used all his artillery to do this, thus paving the way for the successful infantry assault that followed.[23]

At Messines and during the battles of Third Ypres Plumer insisted on one further measure. He placed an Anzac corps (and later, two of them) at the centre of his attacking force, thereby allocating some of the key objectives to 'the most offensively minded' troops in the British armies.[24]

The Battle of Menin Road, which started on 20 September, saw the first of the Plumer attacks. The long delay between this and the previous attack led some German commanders to hope that this particular Battle of Flanders had run its course.[25] Unfortunately it still had a long way to go. After the British artillery had fired 1.5 million shells in a five-day preliminary bombardment, 65,000 men from eighteen brigades advanced from their forward positions. They moved behind five belts of protective fire, three of high explosive, one of shrapnel and one of machine-gun bullets, all fired to a depth of 1000 yards. The objectives were easily taken. This battle is notable for several reasons. For the first time in history two Australian divisions fought side by side, the 1st and 2nd Australian Divisions now fighting as part of I Anzac Corps. According to John Terraine, the battle was 'a model of forethought and precision',[26] a rarity for a Western Front attack at this time. The artillery barrage worked extremely well and was the best of the war to date. 'The power of the attack,' Ludendorff later wrote, 'lay in the artillery, and the fact that ours did not do enough damage to the hostile infantry.'[27] Despite the Menin Road offensive being a success it still cost 21,000 casualties to secure 5.5 square miles and advance the British positions an average of 1250 yards. Pouring rain and the boggy ground across which the infantry had to advance compounded the difficulties.

Polygon Wood was Plumer's next battle, starting on 26 September. This attack aimed to take the wood and Zonnebecke using a shallow advance of around 1000 to 1250 yards on a narrow front of 8500 yards. Seven divisions participated, and, once more, two Australian divisions (the 5th and 4th) fought side by side. It was another success, with nearly all objectives taken, but yet again it was no easy effort and saw much hard fighting as the Germans launched nine counterattacks in an effort to recapture lost ground. The end result was 15,375 casualties and the capture of 3.5 square miles. Polygon Wood passed into British hands and the line advanced to the foot of the main ridge. Ahead lay Broodseinde and Passchendaele.

The two September victories had cost 36,000 casualties to advance some 2750 yards. The British front line was still 4500 yards away from Passchendaele, and with each successive battle, artillery support had grown progressively weaker. Yet the German Army was suffering heavily. General Ludendorff wrote after the last attack that

> the 26th proved a day of heavy fighting, accompanied by every circumstance that could cause us loss. We might be able to stand the loss of ground, but the reduction of our fighting strength was again all the heavier. Once more we were involved in a terrific

struggle in the West, and had to prepare for a continuation of the attack on many parts of the front.[28]

Haig had seen his plans for a great strategic victory evaporate, but he felt delighted by what Plumer had achieved in his two attacks. After three years of almost total disasters, Haig and his headquarters were electrified by two successive victories and believed they had achieved something significant. Haig convinced himself and those around him that the high ground of Passchendaele held the key to victory, that the German Army was near collapse and that he was close to beginning the end of the war. Seizing the high ground, especially that of the Gheluvelt Plateau, would greatly accelerate the British victory. On the eve of the next big attack, Haig's views were expressed by his chief intelligence officer:

> Continued defeats, combined with the long duration of the war, has tended to lower the enemy's morale. The condition of certain hostile divisions was known to be bad. The time may come shortly when the enemy's troops will not stand up to repeated attacks, or when he may not have sufficient fresh troops immediately available to throw into battle. The enemy failed to take advantage of his opportunities on 31 October, 1914, and did not push forward when his repeated attacks had exhausted the British forces on the Ypres front. We must be careful not to make the same error. It was essential that we should be prepared and ready to exploit success on and after the 10th October, and that all the necessary means for this purpose should be at hand.[29]

Twice now Plumer's Second Army had broken clean through the German defence systems. Could they do it a third time? Clearly Haig, Plumer and others believed they could and felt the next attack should follow hard on the heels of the second. It had been noted by the commanders how effective the use of two Australian divisions side by side had been, so it was planned to repeat the formula in an attack on 4 October, but to double the dose. For the final push on to the Passchendaele Ridge, planned for execution in two more phases, there would be an injection of fresh Dominion troops. I Anzac Corps was sidestepped north to allow II Anzac Corps, consisting in part of the untried 3rd Australian Division and the experienced and well-regarded New Zealand Division, to move alongside.

At this stage in the war, the New Zealand Division had not experienced a military failure and, as a result, had a formidable reputation. The Corps Commander of I Anzac wrote to the New Zealand Minister of Defence prior to this attack:

> I know well it will do as well as it always has done and that is saying
> a great deal, for I am not flattering when I say that no division in
> France has a higher reputation than yours.[30]

Before examining the two New Zealand attacks, a brief description of the command structure under which the New Zealanders would be fighting is in order. At the head of the British armies in France was the newly promoted Field Marshal Sir Douglas Haig. Haig's soldierly qualities included determination, industry and resolve, but he lacked imagination and humour and, according to one influential writer, his defects have convinced all intelligent people of today 'of the unredeemable defectiveness of all . . . military leaders'.[31] Yet Haig was not an uneducated soldier. Unlike his peers he had actually devoted considerable time to the study of warfare, and especially the study of military history. But a little learning indeed proved a dangerous thing. As General 'Boney' Fuller wrote of Haig's military education:

> Unlike so many cavalrymen of his day, he had studied war,
> and, strange to say, this was to his undoing, because he was so
> unimaginative that he could not see that the tactics of the past were
> as dead as mutton. We are told that he held that the 'role of the
> cavalry on the battlefield will always go on increasing', and that he
> believed bullets had 'little stopping power against the horse'. This
> was never true, as an intelligent glance at past battles would have
> made clear to him.[32]

From 1916 Haig had become convinced that the war could only be won on the Western Front and by the forces of the British Empire, with the French playing a subsidiary role. He believed the Flanders campaign of 1917 offered his best opportunity for victory. One thing he retained throughout those long months was an eternal optimism that the Germans were almost defeated and one further 'push' would do the trick. Fed intelligence reports by his senior intelligence officer, Brigadier General John Charteris, that bordered on sheer fantasy, Haig believed the German forces in the second half of 1917 were barely hanging on and were ready for the *coup de grâce*. The Germans certainly were suffering under the repeated attacks. Ludendorff recalled after the war: 'The fighting on the Western Front became more severe and costly than any the German Army had yet experienced.'[33] While few Allied commanders shared Haig's optimism, the attack of 4 October did provide reasonable grounds for encouragement.

Under Haig's command were fifty-five British and Dominion divisions organised into five armies. Of these, two fought at Third Ypres: the Fifth Army under General Sir Hubert Gough and the Second Army under Sir General Herbert Plumer. Plumer's unmilitary appearance and age — he was sixty in 1917 and his hair had turned completely white after two years in the Ypres salient — disguised an astute military brain, one that recognised the importance of surprise and of the logistics needed to sustain a large military venture.

Within the Second Army for the attacks at Passchendaele were two Anzac corps, I Anzac commanded by General W.R. Birdwood and II Anzac commanded by General Sir Alexander Godley. Godley had done much to prepare the New Zealand army for war and had established a solid reputation as an administrator and trainer. He was also ambitious, aloof and undemonstrative. New Zealand soldiers hated him. As the popular and astute Birdwood wrote before the New Zealand attacks at Passchendaele, Godley was 'a good soldier, and I am sure means most extraordinarily well, but somehow or other, he does not seem able to command the affection of officers or men'.[34] Godley's unlikable character would provide the New Zealand soldiers of the time, and New Zealand historians ever after, with a convenient scapegoat for the disaster ahead.

The New Zealand Division, under Major General Andrew Russell, formed part of Godley's II Anzac Corps. Though born in New Zealand, Russell was a Sandhurst graduate with five years' service in the Indian army. Since 1892, he had been a sheep farmer in the Hawke's Bay region but had maintained his military knowledge and experience by serving in the Volunteers and Territorial Force. A perfectionist and workaholic, he established a solid reputation as a trainer, administrator and commander who set high standards and ensured they were reached. He was also ambitious and determined to produce the best division in France.[35] To achieve this he drove himself and his commanders extremely hard.

The New Zealand Division at this time was a most unusual military formation. From May 1917 until February 1918, it was a 'superheavy' division with sixteen battalions organised into four brigades, instead of the usual twelve battalions spread across three brigades. This structure had been imposed upon the New Zealand General Officer Commanding instead of New Zealand raising a second division. It proved an unpopular measure. Rather than the extra brigade acting as a kind of super-reserve, it was usually sent away from the division and used as an additional pool of labour. Having an additional brigade also increased the likelihood that the division would be called upon more often than its lighter counterparts. The heavy losses experienced during the forthcoming operations greatly contributed to the short duration of the 'superheavy' experiment. In the long term such a formation proved impossible for New Zealand to sustain.

Preparations for Plumer's next attack were rushed. The British high command knew the current spell of good weather was not going to last and believed the Germans to be staggering under the weight of the British attacks and close to breaking point. For the Germans, October 1917 would be 'one of the hardest months of the war'.[36] The New Zealand Division, out of the front line since the attack at Messines in June, was about to go 'over the top' again. It, too, was about to experience its toughest month of the war.

Chapter 2

Success: 4 October

O N 24 SEPTEMBER 1917, THE New Zealand Division was ordered to move to the Ypres battle area. This meant a six-day trek for most of the 23,000 troops, marching more than 20 miles a day, at the regulation 3 miles per hour. The weather had been fine for the previous three weeks, the longest spell of good weather in 1917, and, as a result, the roads were hard and dusty. The long march severely tested the troops. To ease the strain, the men 'marched easy' and sang songs along the way, but:

> By late afternoon the songs were few and far between. Even conversation lagged. The packs upon our backs in some unaccountable way were fully three times as heavy as when we carelessly hoisted them to our shoulders many, many hours before.[1]

As the New Zealanders passed through Ypres, the ruins of the city made a lasting impression:

> We passed through Ypres, my first time in this town which is perhaps one of the most well-known on the Western Front. It is a great place now, shell shattered and in ruins . . . As I passed through for the first time I marvelled and wondered at the immensity of the war, the ruins of Ypres and the wonderful organisation of the army.[2]

The extent of the destruction of this once proud and beautiful town together with its 'gaunt ruins and deserted streets', according to one New Zealand history, 'suggested some city of the dead'.[3]

If Ypres made a lasting impression on the New Zealanders, the front-line positions had an equally powerful impact:

> The ground is covered with shell holes as close together as pebbles on the beach; the dead from the last two pushes were being buried at half a dozen places en route, but were still lying about the battle front in large numbers, a dreadfully gruesome sight, and the smell struck one forcibly when at least two-and-a-half miles away.[4]

A New Zealand private recorded after the war:

> No words can give any adequate impression of a Flanders battle-field, even the pictured page fails lamentably to adequately impress . . . Picture an expanse of black mud as far as the eye can reach. Shell craters everywhere! There is not a square yard of the Ypres salient upon which a shell has not fallen. The craters have merged one into the other and perhaps a stormy sea, suddenly converted into semi-liquid mud, would hint at the configuration of the land. Every house, every shed has been smashed to splinters, but dotted over the landscape were the squat concrete 'pill-boxes' erected by the enemy. Not a single tree remains, only a few jagged, splintered stumps remaining. Not a leaf, not a blade of grass but everywhere the debris of war, human and inanimate.[5]

Such was the impression made by this war zone, another New Zealand soldier wrote something almost identical:

> . . . nothing but utter desolation, not a blade of grass or tree, here and there a heap of bricks marking where a village or farmhouse had once stood, numerous 'tanks' stuck in the mud, and for the rest, just one shell hole touching another.[6]

It was, as another New Zealander recounted, 'a place where no-one in his right senses would want to venture',[7] while the Commanding Officer of 3rd Wellington Battalion believed that 'the Mark of Cain seemed upon the land . . . Every square yard of it seemed foul with slaughter.'[8]

The New Zealand and 3rd Australian Division, the two attacking divisions of II Anzac Corps, were given just three days to prepare for their next action. One soldier in 1st Auckland Battalion scrawled a hasty note to his sister in New Zealand and caught the mood of the time. He hinted of the important events ahead:

> I am in a terrible hurry so please excuse scribble. Well since long before this ever reaches you we will have been in another 'Dustup' so I most likely wont be able to write to you for a few days.[9]

II Anzac took over its sector of the front on 28 September, only to learn that the attack had been moved forward two days in order to take advantage of good weather. Both divisions lacked familiarity with the ground over which they would have to attack, yet they felt elated that at last the two Anzac corps were to fight side by side.

Nothing was left to chance despite the haste of the preparations. The corps war diary tells of a huge build-up for the coming battle, with 'a continuous stream of lorries and transport taking material to the forward area'.[10] Brigadier Hart of 4th Brigade recorded in his diary that 'convoys of lorries reached as far as the eye could see'. On 30 September he wrote:

> Conference all the morning outlining dispositions and issuing instns for the forthcoming attack. A very busy time all day preparing maps, orders, arranging further moves, obtaining requirements for the offensive, bombs, ammn, flares, rockets, entrenching tools, etc.[11]

By 2 October, all the guns of the New Zealand artillery were forward in their new positions and calibrated ready to fire with plenty of ammunition on hand.[12] The Machine Gun Corps was also well prepared with its firing programme completed and the necessary orders issued on the afternoon of 2 October. To support the infantry in the attack, all five companies of the New Zealand Machine Gun Corps would be used. They would provide a very effective protective barrage, utilising over sixty machine guns and firing some 600,000 rounds on the day of the attack.[13]

The infantry battalions had two days to prepare and used the time wisely. The 2nd Auckland Battalion recorded on 3 October: 'officers and NCOs reconnoitred all ground to the Assembly area and carefully studied the ground of the advance'.[14] All New Zealand battalions did the same. On 2 October, General Russell visited his two brigadiers and all the commanding officers who were to take part in the forthcoming attack. He left the meeting well pleased. He recorded in his diary, 'I fancy we have got most of the work done and everyone seems confident'.[15]

Numerous spurs run from the main Passchendaele Ridge. The two now facing the New Zealand Division were Gravenstafel, the smaller of the two, and Bellevue. These two low hills were to be the scene of the New Zealanders' fighting at Passchendaele. Small streams had drained them but the intense shell-fire had turned the region into one large quagmire in a countryside now bearing the scars of war. Numerous pillboxes peppered both locations, especially amongst the destroyed farms. Broodseinde, the section of the ridge east of Ypres, was the main enemy stronghold and the site of an enemy regimental headquarters and an observation post which overlooked the whole salient. This important feature faced I Anzac Corps and became the main objective of the offensive.

The attack aimed to seize the first low ridge in front of Passchendaele as a preliminary to taking the village on the next ridge in a subsequent push. It would be opened on 4 October by twelve divisions along an eight mile front. For the only time in history, four Anzac divisions, making the main thrust in the centre, would be attacking side by side. They formed 'a single solid phalanx in the centre of the battle-line . . . the greatest overseas force which had ever simultaneously attacked the enemy'.[16] I Anzac Corps would attack Broodseinde on a 2000-yard front, while II Anzac would take the Gravenstafel Spur on a front of 3000 yards. The planned advance varied from 1200 to 2000 yards — 'strictly limited' objectives.[17] The three Australian divisions were to take Broodseinde Ridge and Zonnebecke, while the New Zealanders were to concentrate on taking the Abraham

Heights (the eastern slopes of Gravenstafel) and the spur itself. It was a formidable task because the divisions would have to advance up open slopes chequered with strongpoints. If the final objectives were taken, the British Army would be back on its old line of 1914, which had been lost in the German offensive of 1915.

To preserve the element of surprise, no preliminary artillery bombardment would be used in the attack, but at zero hour a devastating artillery barrage would take place, firing to a depth of 1000 yards. Artillery support for the Second Army, using the field guns of five divisions and some corps and army 'heavies', amounted to an impressive 796 heavy and medium guns, and 1548 field guns and howitzers. While there was no preliminary barrage, practice barrages broke the silence from 1 October and were fired twice a day until zero hour. These swept over the ground of the planned attack and beyond.

The New Zealanders' share of this artillery was generous. They would be supported by one hundred and eighty 18-pounders, sixty 4.5-inch howitzers and sixty-eight machine guns. There were to be four distinct artillery/machine-gun barrages to assist the assaulting infantry. The first would begin 150 yards in front of the start tape, and then lift 50 yards every two minutes for the initial 200 yards. The rate would then change to a lift of 50 yards every three minutes until the Red Line, the first objective, had been reached. A hundred and fifty yards past this the barrage would pause for an hour before moving on at a rate of 50 yards every four minutes until the second and final objective, the Blue Line, had been reached. The barrage would finally halt 150 yards beyond the final objective, during the vital period of consolidation, protecting the infantry while they dug new trenches. The machine-gun group in support of the final advance planned to fire a barrage out to 400 yards from the final objective and then remain ready to offer instant support to the infantry on the Blue Line.[18] As one New Zealand historian noted, this attack was to be 'a limited advance with unlimited explosives to blast out a way. If the weather held it must succeed.'[19]

Few of the unreliable, slow Mark IV tanks were to be used in the attack, but there were none in the II Anzac Corps sector. These steel monsters were not suited to the terrain around Ypres and they were committed to the various attacks in a piecemeal fashion without any consideration of the state of the ground over which they would have to pass. Slow-moving, high-profiled and unreliable, they were easily destroyed by the German artillery, and Ypres became known as the 'tank graveyard'. Sick of being squandered for heavy casualties and no gains, the tank officers protested to GHQ after the 4 October attack about the way their machines were being used. They were not employed again at Ypres, but the tank commanders were given freedom to plan an operation on ground of their own choosing. They found suitable ground some 40 miles to the south-east at Cambrai. Attacking on the misty morning of 20 November on dry, downward-sloping ground, 381 tanks achieved a stunning, though short-lived, victory.

The New Zealand Division was allocated a wide 2000-yard front and would be attacking to a depth of just over 1000 yards. Facing it was the 4th Bavarian Division. The New Zealanders planned their advance in two stages: first, to the Red Line, which ran approximately along the crest of the ridge just short of Gravenstafel village; then on to the Blue Line, at the foot of the Bellevue Spur in the Stroombeek valley, about 500 yards east of Gravenstafel.

Four battalions — 1st Auckland and Wellington from 1st Brigade, and 3rd Otago and Auckland from 4th Brigade — would cross the Hannebeek stream and take the enemy trenches, shell holes and pillboxes as far as the Red Line. They would then be leapfrogged by four more battalions — 2nd Wellington and Auckland from 1st Brigade, and 3rd Wellington and Canterbury from 4th Brigade — which would carry the attack to the Blue Line.

Both brigades were in position on the evening of 2 October and used the next day to carry out last-minute preparations, such as reconnoitring the battleground, establishing approach marches and tapping the start lines. The men were well briefed and understood the task ahead of them despite the short preparation time, which had permitted only two planning conferences. The commander of 1st Brigade was to write after the battle: 'I am satisfied that every man knew his job and the result of recent training was clearly proved.'[20] This would be 4th Brigade's first (and only) action of the war, and it felt determined to prove itself the equal of the other three New Zealand brigades.

On the evening of 3 October, the weather broke, bringing rain and gale-force winds. The long march, followed by the necessity of digging in, had exhausted many of the soldiers, and the dismal weather made for a cold night. With the uncomfortable conditions, and each man's private thoughts focused on what the next day would bring, few of the New Zealand infantry slept well.

On the day of the attack the temperature was 60°F, the sky was overcast and a quarter of an inch of rain fell. Despite the deterioration in the weather the ground underfoot remained firm throughout the day.

At 5.20 a.m., while the whole attacking force was crammed in the front line, a heavy German barrage fell on the front of II Anzac Corps. Most of the rounds fell to the rear of the New Zealand Division, although machine-gun and sniper fire did do some damage, causing about eighty casualties prior to zero hour in 1st Auckland Battalion alone.[21] Many of the sheltering troops believed the shelling indicated the Germans had detected their attack, but the German commander General Sixt von Armin, with three fresh divisions from Ludendorff's general reserve, had also planned a strike for the morning of 4 October, and this was his opening barrage. When massing for their attack, however, his troops were caught in the open by the British artillery barrage which erupted at 6 a.m. They were slaughtered by the tremendous weight of fire, and general confusion followed, from which they never recovered.

The artillery barrage had opened on time and the New Zealand infantry advanced behind it. 'You couldn't hear a thing,' reflected one soldier more than seventy years later, 'the air was just quivering.'[22] A New Zealand writer eloquently expressed the feelings of those taking part in an infantry assault. It was 'the deepest and most soul-searching ordeal that men can undergo'.[23] According to one of the attacking brigades, the artillery barrage 'opened to the second and was very intense'. It was 'excellent and all ranks were full of praise and admiration for it. It was easily followed and very few shorts were experienced'.[24] A New Zealand stretcher-bearer experiencing his first action of the war recalled that the artillery barrage was 'hell . . . let loose . . . The din was deafening and awe-inspiring, just one terrific roar.'[25] A soldier who had found the night of 3 October 'rather terrifying' reflected in his diary:

> Going over the bags in the morning. I am in the hands of God. So are we all. Preserve us Lord.[26]

He died on 6 October from wounds sustained during the attack.

The New Zealand infantry followed the barrage, 'like horses behind the hounds', according to Brigadier Hart.[27] It proved to be an easy advance for the 200 yards to the first enemy line, which had suffered badly during the opening barrage. Resistance was scant and easily overcome.

4th Brigade on the right, covering an 800-yard front, aimed to take the Abraham Heights. Starting with 3rd Auckland and 3rd Otago, it took its first objectives — Duchy Farm and Riverside — with very little opposition. The two battalions were then held up by the large pillbox known as Otto Farm. This was eventually outflanked and then cleared using the powerful Mills bombs. Mills bombs were the perfect weapons against pillboxes. According to Ormond Burton, 'they burst in the confined space with a ghastly effect'.[28] Fifteen prisoners and four machine guns were captured.

A New Zealand soldier, Private Stewart Callaghan, lined up on the tapes at 3.00 a.m. and followed the artillery barrage keeping 50 yards behind the line of shells bursting in front of him. He recorded:

> There were huns getting out of shell holes every where you looked and unless they put up their hands and came in to be taken prisoner they were shot down straight away. I shot one bloke I know of and fired a lot more shots but I don't know whether I got any more or not . . . There were a fair number of our chaps caught it but it can only be expected in an advance such as that was . . . I have wondered since how we got through at all as there were shells and bullets flying everywhere.[29]

Private Callaghan wrote that he came through this ordeal 'without a scratch' and described 4 October 'as a day I will not forget for a lifetime'. Unfortunately he did not have a normal lifetime left to him. He was badly gassed the following year and never recovered, the mustard gas having seared his lungs beyond repair. He died in Trentham Military Hospital in 1920.

One young Otago soldier, Gordon Neill from Outram, found that morning's attack anything but the 'great adventure' he had expected war to be. He recalled it seventy years later:

> Now, at six a.m. that morning we were all lined up on this tape — just in a long row. The barrage came down I would think fifty yards in front of us and it played on there for so many minutes and then it lifted another fifty yards and while it was lifting we moved forward and so barrage after barrage we moved up the hill protected as far as possible by the artillery fire that was in front of us. The idea, of course, is that any enemy between us and our objective was being subjected to heavy destructive fire from the artillery. Right, it was a steady incline. Anybody who was wounded and dropped could very easily perish in the mud. There were times where you had to drag out, almost to your knees, out of soft mud — ghastly conditions. And it pelted rain all the time. There were some spectacular sights, you know you see them painted by the artists. You know you'd see a man throw his hands up and down — finish! That was happening all round us because as we went up the rise we were subjected to heavy machine gun fire from the Germans up the rise . . . As we went up the hill, we encountered heavy machine gun fire from a pill box, a German pill box, and one of my mates, Tommy, received a wound in the thigh and he went down . . . it was in just about the same place that we lost our skipper. He was killed. We had very heavy casualties up at the top. In fact, we made our objective anyway and rooted the Germans out . . . We took our objectives there and we spent the night in the trenches.[30]

3rd Auckland and 3rd Otago had pushed on to the Red Line, where they were covered by a protective artillery barrage. They were followed by 3rd Wellington and 3rd Canterbury, which advanced over the Abraham Heights, suffering heavy casualties from the direct fire of the German machine guns on the high ground to the north and northeast. An officer in one of the following battalions penned in his diary:

> At 5:50 the Bn commenced to move forward. At 6 am our barrage of thousands of guns opened fire and we advanced into the Germans under the cover of their fire. The Germans shelled us fairly heavily. We advanced in company in columns of single file. At 6:20 am Colonel Weston was wounded and a message came to me to take command of the Bn which I did . . . I led Bn Hdqrs and established Hdqrs in a machine gun emplacement. Hundreds of German prisoners coming in . . . Rained at times. Poor Mitchell my batman was killed near me. A great victory.[31]

Both battalions continued their advance down the eastern slopes of the heights to the Blue Line, 3rd Canterbury having to subdue two pillboxes, which slowed its 2nd Company. By 9.10 a.m. Berlin Wood and Berlin Farm had fallen and the battalions were on their final objective. There they immediately began the process of consolidating their hard-won gains.

1st Brigade, on the left, covering a 1200-yard front, planned to advance to Korek. 1st Auckland and 1st Wellington led the way. Both battalions experienced considerable difficulty crossing the bog that had once been the Hannebeek stream but were fortunate the heavy mud softened the impact of the German artillery or they would have suffered severe losses. 1st Auckland drifted to the north in the early stages of the attack, receiving heavy fire from the pillboxes and farm houses, but managing to subdue them one by one with flank attacks and Mills bombs. The battalion ended up fighting in the 48th Division's sector and cleared the entire Red Line in that area. Meanwhile 1st Wellington had also pushed on to the Red Line in its sector and cleared the whole brigade area. As its regimental history states:

> By . . . acts of individual gallantry and by the grim determination
> of all ranks, allied with skilful leadership of officers and non-
> commissioned officers, 1st Wellington pushed on to the Red Line,
> capturing the whole brigade frontage on schedule time.[32]

It was an outstanding feat of arms. But it didn't stop there. With a party
from 3rd Otago, 1st Wellington took the ruins of Korek village 120 yards
beyond the Red Line. Machine-gun fire from two dugouts there had caused
casualties in both battalions and therefore had to be subdued.

Sidney Stanfield, a 16-year-old serving in 1st Wellington, recalled that
the attack was very hard work and that he had a peculiar sensation of
being alone on the battlefield:

> You're loaded down with 220 rounds of ammunition in your
> pouches . . . two bandoliers of fifties, one slung over each way, one
> this way . . . Forty-eight hours' rations, a full water bottle, a shovel
> or a pick shoved down your equipment at the back, and a rifle and
> a bayonet and one thing and another — I think they calculated
> round eighty pounds, so . . . this business of charge boys, charge the
> blighters boys, give them cold steel and all that was a lot of bunkum.
> You just blundered along, blundered along. And . . . if you came
> under heavy fire from a machine gun you'd immediately take shelter
> in a shell hole or something like that, or any bit of broken ground
> you see, to size up the situation. Groups of you in twos and threes.
> You weren't packed close together. It was basic, not to bunch . . .
> Immediately you bunched you drew fire you see. So, there'd only
> be perhaps two of you at most, or three of you, in one shell hole at
> a time . . . with the shell holes nearly all full of water . . . [For] My
> part, in . . . Passchendaele I seemed to be alone mostly. Alone, I felt
> I was alone if you understand, when I think of it now. Although I
> know there must have been men on either side of me.[33]

Little wonder one commanding officer later remarked 'Don Quixote
was not more heavily laden than a modern "digger"'.[34]

The Red Line was consolidated before the leapfrog battalions arrived. These — 2nd Auckland and 2nd Wellington — fought through the German positions beyond Korek to the final objective. While resistance was often strong, especially for 2nd Wellington at Kron Prinz Farm, they were soon in possession of the whole of the Blue Line. Once there, the professionalism of the New Zealand soldiers became evident. With great urgency, they immediately began the process of consolidation and soon had all troops on the final objective well under cover and prepared for the inevitable counterattacks.

The following summary of events is from 2nd Auckland Battalion's war diary:

> Strength Battalion 1 Oct: 26 Offrs, 780 ORs
>
> 3–5 Oct LtCol S.S. Allen wounded and 12 other officers, inc 2IC
>
> Bn CO for most 4 Oct Lt E.A. Porritt A/Adj
>
> 4 Oct: advanced through enemy HE barrage. Casualties not heavy, but direction in many cases badly kept.
>
> 8:05: RED Line reached.
>
> 8:10: Barrage lifted and Bn advanced behind it.
>
> 9:26: BLUE LINE reached and held.
>
> 2:00 pm first counterattack reported and destroyed by arty fire
>
> 4:00 pm enemy again counterattacked in three waves in front of PETER PAN. Artillery barrage was excellently placed completely smashing up counterattack.
>
> Another counterattack at 8:00 pm similarly dealt with.
>
> Total casualties 3–5 Oct
>
> KIA   41
>
> Wounded   179
>
> Missing   40
>
> Strength on 5 Oct: 12 Offrs, 561 ORs
>
> New Major took over Bn at 7 pm 4 Oct
>
> Took 290 POWs, 9 machine guns
>
> Relieved 5 Oct[35]

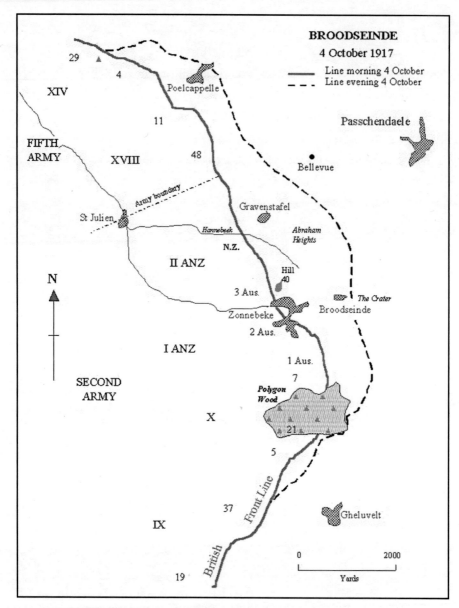

The Battle of Broodseinde, 4 October 1917.

The New Zealand Division had secured all of its objectives by 11 a.m. and was safe behind the wall of artillery and machine-gun fire that protected it in its new positions. The German counterattacks, which came at at 8.15 a.m., 10 a.m., noon and 2 p.m., were 'disjointed and were not pressed home . . . and were satisfactorily dealt with by our artillery'.[36] A New Zealand gunner left an account of the fate of the German attackers:

> We had quite a nice shoot but he [the enemy artillery] spotted us and got onto us with a very fast gun, made rather a mess, but when he counterattacked in force about 10 we were there and I believe they saw the troops get out of the train and form up for it and cut them down in hundreds.[37]

Three more counterattacks in the evening were similarly dealt with.[38] The sixty-eight machine guns of the New Zealanders were all in position to offer instant support to the infantry. They answered three calls on 4 October and another three in the early hours of the following morning. The machine-gunners responded instantly, spraying the entire New Zealand Division front with thousands of rounds. Such support 'won high praise from the infantry'.[39]

The New Zealand attack had been highly successful and advanced the line by 1900 yards. It had taken 1159 POWs from four different divisions, out of a total of 5000 POWs taken that day. The aggressive New Zealanders had also killed many Germans, 800 in 1st Brigade's sector alone. The commander of 1st Brigade concluded his report of the operation by stating: 'I cannot express myself too highly of the work of all ranks. Their dash and elan were magnificent.'[40] The brigade major of 4th Brigade could not 'speak too highly of the splendid conduct of officers, NCOs and men during these operations. Under the most appalling . . . conditions they displayed the utmost perseverance, bravery, endurance.'[41]

New Zealand casualties numbered 192 dead and 700 wounded in 1st Brigade, and 130 killed and 600 wounded in 4th Brigade. The New Zealand Artillery had lost eight killed and twenty-three wounded. Around 200 New Zealand soldiers were listed as missing. While the total of 1853 casualties was regarded by the official historian as 'not excessive',[42] it could hardly be regarded as light. The New Zealanders had experienced a casualty rate of around 25 per cent, or one in four of all participating soldiers. In 1st Auckland Battalion, because of its unfortunate start, the casualty rate had been over 40 per cent. Yet this was a battle in which everything had gone according to plan and the New Zealand infantry had received maximum artillery and machine-gun protection. In their next attack they would not be so fortunate.

Despite the relative ease of the victory — a 'walkover' as one soldier expressed it[43] — the attacking troops were exhausted by their efforts. While looking for his cousin, Gunner Bert Stokes visited 3rd Otago immediately after the attack:

> The poor old boys looked dead beat. Here they were lying asleep in an open paddock, in the rain, wet through. By Jove; they must have had a hard time of it and looked as if they did not care what happened!

Unfortunately, Gunner Stokes learned his young cousin had been killed half an hour after the battalion had gone over the parapet.[44]

Meanwhile, at a regimental aid post (RAP) a New Zealand padre recalled:

> We were going hard nearly all day long. I helped to place in splints I can't tell how many broken thighs, and found at last I could be really useful if given the opportunity.[45]

Removing the wounded from the battlefield proved difficult. Working four men to a stretcher, it took about four hours to cover the 3 miles to safety. Lieutenant Colonel C.H. Weston, Commanding Officer of 3rd Wellington Battalion, was wounded by an artillery shell in the early stages of his advance and had to be carried from the battlefield on a stretcher. He described this experience as 'the hottest corner I had ever been in' and felt it would be 'nothing short of a miracle if we escaped'.[46] Weston did escape, but not unscathed. He suffered another wound when a shell fragment punched a hole through the back of his steel helmet.[47]

After three days of backbreaking work by teams of stretcher-bearers, the battlefield was cleared of the wounded of both sides. As Linus Ryan, one of the stretcher-bearers at Passchendaele, recorded: 'It was the proud boast of the NZ Division that they never left a sector whilst one of their wounded remained.'[48] Once again, this tradition was maintained, although at the end of their ordeal the stretcher-bearers were 'too tired to talk . . . we got back — crawled into our bivvy, sat down and just ached. We were too tired to sleep — very near down and out'.[49]

Gravenstafel Spur, of which the Abraham Heights taken by the New Zealanders formed part, was a good tactical gain. It provided excellent observation of the Passchendaele Ridge and was the logical starting point for any attack on Passchendaele. On the high ground ahead the New Zealanders could see the pillboxes of the Flanders I Line on Bellevue Spur, an obvious objective for the next attack. But not one of those New Zealanders who gazed across to the spur on the morning of 4 October could have guessed that in just over a week's time it would be the site of indescribable suffering and total defeat for their fellow soldiers in the New Zealand Division.

The Australians of I Anzac had taken the Broodseinde portion of the ridge, and for the first time since May 1915, the British held some of the high ground and could look down on the Flemish lowlands beyond. Australian losses had not been light either — 6500, with 3rd Australian Division suffering 1810 of these.

Broodseinde, the name by which this battle is known, and Gravenstafel Spur were vital ground; the Germans had been driven from some of the most important positions on the Western Front. It was a victory of significance, as the Germans had no obvious solution to the step-by-step advances of Plumer's Second Army, especially when the attackers stayed well within range of their supporting artillery. The Germans had been powerless to prevent the attack from succeeding, and the ten counterattacks they had launched that day had failed to regain any ground and had been easily dispersed by the supporting artillery. That their new tactics were failing them was evident to the German High Command:

> Once again the losses had been extraordinarily severe . . . The
> new combat methods had not proved themselves successful on

4 October. The more heavily manned front line which had suffered heavy losses from artillery fire had been overrun by enemy infantry who had attacked in superior numbers with tank support . . . The Army High Command came to the conclusion that there was no means by which the positions could be held against the overpowering enemy superiority in artillery and infantry. Loss of ground in these heavy enemy attacks was unavoidable.[50]

The attack of 4 October was the third hammer blow against the Germans in a fortnight. It was one of the greatest victories of the war to date. Certainly those who had taken part believed they had won a great victory and hoped the Flanders campaign might now reach a successful conclusion. The Germans had been badly shaken. A German regiment on the receiving end of the New Zealand attack recorded in its history after the war: 'The 4th of October arrived. The blackest day in the history of the regiment.'[51] The Australian official historian commented: 'An overwhelming blow had been struck and both sides knew it.'[52] So heavy had the German losses been that Prince Rupprecht considered a general withdrawal from the Flanders front beyond the range of the vicious British artillery.[53]

The reasons for the success were obvious to those who had participated. By attacking without a long preliminary artillery barrage, a tactical surprise had been obtained. Artillery support throughout had been almost perfect, paving the way for the infantry. Despite the change in the weather the ground underfoot had remained firm, so although the infantry's task had by no means been easy, it had not been made harder by having to battle though mud and slush as well. Despite the lack of preparation time, individual units had carried out a thorough reconnaissance of the ground across which they would have to assault and had detected no major obstacles in their way.

Because the Germans had suffered heavily in the attack, many people in the Allied camp believed they were on the verge of defeat. A sense of anticipation of great events mounted in the headquarters of the higher formations. At Corps Headquarters, General Godley's personal messenger recorded the sense of excitement:

Great reports re the advance have been coming in all day. From all accounts they have a great crowd of prisoners . . . The GOC is very pleased with his Anzacs. They did far more than he expected them to do. If only it keeps fine for a few more days Fritz will get the scare of his life but I'm afraid it will rain before long . . . Good reports are still coming in and everyone is excited about the haul of prisoners we have got.[54]

Reflecting this euphoria, on 7 October, General Godley wrote to Allen in New Zealand:

They [the New Zealand Division] took Gravenstafel and Abraham's Heights, and had a wider front and very nearly as far to go as anybody, and, as usual, did it excellently. They took over 1000 prisoners, and I am glad to say that the casualties are much lighter than they had ever been before, and, in fact, are not much more than the number of prisoners taken . . . it will not be long before the other two brigades are attacking again and you will hear of them . . . there is no doubt that the Boche is becoming very demoralised, and if the weather will only hold up for a bit longer and we can deliver a few more blows before the weather sets in, it will go a longway towards the end. The best sign of all was the demoralisation not only of the troops but of the enemy's commanders and staffs . . . The whole of the battlefield of our successive advances is covered with dead Huns, and there is no doubt that a very large number have been killed since the beginning of this third battle of Ypres.[55]

General Monash, the Australian commander of 3rd Australian Division, also believed that the enemy was 'staggering' and that, provided sufficient artillery was in place for the next attack, 'Unless the weather balks me I shall capture P— village on 12th.' Monash felt 'very much elated and not a little excited' by this prospect.[56]

The condition of many of the German prisoners greatly reinforced the view that the enemy was suffering severely and scraping the bottom of the barrel. One New Zealander wrote in his diary:

> At 6:45 am the first of the prisoners started to come in in droves . . . Some of the prisoners, or the majority of them, were very poor types indeed; we managed to find out that some of them were only 17 and 18. One of the little chaps was crying . . . [57]

Gunner Bert Stokes also recorded his poor impressions of the prisoners as they walked past:

> They were a motley crew, some old looking, young boys and all exhausted and worn. A very poor specimen of Germans they were, and all were lacking colour, they were awfully pale and looked as if they had spent some hard times under our bombardment.[58]

Another New Zealander noted:

> The prisoners are a miserable looking mob and one German I was talking to told me that London is a heap of ruins, England was starving and it was impossible to get troops across the Channel — the poor fools.[59]

Leonard Hart regarded the German POWs taken on 4 October as:

> . . . the poorest looking lot I have ever seen . . . Many of them were mere boys of sixteen and seventeen and plenty of them were not an inch over five feet high. This certainly looks as though Germany is falling back to her unfit material to keep up the strength of her armies.[60]

Little wonder, then, that British commanders from Haig down believed the Germans were nearly exhausted as a fighting force and that one more success would finish them off.

Yet the weather had broken, and the heavy rain soon turned the battlefield into a sea of mud. This would save the Germans from certain disaster, and they knew it. A relieved Prince Rupprecht wrote: 'Most gratifying, rain: our most effective ally'.[61]

General Russell felt well pleased with his division and noted in his diary:

> . . . we gained all objectives advancing our line some 1900 yards on NZ front and this division captured 1100 prisoners. Our casualties I estimate at 1500/2000, they make it less. All battns (1st and 4th Bde) fought well especially latter.[62]

In spite of the success of the New Zealand Division, though, and unlike his Australian counterpart, General Russell had a sense of foreboding about his men's future operations:

> We've been having one of our periodic battles today and so far have done well. Casualties not so heavy as at Messines, nor nearly so heavy as the Somme which was the biggest battle, and the hardest fighting that we shall ever see I hope. The more I see of it the less I like it. These big casualty lists, with all they mean, do not lose their effect thro' familiarity. It seems so futile tho' one knows it isn't. Unfortunately it is raining, and the sun hasn't got the power to dry the ground so late in the year. We've got a very muddy time in front of us, and that means a lot. The mud is a worse enemy than the Germans who did not today put up much of a show of resistance, tho' I shall not be surprised if he tries to get us tomorrow.[63]

Exhilarated by the success of 4 October, Haig was keen to follow with another big attack, despite the heavy rainfall and the arrival of fresh German troops. He had wanted to push on to Passchendaele village on 4 October, but as this would have taken the infantry beyond the range of the British artillery, the idea had been opposed by both Plumer and Birdwood. Yet Haig could hardly wait to come to grips with the enemy again and brought the date of the next big attack forward. The offensive would continue, with a fresh attack planned for 9 October.

49th Division relieved the New Zealanders on 6 October, and the exhausted troops had a long march to an area west of Ypres. Brigadier Hart wrote of the relief:

> The night was dark, wet, muddy and miserable troops were weary and worn and had a four mile march to the Goldfish chateau area. We got out as dawn was breaking, the shattered and torn town of Ypres looked extraordinarily sombre and weird at that hour to the eyes of all of us who were winding our weary way back after three sleepless nights and a strenuous battle thrown in.[64]

While this action proved 4th Brigade's only battle of the war, within a week the New Zealand Division would be marching back to the front-line trenches for the attack on Passchendaele village, now only 1½ miles away but still beyond the range of most British guns.

Those New Zealand troops who had taken part in the attack of 4 October were aware of how well they had performed:

> I have not yet seen the newspaper reports of this little 'push' and I don't suppose it will be much more than mentioned but all the same it was one of the most complete successes our side have ever had and even General Godley doled out a little praise to the New Zealanders . . . a thing which must have caused him a severe strain.[65]

Newspaper reports in New Zealand raised the attack to something more than a substantial victory, reporting of 'Thrilling Despatches From Flanders' where the 'Anzacs Fought Like Tigers'.[66] They described it as 'The Turning Point of the War', the New Zealanders' 'greatest and most glorious day',[67] 'Germany's Biggest Defeat' and 'The Most Slashing Defeat Yet Inflicted'.[68]

The New Zealand Division had secured all its objectives and, as far as the troops were concerned, 4 October had been a textbook operation in which everything had gone according to plan. One young soldier wrote after the attack: 'It's marvellous the way these "Stunts" as we call them are got up, everything run like clockwork.'[69] To date the New Zealand Division had not experienced a military failure, and all its members felt immensely proud of this achievement. One soldier, Peter Howden, wrote to his wife after 4 October:

> . . . it is a thing to be proud of being a New Zealander I can tell you when you realise and see and know how our chaps behave over here. People do not perhaps realise that the NZs have the record of being the only troops on our side who have always taken their objectives, who have always done it to time and who have never yet lost a place they have taken. Just think what that means.[70]

A New Zealand newspaper editorialised on this theme on 8 October. Describing the Australian and New Zealand attack on the fourth as 'rivalling Wolfe's ascent to the plain of Quebec', the paper quoted Haig:

> Sir Douglas Haig has said that he looks to the New Zealanders 'to carry out with complete success every task set,' and once more that high confidence has been justified. The division's record is one of which New Zealand is justly proud.[71]

Unfortunately, the New Zealand Division's record was about to end. Its next great attack of the war would prove far from a textbook or 'clockwork' operation. Peter Howden, writer of the proud letter above, would be just one of many New Zealand casualties in the country's worst-ever military disaster.

Chapter 3

Prelude to Disaster: 9 October

FROM 4 OCTOBER, RAIN in Flanders turned the ground into thick, glutinous mud. While the rain turned to drizzle on the fifth, constant showers fell on the sixth and seventh and torrential rain soaked the ground on the afternoon of the eighth. A young New Zealand officer wrote:

> It sure means business when once it does commence to rain in this country. The last two days have been bitterly cold, but now it has set in very wet, such rain as you never see in New Zealand.[1]

The rain obliterated all landmarks and washed away roading and tracks. Three months of constant shelling had destroyed the natural drainage of the region and the thousands of shell holes now filled with muddy water. The entire valley facing the two Anzac corps, and across which they would soon have to fight, became, in the words of one divisional engineer, 'a porridge of mud'.[2] Describing the mud as 'terrible', one Canterbury soldier complained that 'I always thought Oxford was bad enough for mud but it's not a patch on this.'[3]

The heavy rain was also falling on the Germans, who likewise struggled with the mud in their wet trench systems, yet it was easier to occupy high ground from which water would drain. It was also easier, if decidedly uncomfortable, to sit tight in the prevailing conditions than attempt to advance through them. The British Army commander decided this would be the fate of his men.

The state of the road leading to the front line which the New Zealanders had to use was extremely poor and did not reflect the mountain of work being done on it by the engineers and assault pioneers. The war diary of the New Zealand Engineers recorded on 6 October that 'bad weather continues and roads have become too soft for transport. Sappers and Pioneers are working continuously day and night repairing roads.'[4] The New Zealand (Maori) Pioneer Battalion had been struggling since 4 October to make adequate roading for the forthcoming attacks. These experts at road-making, bridge-building, trench-digging and the myriad other manual tasks required of an army at war worked harder than most infantry battalions at these backbreaking tasks and often produced double the output of their more glamorous counterparts. The Pioneers made good progress until 6 October, when the wet weather and the constant stream of mule-drawn supply trains turned earth roading 'into a quagmire'. From 7 to 10 October there was:

> . . . a steady fight with mud. All available men have been carrying fascines [bundles of sticks] . . . BUT guns and horses are bogged everywhere. We have pulled many guns out and into position but the road is in a fearful condition . . . Many of our guns were bogged on the road and never got into action.[5]

Despite their best efforts the road remained 'a shaky bog'. In the Pioneer Battalion's view, the two attacks of 9 and 12 October failed primarily because of 'the failure of roads, light railways and tram lines'. A tram line to Gravenstafel Hill, for example, 'would have been invaluable if only for supply of ammunition and evacuation of wounded'. The overriding lesson of the New Zealand Division's October operations, according to the Pioneers, was the 'vital necessity' of establishing roads, rail and tram lines after an advance 'with all possible speed'.[6]

One of the officers in charge of the road-building teams in II Anzac Corps was New Zealand engineer Stanley Rogers. It was a hard, dangerous and thankless task. Rogers wrote to his brother before 12 October:

> There has never been a stunt like this before; for instance, yesterday we had 42 horses to drag off the road and bury. I phoned for more men, but at the moment manpower is a premium.[7]

Rogers did receive an additional twenty men and was able to have the road cleared and the horses buried in one strenuous night of activity. From 10 October, the priority became shifting ammunition forward for the artillery. To do this, Rogers and his team worked forty hours straight without meal breaks or rest.

Road-clearing also proved dangerous work, and a number of Rogers' men were killed and wounded by enemy shell-fire. Rogers himself had many close calls. One of these occurred while talking to an old friend, Mark Farington, a veteran of the Somme and Messines. A German shell landed between them and catapulted them into the mud. Rogers felt at the time that 'I would suffocate — had I swallowed any mud I would have.' He dragged himself clear of the mud with great difficulty, then located Farington. Rogers pulled his friend from the mud and 'when I went to clear his mouth, his lower jaw was gone and the head split open'. Farington had been killed instantly by the stray shell. Naturally, Rogers felt ill after this very close shave and, being covered in mud from head to foot, he took off the rest of the night. The next day, though, he was back at work and soldiering on.[8]

In this cold, wet, muddy environment the New Zealand Division began to suffer. It was impossible to keep dry and the mud penetrated everything. There was one small comfort. A soldier's diary notes that on 6 October 'the rum ration was recommenced'. This was 'very acceptable too as cold weather set in and we were up to our knees in mud most of the time'.[9] Work still had to be done, no matter what the conditions, and the digging, road-building and shifting of material, especially ammunition, continued. With only one blanket, one pair of boots and two pairs of socks issued per man, the men's health and morale soon plummeted. The end of the war seemed as far away as ever:

> I can't say I feel like writing and saying I am feeling fit and things are going well because that would be lies, but I am a good deal better off than a lot of the fellows as I have the top boots and waterproof overcoat . . . The Army is a queer place at the present moment. I feel pretty fed up. I am really getting rather sick of it. I honestly

believe we are winning but I never do believe now that we will force him to unconditional surrender.[10]

The two commanders, Gough and Plumer, were worried about the bad weather and its effect on the troops. On the evening of 7 October they told Haig that while they could continue the campaign, they would both prefer to suspend it for the winter. Despite their concerns, Haig and others felt so buoyed by the results of 4 October they decided to press their advantage with more attacks in an effort to secure the Passchendaele Ridge as the campaign's last gain. The longer the enemy was left unmolested, Haig believed, the stronger his defences would be and the more rested his troops. After three crushing blows against him, now was the time to strike. The Australian official historian commented:

> Let the student looking at the prospect as it appeared at noon on October 4th ask himself, 'In view of the results of three step-by-step blows, what will be the result of three more in the next fortnight?'[11]

Haig felt convinced, and not without good reason, that the Germans were on their last legs, so Allied pressure must continue. He cited the Germans' failure to push home their attacks at Ypres in 1914 and was determined to avoid making a similar mistake. His enthusiasm proved infectious and easily swayed Plumer. Plumer's Chief of Staff, General 'Tim' Harington, recalled:

> It is, therefore, inconceivable to me that his [Plumer's] agreement with the views of the Commander-in-Chief was anything but one of 'utter loyalty' and desire to carry out his Chief's orders to capture Passchendaele. He knew well what that ridge would mean to his beloved troops and I am sure that once within his grasp, as it was after his successful capture of the Broodseinde Ridge on 4th October, he never gave a thought to stopping and turning back.[12]

General Godley of II Anzac Corps was also an enthusiastic supporter and all for continuing the attack. Haig wrote in his diary on 8 October:

> I called on General Plumer and had tea. It was raining and looked like a wet night. He stated that 2nd Anzac Corps (which is chiefly concerned in tomorrow's attack) had specially asked that there should be no postponement. I ordered them to carry on.[13]

The request that there be no postponement can only have come from General Godley. Ironically, the reckless, impetuous Gough remained unconvinced about continuing the campaign. His experiences in August had filled him with a sense of foreboding and pessimism that made him cautious about forcing troops to fight in heavy rain.

Another factor influenced Haig's decision to continue. The British front could not remain where it was, at the foot of the slope of the most prominent ridge in the region. The choice was to advance or withdraw. A withdrawal would be tantamount to admitting failure and, after so many casualties suffered for the little ground taken, would cause an outcry by the British public, with political consequences. Haig knew the British Prime Minister, Lloyd George, considered him incompetent and wanted an excuse to remove him. Such an admission of failure would provide Lloyd George with just such an excuse. Haig therefore refused to consider the option of withdrawal, instead insisting that the British try to capture the Passchendaele sector of the ridge, where the troops would be able to overlook the Steenbeke valley and winter on higher, dryer ground. At least this would look like some kind of victory. Haig's decision to continue after 4 October when the weather had broken remains 'the most questioned decision of his career'.[14]

The next move was to capture the village of Passchendaele. It was to be done in two steps. The first, in an action that was to be known as the Battle of Poelcapelle, was to occur on 9 October, just five days after Broodseinde, and was to be the shorter of the two advances. It would pave the way for a much larger advance three days later. The main objective of the 9 October attack was to secure two spurs leading up to the Passchendaele Ridge.

Immediately noticeable about the planning for both attacks is the lack of preparation time. They would be very rushed affairs. The first attack by the Second Army, back in September, had taken three weeks to prepare. The third attack, that of 4 October, had been given only eight days, but the attacking divisions still had the maximum artillery and machine-gun protection. For the 9 October push, the attackers had just five days of preparation, while 12 October had only two days, and the vital artillery could not be made ready with such short lead times given the dreadful conditions prevailing in the salient.

The decision to go ahead with the attack on 9 October ignored all the conditions that had led to the previous successes, especially the role of the artillery. Also ignored were the weather and terrain. As the Australian official historian would aptly comment: 'the brilliance of the Second Army's success appeared to be tempting its leaders to forsake their tried methods'.[15] It had taken three years and horrific casualties to perfect these methods. A 'sorry decline'[16] was occurring in the quality of Second Army's preparations and it was about to learn the terrible cost of abandoning its tried and tested formula.

Most soldiers believed that, with the heavy rain, the chance of a decisive, knockout blow had vanished. One Australian subaltern, who would be killed in the attack on 12 October, wrote on the eighth:

> I believe that if the weather had only held over another two or three weeks we would have Fritz well on the run in Flanders, and would have had numerous opportunities of following him up and further knocking him about with our cavalry. Now I fear that it must be a wash-out for the year — tough luck, but we take things as they are and keep plugging away.[17]

On 8 October, General Harington held a press conference. The Second Army, he stated, could not be stopped in its step-by-step approach and the attack the next day would bring further success. The sandy crest of the ridge was 'as dry as a bone' and the cavalry were on standby to pass through the big gap the Second Army would punch in the German positions. Newspapermen listened with scepticism. One later recorded his impression of the conference:

> I believe the official attitude is that Passchendaele Ridge is so important that tomorrow's attack is worth making, whether it succeeds or fails . . . I suspect that they are making a great, bloody experiment — a huge gamble . . . I feel, and most of the correspondents feel . . . terribly anxious . . . The major-generals are banking on their knowledge of German demoralization . . . I thought the principle was to 'hit, hit, hit, *whenever the weather is suitable*'. If so, it is thrown over at the first temptation.[18]

Both British armies would attack on 9 October, the Second Army with six divisions, the Fifth Army with five. In II Anzac Corps, two British divisions would be used: the experienced 49th (West Riding), a veteran formation that had fought in the Somme the previous year, and the untried 66th (2nd East Lancashires). Both divisions planned to use two brigades. I Anzac's 2nd Australian Division would also be used. The brigades of II Anzac were to advance along two parallel spurs towards Passchendaele village. Between the spurs lay the saturated and impassable Ravebeek valley, dividing the formations, which would therefore be unable to offer each other support. The attack aimed to swing the Allied line to the left by taking the Bellevue Spur and the high ground opposite. This was an advance of 600–900 yards, which would take the British line to the foot of the slope just below Passchendaele village. The attack of 12 October would take the village itself.

The attacking divisions of II Anzac had a march of 4 miles through a quagmire of mud and slush just to reach their start line. In fact, this march was so arduous some troops never completed it, and there were large gaps along the jumping-off tapes when the infantry finally moved forward. The effort to get on the start lines in time exhausted both divisions. There was also inadequate artillery support, as few guns had been moved within range. The 66th Division, for example, had only twenty-five field guns in support of its attack. The opening barrage was so weak and patchy it proved impossible for the infantry to establish where the shells were meant to fall. It thus provided no guide, and even less protection, for the advancing infantry.

49th Division attacked from the New Zealand frontage secured on 4 October. Bellevue Spur, facing it, projected north of a sunken road which led to the highest part of the ridge. Uncut wire flanked the sides of the slopes, the steel and concrete walls of pillboxes crowned the spur, and the attacking battalions had to cross the flooded Ravebeek stream, now 50 yards wide and waist deep. The Germans were on the last bit of vantage ground and fought desperately to hold it. The two brigades of 49th Division came under withering fire from machine guns the moment they crossed the start line. The British official history records, ominously: 'No previous attack organised by the Second Army in the War had such an unfavourable start.'[19] Both brigades were then delayed by the dense unbroken wire and pillboxes on Bellevue Spur and suffered heavy losses. They failed to reach their objectives. 148th Brigade, on the right, took no new ground at all, while 146th Brigade, on the left, managed an advance of just 300 yards and held this ground until the next day. The division suffered more than 2500 casualties in this abortive attack.

On the right wing of II Anzac, 66th Division, in its first major action of the war, had a somewhat easier task. Fighting on firmer ground and striking no wire obstacles, its infantry took its final objective, and a patrol from 3rd/5th Lancashire Fusiliers entered Passchendaele village, finding it a deserted ruin. The division had to abandon these hard-won gains, though, to conform to the front of 49th Division and avoid the heavy enfilade fire from machine guns and light field pieces now being poured into both its brigades from the strongpoints on Bellevue Spur. It withdrew to a line about 500 yards in front of its starting line, having suffered more than three hundred casualties.

2nd Australian Division, of I Anzac, also failed to make any progress and suffered 1253 casualties. Only on the left flank of the Fifth Army were the final objectives taken and held. In general, progress on 9 October was slight while casualties were excessive.

Many of the wounded from the attack lay in the open and would not be retrieved until days later, especially those of 49th Division. Some lay on the battlefield for three days and their injuries 'turned septic; in some cases the wounds are filled with maggots'.[20] Many died of exposure or drowned in the shellholes in which they had sought shelter. A New Zealand stretcher-bearer recorded on moving back to the front line:

> In the ordinary course of events we should have been able to spell ourselves until the commencement of the stunt, but we found that the Division who had just left this sector, had left their wounded lying about in shell holes and all our bearers had to set to and clean the place up. We carried out poor little Tommies who told us they had been lying out in shell holes for four days, and their wounds, absolutely black, bore out their words.[21]

There were about two hundred stretcher cases requiring evacuation from the battlefield, no easy task under the prevailing conditions. A New Zealand soldier commented on the task that had been left to him and his compatriots:

> To make matters worse the 49th Division, whom we relieved, went out leaving 200 stretcher cases for us to shift — most of whom had been out 4 or 5 days. Stretcher bearing was exceedingly hard owing to mud and shell holes and the boys were done before the stunt started.[22]

The attack on 9 October was clearly a dismal failure — a 'total repulse', to use the phrase of the Australian official historian.[23] General Russell lamented in his diary:

> Attack this morning a failure — carried out by 49th and 66th Dn on our Corps' front — troops held up early and arrived at Assembly point exhausted.[24]

In three days' time his own troops would be in exactly the same situation.

Losses in both II Anzac divisions amounted to more than 5000, and total Allied casualties for the day to more than 13,000, of which just on 4000 had been killed. Yet enough ground had been taken — even if it was only a paltry 500 yards and none of it vital — to justify, in the minds of the senior commanders, another attempt as soon as possible. Haig, demonstrating no grasp of reality, wrote the briefest entry in his diary:

> Tuesday, 9 October. A general attack was launched at 5.30 am today from a point S.E. of Broodseinde on the right to St. Janshoek (1 mile N.E. of Bixschoote). The results were very successful.[25]

Plumer, presumably after consulting with General Godley, informed Haig's headquarters:

> I am of opinion that the operations of the 49th and 66th Divisions, carried out today under great difficulties of assembly, will afford the II Anzac Corps a sufficiently good jumping off line for operations on October 12th, on which date I hope that the II Anzac Corps will capture Passchendaele.[26]

Not only Haig wanted the attack at Passchendaele renewed — so did General Plumer, despite his earlier misgivings, and Godley. None of these senior commanders, and few divisional commanders, had gone forward to speak to the junior officers responsible for conducting the attack. Even Monash and Russell, both of whom received negative reports, did not check conditions facing their men for themselves, nor did they take any other action. Despite the obviously atrocious conditions, General Godley felt keen for II Anzac to be used and again asked that there be no postponement. His soldiers would attack through the Flanders battlefields, now a sea of thick, glutinous mud resembling in its consistency something akin to lumpy porridge. Relying on second-hand information would cause an appalling tragedy for those at the sharp end of the battle plans. The British official historian admitted after the war that the task given to New

Zealanders on 12 October was 'beyond the power of any infantry with so little support'.[27]

On the eve of attack several senior officers had grave misgivings. Without any change in the weather, and well aware of the difficulties ahead for his troops, General Gough considered asking for the attack to be cancelled. After consulting with Plumer he concluded, however, that it was now too late to do so. The New Zealand Division would have welcomed a postponement, but felt powerless to initiate one. The system of command lacked flexibility and granted little power to subordinates to express their doubts or refuse an order.

Those Anzac divisions responsible for the outstanding success of 4 October were now to be used in another attack on the twelfth. To the objectives of this push would now be added those that had eluded the attacking divisions on the ninth. General Birdwood protested that the conditions on his front, and the exhaustion of I Anzac Corps, meant his troops would be able to do little more than offer flank protection for II Anzac. Yet General Godley said nothing. His silence condemned II Anzac Corps to making the main effort. The New Zealand Division, along with 3rd Australian Division, would again enter the cauldron of battle. The senior commanders, Haig, Plumer and Godley, anticipated another stunning success. They were about to be terribly disappointed.

Chapter 4

Disaster: 12 October

O N THE NIGHT of 10–11 October the attacking brigades of the New Zealand and 3rd Australian Divisions marched from Pilckem to the front line. The march of 5 miles through driving rain proved difficult, and to stray from the duckboards meant becoming stuck in knee-deep mud with the risk of drowning. Progress was slow — 1 mile every four hours. A New Zealand machine-gunner recalled the painful journey:

> We had to go about 6 miles on duck walks and then after leaving the boards it took us 4 hours to go a quarter of a mile. It was raining, we lost the track and the boys were getting bogged. I myself was bogged down to the waist twice. We eventually reached the end of our journey about 4:30 am this morning and as we were in an exposed and dangerous position we had to set to and dig ourselves in.[1]

A corporal of the Rifle Brigade also remembered the march without affection:

> Issued out with bombs, shovels, etc. ready for the attack on Friday morning. Moved off to within 1000 yards of the front line at 6:30 pm. Awful road congested with traffic of all description. Nothing but a veritable sea of mud to walk. Dug a hole to live in that night and next day.[2]

Another rifleman recalled:

> Got on to the duckboards and a few shells dropped near killing three. We took a long time going up, there were constant halts.

Of course Bricky took HQ off the duckboards about a mile from the end of our journey and we had to struggle through mud to Calgary Grange. Arrived there about 11 pm and dug ourselves holes to live in. It came on to rain and Fritz started shelling so we had a rotten night.[3]

Little wonder that a machine-gun officer, a 'valued and trusted leader' of the Machine Gun Corps[4] who died of injuries sustained next day, wrote in his last letter home that moving up to the line was 'more like a nightmare than anything I can think of'.[5] Another soldier accurately remarked: 'no one will ever forget that dark passage amongst the shell-holes and swamps'.[6]

By 3 a.m., most troops were on their start lines ready for the attack, but were thoroughly exhausted. Others had gone astray in the night. One veteran recalled how the troops on his battalion's left flank failed to appear at dawn. He blamed the terrain:

It was broken, not high ridgy country, but broken rolling country with those canals and streams bust up, and it was very easy for people to do a circle almost if they kept going at night, falling into shell holes . . . in the dark it was very hard for the troops to get up if they didn't know the way.[7]

Haig, meanwhile, claimed in his diary on 10 October:

The 3rd Australian Division and the New Zealand Division go into the line again tonight. Gough told me they are determined to take Passchendaele in the next attack and will put the Australian flag on it! The advance will be then over 2000 yards. But the enemy is now much weakened in morale and lacks the desire to fight.[8]

Haig's determination not to miss what seemed a prime opportunity meant the 12 October attack was hurried. The divisions involved not only had much less planning time — just two days — but were given deeper objectives than any of the preceding attacks. The New Zealand Division only took over its sector at 10 a.m. on 11 October but was to attack the next morning. This allowed little time to determine the tape-line for the attack, to draft and issue orders, for commanders at all levels to brief their troops, for artillery barrage tables to be calculated and disseminated to infantry battalions, or to carry out the other vital tasks necessary to prepare an attack of this scale. A British history written shortly after the war caught the mood:

> The sands were fast running out, and if another attempt was to be made to develop the success of October 4 it was clear that it would have to be made quickly. It was decided to attack again on the 12th, a brief two days' interval since our last assault.[9]

A New Zealand junior officer recalled:

> As far as the 3rd Battalion was concerned, the whole affair from the beginning appeared to be rushed. This was seen in the little time allowed officers to impart to the other ranks the meagre information received about the essential features of the attack, and in the belated issue of bombs, flares, etc.[10]

A senior New Zealand officer recorded similar misgivings in his diary:

> We all hope for the best tomorrow, but I do not feel as confident as usual. Things are being rushed too much. The weather is rotten, the roads very bad, and the objectives have not been properly bombarded. However, we will hope for the best.[11]

The hasty preparations affected the troops, including an often ignored unit, the New Zealand machine-gunners. Describing preparations for the attack as 'hasty and imperfect', the official history of this unit clearly indicates plans and decisions were constantly changed until the last minute before the attack. This forced the machine-gunners to prepare three different sets of fire plans and orders, a time-consuming and frustrating task. The final set of orders was not complete until 2 p.m. on 11 October, which meant 'barely thirteen hours were left to the Commanders to get ready for the operation'.[12] Only thirty-eight machine guns participated in the opening barrage, compared with the sixty used on 4 October.[13]

The New Zealanders also knew artillery support would be far weaker than it had been on 4 October. The New Zealand artillery commander, Napier Johnston, was worried and warned Russell that little support would be available to the infantry. Russell noted in his diary on 11 October:

> Napier Johnston came to see me after lunch. The guns are all forward but he evidently feels uneasy about the attack — says preparation inadequate.[14]

The guns were not all forward. The problem was that, as a result of the gains of 4 October, most of the field artillery was now out of effective range (6000 yards) and would have to be moved well forward to be of any use. Because of the haste with which the attack was being thrown together and the dreadful conditions of the front, the enormous efforts being made to move the guns were mostly unsuccessful. The attack would take place with less than half the artillery support provided on 4 October and normally provided in an attack of this nature. Effective counter-battery fire had ceased from 4 October because of limited visibility and bad weather. Johnston plainly stated to Russell that effective artillery support for this next attack was not possible, but Russell ignored the information and did not pass it on to Second Army HQ or GHQ.

Not only were few field guns in position by 12 October, it took seventeen hours to move shells from the rear to the gun lines by pack animal. Each time an animal became stuck, its load of eight shells had to be removed and the animal dragged clear. The shells were then repacked and the animal loaded again for its next few steps. Then the whole exhausting process had to be repeated. A New Zealand sergeant saw a donkey loaded with two 18-pounder shell cases fall into a shell hole where it 'sank like quicksand'. Even probing the hole with 6-foot rods failed to find the donkey. It had sunk without trace.[15] A New Zealand gunner later wrote:

> I knew the ground around our guns as I had been there daily with
> ammunition and I knew how impossible it was to move the guns
> in time for the second attempt. Horses were useless in such mud
> so the guns had to be inched forward by manpower — pulled out
> of the muddy water in one shell hole to slide into another.[16]

Brigadier Hart noted in his diary that many of the guns 'had been
unable to get forward to their proper positions and were stuck in the mud
at all angles along the road between their original and their new lines'.[17]

For an attack of this magnitude each artillery battery usually had
thousands of rounds at its disposal. Yet on 12 October most were lucky to
have a few hundred. This was especially true of the heavy artillery. Captain
Rogers recalled meeting an artillery forward observation officer who was
very concerned about the uncut wire and the lack of heavy ammunition:

> . . . he was of the opinion that the stunt should be held up for two
> days longer. I was of the same opinion and I did get notice that
> the stunt would be on the 14th, but HQ is HQ, and the stunt went
> over on the 12th. I can only say it was a failure, the heavies never
> got up half the ammunition they should have.[18]

With such problems being experienced with the field artillery, there
could be no question of moving the heavy artillery until the ground
hardened.

Another problem was the lack of stable platforms for the forward guns
owing to the state of the ground. Proper gun platforms consisted of a
double deck of hardwood supported by a solid foundation of fascines
and road metal. It took two days to make such a platform and a plank
road connecting it to the main roadway for supplying ammunition. Even
then, many platforms remained unstable,[19] and their guns were useless
after firing a few rounds as the recoil pushed them even deeper into the
mud. Moreover, the limited supplies of ammunition had to be carefully

cleaned before they could be fired — every single artillery shell. Ironically, given the state of the weather, clean water for this purpose was also in short supply.

The attack aimed to take Passchendaele village, a task given to 3rd Australian Division with the New Zealanders protecting their exposed flank. The Fifth Army's 9th Division was on the New Zealanders' left flank. The direction of the attack was north-easterly, and the attacking divisions were allocated unrealistic objectives, requiring an advance of more than 3000 yards, a distance not considered possible even in dry weather. This was 1000 yards more than any of Plumer's previous three advances, and this attack would be made in abysmal weather with only two days of preparation! The Australian official historian was critical of Godley about the depth of the attack:

> Had Godley really known the conditions of October 9th . . . how could he have hoped for success with deeper objectives than any since July 31st, shorter preparation, and with the infantry asked to advance at a pace unattempted in the dry weather of September?[20]

Godley planned the advance in three phases. The first objective, the Red Line, was 1200 yards from the start line. The second, the Blue Line, was more than a mile from the start line and 1000 yards beyond the first objective. The final objectives, the Green Dotted Line and the Green Line, were about 800 yards in advance of the Blue Line and 400 yards beyond Passchendaele village. The 3rd Australian Division would use its 10th and 9th Brigades to take the village, while the New Zealanders used their 3rd (Rifle) and 2nd Brigades to take Bellevue and Goudberg Spurs on the Australians' left flank. Goudberg Spur, which the New Zealanders would not even see on the morning of 12 October, was designated as their main objective. To reach it they would have to advance over the Gravenstafel Ridge, down into the small Ravebeek Valley, cross the Strombeke stream and then advance up the slopes of the two spurs, wading through thick mud and into the driving rain and gale-force winds. Bellevue Spur was

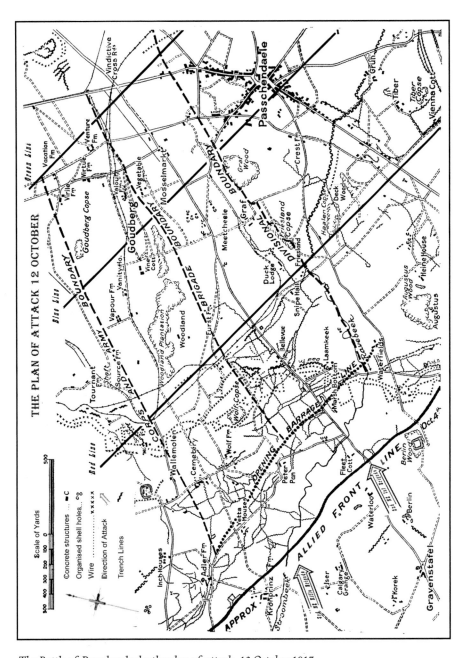

The Battle of Passchendaele: the plan of attack, 12 October 1917.

about 1000 yards from the New Zealand positions and projected from the Passchendaele Ridge into the Ravebeek Valley. The German positions there were well protected by the many concrete pillboxes on the crest of the spur, by concealed machine-gun posts and by two formidable and continuous belts of wire entanglements, more than 30 feet thick. A New Zealand gunner recalled:

> The whole country side was dotted with these Boxes, walls 6 ft thick of reinforced concrete, not many of them were hit. Each one had been a fort on its own with barbed wire right around it and loops for machine guns on each side.[21]

These obstacles were well known to all senior commanders, including General Russell, on the eve of the attack. The day of 11 October was described as 'ominously quiet' by one New Zealand history, which also noted that 'The great belts of wire ahead were apparent to the most casual observer.'[22] Gazing across no-man's-land in the dawn's growing light on 12 October, one New Zealand soldier noted in his diary that 'it was possible to discern the chief details of the slope above us, the broken trees, the torn ground, and on the summit "pill-boxes", black and threatening'.[23] Patrols sent out on the night of 10–11 October by 2nd Otago, including one led by the legendary Sergeant Dick Travis, revealed the extent of the entanglements, but little action was taken. Travis reported:

> No-man's-land is in very bad order — one mass of huge shell holes three parts full of water, a large amount of old wire entanglements scattered about makes it very awkward for patrolling. It is very heavy to patrol on account of the ground being so ploughed up by shell-holes. It is very hard to keep your feet as it is so slippery . . . The enemy posn just below sky line commands a great field of Machine Gun fire and the observation is excellent.[24]

Other patrols revealed the extent of the entanglements: 30 yards thick and well protected by many pillboxes and hidden machine-gun posts along the Flanders I Line. Sergeant Travis detected eight pillboxes in 2nd Otago Battalion's sector alone, the nearest only 150 yards from its forward posts.[25]

This came as bad news to the attacking brigades, and attempts to cut the wire using heavy artillery were half-hearted at best and produced poor results. Prior to the successful attack on Messines in June, General Haig had told Plumer: 'No attack should even commence until the barbed wire has been cut.'[26] Ignoring this sensible precaution would now doom the New Zealanders to failure.

Little wonder morale in the attacking brigades was low. The state of the New Zealand Rifle Brigade illustrates the severity of the situation. Its men were exhausted by a month's backbreaking work, often under fire, burying more than 60,000 yards of cable and constructing more than 30,000 yards of banking 3 to 6 feet high.[27] They had not completed any training whatsoever in preparation for this attack. The brigade's official history reveals:

> It would be idle to pretend that the prospect of an engagement within a few days could be regarded with absolute equanimity. Battalion commanders knew only too well how much their men were in need of both rest and training . . . but since September 4th they had been almost continuously employed at the trying and wearing work of cable burying and road-making, well up in the Ypres Salient. These duties had entailed long marches over difficult shell-hole country; and most of the work had been done at night, and sometimes in gas masks under shell-fire. Exactly 200 casualties had been sustained. The weather, at first fair, became bitterly cold, and as the men had neither blankets nor warm underclothing, they got little sleep. Throughout the period they had literally slaved at their tasks, and now they were almost worn out and certainly unready for immediate combative action.[28]

One wonders whether Russell knew of the condition of this brigade and, if he did, why he foolishly insisted on committing it to the forthcoming battle.

Both New Zealand brigades suffered seriously from the exhausting march to the front, the miserable weather conditions, the sight of the great masses of unbroken wire now facing them and the knowledge that the previous attack had failed, with heavy losses. One New Zealand history noted:

> There was overwhelming and gruesome evidence of the disastrous results of the British attack launched on the 9th. To say nothing of the dead, scores of men, wounded and near to death, still lay out over the country, unattended and without protection from the weather.[29]

Those New Zealanders making the attack on 12 October glumly realised that the difficulties ahead were formidable and their prospects of survival poor. General Gough also knew their prospects of success were minimal. On the evening of 11 October he telephoned Plumer and asked him to postpone the attack until the weather improved. Plumer refused to consider this request and insisted the attack commence on time the next morning.

The New Zealanders again planned to use two brigades: 2nd New Zealand Infantry Brigade, commanded by Brigadier W.G. Braithwaite, and 3rd New Zealand Rifle Brigade, temporarily commanded by Lieutenant Colonel A.E. Stewart. Each brigade was to attack on a narrow front of 750 yards, but the attack was to be made to considerable depth with a battalion being allocated to each separate objective.

2nd Brigade planned to use 2nd Otago Battalion to take the Red Line, to be followed by 1st Otago allocated the Blue Line, while 1st Canterbury received the task of securing the Dotted Green and Green Lines. 2nd Canterbury served as the brigade reserve, with each company allotted a specific task. Each battalion, other than the lead one, was to leapfrog the others once they were established at their objectives. 3rd Brigade, on the far left of II Anzac Corps, also using the leapfrog system, allocated the first objective to 2nd Battalion, to be followed up by 3rd Battalion, with the final objective allocated to 1st Battalion. The assembly for the attack commenced under cover of darkness on the evening of 11 October, so most units were in position by dawn of the twelfth.

The attack opened at 5.25 a.m., 'Barely daylight. A cold, miserable morning.'[30] The opening barrage was so weak and erratic many of the infantry barely noticed it. It was universally condemned by the battalions that took part as 'very feeble'.[31] Worse still, many shells dropped short, landing among the New Zealand infantry and causing death and chaos. One soldier recorded:

> Through some blunder our artillery barrage opened up about two hundred yards short of the specified range and thus opened right in the midst of us. It was a truly awful time — our own men getting cut to pieces in dozens by our own guns. Immediate disorganisation followed.[32]

A sniper with one of the Otago battalions recalled the 'terrible affair' at Passchendaele when the guns of the artillery had sunk into the mire: 'We were firing into our own men, that's how bad it was.'[33] Soldiers in 10th Company of 1st Otago Battalion, for example, were killed by their own artillery shells when still 100 yards behind the starting tape.[34]

This weak artillery protection resulted from the lack of guns forward, the impossible task of establishing stable platforms for the few that were, and the scanty ammunition supply. After firing each round the guns had to be realigned, which affected the density of the barrage. At eight minutes per 100 yards, the rate of advance of the barrage was much too fast for the hapless infantry, and those shells that did land in front of them became buried in mud, showering the pillboxes with fountains of mud but doing little real damage. As one account stated, 'Naturally neither the inaccuracy of the fire nor the scanty sprinkling of shells tended to increase the confidence of the infantry.'[35] General Russell later wrote of the barrage on the New Zealand sector:

> . . . owing to the state of the ground after wet weather, only a proportion of the guns had been able to get into position, so that the fire was weak and patchy, and at places it was almost impossible to see the barrage.[36]

The New Zealand official historian commented: '. . . it was at once apparent that the infantry must rely on their own efforts'.[37] Despite the obvious lack of protection, the infantry advanced from their shelters to be met by a storm of hot metal.

The enemy artillery burst into life as the infantry moved forward. So did the much more dangerous German machine-gun barrage, which sprayed the front of the hillside and the Ravebeek Valley. Each German machine gun spat out between 300 and 450 rounds a minute, and there were hundreds in action that morning. They swept the assaulting infantry from both flanks and from their immediate front. According to an eyewitness, they 'rattled through belt after belt while the New Zealanders fell by the scores'.[38] A veteran of the battle recalled:

> Machine gun fire. That makes your ears ring if you're close to it. When it cracks in your ears it's very close. Both ears were ringing there on Passchendaele.[39]

The official history of the New Zealand Rifle Brigade praises the German defence:

> The enemy's reliance on his machine-gun barrage, however, was not misplaced, for here was a perfect example of the use of machine-guns in the defence, an intense and deadly grazing cross-fire sweeping the front of both the New Zealand Brigades.[40]

2nd Brigade jumped off at Waterloo Farm, on a bend in the Gravenstafel road. 2nd Otago Battalion struggled across Marsh Bottom, waist deep in mud, unable to move beyond a slow shuffle. The attack initially seemed to make progress, and the first farms fell, although New Zealand artillery shells dropping short caused considerable casualties. The Otagos then reached the top of the first ridge and saw, with dismay and shock, the uncut wire at the Gravenstafel road some 25 to 50 yards wide. This wire was well protected by machine-gun fire from undamaged pillboxes beyond. The only gap was on the Gravenstafel road itself, but this was a death trap, protected by heavy machine-gun fire from both sides. It was 'a veritable lane of death'.[41] The wire proved an impenetrable obstacle and many men from this gallant battalion died trying to get beyond it. As one of those who took part recalled with obvious pain:

> What was our dismay upon reaching almost to the top of the ridge to find a long line of practically undamaged German concrete machine gun emplacements with barbed wire entanglements in front of them fully fifty yards deep . . . Even then what was left of us made an attempt to get through the wire and a few actually penetrated as far as his emplacements only to be shot down as fast as they appeared. Dozens got hung up in the wire and shot down before their surviving comrades' eyes.[42]

At the end of the day this soldier's 180-strong company had no surviving officers, one sergeant, one corporal and thirty men. It had been cut to pieces. Other companies in the battalion suffered similar losses. A private soldier who 'hopped the bags' with 2nd Otago Battalion at 5.29 a.m. summarised the day's events:

> . . . attack a failure on acnt [account of] wire encountered. Casualties extremely heavy. Hun machine guns and snipers play havoc. Absolute hell . . . Brigade practically wiped out.[43]

By 6 a.m. it became clear that 2nd Otago could get no further, but 1st Otago joined its sister battalion at the wire and tried to push through. Men tried to crawl under the entanglements, and some actually got beyond the first two belts of wire to within yards of the German pillboxes. Two junior officers died while valiantly attempting to hurl their Mills bombs through the loopholes of the boxes. Very heavy casualties occurred in these courageous attempts to get beyond the wire. The left company of 1st Otago was cut from 140 to twenty-eight men, with every officer either killed or wounded.

To the deadly volume of machine-gun fire was added the crackle of well-concealed German snipers hiding in shell holes and behind tree stumps, who also exacted a heavy toll. A soldier of 4th Company of 1st Otago who survived the attack recalled that 'you couldn't see any enemy . . . never even saw a German there. But they were there and the German snipers were just having a field day.' When his close friend next to him was killed by a sniper, the soldier threw himself into a hollow in the ground and stayed there. This undoubtedly saved his life:

> The snipers just simply had a day out. They were on the alert all the time and any man that moved, I must have seen a dozen men killed that way just dodging to what they thought was a better position.[44]

When the men of 4th Company were able to withdraw under cover of darkness only thirty-four remained of the morning's 140.

The company on the right of 1st Otago suffered heavy casualties from two pillbox fortresses. The Otagos took the pillboxes and over eighty prisoners in hand-to-hand fighting, mainly through the sheer heroism of Second Lieutenant A.R. Cockerell, but his platoon was wiped out in the process.

1st Canterbury Battalion joined the two Otago battalions at the wire, but the New Zealanders could still not break through. The Canterburies lost their headquarters, probably to a New Zealand artillery shell dropping short, a few minutes after crossing the start tape. Wiped out in this one tragic blow were the CO, Lieutenant Colonel George King, the RSM and the entire staff of the battalion's headquarters. One soldier stated that while they could have taken Messines 'with a wet sack', Passchendaele was an entirely different matter: 'In less than no time we were practically extinct — they had wiped us out . . . All our crowd got killed [in] my section.'[45] Another soldier recorded, somewhat laconically, in his diary:

> Arrived 1st position 7 am wet through and covered with mud, latter knee deep. Moved on after spell, across flat swept by Fritz's machine guns which caused a fair amount of casualties. Dug in for life . . .

Things very lively and heavy stuff all around. Raining: retired to
our 1st position . . . at 5 pm and dug in for the night . . . Wet night
and mud nearly knee deep. In open trench but dozed a little.[46]

For Harry Highet, a junior officer of 1st Canterbury Battalion, one
of only seven to survive the attack out of the twenty-three officers of
the battalion who had started, the events of the day had a rather surreal
quality. Describing himself as 'acting entirely by the sub-conscious', Highet
at first thought he was advancing through a large field of pumpkins, then
'realised they were the packs of dead soldiers I could see'.[47] Percy Williams,
a soldier in 1st Canterbury Battalion, recalled seeing dead and dying all
around him at the start line but felt he had left this 'fringe of death' behind
him when he managed to get some yards beyond the starting positions.[48]
He grimly realised his mistake when he reached the formidable pillboxes
and belts of wire on the crest of the slope. He records: 'One saw the
Otago Battalion melt away; then as the Canterbury's moved in, they too
were mown down ruthlessly.'[49] A private in 13th Company witnessed his
whole section 'mowed down to a man, to a man. What a hell of a sight
that was.'[50]

Back at Brigade Headquarters, Signaller Leonard Leary witnessed
an attempt to renew the advance, but 'as soon as the men got to their
feet machine guns opened up and it was just like a scythe going along
the line'.[51] Every unit of 2nd Brigade had now flung itself at the enemy
and suffered in this harvest of death. Party after party of New Zealand
infantry 'undauntedly threw themselves against the impenetrable wire,
raked by the heaviest machine-gun fire',[52] some even reaching as close
as 15 yards from the pillboxes. But not one soldier managed to get right
through the wire. Private David Grant recalled how, during the advance,
'the boys were dropping on all sides' so that he reached the wire with
only one other member of his infantry company, who soon fell victim
to a sniper's explosive bullet. After the attack, only thirty-two of Private
Grant's company remained, and only six from his platoon.[53] The infantry
of this brigade had been cut down in droves and their attack had clearly
failed. The survivors of the three battalions dug in where they could.

The Rifle Brigade, on the far left of II Anzac, led off with 2nd Battalion, which had experienced great difficulty reaching its start line and arrived in a state of exhaustion. It had been on the move since 1 a.m. One soldier later lamented: 'It was raining and things were in a Hell of a mess. I fell down innumerable times and it was all I could do to get up.'[54] The lead troops set off at 5.25 a.m., taking each obstacle one at a time. Rifleman Jervis advanced from the start line at 6 a.m. and noticed 'a fair number had been smacked as I went up . . . Machine gun and rifle fire was very hot.'[55]

After taking the Wallemolen cemetery on the left, Wolf Farm in the centre fell, but the battalion could get no further. Ahead of them lay a line of pillboxes, impervious behind a sea of barbed wire and deep mud, with even more concrete fortresses on the slightly higher ground beyond those to their immediate front. Each pillbox had a strong garrison, and machine-gun rounds poured from the fire positions. These, and enfilade fire from the crest of Bellevue on the right, halted all forward momentum and forced the battalion to dig in at Wolf Farm just after 8 a.m.

3rd Battalion tried to leapfrog this position and made almost 150 yards through the swamp, where it attracted heavy fire, which forced it also to dig in. There were heavy casualties when 1st Battalion reached them. One officer from 1st Battalion managed to penetrate some 200 yards into the German lines before 'he was shot to pieces'.[56] All battalions would remain in these positions for two 'cold, wet and miserable nights'.[57]

An excellent account of the disaster was written by Corporal Harold Green of C Company, 3rd Battalion New Zealand Rifle Brigade:

> At 6 am a tremendous bombardment opened and we went over in a sea of mud. The fire from the German pill boxes was hellish and our barrage failed. The emplacements for the guns were not solid enough and the guns tilted causing trouble in our ranks from the shells of our own 18 pounders. The barbed wire entanglements, the mud and the pill boxes prevented any success. C Company lost heavily and the 3rd Battalion lost about half its number in casualties. Our Colonel, Winter-Evans, was killed. 150 of C Company went

over and casualties numbered 82, including all the sergeants except Goodfellow. The attack was an impossible attempt. The ground was swampy and very muddy and the heavy cross fire from the pill boxes did not give us a chance. The Black Watch on our left were in exactly the same position. The stunt should never have been ordered under such conditions. It was absolute murder.[58]

More than eighty years later, Mr Bright Williams of Havelock North recalled the death of Colonel Winter-Evans. As battalion runner, Rifleman Williams had just been sent by the colonel to locate the adjutant and inform him where the battalion HQ was:

Well I went so far and a machine gun got me. So he [Winter-Evans] said 'All right, I'll see what I can do.' And away he went. And they got him. It cut the artery on the inside of his leg and he was fading away when two of our C Company Signallers came on him and he said, 'You boys stop with me. I might want you'. He was going then. So they went about their own business as soon as he was gone.[59]

A party of six men and an NCO from 3rd Battalion later spent three hours after the attack trying to locate Winter-Evans' body. They never found it.[60]

Some of the casualties in 3rd Battalion resulted from snipers who lay concealed and waited for the infantry to advance before shooting them from behind. Lieutenant George Brunton, the only officer left in the battalion, was hit in the side by a sniper's bullet and initially believed his spine had been shattered:

That's a lovely way to end your life. I'd been shot in the spine from a bullet that had come from the back of me.[61]

Receiving confirmation from his batman that the wound was serious but not life-threatening, Lieutenant Brunton met Lieutenant Colonel

Puttick on the battlefield and was ordered to report to an RAP.

Corporal Duthie, also of 3rd Battalion, recalled in his diary an experience that must have been commonplace:

> We moved forward 6 am through that awful sea of mud until held up by machine gun fire. Hit in left shoulder about 8:30 am. Could not get out until 2 pm. Arrived at dressing station where we had tea and soup. A God send.[62]

While Corporal Duthie suffered an agonising wait of almost six hours until he could receive basic medical attention, he could be counted as fortunate among the New Zealand wounded. Some had to wait days before reaching an RAP.

Corporal A.D. Bridge wrote a detailed account of his horrific experiences in a letter to his wife in New Zealand. He described how 3rd Battalion had been on fatigues for more than a month prior to 12 October 'and this job alone was enough to make the hardest of men tired and knocked up'. The barrage that opened at 5.25 a.m. was 'like all hell let loose' but was obviously inadequate: '. . . we could see gaps in the line of advancing fire even then and guessed that a gun or two was missing'. Corporal Bridge led his section forward behind the other two battalions of the Rifle Brigade. At the foot of the Passchendaele Ridge their problems began:

> All went well until we commenced the incline up the ridge. Then it was that we all became literally bogged. One leg would sink to the knee and many seconds were lost each step pulling it out . . . Our barrage was well ahead of us as we started up the hill. Too far unfortunately and it was seen that it had gone past the Hun 'pill boxes' and left them unharmed. Now was Fritz's chance. He opened on us with every available machine gun and sniper. Comrades fell by the dozen so I decided to plant my section in a shell hole and go forward myself to investigate.

Corporal Bridge found New Zealand troops at the brigade's first objective, but machine-gun fire and poor artillery protection prevented them from advancing further. Realising open movement was suicidal, Corporal Bridge kept his section in the shell hole until it could withdraw to the rear after nightfall. From there he and his section volunteered to help shift the hundreds of wounded men from the battlefield, 'the hardest task in the Army'. Corporal Bridge later stated bluntly to his wife:

> Never before has there been so many casualties to NZers . . . The whole affair was horrible from start to finish and a great sacrifice of life.

Bridge also noted in this revealing letter that he was 'very thankful to God that I am here today able to write to you as a sound and able man'.[63] He had been through the fires of Passchendaele and escaped unharmed, but just over one month later he was not so lucky. The popular and gallant corporal fell to a sniper's bullet while on a minor raid on 25 November 1917.

At 8 a.m. Lieutenant Colonel Puttick arrived at Wolf Farm and immediately grasped the extent of the tragedy. He ordered the three battalions to dig in where they were and decided not to commit the reserve battalion (1st Battalion). He quickly realised progress would be impossible, as any movement brought immediate fire. The battalions dug in along the hill and along Marsh Bottom with fewer than 500 men. The machine-gun fire on the Rifle Brigade's front was so great that, at one stage, all went quiet as the guns stopped for twenty minutes, their supplies of ammunition exhausted.[64]

While the New Zealanders could not pass beyond the wire and the German pillboxes, 3rd Australian Division advanced about 1000 yards but became bogged in the mud of the Ravebeek Valley below Passchendaele, just short of its first objective. There it suffered withering flanking fire from Bellevue Spur. Twenty Australians from 38th Battalion actually reached the ruins of the church at Passchendaele, but were forced to withdraw. General Monash blamed the failure on the state of the ground, the lack of adequate artillery support, the lack of time for preparation and the inclement weather. He believed the plan could have worked only if the weather had been fine and 48 hours of preparation time available to the attacking divisions. He condemned the decision to proceed on 12 October as 'hare-brained'.[65] His 3rd Australian Division casualties numbered 3200, or 62 per cent of those involved, similar to the New Zealand losses. The 4th Australian Division also had 1000 casualties.

New Zealand losses for the morning's action were catastrophic, reaching to nearly 3000 within a few hours. The attack carried the British positions forward from their original line 500 yards on the left and 200 yards on the right. Many New Zealanders had died to make these paltry gains. More than 800 bodies lay in swathes about the wire, buried in the marsh and along the road. The ratio of killed to wounded was unusually high if those listed as missing are added to the numbers killed. Most of those listed as missing had in fact been killed, but their bodies were never located.[66] The death toll reached 846, nearly a third of the total casualty figure, and probably reflects the care taken by the Germans to prepare their killing zone as well as the influence of the well-trained, extremely efficient snipers. One New Zealand soldier testified: 'The marksmanship of the Hun Snipers was deadly.'[67] Over the next week a further 138 New Zealand soldiers died of their wounds.[68] This is 'a loss unequalled by any other disaster in the nation's history'.[69] It makes 12 October 1917 the single bloodiest day in New Zealand's military history.

Despite these losses, the extent of which he had yet to learn, General Russell, believing 3rd Australian Division had secured its objectives and now had a dangerously exposed left flank, ordered the attack to start again at 3 p.m. There now occurred a clash of commanders on the battlefield which many troops believed was responsible for the removal of Brigadier Braithwaite from command of 2nd Brigade. When Braithwaite received the message to renew the attack at 3 p.m., 'all COs in consultation with the Brigade Major . . . were unanimous that such an operation was impossible under the existing conditions'. Two of his COs communicated to him by note and telephone, making it clear their men were exhausted, the ground

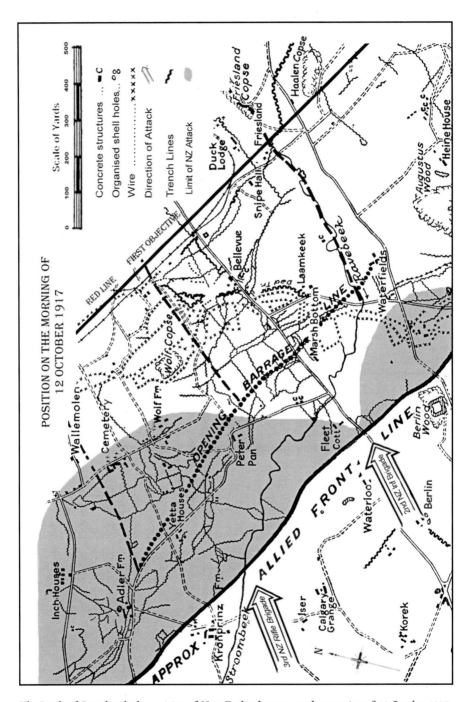

The Battle of Passchendaele: position of New Zealand troops on the morning of 12 October 1917.

was impossible to cross, casualties were very heavy, especially amongst the officers, and the men were trapped at the wire.[70] A battalion war diary recorded: '. . . such an attempt would be absolutely disastrous . . . To advance against it [the uncut wire] would have meant practically annihilation of the Brigade.'[71] One of the New Zealand official histories is also emphatic that those on the spot agreed that 'any attempt to renew the attack would be suicidal'.[72]

Braithwaite told Russell this via a signal at 1.45 p.m.:

> Have consulted my Commanding Officers on the spot and am of opinion that owing to very severe casualties and especially among officers and also to the close proximity of our men to the German wire it is impossible for this Brigade to continue the attack without incurring abnormal additional losses. Reorganisation is absolutely out of the question in daylight owing to snipers and machine gun fire and my men are so closely dug in under the enemy wire that the heavy bombardment of the Pill Boxes is also impossible.[73]

Braithwaite was therefore somewhat shocked when, 'In spite of this message, the G.O.C. Division ordered the advance to take place at 3 pm.'[74] This later changed at 2.10 p.m. to an attack using only 3rd New Zealand Rifle Brigade on the left. The battalion commanders of this brigade, however, 'with their first-hand knowledge of the situation, were unanimous in their opinion as to the fruitlessness of any immediate attempt to get forward',[75] and were relieved when the order to renew the attack was cancelled at the very last minute once the true state of progress on the 3rd Australian and 9th Division front was revealed.

Russell glumly noted the day's results in his diary:

> Attacked this morning at daybreak — we, and indeed all other divisions, were held up from start by M.G. Evidently the artillery preparation was insufficient, the barrage poor, and it goes to show the weakness of haste — our casualties are heavy, Geo King amongst others — I am very sad.[76]

Evidence buried in the New Zealand archives, and the testimony of participants, reveal the Germans almost certainly knew the New Zealanders were to attack on the morning of 12 October and, as a result, the two New Zealand brigades walked into a well-prepared trap. Pinned down in no-man's-land by a German sniper who seemed to take a special interest in him, Lieutenant Harry Highet reflected that the Germans 'had had eight days to set this very obvious trap, his machine guns had the range of every prominent piece of dirt that might shelter an enemy'.[77] Yet there was more than good preparation evident in the Germans' response to the attack. They had been forewarned. A captured German document of 2nd Battalion, 29th Infantry Regiment, reveals in its morning report for 12 October that, 'At midnight a deserter (Scotsman) was brought in by 7 Coy 29 IR. He said that they had been since previous evening in line and would attack at 6 am.'[78] The division on the Rifle Brigade's left flank was the 9th Scottish Division, and the practice of receiving valuable information from deserters was not uncommon on either side.[79] Other evidence supports the view that the Germans were expecting the attack of 12 October and were well prepared to meet it. Brigadier Braithwaite noted in his report that on the night of the eleventh, 'The enemy . . . was very jumpy, and evidently expecting an attack, used a lot of flares.'[80] The intelligence report of II Anzac Corps also suspected the Germans had prior knowledge of the attack:

> It seems evident from a number of prisoners' statements that a large number of Machine Guns were actually in position prior to our attack, but with orders not to fire until the actual assault.

The report also noted that opposite the Corps were two Jaeger regiments, élite, fit troops with high morale and twice the number of machine guns of other German units; that is, seventy-two heavy and seventy-two light machine guns per regiment.[81]

A British newspaper history of the war also commented on the very large concentration of machine guns well prepared for the New Zealand attack and attributed it to a new German method of defence:

The shells thundered with less precision and density than usual along the main road running into Passchendaele village and swept the flanking ridges where the German commander had massed his men and machine-guns in extraordinary number, according to a new method of defence . . . As before explained, he [the enemy] had taken machine-gunners from reserves and supports, and placed them on the hills, hoping that sufficient would survive the British bombardment to check the attack. As the British bombardment was unexpectedly feeble, the German gunners survived in practically undiminished strength. They poured out such a fire between the Lekkerboterbeek and the Ravebeek as made the situation of the attacking troops impossible.[82]

This report is confirmed by a despatch from the distinguished war correspondent Philip Gibbs, which was also reported in New Zealand:

All the machine-guns from the supporting lines were sent to this front. The enemy had never massed so many machine-guns on his front. Many were posted in trees. There were never so many riflemen scattered among the shell craters. The machine-gun fire and rifle fire never ceased for an instant during the attack. Our men, floundering in the bogs, were unable to keep up with the barrage. The German snipers and gunners shot with a cool aim while our men struggled forward.[83]

No German commander would have denuded his reserves and support troops of their main firepower unless he had felt absolutely sure that something big was about to happen and that this firepower would be desperately needed. The evidence is therefore overwhelming that the German commanders knew an attack was due on the morning of 12 October and they had prepared themselves accordingly. One of the New Zealanders in the attack later stated: 'We should never have been sent there. They were so ready for it that we never got any distance . . . Oh, it was slaughter. They had everything all ready.'[84]

The deaths of the two senior officers, Lieutenant Colonel George King of 1st Canterbury Battalion, and Lieutenant Colonel Winter-Evans of 3rd Rifle Battalion, were 'both very great losses' to the Division, according to General Godley.[85] This is especially true of Lieutenant Colonel King, an outstanding commanding officer who had only joined 1st Canterbury at the end of August 1917. King had been the first CO of the New Zealand (Maori) Pioneer Battalion, and only through his outstanding leadership had that disparate organisation become an effective military unit and the great asset it now was to the New Zealand Division.[86] King's death is recorded with some shock and deep regret in the war diary of the Pioneer Battalion, which when the battle was over, recovered his body and buried it in front of the ramparts of the ruins of Ypres. A witness to the tangi recorded:

> I do not think I will ever forget that service, a cloudless sky and an aeroplane scrap overhead, the shallow grave, the body sewn in a blanket and covered with the New Zealand flag, the surpliced Padre, the short impressive burial service and finishing up with the beautiful Maori lament for a fallen chief, 'Piko nei te Matenga' ['When our heads are bowed with woe'] sung by the Maoris present, and with its beautiful harmonies and perfect tune, it seemed to me the most feeling tribute they could offer.[87]

General Russell also attended King's tangi and later described him in his diary as 'a fine good man, one of the best who lies buried in Ypres'.[88] The New Zealand Division had indeed lost many fine, good men in this battle.

Evacuating the thousands of casualties from the battlefield proved a nightmare for the wounded and the stretcher-bearers alike, a slow, difficult task. It took eight men to manage each stretcher on an agonising 3½-mile journey to the nearest dressing station. As one soldier recorded: 'The wounded have had a rotten spin so far, many have died from exposure and a lot were shelled when down at the dressing station and killed.'[89]

The wounded George Brunton, ordered back to the RAP by Puttick, felt shocked on reaching it:

There . . . must have been a hundred men lying there on stretchers and as the shells would come over I could see them shiver. Boy, they could hear the shells coming over and landing.

One particular case haunted Brunton for the rest of his life. A man whose leg had been shot off turned green from gas gangrene:

And I saw him die. [Mr Brunton broke down here.] Oh boy, you know it's a terrible war, a terrible war. To see all those men lying there.[90]

Linus Ryan recalled being sent out as part of a four-man team to bring in a man with a serious leg wound:

Not a dozen steps had we taken before the whole squad were bogged to our thighs in clinging slime. We rested the stretcher on the mud, whilst the two leaders extricated themselves then shoved the stretcher forward a few yards and waited whilst the bearers in the rear crawled out of the slime. It took us over an hour to bring that man a distance of 300 yards . . . Every step you would sink to the knees at least , and when without warning you struck a bad patch, you would feel yourself sink, sink and wonder if you were ever going to stop. Then the struggle would begin and pushing and sliding the stretcher along the surface we would fight to regain the comparative solidity of knee deep mud. It was gruelling heart-breaking work.[91]

Little wonder one New Zealand official history stated that 'the plight of the wounded was particularly pitiful'.[92] The plight of the stretcher-bearers was hardly much better.

The stretcher-bearers of the Army Medical Corps worked the rest of the day and throughout the night to clear the wounded from the battlefield. Yet there were not enough of them. On 13 October, during an informal armistice, more than 3000 extra troops, 1600 from 4th Brigade and 1000 from 49th Division, went forward to remove the wounded of both sides.

One of the bearers from 4th Brigade was the Otago soldier Gordon Neill, who had experienced a rough time in the previous attack. With a party of eight men, Neill stumbled upon a wounded English soldier with both legs broken by shell-fire. He had lain out in the rain and cold for three long days. It took Neill and the others twelve hours to move him to the nearest advanced dressing station, whereupon Neill, himself wounded in the arm, collapsed in the mud and slept for three hours.[93] Neill later learned that his eldest brother, an ambulance driver in the New Zealand Medical Corps, had received a very severe head wound and been left with a mate in a shell hole waiting for the stretcher-bearers to collect them:

> They never found the body of the man who was left behind and my brother was reported missing, missing for ages and ages and ages, and eventually missing believed killed, so eventually the final of it was when he was buried in Tyne Cot cemetery on the Passchendaele ridge.[94]

At the Casualty Clearing Station (CCS) at Waterloo Farm there were nearly five hundred stretcher cases lying around the German pillboxes, sinking into the mud and exposed to the driving rain and hail, 'just dying there where they were dumped off'.[95] Some of these lay in the open for three days. On 14 October Brigadier Braithwaite could not stand to see these men suffer any more. He made a personal appeal to Russell to have the last seventy-five of them moved, which duly happened at noon that day.[96] The same conditions prevailed around the CCS at Kron Prinz Farm.

Gunner Alfred Stratton volunteered for work as a stretcher-bearer and was able to observe the ground over which the infantry had been expected to advance:

> There was a flat muddy bog in front of our trenches and the ground sloped uphill to some pill boxes which completely dominated the position; as our shell fire had not reached these concrete shelters

or the barbed wire entanglements, what chance had our infantry to get out of that mud and climb that bare hill against machine gun fire? It was just pure murder.[97]

Sidney Stanfield, the young boy who had taken part in the earlier New Zealand attack, also worked as a stretcher-bearer after the attack of 12 October. He remembered they 'just carried till you couldn't carry any more. You just went until you couldn't walk really. You just went until you couldn't walk.'[98] By the afternoon of 16 October all surviving wounded had finally been evacuated. It had taken four days of backbreaking work. The stretcher-bearers were physical wrecks:

> Our feet were so swollen and painful that we had to cut our boots off, and not one of us could raise our voice above the merest whisper. Our uniform was concealed beneath a solid casing of mud to our arm pits. Bloodshot eyes shone from haggard faces, so that we could hardly recognise ourselves in a mirrored reflection. Every bone and muscle ached with pain.[99]

Despite the magnificent efforts of the stretcher-bearers, evacuation from the battlefield did not necessarily guarantee survival; it was only the first step. A nurse working at No. 3 Australian CCS, near Poperinghe, noted despairingly: 'I thought I had seen terific [sic] wounds and badly gassed Patients untill [sic] I looked in the resuscitation ward at the CCS. The poor boys came in and died like Flies.'[100]

Both 2nd and 3rd Brigades were relieved on the night of 14 October and the pitifully few survivors faced another weary journey to the rear. One soldier described the relief as 'a hellish experience coming out thro mud, arrive in middle of night . . . Absolutely done when arrived out. Mud from head to foot.'[101]

The responses of Generals Russell and Godley to this tragedy reveal much about their characters. Inspecting the battlefield for the first time on 16 October, Russell felt shocked to see the heavy strands of wire clearly visible on the forward slope and the strength of the German positions on

Bellevue Spur. He was somewhat consoled when General Plumer visited him on 16 October and 'expressed his entire satisfaction with the way our men had fought and attributes no blame for our failure'.[102] Russell condemned the attack on Bellevue Spur and blamed himself and his staff. His diary entry for 24 October recounts a conference at his headquarters, at which he explained the lessons of the two attacks at Passchendaele:

> The chief one [lesson], applying especially to Div. Staff and Self, is that under no circumstances in war is one justified in assuming anything which can possibly be verified — and that where there are certain known conditions necessary to success it is a great risk, however justifiable, to attack before they are fulfilled.[103]

As Russell wrote to Allen, the attack of 12 October, 'though not an entire failure, was very nearly so'. As to its cause Russell frankly accepted a large measure of blame:

> I am confident that our men would have got forward excepting for the insuperable difficulties of the wire. You cannot fight machine guns, plus wire, with human bodies. Without the wire to check them the men would have tackled machine guns in spite of their losses. As it was, they tried to tackle both. This was humanly impossible . . . We, as a Divisional Staff, assumed that the wire had been cut. Assumption in war is radically wrong if by any means in your power you can eliminate the uncertain. This, of course, is pure theory, but we made a mistake.[104]

As a result of an earlier portion of this letter explaining the weakness of the artillery barrage, Allen replied to Russell that: 'We regret this as much as you do, and personally I feel sure that no possible blame can be attached to the New Zealand Artillery.' He went on:

> Rumours have been circulating through parts of New Zealand that the situation was not properly appreciated and that it was known

to some senior officers, at any rate, that it would be impossible for the Artillery to clear up the wire and to preserve the barrage as they had done in previous attacks. I quite understand your position, namely, that your Divisional staff assumed the wire had been cut, and I lay no blame on you, nor indeed do I blame anybody, but there is a feeling of unrest and I have it myself. There is no use denying it.[105]

Russell replied: 'I hope you do not think that I throw any blame on the New Zealand Artillery for our failure on Bellevue Spur. That would be the last impression I would wish to convey.' Russell also reported to Allen with much relief that the New Zealand Division had now left Ypres which he regarded as 'a disgusting spot'.[106]

While accepting some responsibility for the disaster, as indeed he should, Russell also felt there were mitigating circumstances. At a conference of commanding officers held after the Passchendaele operations, Russell stated that the Division had not received timely and accurate information about the enemy's entanglements or the strength of his defences then facing the Division. He added that, even if this information had been available, it would have made no difference:

... even if the position had been known earlier, and it had been possible to make representations to G.H.Q. on the subject, he [Russell] doubted if the likelihood of the non-success of one Division would have effected any alteration in the programme already determined upon in respect of the fronts of two Armies.[107]

Russell was less than frank at this conference. The strength of the German positions and the depth of the German wire were known as a result of the abortive attack of 9 October. As many accounts testify, the wire was clearly visible to anybody who cared to visit the front-line positions. Russell did not do this until after the attack. When doubting whether the attack would be held up because of the qualms of one division, Russell was also on shaky ground. The New Zealand Division had been allocated a key role in the attack, and 3rd Australian Division could not possibly succeed in its thrust at Passchendaele village unless the New Zealanders were guarding its left flank. Before 12 October 1917, the New Zealanders had not experienced a military failure in France and, as a result, General Russell and his division had a formidable reputation. The recent triumphs at Messines and on 4 October at Gravenstafel had firmly cemented this. Any concerns or doubts expressed by Russell then were sure to be taken seriously by GHQ, no matter how unwelcome.

The point is that Russell never raised these doubts, nor did he bother to learn the true conditions under which he was expecting his men to fight. He was adhering to the British imperial system, like all other commanders at the time except Birdwood and Monash, and on 12 October this outdated approach failed the New Zealanders miserably. They were consequently forced to make an attack that lacked any possibility of success.

Godley's response, however, was different. Immediately after the attack he felt deeply affected by the disaster. Sergeant Wilson's diary entry of 14 October shows Godley was 'working day and night in his office lately and looks terrible worried over recent events'.[108] Even so, in his official correspondence dealing with the attacks of his corps at Passchendaele, Godley sought to minimise the casualties suffered while exaggerating the importance of the successes gained. Nowhere in this correspondence does he accept any responsibility for the failures of 9 and 12 October, nor does he acknowledge them as the disasters they truly were. Writing to the New Zealand Minister of Defence on 16 October, for example, he stated that in the 'big fight' of 12 October the New Zealand Division had had to attack 'a very difficult piece of country'. While they had gained about 500 yards of enemy territory, they 'did not quite succeed in getting it all'. He went on:

> . . . so, though not such a big success as Messines or the battle here of the 4th, it was a very good day's work, and the Division again did it excellently. The casualties were about the same as the last time, and the two added up together, though not unduly heavy,

necessitate the provision of a good many reinforcements . . . no troops, except British, could have attacked as our men did over such incredible difficulties in getting to their assembly positions, and starting as tired as they consequently did.[109]

The astute Allen, though, as revealed in his letters to Russell, was not deceived by Godley's dishonesty, and, in fact, remained appalled by the extent of the losses suffered on 12 October.

Writing to Lieutenant Colonel Clive Wigram, assistant private secretary to the King at Buckingham Palace, the ambitious Godley stated: 'I hope it may interest His Majesty to hear something of the performance of my Corps during our share of the advance on Passchendaele.' Detailing the three attacks, Godley claimed them as successes which amounted to a total advance for II Anzac of some 3000 yards. He continued:

> I hope and think [this success] will enable the Canadians, who are now taking over from us, to get into Passchendaele without undue difficulty. We are, of course, very disappointed at not getting into Passchendaele ourselves . . . The courage and tenacity of the men is beyond anything that one can describe. No other troops in the world could have attacked under such conditions as they did on the last two occasions, and, though all four Divisions are very exhausted, their spirit is very high, and in a very short time they will be quite fit to come in again where required.

In this letter Godley either lied or did not know about the true state of the divisions of his corps, especially that of the New Zealanders. With his extensive touring of the battlefield after 12 October, he must have seen the condition of the troops, so the former accusation is probably the correct one. Godley also stated in the same letter that the casualties were 'not unduly heavy'.[110] With the casualty rate for the New Zealand Division and 3rd Australian Division around 60 per cent, and as high as 85 per cent in some New Zealand units, this was an astounding statement to make.

Godley's letter did the trick, though. On 16 October, he received news that must have been music to his ears. Wigram wrote that the King and Queen 'are delighted to hear how well your Corps has done during the recent operations'.[111]

The attack of 12 October should never have gone ahead. It failed for many reasons: poor reconnaissance, the lack of time to prepare, the exhaustion of the troops involved, the weakness of the artillery support, the muddy terrain, and a forewarned enemy who prepared very strong defences utilising a maximum of firepower. That the attack should not have gone ahead under the conditions then prevailing was also the German view. Failing to detect the tragic irony in his statement, Godley had written to James Allen that a German officer, now a prisoner of war, saw the state of the road behind the front line and the lack of artillery and 'exclaimed in astonishment that no troops in the world would have attempted an offensive with such facilities of approach'.[112] The German officer was right. No troops in the world should have been made to attack in such unfavourable circumstances.

In the New Zealand sector the direct cause of the failure can be attributed to the unbroken wire entanglements through which the infantry, despite numerous attempts, could not break. These should have been destroyed by heavy artillery fire, but there were too few shells available for the heavy batteries to do a proper job and, of the few shells available, 'the heavies . . . had concentrated on the pill boxes and not the wire'.[113] General Russell remained adamant on the matter:

> The direct cause of failure was strong and continuous wire entanglements . . . the formidable nature of the wire entanglements in BELLEVUE was not known until the evening of the 11th by the Bde holding the line when a patrol report was received which fully disclosed it. This information 24 hours earlier would have been invaluable.[114]

A junior officer closer to the action believed there was another overriding cause for the failure:

There can be no doubt that the sole reason for the failure of the attack lay in the inefficient support given by the artillery in relation to the enemy machine gun positions. The German machine gunners had practically a free hand as they were unmolested by the artillery fire.[115]

Brigadier Hart, while not a participant, was a keen observer of the tragedy. The reasons for the New Zealand failure he recorded in his diary are remarkably detailed and astute:

This attack by the 2nd and 5th Armies on a 12 mile front was the most ambitious of the many made since 31 July last, and must be written down as a failure. Again it was the weather and not the enemy that rendered victory impossible. The country is now so absolutely shattered, ploughed up and pockmarked by shell fire, that movement is impossible beyond the roads trams and duckboard tracks we construct as we advance, unless the weather is dry.

There were 3 attacks within 9 days, the 4th, 9th and 12th. In the meantime much rain had fallen. Tanks, caterpillars, lorries, wagons, guns, mules and ammunition are stuck and were slowly being engulfed in the morass in all directions. Consequently the artillery preparation was incomplete. Uncut wire was met and was insurmountable under such conditions. Mud and wire prevented our men keeping up to the barrage. Hun machine gunners, protected in concrete pill boxes during the bombardment, came out with their machine guns after our barrage passed on and shot down our men while still struggling to get through and over the mud and wire.[116]

The failure of 12 October can never be blamed on lack of courage, tenacity or sheer heroism on the part of the troops who took part. The commander of the Rifle Brigade made this clear:

In conclusion, I cannot speak too highly of the splendid courage and devotion to duty of all ranks under my command, as they went into action in an exhausted condition and did everything that was humanly possible to attain success.[117]

A New Zealand stretcher-bearer remained in absolute awe of the infantry who had 'jumped the bags' on the morning of 12 October. This First Battle of Passchendaele

> . . . tells a story of almost unbelievable courage. Our citizen soldiers faced impossible odds. They knew what they were up against. They saw death staring them in the face — they saw no possible chance of success and with unfaltering courage, Officers and Men walked to their deaths, because it was their job.[118]

As the Australian official historian perceptively commented, given what faced the New Zealanders in the attack of 12 October, 'No infantry in the world could have succeeded.'[119] This was the New Zealand Division's one large-scale failure in Belgium, and the defeat was deeply felt.

The attack had almost mirrored that of 9 October, and was 'surely one of the lowest points in the British exercise of command'.[120] It was an unmitigated disaster without any redeeming qualities. As a British newspaper history described it:

> The result was in effect as serious as the reverse at Aubers Ridge in May 1915 . . . In both cases the urgency of the need for striking at the enemy seems to have prevented adequate preparation . . . there was again a failure in artillery power which prevented some of the most gallant forces in the world from achieving what they had fiercely determined they would do.[121]

What the newspaper history did not detail, however, was how many of these gallant soldiers, many of them Australians and New Zealanders, had died trying to fight this impossible battle.

The extent of the tragedy was never accurately reported in New

Zealand newspapers, which concentrated on the small nation's 'Honoured Place'[122] in the attack and blamed the lack of success on the weather: '. . . had the rain held off [they] would have gallantly reached and held their objectives'.[123] The attack was portrayed as a limited success rather than the absolute disaster it really was. The accounts reported in New Zealand also made light of the dreadful conditions the men were having to endure. A good example of this was a despatch from an Australian correspondent, Keith Murdoch:

> The correspondent of the United Press [Murdoch] says that the rain reduced the battlefield to a perfect quagmire, but the British and Anzacs navigated the mud seas and mud mountains like miracle men. He talked to Sir Douglas Haig yesterday. The British leader was full of admiration for the men, and said that the entire history of Flanders shows that mud is always the soldiers' worst enemy. This is true to a greater extent now than ever, because the natural drainage is stopped. Nevertheless the British troops from all over the Empire, and also the French, were undaunted by either mud or Germans. The Field-Marshal concluded that they were all simply splendid.[124]

Walking to the battlefield three days later with General Godley, Sergeant Wilson was shocked by what he and the general saw:

> I won't forget my experience today if I live for a thousand years . . . As we got further along we began to come to the part where all the recent fighting took place and where no salvaging had yet been done. Immense quantities of fighting material littered the ground. Graves were thick and bodies with only a few shovels full of earth protruded in every direction you looked and the further we advanced over the famous Abraham Heights the worse things got. Such a sight is impossible to describe. The Somme was pretty bad I'll admit but this is worse. I have never seen such destruction. It is hard to imagine that 4 years ago, peaceful people tilled this

same soil and that it was one of the most prosperous districts in Europe. Now, as I saw it today, well it's simply an awful nightmare, a hideous reeking swamp seething with living (and dead) beings. A place that stamps itself on one's mind and memory like a red hot iron.[125]

The New Zealand attack of 12 October 1917 was an intensely emotional and bitter experience for those who survived. Despite this experience now being all but lost to the New Zealand collective memory, the battle did leave an indelible mark on New Zealand, as if made by a red-hot iron. The following pages explore the destructive legacy of Passchendaele.

Chapter 5

The Legacy of Passchendaele

AFTER 12 OCTOBER 1917, THE Australians and New Zealanders were a spent force. Yet General Haig still refused to give up the offensive at Passchendaele. Six days later he brought in the Canadian Corps as the shock troops to finish the job. Haig had finally learned a valuable lesson from the disaster:

> The Army Commanders explained the situation; all agreed that mud and the bad weather prevented our troops getting on yesterday . . . We all agreed that our attack should only be launched when there is a fair prospect of fine weather. When the ground is dry no opposition which the enemy has put up has been able to stop our men.[1]

The Canadians planned to take in three stages what II Anzac Corps had been directed to achieve in just one. Given two weeks of preparation, the Canadians attacked on 26 October and took Bellevue Spur, before, on 30 October, securing Passchendaele village. On 6 November they went on to take Goudberg Spur (which had been the New Zealanders' final objective), and on 10 November they secured the last of the high ground. All attacks proved successful, but cost the Canadians 13,000 casualties, including 4000 killed, to take just over 3000 yards of ground.

The greatest land battle of 1917, a year of almost constant fighting for the British armies, was Third Ypres. There were eleven major attacks, five of them spearheaded by Anzac troops with the final four spearheaded by the Canadian Corps. In good conditions the Germans had no answer to the step-by-step approach employed by Plumer and were defeated each time. Yet by persisting when the weather was bad, and without adequate artillery support, these attacks petered out into costly failures. The six attempts in the mud and slime after 4 October 'made the name of this battle one to shudder at'.[2]

The fighting around Ypres in the third battle to bear the town's name advanced the British line by almost 6 miles towards the objectives that had been set for the first two weeks of the campaign. The cost to achieve this ground was 275,000 casualties, of which 70,000 were killed. The British Army lost the equivalent of ten to twelve divisions from its total of sixty. Many of those divisions still intact after November 1917 were in no fit state to continue fighting. Persisting with the battle after the success of 4 October produced effects opposite to those intended. The British armies were worn down after the fourth, and, as a result, German morale rose while that of the attackers — British, Australian and New Zealand — plummeted to the depths of despair.

German casualties were also heavy, caused mainly by an insistence on repeatedly counterattacking any time ground was lost. Many forget the Germans were fighting in the same appalling conditions as the British. Ludendorff wrote:

> Enormous masses of ammunition, such as the human mind had never imagined before the war, were hurled upon the bodies of men who passed a miserable existence scattered about in mud-filled shell-holes. The horror of the shell-hole area of Verdun was surpassed. It was no longer life at all. It was mere suffering. And through this world of mud the attackers dragged themselves, slowly, but steadily, and in dense masses. Caught in the advanced zone by our hail fire they often collapsed, and the lonely man in the shell-hole breathed again. Then the mass came on again. Rifle and machine-gun jammed with the mud. Man fought against man, and only too often the mass was successful.[3]

These muddy, freezing, damp conditions took a heavy toll on the German defenders at Passchendaele. Such was the extent of their wastage, it became evident that a change of tactics was required when the weather improved. Ludendorff later stated:

> The Army had come victoriously through 1917; but it had become
> apparent that the holding of the Western Front purely by a
> defensive could no longer be counted on, in view of the enormous
> quantity of material of all kinds which the Entente had now at
> their disposal . . . The condition of all allies and of our Army all
> called for an offensive that would bring about an early decision.
> This was only possible on the Western Front.[4]

At the earliest opportunity in 1918, the Germans launched an offensive
which broke the deadlock of trench warfare on the Western Front and
almost won them the war. The experience of 1917, especially around
Passchendaele, 'had given us valuable hints for an offensive battle in the
West, if we wished to undertake one in 1918'.[5]

The disasters at Passchendaele caused the British Army, the New
Zealand Division included, to lose its confidence and optimism. Its
good spirits were replaced by a 'deadly depression'.[6] For the survivors
of Passchendaele the war seemed never-ending and ceased to have a
purpose. As one New Zealand soldier wrote after the battle: 'I can't see
Unconditional Surrender in the Peace Terms or the end even in sight.'[7]
Soldiers had long ceased betting the war would be over by Christmas. Now
they believed it would last a lifetime and sardonically joked that 'The first
seven years will be the hardest.'[8] A future major general in the next great
conflict, but a captain in the Machine Gun Corps when he witnessed the
fateful attack of 12 October, wrote to his fiancée in New Zealand that his
'secret self' wished to get a minor wound that would finish his war 'and
take him back to all the things he longs for'. Lindsay Inglis confessed: 'I
hate the war, I'm sick of it, I have had enough; but I can't leave til I'm
forced to.'[9] In his next letter he regained his composure and apologised to
his fiancée for being so sentimental, but his letter of 26 October reveals
his true feelings and is indicative of how the Passchendaele experience
affected those who fought there. George McLaren, the soldier who had
hastily scribbled his sister a note on the eve of the 4 October 'dust-up',

wrote in his first letter to her after Passchendaele:

> It will soon be three years since I left NZ, there was a time when I thought I would have been home by now but I don't know what to make of it just now. The old Hun is still going strong in places and at present is wading into Italy at a great pace. I often wonder when he is going to give this front one of his wild visits . . . at any rate I am darned lucky to be alive ain't I . . . a man might have been pushing up the cowslips lots of times only for a terrible run of good luck.

His next letter contained more doubts about the direction of the war:

> it is hard to say at times who is winning, but never mind Tina there is no question about who is going to win in the end, the only question is how long it is going to take the Allies to win.[10]

At the end of 1917, a year of disasters and huge sacrifice on the Western Front, this was the question to which no answer was immediately apparent. Morale in the whole British Army suffered as a result. Victory was far, far away; death near and probable.

Yet the British Army soldiered on, and, remarkably, no large mutinies occurred within its ranks. As the British official history freely admitted:

> The chief cause of the great discontentment during this period of the Flanders fighting was, in fact, the continuous demands on regimental officers and men to carry out tasks which appeared physically impossible to perform, and which no other army would have faced . . . That the attacks were so gallantly made in such conditions stands to the immortal credit of the battalions concerned.[11]

The historian is quite right. Such gallantry, while carelessly wasted at Passchendaele, should not be forgotten.

One of the divisions most affected by the horrors of Passchendaele was the New Zealand Division. The New Zealanders had suffered a huge defeat and they knew it. Ormond Burton accurately described the 12 October attack:

> The Huns kept their nerve, and the result was the inevitable massacre. For the first time New Zealand Brigades had completely failed, and their defeat had cost them as tragic a price as the barren victory on the blood-stained slopes of Sari Bair.[12]

As Stewart has commented, 'it is difficult to describe the troop's mortification and chagrin' at this failure.[13] One soldier noted:

> This is the first occasion when NZ troops have failed. The whole affair failed on account of the awful weather conditions and also through lack of sufficient preparation and coordination with the artillery.[14]

The casualties had been very heavy, but that alone had not caused the damage to morale. After the experience of two world wars, General Freyberg aptly commented:

> We had taken part in two forlorn hopes [Greece and Crete] . . . It was most important that we did not have another failure. It is a fact in war that troops can have heavy casualties, so long as the heavy casualties are not linked with failure.[15]

No longer able to boast of their proud reputation of always securing their objectives, the men of the Division felt bitter at the losses associated with this futile attack. They were also much relieved when word came they were to leave the accursed Passchendaele swamp. Bert Stokes wrote:

> We suffered fairly heavily and I can tell you nobody was sorry when orders came to move out of the line. We had been looking

forward to this day ever since we pulled in and all our eyes sparkled and we smiled a treat when we turned our backs on that part of the line which had treated us so badly.[16]

A gunner recorded that, while they didn't withdraw until 4 November and had to leave their guns behind for the Canadians to use, it was 'a happy day for us all, we were not sorry to leave the Ypres sector'.[17]

Morale in the New Zealand Division after its attack of 12 October reached an all-time low. All brigades were exhausted, and sickness within the various units was rife. The Division had been pushed to the limits of endurance. General Russell's aide-de-camp recorded after Passchendaele that the New Zealanders were 'a Division somewhat shattered, dismally looking ahead to winter in frozen and damp trenches'.[18] One veteran believed that as a result of Passchendaele the New Zealand Division had slipped to being a C-class division, which was only to be expected. He stated years later: 'We'd been hammered too hard and of course your morale got low.'[19] The official history of the Machine Gun Corps readily admits that, after spending five days in the front line of Passchendaele under appalling conditions, combined with the 'nerve-wracking experience' of 12 October, its troops left the line 'completely exhausted . . . broken and worn out'.[20] In early November Russell witnessed the Rifle Brigade marching along a road and recorded that they were 'a sorry sight — this Bde wants looking after'.[21] Before Passchendaele, such a comment about a New Zealand infantry or rifle brigade was unthinkable. Passchendaele, the Division's first and greatest failure of the war, when combined with the heavy winter of 1917, almost destroyed it. The Division reached the nadir of its fortunes, similar to that suffered by 2nd New Zealand Division at Monte Cassino in March 1944. Ormond Burton later wrote: 'There is a limit to what men can endure and during the winter of 1917–18 this limit was very nearly reached.'[22]

The extent of the disaster is reflected in the admission rates of the main New Zealand hospital in the United Kingdom, the No. 1 New Zealand General Hospital at Brockenhurst, Hampshire, 14 miles from Southampton. This hospital had been established to receive sick and wounded New Zealand soldiers in June 1916, and most New Zealanders in need of hospitalisation found themselves there. The hospital continued to receive New Zealand soldiers until it closed in 1919. With a peak capacity of 920 patients, its monthly admission rates for 1916 and 1917 were:

1916 Admission Rates

July	522
August	422
September	1306 (Somme)
October	662
November	389
December	545
Total	**3846**

1917 Admission Rates

January	661
February	368
March	348
April	215
May	275
June	1303 (Messines)
July	529
August	815
September	458
October	1451 (Passchendaele)
November	719
December	720
Total	**7862**

The admission rate for October 1917 was the highest in the hospital's history, and Brockenhurst ran out of bed space, having to set up an additional fifty beds in the local YMCA. Private Gwynne Potts was sent to Brockenhurst in early October suffering the effects of breathing mustard gas. He wrote home at the end of the month:

The Hospitals are full up after this last stunt, suppose you have seen the casualty lists by now, the biggest smack New Zealand has had in some time. I don't think I have a mate left now, I was very lucky to miss it.[23]

The highest rate for 1918 was in September, with 1308 admissions. Total admissions during the hospital's life amounted to 9701.[24] What is also notable about the last three months of 1917 is that not only was the hospital's admission rate at its highest, but in the first two months of 1918, the admission rate was also well above the 1917 average of 655. The impact of Passchendaele was still being felt, these figures giving an indication of the health of the New Zealand Division. One historian has estimated that when the wastage rates from sickness are added to the battle casualties, the figure for New Zealand's losses reaches as high as 7500 men for the month of October 1917, a figure confirmed by a New Zealand government publication of 1919.[25]

Major General J.F.C. Fuller, one of the most influential military thinkers of the twentieth century, believed Third Ypres was 'a tactically impossible battle' and that to persist after August 1917 'was an inexcusable piece of pig-headedness on the part of Haig'.[26] Certainly many people have blamed Haig for the Passchendaele debacle, one New Zealand writer going so far as to claim: 'As the officer in overall command, Field Marshal Sir Douglas Haig was responsible for the death of every New Zealander (not to mention the British casualties).'[27]

It is, therefore, a tragic irony — one almost impossible to explain — that on 15 October the British War Cabinet decided to send a message of congratulations to Haig, which he duly received on the sixteenth. The message declared the Cabinet's desire 'to congratulate you and the troops under your command upon the achievements of the British Armies in Flanders in the great battle that has been raging since 31 July'. Even Haig was puzzled by the message and its appalling timing:

This is the first message of congratulation on any operation by the War Cabinet which has reached me since the war began! I

115

wonder why the Prime Minister should suddenly have sent this message.[28]

As if to confirm the words were real, Haig copied the entire message into his personal diary.

While Haig must take a fair degree of the responsibility for the disaster of 12 October, there were plenty of other 'guilty men'. Many New Zealand soldiers believed Godley, not Haig, was personally to blame: 'A bad thing it was. You can thank old General Godley for that lot . . . One of Godley's mistakes. Everybody hated Godley. He was severe.'[29] Certainly the aloof, universally unpopular Godley made a convenient scapegoat. Most New Zealand soldiers after Gallipoli had come to regard him as both incompetent and foreign, a true-blue British officer in command of a division that by 1917 was largely anti-British. One soldier believed Godley had personally ordered the renewal of the attack on 12 October and that 'it was absolutely, utterly impossible. There wouldn't have been one of us left if we'd tried to do that.' Braithwaite, he believed, had refused to obey this order, and Godley had then had him sent home: 'That was Godley. I have no time for Godley at all. The troops didn't have much of an opinion of him.'[30]

While Godley, certainly not blameless, was the object of much criticism, General Russell, not blameless either, seems to have escaped the hatred and disdain of the troops who had suffered through his lack of action at Passchendaele. There were, however, some extenuating circumstances. Russell's diary reveals that from 5 October he was suffering from a severe cold which he could not shake off and which grew increasingly serious.[31] Years later his aide-de-camp recorded that:

> The severe winter — the strain and the sorrow of the Battle of Passchendaele — the continuous work of building up the Division — the preparation for the Polderhoek Chateau assignment must have told on General Russell's health. He went to medical specialists . . . The General's chest was suspect and bronchitis was diagnosed.[32]

Despite this, General Russell must share much of the guilt for the events of 12 October. He had not gone forward prior to the attack to examine the ground over which he was about to send his soldiers, and, while he knew obstacles faced them, had naively assumed these would be destroyed by the heavy artillery. It was a dangerous assumption to make, and it proved a fatal one for many of his soldiers. If Russell had any doubts about the viability of the attack, he certainly did not voice them openly to his superiors. On the day of the attack he was not forward with the action, did not appreciate the huge difficulties facing his New Zealand troops — the terrible mud, the depth of the enemy wire, the withering machine-gun fire cutting them down en masse — and did not fully grasp the extent of his losses until well after the battle. He, not Godley, ordered the renewal of the attack at 3 p.m., before calling it off at the last minute when he learned the Australian division had also failed to secure its objectives and did not need flank protection from the New Zealanders.

Certainly many of the senior British commanders remained haunted by the experience of Passchendaele. General Harington, Plumer's Chief of Staff, later recalled:

> Those stages up to Passchendaele have always been a nightmare to me as they were to my Chief. They were all right up to and including Broodseinde, 4th October. After that Fate was very cruel to us. It is easy to say now that everyone knew it was going to rain like that except those at G.H.Q. and that the whole operation was an 'unjustifiable gamble.' I do not know how any operation of war can be anything else but a gamble unless the enemy tells you what he has got the other side of the hill and in what state his troops are.[33]

So painful a memory did this battle become that twenty-seven years later, in the third attempt to take the town of Cassino in southern Italy, Lieutenant General Sir Bernard Freyberg had only to utter the name 'Passchendaele' to bring all current operations to a close.[34]

Godley, Russell and Haig were only the most obvious of those to share the blame, but there were others. Above all, it was the British imperial system of command — a system that did not insist higher commanders lead from the front, and in which any doubts about the viability of an attack had to be locked away and internalised rather than openly voiced — that was at fault. This system failed the New Zealanders making the attack on the morning of 12 October 1917. Men like Godley, Haig and Russell were steeped in its culture, were products of it and could not escape from it. On the fields of Passchendaele, just below the Bellevue Spur, a great many New Zealanders paid the ultimate price for its inadequacies.

In early November 1917 Russell wrote to James Allen of the Passchendaele disaster:

> We cannot always expect to succeed, but I feel very sorry about it all when I think of the numbers of men who were lost. My chief fear is that the men may lose confidence in the arrangements made for them as they had always been taught that, provided the Staff arrangements are good, they are able to do anything that is asked of them.[35]

Russell's fear was justified. An angry entry in Gunner Ward's diary caught the general mood of the New Zealand troops:

> Our boys went over at 6 AM . . . A bad, bad business — someone has blundered and our boys pay the price.[36]

Leonard Hart also believed a whole series of blunders were made and would never be brought to light:

> Some terrible blunder has been made. Someone is responsible for that barbed wire not having been broken up by our artillery and Someone is responsible for the opening of our barrage in the midst of us . . . Someone else is responsible for those machine gun emplacements being left practically intact, but the papers will all report another glorious success, and no one except those who actually took part in it will know any different.[37]

Indicating the huge gap between the commanders and the commanded, Gunner Stratton in his 'Recollections' was savage about the person who ordered this second attack:

> It was stated sometime later that some General or high person gave the order for us to attack the second time. Obviously he knew NOTHING at all about the conditions there nor did he heed the warnings of those that did know. Strange that we never heard when they shot him.[38]

Leonard Hart, whose infantry company lost 148 of its 180 members on 12 October, wrote to his parents:

> . . . we have nothing to be ashamed of as our commander afterwards told us that no troops in the world could possibly have taken the position, but this is small comfort when one remembers the hundreds of lives that have been lost and nothing gained.[39]

Such an admission, if true, must have led many survivors to ask why their commanders allowed the attack to take place at all. It did not help matters either when the popular Brigadier 'Bill' Braithwaite left the New Zealand Division in December 1917 and did not return. Braithwaite was in a state of nervous exhaustion after Passchendaele, but had to command the Division in its next action — the failed attack at Polderhoek Chateau. After Polderhoek, Braithwaite's health broke down and he was evacuated to England and hospitalised there. Yet rumours soon circulated that he had been sacked because of his refusal to sacrifice more of his men on the afternoon of 12 October:

> Finally he [Braithwaite] refused to order his men to be murdered and of course that was the end of his military career. He was returned to England and we never saw him again.

This soldier added that 'the older we get the more bitter we feel about the needless suffering and the loss of so many of our friends'.[40] Another soldier, who lost a brother at Passchendaele, reflected in his old age: 'In many respects it makes me so angry when I think of the terrible loss of life and the things we had to put up with in war.'[41] Survivors of the battle took this bitterness back to New Zealand, where it took root and grew.

Anger generated by the Passchendaele attacks never died and, in Britain, some fifty years later, an 'explosive and abrasive' debate was conducted in the daily newspapers, with one contributor summing up the attitude of most veterans: 'The useless sacrifice is remembered by all those still living who took part in the actual fighting.'[42] This bitterness felt at the time grew dramatically when the ground won with so much blood and suffering in 1917 proved impossible to hold the following year. What had taken four months and 275,000 casualties to win was lost in just three days.

The experience was so painful for one soldier that even to this day he does not acknowledge that the battle of Passchendaele on 12 October was a disaster or could have been avoided:

> It was the fortunes of war. Once it starts, it's got to go ahead doesn't it . . . I never heard it discussed that it had gone wrong. I think that is the armchair critics myself. I don't consider, never did consider it went wrong. It was a well-planned battle![43]

At least one participant believed Passchendaele was a positive experience, as painful as it had been:

> In one way . . . when we came out of Passchendaele, we knew from the general higher authorities, we can't risk that again. So you knew you weren't going to be put in the same conditions . . . The troops at Passchendaele could talk about the hard times if they got out of it. But they didn't want it again!![44]

While the next New Zealand attack was also a failure, albeit on nowhere near the scale of 12 October 1917, there were no more Passchendaeles for the New Zealand Division.

In his letter of 7 November Russell had warned Allen: 'In these days of Parliamentary criticism, questions may be asked as to the operations I refer to.'[45] This did not happen. Allen spoke of the Passchendaele casualties in the House of Representatives on 1 November 1917. The number of New Zealand casualties suffered from 4 to 30 October appeared as 957 dead, 3052 wounded and a further 1300 unaccounted for. Allen stated that he 'regret[ed] very much this heavy casualty list', but no comments or questions emerged about the figures given. Allen's short comment is the only mention of the battle in the House records.[46] Despite Russell's concerns, Passchendaele did not provoke a political reaction in New Zealand. It did, however, provoke a reaction of another kind, one that has left an enduring legacy.

Passchendaele remains New Zealand's worst military disaster and as such is a pivotal moment in the country's history. Military history is not just about generals and battles in faraway places; it is also, in every sense, family history. The distinguished military-social historians of the First World War, Jay Winter and Blaine Baggett, have commented: 'War is always the destroyer of families, and the Great War was to date the greatest destroyer of them all.'[47] This catastrophe at Passchendaele affected more New Zealand families and shattered more lives on a single day than any other event in the nation's history. Two stories, neither unusual, encapsulate the extent of the tragedy.

Private Wilfred C. Smith, a carpenter from Wellington, was a young New Zealander separated from his beloved wife and four young children. On the journey from New Zealand to England and France he wrote many long, tender letters to his family. Writing to 'My Dearest Ethel' on 23 September 1917, Private Smith mentioned the 'special training' the New Zealanders had been receiving and described how they would soon be in action:

> . . . we are expecting marching orders any hour and it is for something big too dearest and my only hope dear is to be spared to return to you all. The prospects of an early peace are much brighter now as we have been giving 'Fritz' a good thrashing right along the line.

Smith's letter also reveals a strong awareness of his children pining for an absent father and how deeply this must have affected them:

> Poor old Noni. I expect that she is tired of her Daddy being away from home for such a long time, and I can assure you dearest that I am tired of it too and would give anything if I knew for certain when I was going back to my own home.

Smith concluded by putting into words what many other soldiers must have felt at the time but lacked the ability to express:

> I am not afraid dearest and am certain that I will come through all right — But if I don't dear you will always have the satisfaction of knowing that your Husband has done his duty and that his last thoughts were of his wife and children.[48]

One is left to speculate whether this last letter was of much comfort to Ethel Smith. Private Smith never got to fire a shot at the enemy. He suffered a grievous wound from shell-fire while moving up to the line on the evening of 3 October 1917 and died five days later at the 44th Casualty Clearing Station. Ethel and her children spent the rest of their lives aching for a lost husband and father who had done his duty to New Zealand, but for which this family had paid an almost unbearable price.

The Knight family, farmers and sawmillers from Dannevirke, was large, with ten children. The three elder sons, being of military age, went away to the Great War to do their bit. Not one of them survived to return home. We are able to gauge the extent of this terrible family tragedy through the letters of Mrs Ellen (Nellie) Knight, which have survived and are housed at the Alexander Turnbull Library.

A letter written to George, the second son, shortly after the boys had enlisted reveals Mrs Knight's sense of duty, her fears, and her perhaps naive hope that the family's dreams would not be interrupted by the war. She wrote:

I tried to write last night. I had to tell Dad I could not face it alone. I had a good blub and feel better. Of course I knew we could not hope to keep out of it, nor did I want to as I told the others, if you were needed and you felt you ought to go, it will be very hard to part with any of you and I dare say it will mean all three, but I am ready to do my duty always, as you are to do yours . . . The land won't be much use to us if you boys are not there to work it but please God you may not be wanted or if you are you will be spared to come back 'hero's' and take up your work again and we can all do the things we have planned together to make a lovely garden home.[49]

Both Herbert, the youngest of the brothers who went away, and George joined 2nd Otago Infantry Battalion and served at Gallipoli. There Herbert was killed early in the campaign by a sniper. Mrs Knight's loss and sense of helplessness is revealed in another letter to George:

He did not get long to do his little bit, I would have felt happier, could he have had a chance to shoot a few more goals, but perhaps he did something worth his brave young life. I prayed so hard that you might both come back to me, but it is part of God's great plan and we must bear it, but it is a hard task to be the mother of soldiers . . . We feel so helpless here, there is nothing to do but weep and I try not to.[50]

George Knight survived Gallipoli and served with his battalion in France. He took part in the Somme battles and started to rise through the military ranks. A natural leader with ability and charm, he seemed to influence all around him, as many letters written to Mrs Knight testify.

In March 1917, George was promoted to the rank of sergeant and went to complete his officer training. He returned to the Otago Battalion as a Second Lieutenant in June 1917. 2nd Otago Battalion was allocated a key role in the 12 October attack at Passchendaele. The young, newly promoted George found himself leading a company up Bellevue Spur, where he and the men who remained tried to get beyond the impenetrable wire they found there. The task proved impossible, and George was cut down by a burst of machine-gun fire only feet from the enemy positions. His body was never recovered.

After George's death Mrs Knight received many letters of sympathy. One of his fellow soldiers wrote to her:

> Believe me lady he was a NZer through and through and a boy that any parents can be proud of. He was as good a soldier as ever left New Zealand.[51]

Another soldier described George as 'brave and fearless' and as the 'best officer' in the battalion.[52]

From George's battalion commander came a very special letter:

> I cannot speak too highly of him: he was killed on October 12th while leading his company of which he was in command, both he and the other two officers were killed and a large number of his men: they did magnificent work and you must be proud of him.

Describing how George's company commander had been seriously wounded at the start of the battle, the colonel explained: 'I had such confidence in your boy that I at once put him in Command and most nobly he carried out his duty on that terrible morning.' The colonel also stated that all the men had equal confidence in George, and, in an unusual admission, added:

> Personally I have lost a great friend as he had endeared himself to us all. A splendid example of a soldier and a Gentleman.[53]

This letter clearly meant a great deal to Mrs Knight, as she copied it out in full as if hanging on to every word. At the top she wrote:

> Copy of letter which I can justly be proud of and put by with my other treasures.[54]

In another unusual measure of George's popularity, Mrs Knight also received a letter of sympathy from Brigadier Braithwaite, the commanding officer of 2nd New Zealand Infantry Brigade. Describing George's record of service as 'a brilliant one', Braithwaite wrote:

> I am well aware that no words of mine can be of the slightest comfort to you and yours at such a time, but although a stranger to you, I would like to tell you how much I feel for you in your great sorrow.

While trying to comfort Mrs Knight, the brigadier added something that probably had the opposite effect:

> The 2nd Brigade and especially the 2nd Otago Battalion suffered grievous losses that morning and experienced desperate fighting under the most intense machine gun fire.

Braithwaite then told Mrs Knight how her son had led his company very bravely and had died only yards from the enemy.[55]

One is to left to wonder how many other George Knights perished in the two attacks at Passchendaele and throughout the course of the war. For Nellie Knight the suffering was far from over. In 1918 her eldest son William (Douglas), serving in an Auckland Infantry Battalion, was killed in France during the great advances made by the New Zealand Division in the second half of that year. His experience is examined in detail in the third battle covered in this book. His last letter to the family at home arrived after the news of his death and was never opened. Nellie Knight's dreams of 'a lovely garden home' shared with all her children were destroyed by the Great War.

Yet there was a further 'bitter blow' to come.[56] The youngest of the children, Maurice (Marty), a masters graduate of Canterbury University with a doctorate from London University, while serving as an officer in a British anti-aircraft battery in the Punjab, contracted malaria and died in 1944, only weeks before he was due to return to New Zealand. War certainly destroyed a large part of this family, and we can only guess how Nellie Knight, who died in 1966 aged 94, suffered because of it.

Nellie Knight's case is certainly not unique. Mrs Mary Ann Newlove of Takaka, near Nelson, suffered similar agonies when the casualty figures from Passchendaele reached New Zealand. Three of her sons had enlisted in 1916. One, Leonard, was killed on 4 October. The other two boys, Edwin and Leslie, were killed on 12 October. Not one of the Newlove boys has a known grave, their names being recorded on the New Zealand Memorial to the Missing at Tyne Cot. All words are inadequate to describe the extent of this family's suffering.

Chaplain G.H. Gavin, who spent most of 12 October 1917 assisting a medical officer in dressing the stumps of a man with both legs shot away at the knee — 'the most distressing case I have ever seen' — devoted the following days to writing to the families of the deceased. He received numerous replies and noted that the families back in New Zealand 'are so grateful for the least news one can give them of their lost sons and brothers'.[57] Nearly every New Zealand family was affected by Passchendaele, or knew someone who was. By now New Zealanders knew first-hand the maiming, death or uncertain fate of loved ones that had become the terrible price of the war. The heady days of 1914, with their innocent illusions of glory, had long gone. In October 1917, New Zealanders 'did not need to be told that the angel of death had passed over the land: they had heard the beating of its wings'.[58] With the passage of time, the reasons for going to war faded from memory, but the loneliness and heartache never did. The sense of loss endured. The pain of the losing of loved ones was all the greater for the fact that the ultimate separation occurred at such a distance, with families isolated from the events that caused it. Denied the rituals that usually accompany death — the funeral, the church service, the mourners, a grave with a headstone that could be visited and tended — no sense of closure accompanied the loss. Empty places around family dinner tables could never be filled and were a permanent reminder that life would never be the same again. The Great War created a huge chasm between then and now.

The suffering did not end in 1917 or with the end of the war. The distinguished Australian historian Professor Sir Ernest Scott believed the Great War had a lasting impact on Australia and Australians, cutting 'deep furrows' in the political and social fabric of society that would still be evident in one hundred years' time.[59] The disaster of Passchendaele cut equally 'deep furrows' in the political and social fabric of New Zealand, especially through the experiences of those who had been through the fires of Passchendaele and survived. Lieutenant Colonel C.H. Weston, wounded on 4 October and graded PU (Permanently Unfit) as a result, certainly believed the war left an imprint on him. He reflected when packing his neatly pressed uniform away for good: 'Will Time then set to work with his iron, to smooth out the furrow made on my brain by the war?'[60] Whether Time ever did or could remove the deep furrow from Weston's brain will remain an unanswered question. For many New Zealand soldiers, the furrow made by war lasted a lifetime and was never erased.

Stanley Herbert, wounded at Messines, admitted he was an emotional wreck coming back from the war. He even burned his discharge papers because he was 'full up with war'. What saved Herbert was a good marriage that lasted sixty-one years. Without his wife Herbert would have been a lost soul and a victim of his war experience:

> I would have been just a hobo. Because I was a hobo. Because I had learnt many things too young. I was a good boy and a good worker. But she [his wife Beatrice] made me . . . My wife got the war out of my mind.[61]

The suffering was not confined to war veterans. Jeremy Rees, reflecting on the death of a great-uncle at Passchendaele eighty years later, recalled:

> Back home his death was devastating. His mother lost two sons in the war, a third died soon after. Some times her pain burst forth. She would cry at the dining table, weeping and railing against the injustice of war.[62]

Many returned soldiers were not as lucky as Stanley Herbert in being rescued by a good marriage. A section in Robin Hyde's *Nor the Years Condemn* reveals much about the cost of the war, and Passchendaele in particular, to New Zealand:

> Those [men] that came back from the war had ventured over the hills somewhere, restless, trying for adventure; or they had picked up chest trouble at the front, or worse. You could get engaged, triumphantly, to a good-looking, fine-faced returned man, give trousseau parties and indulge in the pride of showing your silk and semi-silk things to your girl friends. Then, perhaps on the eve of the wedding, there would be an incoherent note, a policeman around in the morning, and an inquest on a man who had put a bullet through his head. Somebody would explain that he had been badly shell-shocked at Ypres, badly gassed. Poor old Jack, everybody said. Yes, but nobody thought, in the same degree, poor young Laura or Mavis.[63]

Jack was a victim of Passchendaele, but so were Mavis and Laura, their parents, Jack's parents and the community where these various tragedies unfolded. As the New Zealand writer John Mulgan, a casualty of the next war, testified:

> We had never . . . outgrown the shadow of that earlier war . . . We felt the tragic waste and splendour of this first Great War, and grew up in the waste land that it produced.[64]

For many New Zealanders, the 'scars of war' would never heal.

In many ways the mistrust, suspicion, hostility, almost contempt, that New Zealand has demonstrated in the past towards its military can be traced back to the disaster of 12 October 1917. According to A.J.P. Taylor, the Somme battle 'set the picture by which future generations saw the First World War: brave helpless soldiers; blundering obstinate generals; nothing achieved'.[65] For New Zealand, though, relative latecomers to the

Somme battle, the Passchendaele attack of 12 October dominates public memory of the Western Front, even though few New Zealanders are familiar with its details. Certainly one veteran of the war believed the Passchendaele disaster awakened New Zealanders to the dreadful reality of total war, and that all the 'wild enthusiasm' for the war in New Zealand ended when the long casualty lists from the Passchendaele battles finally reached here.[66] The stark reality of war hit home with a crushing blow, and New Zealanders, deeply hurt by the massive casualties, looked for ways to vent their anger and turned against anything military.

The New Zealand army still lives with this legacy of Passchendaele. Those who doubt the existence of a deep-seated hostility towards the military need only read Oliver Duff's account of how military personnel were viewed during the interwar years to realise how widespread it was. Duff wrote in 1941: 'No one was so ridiculous in those days, so derided and so despised, as the man who ventured out in uniform.'[67] This attitude has persisted throughout most of this century, and it was not until the late 1970s that the New Zealand army permitted its soldiers posted to Auckland and Wellington to appear in public in their uniforms. Even then old attitudes died slowly. One senior officer who retired from service in 1997 recalled how, when he first appeared in uniform in Auckland's Queen Street, he was spat on by a member of the public who would not have given him a second glance had he been dressed in plain clothing. 'We all felt besieged all the time,' he recalled.[68]

The negative attitude of many New Zealanders towards their soldiers, fuelled by the experience of Vietnam, has continued to this day. Those in uniform, especially officers, are derided by many New Zealanders as unthinking, uncaring militarists who might send 'brave, helpless soldiers' to their deaths without giving it a second thought. As with most stereotypes — this one derived from the experience at Passchendaele in 1917 — it is wide of the mark.

In New Zealand, memories of the Great War have been repressed for eighty years. No detailed, popular history of the New Zealand experience in the Great War has been written, unlike the twelve volumes of the Australian official history. In his volume on the Australian home front,

Professor Scott wrote that the Great War was an ordeal unlike any other that Australia had faced and that it was 'a stirring and straining run of experience which required to be studied and recorded'.[69] This is equally true for New Zealand, but New Zealanders have barely scratched the surface in studying their Great War experience. Why is this so? There is probably no definitive answer, but three possible reasons spring to mind.

The first is that the men who returned from Passchendaele and other battles like it were unable to talk about their experiences for some time, and when that time finally came, towards the end of their lives, few people seemed prepared to listen. Many participants felt extremely unwilling to talk about experiences that were mostly brutal, painful and horrific and which they wanted to leave far behind them. One veteran succinctly expressed this reluctance:

> There was a lot of things that happened that I would like to forget.
> I didn't tell my mother, I didn't tell my family.[70]

Vic Martin, a sniper with the Otago Regiment who was himself wounded in the arm at Passchendaele by an enemy sniper, saw a friend's face shot away by a sniper's hollow-point bullet. His friend was standing alongside him, yet Martin paid little attention to the incident at the time: 'In war time, there is no effect. You are looking out for number one, aren't you?' But after the war the image of his friend's shattered face haunted Vic Martin, who often thought of him. He remained unable to talk about it even to those closest to him: 'You couldn't explain it . . . It was a big mistake . . . They should never have sent us over, not under the conditions . . . It was over as far I was concerned . . . I just wanted to forget about it.'[71] Unfortunately, such an experience burns itself deep into an individual's memory and those affected cannot easily dismiss it, as Vic Martin found out during his lifetime.

John A. Lee, returned soldier, writer and maverick Labour MP, described the reluctance to discuss the war in his autobiographical novel:

Looking at those glittering crosses, he had realized that the front, the suffering out of which this wreckage had stumbled to die, was beyond description, something men could know, something men could feel, something men could talk about only to those who had known and felt.[72]

Even on those occasions when veterans did get together, such as Anzac Day or reunions, their memories were selective. On such occasions rarely was there talk of the pain and suffering endured, or of the death and destruction that are a part of war.

In his influential work on the Great War and the modern memory of it, Professor Paul Fussell astutely noted:

But even if those at home had wanted to know the realities of war, they couldn't have without experiencing them: its conditions were too novel, its industrialised ghastliness too unprecedented. The war would have been simply unbelievable. From the very beginning a fissure was opening between the Army and civilians.[73]

A Passchendaele veteran reflected this attitude when he stated: 'A terrible thing war, isn't it? You've got to be there to understand it.'[74] Another, when asked why he had been unable to talk of his experiences, reinforced this view:

I just didn't bother. I didn't lock it away. It was there but you just didn't bother. How can you explain to a civilian that has never seen anything like that, what it was actually like?[75]

Writing home just after the Passchendaele attacks Bert Stokes almost started to explain what he had been through, but caught himself just in time:

This is war, grim warfare, and some of the sights I've witnessed have hit me very hard, various things have taken place right under my nose that I'll never forget, a chap has to have a stern heart and a strong nerve. But we won't say any more of these things, there's a cheerful side to all our experiences, so let's look at that side.[76]

The second reason why New Zealand has not examined its war experience is, as Jock Phillips has written, the overwhelming image of the New Zealand soldier. This image, a powerful social force, is that of a 'hard man' — physically tough but also 'emotionally hard as a man who will never admit to pain or fear or weakness'.[77] Most New Zealand soldiers of this century have believed it their duty not to inflict their personal pain upon others. The pain must be borne in silence and no one speaks of it. But in most cases, the silence does not indicate all is well; far from it. The silence is that of an unrelenting personal despair.

Most psychologists agree that repression of unfavourable memories is very unhealthy for individuals, and in post-1918 New Zealand it seems to have occurred on a vast scale. There are four individual responses to a traumatic experience. They are:

1. Mild reaction to stress: a slight reaction occurs but natural coping mechanisms take over.
2. Memory shutdown: a physiological response in the subconscious or deeper.
3. Conscious suppression: the individual makes a deliberate effort to suppress the memory.
4. Mental and/or physical breakdown.[78]

For the majority of New Zealanders returning from the war, the response to experiences like Passchendaele was either 2 or 3 — a deliberate or subconscious attempt to forget. Few New Zealand soldiers fell into categories 1 and 4.

There are, however, significant behavioural outcomes associated with memory suppression and shutdown. In increasing order of severity, these can include slight maladjustment, being mildly dysfunctional, mental illnesses such as mood and/or sleep disorder and compulsive behaviour, post-traumatic stress disorder, physical illnesses, relationship problems, social, economic and work problems, survivor's guilt, suicidal tendencies and suicide itself. Most New Zealand soldiers who returned from the Great War experienced some kind of adverse reaction. In the main, though, this ranged from being slightly maladjusted to experiencing considerable guilt for having survived.

Widespread memory repression also affects the development, maturity and health of a nation. If not dealt with openly through public policy or some form of national healing process, the end result is collective guilt, denial, the suppression and distortion of the nation's history and the damaging of the nation's social institutions — all consequences borne by New Zealand after the Great War.

The third explanation for New Zealand's unfamiliarity with the Great War, one particularly relevant to Passchendaele, has to do with the country's attitude to its military past. Canada's experience of Passchendaele, because of the Canadian Corps' success there, has become part of the national mythology of Canada as a nation of super-soldiers, that country's version of the Australian 'digger' legend. New Zealanders, by comparison, uncomfortable when talking about military successes, have tended to focus on heroic failures, when success came so tantalisingly close but never materialised. This certainly applies to the three actions on which, according to Michael King, New Zealanders have 'dwelt most considerably in retrospect': the actions at Gallipoli, in Crete and at Monte Cassino.[79] Neither of the New Zealand attacks at Passchendaele in October 1917 falls into this category. The first was an outstanding success, described by the German records as 'a black day' for their army. The second was such an abject failure it was best forgotten, and never spoken of. Both attacks are recorded only on the silent war memorials where the name Passchendaele undoubtedly puzzles many who read it. The New Zealand experience of Passchendaele deserves much better than this. It should become at least as well known as Gallipoli, the only battle of the Great War to occupy a prominent place in the imagination of most New Zealanders. The battles at Passchendaele — the textbook success and the bloody failure — rate as highly as any of New Zealand's military encounters in their significance to the nation.

In his official history of the Australian home front during the Great War, Sir Ernest Scott regarded the conflict as a pivotal event in Australian national life.[80] He believed this because of the terrific losses associated with the war (nearly 60,000 dead) and the social upheaval and economic dislocation which followed its conclusion. Many other Australian historians agree with Scott's assessment. For New Zealand, with its own civil war in the nineteenth century and its heavy commitment to the Second World War, it is difficult to make this claim about the Great War. There is little doubt, however, that the First World War deeply affected New Zealand in ways we haven't yet begun to understand. The losses of men were as proportionately high as Australia's, and New Zealand suffered equally from postwar dislocation. Life for all New Zealanders could not turn back to 1914. Too much blood had been shed and too much pain, often borne in silence, endured. The shadow of death had fallen across the land and it would remain for some time to come. And Passchendaele lies at the heart of this experience.

From a population of slightly more than one million people, New Zealand suffered some 17,000 killed during the war and another 41,000 wounded. New Zealand's casualty rate was 59 per cent of those who served, second only to that of Australia (65 per cent) in the British Empire. This was an enormous price to pay. The significance of Passchendaele, New Zealand's one great military failure in Belgium, can be measured when one considers that 6 per cent of New Zealand's total casualties occurred in just one morning of action on 12 October 1917. This day of tragedy has to be ranked as the very worst in New Zealand's path towards nationhood.

Conclusion

IN OCTOBER 1917 there were compelling strategic reasons for continuing the Flanders campaign. These included the state of the French Army coupled with problems on the Italian front culminating in the disaster of Caporetto at the end of the month. Caporetto would necessitate sending the most able army commander, Plumer, to the Italian front in November. The total domination of the German Army on the Eastern Front meant the Flanders region was one of the few places where the Allies could pin down and seriously damage the German Army. On every other front the Germans were winning the war, and there was only one army on the Western Front capable of mounting a large-scale offensive in the second half of the year. An American army study of the campaign completed in 1922 concluded that, for the reasons mentioned above, 'to let the new British conscript armies sit in the trenches and lose the offensive spirit would have been a blunder'.[1]

Many of the senior commanders, therefore, felt they had no alternative but to continue attacking the Germans in 1917 no matter what the conditions. The tragedy that occurred at Passchendaele had a sense of inevitability about it. Major General Sir Charles Harington:

> I have knelt in Tyne Cot Cemetery below Passchendaele on that hallowed ground, the most beautiful and sacred place I know in this world. I have prayed in that cemetery oppressed with fear lest even one of those gallant comrades should have lost his life owing to any fault or neglect on the part of myself and the Second Army Staff. It is a fearsome responsibility to have been the one who signed and issued all the Second Army orders for those operations. All I can truthfully say is that we did our utmost. We could not have done more. History must give its verdict.[2]

This view was not shared by those at the receiving end of those orders. One soldier summarised their opinions in his response to a historian's questioning:

Question: Just to come back to Passchendaele. Looking back at it, do you think that the attack could ever have succeeded?

Answer: Is there ever any success? Is there any success when you throw men's lives away like that? I'm not answering your question, but I'm posing another one.[3]

While there was indeed a strategic imperative to mount a large-scale operation on the Western Front, there was considerable flexibility in the way it could have been executed. There was no reason to keep plugging away at the Germans in the same area and in the same old manner, especially when this had failed as dismally as it had on 9 October. A principle of war is not to reinforce or repeat failure, as this will only compound the scale of the disaster that inevitably results. General Ludendorff wrote an accurate description of the British methods of attack after 4 October:

The enemy charged like a wild bull against the iron wall which kept him from our submarine bases. He threw his weight against Houthulst Forest, Poelcapelle, Passchendaele . . . He dented it in many places, and it seemed as if he must knock it down. But it held, although a faint tremor ran through its foundations.[4]

Rather than learning from the first charge at the iron gate that this type of attack hurt very much, and despite having adopted new tactics in 1916–17, the British commanders failed to adapt and innovate. They seemed lost for new ideas after 4 October. Instead, it would be the Germans who came up with the next major innovation of the war in their spring offensive of 1918, and it caught the British armies completely by surprise.

It is obvious in hindsight, as it was to many of the junior and senior commanders at the time, that the attack of 12 October should never have gone ahead. Certainly there was considerable doubt about the viability of the operation in the minds of General Russell and his brigadiers. That these commanders did not express their doubts more forcefully and allowed the attack to continue is an indictment of the military system of the time. The attacks at Passchendaele after 4 October were not based on detailed analysis and accurate intelligence. Rather, they rested on little more than wishful thinking, on 'hoping for the best' when all the available evidence suggested overwhelmingly such hope would prove vain and cost lives.

Two senior American army officers have recently written: 'Hope is not a method.'[5] Hope should never be a substitute for sound, realistic planning based on accurate intelligence; that is, a substitute for a proper appreciation process. Such a process was clearly lacking for the attack of 12 October 1917.

A New Zealander who took part in the attack on 4 October, and in the massive recovery effort following the disaster of 12 October, encapsulated the infantry soldier's experience many years later:

> An ordinary infantryman at Passchendaele was a pretty dumb beast. That's how he's treated you see. He was only gun fodder and when all is said . . . that's what I feel. We were pretty dumb beasts you see, or we wouldn't have been thrown into that sort of warfare, because it was hopeless before you started. We all knew that. We all felt it couldn't [succeed] . . . But you'd go on, you know, if you could, and if it was possible to get through the wire, they would have got through the wire all right. Fellas did try to get through, crawled under it and did all sorts of things to get through, but you'd get shot as soon as you stopped.[6]

Certainly the men forced to attack knew they had been given an impossible task. That they still tried to do it regardless of the cost was an abuse of their trust.

New Zealand commanders in coalition wars now have the authority, and, one hopes, the moral courage, to say 'No!' to operations they consider too risky for troops under their command. It is their paramount duty as national commanders to do so. This was the rather painful lesson Major General Bernard Freyberg had to learn after the debacles of Greece and Crete in the next world war.

New Zealand commanders are now also expected to demonstrate inventiveness, and are required to complete a complex course of military education that provides them with the analytical skills required to achieve their objectives at a minimal cost to young New Zealand lives. If we take any lesson from the tragedy of Passchendaele, this one is fundamental. Given the right training and junior leadership, New Zealand's soldiers are superb, with 'a reputation as the best soldiers in the world in the twentieth century', according to John Keegan.[7] But this should not be taken as a licence to squander them in futile frontal assaults. The days of ordering New Zealand soldiers to do the impossible should be long gone.

It is a tragedy that the events of Passchendaele are largely unknown to the majority of New Zealanders. As a nation we have inherited a reluctance to explore fully our war experiences, and thus we emulate those silent soldiers of the Great War. Consequently, what should have been an unforgettable experience has all but disappeared from our collective memory. What citizen of the United States of America, for example, would not know of the events surrounding the Alamo, Valley Forge, Gettysburg or Omaha Beach? New Zealand's military history is a vital part of the nation's past and has affected countless New Zealanders and their families. Yet it is a part of the nation's heritage that is all too often forgotten. That so few New Zealanders know anything about the battle of Passchendaele, New Zealand's worst-ever disaster, only emphasises how much we have forgotten.

Writing eighty years after the battle, one New Zealander did remember, and reflected on the sacrifice his great-uncle made on 4 October 1917:

> He was no hero, my great-uncle. But I admire his courage. He kept going amid the slaughter and the mud. Other armies mutinied or fell apart . . . At Passchendaele, Arthur Brown and his fellows did the hard yards, yard by sodden yard. That's courage of a kind. It's something to hold on to 80 years later.[8]

It certainly is.

Spring Offensive

Introduction

Storm Warning

O N 21 MARCH 1918, AT 4.20 a.m., a storm of fire and steel was hurled against two British armies on the Western Front. The German artillery that unleashed this onslaught had been secretly assembled around St Quentin in the southern sector of the British front line. The concentration of military force for this operation was massive: some seventy-four infantry divisions, a number greater than the entire British Expeditionary Force, and more than 6000 artillery pieces. German morale was high and they were confident of success. One fanatical young German stormtrooper, Lieutenant Ernst Junger, felt that with this huge artillery barrage and the hundreds of thousands of infantry ready to surge forward, victory was a foregone conclusion.

> When I saw this massed might piled up, the break-through seemed to me a certainty. But was there strength in us to smash the enemy's reserves and hurl them to destruction? I was convinced of it. The decisive battle, the final advance had begun. The destiny of the nations drew to its iron conclusion and the stake was possession of the world.[1]

This battle, the *Kaiserschlacht* (Kaiser's battle) or the Michael Offensive as it is also known, was to be the Germans' supreme effort to win the war. Its initial success brought the Allies on the Western Front to the brink of defeat.

The German artillery that opened fire on the British lines that morning numbered nearly 6500 guns of all calibres and more than 2000 trench mortars. It was the heaviest artillery barrage of the war and one of the largest ever used. In the first two hours the German artillery drenched the British gun positions in front of them with mustard gas. Then for the next three hours they fired a mixture of high explosive and gas shells that targeted the British infantry's forward positions. It was indeed, as the Germans labelled it, the 'Devil's Orchestra'.[2]

This bombardment lasted five hours. It was designed to stun the defenders, destroy the front-line communications, and silence the enemy artillery by its sheer weight and ferocity. It was totally successful. Ernst Junger, one of only fourteen lieutenants to win the *Pour le mérite*, Imperial Germany's highest military decoration,[3] left a vivid description of this action:

> At once the hurricane broke loose. A curtain of flames was let down, followed by a sudden impetuous tumult such as was never heard, a raging thunder that swallowed up the reports even of the heaviest guns in its tremendous reverberations and made the earth tremble. This gigantic roar of annihilation from countless guns behind us was so terrific that, compared with it, all preceding battles were child's-play. What we had not dared to hope came true. The enemy artillery was silenced, put out of action by one giant blow. We could not stay any longer in the dugouts. We got on to the top and looked with wonder at the wall of fire towering over the English lines and the swaying blood-red clouds that hung above it.[4]

Young British officer Lieutenant E.C. Allfree was on the receiving end of this wall of fire:

> So intense was the bombardment that the earth around us trembled. It was a dark night, but the tongues of flame from the guns — 2500 British guns replied to the German bombardment — lit up the night sky to daylight brightness. Mixed up with the high explosive shells crashing on our trenches, were the less noisy, but deadly gas shells. Trenches collapsed, infantry in front-line positions, groping about in their gas masks, were stunned by the sudden terrific onslaught . . .

Machine-gun posts were blown sky high — along with human limbs. Men were coughing and vomiting from the effects of gas, and men were blinded.[5]

At 9.40 a.m. the bombardment was replaced with a creeping barrage behind which advanced specially trained storm troops, equipped with numerous flame-throwers and light machine guns. Their tactic was to push forward and bypass centres of resistance. This deadly artillery and infantry combination soon overwhelmed the dazed, outnumbered British defenders in the front lines who bore the brunt of this ferocious storm. At the end of that long day the British situation on the Western Front was critical. The Fifth and Third Armies suffered 38,000 casualties and lost 500 guns. When an army loses its guns, it is a sure sign that the military situation is desperate. On 21 March the German stormtroopers managed to penetrate the front lines to a depth of 5 miles, forcing the two British armies to fall back in some confusion. Over the next six days they would be forced, in the face of renewed attack, to withdraw further, to a distance of nearly 40 miles.

In a theatre of war where gains measured in a few hundred yards were considered successful, the German rate of advance in these early days of the *Kaiserschlacht* was regarded as staggering. A withdrawal in the face of an aggressive enemy is the most difficult of military operations to perform. In the process of withdrawing the two armies, huge gaps opened up in the British lines between army and corps boundaries. The German storm troops were expert at spotting these gaps and exploiting them to the maximum. They drove through them in force, prompting further British withdrawals. The French, on the left of the British line, became so alarmed at the extent of the British casualties and at the ground being lost to the Germans that their commander considered abandoning his front-line positions and moving his armies back to protect Paris. For a time, the whole Allied line on the Western Front was in danger of collapsing. As leading First World War historian Gary Sheffield has written, the German spring offensive of 1918 'brought the allies face to face with defeat'.[6]

In order to plug these gaps in the British lines and in an attempt to stem the German advance, nine divisions were plucked from other sectors and rushed to the endangered areas. It was a last-ditch effort to hold the Germans at bay. Included were three Australian divisions and the New Zealand Division.

In March 1918 the New Zealanders were in rest areas around Cassel and Hazebrouck as part of the Second Army reserve, as described in the previous section of this book. The previous few months had not been good ones for the New Zealanders. In October 1917 they had taken part in two large offensives in the Ypres salient at Passchendaele. The second of these, on 12 October 1917, had been an absolute catastrophe; in terms of human suffering it is the greatest disaster New Zealand has ever experienced. The massacre at Passchendaele very nearly broke the spirit of the New Zealand Division. Then, in December 1917, came another failed attack at Polderhoek Chateau, with heavy casualties. From December 1917 through to February 1918 the New Zealand Division was in the Ypres salient, a period one writer has aptly described as 'dreary weeks of trench fighting in desolate wintry places'.[7] Though little fighting occurred during those two months, New Zealand battle casualties numbered 877 — 25 per cent of them were the result of poisonous gas. But evacuations of New Zealand soldiers who fell sick during this period were much higher: some 1788, 730 of whom were suffering from trench fever.[8]

From late February 1918 the soldiers of the New Zealand Division were rested and began to recover their health and spirits. The fine weather in early March 1918 helped considerably, as did the fact they were now out of the terrible Ypres salient. Time for personal administration and periods of moderate physical training also provided welcome relief. Unfortunately it was all too brief. On the first day of the *Kaiserschlacht* the New Zealand Division was placed in Army Reserve, and two days later, on 23 March 1918, it began a long trek towards the threatened areas of the British front line. Just three days after starting this march towards the sound of the guns, the first New Zealanders were in action against an enemy flushed with victory.

So, after suffering New Zealand's worst ever military defeat five months before and spending a 'winter of discontent' in the most dangerous sector of the line, and with only a few weeks of rest from this ordeal, the New Zealand Division was facing Germany's greatest offensive of the war. Once there, it was asked to plug a huge gap in the line. This section of the book concentrates on the Division's experiences and the actions it fought against the Germans in the valley of the Ancre River in March–April 1918. It was here that the New Zealanders made their most vital contribution to the Allied victory, yet, like so many New Zealand experiences in the First World War, their ordeals and achievements during those weeks remain unknown to most New Zealanders. These New Zealand soldiers played a decisive role in stopping the German storm of fire and steel that erupted on 21 March 1918. Here, for the first time, is their story.

Chapter 1

Storm Clouds

NINETEEN-SEVENTEEN WAS the hardest year of the war for the European Allies, a time of disasters and defeats. So severe were most of these setbacks that they altered the strategic situation in favour of Germany. All of the four major Allies — Britain, France, Russia and Italy — were seriously weakened and, in the case of Imperial Russia, the wounds inflicted proved fatal.

In 1917 Russia suffered the twin evils of disastrous defeat on the battlefield and revolution on the home front. It was more than the fragile Romanov Empire could stand. Most of Russia's armies had dissolved by the middle of 1917 and, at the end of November, the new revolutionary government, which the Germans had helped to create, formally requested an armistice. At the start of 1918, as General Max Hoffman, the German Chief of Staff in the East, so graphically put it, 'The whole of Russia is no more than a vast heap of maggots.'[1] The collapse of Russia altered the military balance of power in the war. Masses of men and artillery could now be released for service on the Western Front and armaments captured from defeated Russia and Romania could also be used. From November 1917, General Erich Ludendorff, the man effectively running the German war effort, was able to transfer land forces to the Western Front at the rate of two divisions a week. This would give Germany numerical superiority and the initiative on the Western Front, something they had not held since launching the Verdun offensive at the beginning of 1916. According to Cyril Falls, the elimination of Russia 'gave Germany her first and only chance of redeeming the loss of the Battle of the Marne in 1914 by winning the war on land'.[2]

There was something especially sinister about the defeat of Russia on the Eastern Front. Hostilities between Russia and Germany were not formally concluded until the signing of the Treaty of Brest-Litovsk in March 1918. Brest-Litovsk was a conqueror's peace and it was harsh. Russia lost 34 per cent of its population, 32 per cent of its agricultural land, 54 per cent of its industry and 89 per cent of its coalmines. The treaty showed the Allies the type of peace they could expect if Germany won the war. As John Terraine has aptly commented, 'Brest-Litovsk, too often forgotten now, was, in fact, what the war was about'.[3]

If Russia's condition was terminal at the end of 1917, it appeared to many that Italy's situation was not much better. After more than two years of costly, inconclusive battles on Italy's Isonzo Front, on 24 October 1917 an Austro-Hungarian army, backed up by the German strategic reserve of six divisions, launched an offensive that routed the Italian Second Army and completely ruptured the Italian front line. Italian casualties were heavy, more than 300,000, and the Second Army lost over half its strength in less than a week. The Battle of Caporetto, as this offensive is known, came close to knocking Italy out of the war. The crisis was averted largely due to poor weather, which made it impossible for the Germans and Austrians to sustain their offensive. In an effort to prop up an ally on the verge of collapse, five British and six French divisions were sent from France to Italy, along with a large number of heavy guns, planes and other materiel. Such a large diversion of troops came at a very dangerous time. The Western Front was the decisive theatre of operations in this war. Not only were the Germans increasing their numbers there as a result of their victory over Russia, but the French and British armies were in poor shape and stretched dangerously thin.

In 1918 the French Army was recovering from three years of butchery and bloodshed. The French had suffered massive casualties since the start of the war and the failure of the much-publicised Nivelle Offensive of April 1917 was the final straw. It had promised so much but delivered so little and, as a result, the French Army was seriously damaged. Soldiers in fifty-four divisions, nearly half the army, demanded better treatment for the rank and file and an end to the butchery. They refused to take part in further offensive actions. These mutinies meant that, for a considerable period, the French Army was incapable of any more large-scale offensive operations. General Henri Pétain took over the running of the French Army during this troubled time and slowly nursed it back to health. By the beginning of 1918, French military morale had improved but the army had lost its fighting spirit. Its poor condition was reflected in Pétain's strategy for victory: to wait for the Americans and the tanks.[4]

After three failed and costly British offensives on the Western Front in 1917 the British Expeditionary Force (BEF) was also in a bad state. In January 1918, after losing the equivalent of half an army to the Italian Front, the BEF consisted of four field armies. These comprised forty-seven British divisions, four Canadian divisions, five Australian divisions and the New Zealand Division. There were also five cavalry divisions, of limited use in this war, each about a third of the strength of an infantry division. The key problem, which was especially acute at the beginning of 1918 and would plague the BEF for the rest of the war, was shortage of men. At the end of 1917, the British Army Council asked for an immediate draft of 250,000 men, 95,000 of whom were needed to bring the infantry battalions in France up to strength. A further 350,000 men were required to cover wastage over the next seven months. The council was told that these numbers were excessive and that it probably would not get them. Called home to consult the War Cabinet on 7 January 1918 about his manpower requirements, Field Marshal Douglas Haig, the BEF commander, committed a crucial blunder. As Field Marshal Sir William Robertson, the Chief of the Imperial General Staff, explained to him:

> For a long time past they [the War Cabinet] have been trying to persuade me to say that the Germans may not attack this year. Unfortunately you gave as your opinion this morning that they would not do so, and I noticed as Lord Derby also did, that they jumped at the statement . . .
>
> The long and the short of it is that the cabinet think that by giving us a hundred thousand men this year in place of six hundred thousand we have asked for, you will be able to hold your own. Personally, I think that it is doubtful. My belief is that the Germans will make the heaviest attack possible this year.[5]

Two days later the notoriously inarticulate Haig[6] attempted to recover from this blunder by reversing his view. The damage was already done, however, and Haig's volte-face was exploited by a hostile Prime Minister, David Lloyd George, who asked his Cabinet, 'What is the value of a man's opinion who says one thing one day and the opposite the next?'[7]

Haig did not get the 600,000 men he requested. The Royal Navy, the newly created Royal Air Force, ship-building, munitions and food production were all to have priority in terms of manpower allocation. Haig was given 100,000 Category A men, with another 100,000 available from lower medical categories should they be needed. The irony was that the men Haig required were readily available. There was an enormous Home Army in Britain supposedly necessary in the most unlikely event of a German invasion — 1.5 million men, 449,000 of whom were medically fit and over nineteen, the official minimum age for overseas service.

There was also another barb to the War Cabinet's January decision. As Anthony Farrar-Hockley has pointed out, though he was aware of the dangers presented by the collapse of Russia, Lloyd George was 'blinded by his mistrust of Haig and Robertson . . . He fell back on the age-old remedy of administrators lacking original ideas: reorganisation.'[8] The War Cabinet directed Haig to make up his shortfall by reducing the number of cavalry divisions in the BEF and by cutting the number of battalions in an infantry division from twelve to nine. In 1916 the Germans had reorganised their divisions to contain only nine battalions and the French had soon followed their example. But Germany and France had made this change in order to form new divisions from the withdrawn regiments (of three battalions). When the BEF was ordered to carry out this reorganisation in 1918, it was not done to create new military formations, but to beef up those that remained.

The British Army Council protested about being forced to make these changes, warning of the dire consequences:

> There is every prospect of heavy fighting on the Western Front from February onwards, and the result may well be that even if the divisions successfully withstand the shock of the earlier attack,

149

they may become so exhausted and attenuated as to be incapable of continuing the struggle until the Americans can effectually intervene. In short, the Council would regard the acceptance of the recommendations in the draft report, without further effort to provide the men they consider necessary for the maintenance of the forces in the field during 1918, as taking an unreasonably grave risk of losing the War and sacrificing to no purpose the British Army on the Western Front.[9]

The War Cabinet remained unmoved and ignored the warning, ordering the reorganisation on 10 January 1918. Effectively, 145 battalions would disappear from the British order of battle. Many British historians have been scathing about these forced changes, and their timing. John Terraine's comments are typical:

So, as the German preparations for the greatest battle of the war remorselessly proceeded, the British Commander-in-Chief found himself forced to disband two of his five cavalry divisions (another Cabinet Committee edict) and was given a list of 145 infantry battalions out of which he was permitted to select the four which might survive and the 141 which must go.[10]

It took some time to implement these alterations. The disruption and the effect on the morale of those whose units were disestablished can only be imagined. Esprit de corps built up over years of fighting was killed off overnight with the stroke of a pen. Three of the British armies were reorganised during the last two weeks of February 1918 but the changes in the Fourth Army were not complete until 4 March, only two and a half weeks before the *Kaiserschlacht*. In all 115 battalions were disbanded, 38 were amalgamated to form nineteen new units and seven were converted to pioneer battalions. (These provided labour for digging trenches and other duties.) The British Army's peacetime training had been based on their divisions containing three brigades with four battalions in each. For three years the British had fought all their battles in this formation and now 'on the eve of the impending German offensive, they had to reorganise their thinking'.[11] They would not have had time to do so.

Even then, British divisions remained significantly understrength and the BEF was certainly incapable of mounting the large-scale offensive that was the hidden purpose behind this reorganisation. Those battalions that survived were supposed to number around 1000, but the lack of reinforcements meant that, in 1918, most were down to 600 men.

Of the ten dominion divisions, only the Australians were forced by severe manpower shortages to disband individual units, a price paid for Australia's refusal to introduce conscription. By the end of 1917, as Jeffrey Grey has noted, 'The effort of maintaining a field force of approximately 117,000 men in France was becoming too great for Australia to bear.'[12] The Canadians and New Zealanders retained twelve battalions in their infantry divisions, making them significantly stronger than their British counterparts. The New Zealand Division did disband its fourth infantry brigade but used it to provide a pool of reinforcements and to form three entrenching battalions as a divisional reserve. This restructuring made the New Zealand Division the strongest on the Western Front.[13] (For a breakdown of the structure of the New Zealand Division, see Appendix 1, pages 522–23.)

Another factor added to the weakness of the BEF in 1918. From the last few months of 1917 Haig was under increasing pressure to extend the British line by taking over an additional sector from the French, who wanted a more equitable share of the front line. At the beginning of 1918 the French armies were holding 350 miles of trench lines with 108 divisions, each equipped with nine infantry battalions, making a total of 972 battalions. The BEF was holding 100 miles of trench line with sixty-two divisions, but each British division had twelve infantry battalions and a pioneer battalion, making a total of 806.[14] On paper it looked grossly unfair, but the reality was different. A large section of the French line, some 150 miles to the east of St Mihiel, was virtually inactive and only one-seventh of the French Army was garrisoned here. The British sector in northern France and Belgium was an extremely active part of the front: sixty-nine German divisions faced the British across no-man's-land.

The long French front line faced seventy-nine German divisions. Since May 1917, the BEF had done the bulk of fighting on the Western Front; the French armies had not fought a major action. Also, a French soldier enjoyed three times the leave entitlements of his British counterpart, so the French divisions in the line were never at their full establishments.

Yet the French felt they were being cheated and that Britain was not doing her fair share. On one occasion, French Prime Minister Georges Clemenceau, known as 'The Tiger', even threatened to resign if the BEF did not extend its front line. Since increased responsibilities in France also suited the British government, it did not resist this pressure as firmly as it could have and Haig again lost the argument. On 14 December 1917 the Supreme War Council decided that Britain would take over an additional 26 miles of the French front, covering the sector opposite St Quentin and south towards Barisis. General Sir Hubert Gough, whose Fifth Army later had responsibility for this new sector, was scathing about the logic behind extending the British line and the pressure to 'equalise' the burden:

> This was an extremely superficial way of deciding on the disposition of troops. A sound consideration should naturally take into account the strength of the enemy in front and the importance of the bases it covered. In January 1918 there were nearly twice as many German divisions massed opposite the smaller British front, than there were opposite the French front. Moreover, behind the English front, within easy striking distance, lay the Channel ports — all vital bases of supply for our Army.[15]

The extension of the line, which was completed by the end of January, entailed the creation of a new army, the Fifth Army, under the command of General Gough. When the Fifth Army took over the additional 26 miles from the French, they found the state of the trench system extremely poor. The French assured them, however, that this was a quiet sector and that swamps on either side of the Oise River guaranteed no danger of attack. The extension meant that the BEF held the line very thinly, especially in this new sector. The Fifth Army was to hold a front of 42 miles, much longer than any held by the other British armies. The Fifth Army had the smallest number of infantry divisions — only twelve. Its 58th Division, the last BEF division on the right flank, was holding a front of 10 miles, the longest held by any British division. Spread so thinly, and without adequate reserves, the Fifth Army was an exceptionally soft target, and it would bear the brunt of the German offensive.

Why had the British government agreed to all these measures which they knew must weaken the BEF in France? The answer lies in the total breakdown of trust and confidence between the military commanders represented by Haig and Robertson, and the British government headed by Lloyd George. By the end of 1917 Lloyd George was convinced that Haig was incompetent as a military commander, yet he lacked the power to remove him. In his view, and it was not without foundation, Haig had squandered men's lives on the Somme and at Passchendaele. If Haig had his way, he would do it all again in 1918: his preferred strategy was to continue the Flanders offensive when the good weather arrived. This would renew the series of attacks that had ground to a bloody halt in the mud of Passchendaele in November 1917. Haig believed, and he was almost alone in this, that the Germans' morale was close to cracking and that one more great offensive would break them. The senior officers of France, Italy and Belgium, however, favoured remaining on the defensive in 1918 until a large United States Army was ready to take the field in 1919. This was the policy Lloyd George also favoured. Rather than more attritional stalemates on the Western Front, with their huge and politically damaging 'butchers' bills', Lloyd George wanted to concentrate on sideshows and to knock away Germany's props of Turkey, Bulgaria and Austria. British strategic plans for 1918 were decided at the Supreme War Council in January 1918. There would be no major offensive on the Western Front until 1919 when the Allies would have masses of tanks, planes and guns and the armies of the United States. In 1918, the British would make Palestine their main offensive. The British armies in France were deliberately being kept weak in order to prevent a renewal of the offensive in Flanders.

There were several problems with this strategy. The first was that

Germany was propping up its allies; they were not vital to her war effort. The second was that the Western Front, as Haig and Robertson recognised, was the decisive front of the war. Haig was also correct in his assertions that the Somme and Ypres Offensive had seriously damaged the fighting quality of the German Army. Yet now, while the Germans were concentrating their efforts on the Western Front, the BEF was being reduced in strength. Third, this strategy required the BEF to stand on the defensive for all of 1918, requiring tactics with which they were wholly unfamiliar. According to the British official war historian, Sir James Edmonds, after two-and-a-half years of offensive warfare the BEF 'were not well trained to stand on the defensive and to deal with attacks by infiltration; they were totally untrained in the carrying out of a retreat'.[16] Finally, as the historian of the New Zealand Rifle Brigade recognised, 'It was clear that for a time the initiative must pass from the Allies to the Germans. A defensive policy was therefore adopted, and preparations were made to meet a strong and sustained hostile offensive.'[17]

The initiative did not automatically pass to the Germans on the Western Front in 1918; it was gifted to them by the Allies' chosen strategy. Though the British government was fully aware of the growing German concentration against the Allies on the Western Front, they accepted the risks associated with keeping the BEF in a weakened state. Part of their risk assessment was based on recent British failures. According to Winston Churchill, at the time munitions minister in the War Cabinet, the British government 'believed that the Germans if they attacked would encounter the same difficulties as so long baffled us, and that our armies were amply strong enough for defence'.[18] Seeking to restrict Haig's activities on the Western Front by subterfuge rather than by direct instructions to him would seriously impair the fighting effectiveness of the BEF in the early months of 1918. This was 'unlikely to avoid the merited censure of posterity'.[19]

The strategy decided upon by the Allies in 1918 recognised that the United States would eventually become a key player on the Western Front. The entry of the Americans into the war in April 1917 compensated in some respects for the Russians leaving the war at the end of the year.

Historian John Mosier has christened the period from April 1917 to April 1918 'the Great Race': could the United States Army take the field before the Germans won the war in the west?[20] At the beginning of 1918, though, the Germans were clearly winning. In 1917 the United States was in no state for decisive and immediate intervention. It possessed a formidable naval fleet that could be used immediately, but its army was 'only a skeleton and to put flesh upon it was going to be a long task, which would show no results at all for some time'.[21] Raising, equipping, training and sustaining a large field army would take considerable time and effort. In April 1917, the United States Army did not have even a single division and there were serious shortages in the most basic of equipment. The American military possessed no aircraft or trained pilots and industry was not geared for war production. Added to the problems of creating a field army from scratch were the difficulties of getting this army to France. Shipping space was at a premium and added to the length of time before the United States could deploy its armies. At the beginning of 1918, there were only four American divisions in France — the 1st, 2nd, 26th and 42nd Divisions, totalling 130,000 troops. But these men had to be equipped and trained before they could take to the battlefield, and even then they could not be used. Unless it was a dire emergency, the American commander General John Pershing refused to allow his troops to be committed piecemeal. These newly raised American divisions would be allowed to fight only as part of a United States-led army. Given that it had taken Britain almost two years to raise an army capable of large-scale offensive action on the Western Front, little could be expected from the Americans until the second half of 1918.

In his brilliant history of the First World War, Cyril Falls neatly encapsulated the strategy forced upon the belligerents on the Western Front. According to him, the stronger side had no option but to carry out offensive operations: 'And if the stronger side did not attack on the Western Front it played into the hands of the weaker, which asked nothing better than it should be left in peace during the phase of weakness.'[22]

By the early months of 1918 Germany had the strongest army in France, but her military leaders knew this would not long be the case.

They were determined, therefore, to exploit this temporary position of strength. General Ludendorff would make the strongest possible attack against the BEF where it was weakest. Victory here could split the Allies and win the war.

Although the German Army possessed some of the world's most talented military intellects, by 1918, its fate lay in the hands of one man, the First Quartermaster General, Erich Ludendorff. A man of mixed ability and unstable temperament, he alone dictated the army's strategy and tactics. As Churchill wrote of Ludendorff's influence in 1918, 'We must regard him at this juncture as the dominating will.'[23] Though Ludendorff was nominally subordinate to Field Marshal Paul von Hindenburg and the Kaiser, he had almost unfettered powers of command over the German Army. As he stated frankly in his memoirs, 'My sense of responsibility was far too great. I alone had to decide, of that I remained conscious throughout.'[24]

In 1918, the German Army was in a paradoxical situation. Numerically it had never been stronger, yet in terms of quality it was 'in palpable decline'.[25] The collapse of Russia and Romania meant that, for the first time, the Germans outnumbered their opponents on the Western Front. As Ludendorff later recorded, the military situation was 'more favourable to us . . . than one could have ever expected'.[26] However, three years of attritional warfare had taken a heavy toll on the German Army. Its best soldiers had become casualties and it was riddled with what Ludendorff called 'skulkers', men who disappeared during dangerous periods and reappeared when things had quietened down.[27] There was an acute shortage of men caused by an 'uncommonly high' desertion rate.[28] Tens of thousands of German deserters had fled to internment in neutral Holland and an equal number were living in Germany where sympathetic local authorities seemed happy to turn a blind eye.

It seemed, then, that the strategy of attrition initiated by the Germans at Verdun and adopted by the Allies on the Somme in 1916 and in several offensives in 1917 'was at last bearing fruit'.[29] The last thing the German High Command wanted in 1918 was a repeat of the Allied offensives of 1917, which had inflicted heavy casualties and, more importantly, drained the army's morale. In order to survive, the German Army needed to attack and now had the numbers to do so, as Ludendorff made clear in his memoirs:

> Against the weight of the enemy's material the troops no longer displayed their old stubbornness; they thought with horror of fresh defensive battles and longed for a war of movement . . . As they were depressed by defence their spirits rose in the offensive. The interests of the Army were best served by the offensive; in defence it was bound gradually to succumb to the ever-increasing hostile superiority in men and material. This feeling was shared by everybody. In the West the Army pined for the offensive . . . It amounted to a definite conviction which obsessed them utterly that nothing but an offensive could win the war.[30]

Ludendorff made the decision to launch a major offensive in the spring of 1918 at a conference at Mons on 11 November 1917. As we have seen, from November 1917 the German Army started transferring infantry divisions from the east to the west at the rate of two divisions a week and by mid March 1918 had an additional forty-six divisions on the Western Front. These were fresh and at full strength. When the Germans began the offensive on 21 March they had a total of 192 divisions;[31] the Allies could field only 175. By May 1918 the number of German divisions had peaked at 208 while that of the Allies had fallen to 173.[32] In addition, the Hindenburg Industrial Scheme enabled Ludendorff to recall 123,000 men from industry to the army. By the opening day of the attack 136,618 German officers and 3,438,288 other ranks were crammed into the Western Front ready for action.[33]

A significant number of guns accompanied the million men who came from the east. These included German and Austrian artillery pieces now regarded as surplus, as well as weapons recently captured from the Russians and Italians. Some 3000 of these guns, 1000 classified as heavy, now appeared on the Western Front ready for action.

How was this mighty array of military force to be used? Though the

decision about a major offensive was made on 11 November, the plans for
how that offensive would unfold were not finalised until 21 January 1918.
The reason for the delay was the number of options open to Ludendorff,
which made it difficult to decide where to attack. There were three obvious
sectors: in Flanders in the north between Ypres and Lens, on both sides of
Verdun in the south, and between Arras and St Quentin in the centre of
the line. After consideration Ludendorff decided to attack on both sides
of the town of St Quentin. There were compelling strategic and tactical
reasons for attacking at this point:

> . . . here the attack would strike the enemy's weakest point, the
> ground offered no difficulties, and it was feasible in all seasons . . . If
> this blow succeeded the strategic result might indeed be enormous,
> as we could separate the bulk of the English Army from the French
> and crowd it up with its back to the sea.[34]

The objective of the attack was to separate the French and British
Armies at their junction some 30 miles south of Cambrai. The BEF would
be then forced back to the Channel with 'little room for manoeuvre and
none for escape'.[35] It would be hemmed in against the coast, leaving the
Germans free to deal with the French. Both armies would be tied to their
critical vulnerabilities — the BEF to the Channel ports and the French
to Paris. There they could be isolated and defeated. It was hoped that
the BEF and the French armies would become so exhausted during the
offensive and subsequent withdrawal that they would sue for peace. An
ambitious timetable was set for the offensive. It aimed to push the British
back over the Somme on the first day, enforce a general retreat down the
Somme Valley on the second day and take the strategic town of Arras
by the third day.

This attack, given the name Michael, was to be the main effort of
the German offensive and other attacks (named Mars and George) were
planned to supplement it. Michael was to be an immense undertaking
involving seventy-four divisions, three armies and a combined soldiery
larger than the 1918 population of New Zealand. Orders for Michael

were issued on 10 March 1918. Attacking across an enormous front of 50 miles, from the Oise to Croisilles near Arras, were three armies divided between two army groups. In the north was the Seventeenth Army, newly arrived from Italy and commanded by General Otto von Below. In the centre was General von der Marwitz's Second Army. Both these armies were in the Army Group of Crown Prince Rupprecht of Bavaria and they were to make the main inroads in this attack by cutting off the Cambrai salient on each side and pushing through to Croisilles and Péronne. Protecting the left flank of Rupprecht's armies was the Eighteenth Army under General Oscar von Hutier, who had only recently arrived from the Eastern Front where he had a formidable reputation. He had been instrumental in breaking the Russian Army at Riga in September 1917 and had pioneered new artillery techniques to do so. When given his new command von Hutier insisted on bringing his artillery expert from the Eastern Front, Lieutenant Colonel Georg Bruchmüller. Von Hutier's Eighteenth Army was in the Army Group of the German Crown Prince.[36] The Seventeenth Army would attack in the Arras area against the BEF's Third Army. The other two armies, numbering forty-three divisions, would attack the weakest of the British armies, the Fifth, then comprising only twelve divisions. Michael was an undertaking deserving of the name *Kaiserschlacht*.

The offensive aimed to pierce and break through the Allies' front line, sending them reeling back in defeat. This was what both sides on the Western Front had been attempting to do for the past three years, without success. Solving the problem of endemic trench warfare required a new sort of offensive tactics. At the end of 1917 the German Army came up with an innovative set of solutions, quite an achievement given that the Germans had not taken offensive action on the Western Front for more than a year. Reviving some of the earlier principles of offensive operations and combining them with the recent lessons of the failed Allied offensives, the Germans introduced several tactical innovations aimed at breaking the deadlock of trench warfare. As Ludendorff explained in a set of notes issued in January 1918, the success of any offensive operation depended on skilful leadership at all levels and on adaptability:

our attack must differ essentially in this respect from the attacks hitherto undertaken by the British. The British believed in the efficacy of their skilfully worked out but rigid artillery barrage; this was to carry forward the infantry attack, which advanced without any impetus of its own. The subordinate and, still more, the higher commanders ceased to have any further influence.[37]

Although the recent British attacks — Somme, Arras, Messines, Flanders and Cambrai — had caused considerable alarm,

> . . . the initial tactical successes, which were frequently very considerable, were not seized upon and were not usefully exploited. A defeat was eventually the outcome of this narrow-minded principle on which the conduct of the battle and the leadership was based.[38]

As British novelist, biographer and military historian John Buchan wrote of the 1918 offensive, Germany 'deserves all credit for a brilliant departure from routine, a true intellectual effort to rethink the main problem of modern war'.[39] The novel use of infantry soldiers and some innovative employment of artillery amounted to a revolution in military firepower.

In the German infantry companies, the light machine guns ceased to be regarded as auxiliary weapons and became standard infantry weapons. This increased firepower was further enhanced by quick-firing weapons of all kinds, plus various sorts of rifle grenades and the flame-thrower. The infantry units and sub-units were augmented by sections of heavy machine guns and light trench mortars. German infantry units were classified into three types. The best soldiers, in some cases whole battalions of them, were chosen as *Sturmabteilungen* or storm troops. Divided into mobile teams armed with light machine guns, mortars and flame-throwers, they had the task of penetrating the enemy lines where they were weakest. They would lead the assault but not in packed ranks. They acted more like skirmishers, except that there were large numbers of these small groups all closing on the enemy at speed. They would head the assault, pressing on through weakly held positions and past any centres of resistance, which would be left to the waves of infantry following them. If possible, the storm troops were to break through and threaten the enemy's artillery positions. As the vanguard of the assault, the storm troops were to be constantly kept up to strength by reinforcement and they received priority for all vital equipment — stores, horses, support weapons and rations. Behind the storm troops came the battle units. These were composed of regular infantry units, machine guns, trench mortars, engineers, field artillery and ammunition carriers. Their task was to mop up the strongpoints bypassed by the storm troops. In the third category were the poorer quality soldiers whose sole job was to occupy trenches.

The other main innovation involved the use of artillery, the focus of the storm troops' tactics. The German artillery for this offensive was concentrated in numbers 'in a quantity never before dreamed of, and used with great sophistication'.[40] They would be controlled by the outstanding artillerist Colonel Bruchmüller. All guns to be used in the offensive were tested for individual errors behind the lines and a simple table was constructed for each one, explaining how to adjust it when firing on a target. Ranges were accurately measured. Maps were made as accurate as possible and targets plotted on them using the techniques of flash spotting, sound ranging and aerial photography. A great deal of work had to be done before the attack. The artillery bombardment unleashed to support the offensive would be short, only a few hours long, but it would be enormous and ferocious. Ludendorff's 'battering ram' consisted of 3965 field and medium guns, 2435 heavy and seventy-three super-heavy guns and howitzers. By comparison, on the opening day of the Somme the BEF had used 149 heavy and eighteen super-heavy guns.[41]

Once the German artillery had had sufficient time to pound the British artillery and front-line trenches, the German infantry in its forward positions would then advance behind a powerful creeping barrage. The offensive would be supported by over 700 aircraft but by very few tanks. In the vital sector of the Third and Fifth Armies there were 730 German planes, 326 of which were single-seater fighters. Opposing them was the

Royal Flying Corps with 579 machines, including 261 single-seater fighters. These numbers are significant. As the British official historian later stated, 'For the first time, the German air concentration for battle on the Western Front was greater than that of the Royal Flying Corps.'[42] Tanks were a different matter. In March 1918, the German Army possessed only fifteen tanks of their own design and a small number of captured English ones. Tanks would be used on only one sector, near St Quentin. Ludendorff did not rate tanks highly as weapons of war and therefore he 'had not recognised their value or ensured their provision'.[43]

So, in essence, the German assault of 1918 involved no preliminary massing of troops. Men would be brought up by night marches only just before zero hour, thus achieving a tactical surprise. There was to be no long artillery preparation to alarm the enemy. The attack would be preceded by a short, intense bombardment that would deluge the enemy's back areas and support lines with gas shells. The infantry assault, following hard on the heels of a creeping barrage, would be made with picked troops, in small clusters, armed with many automatic weapons. Their aim was to punch small holes in the front line through which they could infiltrate, outflank and encircle. A system of flares and rockets would let the battle units know where the gaps had been made. The storm troops at the front of the offensive had unlimited objectives, rations and ammunition to last them for several days. When one unit of the storm troops tired or suffered heavy casualties, another took its place, 'like a continuous game of leap-frog'.[44] Ludendorff's tactical notes were emphatic on the use of reserves.

> [They] will . . . not be thrown into the battle at points where the attack has been held up by strong points and centres of resistance, and where unnecessary sacrifice is involved, but at points where the attack is still in movement and its progress can be facilitated with a view to breaking down the enemy's resistance in the neighbouring sector by rolling it up from flank and rear.[45]

Acknowledging that the position of all commanders was 'of considerable importance', Ludendorff directed that 'All staffs, including

Corps staffs, must be on the battlefield, the divisional staffs being pushed well forward'.[46] In many respects, with the exception of the absence of tanks, this new method of attack had a 'modern' look.

For the last two months of 1917 and the first two months of 1918 the German Army was trained in these new techniques, 'another tremendous task', according to Ludendorff.[47] There was no time to prepare every division: only the 56th, and a large proportion of the German artillery, underwent this training. But all levels of command were involved, including the higher level commanders, staff officers, officers and soldiers, and it was comprehensive. In his autobiographical account of the war, Ernst Junger described the training scheme for this offensive as 'marvellously clear', with Ludendorff's directive being distributed 'even to company commands'.[48] Fourteen of the storm troop divisions trained with aircraft and practised new techniques of close air support. The training culminated in live firing exercises which included having the infantry advance behind a creeping barrage. With nearly every available slope behind the front line being used as a firing range it was little wonder that there were many casualties. Junger described the bullets as 'whistl[ing] about the country very much as in a battle' and admitted that a machine-gunner in his company accidentally shot the commanding officer of another unit from his horse while that unfortunate man was reviewing his troops. 'Fortunately the wound was not mortal, and equally fortunately the deed was not clearly brought home to us.'[49] By the end of February the trained units began the lengthy process of moving into position for the attack. As Junger wrote, 'Training was over; and now we came to the business, not a wheel of the machine was to be checked.'[50]

According to John Terraine, the 1918 German offensive was 'the decisive battle of the war'.[51] The Germans understood the importance of the forthcoming offensive and the stakes involved. As Ludendorff was well aware, it was a huge gamble that would either win or lose the war.

> All that had gone before was merely a means to the one end of creating a situation that would make it a feasible operation . . . That the attack in the West would be one of the most difficult operations

in history I was perfectly sure, and I did not hide the fact. The German nation too, would have to give all it had.[52]

When Ludendorff met the Kaiser and the Imperial Chancellor at Hamburg on 13 February 1918, he told them:

> The battle in the West is the greatest military task that has ever been imposed upon an army, and one in which England and France have been trying for two years to compass . . . I believe too, that I, who have to furnish the Field Marshal with the foundation on which he bases his request for His Majesty's decision, am more than anyone impressed by the immensity of the undertaking . . . The Army in the West is waiting for the opportunity to act. We must not imagine that this offensive will be like those in Gallicia or Italy; it will be an immense struggle that will begin at one point, continue at another, and take a long time; it is difficult, but it will be victorious.

Ludendorff concluded by reporting to his emperor 'that the Army was assembled and well prepared to undertake the biggest task in its history'.[53]

Because of the enormity of the task before them, the German troops were told that the Emperor was in command — this would be the *Kaiserschlacht*, his battle. It was for this reason that von Hutier's army was placed under the German Crown Prince (and would in the course of the battle compete with the other armies for the lion's share of the glory). The Kaiser and his generals were also hoping that, by giving the German people the decisive victory they craved, they would restore the waning prestige of the royal house. The future of the House of Hohenzollern and the fate of the German nation were the ultimate stakes in Ludendorff's massive gamble. To paraphrase Gary Sheffield, in 1918 the German Army risked everything to obtain victory on the Western Front. Failure could cost them everything.[54]

That there would be a great German offensive in the early months of 1918 was the worst kept military secret of the war. For example, on 16 March 1918, the German Minister of the Interior, Karl Helfferich, delivered a public lecture on Germany and England. He told his audience that the outcome of the war would be decided very soon on the battlefields of France:

> Where is Hindenburg? . . . He stands in the West with our whole German manhood for the first time united in a single theatre of war, ready to strike with the strongest army that the world has ever known.[55]

Allied military intelligence detected the German build-up of troops and material. In the first week of February 1918, for example, the Fifth Army's intelligence section reported that the Germans had sixty-four divisions, all trained and rested and within three nights' march of St Quentin, the town opposite the centre of their line. This was how the Germans had massed their forces before their successful attacks at Riga and Caporetto. The Army Commander, General Gough, passed this information on to GHQ and to his corps commanders. Gough had also discovered that von Hutier, new to the Western Front, was commanding the Germans.

Warnings also came from other sources. Early in the year, the King of Spain informed the French military attaché in Madrid that 'a great blow to end the War was intended, and that it was already imminent and likely to be struck in February'.[56] As Ludendorff noted in his memoirs, 'All the world, including the Entente, knew we were going to attack in the West.'[57]

The problem for the Allies, though, was that they did not know where or when the attack was coming. An elaborate German deception plan gave their entire front the appearance of preparing to mount a large-scale offensive in the immediate future. Meanwhile the real build-up continued, well concealed from the Allies. The Germans occupied an area of France well served by an intricate railway network, which meant they were capable of strategic surprise.

So what did the Allies, and in particular the British upon whom the mighty blow was soon to fall, do to prepare for the imminent offensive?

Forced on to the defensive by a lack of reinforcements, the British Army had some serious problems. It had fought defensive battles in 1914–15, but by 1918 the men who had conducted them were mostly gone. From 1916 to 1917 the BEF had concentrated its education and experience on offensive action. Now training and education for a defensive role was urgently required. But preparing for a withdrawal over many miles 'never entered anyone's mind'.[58] To ready itself for this new role the British Army attempted to copy the German methods of defence that had successfully thwarted their efforts over the last two years. In doing so, they misunderstood the key principles behind the German methods and applied them wrongly.

The British had captured German manuals of defensive techniques soon after they were issued in August 1917. On 14 December the BEF's GHQ issued instructions as to how their front line should be defended using the 'German' methods. The line was divided into three zones of defence: the Forward Zone (called the Outpost Zone by the Germans), the Battle Zone and the Rear Zone. The Forward Zone was the apex of the front line. Supposed to be lightly held, it relied on many machine guns for its firepower. Its task was to guard against surprise and compel the enemy to deploy strong forces in order to capture it. It was intended to drain any attack of its momentum. Behind the Forward Zone, on the ground most suited to defensive warfare, was the Battle Zone. It could be anywhere from 600 yards to as much as 3 miles from the Forward Zone but was usually 1 to 2 miles behind it. The Battle Zone was about 3000 yards deep. Designed to repulse whatever attack the enemy might make, it was heavily fortified by mutually supporting redoubts and machine-gun nests. This ground was to be held at all costs, even if meant deploying corps or army reserves.

An attack should be halted in the Battle Zone, but in case it wasn't a Rear Zone was also to be constructed as the ground of last resort, the area to which the defence could fall back if necessary. The Rear Zone was to be about 4 to 8 miles behind the Battle Zone. Owing to a shortage of labour, in 1918 the Rear Zone had only been reconnoitred and marked out for construction. In some parts of the British line, it consisted of 'the removal of a spit of turf to show where the trench should be dug'.[59]

Simply copying the enemy's methods without understanding why they worked eventually proved disastrous for the BEF. The January 1918 change of name from Outpost Zone to Forward Zone indicates how little the British understood of the German methods of defence. An Outpost Zone implied that the ground was not to be seriously contested and that there would be a withdrawal only when things got too hot for the defenders. Yet in March 1918 some of the BEF's Forward Zones were more than 2 miles wide, impeding a hasty withdrawal, making support from the Battle Zone difficult and allowing the Forward Zone to be surrounded. The troops holding the Forward Zone were instructed to 'do all in their power to maintain their ground against attack'.[60] The danger was, and it did eventuate, that good troops would be sacrificed trying to hold ground of no vital importance.

The German method of defence in depth relied on a decentralised method of control which the British, in early 1918, were ill prepared to practise. As an American historian has recently commented:

> On the one hand, the British failed to grasp the key basis of German defensive success, the holding back of most of the infantry so the attackers would be sucked into a trap, blasted by artillery, exhausted by their trek, and then wiped out by the developing counterattack. In actual practice, most British infantry were too far forward. On the other hand, British practice was such that there was no possibility of giving low-level unit commanders the authority they needed to determine when and where to fight. German tactics worked because the Germans decentralized decision making downward. Simply copying their troop dispositions hardly solved the problem.[61]

In March 1918, the British attempt to emulate the German system of defence proved a total failure.

On 10 January 1918, XVIII Corps of the Fifth Army, under Lieutenant General Sir Ivor Maxse, began the takeover of a sector of the line previously held by the French Sixth Army. This meant that the British front line was now 26 miles longer. The newly acquired portion of the front did not have the three zones of defence. Only a belt of wire marked the second, vital zone. To hold this 126-mile line, Haig had fifty-nine divisions consisting of forty-seven British divisions, four Canadian, five Australian, one New Zealand and two Portuguese divisions. He also had three cavalry divisions, each the equivalent in size of an infantry brigade. Haig's dispositions showed that his main concern was his left flank and the Channel ports. From the coast to the link with the French Army Haig spread his forces as follows. The Second Army, nearest the coast, held 23 miles of front with twelve divisions. Next came the First Army, stretching to Vimy, a distance of 33 miles which it held with fourteen divisions. Third Army held its 28 miles of front with fourteen divisions. Anchoring the British right flank was the Fifth Army, which had twelve divisions (plus three cavalry divisions) to hold 42 miles of front. In addition there were eight divisions in GHQ reserve, parcelled out two behind each army.

These reserves were wholly inadequate to cover such a long front, but there were other serious concerns for the British commanders. Not one division was at full strength. Those in General Gough's Fifth Army were typical. As Gough recorded when the attack came, 'Instead of strength of 12,000 men, none of them [his infantry divisions] could produce more than 6000.'[62] The divisional frontages of British armies were too long for the number of divisions they contained. In the Fifth Army, the average front for a division was 6750 yards. In the Third Army it was 4700 yards. The average length of frontage for German divisions at this time was 1200 yards.[63] Then there was the appalling disposition of the Fifth Army, which would soon bear the brunt of the German offensive.

Despite being one of the weakest of the British armies and still recovering from its battering in the Third Battle of Ypres, the Fifth Army held the largest portion of the line. When Gough took over in 1918 it was 42 miles long and had only one line of defence, based on the old British and German trenches of 1916. It possessed only one natural feature that could be a useful obstacle in defence: the water line of the River Somme and canal, and its extension to the Oise River known as the Crozat Canal. General Gough estimated that he needed seventeen divisions as a minimum to hold this line. As William Moore noted, 'Never, during the

First World War, had a British Army been spread so thinly.'[64] When Gough asked Haig to explain why he was being kept so weak in the south Haig replied that he expected the French to assist the Fifth Army in the event of a serious German attack. Also, the marshes of the Oise were impassable and provided Gough's army with good flank protection. Haig explained further that he considered his north and central sector vital. The loss of the Channel ports in the north, he said, 'would be absolutely fatal to the British Army and probably decisive to the war'.[65] The nearest point of strategic significance in the Fifth Army's sector was the great railway centre of Amiens, nearly 40 miles behind Gough's front. This, Haig felt, could not be threatened in the foreseeable future.

During the months of February and March, Gough became increasingly uneasy about the front he was holding and the forces allocated to him. His intelligence sources detected in this area a huge build-up of the German Eighteenth Army. The current spell of excellent spring weather had dried out the swamps around the Oise, making them no obstacle at all to advancing troops. Gough knew that, in their current state, his troops were sitting ducks. A huge front to defend, an acute shortage of men, a German defensive doctrine hastily adopted and poorly understood, limited time for training especially in defensive tactics, lack of time to add depth to their defensive positions — little wonder Gough and other British commanders viewed the coming of the German offensive with foreboding. It is hard not to agree with the New Zealand historian who wrote that the British front in March 1918 was 'thinly held and inadequately organised'.[66]

On the night of 20 March 1918, a gentle rain, the first for eight weeks, started to fall on the British soldiers in the front line. A major in the London Regiment recalled this pleasant evening, the last that many British soldiers would ever experience:

> . . . strangely still and peaceful; few of war's usual discordant sounds disturbed the last quiet hours of the departing day. The whole country was instinct with the sweetness and vigour of approaching spring . . . Yet over all there was a presage of impending disaster.[67]

Chapter 2

A Brief Interlude

OCTOBER 1917 THROUGH to the middle of February 1918 was the worst of times for the New Zealand Division. A military disaster at Passchendaele on 12 October, another failed attack at Polderhoek in November and then three months wintering in the Ypres salient had taken a fearful toll, and Christmas provided no respite. On 24 December the New Zealanders were shelled for more than two hours. As Oscar Reston, a signaller in one of the Canterbury battalions, recalled many years later, 'After you stood up to that for a couple of hours, you just felt like a jelly. It's a horrible feeling I tell you.'[1] A Christmas dinner of iron rations — bully beef and biscuits — did little to improve the men's spirits. The conditions in the Ypres salient were almost indescribable. For Reston, it was

> . . . the worst place ever I was in. It wasn't like going over the top . . .
> You were sort of pinned down by shellfire all the time. You never
> got rid of it. It was there all the time and you were likely to get
> blown up. You never knew when a shell was coming.[2]

Many years later Thomas Eltringham, a Lewis gunner from the 2nd Auckland Battalion, remained incredulous about the conditions he experienced in the Ypres salient:

> Mud, slush. You imagine a strip of land from the Belgium border
> to the Swiss border — but in the middle . . . nothing but mud &
> slush, dug up by shellfire . . . not a green blade of grass, not a leaf
> on a tree not a cat or a dog or any sort. Just mud and slush. And
> we had to live in it. Now that was the Ypres front . . . And we lived
> in that. If anyone had told me when I went to war that I would be

able to stand up to that, I would have laughed at them. I would have said it's impossible.[3]

After three months of this hell on earth the New Zealanders were in a poor state. According to James McWhirter, a veteran of the Auckland Infantry Regiment, by the beginning of 1918 the Division was 'trench weary' and overdue for 'a well-earned rest'.[4] Leaving the men for so long in this sector of the line nearly broke their spirit. As the historian of the Otago battalions admitted:

> Continuous fighting under the worst possible conditions of ground and weather, such as had been experienced in the salient over the preceding few months, had produced a state of complete exhaustion.[5]

'They'd had it', Oscar Reston recalled. 'Those who were fit to stay on, by the time they got out of Ypres and got shifted down to the Somme, they were due to go out. They'd had plenty.'[6]

On 24 February 1918, the New Zealand Division handed over its sector in the Ypres salient to the British 49th Division and passed into the Second Army's rest area. The New Zealanders did not know it then, but the Division's period of active service in Flanders was over. Not all the Kiwis experienced this fortunate change of circumstance though. The Maori Pioneer Battalion remained at Ypres digging trenches and laying belts of barbed wire to protect them — a backbreaking, laborious task. They also spent some time strengthening the pillboxes. The Maori continued this work uninterrupted until 21 March 1918, when news of the German offensive reached them. The next day, after three months in the salient, the battalion was on the road heading south. Their experience was shared by the New Zealand artillery brigades, who also remained in the line at Ypres supporting the divisions of the Second Army. It would take them three to four days to pack up and start their journey south.

At the end of February 1918 the bulk of the Division was billeted in pleasant villages around Cassel and Caestre. The first few days were devoted to what the army calls 'interior economy': cleaning equipment, refurbishing missing or lost equipment and reorganising individual units so that their numbers approximated what the establishment levels indicated they should be. James McWhirter, who was a member of a machine-gun crew, noted in his diary that although warned to move at five minutes' notice, 'Our first undertaking was to overhaul all our guns, spare parts, ammunition, belts, ropes & other gear'.[7] The light workloads, coupled with a spell of glorious spring weather and the attention of friendly villagers, soon revived the exhausted men's spirits. Great efforts were made to remove all traces of the Flanders mud.

> All this cleaning had its effect. As clothing and equipment became spotless and shining, the stain of the mud and blood of the autumn and winter from the salient commenced to fade from the men's minds.[8]

After the first three days out of the line, the cleaning was combined with some light training designed, as the war diary of the 2nd Brigade explained, with 'the object of smartening the men up'.[9] Other activities included inspection parades by the ever-watchful divisional commander, Major General Andrew Russell, and sporting competitions. On 9 March a football match was held between New Zealand and their great rugby rivals of the day, the Welsh. As the war diary of the 2nd Otago Battalion shows, some things never change: 'In afternoon Football match, WALES V NEW ZEALAND was held at HONDEGHEM. Game was very ragged at times, although full of incident. Wales won by 13 points to 9 and on the play deserved their win, although the referee's decisions were at times peculiar.' The New Zealanders thoroughly enjoyed being out of the line, but there was a nagging suspicion that the respite would not last very long. As Ezekiel Mawhinny wrote to his sister Laura in New Zealand on 10 March:

> . . . as usual there isn't anything to say. We are still out for a spell and things are going all right as long as Fritz doesn't get too ostropulus somewhere and cause us to get sent back into the line again.[10]

By the middle of March, the training programme was in full swing and it had a new focus. As well as the standard, repetitive musketry training with rifles and Lewis guns, emphasis was now placed on the use of infantry weapons in the open, in combination with machine guns, mortars and artillery fire support. Various war diaries record training for an 'attack in open warfare',[11] attacking trenches across open ground and various tactical schemes illustrating the 'Principles of Fire and Movement'.[12] The New Zealand Division, under Russell's guidance, had begun to train in the techniques of open warfare, which had not been seen on the Western Front since the opening months of the war.

Despite Russell's prescience in initiating this type of training, it was a case of too little, too late and he was unhappy with the standards reached by his division. When, on 8 March, Russell watched two battalions of the 2nd Brigade training for an advance in open country he was disappointed: it was 'extraordinarily difficult to get the right idea of fire and movement carried out'. Three days later, and only ten days before the start of the German offensive, he watched the same brigade undergoing company field training. 'I was frankly disappointed, and think that it is doubtful if we can get the division up to anything like a decent standard in open warfare.' On 21 March, the day the German spring offensive began, Russell paid a surprise visit again to the 2nd Brigade 'to see what work the units of the 2nd Bde were doing — not much, chiefly competitions, instead of taking advantage of fine weather and good training ground'.[13]

The New Zealand historian of the division was in no doubt about the state of the New Zealand Division barely a month after leaving the Ypres salient: 'By the middle of March rest and training had reforged the Division into a weapon of sterling quality'.[14] The war diary of the 2nd Infantry Brigade echoed this view, although it was not quite as emphatic: 'the Brigade on the eve of offensive operations, is in the best of form, and as well trained as is possible under present conditions'.[15] Even General Russell was occasionally pleased by what he saw. On 1 March he had described the men of the 3rd (New Zealand Rifles) Brigade as 'looking well, and full of go'. On 5 March he had found the two Otago battalions 'quite satisfactory' and he felt 'quite cheered and encouraged'.[16]

Yet there are several warning signs that the New Zealand Division was not as well prepared for the ordeal ahead as several commentators have suggested.[17] First, those who had been through the hell of Passchendaele were physical and emotional wrecks: 'They'd had it. Exhaustion.'[18] Then the period spent in training for open warfare was too brief — only nine days — and the division had not reached a high standard. Finally, the effects of the disasters of Passchendaele, Polderhoek and the winter in Ypres should not be underestimated. As Ormond Burton recalled, 'There is a limit to what men can endure and during the winter of 1917–18 this limit was very nearly reached.'[19] Some units in the Division had been seriously affected. On 4 March Russell inspected the two Canterbury battalions and found mixed results.

> 1st Canterbury was . . . distinctly good . . . 2nd Canterbury distinctly bad — this latter suffers from a complete change of officers including C.O. who is only temporary — Stewart on leave — In everything they require bracing up — Heavy casualties in bde and at Polderhoek account for deterioration.[20]

A unit in such a poor state could not recover its fighting spirit in less than a fortnight. The New Zealand Division had no doubt benefited from its time out of the line, but it was certainly not in peak condition.

On 14 March, the New Zealanders were issued a warning order preparing them for rapid movement in case of an emergency. On 21 March the men learned that the Germans had opened their massive offensive and seemed to be carrying all before them — 'Wild stories of impossible captures and impossible losses were passed from mouth to mouth'.[21] These rumours were soon confirmed. The German Army had broken through on a wide front, the Fifth Army was falling back on the Somme and the Germans were in pursuit, surging towards Amiens in an attempt to cut railway communications, isolate the Channel ports and destroy the British Army. Edward Bibby and the rest of the Division could see what lay ahead:

We knew that the Russians had surrendered and the Germans were bringing back all their Eastern troops and massing them along the border. They knew and we knew, even the ordinary private soldier, that once the Americans got over in force they could stop the Germans. So the Germans must act quickly in spring and we knew that we would be involved. They told us that within a month we would be in a major conflict.[22]

On 21 March the Division was ordered to be ready for immediate movement. The next day Russell received his instructions: 'Word has come that we are to be ready to move south at once to the Somme, to help hold up the German offensive which has been let loose on a 50 mile front — the men very pleased, I hear'.[23] Amid the laughter, tears and prayers of the local villagers, the first New Zealand units set off for the Second Battle of the Somme at dawn the following day. Up to this time the Division had experienced only offensive operations in France — they had been involved in attacking the Germans. Now, for the first time in the war, they would be on the receiving end of a German Army flushed with victory. They would have their first experience of defensive operations in one of the decisive battles of the war, and it would test them to the limits.

The New Zealanders were not the only soldiers called to assist the beleaguered British divisions on the Somme. Three Australian divisions were also on the way. Brigadier W.R. McNicoll, of the 10th Brigade, made a stirring speech to his officers on the road at Campagne in Flanders:

with his map before him, he put the position plainly. He told us that the Fifth Army had been driven back, and were retreating everywhere, and that the British front was broken and the British and French Armies were in danger of separation; that the German divisions were pushing forward with great rapidity; and he added the surprising information that a long-range gun was shelling Paris. He finished by saying that we would entrain the following morning, and would go straight into action and that we would have the fight of our lives as the fate of the war now hung in the balance.[24]

Chapter 3

The Storm Breaks: 21–25 March 1918

FROM THE EVENING of 18 March 1918, those German divisions selected to open the offensive began to move into position. To avoid detection they marched by night and rested during the day. After weeks of intensive training, and with the might of the German Empire on display all around them, the marching men were full of confidence. As one German officer recorded:

> The preparations have been so thoughtfully planned that failure is almost an impossibility . . . moral and general condition is very satisfactory . . . We have a colossal amount of artillery at our disposal; for instance, in our own division, of which only two regiments will be in line, we have 68 batteries and several hundred trench mortars of various calibres. Gas is to be freely used.[1]

This battle was to be a true *Materialschlacht*, involving a prodigious amount of men, materiel and heavy weaponry, artillery in particular. It 'enveloped the battlefield in a "storm of steel"'.[2]

By the evening of 20 March 1918, the German Army was ready. That night its officers read a special signal to the soldiers: 'H.M. the Kaiser and Hindenburg are on the scene of operations'. Some of the old hands muttered that they would rather have had an extra issue of cheese, a remark tactfully ignored by the officers, who recorded that the message was 'received with enthusiasm'.[3] Close to a million German troops were in position, as was a massive concentration of guns and ammunition. It was a masterpiece of planning and precision, of which Ludendorff remained justifiably proud. 'It was a remarkable achievement,' he wrote later, 'and at the same time a marvel that the enemy had neither seen anything nor heard any movement at night.'[4]

Meanwhile, back in New Zealand on this very day, a newspaper report assured its readers that the German offensive would be delayed for some considerable time. The *Otago Daily Times* reported that:

> The delay in the German offensive is probably due to the failure of their gunners to gain the ascendancy over the British batteries, which for several weeks have returned blow for blow. It is a repetition of the German failure in the air, for we have completely smashed every strong German serial offensive for the past fortnight. There has been a remarkable increase in the enemy's gun-power since Christmas, owing to the reinforcements from Russia, but the enemy's full strength in artillery has not yet been disclosed.
>
> A significant feature of the new situation is the promptness with which the British recognise and counter every manoeuvre of the German gunners in their attempt to silence our guns. British shells immediately strip the camouflage from the carefully hidden German batteries, and drench their gun crews with gas.[5]

In just a few short hours German gunners would demonstrate that they had gained absolute ascendancy over the Third and Fifth Armies.

At 4.20 a.m. on 21 March, the 'Devil's Orchestra' of 6608 artillery pieces and an almost equal number of trench mortars opened up along the entire front of the Fifth Army, along two-thirds of the Third Army and, as part of a deception plan created by the innovative Bruchmüller, along the front of the First Army too, hammering the British defenders to the full depth of their positions. By the standards of the First World War the artillery barrage was short, lasting only five hours. But it was the heaviest artillery barrage of the war and to date 'the most concentrated artillery bombardment the world has yet known'.[6] By the end of the day the German gunners had fired 3.2 million rounds, a third of which were gas shells.[7] This was ten times the number of shells that had been used on the opening day of the Somme.

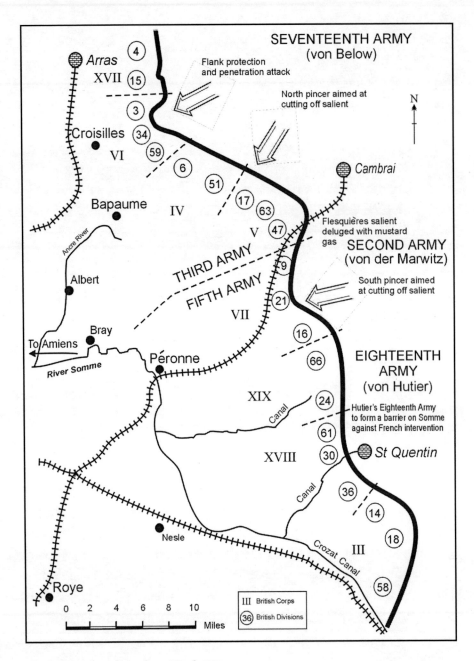

The German plan of attack, 21 March 1918.

The artillery fire programme had been meticulously planned. The first two hours of bombardment was devoted to neutralising the British artillery primarily by firing gas shells on their positions. Also targeted were command centres, various unit and formation headquarters, telephone exchanges, railheads and arterial roads. The Germans had spent the previous month pinpointing most of these important locations and all received direct hits. In the next three hours the weight of fire was directed against the infantry positions in the Forward and Battle Zones. It culminated in a concentration on the front-line trench positions. Halfway through this fire programme, there was a deliberate respite when the firing paused for half an hour. It was a ploy: the Germans were hoping to lure reinforcements into the open where they could also be destroyed. After this the medium and field batteries opened fire on the British infantry positions with shrapnel and gas shells.

When the attack opened Winston Churchill was in France attending a chemical warfare conference at St Omer. He had stayed overnight with the 9th Division, commanded by Major General H.H. Tudor. (In 1916 Churchill had commanded a battalion of this division.) Waking in the early morning, Churchill was an eyewitness to this storm of steel:

> Suddenly, after what seemed about half an hour, the silence was broken by six or seven very loud and very heavy explosions several miles away. I thought they were our 12-inch guns, but they were probably mines. And then, exactly as a pianist runs his hands across the keyboard from treble to bass, there rose in less than one minute the most tremendous cannonade I shall ever hear . . . Far away, both to the north and to the south, the intense roar and reverberation rolled upwards to us, while through the chinks in the carefully prepared window the flame of the bombardment lit like flickering firelight in my tiny cabin.

So loud was the noise of the German barrage that when the 9th Division's 200 guns fired in reply, Churchill could not hear them:

> From the Divisional Headquarters on the high ground of Nurlu one could see the front line for many miles. It swept around us in a wide curve of red leaping flame stretching to the north far

along the front of the Third Army, as well as of the Fifth Army on the south, and quite unending in either direction. There were still two hours to daylight, and the enormous explosions of the shells upon our trenches seemed almost to touch each other, with hardly an interval in space or time. Among the bursting shells there rose at intervals, but almost continually, the much larger flames of exploding magazines. The weight and intensity of the bombardment surpassed anything which anyone had ever known before.[8]

Many of the waiting German troops were so impressed with the destructive might of their artillery that they left the safety of their trenches and dugouts and stood high on the parapets to watch the effect as the shells fell on the British lines.[9] The barrage awakened the Fifth Army commander. To Gough the artillery fire was 'so steady and sustained that it gave me an immediate impression of some crushing, smashing power'. He immediately rang his four corps commanders to find out where the artillery fire was directed. He learned that its target was his entire front.[10]

At 9.40 a.m., five hours after the opening of the bombardment, the German infantry advanced behind a creeping barrage. Thousands of machine guns had joined in the barrage, though they could scarcely be heard above the din of the artillery fire. They swept the British Forward Zone 'with swarm upon swarm of lead'.[11] The Kaiser, staying with his son in an Eighteenth Army observation post, watched his infantry soldiers stream past in the thick fog. All four corps of the Fifth Army and two corps of the Third Army were subjected to this attack. The Fifth Army's Forward Zone was swamped and overrun. The storm troops swept on though, leaving posts and redoubts still holding out in the Forward Zone. These were to be dealt with by the battle troops following them. Some of these British strongholds held out for two days; most survived for only a few hours. This opening phase of the offensive was a real soldier's battle on a vast scale. All told, 127 British battalions met the onslaught that morning in their Forward and Battle Zones. Each fought its own individual, disjointed battle, often as isolated companies or platoons.

Against such overwhelming odds, though, gallantry was not enough and the British front crumbled in the face of the sheer weight of high-explosive shells and innovative infantry tactics.

The war diary of the 51st Highland Division is typical in its record of the day:

> **21 March Midnight to 5:00am**
> No Man's Land on Div front was patrolled continuously, but no unusual enemy movement was heard. Morning reports by all three Inf Bdes & by flanking Divs . . . stated that all was quiet.
>
> **5:00am**
> Very heavy bombardment opened by guns and howitzer of all calibres up to 8' on our front & also on our back areas as far as FREMICOURT. Front, support & all Intermediate line & bty posns heavily gas-shelled.
>
> **9–9.30am**
> Large numbers of enemy infantry appear on left flank.
>
> **11.30am**
> Left flank withdrew.
>
> **1pm**
> 1/6th Black Watch launch counter attack — 50% casualties already.
>
> **5pm**
> Withdrew to Corps line that night.[12]

General Gough received the first situation reports from his four corps at 10.00 a.m. All spoke of heavy fighting, but only III Corps on the right flank appeared to have lost significant ground. There the Germans were clear of all obstacles and making significant progress. The Oise marshes had not impeded them at all. Gough was not too concerned: 'If that is all we've lost it'll be a miracle'.[13]

There was to be no miracle though. On 21 March the Fifth Army had 20 battalions manning the Forward Zone. Blinded by fog, they were too far apart to support one another and their orders did not envisage a retirement. In Gregory Blaxland's words, they were 'doomed from the start'.[14] Some idea of the extent of the losses can be seen in the fate of XVIII Corps: of the eight battalions in the front line on 21 March, only fifty men survived the day to retire to the Battle Zone where half of them quickly became casualties.[15] Some battalions disappeared without trace. The fate of two battalions of the King's Royal Rifle Corps was not discovered until the end of the war when a few survivors were found in German hospitals recovering from their wounds.[16] By mid morning the Forward Zone of the Fifth Army had ceased to exist.

That evening the situation was critical. The Germans had taken the Forward Zone along the front of both the Third and Fifth Armies. In the south, von Hutier was almost through Gough's Battle Zone, which had necessitated a retreat to the Crozat Canal. The Germans had penetrated the British positions to a depth of nearly 5 miles. The Fifth Army was falling back in considerable confusion and the Third Army would have to withdraw also or face the danger of being outflanked and encircled. Both armies were now forced to implement a withdrawal — a difficult manoeuvre for which the British were wholly untrained. On the opening day of Ludendorff's offensive, the BEF had lost 500 guns and suffered 38,000 casualties, most from the Fifth Army.

Yet the day was not the overwhelming success the Germans had been seeking and Ludendorff was disappointed with progress.[17] The soldiers on the ground doing the actual fighting certainly felt elated with their success, as one officer noted in his diary:

> The attack was a complete success and the enemy entirely taken by surprise . . . The spirits of the troops are high . . . As Michael's attack succeeded, it seems highly probable that the further planned attack by Mars (to whom we belong) will take place.[18]

But though the Germans had inflicted heavy losses on the British and taken an unprecedented amount of enemy territory, their own losses were substantial. As Ernst Junger noted, the machine-gun nests caused particularly heavy casualties. Some positions surrendered easily, but in most cases the British defenders 'put up a superb show'.[19] The advancing storm troops also suffered heavily from the efforts of the British airmen, who met little resistance in launching their attacks. Later, the German air arm came in for much criticism for its inactivity. As William Moore has written, 'It was a mercy for the hard-pressed British ground troops that Ludendorff did not possess an aeronautical Bruchmüller to advise him.'[20] British resistance meant that the Germans were nowhere near reaching the Somme as far north as Péronne, which had been their objective on this day. In the north, the Seventeenth Army, attacking the strongest part of the line, had made little progress, barely reaching the second line of defence. In the centre the Second Army had made better progress and had actually penetrated the Battle Zone. Von Hutier's Eighteenth Army was the real success story, however, taking all its planned objectives. Despite initially having only a subsidiary role, the Eighteenth Army had made the greatest progress and Ludendorff now considered exploiting this success at the expense of the main thrust. His decision would depend on the progress achieved by the other two armies the next day.

Fighting was continuous on 22 March as fresh German troops entered the battle. The Fifth Army was in poor shape. Its withdrawal had actually increased its line by 4 miles but heavy casualties had reduced the infantry divisions to below half strength. By the evening of 22 March the Fifth Army had been driven completely beyond its Battle Zone and half was beyond its last prescribed defensive line. The Third Army was still fighting in and around its Battle Zone. British casualties now exceeded 100,000 men. German losses were also heavy but could be replaced by the reserves close at hand. By midday on 22 March the Germans made their first breach of the Somme, the water obstacle that was supposed to be the Fifth Army's last line of defence. This happened on the extreme right near the junction of the Oise with the Crozat Canal.

On the night of 22 March General Gough ordered the Fifth Army to withdraw behind the Somme River. The ordering of this retreat was thoroughly justified but entailed considerable risk. It would leave the flank of the Third Army exposed unless it also withdrew in concert and, as Churchill wrote, 'once the retreat of so thin a line on such a wide front had begun, it was very difficult to stop as long as the enemy pressure continued'.[21] Because the armies were withdrawing at different rates, the first significant gap in the British line opened that night. A German colonel detected the gap, sent through a sizable force and seized the village of Fins, astride an important supply route used by the Third Army. Over the next few days many more gaps would appear.

Most withdrawals were poorly handled because the British had not trained for them, but on the morning of 23 March the 50th Division carried out a textbook one. After fighting a hard and costly action on the previous evening, the troops disengaged from the enemy on the night of the twenty-third without detection and had an easy passage back to the Somme. It was, according to Blaxland, 'a manoeuvre that begged more frequent use'.[22] In a retirement of this magnitude the general policy should have been to hold on to positions by day, then slip away a couple of miles or so to a new position under cover of darkness, leaving a screen behind to cover the withdrawal. It was courting disaster to remain in established positions and be found in them in the morning once the enemy knew of the location and had registered it with his artillery. The BEF learned this painful lesson, and another. When two armies withdraw, their movements must be carefully planned and coordinated. This did not happen during the Michael Offensive. Generally, the Fifth Army withdrew too quickly, while the Third Army was much too slow in leaving non-vital ground such as the Flesquières salient, which had been formed in the Cambrai Offensive. When the Third Army did withdraw, it tended to head due west without extending its flanks in an effort to maintain contact with the Fifth Army. Inevitably contact was soon lost and large gaps began appearing in the British lines. For the Germans, though, the battle had now developed into a race to cut off as many British units as possible on the east side of the Somme and, if possible, prevent the British from destroying the bridges across the river.

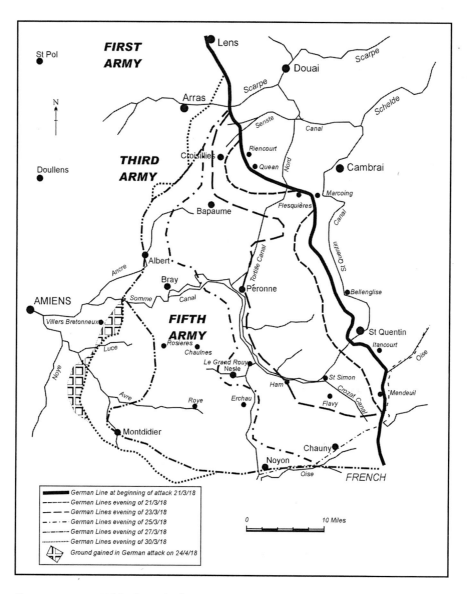

German progress, 21 March–24 April 1918.

General Haig visited Gough briefly on the morning of 23 March, the only person from GHQ who did so during 'Michael'. Haig was surprised to learn that much of the Fifth Army was already behind the Somme and Tortille Rivers. He was calm and cheerful and his only comment to Gough was a philosophical 'Well, Hubert, one can't fight without men'.[23] That night, back at GHQ, Haig sent an order to Gough:

Fifth Army must hold the Somme at all costs. Third and Fifth Armies must keep in close touch in order to secure their junction and must mutually assist each other in maintaining Péronne as a pivot.[24]

But events were moving too quickly for Haig to keep up. By the time he had finished writing the order the Germans were already across the Somme in force and had taken the important railhead and communication centre of Péronne.

Worry over the gap between the two British armies forced further retirements. But the gap widened and another one of some 2 miles occurred between VII and XIX Corps in the Fifth Army. This day, 23 March 1918, was 'perhaps the most difficult in the whole annals of the British Army . . . It was open warfare with a vengeance, and often it seemed that the whole British line had lost cohesion, and had been jolted into a number of isolated detachments.'[25] That evening, German news bulletins announced the end of the first stage of the battle and claimed that a large part of the British Army had been defeated. In three days since the start of the offensive the Germans had advanced 9 miles at their deepest point.

Dawn on 24 March revealed that the Fifth Army was in a perilous position. The previous day it had been forced back an average of 4 to 6 miles everywhere along its line. Most of the Fifth Army was now behind the Somme and it had been driven back from the Crozat Canal. Its line contained several gaps and the situation was chaotic. The left flank was not in touch with the Third Army whose nearest troops were at least 3000 yards further north. The retreat of both armies continued on 24 March and, according to the official history, 'a considerable amount of ground was lost, both in the Fifth and Third Army areas'.[26] The Germans were able to cross the Somme at several places and now gained a strong foothold west of the river. After three days of battle, with constant fighting and much forced marching, German and British troops 'were tired almost to the limits of endurance'.[27] Short of food, ammunition and sleep, the British were so exhausted that many managed to snatch some sleep even while under artillery bombardment.

On the evening of 24 March the Germans found a gap between the two armies and launched a powerful attack on the flank of the Fifth Army, driving a deep wedge into the centre of the British front. By 10 p.m. there was a gap of more than 4 miles between the two British armies. To avoid disaster the Third Army was forced to swing its right wing back to the line of the River Ancre. Bapaume, an important junction town, had to be abandoned. This meant that, by the end of the day, the southern flank of the Third Army was nearly 17 miles west from where it had been that morning. In the north, where contact was maintained with the First Army at Arras, its line had barely moved at all. The situation was perilous. There were other gaps between IV and V Corps of the Third Army, and between many of the divisions. The Germans were freely exploiting these breaks and there was a real danger that the British front would collapse.

During the night of 24 March, the BEF underwent a dramatic re-organisation in which General Gough lost three-quarters of his army. As it was north of the Somme, VII Corps of the Fifth Army was transferred to the Third Army and XVIII and III Corps were placed under operational control of the French, leaving Gough with just XIX Corps under his direct command.

The day of 25 March was one of crisis in the Third Army as seventeen German divisions crashed into its fragile defences.[28] Another long withdrawal was needed and that afternoon the Third Army fell back to the line on the Ancre River, a tributary of the Somme and the location of the old British front of July 1916. There it would hold a line running from Bray-sur-Somme to Albert, Beaumont-Hamel, Gommecourt and through to Arras. Any reserves on hand were to occupy this line forthwith. On the evening of 25 March, in the most unfavourable of circumstances, the Third Army carried out another general retirement. The troops had to break contact with the enemy at short notice, they were already thoroughly exhausted, and the weather was stormy, with much hail and sleet. All around them buildings were on fire and the roads were congested with traffic. It was the stuff of nightmares. As the official historian commented, 'Few who took part will forget the horrors of the all-night march by the light of burning dumps and aerodromes'.[29] That night the Germans captured the town of Albert and the Third Army withdrew to take up defensive positions on the left bank of the Ancre.

By the morning of 26 March the Third Army managed to reach the new positions assigned to it, but the revised line was far from intact. Between 62nd Division of IV Corps in the north at Bucquoy and 12th Division of V Corps just north of Albert there was a dangerous gap of 5 miles stretching from Puisieux-au-Mont south to Hamel. If it could not be closed before the Germans exploited it further retirements were likely. The New Zealand Division and the 4th Australian Brigade would eventually be given the task of closing this gap. The British had now lost most of the gains on the Somme battlefield that had cost them so dearly in 1916 and the enemy seemed to have Amiens within its grasp. However, fresh reinforcements were arriving and it was evident that the German thrust was weakening. The German élite units were tiring and their artillery and logistics support could not keep pace with the rapid advance.

Several other significant events occurred during the week-long retreat. First, on Saturday 23 March, Ludendorff, believing that he had decisively beaten two British armies, changed his plan of attack. He had earlier told Prince Rupprecht: 'I forbid myself to use the word strategy. We chop a hole. The rest follows.'[30] This was the method of a military opportunist. The hole (actually several) had been cut and here was an opportunity. That evening Ludendorff issued new orders to his armies:

> A considerable part of the British Army is beaten . . . The object now is to separate the French and British by a rapid advance on either side of the Somme. The Seventeenth will conduct the attack against the British north of the Somme to drive them into the sea. They will keep attacking at new places in order to bring the entire British front to ruin.[31]

Instead of cooperating in a gigantic turning movement against the British, the three German armies were now to do their own thing. Von Hutier's Eighteenth Army, originally there to provide flank protection and stand on the defence, was now to press further to the south-west and carry the offensive to the French. Von der Marwitz's Second Army was to advance on Amiens along both banks of the Somme, forming the blade that would sever the British from the French. Von Below's Seventeenth Army, reinforced by three new divisions, was to attack through Arras towards St Pol with the rather forlorn hope of driving the British into the sea. As Blaxland puts it, 'the three German armies were now to sprout forth in divergent directions like the leaves of a *fleur-de-lys*'.[32] The main thrust now was to separate the British and French armies by capturing the important junction town of Amiens. This change of plans, so soon in the offensive, was a considerable contraction of the original aim and it violated two crucial principles of war: selection and maintenance of the aim and concentration of force. Ludendorff's new direction would prove a major mistake.

Second, on the same day, as part of their policy of *Schrecklichkeit* ('frightfulness'), the Germans began shelling Paris with their long-range guns. These huge weapons, 8.26 inches in calibre, were firing from 75 miles away. This shelling was meant to demoralise the French people and demonstrate German resolve to win this war. The New Zealand newspapers reported that firing shells at such a great distance 'seems incredible'.[33] In his memoirs, Ludendorff wrote proudly of this action. The guns, designed by Krupps, were

> marvellous product[s] of technical skill and science . . . They made a great impression on Paris, and on all France. Part of the population left the capital, and so increased the alarm caused by our success.[34]

New Zealand Brigadier Herbert Hart had been convalescing from illness in the south of France when news of the German offensive reached him. He immediately set off for the front, passing through Paris on 29 March where he witnessed the effect of the long-range shelling.

> Business as usual was the password here although there was sufficient reason to be otherwise. A fortnight ago the whole town was shaken by a munition explosion, one of the biggest in France.

The town has been bombed nightly all the month, — a week ago the offensive commenced and the advance of the Germans threatens both Amiens & Paris, and at the same time Paris was bombed by the extraordinary long range gun firing a 4.5 inch shell a range of 75 miles. Each day it has fired regularly one shell every 15 minutes. Today 29 March, Good Friday, one shell hit a church at the moment the congregation was at prayer, killing 77 & wounding 90. Otherwise the casualties from the gun average about 18 daily.[35]

This shelling of a nation's capital by guns that could not be seen was a new development in the war. It was a feat that had been possible for some time, but it took a ruthless and determined enemy to perform it. As Churchill wrote, 'it was a warning to the Allies that Germany was devoting every energy to her final offensive, and would leave no method untried to break her foe'.[36]

Third, one of the many units of the BEF swallowed up by the Germans in the long withdrawal was the only formation South Africa had sent to the Western Front. The South African Brigade was part of the 9th Division, which Churchill had visited on the eve of the attack and which fought extremely hard during the German offensive. The South Africans had been given the order to 'hold at all costs' the ground west of Bouchavesnes and they 'carried out this duty to the letter'.[37] Though their commander, Brigadier General F.S. Dawson, had serious doubts about the wisdom of this order, it had been given to him personally by the divisional commander, General Tudor, so that he felt compelled to obey it. Dawson confided in his diary:

I cannot see that under the circumstances I had any option but to remain till the end. Far better to go down fighting against heavy odds than that it should be said we failed to carry out our orders. To retire would be against all traditions of the service.[38]

The South Africans were supposed to have a brigade on each flank in support. When the Germans attacked the position in force from 9 a.m. on

24 March, the two flank brigades, perhaps less worried about traditions of the service than keeping their units intact, withdrew in the face of the onslaught. The South Africans fought on and by noon the brigade was surrounded. The 35th Division sent to relieve them got within 2 miles of their position but could get no further. At 4 p.m. there were only 100 South Africans left unwounded and to compound problems they had run out of ammunition. When the Germans charged the position shortly afterwards the brigade's survivors had no choice but to surrender. That evening the South African brigade ceased to exist on the BEF's establishment.

Finally, there had been a resolution of a crisis that threatened to split the alliance between Britain and France, thereby assuring a German victory. During the withdrawal in the face of the *Kaiserschlacht*, there was a meeting between the commanders of the British and French armies that caused considerable alarm. On 24 March, an 'upset and very anxious . . . almost unbalanced'[39] Pétain visited Haig at Dury. Haig tried to cheer his French counterpart with some good news, as a French account of the meeting stated:

> Although his [Haig's] Third Army had, during the day, made a considerable withdrawal, he was concentrating behind it all his reserves — in the first place five divisions, of which four were solid Australian ones. Thanks to this reinforcement he was hoping to stop the enemy's progress on that front at least temporarily.[40]

But Pétain was not convinced and remained gloomy. In his view the current battle was not going to be the principal German offensive. This would be made against his front soon. Then he dropped a bombshell. If the Germans continued to press towards Amiens, Pétain would withdraw his armies to the south-west in order to cover Paris. If this had occurred, the Germans would have been successful in their aim of splitting the two armies. In Geoffrey Blaxland's words, 'It was tantamount to admitting that the war was lost.'[41]

At Haig's urgent request, a meeting of political and military leaders from both nations took place at Doullens on 26 March. As it was just 20 miles from Albert, which had fallen to the Germans the previous evening, General John Monash's 3rd Australian Division was used to provide a protective screen around the town. Described as 'a milestone of the war',[42] the meeting got off to a bad start. General Pétain — who, according to Haig, 'had a terrible look. He had the appearance of a commander who had lost his nerve'[43] — began by insulting the quality and performance of British soldiers over the last few days. 'Alas, it [the Fifth Army] no longer really exists. It is broken . . . From the first they have refused to engage the enemy . . . They have run like the Italians at Caporetto.'[44]

Pétain, however, was sidelined for the rest of the meeting. A crucial decision was taken to appoint the French general, Ferdinand Foch, as the coordinating authority for the Allies on the Western Front, in effect a supreme commander. Foch, renowned as a fighting general, immediately overruled any suggestions of falling back to Paris or of separating the two armies: 'We must fight in front of Amiens, we must fight where we are now. As we have not been able to stop the Germans on the Somme, we must not now retire a single inch.'[45] It was a policy welcomed by Haig, who had informed the meeting that he had no intention of giving up any more ground. He was determined to hold the enemy on the Somme and he was bringing forward every division he could spare. This battle would be won or lost on the line the BEF was currently holding. With Foch directing the Allied war effort, unity of effort and purpose would be achieved.

Pétain's plans to abandon the front and fall back to Paris were not the only casualty at this meeting. At Doullens Haig was told that, in order to appease the British public, the commander of the Fifth Army, General Gough, had to go. Haig defended Gough, protesting that 'Whatever the opinions at home might be, and no matter what Foch might have said, I considered that he [Gough] had dealt with a most difficult situation very well. He had never lost his head, was always cheery and fought hard.'[46] Haig was correct. In many ways his handling of the Fifth Army during this difficult withdrawal was Gough's finest military performance. This did not save him, however. The situation demanded that heads must roll and it was Gough who was unfairly made to pay the price.

It should be clear that from 21 to 26 March 1918 the BEF had suffered 'a grave disaster'.[47] There was no other way to view being forced back a distance of 15 to 20 miles to positions held at the beginning of 1916 and suffering more than 100,000 casualties in an army strapped for manpower. Yet by 26 March, the British were not beaten in the field, as Ludendorff prematurely believed. By 26 March, after six days of heavy fighting, the BEF had taken a severe battering. Even the British official history admitted that 'the opening of a breach between the French and British Armies appeared inevitable'.[48] However, in spite of the heavy casualties and the lost ground, the Allies' front line remained intact. And it was clear to many observers that the German offensive was losing momentum. The situation was precarious for both sides. Success was finely balanced, as if on a sabre's edge. It could go either way.

How had this grave disaster been reported in New Zealand? Were New Zealanders aware that the outcome of the war hung in the balance? The metropolitan newspapers stressed three main themes about Michael: that though the Germans had taken considerable ground from the British, none of it was of vital importance; that the Germans had suffered massive casualties taking this useless ground; and that the British Army had retired in good order at a rather leisurely pace. The *New Zealand Herald* of 25 March is a good example. The thundering headlines were followed by a Reuters account, sent from London three days before:

ENEMY GAINS OF NO GREAT STRATEGIC IMPORTANCE

WITHDRAWALS, AFTER EXACTING FEARFUL PRICE

DIVISIONS MELT AWAY UNDER TORRENTS OF SHELLS

. . . A correspondent at British headquarters writes: 'The offensive is proceeding. The weather is glorious. Definite details are still unobtainable. Despite our giving ground under the unprecedented weight of men and guns, the enemy gains are nowhere of real strategic importance. The withdrawal was carried out in an orderly manner, at all points, after a fearful price had been exacted. The airmen report that the ground in the enemy's rear is strewn with grey corpses.'[49]

The next day's headlines were in a similar vein:

HOMERIC FIGHTING

INCREASING RESISTANCE

TERRIFIC GERMAN LOSSES

BRITISH ON NEW LINE

OPENING OF TITANIC BATTLE SOUTH OF ST. QUENTIN[50]

On the same day the *Dominion* told its readers:

BRITISH RETIRE FROM BAPAUME

LINES STILL INTACT

FEARFUL SLAUGHTER OF ENEMY TROOPS

GERMANS DRIVEN BACK OVER SOMME

Today's reports dealing with the tremendous conflict in France show that the Allies are still slowly retiring on a considerable part of the battlefront, but with lines intact and with artillery and machine-guns taking unprecedented toll on the advancing enemy masses.

TITANIC STRUGGLE CONTINUED

London, March 25

Sir Douglas Haig reports: 'The battle continues with great violence on the whole front. We heavily repulsed powerful attacks yesterday morning and last evening north of Bapaume. The Germans only at one point reached our trenches where they were immediately thrown out.'

BRITISH RETIRE VOLUNTARILY FROM BAPAUME

GERMANS BLEEDING AT THE MAIN ARTERIES

BRITISH RETAIN COMPLETE POWER
TO COUNTER-ATTACK

London, March 25

Even if the German claim of prisoners and guns is true, it does
not justify the despondency on our part or jubilation on the part
of the enemy. We do not hear of any division being cut off. All
the accounts suggest that the Germans are bleeding at the main
arteries. The Kaiser has apparently announced the end of the first
stage of the battle because the Germans want breathing time.[51]

Despite the positive 'spin' being placed on the events occurring in
France, most New Zealanders must have been aware of the gravity of
the situation. Buried among the optimistic accounts were some disturbing
facts. 'GERMAN LOSSES ENORMOUS; BRITISH CONSIDERABLE'
conceded a headline in the *Press* of Christchurch.[52] On 30 March the *New
Zealand Herald* carried a surprising admission that must have alarmed its
readers. Its headlines stated that the German advance was slowing and
had outpaced its artillery support, but the paper continued:

What the German papers call the great Kaiser battle continues in
full force. The Germans in five days wiped out the results of the
eight months' battle of the Somme, which cost ourselves and the
Germans a million and a quarter casualties. Nevertheless the latest
news shows that the German advance is slowing down.[53]

In a ministerial statement made in the House of Representatives on
Monday 15 April 1918, Prime Minister William Massey admitted that,
during the first few days of the German offensive, he had feared that the
British were losing the war. Referring to a new German offensive against
the BEF in Flanders, Massey said:

There can be no doubt in the minds of any of us who have watched
what is going on but that is the intention of the Kaiser and those
who are acting with him. Their intention is to smash the British
during the next two or three weeks, or during the next two or

three months; but we can say so far that he has not been able to accomplish his object, and I do not for one moment imagine that he can succeed. It is his last effort. I believe that to be the case, and I feel that he knows it. Field-Marshal Sir Douglas Haig issued that famous order that we all read a few days ago — an order no doubt necessary, and issued at the right moment — in which he said to his soldiers, 'Stand fast; stop the enemy; die at your posts if necessary, but do not allow the enemy to advance.' That, Sir, was the tenor of his order. I have no doubt they will stand fast; and it is not the first time that British soldiers have been called upon in the same way, and they have never failed in hundreds of years. I am quite satisfied they will not fail now. At all events, I have a very confident feeling with regard to the outlook. I can speak for myself, and I am sure my experience is the experience of many others. I have a very different feeling with regard to the outlook to-day as compared with that I experienced some days ago.

This frank admission earned Massey an interjection from the floor:

Mr. PAYNE.— You should not give way to hysteria.

Massey retorted:

I am not in the habit of giving way to hysteria; I take things as they come along.[54]

Certainly many in New Zealand in March 1918 shared Massey's unease about events in France and their concerns only increased when they learned that the New Zealand Division would soon be involved in the fighting.

By 26 March, twenty-nine British divisions had been fighting almost constantly since the start of the offensive. After six days of continuous action the men were reaching a state of exhaustion and numbers were much reduced as battle casualties, sickness and straggling took their heavy toll. Despite several large gaps the British line was still in place and the survivors of these decimated formations were determined to see that it remained so. Nine fresh divisions had arrived to help: four from the GHQ reserve and five being released by the other British armies. The first three of these reinforcements arrived on 22 March, to be followed by three more the next day. From 24 March a fresh division arrived each day and was immediately committed to the battle. Eight of the nine divisions were sent north of the Somme in order to keep the Third Army in existence. Especially significant were the arrivals of the 5th Division from Italy, of the 1st, 3rd and 4th Australian Divisions and of the New Zealand Division. None of these had undergone the reorganisation enforced on the BEF and all were thirteen battalions strong.

In 1918 the New Zealand Division was the strongest on the Western Front. It had been released from the Second Army and placed in GHQ reserve on the evening of 21 March. The next day it was marked for transfer to the Third Army. On 23 March the New Zealanders began their march to the Somme front, uncertain about where and how they would be used. All they knew for certain was that when the marching stopped, the fighting would begin.

Chapter 4

A Hurried Journey: 22–26 March 1918

G ENERAL RUSSELL'S DIARY entry for 21 March had noted that the New Zealanders were pleased at the prospect of being involved in this deadly struggle. John Harcourt of the 1st Canterbury Battalion agreed. In his diary for 23 March he wrote: 'we expect to move any day, probably tomorrow. Everyone excited and keen. News of attack down South very scarce.'[1] The next day, however: 'News from the front rather disquieting. We heard with incredulity of the shelling of Paris by long range gun.'[2] Writing from the No. 1 General Hospital at Brockenhurst in England, a wounded Lieutenant Kenneth Luke, on the headquarters staff of the New Zealand Rifle Brigade, recalled the soldiers' reaction when they learned they were to play an active role in halting the German offensive:

> It was about Thursday 21st that we received word that we were to
> be withdrawn & thrown into the big scrap. At this time we were
> getting very meagre details of the fighting, but we were delighted
> at the prospect of the change as we were thoroughly sick of Ypres
> & its environments, having been there for six months during the
> worst part of the year. We gave three cheers when we heard of the
> change & eagerly awaited detailed orders for the shift.[3]

All unit and formation war diaries of the New Zealand Division recorded the news of the opening of the offensive on 21 or 22 March and receiving a warning order to be ready to move at short notice. The diary of the 3rd Battalion New Zealand Rifle Brigade was typical:

22 March
Sent out 200 O/R [other ranks] on Working Parties from WEST

FARM CAMP. Quiet day in camp and no enemy shelling as on previous days. At 6 pm warned to be in readiness to move at 3 hours notice. Issued order for all ranks to be ready to move out at 1 hours notice and all gear for transport to stand ready for loading from 8pm onwards.

7pm. All night work parties cancelled by Brigade. Received orders at 8.30 p.m. to be clear of WEST FARM CAMP by 9.30 p.m. Company Commanders called up and orders issued for march to WINNIPEG camp. All Companies cleared camp by 9.45 p.m. Whole Battalion in WINNIPEG CAMP by 2am 23rd March.

23 March

Instructions for Brigade to be ready to move at 4 hours notice by bus, train or route march. Day spent in equipping whole Battalion for battle and all equipment complete by 5pm. Conference of Battalion Commanders held at Brigade at 3 pm. Our period of rest as Corps Troops cut out but men in good fettle. Had a decent night's rest without interruptions from enemy shelling. Lorries passing through the whole night with troops for the Battle Front.[4]

The New Zealand Division's artillery brigades and the Maori of the Pioneer Battalion still working in the Ypres salient also received the word to move. According to its war diary, the readying of the Pioneer Battalion for the march south presented additional problems:

On 21st March news came through of the Germans offensive in the Cambrai Area. From the reports it appeared they had met with little success but we got orders to stop all work and prepare for an immediate shift. Steps were taken at once to get ready for the road and the amount of extra blankets and gear our young gentlemen had collected round themselves during our nearly three months stay in Ypres was appalling. We got it all away and were ready waiting first thing on the morning of the 22nd.[5]

The Pioneer Battalion set off for the Somme at 7 o'clock that evening. The next day the diary recorded that 'Ammo was brought up to strength and officers kits down to reasonable proportions'. Joining up with the Rifle Brigade on 24 March the Maori troops learned that the first reports were wrong: 'News from the South much more serious'.[6]

Bombardier N. Bailey from Little Akaloa on the Banks Peninsula was a member of the New Zealand Field Artillery, responsible for the loading and distribution of ammunition for the New Zealand guns. On 21 March 1918, he wrote in his diary:

> This evening at about 7.pm we got word to prepare to move out early in the morning to an unknown destination to entrain in the near future. Rumoured that Fritz has broken through on the 3rd & 5th Army fronts and also on part of the French Front. Plenty of work and preparation going on.

The artillery units moved out of the front line the next day, which was beautifully fine and warm. 'At 9.30 am we had a mobilization parade, and all spare gear, extra blankets etc were collared and sent to salvage . . . We are down to summer issue and marching order kits.' On 24 March the artillery ammunition arrived and was loaded on horse-drawn wagons. Bailey's unit set off to Caestre at 1.30 p.m. 25 March. 'There are all sorts of rumours flying around that Fritz has advanced for miles and that he has bombed the railway bridge at Amiens, hence the delay in trains.' The ammunition was loaded on to a train in the early hours of 26 March. That afternoon Bailey and his comrades reached Ailly-sur-Somme where the ammunition had to be unloaded. 'All along the road we passed Frenchies fleeing for their lives away from Fritz. Rumours galore floating around.'[7]

These fresh reports from the battlefront, 'which alters rather too fast' as Russell noted in his diary on 24 March,[8] caused the New Zealand Division to be issued four different sets of orders in the first 24 hours of the march. At first the Division was to concentrate on the left flank of the Third Army at Le Cauroy, some 12 miles east of Arras. They would be part of that army's XVII Corps. On 24 March this order was cancelled and the New Zealanders were diverted to the Fifth Army area where they would concentrate at Bray as part of VII Corps. Russell set up his divisional headquarters at Corbie in preparation for this move. At 1 a.m. on 25 March the orders were changed again: the Division was to concentrate around three small villages on the outskirts of Amiens. At 10 p.m. came fresh instructions. As Russell recorded, 'Orders came late in the evening that whole Div was to move northwards and shifted HQ to Hedauville, where we concentrate to fill a gap to the North.'[9]

Even these orders were altered. The 10 p.m. orders stated that Russell was to establish a line from Hamel to Puisieux, where there was a gap in the line. At 2 a.m. on 26 March, though, fresh orders arrived from Lieutenant General G.M. Harper, whose IV Corps now included the New Zealand Division (see Appendix 2, page 524). The division was to move further north through the village of Mailly-Maillet to the line of Hamel-Serre and close the gap there. If the Germans reached this line first they were to be pushed back and every effort was to be made to connect the line up with the right flank of 62nd Division. If the Germans could not be pushed back then the New Zealanders were to check their advance and establish and hold a line from Colincamps to Hébuterne, some 3 miles to the rear of Hamel–Serre. Russell did not need to shift his headquarters again; he remained at Hédauville, some 4 miles north-west of Albert, which was now held by the Germans. He eagerly awaited the arrival of the units of the New Zealand Division.

The constantly changing orders clearly reflected the fluctuations of battle. The Germans still retained the initiative and the British had to react to the shifting situation. They also reflected a degree of panic in the higher levels of the BEF and a lack of clear direction. So many different directives in one day also had an adverse effect on the New Zealand Division. They caused much confusion and anger, as well as additional fatigue, and ensured the Division was strung out over many miles. This contributed to the delay in concentrating it for action.

Getting to Hédauville proved a nightmare for most of the New Zealand soldiers. The men travelled to the Somme by train, then by lorry — the first time large numbers of Kiwi troops had moved on operations in motorised transport — and then by forced march. The train journey was uncomfortable. The soldiers travelled in cattle cars displaying a sign that indicated they were suitable for carrying either 40 men or eight horses. Ira Robinson of the Rifle Brigade described the experience to his sister Lizzie:

> Well, we marched out of that camp and after walking most of the night we reached another camp near the railway and the town of Poperinghe. There we rested all one day and those who had not made wills were compelled to make one out. The following, or at least the same night, we packed up and marched out again, and after walking two or three miles we entrained and started on an all night ride. It was not by any means a pleasant one as we were told off in lots of thirty and bundled into covered vans and told to make ourselves as comfortable as possible on the floor. It was one tangled mass of legs, arms, boots, rifles and equipment, steel hats and gas helmets, but in spite of all that I managed to get a few hours' sleep. I can sleep on a brick now and not even get a little bit stiff. The only thing that would keep me awake would be a decent bed, which I have not seen for months and months.[10]

Captain George Tuck of the 2nd Auckland Battalion travelled with the battalion's headquarters group. 'In the train on the way south towards Amiens. Have been travelling all night & still a long journey before us . . . In the carriage with Hdqtrs are Col. Allen, Major Shepherd, self, Wolow, Padre, Lts Stewart & Eccles. How many of us will return I wonder.'[11] His commanding officer, Lieutenant Colonel S.S. Allen, had had a similar thought during the church parade on Sunday 24 March. That service was 'unusually impressive from the thought that must have been present with everyone that to many it would be their last'.[12]

The march to the Somme front was a long, hard one for men who had wintered in the trenches of Flanders. The lack of available transport required most of the New Zealanders to march a considerable distance —

between 25 and 30 miles if the trains had deposited them south of Amiens. The men marched in light fighting order, which required them to leave their packs, blankets and greatcoats behind. They carried 220 rounds of ammunition, extra ammunition for the Lewis guns and three days' water and rations. For the next two weeks the New Zealanders had to live, sleep and fight in their uniforms. They lacked shelter and warm clothing and the spring weather was unpredictable, with extremely cold nights. The war diary of the 2nd Otago Battalion summed up the conditions:

> Battalion detrained at HANGEST at 4 p.m. and received orders to proceed in fighting kit at once. All surplus gear dumped and left under charge of guard. Had evening meal and set off at 8 p.m. Bivouacked for night near BRIELLY — bitterly cold, no blankets or overcoats and hence little sleep.[13]

As they marched through the Somme district the New Zealand soldiers were struck by the beauty of a landscape which, so far, had escaped the damage of war. This would soon change, as one veteran recalled many years later:

> When we went up to the Somme, there was grass that high, whole of the Somme country, grass all over it. When I went out of the line there wasn't a bit of grass left, it was all mud with bombs, so you'd wonder how anybody lived there.[14]

The soldiers also thought it strange that the countryside 'appeared to be curiously deserted',[15] but this altered as they reached Hédauville. Large fires in the direction of Albert were visible throughout the night. As one diary recorded, on the morning of 26 March, 'The whole countryside is aglow with burning villages and the roar of the artillery is awful.'[16] Along the road one of the Auckland battalions experienced an unusual event which William Knight, one of three brothers killed in the war, described to his parents:

I have been trying to write before but we are in for very hard times from pillar to post but we are to settle here to dig trenches in case we had to fall back . . . As we were having dinner on the road side, coats off, boots off etc, the King, on a tour, got out of his car, & walked along past us & we gave him a cheer for company as he went past.[17]

Every account of this journey describes it as extremely tough. For example, Corporal Gerald Beattie of the 1st Otago Battalion recorded in his diary for 25 March that:

We marched in Battle Order not even carrying greatcoats. Were issued with extra ammo and rations and then marched on until 8.30 when we were billeted in a row of crippled motor lorries along the roadside . . . It was a hard frost and we were very miserable without any blankets, but we had to make the best of a bad job.

On the next day came a forced march of 25 miles, 'a record for the New Zealand Division'. That night the battalion 'had to doss down in an open field in a heavy frost with only an oilsheet . . . Another most miserable night.'[18]

Another soldier recalled:

Hell! But I am weary this morning! Had a most wearisome march last night. We seemed to cover fifty miles or so, but we learned this morning it was only eighteen . . . Half the boys dropped out of the ranks during the night, and ducked into the hedges for a rest and sleep. I plodded steadily, or perhaps I should say unsteadily along the weary road, but I must say it was hard going made harder by the officers informing us every now and again that there was only a kilometre or two further to go. After about five more kilometres had been covered the same would be told; the march seemed endless. At some unearthly hour during the night, we halted on the cobblestones in some dingy dark town, where we remained for perhaps an hour, while there was bustling to and fro by the officers who seemed to be completely at sea to us as to where we were or where we were going and when. Discipline went by the board and the boys were in an evil temper, shouting and calling the officers all the B.B.B.'s they could lay their tongues to.[19]

John Coleman neatly captured the experience in a letter to his sister Mary:

Our company was out in billets for a few weeks' spell, but old Fritz started making things pretty merry, and we were moved away in rather a hurry to quite a different part of the line. We had about eighteen hours' train journey, stayed the night in a village, where we got off the train. Spent most of the night waiting for transport. We made huge fires in the streets and sat around them until I went to sleep, and when I woke up again our fire was out and all the fellows were asleep, huddled up to each other in all sorts of attitudes. Well, we had a good rest in the morning and finally got in the motor lorries at two in the afternoon. We travelled in the lorries for about two hours and then marched about ten miles, where we camped in an open field for the night, but were fortunate enough to get some straw which we nestled in like pigs. There was a fairly hard frost, but we cuddled up close to each other and kept fairly warm.[20]

Such a difficult journey meant that the New Zealand soldiers arrived at Hédauville footsore, tired and hungry. They were exhausted before they had even met the Germans. As the War Diary of the 2nd Auckland Battalion admitted on 26 March:

2 a.m. Battalion proceeded by motor lorries to PONT NOYELLES debussing at 5 a.m. and marched to HEDAUVILLE . . . where the Division assembled. Arrived at 12.30 p.m. During this march which was very long the Battalion displayed the greatest endurance.

Only one man fell out. The men were very tired after travelling constantly without sleep for 38 hours.[21]

It was certainly not an ideal state for soldiers who were about to have the fight of their lives.

As the New Zealand and Australian soldiers neared the front line they came across thousands of retreating soldiers, mainly from the Fifth Army. They were not at all impressed by what they witnessed. Bernard Cottrell wrote home to his father:

> I suppose you have wondered at how events have shaped recently, well we also were very surprised, you will get details later & will be in a better position to judge still there was some damnable mistakes somewhere, as we came up everyone was clearing for their lives, many did not know what was doing, others gave very vivid descriptions, but one look at their clothes was sufficient. They had never been in the line. They were told what was thought of them in very forcible language.[22]

Charlie Lawrence from Greymouth served in 13th Company, 1st Canterbury Battalion, which encountered a large group of retreating British soldiers.

> They said to us: 'Don't go over there chum, you'll get killed.' That's what they said: 'Don't go Chum, you'll get killed.' We said: 'Turn around, you bastards and go the other way.' . . . It was a bad affair that was.[23]

Although he moved to the Somme behind the infantry, Sergeant Leonard Hutchinson of the 15th Howitzer Battery New Zealand Field Artillery still formed a thoroughly negative impression of the British soldiers.

> Our batteries moving up fast & will go into action tonight . . .

Civilians evacuating all along the road from Amiens to Picquigny. The sight is awful. Old men and women carrying packs & almost praying of the lorry drivers to give them a lift. We were full up, but carried 4 ladies & 2 children on the back. They were that thankful that they wanted to pay us, but we refused. The Tommy soldiers have behaved shamefully, deserting the line and going into the civilian's houses & looting — absolutely wanton destruction.[24]

Corporal Claude Wysocki of the 2nd Battalion New Zealand Rifle Brigade was disgusted with the soldiers of the Fifth Army and had no sympathy for them.

It was General Gough's Fifth Army, God Bless 'em. General Gough's Fifth Army was the most disorganised, out-of-tune, poor silly sips that you ever had anything to do with . . . At 3 o'clock in the afternoon at Amiens, that's when the war really started on the Second Somme. Previous to this, all you had was General Gough's Fifth Army in disarray. They'd been running all night long from the front line, which was the front line in their case, . . . you never saw such a spectacle in all your life. Nothing ever appeared in the newspapers concerning that. They had absolutely no heart for it and they were the cause of more trouble than enough . . . They never marched past, they ran![25]

In a letter to his sister, John Bartle recounted a popular joke in the New Zealand Division.

A Tommy O. [officer] asked a Maori what he was doing here one day, & he said, 'Oh putting up plenty of barb wire to stop the Germans getting through & stop the Tommy's from running back'. He got seven days CB [confined to barracks].[26]

Vincent Jervis of 12th Platoon, C Company, 2nd Battalion New Zealand Rifle Brigade was in hospital with a high temperature when the New

Zealand Division marched to the Somme: 'I wonder what the NZ Div is doing. I should like to be with the boys if they go into it.'[27] As he had more news from the wounded New Zealand soldiers passing through his hospital, Vincent Jervis formed a poor opinion of the British soldiers' performance. He would not have been alone.

> Very nice day. Fritz seems to be doing what he likes. I don't believe the British are putting up as big a stand as they might . . . Saw Fitzsimmons out of C Coy. Hear Sgt Dobson & Mick Dellow were killed. When our division went into the line down Amiens way they reckon they had to fill a gap of about 6000 yds. The Aussies and NZ's have been sent up to the Bailleul front, they get shoved into all the hot spots. I'll bet it is because they don't run away.[28]

Some New Zealanders, while not excusing the retreating British soldiers, did express some sympathy for them. William Jamieson, a runner in the New Zealand Field Artillery, was one:

> Some of them came down the road as we were going in. They said to us: 'They're coming over in thousands. They're coming over in thousands.' But a lot of these little blokes, they were not much more than schoolboys. The Tommy Army had been there for four years and they were just about wiped all out, by that time they were not much more than damn kids. At least that's what they looked like to me.[29]

Corporal Gerald Beattie of the 1st Otago Battalion, who survived the war and lived to the age of 103, dying in Rangiora in 1994, recorded the popular opinion of the British two days before he was wounded by a German artillery shell:

> The Froggie flight from these parts had been very precipitate, showing the speed of the Huns advance . . . The Tommies put up no fight at all against Fritz, but turned and fled, and our Dinks

[soldiers of the New Zealand Rifle Brigade] coming up on Monday
when just about 400 yards beyond Mailly Maillet, met a battalion of
Fritzies marching in column of route with a band playing, the dinks
spread out and got well sunk into Fritz and he turned round and got
chased back a mile or so. Prisoners said the New Zealanders were
the first to offer any resistance. Fritz is a fine soldier when the enemy
is running away, but he won't have a go at us in the open at all.[30]

According to C.E.W. Bean, the Australian war correspondent and official
historian, the widespread judgement that British soldiers were greatly
inferior to Australians and New Zealanders derived largely from these
experiences of 1918. Unfortunately the Anzac soldiers took this harsh view
back to their respective countries where it gained a widespread following.
As Bean himself recognised, the verdict was inaccurate and unfair:

It may be taken as an axiom that, when an army is in the grip of a
desperate struggle, any one moving in its rear tends to be unduly
impressed with the disorganisation, the struggling, the anxiety of
the staffs, and other inevitable incidents of such a battle; he sees
the exhausted and also the less stubborn fragments of the force,
and is impressed with their statements, while the more virile and
faithful element, mainly fighting out in front, ignorant or heedless
of all such weakness in rear, is largely beyond his view.[31]

As the New Zealanders marched south and then east the roads were
crowded with stragglers, vehicles and French refugees fleeing from the
advancing Germans. The refugees were dressed in their best clothes and
carried their most valuable possessions. They were worn out, frightened
and in a state of bewildered despair as their world tumbled into ruins.
John Coleman described them to his sister:

We marched the next evening to a village that the French had just
deserted for the second time, poor beggars. You see some rotten
sights on the battlefield, but one is so hardened to them now that

you really don't take much notice of what occurs now. All along the road as we came up here we passed continual streams of these poor peasants beating a hasty retreat. This is what touches the soft part of a fellow's heart, to see the poor women and children hurrying along the road with terror-stricken faces. They have all sorts of old-fashioned vehicles moving their happy homes, some with mules drawing them, others horses and some smaller carts drawn by dogs. And what a collection are in some of the carts, furniture, poultry, calves and the cows are generally tied behind like we would lead a horse. Other women might have four or five cows tied coupled together, leading them. Lots of old people, who might be seventy or eighty years old, were wheeling barrows with their goods and chattels. Women, too, and they must have travelled miles.[32]

As Lieutenant Kenneth Luke remembered, near Amiens

along the high road beyond one saw evidence of the big push coming our way. We met hundreds of refugees pushing, wheeling & carrying their scanty possessions. Some of their valuables would make you laugh, at other times make you feel mad with the hideous war.[33]

All surviving accounts of New Zealand soldiers comment on the refugees' plight. Harold Muschamp of the Machine Gun Battalion: 'We saw some pitiful sights on our march. Old men and women and children all fleeing for their lives.'[34] And Corporal Beattie, writing on 26 March: 'on the road we passed dozens of people moving back with all the possessions they could carry. It was truly a pitiful sight'.[35] For Padre Ronald Watson of the 1st Otago Battalion,

Two of the saddest things I have seen lately have been the plight and sorrow of refugees and destroyed homes. New Zealand is indeed a happy country to be spared the sight of so much sadness and desolation as poor old France has known.[36]

Cecil Jepson of the 2nd Wellington Battalion wrote in his pocket diary that 'Heartbreaking sights are here seen' but added that 'many of our boys are wheeling barrows and carts and carrying bundles for the refugees who are passing through here day & night'.[37]

This was the first time ever that New Zealand soldiers had seen refugees fleeing from a war zone and it made a lasting impression on them. According to Ormond Burton, the New Zealand soldiers felt compassion for the suffering French, but also a hardened resolution to halt the Germans.[38] As Ira Robinson told his sister Lizzie:

> Man, it made regular savages of our boys and Fritz has paid the price since . . . This last stint has made me very bitter towards Fritz and I will never think of him as anything but a savage again and will treat him as such. I am on a gun capable of firing 700 shots a minute and if it would fire 1400 shots a minute it would not be going too quickly for me.[39]

For many New Zealand soldiers this was also a chance to avenge their suffering at Passchendaele the previous year. This was certainly James McWhirter's thought as he watched a large group of Germans march into the killing zone of his machine-gun crew. 'Oh what a target, men & transport in marching order, we were all eager to have a bit of our own back for what we got at Passcendaele [sic].'[40]

A considerable mythology has arisen, especially in Australia, about the role of the four Anzac divisions that arrived to help stem the German advance. Some accounts have exaggerated their role, suggesting that they were almost solely responsible for the German offensive grinding to a halt.[41] Nearly every Australian account of the *Kaiserschlacht* contains two quotes from Bean's official history that have passed into Australian folklore. As the men of the 4th Australian Division moved south-west of Arras, they were recognised despite the fact they had never served in the region before. At Barly, the villagers were loading their most precious possessions on to wagons and carts and making ready to abandon their homes to the Germans. When they saw the Australians, they stopped and took up the call, 'Les Australiens'. One old man said to the soldiers of the 13th Battalion, whose lorry had halted, 'Pas necessaire maintenant — vous les tiendrez.' (It's not necessary now — you'll hold them.) A digger is said to have replied, 'We'll have to see the old bloke isn't disappointed.'[42] Similarly, a 'grim digger' of the 3rd Australian Division, cleaning his rifle in the village of Heilly, said to a woman in broken French, 'Fini retreat, Madame. Fini retreat — beaucoup Australiens ici.'[43]

Contemporary New Zealand accounts carried similar tales although they did not receive as wide an audience as the Australian ones quoted above. When asked why the French civilians had halted their flight from the Germans at Amiens, the answer, attributed to a French general no less, was obvious:

> they had learnt that the troops they had just passed were the New Zealanders moving in and so there was no need for them to move out & so the evacuation came to an end. Yes, he [the French general] said, such was the reputation of the New Zealanders.[44]

In a letter to his father, Bernard Cottrell emphasised the role of the New Zealanders:

> The most pitiful sight was the poor French people getting out of it with their worldly goods stacked on a cart followed by cows, pigs & goats. By the way the French authorities are supposed to be taking this retreat pretty badly (and every reason) & French papers give us the credit for stopping the 'British rot'. I haven't seen the English equivalent for it yet though I think a certain amount of credit must come eventually to us.[45]

Newspaper reports in Australia and New Zealand echoed the theme that Australia and New Zealand had saved the situation on the Western Front, and tended to exaggerate their performance. The account featured in the *Otago Daily Times* by the distinguished correspondent Philip Gibbs is typical. It is featured below with its evocative headlines:

A BREATHING SPACE

AUSTRALASIANS IN BATTLE-LINE

MR PHILIP GIBBS ENTHUSIASTIC

DASHING ATTACK BY NEW ZEALAND

BRILLIANT SUCCESS ACHIEVED

ENEMY SURPRISE ATTACK FORESTALLED BY
AUSTRALIANS AND NEW ZEALANDERS

EAGER WELCOME BY THE VILLAGERS

THEN 'THERE WAS SOMETHING DOING.'

. . . The enemy in the next tussle will meet men who are not tired, whose resolution is as great as that of those they met in the first on-slaught. The Australians and New Zealanders have come into the line, fresh and keen, uplifted by a fierce enthusiasm, stirred by emotions which make these fellows very dangerous. I saw them coming to relieve hard-pressed troops, and the sight made the pulse beat. It gave a sense of security. The Australians came swinging down towards the old Somme battlefield with the spirit of men coming to the rescue of a great cause. Is not this blasted field of Pozieres hallowed to them by memorials of their own dead and the graves of many comrades? 'We will take Pozieres back,' they said; 'it is our job.' News that the enemy had come pouring back over the ground at Bapaume and Le Sars, where the Australians bitterly fought a year ago, was a shock and a challenge. They waited impatiently for the call to come, saying, 'It's a damned shame we are not on the way.' . . .

The New Zealanders followed spick and span, debonair lads who have already seen many adventures. It was a glorious night on the road.

After reaching the battle line there were things doing. They sent out patrols, clearing 'No Man's Land,' caught the Germans in ambushes, raking stragglers with bullets; slaughtered the enemy in several small attacks; drove them out of woods and villages, scaring them horribly day and night.

Mr Gibbs says he saw slightly wounded Australians and New Zealanders, who remarked: 'We were a bit rash to put our heads into it.' All are certain the enemy will not get further.[46]

Yet, as with most mythology, there is some truth in these accounts. Certainly by 1918 the Australian divisions in France had established a formidable reputation, while the New Zealand Division, as Keith Murdoch reported in the *New Zealand Herald*, 'is known everywhere as one of the hardest-working and hardest-fighting Divisions in France'.[47] There is plenty of evidence to suggest that soldiers of this calibre must have been welcome during the Allies' darkest hour.

On 24 March two official Australian correspondents (probably Bean and Murdoch) went to the press headquarters of the BEF, now at Amiens, to gain information about the progress of the German offensive. There the chief censor, Major the Honourable Neville Lytton, and a press officer, Lieutenant Colonel C.R. Cadge, gave them an overview of the situation. Both Australian correspondents were shocked to learn that the Germans were now past Combles and on the old Somme battlefield. Part of the conversation went as follows:

'Where's the nearest point they have got to?' I asked.
'Delville Wood,' he [Lytton] said.
That was a staggerer.
'Haven't we any reserves — surely we must have!' I asked.
'No — I don't think there's a division between the Germans and here,' Cadge said.
We said our divisions would surely be coming and the N.Z.'s.
'How can they get here in time?' he asked.

Both Australian correspondents were somewhat despondent on hearing this news. But the next morning (25 March) troops were passing through Amiens heading towards the advancing Germans and one of the correspondents recorded in his diary: 'They were New Zealanders. I can't say how glad I was to see them . . . They are the solidest, calmest looking troops in France.'[48] An Australian battalion history reported a similar experience. On the trip south the Australians stopped at Doullens, where they saw many British wounded and stragglers.

> There was a most depressing atmosphere of hopelessness about them all, but we saw some New Zealanders who told us that their division had gone down, and that the 4th Australian Division was also on the way, so we bucked up considerably.[49]

Kenneth Luke described the effect of the Anzac troops arriving to plug the gaps in the line:

> We met remnants of the Divisions that had fought from the beginning of the terrible battle struggling along the road, & everywhere our peaked hats were espied the anxious question was asked 'Are the ANZACS coming?' and cheers & smiles met us everywhere.

Watching the troops of his brigade's 1st Battalion go into action was inspiring: 'It did my heart good & stirred my blood to see our boys swing by. They did look a fit lot after their month's rest and went in to fight with great spirit.'[50]

At 10 p.m. on the evening of 25 March General Russell received orders from the Third Army to move his division into the ever-widening gap between IV and V Corps. The New Zealanders were to establish a line running from Hamel in the south and bending north-east through Beaumont-Hamel to Puisieux-au-Mont, a distance of just over 4 miles. This would place the Division on high ground overlooking the Ancre Valley and facing almost due east. It was also 'the most vulnerable and fluid part of the front'.[51] There they would be part of IV Corps under command of Lieutenant General G.M. Harper and provide the link between 62nd Division of IV Corps at Puisieux and 12th Division of V Corps at Hamel. In a further complication, the 4th Australian Brigade was allocated to the depleted 62nd Division in order to help with securing and holding the important junction town of Hébuterne. The command arrangements were complicated, but the task allocated the New Zealanders was not:

1. Gap exists in line from Hamel to Puiseux au Mont. The NZ Division will occupy this gap, both villages inclusive — second Brigade on the right, 1st Brigade on the left. Dividing line L of BEAUMONT HAMEL.

2. All units in the Brigade Group . . . will proceed by shortest route forthwith, to HEDAUVILLE.[52]

Orders issued to the individual units contained more information and explained what their task would be once they were involved:

The enemy last night reached the line of the ANCRE from MIR-AU-MONT to BEAUCOURT where he is believed to have crossed the river. The 12th Divn. has been ordered last night to occupy the line of the ANCRE from ALBERT to HAMEL. The 62nd Divn. are retiring from the ANCRE North of MIR-AU-MONT to the line PUISIEUX-AU-MONT–BOCQUOY, where they will fight today remnants of 5th Corps on collecting about ANGEL BELMER and of the 4th Corps at SAILLY AU BOIS. N.Z. Division will occupy and hold the line HAMEL–SERRE and close the gap between the right of the 62nd Divn. and the left of the 12th Divn . . .

Should the enemy be encountered he must be pushed Eastwards and every endeavor made to get touch with the Right of the 62nd Divn. and cover their flank.[53]

By the early morning of 26 March Russell had established his head-quarters at Hédauville and the first of the New Zealand units was arriving. But the Division was strung out on the road for many miles so that, as they arrived at Hédauville, the units had to be committed piecemeal to the battle. There was no time for reconnaissance and a lack of information about the exact location of the advancing Germans and their numbers.

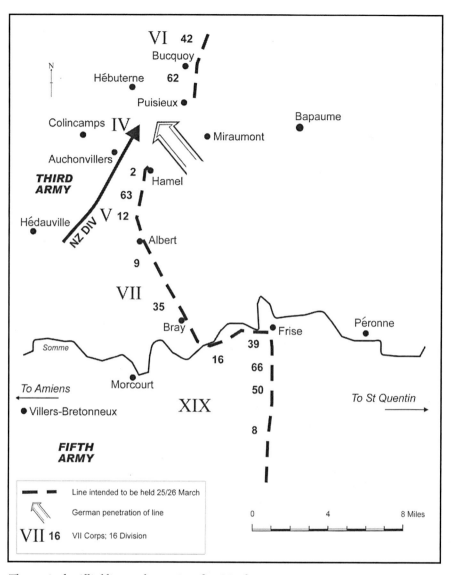

The gap in the Allied line on the evening of 26 March 1918

A plan was hastily worked out. The first battalion to arrive at Hédauville would be sent through the village of Mailly-Maillet to occupy an outpost on the dominant Engelbelmer–Auchonvillers Ridge. Here it could protect the New Zealand Division's right flank as it advanced to contact the Germans. Then two infantry brigades would make the main advance to Serre and Hamel — one to occupy Hamel and link up with V Corps, the other to secure the road north from Beaumont-Hamel to Hébuterne, swinging back to Serre and linking up with IV Corps at Puisieux. When it arrived the third brigade would extend the line north to hold the high ground from Colincamps to Hébuterne. It was an ambitious plan and Russell soon realised that he lacked the resources to carry it out. He stressed, however, that if the New Zealand brigades encountered superior numbers of the enemy they were to check their progress and manoeuvre to establish a solid line of defence on favourable ground.

> The definitely affirmed principle on which these operations were based was that whatever the development of the enemy offensive, the New Zealand Division was to set itself as an impassable barrier to the German onslaught.[54]

The first unit to arrive at Russell's new headquarters, at 2 a.m. on 26 March, was the 1st Battalion New Zealand Rifle Brigade (1st Rifles), after a 10-mile march from Pont Noyelles. After resting for four hours, the battalion set out at 6 o'clock to occupy Englebelmer and Auchonvillers and the connecting ridge line. This, it was hoped, would cover the advance of the rest of the Division. By mid morning only four other complete battalions had reached Hédauville: the 1st and 2nd Auckland, and the 1st and 2nd Canterbury Battalions. Three companies of the 2nd Battalion Rifle Brigade (2nd Rifles) and two machine-gun companies had also arrived. Russell, aware of the urgency of the situation and how little time he had to concentrate his division, formed these battalions into two composite brigade groups, each containing two battalions and a machine-gun company. The 1st and 2nd Canterbury Battalions were designated the 2nd Brigade; the two Auckland battalions and the companies of the rifle battalion formed the 1st Brigade. In the afternoon both brigades moved forward to fill the gap between Hamel and Puisieux.

The New Zealand soldiers were heading for a large hole in the British lines through which the Germans were advancing. For four days now the Germans had met with no serious opposition and they were 'flushed with victory'.[55] They had now passed the old front lines of 1916 and were capturing new French towns and villages. The city of Amiens was within their grasp. Shortly, without its artillery support, the New Zealand Division would have to fight the advancing Germans with only the weapons it carried. The two infantry brigades were at half their normal strength and the Division's flanks were exposed. As soon as the marching stopped, a hard fight could be expected. All told, it was a very risky prospect as General Russell well recognised. 'The Division came on in the nick of time. There was a big gap and by dint of hard marching we managed to fill it just in time . . . I was not sure that we were not in for a catastrophe.'[56]

Russell was certainly risking the fate of his prized division, but the situation was desperate. Though the German offensive was slowing, it was far from a spent force. Pushing the New Zealand Division piecemeal into the large gap in the Third Army was a leap in the dark. If the Germans could not be halted on this new line the New Zealanders might well suffer the same fate as the South African Brigade.

Chapter 5

Into the Storm: 26 March 1918

T HE 1ST RIFLES had a number of important tasks to perform on that
fine spring morning in March 1918. First, it was to advance through
Mailly-Maillet, in the scenic Picardy region of the Somme, ensuring that
the village was clear of enemy troops. Then the battalion had to establish
an outpost line on the Auchonvillers Ridge, an important piece of high
ground. In doing so it was to establish contact with 12th Division of
V Corps at Englebelmer, while covering the deployment of the 2nd and
1st Infantry Brigades in their advance to Hamel and Serre. To help them
achieve these tasks the 1st Rifles had been allocated two sections of the
Canterbury Company of the Machine Gun Battalion. By the end of the
day these two sections would more than prove their worth.

At 6.30 a.m. the 1st Rifles, with its two sections of machine guns,
moved from Hédauville, up gentle slopes north-east towards Mailly-
Maillet. Using a company well in advance as a protective screen the
battalion advanced in open formation; it passed through Mailly-Maillet
just after 9 a.m. An advanced brigade headquarters was established in the
village. It was not until 11 a.m. that the New Zealanders encountered the
Germans, some 500 yards east of Auchonvillers. The battalion's screening
company bumped into several German patrols which had skirted around
the open flank of 12th Division and were pushing westward. These patrols
were easily driven off by Lewis gun and rifle fire from the centre platoon
of the screening company. Many casualties were inflicted on the fleeing
Germans. This company then pushed forward to the road leading to
Hébuterne and started to advance along it. At the major crossroads to
Serre stood a sugar refinery and here the company engaged a strong
enemy position. The fighting was fierce and at close range — sometimes
less than 20 yards separated the combatants. One rifleman accounted for

fourteen Germans, including two officers, while the Lewis gun section of this company accounted for a further ninety enemy soldiers.[1]

The odds, however, were against this isolated company and it was nearly overrun. At the last moment, two other companies of the 1st Rifles arrived and occupied the high ground of the Auchonvillers Ridge, meeting little resistance. One company of the battalion was held in reserve. The company occupying the right portion of the ridge pushed out patrols to a distance of 2 miles and easily linked up with 12th Division of V Corps at Hamel. Things remained relatively quiet on this right flank and in the centre of the ridge. Meanwhile, though, the two rifle platoons on the extreme left were fighting for their lives, trying to prevent the enemy from advancing up the sunken road from the sugar factory. Machine-gun and rifle fire coming from Hébuterne was also severe. The enemy surrounded the sugar factory in force. There were about 300 Germans now in position across the Serre road and fresh troops could be seen marching westwards from Serre. The Germans called upon the platoon on the extreme left to surrender. Though cut off from the rest of the company, this platoon refused to give in and kept fighting. Only the support provided by two machine guns prevented the New Zealanders from being routed. By 1 p.m. the situation was desperate and the battalion commander committed half his reserve and his support company to hold this flank open. The Germans were held up at the sugar factory, but they remained a potent threat.

Rifleman Fred Avery of the battalion's C Company was hit in the shoulder and hand by a German machine gun while fighting at the factory. From a strict Catholic family, he had departed New Zealand with a stern warning from his father: 'The Germans won't be your enemy, it will be women, so be careful'. On the Serre road, Rifleman Avery learned that the Germans were equally dangerous:

> Well, it [was] mostly a train ride, and then a long walk. I remember I had a sleep . . . on the steps of the Amiens Cathedral. And we were there till we got the orders to go in. Into a bit of a ditch and the sunken roads. We'd call them a hollow here . . . Then we had to attack a sugar refinery near Colincamps. And that's where I

got my [wound]. There was so much stuff flying you don't know what hit you. You don't know whether it was machine guns or shell burst. You couldn't tell what hit you. It was raining and mud & slush at the time. I didn't come conscious until I woke up in Walton-on-Thames, London . . . It was wet & cold and I was in a lot of pain.[2]

Between 3 and 4 p.m. the two Canterbury Battalions of the 2nd Brigade advancing to their objectives passed through the positions of the 1st Rifles and turned the tide against the Germans on the sunken road. With 1st Rifles' left flank now secure, the New Zealand Division's outpost line was firmly established and doing its job of covering the deployment of the two infantry brigades. As well as this, the Division's right flank was anchored to V Corps.

During this hotly contested engagement, the Germans, a battalion of the 4th Division, had attacked with great courage and their losses were severe. As the historian of the Otago Regiment recorded:

The fearlessness displayed by the German leaders evoked the unbounded admiration of our men. Possibly they were unduly flushed with the victories of the past few days, for they repeatedly dashed forward with what appeared to be the utmost foolhardiness, and it was clear that a realization of the fact that they were now striking at a line practically immovable had not yet dawned upon their minds.[3]

The 1st Rifles had had a remarkable day. It now became part of the 2nd Brigade.

The New Zealand infantry brigades that advanced to meet the Germans on the afternoon of 26 March had been cobbled together from units as they arrived at Hédauville. The first brigade to set off was the 2nd Brigade (temporarily designated A Brigade) under the command of Brigadier Robert Young. It consisted of the 1st and 2nd Canterbury Battalions plus a machine-gun company, about half its normal battle strength. After the redistribution of equipment and ammunition, the insertion of detonators into the Mills bombs and a hot meal hurriedly eaten, the brigade set out from Hédauville at noon. Its task was to occupy the ridge line overlooking the Ancre from Hamel in the south, north-west to Beaumont-Hamel.

The 2nd Canterbury Battalion led the way, advancing in artillery formation with platoons spread out at 100-yard intervals and with a protective screen of scouts in front. The battalion advanced down the Mailly-Maillet road, reaching the village without opposition. Knowing nothing of the situation to its north and with many enemy troops in the sunken road, 2nd Canterbury sent one company down the Serre road to assist the hard-pressed left flank of the 1st Rifles. This company took up a position on a stretch of high ground known as the Apple Trees, about a half-mile northeast of Mailly-Maillet. It would protect the left flank of 2nd Brigade as it advanced.

Meanwhile the 1st Canterbury Battalion, also in artillery formation, moved south-east of Mailly-Maillet in an attempt to link up with the 12th Division on the New Zealand Division's right flank. Young Lieutenant John Harcourt found this movement impressive. It was 'carried out exactly as if on parade and was a great sight — must be about the only occasion on record that such a stunt had been carried out according to textbook'.[4] At 4 p.m. 1st Canterbury moved through the outpost line established by the 1st Rifles and on to the brigade's objective, establishing a line west of Hamel and south-west of Beaumont-Hamel. It experienced some light shelling, but took its objectives easily. Harcourt, a platoon commander of the 13th North Canterbury and Westland Company, recorded the experience in his diary:

> On our left we could see the 1st Bde [it was actually the 1st Rifles] having a good scrap but we found a few Tommies holding some old trenches (the old British Line on the Somme) in front of us. Occupied these. The Hun could be seen retiring over a hill some distance in front and we peppered him with rifle & MG fire. At the time we could have advanced almost unopposed but the 'Heads' decided to stay there.[5]

The 2nd Canterbury Battalion attempted to do the same on the left of the line but experienced considerable difficulties. At Auchonvillers the battalion came under heavy machine-gun fire and light shelling. It took the village, moved through it and continued to its objective, the old British trench line of 1916.

Private William Morris of the 12th Nelson Company remembered this day more than 70 years later. The time spent in training for open warfare had been well worth the effort. After three days on the march:

> We ended up on a hillside like that one there and it was a nice sunny day . . . and we had our first hot food — a plate of porridge. Not much of a feed, was it? Then we started off and it was all rolling downs . . . And there were Australians on that side and New Zealanders on this side. All in order, one section here, one here and so on. I said to the bloke in front of me, 'Good Lord, it doesn't look like there is a war on'. I just got the words out of my mouth and old Jerry turned a machine gun on us. Well, there wasn't a second and there wasn't a bloke standing up, they all went down like a shot. We were trained to do that, you see. We never got any casualties then.

When his company reached the old British trenches, Private Morris was confronted by a German soldier there and was forced to bayonet him. 'It was the only time I used a bayonet. I'm glad it was the last. I was nearly sick. It was a terrible thing to do.'[6]

A new defensive line had been formed, about 3000 yards in advance of the outpost line of the 1st Rifles and about 1000 yards north-east of Auchonvillers. On the left the 2nd Canterbury Battalion was occupying a portion of the old British trenches while further south, 1st Canterbury was on the high ground and had linked up with the 12th Division. The situation was far from secure, though. From the ridge they now held the New Zealanders overlooked the Ancre Valley as far back as Thiepval. It was full of German soldiers on the move. To their north, they could see the 4th German Division in Beaumont-Hamel and heading towards

Auchonvillers. The New Zealand machine-gunners soon took a heavy toll on the advancing Germans, forcing them to take cover. The left flank of 2nd Canterbury, resting on the Apple Trees, was 'up in the air'. Its casualties were few but 'flank connection was not good'.[7] The Germans were in possession of One Tree Hill between Beaumont-Hamel and Colincamps, which was reported to be in enemy hands. There was considerable opposition on the left flank and the brigade lacked a reserve to deal with it. Fresh New Zealand units were eagerly awaited.

The 1st Canterbury Battalion had had a much easier time, as its war diary reveals:

> Reveille: 2 a.m. Marched to HEDAUVILLE, where we arrived about 9 a.m., and where we found the greater portion of the Division already assembled. A hot meal, and a short rest, and orders for the attack were explained to all ranks. One bomb per man was issued, 'B' Teams told off and final preparations made. The task allotted to this Battalion was that of filling the gap which existed between BEAUMONT HAMEL on the left and the village of HAMEL on the right. 2nd Canty. were on our left. Shortly after noon the Battalion moved off by Platoons at intervals . . . On coming under close range Artillery and Machine Gun fire the attackers deployed and arrived at the objective with practically no casualties. Consolidation was not difficult as a complete system of trenches in good order already existed and almost coincided with the proposed line. Touch was secured on both flanks, and with three platoons per Coy. in the front line and a reserve platoon some 200 yards in rear the night passed quietly. The general situation to the right of HAMEL was obscure. Battalion H.Q. was established at . . . with Brigade H.Q. at a Chateau in MAILLY-MALLET [sic]. There was no covering artillery. Much movement on the part of the Enemy could be observed across the ANCRE on the opposite crest.[8]

The 2nd Brigade had advanced just in time to prevent the Germans from occupying the old British trenches in considerable strength and thereby holding much of the high ground in the area. As Brigadier Young recorded, 'It was apparent that I had occupied my position only just in time, as the enemy had crossed the ANCRE in places, and occupied part of the trench system in the vicinity of the Northern half of my objective'.[9] The 1916 trenches were in reasonably good condition, considering that they had been abandoned for twenty months. The precarious situation north of the 2nd Brigade was resolved by the arrival of the 1st Brigade in the early evening of 26 March. This brigade linked up with 2nd Canterbury's left flank and it was 1st Brigade's turn to have its flank 'up in the air' for a while. The night of 26 March 'passed quietly'[10] for the 2nd Brigade. It faced some light shelling and machine-gun fire but consolidated its line by intensive digging and by sending out fighting patrols. As John Harcourt noted in his diary, 'The night passed uneventfully except for a smoke bomb dump left over from the 1916 [battle] being exploded by a Lewis gun shot & rather putting the wind up everyone including the Hun.'[11]

The 1st Brigade, consisting of the 1st and 2nd Auckland Battalions, three companies of 2nd Rifles and a machine-gun company (and temporarily designated as B Brigade), and under the command of Brigadier General C.W. Melvill, did not set off from Hédauville until 2 p.m. This brigade was delayed from joining the other New Zealand units on the high ground because of the news that the Germans had taken Colincamps. The village had to be cleared because it was well to the rear of where the New Zealanders were attempting to establish their new line of defence. Once Colincamps was free of the enemy, 1st Brigade could continue its advance. It hoped to reach as far east as Serre, some 3½ miles from Mailly-Maillet.

The brigade set off with 1st Auckland on the right, 2nd Rifles on the left and with 2nd Auckland in support. The road to Serre provided a clear direction of the attack and was the dividing line for both battalions. When the 1st Brigade reached the flank of 1st Rifles on the Auchonvillers Ridge it came under heavy fire. There was fierce opposition at the sugar factory and the enemy was across the Serre road and holding it in force. Both leading battalions of the brigade immediately went into action.

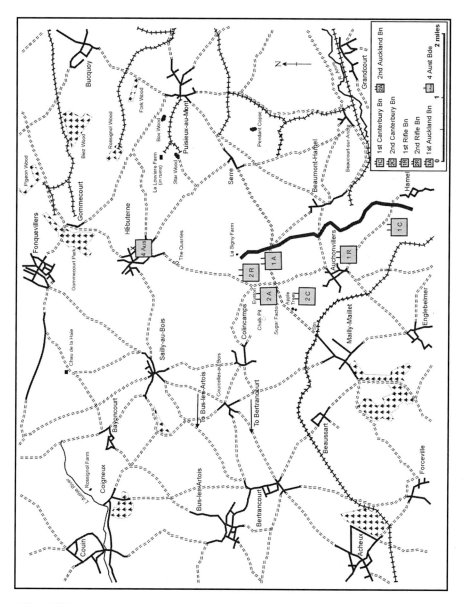

Where NZ Division was committed on 26 March 1918.

The 1st Auckland Battalion had been advancing cautiously along the Serre road. As the men neared a large windmill two German machine guns fired on them. The Aucklanders immediately swung half-right and moved into position to attack this threat. With two infantry companies leading and another holding the Serre road as its left flank, they advanced in artillery formation towards the Apple Trees and a long hedge running in front of them. The German machine-gun fire was intense and a number of men were wounded. From the hedge the ground fell away for some distance and then, after a small level section, rose again to the Serre Ridge. At the foot of the ridge, just to the right of the sugar refinery, one of the Auckland companies was checked in its advance. The machine-gun barrage was too heavy to continue the assault, so the company halted in the sunken road. The men gained a short respite while their officers looked for a way to continue the advance. Meanwhile the other company had been successful in their attack and were well forward and deep into the enemy positions. They took three machine guns, killed many Germans and put the rest to flight.

Private Jesse Stayte, who was 43 years old in 1918, wrote a vivid account of this attack in his diary. The battalion had moved out from Mailly-Maillet at 4.30 p.m. and was just past the windmill when the men were ordered to fix bayonets and move into artillery formation. They advanced up a gentle crest with a hedge running across its top. They had just broken through the hedge when

> all at once we were under arty fire from Fritz's guns. The shells dropped right amongst us & we at once got the order to charge. Many were hit before we left the assembly place, but soon we were off got to the hedge and trees and it was here that we first got into the fight proper. Fritz seemed to have the range to a yard and his shells and bullets from machine guns and rifles simply deafened one. The screech of bullets was awful and our men began to fall rapidly. We had 800 yards to go down a slope before we could get cover. Fritz was on the ridge in front. However we went on and got to the bottom where there was a trench which was our objective and we took it but we left a trail of dead and wounded all down that slope.

Then came word that the Germans were preparing a counterattack so another bayonet charge was needed, and we went over to them again and this time we were on more even terms and got among them with the Bayonet and drove them back and so spoiled their chance of a counter attack just then.

These attacks were nerve-wracking experiences for Private Stayte.

This was my first time over the top and I hope I may never again have to go over. We were all naturally nervous at the start but once we started and saw our mates going down all fear vanished and our aim was to get to them with our Bayonets, and when we did get there they ran like a flock of sheep and it was simply a matter of shooting them as they ran.[12]

Jesse Stayte, whose brother Ollie had been killed in January 1918, did not see the end of the war. He fought at Bapaume and his account of that battle appears in the last section of this book. Having survived 'Bloody Bapaume', Jesse Stayte was killed on 1 October that year, leaving a wife and six children in New Zealand to cope without him.

After more than seventy years of reflection Thomas Eltringham, a Lewis gunner in the 2nd Auckland Battalion, knew what had sustained him and the other soldiers during the terrible ordeal of close combat:

I was never fitter in my life than when I was training . . . that stands you in pretty good stead . . . helps you a lot later on . . . and you could never find better cobbers than the jokers you were in the line with . . . Never let your mates down, that was a good motto . . . People used to say to me, 'Was you scared?' Yes, who wouldn't be? But, I said my biggest worry was not to let my mates think I was scared. Mustn't let them down.[13]

The 1st Auckland was in a precarious position. One of its rifle companies was now well ahead of the other and isolated in enemy territory. It could withdraw or the other company could renew its attack. The latter option was chosen. The stalled company was reinforced and preparations were made to renew the attack at nightfall. By dusk, everything was ready.

As darkness fell, the company commander, Captain H.R. Vercoe, gave the signal to attack and led the way, yelling, 'Come on, boys; rush them, rush them!' The men surged up the gentle slope and pressed their attack hard, despite heavy machine-gun fire. 'The Aucklanders closed in with the cold steel, and in a few moments the Huns were a crowd of panic-stricken fugitives. It was in vain that their officers endeavoured to rally them — a few were taken prisoner, many were killed and the remainder ran.'[14] The battalion's war diary simply recorded that 'The 16th and 3rd companies advanced & took this point, capturing 40 prisoners & 8 MG's [machine guns] . . . Our line was now reasonably secure and the MG fire slackened considerably.'[15]

Between the sunken road and the Serre Ridge lay only 120 yards of open gentle slope. Yet this attack demonstrated the fighting spirit and great courage of the New Zealand officers and soldiers. Taking the ridge was a significant achievement as it enabled 1st Auckland to link up with the 2nd Canterbury Battalion on its right flank.

North of the Serre road, 2nd Rifles tried to advance to a road just north-west of Serre village. Its advance was rapid and steady until it struck heavy enemy opposition at the sugar factory. This German stronghold had been a thorn in the New Zealand Division's side all day. The 2nd Rifles' advance was concealed by the smoke of a burning ammunition dump, so that it was able to advance to a prominent hedgerow about 1000 yards east of the refinery, finally in New Zealand possession, and just south of La Signy Farm. The Germans made two unsuccessful attempts to force 2nd Rifles off this site. The left company managed to clear the Germans from the Hébuterne road where, as a measure of protection, it established a flank guard along the road from Colincamps. The 2nd Rifles captured thirty-seven prisoners and four machine guns in the fighting that night. The sugar refinery, scene of intense fighting all day, was set on fire by German artillery, and burned luridly, making for 'a wild night'.[16]

At 7 p.m., the left flank of 1st Auckland moved forward some 300 yards to connect with the right of the 2nd Rifles. At 10 p.m. the 2nd Auckland Battalion joined its sister battalion on the ridge line. 'The night was bitterly cold and all ranks were in battle order without greatcoats a very trying time was experienced.'[17] Years later Thomas Eltringham remembered this advance:

> Our battalion pushed them back and came to a stall at La Signy Farm which happened to be on higher ground and easily defended . . . That is where we had to dig in & settle and reorganise and wait for the next attack . . . La Signy Farm was of such a value, being on higher ground and with a good view right to the rear of whoever held it. We must have it or else.[18]

During the morning of 26 March, fourteen Whippet tanks had cleared Colincamps. This was the first time these light tanks had been used in action and their success meant that the New Zealand Division did not have to devote large numbers of soldiers to its rear security. It could focus solely on the enemy in front.

Despite 1st Brigade's achievements, the New Zealand commanders could see instantly that reaching Serre that night, or in the immediate future, was out of the question. The New Zealand line was linked up, but no connection had been established with 4th Australian Brigade, now at Hébuterne. The heights of La Signy Farm, a significant weak point in the New Zealand position, also required urgent attention.

Just after 2 p.m. on 26 March, 4th Australian Brigade of the 4th Australian Division was ordered to Hébuterne, which was reported to have fallen to the Germans. The brigade commander, Brigadier C.H. Brand, directed his four battalions to concentrate near an old windmill while he went forward on horseback to the village with a small reconnaissance party. It was a courageous move. Hébuterne was thought to be in German hands and there were rumours of German armoured cars raiding all along the roads of Picardy. At 3.30 p.m. Brigadier Brand came cantering back and gathered his men around him. He had ridden right into Hébuterne and the village was empty. But, well aware that his troops had not eaten all day, Brand ordered up the brigade cookers and gave his soldiers a hot meal before ordering them to take the village. So the soldiers of 4th Brigade did not set off to occupy the village until 5.40 p.m. C.E.W. Bean was critical of this delay: 'considering the tension of the situation and the vast issues at stake, he [Brand] was indeed a cool commander — the future student may think too cool'.[19] It was well after nightfall when the 4th Brigade reached Hébuterne and the Germans had beaten them to it. They were not there in force, however, and were easily driven out. The fighting that night and in subsequent days completely destroyed what had been a large village. As one New Zealand soldier recorded in his diary, Hébuterne 'is just a heap of ruins now'.[20] By midnight on 26 March, Hébuterne had been taken by the Australians and would provide a solid left flank for the New Zealand Division.

Brigadier Brand's 4th Brigade now became part of the 62nd Division. Brand was informed that the New Zealand Division was immediately south of him and would attempt to swing up and close the gap on his exposed right flank. The brigadier directed his 16th Battalion to swing round towards the east and extend the brigade's flank towards the New Zealanders. The link should be made in the next few hours. Until that gap was closed, it was a cause for considerable anxiety.

The night of 26 March was a quiet one for the New Zealanders now forming part of the Third Army's new line of defence. But the spring temperatures were bitterly cold and there was plenty of work to do as the New Zealanders consolidated their new positions. Fortunately the old British trenches most occupied did not require much repair work. As they always did when occupying new territory, the New Zealanders sent out fighting patrols along the whole of their front to establish where the Germans were and to learn what they were up to. The enemy was occupying Beaumont-Hamel and using its 1916 front-line trenches, but it was up to very little. This was a situation that was not expected to last.

At the end of this first day of action the New Zealand troops committed to the fray occupied a strong and continuous line from just west of Hamel to north of the Serre road. The southern portion of the gap between IV and V Corps was closed. Observation on the 2nd Brigade front, based primarily on the Auchonvillers Ridge, was excellent, but north of Serre road it was poor. Here the Germans still held the high ground and overlooked the New

Zealand positions. At La Signy Farm the situation was particularly bad.

The main problem for the Allies was that, though much reduced by the day's activities, the gap had still not been closed. Between 4th Australian Brigade at Hébuterne and the left flank of the New Zealand line at La Signy Farm its northern portion was now about a mile and a half long. If the Third Army was to make a stand on its current lines of defence, this gap must be closed without delay. This task would be the responsibility of those New Zealand units not yet committed to the battle.

On 26 March things improved dramatically for the British Army. Though the twenty-nine British divisions that had been in the line since 21 March were exhausted and their numbers much reduced, the spirit of the survivors remained strong and there was considerable fight left in them. This was remarkable given the force that had been thrown against them. But the key to survival for the British was the nine fresh divisions, all of which had been committed to battle by 26 March, eight of them north of the Somme. There they were making a telling difference. The new line they had helped establish was almost continuous and was holding well.

> The battle was now becoming stabilised, and after the 26th March the enemy, although he made desperate and despairing efforts, gained from the British no ground worth mentioning. Reinforcements had now appeared and the idea of defeat, never very potent, was fading away.[21]

The same could not be said for the Germans. There were plenty of indications that they, too, were tiring, lacked food and ammunition, and had outpaced their artillery support. As each new German attack failed, with ever-increasing casualty lists, morale began to plummet. For the first time the German soldiers began to doubt whether the *Kaiserschlacht* would succeed.[22]

There is little doubt that the New Zealand Division played a key role in this reversal of fortune, though the credit for halting the Germans on 26 March has to be shared with other divisions in the line. John Coleman was correct in his assessment:

So the little New Zealand division has again made history in this rotten war. I may tell you that there was absolutely no defence on the two-mile front against old Fritz, which we are at present holding. So our boys did not know where the enemy was, one just had to march on until they ran right into them. Then the fight began and our boys must have absolutely cut the Hun to pieces. Our company was supposed to be up here first, but we were delayed on the way. When we went in to hold the lines there were Huns lying dead in all directions.[23]

Initially the Germans were delighted by the progress they were making in their offensive and believed that the British Army was in a state of collapse. 'If it goes on like this, in 14 days we'll reach the sea,' noted a German officer of the 49th Infantry Regiment on 24 March. But two days later, near Bucquoy and Serre, it was a very different story:

Now we lay close to the edge of the devastated zone and could already gaze on the promised land. To the right ahead of us, lay the village of Hébuterne. But two kilometres before this region untouched by war the Englishman holds his last trench ahead of us with colossal toughness . . . The resistance had so strengthened that we could no longer generally break it down. Unfortunately neither could the troops who relieved us.

As Charles Bean concluded, 'The "colossal toughness" was presumably largely that of the New Zealand Division, and the adjective does not exaggerate its quality.' He was, however, quick to point out that the German was also referring to the defensive efforts of 19th, 62nd and 42nd British Divisions.[24] It would be another twenty-two years before an advancing German Army finally reached the sea and the New Zealand Division had indeed helped to make history on 26 March 1918. It had, though, already lost 150 men while doing so.[25]

Chapter 6

Stopping the Storm: 27 March 1918

O N THE NIGHT of 26 March there was still a large gap in the newly established line. More than a mile wide, it stretched from the New Zealand 1st Brigade position at La Signy Farm to the 4th Australian Brigade now firmly established at Hébuterne. The importance of closing this gap was obvious to General Russell and the New Zealand staff officers. As more New Zealand battalions arrived at Hédauville they were immediately gathered up and formed into a composite brigade under the command of Lieutenant Colonel A.E. Stewart of the New Zealand Rifle Brigade. A real mixture of units, the brigade consisted of the headquarters of the Rifle Brigade, the 3rd Battalion New Zealand Rifle Brigade (3rd Rifles), the 2nd Wellington and 2nd Otago Battalions. The Wellington Machine Gun Company was also part of the brigade. General Russell kept the last two battalions to arrive at Hédauville that night as a divisional reserve. They would be sorely needed in the following days. Stewart's orders were to extend the New Zealand line north to the Hébuterne road and link up with the Australians there. At 1 a.m. on the morning of 27 March Stewart's composite brigade set off to find the Australians and close the gap.

The night was perfect for marching. It was cold and clear, the moonlight so bright that maps could be clearly read. There had been no time to issue written orders, so each unit was given its instructions while on the move. The brigade marched through Mailly-Maillet and reached Colincamps safely at 4 a.m. There, headquarters were quickly established. The moon had now set so that the battalions, led by the 2nd Otago, moved out from Colincamps quickly in order to take advantage of the short period of darkness. The 2nd Otago Battalion marched directly east in order to screen the advance of the rest of the brigade. The 2nd Wellingtons on the right was to link up with the 1st Brigade at La Signy Farm while the 3rd

Rifles, marching north-east along the road to Hébuterne, would provide the link with the Australians. Once past the outskirts of Colincamps the New Zealanders came under heavy machine-gun fire that forced them to deploy in skirmishing order. In other words, they thinned out the numbers with gaps between individual soldiers and larger spaces between sections of infantry.

After spending only fifteen minutes in Colincamps, the 3rd Rifles moved off as fast as they could. After making contact with the Australians at Hébuterne, the riflemen would turn to the right. Two companies would then be sent in attack formation to the high ground east of the Hébuterne road while the other company formed a support line in a strong defensive position 100 yards east of the road. There it could cover the whole battalion front with fire. According to the history of the Rifle Brigade, the plan 'was carried out with clockwork precision'.[1] The 3rd Rifles, under the command of Lieutenant Colonel Edward Puttick, who would be severely wounded just after midday, advanced in perfect order against machine-gun and rifle fire of moderate intensity. When the battalion linked with the Australians just south of Hébuterne, two companies set off for the high ground east of the village. The company on the left gained the crest of a ridge some 600 yards away. With this flank extended, the other advancing company came up level with it so that by 6.45 a.m. the battalion had secured its objective. This important ridge was in New Zealand hands and the link-up with the Australians was secure. The fighting had not been severe despite the enemy outnumbering them. The Germans had not been expecting an attack and most fled from the ridge. Only at one point had there been any resistance and the determined riflemen charged this location with fixed bayonets, which soon dispersed the German defenders.

Bernard Cottrell witnessed the attack and described it in a letter to his parents:

Just a few lines, not so hurried this time, but still am not yet able to write much, censorship will now be very strict on account of the serious position we were in, how serious very few realise . . .

The battle & situations leading up to it I will leave later, but we spent 3 freezing nights up in the trenches & that together with travelling made 4 or 5 nights without rest. Many things happened one outstanding feature was a bayonet charge, quite like a moving picture show & quite the old style of things, it resulted in bringing in 17 machine guns. I viewed it from the front line, it was as bright as day, moonlight & Fritz light the dry grass in front so everything stood out very vividly. Our losses were not great in killed but taken together with wounded amounted to a fair number. Things are not all finished yet, but wait & you will get all news, & don't worry for me as things are quite alright with me now.[2]

The 3rd Rifles' attack succeeded because of the speed with which it was launched and the tactical surprise it achieved. By 7 a.m. on 27 March the northern portion of the gap had been closed.

Unfortunately, the 2nd Wellington Battalion on the brigade's right flank had a much tougher time and failed to reach its objective. It ran into heavy German machine-gun fire from near La Signy Farm. One of the companies attacked an enemy outpost there, killing fourteen Germans and capturing fifty-three others. But the intensity of the fire from the ridge in front of La Signy Farm halted further progress and 2nd Wellington was forced to dig in some 400 yards west of the Hébuterne road, which had been its final objective. Though the Germans still held the high ground and overlooked Colincamps, it made little difference to the final outcome. Despite falling short of its final objective the 2nd Wellington Battalion managed to link up with the 3rd Rifles on its left and the 2nd Rifles on its right at the road junction.

The composite brigade hastily formed on the night of 26 March had fulfilled the task assigned to it with relative ease. It had made contact with the Australians and secured the important ridge between La Signy Farm and Hébuterne. The dangerous gap on the division's northern flank had been closed. More significantly, the new British front now extended in an unbroken line from Hébuterne to Hamel. The open gate had been slammed shut. Now it needed to be firmly secured.

On 27 March, except for the area in front of La Signy Farm, the

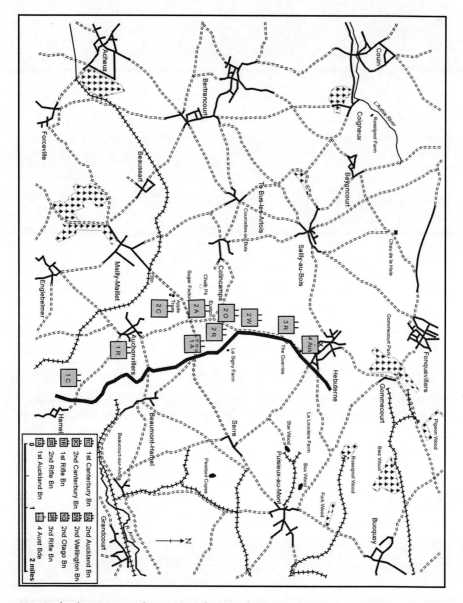

New Zealand positions on the morning of 27 March 1918

Australians and New Zealanders occupied a considerable portion of high
ground overlooking much of the old Somme battlefield. They had an
especially good view over the several spurs and gullies leading towards the
hidden valley of the Ancre, despite the long grass that was now growing
there. The village of Hébuterne, now occupied by the Australians, was

also on high ground. Due south on the same ridge as Hébuterne was Auchonvillers, now held by the New Zealand Division. South-east, 2 miles away on the plateau beyond the nearest depression stood 'the bare stump of Serre'.[3] A mile north-east of Serre in a gully leading to the Ancre was Puisieux. On the heights, 1½ miles north-east of this lay Bucquoy, held by the remnants of the British 62nd Division. So the Australian and New Zealand soldiers had the distinct tactical advantage of being able to see for some considerable distance to their front. Everywhere they looked on the morning of 27 March, their front was alive with the movement of German troops making ready to resume their advance. The Germans were exposed and vulnerable. As Bean noted, this was a sight 'such as Australian infantry had never before watched from their front trenches',[4] and New Zealand veteran and historian Ormond Burton wrote that 'Such an opportunity had not come to most of them [the New Zealand soldiers in the line] during the whole war'.[5]

The Germans must have believed that the gap in front of them was still open: they began advancing towards the New Zealand and Australian positions as if on parade and 'without the slightest attempt at concealment'.[6] For a brief moment the New Zealanders and Australians were stunned by the sheer audacity of their opponents. 'Look at the bloody bastards coming up the road,' shouted a soldier in the 2nd Auckland Battalion as the Germans marched in four columns down the Serre road.[7] Then every man capable of firing a rifle or machine gun opened up on the advancing Germans. They took a fearful toll on their enemy that morning and inflicted thousands of casualties in the space of a few minutes, as James McWhirter recorded:

> As we watched we could see the enemy coming marching up the road, some smoking, some laughing, as if they were marching on to Paris. What an eye opener they would get in a few minutes, everyone was eager to shoot, but we must wait till we get orders.

The Germans were allowed to get to within 50 yards of the New Zealand front line before the order was given to open fire:

It was like corn before the sicle [sic], machine guns cracked, every one of the enemy fell like ninepins, horses struggled on the ground, those who did escape flew in a panic and there was congestion all along the road. The dead were heaped on top of one another, the German red-cross were carrying away the corpses for three days afterwards.[8]

Oscar Reston, a signaller in one of the Canterbury battalions, told a similar story. On the morning of 27 March 1918, his battalion

met Fritzy coming up the road in columns of four. We got stuck into them with machine guns and rifles . . . The New Zealanders had the drop on them. We were waiting for them to come down the road. We kept quiet until they got within shooting distance and then tore into them.[9]

And William Morris of the 12th Nelson Company, 2nd Canterbury Battalion, was haunted for the rest of his life by the killing that occurred on that fateful morning.

The Germans come over three times. Three times the next day in close formation. As close as you and I. And they just wiped them down. Wiped them down. And he sent another lot and he got wiped down the same. Terrible! One lot of Australian soldiers when we were going up there, they met a whole regiment of Germans coming along a sunken road — they had the Colonel right along in the front coming along the sunken road and they came to the top of the hill and there they were. They just wiped the whole lot out. They had four deep, cleared the whole thing. Terrible! A terrible thing to happen, isn't it? Just murder.

But, as Morris realised, 'It was you or them.'[10]

The killing continued throughout the day. In an attempt to get their advance moving again, the Germans abandoned their tactics of infiltration in favour of full frontal infantry attacks supported by heavy artillery and machine-gun fire. The New Zealanders were aided by the fact that their position formed the boundary line for two German armies — the Second and the Seventeenth — so that, according to the British official historian, 'the enemy's efforts were not well combined'.[11] Still, the New Zealanders in the front line on that day knew they were in for a tough time, but they were determined not to be ejected from their newly established positions. Captain George Tuck of the 2nd Auckland Battalion kept a detailed diary of events. That crucial morning he caught the determination of the New Zealand troops:

> We took a section of trench over this morning at 5 am. Fritz has been massing all morning in our immediate front where he had been allowed to cross the Ancre. Consequence is he intends to develop his advantage here where we threw him back some distance yesterday & closed the gap. The preliminary bombardment is down on us, we ourselves have practically no artillery & we expect him to launch his offensive at any moment. He will get the surprise of his life.[12]

The fighting was continuous from midday, but the Germans launched four large counterattacks against the New Zealand positions that afternoon. The first came just after noon; the others followed at 1 p.m., 3.30 p.m. and at 7 p.m. Only in the last counterattack did the Germans succeed in capturing any ground from the hard-pressed New Zealanders. They attacked on a front of 1500 yards midway between the sugar refinery and Hébuterne. The 2nd Wellington Battalion was forced back off its defensive position to a distance 500 yards from the road. At 8.50 p.m. the reserve company, from Hawke's Bay, tried to counterattack in an effort to regain the ground, but it made little headway against the enemy party now well established on Wellington's old position, protected by machine guns and holding a section of the Hébuterne–sugar factory road. The New Zealanders fought hard, killing about sixty of the enemy and capturing five machine guns. But their own casualties were heavy and they could not re-establish 2nd Wellington's original line. The battalion's casualties on this day were four officers and sixty-nine soldiers.

This loss of ground had the potential to cause a huge disruption along the New Zealand line. That it did not was the result of fast and courageous action by the men of the 3rd Rifles. The forcing back of 2nd Wellington's position had left the flank of the 3rd Rifles exposed. The latter immediately altered its position to form a defensive flank, but it could spare only one platoon to carry out this vital task. This soon came under intense pressure from the Germans and the platoon's officer was killed in an early exchange of fire. A sergeant and then a corporal took charge of the platoon and held the Germans at bay. This pressured flank was reinforced first by the reserve platoon, then by the bulk of C Company, which had been detained on duty at Amiens. The exposed flank was now secure and managed to regain contact with the 2nd Wellington Battalion.

There were other times throughout the day when the situation hung in the balance. One occurred in the centre of the line at La Signy Farm. There, a young, inexperienced officer in the 2nd Auckland Battalion, after an attack where his platoon's position had been pelted with German stick grenades, decided it was time to withdraw, despite the fact that his men had not suffered any casualties.

> It was a critical moment. The whole army was depending on the New Zealand Division to hold its ground. 2/Auckland were holding the most delicate portion of the divisional front, and the left post of the 15th Company was the key to the whole position.[13]

The situation was soon restored. Captain George Tuck, from the battalion's headquarters, saw the retirement, ran from his position and ordered the men to turn back. He was obeyed and with the sergeant now leading it, the platoon rushed back and retook its trench from the enemy who had just arrived in it. A new officer was immediately assigned and the platoon put up a determined resistance for the rest of the afternoon.

Because the fighting was continuous and the New Zealanders occupied most of the high ground, German casualties mounted steadily throughout the day. In the absence of any artillery support, the New Zealand machine-gunners provided the infantry with much-needed fire support and inflicted the bulk of the casualties. For the New Zealand machine-gunners, 27 March 1918 was a red-letter day. The Wellington Company in support of the composite brigade opened the account. It was occupying a superb position on the division's left flank with a commanding view over the whole brigade front. At 10.30 a.m. an enemy battalion was observed at 1800 yards' range moving from near Hébuterne. The Wellington Company's machine guns at once opened up on them and soon found the range. This

> had the effect of scattering and thoroughly disorganising the enemy. Casualties could not be observed but the action of the enemy in breaking and scattering in all directions made it evident that casualties had been inflicted.[14]

At noon the situation was repeated, though this time the deadly effect of the machine-gun fire could be observed:

> Two guns at a range of 700 yards engaged two companies of the enemy in mass formation. The enemy was literally mowed down and stretcher-bearers were observed working at the point for three hours afterwards.[15]

The latter were not fired upon as they went about their life-saving work.

But still the Germans kept coming. Mid afternoon the next target appeared: two long advancing columns of enemy infantry 1600 yards away and gradually converging over the Serre Ridge. Although the Germans were well within the range of the New Zealand machine guns, the order was passed not to open fire until the enemy was within 1000 yards. 'Probably no better target presented itself to the New Zealand Machine Gun Corps in France, and the fullest advantage was taken of it.'[16] The machine guns played havoc.

With the second burst of fire about 50 of the enemy were seen
to fall, a long burst was then fired into the mass and a very great
number fell, the remainder broke and took cover in shell holes or
undulations. As a meagre estimate 300 casualties were inflicted
in this instance and until nightfall the ground was observed to be
littered with bodies.[17]

The Germans now turned their full attention on these troublesome
machine-gunners. Twelve enemy machine-gun crews attempted to move
across the open towards an old trench, presumably to establish a machine-
gun nest there. They were seen and fired on. Some teams were killed out-
right; the rest fled, leaving behind their precious guns. When the Germans
tried to recover their weapons, more were killed and wounded.

Just after 2 p.m., under cover of artillery fire, some small groups of
Germans advanced through an old communication trench and rushed
three of the Wellington Company's guns. The commander of A Gun
stood his ground and kept firing as ten Germans attempted to seize
the weapon. All were killed. C Gun managed to carry out an orderly
withdrawal but a party of thirty Germans rushed B Gun. Ten of the
attacking Germans were killed before the New Zealand firer was wounded
and the gun taken. This was the first time a New Zealand machine gun
had fallen into enemy hands, but not for long. A sergeant and some men
of the Ruahine Company of the 2nd Wellington Battalion charged the
Germans, killing most of them and regaining the lost weapon. In the
process the Wellington soldiers captured a German light machine gun.

Still the Germans came on. At 3.30 p.m. they again attacked the
composite brigade's position, this time taking the precaution of
advancing in open order. They were seen as they came over the ridge
some 1200 yards away. The Wellington Company's guns opened up and
many of the enemy fell immediately. The rest took cover. For some time
afterwards, isolated groups of Germans were seen trying to crawl back
over the ridge.

At 4 p.m., when 2nd Wellington was forced back, the gun on the right
flank of the Wellington Company was ordered to withdraw. The whole

gun team was wounded while doing so and the gun was dismantled and left behind, minus its crucial firing mechanism. This was recovered the next day. The machine guns and rifle fire had inflicted massive casualties on the Germans. '[U]ntil nightfall' the ground in front of the composite brigade was 'littered with dead Huns'.[18]

At 9.10 p.m. on 27 March 1918 Captain George Tuck wrote an entry in his diary that neatly summed up what had been 'a stressing day':

> The Hun has been attacking us all day by all means. Things happened of which I dare not write. Haven't had 10 seconds to myself all the time. We are just holding the bounder but we have suffered pretty heavily — but he more so. If he doesn't put in an attack before the next hour I think all will be well. A thousand pities he was allowed to cross the line of the Ancre.[19]

It had been a real soldier's battle, in which nearly every New Zealander then in the line took part. It was their tenacity and courage as well as the superb leadership skills shown by non-commissioned and junior officers that held the New Zealand line intact. 'The bravery display by all ranks . . . during these attacks was beyond all praise and it was purely due to this that the Hun failed entirely in his efforts.'[20]

Captain Harry Highet was the only officer of his battalion to survive the Passchendaele disaster. Even then he had required hospitalisation in England, having suffered gas inhalation. He returned to the New Zealand Division in time to serve on the Somme in 1918, where his company was occupying part of the old British trenches in 'a very nasty position'. On the morning of 27 March, his company seemed to be alone on the battlefield.

> I got up to this place and there wasn't anybody on the left. So I set out with a man to go way out on the left which I shouldn't have done. I should have sent someone else. But I wanted to have a look. Didn't see anybody. On the way back suddenly the chap with me found that he had a big splinter taken off his rifle, the woodwork

of his rifle. Sniper! From then on it was 'Up', go for your life, and down again, until we got to a place out of sight of the sniper. That was a pretty near squeak that was.

Highet's company was under considerable shell-fire but his orders were explicit: 'We had word not to move'. But a runner from a Scottish battalion in front of his position brought word that his CO wanted the New Zealanders to move close to the Scots' position as the Germans were going to attack. 'What the hell do we do?' asked Highet. So off he went to the Scots, again risking artillery and rifle fire. By checking the situation personally, Highet decided that there was no need to move his company. The return trip was extremely dangerous. 'On the way back, shell fire was pretty tough. I reckon I was doing 100 yards in 10 seconds.' Highet reached the safety of his trenches just as a shell did. He was covered with dirt, but unscathed.[21]

Like Harry Highet, James Frederick Blakemore was a Passchendaele survivor. In March 1918 he was a sergeant major in one of the Canterbury battalions. On 27 March an incident on the Serre Ridge stirred him to action:

> The Germans were waving a white flag. And when they [New Zealand soldiers] hopped out, three Sergeants got shot. It was a gag, to show themselves. That made me really mad. I lost control of myself. We went from shell-hole to shell-hole . . . to within 30 yards of this strongpoint . . . I had one bomb . . . Mills grenade — I rushed to this crowd . . . and I shot a pair in the head . . . Some were wounded . . . they surrendered.

Blakemore's company commander then came up, called him 'a bloody fool' and recommended him for the Military Medal. It was subsequently awarded.[22]

Conditions in the front line were hard. The day was clear but, in John Harcourt's words, 'dull and cold'. In an effort to keep warm he wrapped a thick towel around him and wore it under his tunic.[23] Private Jesse Stayte of the 1st Auckland Battalion, dug in forward of Mailly-Maillet, described the conditions in his diary:

> The weather is fine and cold, but we have no greatcoats. The food is very poor and water we have none . . . We have not had a cup of tea or anything hot since Sunday morning and we have been shivering all day.[24]

Over the next few days, conditions in the front line would get worse.

The German attacks along the front of IV Corps were unsuccessful, except at Rossignol Wood, north of Hébuterne, and on the corps' right boundary where ground near the village of Hamel was lost. As a result of this development, the 2nd Brigade reinforced its right flank and extended it towards Hamel. Elsewhere along the British front the situation was much the same. On 27 March, the Third Army had been attacked all day by two German armies (the Second and Seventeenth). Losses were heavy on both sides but the Germans did not take a single objective. Ground, none of it significant, had been lost in only four places — north of Albert, north of Ablainzevelle, west of Serre and at Rossignol Wood. The price of these minor gains was dead and wounded German soldiers numbering in their thousands. In most New Zealand units casualties were light. The 2nd Wellington and both Canterbury battalions had suffered the heaviest losses: more than seventy each. In the evening of 27 March, the New Zealand wounded collected from the regimental aid posts (RAPs), the first-line medical treatment centres, numbered just under 300. Also collected from the RAPs were about a hundred wounded British soldiers and an equal number of wounded Germans.[25] All the wounded were sent for further treatment and processing at the New Zealand advanced dressing station (ADS) at Mailly-Maillet.

The New Zealanders were elated with their success on 27 March. The 1st Brigade held the difficult centre section of the line and had taken more than a hundred German prisoners from five different regiments. Though its left flank had suffered badly, the brigade's war diary could record that 'The operation has left our men in excellent spirits with absolute confidence in themselves and their leaders'.[26] The New Zealand soldiers had every reason to feel this way.

During the night there was a considerable lull in activity along the New Zealand front. General Russell was able to reorganise brigades so that each unit was in its proper parent formation. In the northern sector of the line the rifle battalions were now in the New Zealand Rifle Brigade. Brigadier H.T. Fulton arrived that night to take over command from Lieutenant Colonel Stewart. In the centre of the line the North Island units formed the 1st Brigade, while in the south the battalions from the South Island formed the 2nd New Zealand Infantry Brigade. During this reorganisation, Russell was able to relieve those units that had suffered most from the German attacks and replace them with fresh ones. The 1st Otago Battalion, for example, moved into the line on the Englebelmer–Auchonvillers Ridge to relieve the 1st Rifles, the first New Zealand unit committed to action. As the medical officer of the 1st Rifles noted, this relief was welcome.

> Wednesday 27 March
> Worked all thru last night & got to bed this morning about 3 and rested until nine. Our chaps continue to hold on and casualties are somewhat less. The Battalion was withdrawn during the afternoon and we changed our position . . . now going to bed in hope of a good night's rest.[27]

Many years later Private Edward Bibby, a battalion runner with 1st Otago, remembered how difficult this relief was. The first task of Otago soldiers was to deepen the trench the 1st Rifles had been holding. According to Bibby, it was 'one of the hardest jobs I had, you see, being really hungry and trying to dig this gummy stuff on the bottom of the trench'. But by dawn on 28 March the task had been accomplished just in time to put the trenches to good use.[28] Further north at La Signy Farm the 4th Rifles, the last infantry unit to reach Hédauville, took over from the depleted 2nd Wellington Battalion. In the following days the 4th Rifles would make four attempts to recover the lost ground and take the heights of La Signy Farm.

The lull also permitted the completion of a reserve line of defence known as the Purple Line, which would add considerable depth to the New Zealand line. The soldiers from the New Zealand Engineers, the Pioneer Battalion and from three Light Trench Mortar batteries started work on the new position on the afternoon of 27 March and worked throughout the night. The Purple Line ran to the rear of Mailly-Maillet, Colincamps and Hébuterne. Lack of time and manpower made it impossible to build a continuous line of defence so the units allocated to this task concentrated on establishing a series of strongpoints that offered mutual support. Each could hold forty men and had at least six firebays, and included adequate drainage, duckboard flooring and barbed wire obstacles to their front. This was backbreaking construction work in uncomfortable and often dangerous conditions.

William Milne was a sapper in the 1st Field Company New Zealand Engineers. After stand-to on the morning of 27 March, his company marched from Bertrancourt to Mailly-Maillet, where they began to dig five strongpoints. The task was finished just after 10 p.m. and then the company manned the strongpoints until dawn. As Milne noted in his diary, 'All in light marching dress — bitterly cold night & all practically frozen.' The company was relieved by an infantry company the next day and marched back to Bertrancourt to collect their packs. By then Milne recorded he was 'Feeling unwell — probably cold & lack of sleep'.[29] For the next few days he was sick and confined to bed.

William Bertrand (also known as William Tume), of Ngati Awa descent, served in the Maori Pioneer Battalion. He was wounded on the Somme by German artillery fire. 'I got wounded in the hip . . . How did it happen? If you are out in the rain and a drop of rain hits you, you don't describe it. You just take it for granted.' Digging the strongpoints on the night of 27–28 March remained a vivid memory:

> I had to lie down, I don't know how many times, to avoid the bullets from machine gun fire sweeping across. The Germans knew we were there. Every chance we got, they'd have flares up in the air. It was just like daylight. When there was a chance came, you hopped out and dug. Dug a hole. When you can get into this hole well you're

right. You can carry on digging. It didn't take long to dig a hole that you can get down into when there's bullets flying about.'[30]

Bill Bertrand survived the war but returned to New Zealand to find that his guardians, the Tumes of Urenui, had died in the influenza epidemic. 'It wasn't a very happy home-coming.'

The initial plan had been for the Purple Line to be completed by 5 a.m. on 28 March and be capable of holding two infantry battalions and a machine-gun company. All the strongpoints were completed well ahead of time, before midnight on 27 March. Within the next four days some sixty such posts were constructed.

The New Zealand position was further strengthened by the arrival of the first units of the division's artillery: four 18-pounder batteries and one howitzer battery. The Divisional Ammunition Column had been hard at work on 26 and 27 March moving a total of 10,000 artillery rounds into the New Zealand front line. As the war diary of one of the artillery brigades states, 'Headquarters and Batteries moved into line at Mailly-Mallet [sic]. All Batteries reported in action by 11 pm.'[31] The artillery had not had time to register their guns so most of this firing was for the psychological effect it produced on both sides. The New Zealand guns kept up a harassing fire on the enemy's forward areas all night, targeting likely German concentration areas around Serre. At 4 a.m. the next day the gunners fired the first counter-battery fire, which lasted for just over two hours. As soon as dawn broke on 28 March the New Zealand artillery lost no time in registering their guns along the whole New Zealand front. With excellent observation over the enemy line the New Zealand gunners made their deadly presence felt, especially as the Germans 'showed themselves very freely during the first few days, and could even be seen in bivouacs on the slopes of the ridges behind Beaumont-Hamel'.[32] The early hours of 28 March permitted 'some splendid shooting, which no one enjoyed more than the infantry in the line'.[33]

During the night of 27 March, General Russell moved the New Zealand Division's headquarters from Hédauville to the Chateau at Bus-lès-Artois. Almost directly west of Colincamps, Bus-lès-Artois was only 4 miles from the New Zealand front-line positions. Russell also took the opportunity to inspect his men. In general he was happy with the New Zealanders' position, though he was concerned about the ground lost near Hamel on the division's southern flank:

> 27 March
>
> Attacked in two places but held them off — visited Colincamps and looked over position — it is, here a strong one. To the South not so good, and down on left not sticking well — Confusion, some great, on detraining at odd places and altered destination, now being overcome. Artillery of Div just up tonight.[34]

The Germans had far greater reason for concern. Only one German Army, the Eighteenth, made any significant progress on 27 March. The Second Army, which had been expected to make the greatest inroads on this day and 'on whose advance the operation mainly depended',[35] made no progress at all. The Second Army had been expecting to find only weak rearguards in its path, but had crashed into a new line defended by fresh New Zealand and Australian troops. The Germans had been made to pay dearly for this wishful thinking. As William Moore has written, 'What had been the most dangerous spot on the front of the Third Army now appeared to have been sealed.'[36] Many German sources regard the lack of progress on 27 March as the decisive moment in the Michael Offensive. This was certainly the view of the commander of the northern group of armies, Crown Prince Rupprecht of Bavaria.[37] When Rupprecht learned of the Second Army's lack of progress he ordered three of the German High Command's reserve divisions to attack Hébuterne the next day with the aim of breaking through to Doullens. No sooner had Rupprecht issued this order than Ludendorff countermanded it, sending the three divisions south of the Somme instead. On learning of this decision the prince cried, 'Then we have lost the war.' Ever after he referred to 27 March 1918 as 'this fateful day'.[38] But though the storm had been stopped in its tracks, it was far from a spent force.

Chapter 7

Holding the Storm: 28–30 March 1918

W HEN IT BECAME evident that their offensive was slowing down, the Germans launched a new attack north of the Somme on 28 March with the codename Mars. The British know this offensive as the First Battle of Arras 1918. First, the Germans wanted to split the two British armies defending the Arras sector of the line. Second, they wanted to recapture the vital position of Vimy Ridge that they had lost to the Canadians in April 1917. This would lead on to taking more significant ground. The final 'astoundingly ambitious' objective given for Mars was the city of Boulogne, some 72 miles from Arras.[1] Ultimately, though, the Germans wanted to reinvigorate their Second and Seventeenth Armies fighting on the Somme in order to restore the momentum of the *Kaiserschlacht*. According to Cyril Falls, 'If this had gone as well as the attack of March 21 the war might have been as nearly good as won.'[2]

There is considerable confusion in the many accounts of this battle over how many divisions the Germans used and what area they attacked. These range from twenty-nine divisions (with another sixteen in support) over a 33-mile front to just seven divisions along a front of 8 miles due east of Arras.[3] Churchill's history of the war has a twenty-twenty formula stating that twenty German divisions attacked a 20-mile section of the front then held by eight British divisions.[4] All the histories agree, however, on the outcome of the battle. In a static defensive battle of this kind the advantage lay with the defenders and the British made full use of it. The weather on 28 March was clear, allowing the Germans no chance of concealment. The British had learnt from the mistakes of a week before and used the new system of defence perfectly. The defences of the British Third and First Army divisions were elastic, well prepared and resolute. British artillery and machine-gun fire cut the attacking Germans to shreds.

Though the German infantry managed to penetrate the British Forward Zone in places they made no impression on the main line of defence. The Battle Zone remained untouched.

> The Germans came on time after time with the greatest bravery, sometimes almost shoulder to shoulder, assured that it required but one more effort to break the British front, only to be held and repulsed by the combined fire of guns, machine guns and rifles. They suffered severe losses, the total of which has never been divulged.[5]

For the British, the Mars Offensive was a model defensive battle; for the Germans it was a dismal failure. That evening a bitterly disappointed Ludendorff called it off.

It was not only the Germans who carried out an attack on 28 March 1918. On the night of 27 March, the New Zealand infantry carried out an offensive of their own, albeit on a much smaller scale and on the morning of 28 March they made two local attacks in an attempt to improve their line. The two attacks had quite different outcomes.

On the left flank of the New Zealand position, the 3rd Rifles had sent out reconnaissance patrols during the night and in the early morning of 28 March. As a result of the knowledge gained, 3rd Rifles decided to attack the German position in a series of quarries 500 yards south of Hébuterne and a short distance in front of their lines. The Battalion's D Company carried out the attack in the late morning and was supported by the machine guns and trench mortars of the Australians on its flank. The quarries were easily captured, along with a quantity of arms, provisions and equipment. It was an important success as the quarries gave excellent observation to the south-east for up to 3000 yards. This new position was large enough to hold a full company in its defence and had a good source of water, an important consideration in defensive warfare. The dead Germans at the quarries were searched for documents (and were also 'ratted' for warm clothing, food and souvenirs). The information obtained revealed that they came from two German divisions, the 20th and the 4th. This company attack by the 3rd Rifles had been a relatively easy affair: the objective was taken quickly and without loss. The other New Zealand attack did not meet with anything like this degree of success.

In the early morning of 28 March, the 4th Rifles had replaced the 2nd Wellington Battalion in front of La Signy Farm. The position was a poor one. The battalion did not hold any of the Hébuterne road, which was a prime defensive position; the Germans on the high ground at La Signy Farm overlooked it and the connection with the 3rd Rifles on its left flank was tenuous. An attempt by 4th Rifles to close the gap on the Hébuterne road soon after its arrival ground to a halt some 50 yards from the start line.

On the afternoon of 28 March, the 4th Rifles tried again to capture the high ground at the Hébuterne road. The attack began at 4 p.m., just as heavy rain started to fall. The 4th Rifles used three companies for this attack: B Company was on the right, A Company on the left and D Company was held in reserve. The 3rd Rifles on the high ground was to assist in the attack by extending its line south to make it easier to establish the connection between the two rifle battalions.

The attacking infantry had good artillery protection provided by the New Zealand gunners, but from the moment the two companies set off they encountered withering machine-gun fire. On the right, B Company was successful in gaining part of the ridge along which the road ran, but a small party of Germans from the 24th (Saxon) Division, strongly entrenched along a huge timber dump, held up its left flank. Meanwhile A Company on the left experienced problems too. Two platoons on the right flank were held up while the remaining two attempted to storm the ridge. It proved to be a difficult task. The machine-gun fire had been so intense that only two officers and twelve men were left to assault the ridge, held by at least fifty Germans. The New Zealanders pressed home the attack, though, and drove the Germans out, capturing six heavy and two light machine guns. This success allowed the 4th Rifles to make contact with the 3rd Rifles on the ridge. But the situation was far from satisfactory, since the two platoons on the right were still held up, leaving those on the left flank isolated and exposed. The much-depleted platoons on the ridge stayed put, however, and dug a trench along their exposed flank to give a measure of protection. The attack had been only partially successful, reducing the enemy salient on the high ground and taking about another 100 yards of the Hébuterne road. But the 4th Rifle soldiers now on the ridge were weak in numbers and terribly vulnerable with their open right flank. Clearly, another attack would soon be necessary.

The Mars Offensive around Arras and the two New Zealand attacks should not imply that the Germans were inactive across the IV Corps front. They had used the night of 27 March to send out many patrols that pressed up against the British front looking for weak spots. On 28 March, the remnants of nine German divisions attacked the four divisions of IV Corps, holding the 'great re-entrant' in the line around Hébuterne. A further five German divisions were held in reserve in case the front could be cracked open. The whole IV Corps front was harassed by German artillery and machine-gun fire and the British official history describes 28 March as 'a hard day's fighting' for the corps.[6]

The New Zealand sector of the front was under almost constant attack throughout the day until 10 o'clock that night. The New Zealand artillery and machine-gunners repulsed all attacks, inflicting heavy casualties on the Germans. As the war diary of the 3rd Brigade New Zealand Artillery reported,

> All Batteries fired counter preparation for 2 hours as per instructions from DA [Director, Artillery]. During the day all Batteries engaged in registration and much harassing fire carried out. All Batteries reported being shelled intermittently throughout the afternoon.[7]

In the early afternoon, two brigades of German infantry were reported moving down the valley from Serre towards the Ancre. They were immediately subjected to an hour-long barrage from every available New Zealand gun. As the artillery history records, the German infantry 'were not seen again'.[8]

The 2nd New Zealand Infantry Brigade experienced most of this

German activity and was thankful for the support provided by the gunners of the 3rd Brigade, who

> during the day did some very good shooting, which was much appreciated by all ranks in the line. During the later part of the day all enemy was much more cautious in his movement than formerly thus proving the efficacy of our artillery fire.

But the German artillery was 'much more active, especially during the afternoon'.[9]

The New Zealand machine-gunners started the day quietly but spent a busy afternoon firing on numerous targets. The Germans again captured a New Zealand machine gun, but once more it was recovered by the machine-gunners. There were attacks at 10 a.m., noon and 3 p.m. All were repulsed. When the machine gun was captured, 'Bombs were obtained and the gun team bombed up the sap and recovered the gun . . . Many casualties were inflicted upon the enemy during these advances.'[10]

One of the busiest sections of the line was at the troublesome La Signy Farm, which actually formed part of a brigade boundary for the New Zealand Division. The Germans here were in superior numbers, well supplied with bombs, machine guns and mortars. The 2nd Auckland Battalion shared responsibility for this unhealthy sector with the hard-pressed 4th Rifles. The Aucklanders' war diary reveals that 28 March was a busy day:

> During the day the Hun made repeated attacks on our right from the direction of LA SIGNY FARM. Approximate times — 9 a.m., 12.30 p.m., 1.30 p.m., and 4 p.m. During these attacks the enemy suffered severe casualties. Ours were light . . . At 10 p.m. another attack was beaten off, his tactics being slightly different on this occasion. He attacked both up the saps and over the top. He was beaten off and left several dead in our hands. His machine gun barrage was very heavy. An inter-company relief took place on the night of the 28th/29th . . . Relief was carried out satisfactorily without casualties.[11]

Heavy casualties made it necessary for the battalion's 15th Company to be relieved that night.

German attention was not confined solely to La Signy Farm. The New Zealand right flank at Hamel was another obvious weak spot and here the 1st Canterbury Battalion also experienced a tough time.

> 28 March
>
> At about 1 a.m. our right was reinforced by 6 Officers 50 OR, and 10 Lewis Guns, of the Eighth Battalion Tank Corps. This was made necessary by reason of the obscure situation existing South of HAMEL. During the day the Enemy pounded our trench system from close range inflicting fairly heavy casualties. 10 O.R. Killed, 2nd. Lt. G.J. Hawkins and 45 O.R. Wounded. Much movement of Artillery, Transport and men, on the Enemy's side was noticeable, but the situation was relieved by the arrival of part of our own Artillery, and offensive action by Lewis Guns and Snipers.[12]

The New Zealand Rifle Brigade, holding the northern sector of the New Zealand position near the Australians at Hébuterne, also shared in the action. Gallipoli veteran Les Hearns remembered this day forever. The artillery and machine-gun fire was deafening: 'I never heard such a racket in all my life. It was terrible. That's when I was wounded.'[13] Around 11 o'clock that morning Hearns was hit in the leg by shell fragments. That night he was evacuated from the front line and eventually reached a field hospital that consisted of one big tent. There his leg was operated on. It was the end of Les Hearns' war.

Throughout the night the New Zealand casualties continued to mount and tragedy soon struck the New Zealand Rifle Brigade. A 5.9-inch German shell scored a direct hit on the brigade's headquarters, which had been established in a cellar in Colincamps. The whole headquarters was wrecked, eleven men were killed and another fourteen were wounded. One of the officers killed instantly was one of the most popular and talented officers in the division, Major R.G. Purdy, aptly described as 'fearless in the presence of danger, and every inch a soldier'.[14] Brigadier Fulton died of concussion the next day while being conveyed to the casualty clearing station (CCS) at Doullens. He was the third and last of the New Zealand Brigadiers to fall in action. As General Russell noted in his diary, 'Fulton & Purdy killed by an unlucky shell . . . Both a severe loss to the division. Stewart replaces Fulton.'[15] Writing to Defence Minister Sir James Allen in New Zealand, Lieutenant General Alexander Godley, commander of the New Zealand Expeditionary Force of which the division was a part, showed a little more emotion about the loss of Purdy and Fulton:

> I am very sorry about Fulton. He was an excellent Brigadier, and his loss is keenly felt by us all. Also young Purdy . . . one of the most promising officers of the Staff Corps.[16]

Lieutenant Colonel Stewart again assumed command of the Rifle Brigade, shifting its headquarters from Colincamps to Courcelles.

While the New Zealand infantry were in action on 28 March, soldiers from the Pioneer Battalion and the Engineers continued the tough task of building strong posts behind the New Zealand front line. By that night 'there was a line of posts dug right across the New Zealand Divisional area'.[17] The sappers and Pioneers then started converting these posts into continuous trench lines, preparing deep dugouts for various headquarters and siting and digging machine-gun posts all over the divisional back area. The New Zealanders were not about to be easily shifted from their current location.

The situation on the Third Army front was now much improved though it 'remained full of anxiety'.[18] On the IV Corps front the situation was relatively stable, as a message to the troops on the evening of 28 March indicated:

> The Corps Commander congratulates the 42nd, 62nd, and the New Zealand Divisions and the 4th Australian Brigade on their magnificent behaviour during the last few days' fighting. Numerous heavy attacks by the enemy have been completely repulsed with heavy loss and the capture of prisoners and machine guns. He

heartily thanks the troops for their courage and endurance and is confident that they will continue to hold the line against all attacks.[19]

British confidence was high, but the Germans opposite them were plummeting to the depths of despair. The diary of a German officer who would be killed on 5 April described his men as 'dog tired' and the German attacks on IV Corps as in a state of 'much confusion and great disorder'. With the enemy in front of him in strong defensive positions and in considerable numbers, he lamented, 'It seems that there will be a return to trench warfare.'[20]

The German officer was right. On the evening of 28 March heavy rain set in, bringing with it the inevitable mud and the misery of trench warfare. Those troops using the old British trenches suffered the most. After nearly two years these trenches were still reasonably intact but in no condition to withstand a deluge and it was too late to construct adequate drainage. Some collapsed in on the men sheltering in them. Those that did not soon flooded so that sentries standing at their posts, usually for two, but sometimes for up to four hours, had to do so in thigh-deep mud and water. Food was scarce and the New Zealand soldiers were without their cold weather clothing. When relieved, craving rest and sleep, they crawled into filthy, shallow holes scooped out of the sides of the trenches. It was a nightmare existence like that endured in the Ypres salient.

Wrapped in an old bag or blanket or dead German's ground-sheet, unshaven, and caked with mud and filth, men lumbered heavily along the trenches by night or lay huddled in these holes in the ground, more resembling beasts than human beings. The written impressions of a French correspondent during a visit by night to a front line trench fairly describe the conditions obtaining in this unwholesome place. 'A sinuous ditch bottomed with mud, and fould [sic] with human refuse. There are holes in its sides from which as you lean over there comes a foul breath. Misty, shadowy things are emerging from these side caverns, and moving about in shapeless bulk like bears that shamble and growl. They are the squad.' With the substitution of the word platoon for squad, the description stands.[21]

The early morning rum ration was regarded as a lifesaver.

The New Zealand soldiers did not allow these deplorable conditions to affect their morale. They also resorted to searching the deserted French houses looking for food and warm clothing. This was often a dangerous practice, as Bernard Cottrell soon found out:

> I wondered what you did Easter Sunday. As for me, well as tucker was running pretty low two other chaps & myself decided to visit an evacuated house and made some chips and some stray rice . . . Everything was going swimmingly till Jerry lobbed one outside and killed two soldiers and a horse, we bolted for the cellar.[22]

Food was desperately short, as Private Edward Bibby of the 1st Otago Battalion remembered: 'We were down to one loaf for 10 or 12 men'. The soldiers were also issued with iron rations — a quarter of a pound of hard biscuit, some bully beef, tea and sugar — to be used only in an emergency. Bibby was with a group of soldiers sent to Mailly-Maillet to forage for food. They found some tins of bully beef, then entered a French house and looked in the cellar for food. There they got the shock of their lives: 'And didn't we get a blast. There was a French Family there taking refuge. We withdrew hastily.' When they left the trenches some days later they were 'covered with mud'.[23]

Compared with what had come before it, 29 March was a quiet day for the New Zealanders, but it was by no means easy. Conditions in the front-line trenches deteriorated further as the bad weather continued. Food remained in short supply, and the enemy, although quieter, was still active. The 4th Rifles again carried out an attack to improve its position at La Signy Farm.

At 11 a.m. a large working party of Germans was seen on a ridge in front of the New Zealand position. The Germans were 2500 yards away, well within range of the New Zealand machine guns which opened fire. There were some German casualties; the rest of the working party scattered. The New Zealand artillery continued harassing fire throughout the day and received plenty of the same in retaliation. The war diary of the 3rd New Zealand Field Artillery described the German artillery fire as '"lively" especially in village Mailly-Mallet [sic]'.[24] Bombardier Bailey and his unit took much-needed ammunition to the infantry brigades in the front line. 'Altogether we carted 575,000 rounds of SAA [small arms ammunition] and about 3000 hand grenades to the infantry.'[25]

The village of Mailly-Maillet suffered heavily during this offensive, and not all the damage was caused by the Germans. William Robson of C Section, 2nd Field Ambulance, walked around the village on 29 March, looking for food. 'It has been knocked about a good deal by Fritz but the place has been wrecked by the Tommy in search for booze and money. Houses have been pulled inside out and it is an absolute disgrace.'[26] But New Zealand soldiers were responsible for a large proportion of the havoc, as John Coleman explained to his sister:

> All the fellows had a pretty gay time as, of course, they ransacked the place, and in lots of the cellars there was champagne and wine galore, so you can imagine all hands had a royal time. Of course, I daren't say where we are, but no doubt you have seen in your papers.[27]

The village was Mailly-Maillet.

Harold Muschamp of the Machine Gun Battalion had a similar experience of looting.

> There is plenty of wine & champagne in the villages & some of the boys are making a welter of it. Also the hen & pigs are getting a sad hearing from our boys, we are living high, a piece of good fresh pork is a great change these times. Vegetables are plentiful too.[28]

Just after daylight the 4th Rifles made a renewed effort to improve their position at La Signy Farm and establish a firmer link with the 1st Brigade.

Bitter fighting ensued with heavy casualties on both sides. The 4th Rifles made little progress. An attack by a bombing section cleared 200 yards of trench towards the junction of the farm track and the Hébuterne road, but the men ran out of bombs and could not hold the ground. Later in the morning a German bombing party from La Signy Farm attacked the 2nd Auckland Battalion, which repulsed the enemy. But this action, coupled with the failure of the 4th Rifles to improve its position, prompted the two battalion commanders to plan for a larger, concerted attack next day to deal with the troublesome La Signy Farm once and for all.

The day in question was 30 March 1918, Easter Sunday. The New Zealanders had carried out valuable reconnaissance work the previous night to pinpoint where the deadly German machine guns were. The day dawned mild but there were constant rain showers. Little activity from the Germans during the morning left the New Zealanders free to prepare their attack. Although only a small-scale venture in comparison with others on the Western Front, it was a significant action and the stakes were high. Three brigades of field artillery and three battalions of infantry would be used in this attack. Before it was over another two infantry battalions would also be used. If the New Zealanders succeeded, the important position of La Signy Farm would be theirs. The spur dominated the left brigade's sector and, as the highest ground for many miles, it gave the Germans a wide field of observation. On the crest of the spur ran the hedge that the 2nd Rifles had reached on 26 March. The hedge ran for 1000 yards from north-west across La Signy Farm to the Hébuterne road. In front of the hedge was a system of dugouts and trenches riddled with German snipers and machine-gun nests. This trench line was only 300 yards in front of the New Zealand positions; taking it would not be easy. The German defenders were mainly from the 20th Division, though remnants of several other formations were also present. By 30 March, however, the German defenders were tired and short of supplies. Their own food had long been exhausted and for the last few days they had been living on captured British iron rations. The last thing they expected on Easter Sunday was a daytime attack by the enemy to their front.

The New Zealand plan was for the three infantry battalions to advance on a front of about 1200 yards up the slopes to La Signy Farm. This would occur after a short artillery barrage designed to drive the German defenders underground. The 1st Wellington would be on the right, some distance from the farm. Its advance was to provide a solid platform for the attack by protecting the flank of the 2nd Auckland Battalion, who would be in the vulnerable centre of the attack and directly facing the hedge trench. The 4th Rifles on the left planned to advance to the Hébuterne road, capture the section held by the Germans and link up with the 2nd Rifles on its left flank.

At 2 p.m. a 'beautifully accurate' shrapnel and machine-gun barrage forced the German defenders to take cover in the trenches.[29] The German sentries were careless. Not expecting an attack, they all took cover, keeping their heads well below the parapet as the shelling continued. The German defenders not on duty were asleep in their dugouts. As Ormond Burton has commented, 'It was the most impossible and most improbable time for an attack to take place.'[30] When the German sentries emerged after the barrage, soldiers from three New Zealand infantry battalions had crossed the dangerous open ground and were right on their positions. It was too late to organise effective resistance. On the right, the centre and left companies of the 1st Wellington advanced their line 500 yards from One Tree Hill to the southern point of the hedge above the Serre road. This was an important gain: now the New Zealanders were nearly 1000 yards east of the sugar refinery and with an uninterrupted view along the valleys south and west of the Serre. During their advance 1st Wellington had taken seventy-four prisoners and twenty-two machine guns.[31]

In the centre of the attack, two companies of the 2nd Auckland Battalion advanced towards the hedgerow under cover of machine-gun and artillery fire 'as if on parade'.[32] Their attack completely surprised the enemy and the Auckland battalion took most of the objective within seven minutes. The 2nd Auckland infantry entered the trenches with rifles, bayonets and bombs at the ready and the slaughter of the surprised Germans was fearful. Many were killed in the trenches, some surrendered, others bolted. The Aucklanders encountered strong opposition in only two places. In the centre of the line a redoubt sheltering a machine-gun crew held out and resisted all attempts to take it, preventing the 2nd Auckland Battalion from linking up with the 1st Wellingtons on its right. A platoon from the Waikato Company tried to take this redoubt but its line of advance was exposed to direct fire from the German machine guns and fourteen men fell, every one of them shot through the head. For Lieutenant Colonel Allen of 2nd Auckland, it was 'the most ghastly sight I have ever seen in all my experience in the war'.[33] When more men were killed and wounded, including the company commander, Allen moved forward, bringing with him a trench mortar officer who managed to bring one of the mortars into action. The Germans in the redoubt soon surrendered. The other problem area was on the extreme right near the Serre road. A German machine-gun post held out for a considerable time until subdued by a bombing party. The New Zealanders took La Signy Farm. More than 140 dead Germans were counted in the 2nd Auckland Battalion position and a further 156 were taken prisoner. Captured war materiel included forty-three machine guns, two mortars and three bicycles.[34]

It had been a hard fight and the Aucklanders were exhausted. Lieutenant Colonel Allen feared they were ripe for a German counterattack 'but none came'.[35] Just after 6 p.m. he reported the situation to his brigade headquarters:

> We are now in touch with 1/Wellington having captured the strong point on our right. We are not quite in touch with 4/N.Z.R.B. but expect to be soon. Our line now runs from . . . along fence to . . . The line is strong, well wired in front and with good observation. The dangerous flank is the right, where enemy can collect in . . . under cover of hedge and I should like artillery to strafe it periodically during the night and occasionally with a few on LA SIGNY FARM. We have captured a large number of machine guns estimated at 30 and at least one light Minenwerfer [trench mortar]. I have all my men in the front line except about three platoons. 2/ Wellington are going to carry for us and I shall keep two platoons of theirs here for the night. The men are very tired and will not stand many heavy counter attacks. Communications with you are

very bad. The Hun is now shelling us heavily without doing much damage but is probably working himself up for a counter attack. If he does I shall make for Brigade Headquarters as I have no reserves to fall back on and will leave my staff to master the situation . . . Our casualties during the attack were 7 Officers Wounded, 30 O/Rs Killed and 75 O/Rs. Wounded . . . The enemy's casualties were very heavy 140 dead being counted in the trench. All the wounded were evacuated during the attack without further mishap.[36]

Meanwhile, on the left, the 4th Rifles were experiencing considerable difficulties. Only after hard fighting all afternoon was the battalion able to link up with the 2nd Auckland Battalion on the spur and this did not occur until after 11 p.m. During this attack the 4th Rifles was dogged by persistent bad luck. Like the other battalions, it attacked with two companies of infantry, but because of its depleted strength through the previous attacks, both had to be strengthened with a platoon from the 3rd Rifles. The lone group in touch with the 2nd Rifles from the previous day stayed put on the ridge while the rest of the battalion tried to end its isolation. From the start of the atttack there was extremely heavy resistance from bombs and machine guns about La Signy Farm. Part of the company on the right reached its objective, but the remainder was held up by many Germans on the feature called Woodstacks just short of the Hébuterne road. Again the riflemen ran out of bombs and were forced to take shelter in the shell holes there. There was another attempt at nightfall with a fresh company supported by soldiers of the 2nd and 3rd Rifles. In the face of this pressure the Germans finally abandoned the position and withdrew. The crest where the La Signy Farm track left the Hébuterne road was occupied at last.

That night, the 2nd Rifles extended its flank by carrying out a 'brilliant minor operation'.[37] Under Captain H.E. Barrowclough, who would serve as a major general in the Second World War, two platoons struck out to their south and east to clear the gap on their right flank and gain the last of the high ground on the spur. After a brief, intense firefight the Germans fled. The 2nd Rifles managed to recover the whole of the position lost on

27 March and then took even more ground to its front. In doing so it killed many Germans, captured twenty-two and also took sixteen machine guns. Two New Zealanders were wounded in this venture; one subsequently died of his wounds.

The net effect of these different operations was some 300 dead Germans plus 300 captured. In fact, the 20th Division's losses were so heavy that it was withdrawn from the German front line and later disbanded. A significant amount of war materiel was also captured, including 110 machine guns and fifteen mortars.[38] Most important, the New Zealanders had significantly altered their tactical position. Their line was no longer broken and overlooked by the Germans. Instead it ran continuously from One Tree Hill in the south along the ridge to the quarries near Hébuterne. Occupying all the high ground in the location, the New Zealanders now had excellent observation over the Germans who had been forced down into the valley. A report by the Brigade Major W.I.K. Jennings of the 1st Brigade emphasised the importance of these gains:

> Yesterday's operation has improved our line out of all knowledge and we now completely dominate the enemy's positions along two thirds of our front . . . The success of our attack seems to have been due to the speed with which it was carried out. Our men state that in many cases the enemy were lying down in the trench and that they were on top of them before the enemy could stand to. The men themselves are in great heart and only ask to be allowed to go on and push the enemy back again.[39]

The New Zealand history of the division in France emphasised that, apart from the 4th Rifles, who had experienced the greatest difficulties during its part of the operation, losses in the other battalions were light. When John Coleman wrote home of this attack, he stressed its success and how few New Zealanders were lost:

> After we had been there for a couple of days there was a piece of the line wanted straightening, so the boys 'hopped the bags' at

two o'clock in the afternoon and caught old Fritz napping. They captured some over a hundred machine guns, 200 prisoners and Lord knows how many were killed, as they were lying about in all directions. Lots of them must have been killed whilst asleep in their bivvys. This was, I think, the most successful little stunt our boys have had, as our casualties were extremely low — small, considering what we gained.[40]

But the three attacking battalions had suffered and they would have to be withdrawn from the line over the next two days. A good many New Zealanders had been killed or wounded to secure La Signy Farm, as Ira Robinson acknowledged in a letter home:

Of course we lost a lot of good men and also officers, but not as many as one might expect under the circumstances, and we have been reinforced a good deal since and are now stronger than ever. So far I thank God I have not received a scratch, although five of my mates were killed by one shell and I was standing in the middle of them, so you see your prayers are not in vain after all.[41]

The 2nd Auckland Battalion had suffered 130 casualties, thirty of whom had been killed. Captain George Tuck had been up most of the previous night writing the battalion's operation order for the attack, finally finishing it at 2.30 on the morning of the assault. That evening he reflected on its success in his diary:

All is over for the time. We lost severely; the poor Waikatos losing more than 70% of their men. In one sap there are several Waikato jambed shoulder to shoulder all shot thru the head. We hold all the line attacked. It is a much improved position & is well wired with a splendid field of view. Fritz was determined to hold it as it is such a fine defensive position for us. There was a mg [machine gun] every 10 yards & we captured about thirty or more. We also took 160 prisoners and killed hundreds of Huns. It was costly but well worth it. A splendid position which he will no doubt make a big effort to recapture if he can organise in time. We took men of many units so he must be a bit mixed after his great advance.[42]

The casualties of the 4th Rifles numbered almost 200; over fifty men had been killed. The 1st Wellington Battalion, allocated a minor role in this attack, lost twenty-two men and had more than fifty wounded.[43]

One of the 4th Rifles' deaths was that of Second Lieutenant George Malcolm. His brother, William, a soldier in the 2nd Auckland Battalion, had reached the Somme on 30 March, the day George died. William Malcolm did not, however, learn of the tragedy until 3 April 1918 and then spent hours trying to locate his brother's grave.

Poor old Mum & Dad. I don't know how you can bear it but remember that George was a son who was an honour to you. Even although I am his brother I must tell you that I know very few boys who lived a cleaner life . . . We were camped near an old sugar refinery or what was left of it. McKenzie had told me that George's grave was about 500 yds north along a sunken road. On three different days I searched for nearly a mile along and in from the road, but although I found many 4th Bttn chaps there I could not find him. I found Harry Cottingham within a couple of hundred yds of the factory. He was knocked out on the 6th. Poor old Harry. I had seen him about a week before.[44]

It was to be another two months before William Malcolm located the site where his brother was buried. He erected a cross over George's final resting place.[45]

The result of this attack on 30 March offered a much better view over the Ancre Valley to Thiepval, Pozieres and the Albert–Bapaume road. Ahead lay the town of Flers, so well known to the New Zealand soldiers of 1916 and now only 7½ miles away. To the north-east, about the same distance away, was the large town of Bapaume, which would become very familiar to the New Zealanders later in the year. The New Zealand

Division had carried out an attack of some significance and congratulatory messages flowed in from Generals Birdwood, Plumer, Godley, Monash and many others. As Ormond Burton wrote:

> This operation was surely one of the most successful surprise attacks of the war. When it is considered that the attackers were greatly fatigued and were part of an army that had been heavily defeated, and that the Huns were flushed with victory, the full merit of the achievement becomes obvious. Small as the operation was, compared with the mighty happenings of those critical days, it was yet the first successful attack made by Allied troops since the opening of the German offensive.[46]

Yet the New Zealand history of the division was almost dismissive of the success of this attack and downplays its significance:

> Care must be taken not to overestimate the general moral effect of this success. In conjunction, however, with the stiffening resistance all along the front and with the gallant and remunerative enterprises carried out by the Australians at Hebuterne and by the 32nd Division 6 miles at Ayette a few days later, it was unquestionable opportune and acceptable to the British Staff after days of unrelieved if stubbornly resisted reverses. It helped too, to demonstrate to the German Army that north of the Somme the British line had become established.[47]

Though such caution is an admirable quality in a military historian, the significance of the New Zealand attack on 30 March was lost in his restraint. This attack was the first offensive taken by the BEF on the Western Front since the start of the Michael Offensive nine days earlier. Its success stunned the Germans and provided considerable encouragement to the soldiers of the Third Army. The Australian official historian, the astute Charles Bean, recognised the importance of the New Zealand attack: 'small though the operation was, the news of it came in those dark

days like a tonic to the whole of the British Army and to the Empire'.[48]
James Edmonds, the British official historian, wrote:

> at the time it was said that, simultaneously with the arrival of the
> Australians and New Zealanders, as a result of the heavy losses
> inflicted by Fifth and Third Armies the initiative had passed out of
> the hands of the enemy.[49]

The successful New Zealand attack was the first indication that this
was so.

By the end of March 1918 Ludendorff knew that his offensive was
failing. One reason for this was that the German storm troops and battle
units had outpaced their artillery and logistical support. Ludendorff
therefore ordered a postponement of further operations until 4 April.
He also announced another change of strategy: the city of Amiens was
now the objective of the attack. There would be a pause of three to four
days while newly constructed light railways took stores forward to feed
the war machine. Battlefield communications would also be restored and
the vital artillery moved forward with thousands of shells stockpiled for
their use. This, it was hoped, would get the offensive rolling forward again.
When he was ready Ludendorff would hurl his armies forward again to
take Amiens. Now occupying a solid defensive position less than 20 miles
north-east of this city, the New Zealand Division and the other divisions of
IV Corps would be on the receiving end of a renewed German offensive
within a matter of days.

Major General Andrew Russell inspects a New Zealand Brigade. Colonel Young of the Auckland Regiment is on the General's right. A Sandhurst graduate, Russell had a reputation as a perfectionist who was determined to produce the best division on the Western Front. His performance and judgement at Passchendaele in October 1917 fell well below his usual standards and he remained largely ignorant of the conditions facing the New Zealand brigades on Bellevue Spur. (H11, Kippenberger Military Archive and Research Library, Army Museum Waiouru)

General Sir Alexander Godley reviews New Zealand troops and congratulates them on their success at Messines. Godley was a fine trainer and administrator but universally disliked by New Zealand soldiers. (H71, Kippenberger Military Archive and Research Library, Army Museum Waiouru)

The ruins of Ypres village in 1917. The destruction made a deep impression on the New Zealanders. Every building had been destroyed suggesting to some a 'city of the dead'. (1999-1951, Kippenberger Military Archive and Research Library, Army Museum Waiouru)

An advanced signaller on a German dugout receiving and sending messages. Signallers were a crucial link between the forward positions and the artillery and Headquarters to the rear. (H302, Kippenberger Military Archive and Research Library, Army Museum Waiouru)

A disabled tank on Messines Ridge. The Flanders region was not good tank country, especially in the winter. (1999-1951, Kippenberger Military Archive and Research Library, Army Museum Waiouru)

New Zealand victim of a German gas atack in the Ypres salient. (1999-1951, Kippenberger Military Archive and Research Library, Army Museum Waiouru)

A German pillbox or 'field fortress'. Each pillbox was a miniature fortress that was impervious to field artillery. There were thousands of these pillboxes around the Ypres salient. (H299, Kippenberger Military Archive and Research Library, Army Museum Waiouru)

New Zealand pioneers lay new road immediately after an advance, a backbreaking, laborious and dangerous task. (H61, Kippenberger Military Archive and Research Library, Army Museum Waiouru)

A constant struggle with the mud. Horses in difficulty. (1999-929, Kippenberger Military Archive and Research Library, Army Museum Waiouru)

The way most ammunition reached the firing line. Pack mules moving through the mud, each loaded with eight artillery shells. (1999-929, Kippenberger Military Archive and Research Library, Army Museum Waiouru)

Jacking up a field gun at Passchendaele in an attempt to move it forward. (1999-929, Kippenberger Military Archive and Research Library, Army Museum Waiouru)

Casualties of war too. Dead horses after an ammunition column was hit by German artillery. (1999-929, Kippenberger Military Archive and Research Library, Army Museum Waiouru)

Artillery position at Passchendaele.
(1999-930, Kippenberger Military Archive and Research Library, Army Museum Waiouru)

'A hard task to be the mother of soldiers.' Nellie and Herbert Knight (second and third from the left) who lost three sons in the war. This photograph was taken in Dannevirke in 1916. (Nancy Croad Collection)

Second Lieutenant George Knight was a natural leader of considerable ability and charm. He was killed at Passchendaele on 12 October 1917. (Nancy Croad Collection)

'Piko nei te Matenga.' (When our heads are bowed with woe.) The tangi of Lieutenant Colonel George King, killed at Passchendaele, 12 October 1917. (H347, Kippenberger Military Archive and Research Library, Army Museum Waiouru)

New Zealand soldiers on their way to the NZ No. 1 General Hospital, Brockenhurst, Hampshire, England. (Anne Smyth)

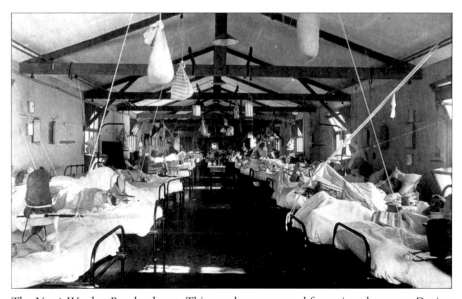

The No. 1 Ward at Brockenhurst. This ward was reserved for serious leg cases. During October 1917 the hospital ran out of bed spaces, having to set up an additional fifty beds at the local YMCA. (Anne Smyth)

Winter in Passchendaele, Christmas 1917. The two soldiers are standing on the ice sheet over a shell crater. (1999-1951, Kippenberger Military Archive and Research Library, Army Museum Waiouru)

Private Linus T.J. Ryan. A keen observer of events at Passchendaele and one of the long-suffering stretcher-bearers of the New Zealand Army Medical Corps. (Anne Smyth)

The Gravenstafel (Passchendaele) Memorial in Belgium, a corner of a foreign field dedicated to New Zealand soldiers. (1999-1708, Kippenberger Military Archive and Research Library, Army Museum Waiouru)

General Russell inspects an Otago Battalion on 5 March 1918. He wrote in his diary that the two Otago Battalions were 'quite satisfactory. I feel quite cheered and encouraged.' From Russell this was high praise indeed. (H439, Kippenberger Military Archive and Research Library, Army Museum Waiouru)

The caption to this cartoon in *Chronicles of the N.Z.E.F.* read 'Trouble is blooming in Picardy'.
The New Zealand Division were to find themselves in the thick of that trouble.

New Zealand machine-gunners, such as these men in the fields near Colincamps, inflicted
massive casualties on the advancing Germans. (RSA Collection, Alexander Turnbull Library, G-13258-½)

That a great German offensive was coming in 1918 was the worst-kept military secret of the war. Yet the Allies were still not prepared for it when it happened. As this cartoon shows, some people had become a little blasé about the coming offensive. By the time this cartoon appeared in New Zealand the offensive had started and the Allied line was crumbling under its weight. (*New Zealand Herald*, 23 March 1918)

Their world 'tumbling into ruins', French refugees, wearing their best clothes, flee from the advancing Germans. This was the first time New Zealand soldiers encountered refugees in a war zone, and it made a deep impression on them. (Kippenberger Military Archive and Research Library, Army Museum Waiouru)

New Zealand engineers dig a strong point at Colincamps. (H465, Kippenberger Military Archive and Research Library, Army Museum Waiouru)

Wounded New Zealand soldiers are placed into an ambulance at a Casualty Clearing Station. (H479, Kippenberger Military Archive and Research Library, Army Museum Waiouru)

A New Zealand soldier using a captured German machine gun at La Signy Farm. (H484, Kippenberger Military Archive and Research Library, Army Museum Waiouru)

Bringing in the wounded under shelling near Courcelles village in early April 1918. (H485, Kippenberger Military Archive and Research Library, Army Museum Waiouru)

Loading a New Zealand trench mortar near Colincamps. Trench mortars were deadly over a short range. (H504, Kippenberger Military Archive and Research Library, Army Museum Waiouru)

This building in Colincamps had been the headquarters of the New Zealand Rifle Brigade. On 28 March 1918 it received a direct hit from a German artillery shell, killing Brigadier Fulton, Major Purdy and several others. (H491, Kippenberger Military Archive and Research Library, Army Museum Waiouru)

The work of the military chaplains was useful in maintaining morale. A padre of the Rifle Brigade has set up a canteen only 300 yards from the front line. Note the stretchers in the right of the photograph, ready for action. (H473, Kippenberger Military Archive and Research Library, Army Museum Waiouru)

Meal time for the New Zealand Rifle Brigade. This trench is at La Signy Farm and is only 250 yards from the German front-line positions. (H468, Kippenberger Military Archive and Research Library, Army Museum Waiouru)

New Zealanders in a strong point near Mailly-Maillet. The soldiers in the foreground are preparing a meal while a single man keeps watch, the Lewis gun ready for action. (H461, Kippenberger Military Archive and Research Library, Army Museum Waiouru)

New Zealand medics help themselves to some milk at Courcelles village. (H462, Kippenberger Military Archive and Research Library, Army Museum Waiouru)

A batch of German prisoners taken by the New Zealand Division at the end of March 1918. (H452, Kippenberger Military Archive and Research Library, Army Museum Waiouru)

War trophies. Captured German machine guns being inspected by officers from New Zealand Division headquarters. (H482, Kippenberger Military Archive and Research Library, Army Museum Waiouru)

The ruins of Hébuterne village, May 1918. (H578, Kippenberger Military Archive and Research Library, Army Museum Waiouru)

Marcus David Smith soon after his return from the war and prior to taking up his law practice in Dannevirke in 1920. Lieutenant Smith was a newly commissioned officer thrown in the deep end at the Somme in 1918. (Alastair E.B. Jones)

The Very Reverend Ronald G. Watson, MC, ED, MA, padre to the 1st Otago Battalion, and one of the 'happy band of brothers' on the Somme. This photograph was taken in 1939, prior to several periods of Home Service in the Second World War. (Malcolm H. Watson)

The New Zealand soldiers were aware, even if it is typically understated in this cartoon, that they had played a key role in stopping the German spring offensive.
(Chronicles of the N.Z.E.F.)

A play on the word Somme. This cartoon indicates that morale was high in the New Zealand Division in August 1918. (*New Zealand at the Front, 1918*)

Drawn by Corporal W. F. Bell

The Modern Infantryman: "A thing to hang things on"
Drawn by Private J. O'Grady

The New Zealand soldiers discover a universal truth. (*New Zealand at the Front, 1918*)

STUNG !
Drawn by Lieut. G. P. Hanna

From April to July 1918, units from the United States Army were attached to the New Zealand Division for training. In most cases the arrangement worked more smoothly than is indicated here. (*New Zealand at the Front, 1918*)

Australian troops pass through the ruins of Bapaume in May 1917. The Australians had captured the town on St Patrick's Day that year. (Alexander Turnbull Library, P.C. Norman Collection, F-92073½)

A New Zealand RAP set up in a captured German trench. This is on the first day of the battle, 21 August 1918, near Puisieux. (H922, Kippenberger Military Archive and Research Library, Army Museum Waiouru)

New Zealand soldiers shelter in shell holes during a German bombardment. This is north of Achiet-le-Petit on 22 August 1918. (H957, Kippenberger Military Archive and Research Library, Army Museum Waiouru)

A Whippet tank in action near Grevillers, 24 August 1918. (H967, Kippenberger Military Archive and Research Library, Army Museum Waiouru)

A wounded and very worried German soldier at Grevillers, 24 August 1918. (H942, Kippenberger Military Archive and Research Library, Army Museum Waiouru)

Brigadier Herbert Hart (right) near Bapaume. Hart's diary is one of few kept by a senior officer of the NZEF. It is remarkable for its lucidity and frankness. (1993-1293, Kippenberger Military Archive and Research Library, Army Museum Waiouru)

New Zealand machine-gunners in a captured German position. (H923, Kippenberger Military
Archive and Research Library, Army Museum Waiouru)

Captured Germans have their details recorded by the battalion Intelligence Officer. (H939,
Kippenberger Military Archive and Research Library, Army Museum Waiouru)

A German machine-gun position photographed just after its capture. (H934, Kippenberger Military Archive and Research Library, Army Museum Waiouru)

'The best pioneers in the Army.' New Zealand pioneers digging defences near Bapaume, 27 August 1918. (H969, Kippenberger Military Archive and Research Library, Army Museum Waiouru)

Success at last. New Zealand troops advance towards Bapaume, 29 August 1918. (H972, Kippenberger Military Archive and Research Library, Army Museum Waiouru)

New Zealand soldiers searching the Bapaume sugar factory. This had been a particularly strong point of resistance. (H975, Kippenberger Military Archive and Research Library, Army Museum Waiouru)

A section of the 3rd Rifles, the first group of soldiers to pass through the abandoned town of Bapaume. This photograph was taken on the town's outskirts on 29 August 1918, the day the town was finally captured. (H981, Kippenberger Military Archive and Research Library, Army Museum Waiouru)

A German artillery observation post on high ground overlooking Bapaume. It is easy to see why the town was described as 'a grim and pathetic spectacle of almost entire destruction'. (H986, Kippenberger Military Archive and Research Library, Army Museum Waiouru)

Douglas Knight, an officer in the 2nd Auckland Battalion, killed in action on 1 September 1918. Douglas was the third member of the Knight family to be killed in action during the war. (Nancy Croad Collection).

Leslie Cecil Lloyd Averill, Second Lieutenant, 4th Battalion, New Zealand Rifle Brigade. A medical student prior to the war, Averill played a prominent part in the Battle of Bapaume and left a vivid record of his actions. In early November 1918 he again distinguished himself, this time during the liberation of Le Quesnoy. The town's walls had to be scaled by climbing up ladders, an action described by the New Zealand official historian as 'one of the most dramatic moments in the Division's history'. Averill was the first man up the ladder. (Colin Averill Collection)

New Zealanders advancing through a recaptured village near Bapaume. (Alexander Turnbull Library, G-3558-½)

A New Zealand battalion re-entering Bapaume to rest. (Alexander Turnbull Library, G-3604-½)

Chapter 8

A Lull: 31 March–4 April 1918

COMPARED WITH THE frantic period of 23–30 March 1918, the next five days were quiet, a time of minimal activity. The lull was a welcome relief. It gave the New Zealand soldiers in the front line a chance to catch their breath and to consolidate their hard-won positions. Both sides used 31 March, a day of heavy rains and thunderstorms, to bury the dead whose bodies could be retrieved without risk. Those who had been killed in the narrow no-man's-land remained where they had fallen.

The 2nd New Zealand Infantry Brigade was holding the line west of Beaumont-Hamel with the two Otago battalions in the line and the two Canterbury battalions in reserve. On 1 April its war diary recorded that 'The enemy's inactivity was most marked during the day, no movement being seen and only very scattered shelling experienced'. The next day was the same. There was the 'Usual scattered shelling', but no enemy movement. The diary made a prescient comment: 'The situation has developed almost into trench warfare'.[1] On 1 April the 1st Otago Battalion

> was in the line in front of Auchonvillers and the day passed quietly. Our artillery periodically shelled targets in enemy's forward areas, the Serre road and Beaumont Hamel receiving special attention. A number of Stokes shells were fired at the crater, silencing an enemy machine gun which had been causing trouble to our front line. Enemy artillery was fairly active — periodically shelling our front line with 77 m.m guns, and heavier shells to the Bowery and Auchonvillers. During the afternoon rain again fell, making movement in the front line and communication trenches very difficult.

On 2 April:

> Our artillery was much more active particularly on the Serre road
> and on village of Beaumont Hamel. Enemy artillery was normal,
> periodically during the day, shelling our right Coy in the front line.
> Heavier shells were used on Auchonvillers, the Bowery, Sugar
> Factory, and Mailly-Maillet. Enemy snipers, were much quieter,
> and except for an occasional burst from an enemy machine gun in
> the crater, they also were much below the normal activity. Enemy
> movement in the forward areas was very scarce — Rifle and Lewis
> Gun fire being brought to bear as soon as any targets presented
> themselves.[2]

Its sister battalion in the line also reflected the drop-off in German
activity. On 3 April, for example, its war diary recorded 'Enemy activity
below normal. Usual sniping from our side, several hits being claimed.'[3]
Lieutenant Roderick Toomath, the Medical Officer of 1st Rifles, had found
the front-line trenches 'in a bad state', but he described the 1 to 4 April
period as 'very quiet'. He described 1 April as 'an awfully lazy time'.[4] After
the frenetic activity of 26 March and the days that followed, the 1st Rifles,
the first infantry battalion to encounter the advancing Germans, certainly
deserved a peaceful spell in the trenches.

The Germans may have been quiet during this period, but they were
far from inactive. At a IV Corps conference on 2 April, the silver-haired,
avuncular Lieutenant General Sir George Harper (his nickname was
'Uncle') succinctly outlined the current tactical situation:

> The enemy in front are much messed up and disorganised. He
> is at present quiescent, reorganising and waiting to see what will
> transpire to the south and north. When ready he will attack.

Harper believed that the Germans would most likely attack at Bucquoy
and Hamel.[5]

From 1 to 3 April there was much activity behind the German lines as they prepared to launch a fresh attack in the Somme region. Some sixty German railway construction companies laboured day and night to build, repair and restore the communication and transport facilities necessary to support a large attack on Amiens, described by one historian as 'one of the major cities of France'.[6] The Germans planned to advance on both sides on the Somme River in an effort to take this vital rail and supply centre. The New Zealanders were sure an attack was looming when they saw German observation balloons rise into the sky. Nor was this attack the only one the Germans were planning. Aware that the British had moved a number of divisions down from Flanders to the Somme in order to cover the vulnerable sectors exposed by their offensive, the Germans were also preparing to strike a new blow in the north.

The New Zealanders were not inactive either. Daylight patrolling began early on 31 March in order to pinpoint the forward positions of the enemy. Units also pushed out forward posts to cover any dead ground, that is, ground that could not be seen from the ridge line, and strengthened them with barbed-wire obstacles. They were eventually connected up to form a continuous trench.

West of La Signy Farm a lone daylight patrol by Lance Corporal R. McMurray of the 1st Rifles captured a German sentry who, under interrogation, revealed the location of two German strongpoints. These were attacked and captured that evening. Over the next two days more New Zealand posts were established all around the farm and 150 yards east of it. There was also activity to the south of the New Zealand line. On 1 April the war diary of 1st Otago recorded that:

> A very good and daring daylight patrol was carried out by Cpl. Marshall of 8th Company and a comrade, from the left of 8th Corps Sector. The patrol worked up a C.T. [Communication Trench] leading from our line, in enemy's direction, for about 250–300 yards. After working up and down a number of C.T's and gaining valuable information about this ground, the patrol suddenly saw an enemy block a short distance away. Cpl Marshall worked up to within 12 yards of sentry, who was guarding the block and shot him.[7]

As a result of the patrol, 1st Otago rushed a German trench and easily captured it. Further north a patrol from 1st Wellington captured six prisoners, including a wounded German officer. Private Jesse Stayte was given the task of escorting the German prisoners to the brigade headquarters at Mailly-Maillet.

> When I got them there some of our Boys souvenired them thoroughly. They made them empty their pockets and took all they (the Fritzs) had. I could not bring myself to rob a man's pockets even though he is a Fritz, but some of the Boys did it with as little regard as though that was their trade (and perhaps it was). I don't mind looking him over after he is dead but not till then. I even saw them take Family Photos away from the Fritz.[8]

The minor engagements fought by the New Zealanders in the first four days of April 1918 were both successful and important. Though they made only a slight improvement to the New Zealand line, they did ensure that the New Zealand soldiers did not lose their hard-won initiative.

From 31 March the New Zealanders were in a fairly positive position. Their line was regular and continuous and the advantage of being on high ground was all too obvious. Observation was good, especially in the northern sector of the line from One Tree Hill to Hébuterne where the New Zealanders completely overlooked the enemy opposite them. Their line, however, was a long one and it needed all three New Zealand brigades in line to hold it. This situation could not be sustained. Accordingly, on the night of 2–3 April, the 4th Australian Brigade extended its flank so that it was now 500 yards south of the quarries and completely covering Hébuterne. On the night of 4–5 April, the 1st Brigade in the centre of the New Zealand position was withdrawn and became the reserve brigade. The Rifle Brigade sidestepped to the right and took over the sector vacated by the 1st Brigade. The latter's new line was now 3200 yards long. The Rifle Brigade placed the 3rd Battalion on the right from One Tree Hill to the Serre road, the 4th Battalion in the centre with its flank on the hedge trench north of La Signy Farm and the 1st Battalion on the left linking with the Australians at Hébuterne. The New Zealand Division now had a normal two-brigade front and the changes were completed just in time to meet the next German attack.

The lull also provided an opportunity to rest the units that had borne the brunt of four days of heavy fighting. On 31 March, 2nd Wellington relieved the 2nd Auckland Battalion, who had not had their boots off for over a week and had not slept during their time in the trenches because the fighting 'had been severe and continuous'.[9] Many were suffering from the first stages of trench foot; they were hungry and dog-tired. Captain George Tuck caught the mood in his diary:

> 1/4/1918
>
> Out at last. Tho' we have been in only 4 days the Battalion has spent just about the hardest week in its history. Practically no sleep from Sunday to Sunday. No blankets or overcoats. Raining the last two days which turned the trenches into clay baths. How the men stood the terrible strain I cannot tell. There were forty-two machine guns in the trench we took and more put out of action just in front.[10]

The 4th Rifles had also experienced heavy fighting. After nightfall on 31 March they were relieved by the 1st Rifles and enjoyed a three-day break from the trenches.

> 1 April
>
> Took over from 4th Battn. N.Z.R.B. in Right Subsector of Brigade Front at COLINCAMPS during last night. Very large number of enemy dead lying about as the result of the raid recently. Very active patrolling being carried out. Received reports from Australian Brigade on our left that the enemy was assembling, but nothing came of it. Battn. and Company Snipers and Observers very active and have accounted for many of the enemy. Transport is able to get up quite close to Companies so that water and rations are distributed with little trouble.[11]

During April the Maori Pioneer Battalion spent nearly every day constructing defensive works around the New Zealand front line. The men dug many miles of trenches, built strong posts and drainage and carried out a host of other tasks associated with 'all the paraphernalia of the filthy trench warfare'. As the battalion's war diary stated, it was 'not an exciting job at all as we have been for the most part working on reverse slopes and away from the enemy's observation'. It was also one that involved considerable risk. That month there were forty-five casualties: four men were killed and two more later died of their wounds.[12]

The rain that had started to fall on the evening of 28 March continued unabated in the early days of April. The conditions of the trenches remained deplorable and it was an ordeal to remain in them for any length of time. In Jesse Stayte's words, 'The trenches are in a shocking condition with mud and rain . . . The place is littered with dead Fritz and the stench is very bad. It rained all evening.' After his battalion relieved a Rifle Brigade unit in the line on 2 April he and his fellow soldiers were only 70 yards from the German trenches. On Wednesday 3 April Stayte wrote, 'There is nothing doing during the day only sniping so we live like wild beasts, we sleep in our holes or trenches at day and go out to maim and kill at night.' That evening Stayte was on guard duty watching over a sap. He stood on a platform made from dead bodies and covered with earth.

> It is a good stand but rather gruesome when one is on guard standing on it through the night. There is a dead Fritz officer just on the other side of the block and about 50 yards further on Fritz has a block in the same sap and I suppose his sentry is watching me from his block.

On 4 April Stayte noted that 'It has been raining nearly all day and things are very dirty in the trench'. That night, though, the Aucklanders were relieved by a battalion from the Rifle Brigade and trudged wearily back to Mailly-Maillet. 'We were wet through and quite exhausted when we got to the place. We had a good feed and a nip of rum and lay down anywhere and went to sleep.'[13]

All brigade and battalion war diaries commented on the poor state of the trenches and the terrible living conditions. The 2nd Otago Battalion found its trenches 'very muddy and dirty — very shallow in places. Poor accommodation. Posts very scattered owing to large frontage. Dispositions: — 4 Companies in line, one platoon of each company in close support.' The diary also noted that there was a 'Considerable amount of enemy movement. Much sniping on our side. Enemy snipers fairly active.'[14] The war diary of the 2nd Canterbury Battalion recorded a similar experience:

> Trenches and C.Ts in very bad condition, both falling in on slightest provocation. Sniping active from our side. Hun using Light Minnenwerfer and Granatenwerfer [grenade projector] from the crater in front of Centre Company Sector. There is an occasional Pineapple [finned mortar bomb].[15]

The 2nd Wellington Battalion spent a quiet few days in front of La Signy Farm although they could see considerable German activity behind the front line. The state of the trenches caused them some concern:

> Weather fine . . . Battalion in line . . . in front of LA SIGNY FARM. Enemy quiet all day, but a lot of individual movement seen in back areas. Owing to recent rain trenches very muddy and difficult to walk through. Casualties Nil. Evacuations Nil. Reinforcements Nil. Ration strength 28 Off. 748 O/Ranks.[16]

New Zealand gunner Bert Stokes hinted at the unpleasant conditions in a letter to his parents:

> I'll just tell you that during the past three or four days I had had a touch of the 'Flu' & have not felt too bright . . . These times particularly we get no time to ourselves at all, and conditions are not too good either. I am writing this in a small bivvie, just a canvas one, round us is our ever present enemy — MUD. It has rained

incessantly for days & days, consequently things are in a horrible mess. But of course I forgot, you don't want to hear all this do you now? I expect you imagine all too vividly as it is.[17]

Surprisingly, though the men's health suffered, their morale remained high throughout the German offensive. This is confirmed by both official and private sources. For Brigadier R. Young of the 2nd New Zealand Infantry Brigade:

> The behaviour of the men throughout these operations has been excellent. They have maintained a cheerful spirit throughout, and have been eagerly awaiting an attack by the enemy, being quite confident in their ability to repel such an attack with their machine guns and rifles. This feeling of superiority became more apparent than ever when the attack on the 27th had been successfully beaten off. The men are still in good spirits, but the exposure to the mud of the trenches is beginning to affect their feet.[18]

The brigadier finished his report by noting that the battalions were using whale oil and clean socks to fix the problem of the men's feet.

Ronald Watson was the padre of the 1st Otago Battalion. Later in the year he would win the Military Cross for his bravery in caring for the wounded at Bapaume. Padre Watson's correspondence supported Young's assessment. A letter written on 9 April 1918 described the terrible condition of the trenches and the men's unbroken spirit:

> In the Field.
> Tuesday, April 9th. 1918.
> My last budget was dated the 1st April. We have had quite a deal of rain lately, and there is plenty of mud about. Life is very full of incident, where we are. You will know now by the papers of our sector. Our boys are doing most excellent work. Really their spirit is a thing to marvel at — their cheerfulness in spite of all the mud and uncertainty. I do love these chaps. They are so

supremely worthwhile. Nothing that one can attempt seems too much. I am trying to do all I can for them. Here is a typical day of mine yesterday — Plenty of rain in morning. In the morning, I buried one of our boys, and then Campbell (my batman) and I went into a village in our rear, to see what I could fix up with the Y.M.C.A. for the boys. I landed some cigs., chocolate and toffee. I saw Frank Cameron in the Y.M. there. In afternoon, Campbell and I went the round of one company and distributed the gifts. In places, I went into mud up to my knees. It took us 4½ hrs. to do the trip. Men in great heart and very pleased to see me, and I them. A smile is a big thing, I am certain. I came on a section of one company in the Line the other day. Evidently someone said, 'Here's the Padre.' I heard, 'And I bet he's smiling.' I don't like going around empty-handed. I believe in laying hands on all I can to give away. By all sorts of means and from different sources I get newspapers, mags. (new and old), cigs., sweets, etc. and dole them out. One feels that these chaps deserve such a great deal. Several days ago, we had some hours of a fearful strafe from Fritz. I sheltered for several hours, then Campbell and I went out with a stretcher round two of our companies to see what we could do. We were out and managed to dodge everything for 3–4 hours. I am getting my nerve very much improved, I am glad to say. Our casualties have been very light, considering. We seem to have the upper hand of Fritz in these parts. Already our boys have shaken him up goodoh. Please don't expect too much in the way of letters. I find so very much to do these days. Time is not nearly sufficient for all I see I can do up here. We are a happy band of brothers.

Cheeroh.

Much love from

RONALD[19]

Echoing this view, Major Lindsay Inglis, an officer with the machine-gunners and a major general in the next world war, found the spirit of the men infectious. As he wrote to Agnes May Todd, his fiancée in New Zealand:

> Nobody seems to be worrying his head about the Hun much, everybody in the best of spirits — even to one company that lost two thirds of its strength from MG fire a couple of days ago. Our outfit has never been more full of fight. Beginning to catch the atmosphere myself again and feel like a warhorse once more. Wish they'd finish it off though.[20]

One letter, however, hinted that things were not quite as rosy. Bernard Cottrell wrote to his father on 10 April 1918:

> Things are somewhat 'patchy' as yet. Tucker a bit low & everything messy & muddy and we are doing more than our share in holding on, consequently everyone discontented, we haven't been paid yet, still that doesn't matter much seeing that there are not any places to buy anything at.[21]

Private Ernest Painter's diary also showed the reality of trench warfare for the New Zealand soldiers.

> Still in the trenches. I am tired, sore and heart broken of this Hellish life. Just one continual roar of guns and shell and bullets flying all around everywhere . . . I have not had my clothes off for 2 months or more now, no blankets now only Great coats and as lousy as a coocoo [sic]. God knows when it will come to an end this Hellish life.[22]

With the poor conditions in the trenches, limited food, no pay or creature comforts, it is not surprising that the New Zealand soldiers were discontented. Soldiers can, however, be inveterate grumblers and grumbling should not be mistaken for a low state of morale. Both the evidence and the subsequent performance of the division indicate that the spirits of the New Zealand soldiers remained high throughout 1918. Even months of 'filthy trench warfare' could not change this.

Soldiers who joined the division in the middle of this operation found the experience hard. Rifleman Arthur Leslie Ross, known as Les, who eventually joined B Company of the 2nd Rifles, had left Etaples on 1 April and, with other reinforcements, travelled by train to the Somme. Then came a hard march of 16 miles to join the New Zealand Division. Their loads were heavy and food was scarce.

> Our rations were poor, a lot of the bake houses had been lost and bread was scarce. We found a stack of beans, they were a bit mouldy but we ate the lot we were really hungry, the troops holding the line got preference and rightly so.

On an overnight stop Ross set off with three friends in an attempt to buy some bread.

> We could not talk French but old Jack said he could make himself understood but there was a surprise in store for him. A woman was standing at a door and Jack went up to her he took a ten franc note out of his pocket gave it to her and said bread, bread. She nodded and motioned him in & we could almost taste the bread, but Jack was out in ten seconds. She had thought he wanted to go to bed and Jack was not having any.

The reinforcements finally reached the New Zealand Division where Les Ross ended up in a trench at La Signy Farm. It had been raining solidly for two days and 'the result was that we were in a foot of mud and water.' The New Zealanders did not, however, lose their sense of humour. A suspected German spy in a British officer's uniform had inspected the front at La Signy Farm and advised a corporal there to pull his men back 100 yards if they were shelled by the Germans. After this security scare the men instituted the use of a nightly password which all their soldiers had to remember.

Some of the passwords were really funny. They would start to undress a girl. The first night the word would be Blouse, the next, skirt, petticoat, chemise, stocking panties would all follow, we would have the poor girl stripped in ten days. Then the reverse, it took longer to dress her as she would have a overcoat and hat on.[23]

Rifleman Ross and the newly arrived reinforcements remained in the front line at La Signy farm for two weeks.

If it was hard for reinforcements to slot into their units while they were in action, it was doubly so for newly commissioned officers. Lieutenant Marcus Smith, a lawyer from Sanson near Palmerston North, had not reached Britain until mid December 1917 and there he remained for the next two months. On Sunday 17 March he wrote a reassuring letter to his widowed mother in Waipukurau:

I believe I am to go overseas with a draft next Weds which will mean some time at our base in France as they don't seem to require officers at present, our division will probably be put in a quiet sector . . . we may not be in a big fight again, the Division could not stand another Passchendaele.[24]

Normally, Lieutenant Smith would have spent some time at the base camp, as he indicated in his letter. But these were far from normal times. By the time Marcus Smith reached France the New Zealand Division was again in the thick of the action and the Rifle Brigade was desperately short of officers. His next letter to his mother was written in pencil on two pages of a field notebook rather than with the fountain pen and fine writing paper he had been recently using.

I wrote to you just after reaching France & was pushed straight into it, did some heavy marching & suddenly found myself in an attack . . . I feel very lonely among strangers & the conditions are awful, at present I have just moved back from the line & am in a fairly dry dug out. Fritz is straffing all round with shells & my nerves are on edge, he occasionally gets a dugout, one landed a few yds from mine yesterday & shook me up, also had a bullet through my coat sleeve on the first stunt, oh if it had been a blighty.

This morning while walking through a newly captured trench I saw poor Mathew lying dead in the mud, he was killed in a raid the day before, he was one of my original subalterns & went right through with me, he was a very brave man in the line. I took a cigarette case from him & will send it to his wife if I get the chance. A 'q' [small artillery shell] just landed very closed, it is hard . . . not having had a chance to get used to it first & being shoved right into bloody fighting . . .

Another shell very close, I suppose I shall get used to it. Much love to you all. I will write from Blighty.

Marcus[25]

It was certainly a tough experience for a young officer. It was not surprising, perhaps, that Marcus Smith's next letter to his mother was written from the Medical Depot at Etaples, far from the fighting on the Somme.

On the morning of 4 April a heavy German bombardment announced an end to the quiet period. It also marked the beginning of the last stage of the great March offensive. The attack on 4 April was not made on the front where the New Zealand Division was situated but rather south of the Somme on a 15-mile front. The Germans used seventeen divisions, six of them for the first time in the offensive. Twelve divisions attacked the French Army on a 9-mile front while five divisions attacked the remnants of the British Fifth Army, now renamed the Fourth Army, on a front of 6 miles. The very muddy ground the Germans had to cross greatly inhibited their movement, but they still managed to drive back the British Fourth Army along its entire front, in some places for nearly 2 miles. The French XXXVI Corps was also driven back as far as 2 miles beyond the Avres River to Senecat Wood from where the attacking Germans could clearly see the outskirts of Amiens. The Germans captured Hamel in the morning, but a new defensive Allied line was formed west of the village. A renewed attack that afternoon reached the outskirts of Villers-Bretonneux, less than 10 miles east of Amiens and the key to the defence of the city. For a time it seemed likely that the town would fall to the Germans, but a spirited charge by the 36th Australian Battalion and the remnants of two British companies saved the day. The Australians had been lying in wait in a hollow south of the town and on sighting the Germans made 'a spectacular charge' with fixed bayonets.[26] The Germans hesitated, then ran, taking up a new position in old trenches a mile from the town. The 36th Australian Battalion lost 150 men in this attack — a quarter of its current strength and more than half of its officers.[27] For a time the situation hung in the balance, but reinforcements arrived to plug the gaps in the defences. The southern approach to Amiens remained blocked.

Though significant ground had been taken the Germans finished the day well short of their objectives and their casualties were heavy. Yet this limited success was enough to encourage them to renew their attempts the following day. Believing that the front south of the Somme would crumble if subjected to enough pressure elsewhere, the Germans planned to strike on 5 April at various points north of the Somme in an effort to take Amiens from that direction. One of the areas selected for close attention was the village of Hébuterne and the region immediately to its south.

Chapter 9

Weathering the Storm: 5 April 1918

O N 5 APRIL 1918 THE Germans made a last desperate effort to open the road to Amiens. Though the Second and Seventeenth Armies planned to launch a general offensive against the whole front of the British Third Army, such a large-scale operation proved impossible to mount so only isolated attacks took place. Between Dernancourt and Bucquoy, using ten infantry divisions heavily supported by artillery, three main attacks took place on 5 April at Colincamps, at Albert against the 12th and 63rd Divisions, and at Dernancourt, where the hardest fighting took place. At Dernancourt, two brigades of the 4th Australian Division held three German divisions at bay, suffering more than 1000 casualties while doing so. For the entrenched Australians, 5 April began with the heaviest artillery bombardment they had experienced 'since the worst days of the Somme'.[1] The depleted Australian brigades were forced to give ground, though the Germans gained only about 2000 yards by the end of the day. The extent of the Australian losses made it necessary to withdraw the 4th Division from the line when the fighting died away that evening.

The New Zealand Division and the 4th Australian Brigade also had their share of heavy fighting on 5 April. One of the locations singled out for attention by the Germans was just south of Hébuterne, where two German divisions attempted to batter their way through the defences. Their immediate objective was the long stretch of high ground behind the New Zealanders, the site of the village of Colincamps, just over a mile behind the New Zealand front line. Pencil sketch-maps found on the bodies of German officers showed where the enemy would locate their brigade and battalion headquarters once Colincamps was taken. A German prisoner taken that morning confirmed that their intention was to capture and hold Colincamps. The German soldiers at Hébuterne were carrying full packs loaded with ammunition and enough rations to last three to four days. As one New Zealand historian has commented, these maps and the loaded packs suggested that 'a successful issue was, in his [the enemy's] mind, a foregone conclusion'.[2] If this was the case, then the German commanders were about to be bitterly disappointed.

Around 5 a.m. on that day, in a blanket of mist and light rain, the storm erupted again on the New Zealand Division as the Germans attempted to revitalise their flagging offensive. It was a cold, dull day with low overhanging clouds. This bleak weather tended to favour the defenders as it prevented the Germans from using their observation balloons. The German attack started with an 'extraordinarily vehement'[3] artillery bombardment, probably the heaviest and most sustained barrage the New Zealand Division experienced during the war.[4] The German artillery fire was constant throughout the day, but the initial barrage lasted for three hours and extended across the whole New Zealand front line and on the right half of the 4th Australian Brigade at Hébuterne.

The Germans used guns of all calibres, including some as heavy as 21 centimetres (12 inches). The main areas targeted were the forward trenches, the support and rear positions as far back as Bertrancourt, Colincamps and Bus-lès-Artois. The German gunners paid particular attention to the dead ground and valleys in front of the New Zealand line where strongpoints had been recently constructed. These areas 'were almost deluged with high explosive, and swept with shrapnel'.[5] In an attempt to neutralise the division's artillery batteries, the New Zealand artillery positions were hit with a high proportion of mustard gas shells.[6] This 'storm of steel' severed all the ground wires from the various observation posts to the battalion and brigade headquarters. Throughout the day communications remained 'difficult and uncertain'.[7] Despite this, the New Zealand artillery was soon active, firing on known troop concentration points and engaging in some counter-battery fire of their own.

All those on the receiving end of this barrage commented on its severity. According to James McWhirter, 'the shells seemed to drop like hail, it was terrific and caused many casualties'.[8] Captain George Tuck found little rest away from the front line on this 'very tiring day':

> At about 4.00 a.m. this morning, the Hun started to shell these areas with every kind of gun including our own 18 pounders. He never stopped for 11 hours and then continued intermittently. All windows were blown in my orderly room the sashes came in with the windows and much stuff was knocked off the ceiling and walls. We were very lucky though.[9]

The war diary of the 2nd Canterbury Battalion reflected Tuck's thoughts:

> 5 April
> Dirty day. At 6 a.m. enemy commenced to shell AUCHON-VILLERS with guns of all calibres, and to a lesser extent, the Front and Support Lines. This continued without a lull until 4.30 p.m. Casualties were light — but AUCHONVILLERS torn to rags. Night was quiet. Patrols reported no enemy movement.[10]

Despite the intensity of the barrage, the New Zealanders were indeed lucky: casualties were surprisingly light, as all unit and formation war diaries recorded with a sense of relief. That of the 2nd Auckland Battalion, Captain Tuck's unit, is typical:

> 5 April
> Early in the morning of the 5th the enemy unsuccessfully attacked the Rifle Brigade in the front line positions and from 5:30 a.m. until 2.30 p.m. our positions in Divisional Reserve were heavily shelled, especially COURCELLES AU BOIS and the positions occupied by the 16th Coy. However in spite of the heavy shelling our casualties were very slight.[11]

The diary of the 1st Canterbury Battalion, which had borne the brunt of the German barrage in the southern sector of the line, recorded: 'Our casualties, in face of so heavy a bombardment, were very light'.[12] Lieutenant John Harcourt was a company commander in the 1st Canterbury Battalion. Like most of the New Zealander officers that day, he was both surprised and delighted that the battalion's casualties were not heavier and he had a convincing explanation:

> 5 April
>
> A memorable day which broke very chill. The trench was full of mud & movement along them difficult in consequence . . . I had two men wounded, both lightly, but how I got off so lightly, still remains a miracle. McFadden on my left had 5 or 6 killed and several wounded. This artillery barrage was one — if not the most — prolonged bombardment with big shells yet experienced by the New Zealanders and our casualties were very light. For this we can thank the soft ground and the bad shooting of the enemy most of whose artillery had been brought up secretly and was firing without having registered on our trenches.[13]

One New Zealand soldier wounded that morning was Edward Bibby. When recalling the experience just over seventy years later he was in no doubt that the German barrage of 5 April was the 'heaviest bombardment of the war . . . they hammered us all day'. In front of the 1st Otago billets was a paddock of thick grass. At the end of the day, not a blade of grass remained: 'it had been ploughed'. A shell splinter hit Bibby early in the morning, but he could not be moved until just after 2 p.m. when there was a slight decrease in the barrage's intensity. Bibby set off for Mailly-Maillet where he found things 'a real classic, it would suit the war pictures. There were ambulances coming and going. There were shells going off, the wounded streaming in . . . It was an interesting experience.'[14]

The depth and intensity of the opening barrage indicated that the Germans were likely to launch an attack soon, so the New Zealanders in the front line steeled themselves. 'The enemy could be plainly seen in his trenches watching the effect of his shelling and in such numbers as

to suggest his following up the bombardment with an infantry attack.'[15]
After three hours the German barrage began to creep forward, a sure sign
that the infantry were advancing behind it. The New Zealanders did not
have to wait long until their suspicions were confirmed.

In line that morning were the 2nd New Zealand Infantry Brigade on
the right and the Rifle Brigade, linking with the 4th Australian Brigade
on the left. German infantry attacked both New Zealand brigades on two
separate occasions. The German commanders had intended to synchronise
these attacks, but owing to the disorganisation on the German front,
they were launched at different times. In fact, the last two attacks were
separated by as much as four hours.

The first German infantry attack was made just after 8.30 a.m. when
a regiment from the 26th German Division advanced against the Rifle
Brigade, barring their way to Colincamps. The German infantry suffered
heavily under the New Zealanders' withering machine-gun and rifle fire.
As they closed in on the Rifle Brigade, New Zealand bombers operating
from the saps also took a heavy toll on the German infantry. Still they
came on, managing to get within 30 yards of the Rifle Brigade's trenches
before they were finally driven off. The war diary of the 4th Rifles records
the details of this attack:

> The night of 4/5th April was quiet except for sounds of talking
> and whistle signals coming from the enemy lines. Patrols reported
> nothing else unusual.
>
> At about 5.15 a.m. on the 5th April the enemy commenced a
> heavy shelling of our front line which continued without cessation
> until about 8.30 a.m., when the barrage lifted to the hollow and
> ridge in rear of the front line. Shortly afterwards the enemy were
> seen through the haze all along the line advancing to the attack. It
> was general on all three front Company sectors but he appeared
> to be in greatest strength on the right in the direction of RED
> COTTAGE to LA SIGNY FARM.
>
> The S.O.S. rocket signal was put up and the artillery response
> was good.

Our three Companies had the situation well in hand from the commencement. In no case did any advanced posts give way, but there were several cases of individual and collective movements forward to meet parties of the enemy. Waves in the open made excellent targets and bombing forward down the C.T's was exceedingly well done, the enemy being driven back through these or forced to leave them and be dealt with by Lewis Gun and Rifle fire. In every respect our men displayed fine fighting spirit. It is worthy of note that while the action was in progress, Company Cooks brought up tea for the men in the front line and posts.[16]

The next assault on the Rifle Brigade was made at 10 a.m. and it met with more success. The Germans succeeded in capturing an advanced outpost manned by a small garrison of men from the 4th Rifles. 'An advance post at LA SIGNY FARM was rushed by the enemy under cover of fog. 1 sector with a Lewis gun evaded the flanking movement by the enemy but the remainder of the garrison 14 in all were either killed or captured.'[17]

Using this position as a lever the German attackers went on to take La Signy Farm. Hoping to use the farm as a pivot to capture the New Zealand trenches, the Germans turned trench mortars on the New Zealand positions and then pushed as many parties of infantry as they could up old saps towards the New Zealand lines. The forward posts of the 4th Rifles inflicted massive casualties on the German infantry and foiled their attempt to reach the New Zealand lines. 'Never before had the Lewis gunners of the 4th Battalion had such targets as on this day and of their opportunities they made full use.'[18] With the Germans in possession of La Signy Farm, the 1st Rifles were exposed to dangerous enfilade fire, but the problem was solved by having its C Company form one defensive flank along the hedge that ran beyond the farm and another across the main line in case the Germans launched a frontal assault. Moving forward down the saps and attacking the enemy there could easily defeat any assault made against the front of 1st Rifles.

By noon the situation was restored and this attack petered out. There were no further attacks on the Rifle Brigade that day. From 1 to 12 April 1918, the Rifle Brigade's casualties were recorded as ninety-six men killed, 311 wounded and three missing.[19] Most of these casualties were sustained on 5 April. German losses were higher, conservatively estimated to be more than 500 on 5 April.[20] As the 4th Rifles' war diary noted, 'The enemy losses appear to have been heavy as all that day his stretcher bearers were engaged in carrying out wounded.'[21] German accounts of this action claim that the attack was halted by New Zealand machine-gun fire from the flanks and centre. The 10th Bavarian Infantry Regiment 'lost 190 officers and men. The attack had no prospect whatsoever of success unless the enfilade fire of enemy machine-guns were eliminated by the preliminary bombardment and by the barrage.'[22] La Signy Farm remained in German hands but it was kept under constant fire by the New Zealand artillery. At dusk on 5 April the New Zealanders struck back with the 3rd Rifles south of the Serre road, advancing their line by some 150 yards.

On the right of the New Zealand line, German infantry attacked the 2nd New Zealand Infantry Brigade in the morning and afternoon of 5 April. The brigade was holding the line with the two Canterbury battalions. Of these, only the 1st Canterbury Battalion was attacked that day. The attack in the morning came just on 9 a.m. with German infantry working up the saps leading to the front-line trenches. The 1st Canterbury Battalion established blocking positions in the saps, forcing the Germans into the open where they were overcome with rifle, Lewis gun and machine-gun fire. German losses were heavy. The war diary of the 1st Canterbury Battalion made only a brief mention of this first attack:

> Weather dull. Enemy opened an intense bombardment the whole of our system about 7.15 a.m., which he maintained all day, and during which he concentrated bodies of troops in saps leading towards our Front Line. At 9 a.m. his first attempt to come across was quickly repulsed, our fellows being, if anything, too keen.[23]

Lieutenant John Harcourt of the 1st Canterbury Battalion was visiting battalion headquarters at 9 a.m. when a runner from his platoon arrived to inform him that:

> Fritz was coming over the top. I rushed straight back to the front line and found that Sgt Carter had put up the S.O.S. in my absence and that the Light Trench Mortars had at once opened fire and caught the Hun waves right on the S.O.S. line dispersing them immediately.[24]

Harcourt had missed the German attack against his battalion that morning, but in the afternoon he would be in the thick of the action when the Germans struck again.

The Germans renewed their attack around 2 p.m. If anything, it was more of a non-event than the previous one and achieved nothing but heavy casualties for the Germans. The British official historian described it as a 'final but feeble effort'[25] while the history of the Canterbury battalions said it was launched 'in a half-hearted way'.[26] For a while it seemed as if the Germans might make some progress on the New Zealand right flank, but an enterprising Corporal White of 2nd Company quickly organised a bombing party to halt the Germans and captured ten prisoners. The attack was easily driven off. One of the many German casualties was a plane.

> An enemy Contact Plane, flying low over our front trench system, nearly all the morning, and doing invaluable work for the enemy was brought down by 12th. Company Lewis Gunners. The Pilot, badly wounded, and the Observer, unwounded, were both taken prisoners. Our much esteemed M.O. [medical officer], Dr. Harris was killed about 40 yards from the R.A.P.[27]

Harris was killed by the shell-fire that had continued unabated throughout the attack.

Lieutenant Harcourt's platoon was on the receiving end of an intense bombardment. It caused much damage to his trench but his casualties were light: only two of his men were slightly wounded. Harcourt regarded this 'as a miracle':

> My trench was blown in many places and one section of mine had a circle of big shell holes right around them only a few yards away. I did my best to keep the men cheerful despite the rather rattled feeling I had myself . . . The Hun did not get more than 50 yards before giving it up as our rifle and MG fire was too hot.[28]

The 2nd Otago Battalion was one of the reserve battalions of the 2nd New Zealand Infantry Brigade. Its war diary gave a succinct summary of the day's action on its brigade front:

> 5 April
> Heavy enemy bombardment opened up at 5 a.m. which lasted for 10 hours. Shells of all calibres were used and all villages received special attention. Companies had to quit their bivouac shelters and dig in clear of the village. This bombardment was of a very intense nature and was used to cover his attack further north. Enemy did attempt in a feeble sort of way to attack on our front but it was easily repulsed. Wet. Poor observation.[29]

When it was clear that this last attack had failed, the German artillery fire died down to become almost nonexistent from 3.30 p.m.

Dr Harris of the 1st Canterbury Battalion was not the only Medical Corps casualty that day. At Hédauville the 2nd New Zealand Field Ambulance was in reserve. It had despatched fifty of its stretcher-bearers to the 1st Field Ambulance, which was responsible for evacuating stretcher cases from the ADS at Mailly-Maillet. Although in reserve, the 2nd Field Ambulance had more casualties than the 1st Field Ambulance, operating near the front line. Remaining in the villages behind the New Zealand front line did not mean protection from danger. The German artillery had clearly selected the 2nd Field Ambulance as a prime target and continued shelling the unit throughout the day with a mixture of high-explosive, gas and shrapnel shells. In the afternoon a prisoner of war compound in Hédauville received a direct hit and several captured Germans were killed. The 2nd Field Ambulance suffered six casualties; one soldier was killed.[30] Meanwhile, at Mailly-Maillet, the 1st Field Ambulance, busy evacuating wounded soldiers away from the front line, also came under artillery fire.

> 5 April 1918
>
> Enemy attacked — 230 casualties being passed through A.D.S. RAPs on left flank had to shift back slightly, on account of heavy shelling, but all evacuations carried out satisfactorily. Two ambulance cars put out of action by shellfire. The unit had 3 casualties during the day — all slight wounds.[31]

The New Zealand artillery batteries received considerable attention from the German gunners and some suffered heavy losses, as Bombardier Bailey's diary recorded:

> Fritz started shelling the heavy batteries in the next village of Bertrancourt. He pasted them all the morning. My word the big H.E. [high-explosive shells] did come in . . . There was heavy artillery fire all day and some of our batteries suffered. The news reached us that the 10th Battery was blown out and some of the others had casualties . . .
>
> Fritz is supposed to have made three separate attacks during the day and sent over three waves of infantry with each attack. Our boys must have stopped him alright though we had a lot of casualties; the ambulances being kept very busy.[32]

It would seem that the New Zealand machine-gunners were responsible for most of the German casualties. At 8.30 a.m. the Wellington Company of the Machine Gun Battalion, in support of the Rifle Brigade, caught the advancing Germans with 'a perfect hurricane of fire'.[33] The machine-gunners estimated that they accounted for about half of the advancing force. When the second attack was made on the Rifle Brigade at 10 a.m., the machine-gunners once more assailed the Germans with withering fire. One gun kept up a fire that lasted for more than four hours and prevented the German infantry from reaching an old communication trench. In the southern sector of the line that afternoon, the situation was similar.

> Enemy again attempted to advance and were engaged at a range of 600 yards . . . 70 or 80 casualties were observed . . . Very many small targets were engaged throughout the day and machine gun fire brought to bear upon all approaches and points where enemy might assemble unobserved.[34]

This New Zealand machine-gun fire took a heavy toll on the German infantry and was primarily responsible for the failure of the enemy attacks. In a letter home Major Lindsay Inglis described the effect of his guns in support of the 2nd New Zealand Infantry Brigade:

> Things are much the same as they were in my last letter, the only events of note being a heavy attack by Fritz two days ago — he came a stomacher as we all predicted he would. Two guns of mine had him at 80 to 100 yards range in considerable lumps and the others had him at various ranges — the bag was quite satisfactory and I don't think he'll come at it again here unless at the very greatest strength he can muster. I doubt if it will be worth his while even then.[35]

Captured Germans, too, testified to the effect of the New Zealand machine guns. An officer interrogated at general headquarters gave two reasons for the failure of the 5 April attack:

1. The intensity of our [the New Zealanders] machine gun barrage.
2. The fact that some of the attacking troops did not leave their front line until ten minutes after the assault had been launched.[36]

A German prisoner from the 4th Company, 1st Battalion, 119th Grenadier Regiment, which had been part of the attacking force on 5 April, made a graphic and tragic entry in his diary:

> At 9.am we attacked. Many comrades find a hero's death, others writhe in their wounds. Primarily it was due to machine gun fire from the right and left flanks. The losses are very great. Many wounded are lying in the open. At night the battalion returns to its starting point. During day we are withdrawn to Battalion Battle Headquarters, but here also we are under fairly heavy fire. Thank God we are relieved here.[37]

Those New Zealanders who had weathered the storm of 5 April were full of confidence and relief.

> I do not think any man who was through today's happenings will ever forget it. We were all a bit shaken but our morale was very high after our double victory over the attacking Hun . . . It was a very trying and nerve-racking day — although exciting at times. The men were in great spirits after the show and would have gone after the Boche had they been allowed.[38]

The German onslaught of 5 April 1918 was an event of considerable significance for several reasons. First, according to the historian of the Rifle Brigade, 'The attack was unique in the respect that it was the only one of major importance that the New Zealand Division ever sustained.'[39] Second, for the first time in this war, the New Zealanders were not at a disadvantage in terms of the terrain on which they were fighting. They enjoyed the novelty of dealing with an attack in force while occupying a superior defensive position. Their efforts to secure all the high ground over the previous week had clearly paid off. Third, as a result of the failure of the 5 April assaults, Ludendorff took the painful decision to abandon the Michael Offensive.

These actions were indecisive. It was an established fact that the enemy's resistance was beyond our strength. We must not get drawn into a battle of exhaustion. This would not accord neither with the strategical or tactical situation. In agreement with the commanders concerned, G.H.Q. had to take the extremely difficult decision to abandon the attack on Amiens for good.[40]

So, after sixteen days, the German offensive on the Somme ground to a halt. After experiencing spectacular success at the beginning, it lost momentum and petered out in a series of spasmodic attacks. As in all the Allied offensives that had taken place to date, there was a break-in, but no breakthrough and the situation had deteriorated to the point of stalemate. After the failure of the assaults on 5 April Ludendorff decided that, in order to make any further progress, he needed to attack the BEF elsewhere. This would occur in the north in four days' time. But the Michael Offensive, the *Kaiserschlacht*, 'the most formidable onslaught of the war',[41] was over. The storm on the Somme had caused considerable damage to those who had stood in its path. It remained now to count the cost.

Chapter 10

Damage Assessment

C ASUALTY FIGURES FOR military campaigns are notoriously unreliable. There are often huge discrepancies in the numbers given for dead and wounded, and the German Michael Offensive is no exception. The figures given for German casualties in the *Kaiserschlacht* vary enormously from 105,000 to 300,000,[1] and it is now impossible to be sure just how many Germans were injured and killed in the period from 21 March to 5 April. It is possible, however, to note two significant details. First, the Germans did not lose as many men as the Allies, which was rare for an attacking force during the First World War. Describing his casualties as 'not inconsiderable', Ludendorff took considerable comfort from the fact that his enemies' casualties were higher: 'We had been attacking and had come off well, even in the matter of casualties'.[2] The second point is that though the Germans had fewer casualties than the BEF and the French, they came from those units that had done the heaviest fighting: the élite storm troops and the attack formations that followed them. Germany lost many of its best soldiers, men chosen for their initiative, fitness and ability, men the Kaiser could least afford to lose. As William Moore has commented, 'the losses in numbers could be counted, the losses in quality were incalculable'.[3] This would become all too evident in the later stages of the war.

Losses in the BEF were undoubtedly heavy — around 180,000, of whom half were missing.[4] Unlike previous battles of the war, however, where a high proportion of the dead were never recovered, most of the missing were, in fact, prisoners of war. The British Fifth Army suffered most during the Michael Offensive. It had disappeared from the BEF establishment and needed to be rebuilt as a fighting formation. These losses were indeed serious, but the BEF was not 'virtually finished as a fighting force', as one historian has recently claimed.[5]

New Zealand losses were considerable, despite the extraordinary claim made in the division's history that the casualty list was 'by no means an unduly heavy one'.[6] By 1918, the New Zealand government knew that any involvement in operations in France inevitably meant a large list of dead and wounded would soon follow. The Minister for Defence, Sir James Allen, clearly expressed this point to General Godley in early April 1918:

> I cannot conclude this letter without referring to the great fight that is now on. We are watching from day to day with eagerness for news, and I cannot tell you how much we admire the pluck and staying power of the British Army against the attacks of the masses that are brought against them. We are hoping that you have them held and will soon turn the tables. I fear casualty lists will be heavy, but there is some consolation to us as we are informed at the same time that the lists of our enemies are heavier still.[7]

There is considerable variation in the casualty figures given for the New Zealand Division in this offensive. *The Oxford Companion to New Zealand Military History* fudges the figures somewhat by stating that the casualties were more than 500 New Zealanders killed and 1800 wounded.[8] Stewart lists the casualties as 530 men killed, 1800 wounded and another sixty missing.[9] The British official history offers different figures again: 511 men killed, 1845 wounded and a further sixty-three men missing, making a total of 2419. Carbery's medical history of New Zealand's involvement in the war contains a full list of New Zealand casualties month by month. For the two months of the Michael Offensive the figures are a total of 448 in March (seventy-nine dead and 369 wounded) and a total of 3201 in April (885 dead, 2300 wounded and sixteen missing or captured).[10]

The total casualties for April 1918 are among the highest for the war, surpassed only by the months of September 1916 (the Somme), June 1917 (Messines), October 1917 (Passchendaele) and September 1918. As A.E. Byrne wrote in his history of the Otago battalions, 'This high total affords some indication of the severity of the period.'[11] Carbery's figures are probably the most accurate, especially if measured against the names in the casualty reports for this period. These list all the New Zealand soldiers reported as casualties from 23 March to 30 April 1918: 811 were killed or died of wounds; 2181 were wounded.[12] It should never be forgotten that each of these numbers represents an individual, a New Zealand soldier far from home with dreams and aspirations, plans for the future and loved ones to whom he wished one day to return.

For the Germans, the Michael Offensive was both a success and a failure. It is best summed up in the words of Cyril Falls, as 'a magnificent tactical victory, but not a strategic success to anything like the same extent'.[13] The Germans' success in the *Kaiserschlacht* was outstanding. When Ludendorff broke off the offensive on 5 April, the Germans had seized more ground than the Allies gained during the entire war. They had also inflicted some 250,000 casualties on the enemy. More than this, the Germans had done what many at the time thought was impossible: they had found a way to break the deadlock of trench warfare, something the British and the French had been struggling desperately to achieve for the last three years. Charles Bean summed up this remarkable success:

> If, however, Ludendorff failed to grasp the human problem involved, he solved most brilliantly some of the tactical and strategical ones. By solving the extraordinary difficult problem of achieving a large measure of surprise in one of these great, long prepared offensive, and by inventing a tactical method — infiltration — which freed the German infantry from the rigidity that had hitherto bound the tactics of the Allies, Ludendorff presented his opponents with a problem to which — so far as resistance in their prepared trench-systems was concerned — there was no answer. Even with his army weakened through the policy of Lloyd George, Haig had been confident of at least holding the Germans for many days before they reached the Somme. But Ludendorff, by deceiving his opponents with preparations in three sectors — and more — and then by flinging his whole strength against one of these, had

actually placed it beyond the power even of a Napoleon to stop the rapidity of his advance in the first stages.[14]

Later in the year, the Allies copied Ludendorff's methods while adding some variations of their own. This initiative finally brought them victory on the Western Front.

The German victories shook the British establishment to its core and left its forces in a desperate situation. After 5 April, Haig was left with only a single division in reserve (from a total of sixty). Sixteen of his divisions were being made up with drafts of youths aged eighteen or nineteen. The German triumphs also implied that, for the first time on the Western Front, the British forces in the field had been attacked and defeated. As John Buchan noted, there is no escaping the fact that the days of retreat from 21 to 26 March had all the hallmarks of defeat: 'for defeat it is, when two armies fall back thirty miles with heavy losses, and have the enemy's will imposed on them'.[15] The performance of British troops during those dark days produced a crisis of confidence at home and the demand for a scapegoat, which the government duly provided in the form of General Gough.

The atmosphere and mood in Britain is reflected in the letters that passed between General Godley and the King's private secretary, Colonel Clive Wigram. In a letter marked 'Private and Confidential' Wigram lamented the mood of pessimism that had swept the country and, in his view, had emanated from Parliament:

> The spirit of the men must indeed be marvellous . . . The misery is that with all this sacrifice and keeping up the honour of the Old Country, there is so much bickering and snarling at home, and tendency to decry what the British soldier has done and is doing on the Western Front. Why does not the Prime Minister or some Member of Cabinet get up and tell the people how magnificently our Armies have been fighting against heavy odds, and how thinly the Fifth Army front had to be held, and render to DH [Haig] and his commanders the tribute due to them?

A recent debate in the House of Commons had left the public with the impression that the British and Germans had been equal in strength during this offensive and that the British soldiers, especially those in the Fifth Army, had run away without offering any effective resistance. Wigram deeply resented this insinuation: 'Now you and I know this to be a false suggestion and a suppression of the truth, to which the accounts of all the correspondents now bear witness. I cannot understand the attitude of a Britisher who prefers to think that foreign methods, plans, leadership and staff work are better than our own.' He felt that Lloyd George had misled the British people in an effort to deflect criticism away from the government. 'I think that L.G. is the best man we could have to win the war, but his methods are rather un-English.' What was lacking, according to Wigram, was more military control in the government: 'A war can only be won where there is military control in military affairs, and, alas, the Boches are expert at this'.[16]

Yet, as Ludendorff acknowledged, the Michael Offensive was a strategic failure.[17] Though, in comparison with what had gone before it, Michael had made substantial territorial gains, this was not enough. In war, a withdrawal in the face of enemy pressure does not necessarily lead to defeat, and nor does an advance mean that victory automatically follows. The offensive had not fulfilled any of its key aims. The Germans had not turned the flank of the British armies and had not separated the armies of Britain and France. The strategically important towns of Arras and Amiens were still in British control. In fact, some historians of note came to regard the Michael Offensive as a decisive defeat for the Germans. This was certainly the view of Winston Churchill:

> Contrary to the generally accepted verdict, I hold that the Germans, judged by the hard test of gains and losses, were decisively defeated. Ludendorff failed to achieve a single strategic object . . . What then had been gained? The Germans had reoccupied their old battlefields and the regions they had so cruelly devastated and ruined a year before. Once again they entered into possession of those grisly trophies. No fertile province, no wealthy cities, no

river or mountain barrier, no new untapped resources were their reward. Only the crater-fields extending abominably wherever the eye could turn, the old trenches, the vast graveyards, the skeletons, the blasted trees and the pulverised villages — these from Arras to Montdidier and from St Quentin to Villers-Bretonneux, were the Dead Sea fruits of the mightiest military conception and the most terrific onslaught which the annals of war record.[18]

In a recent publication historian Gary Sheffield echoes Churchill's view, but rather than seeing the March–April battles as defeats, Sheffield views them as successes for the BEF: 'In terms of sheer scale these battles rate as the greatest British defensive victories in history, for victories they were'.[19] If this is so, and there is good cause to argue this case, the British victory during the Michael Offensive, with its loss of territory and heavy casualties, must be described as Pyrrhic — triumph won at too great a cost.

Certainly the New Zealand soldiers in 1918 knew that they had taken part in a victory and their morale was high. The men also felt that, after 5 April 1918, the Germans were a spent force. Though the reality was a little different, as the Germans would soon show in their next attack, this optimism was widespread in the New Zealand Division in 1918. The war diary of the 1st Canterbury Battalion reflected this view in its entry for 6 April — 'Opened fine and quiet. Enemy evidently having had enough of it for the time being'[20] — and on 22 April Captain George Tuck of the 2nd Auckland Battalion told his parents:

> Conditions have not been for the best this last month, but they might have been worse. No one seems pessimistic and I think that most of us regard the present enemy effort as being what is colloquially known as 'shooting his bolt'. Personally I am quite optimistic about the whole state of affairs.[21]

A few days earlier Tuck had written: 'In direct proportion to the Hun's success so the spirit of our men is rising. Everyone is laughing and joking about the whole thing.'[22] Success certainly bred confidence and in April

1918 the New Zealand Division had this in abundance. As Carbery's medical history noted, 'The morale of the Division had never been more exalted and our infantry were well prepared, even eager, to meet any assault the enemy might choose to fling upon them.'[23] Fortunately, though, it would be some months before the Division was again involved in heavy fighting.

The Germans were far from a spent force after 5 April. They had, however, been checked on the Somme and could not break through the hastily formed British defences there. To make any further progress they needed to strike elsewhere. As the Second Battle of the Somme ended the Germans switched their efforts further north to the Lys Valley, south of Ypres. This second drive, codenamed Georgette, lasted from 9 to 29 April. Two days before the attack the Germans launched a massive mustard-gas barrage on the British positions. The New Zealanders' old haunt of Armentières was saturated with more than 40,000 of these shells. Operation Georgette used two armies with thirty-five divisions advancing behind a Bruchmüller barrage that achieved a density of 100 guns per kilometre, their greatest artillery concentration of the war. Like the Michael Offensive, Georgette had initial tactical success but soon lost momentum. None of its aims were achieved either. The German attack advanced about 9 miles before grinding to a halt at the end of April.

The ground captured by the Germans included much of the Ypres salient, including Messines and Passchendaele. News of the loss of these two ruined villages, scene of much savage fighting the previous year, greatly distressed the New Zealanders.[24] Writing from the Medical Depot at Etaples, Lieutenant Marcus Smith caught the mood of the New Zealand soldiers:

> The position is right on the edge & if Fritz gets another mile or two we may have to withdraw from the historic Ypres Salient, already the line has withdrawn from Passchendaele Ridge where one cannot put a spade in without digging up an Australian, New Zealander, or Canadian & is the place of our enormous casualty lists of October last year. As I have told you before we were pushed

up to stop a rout & have learned a lot since then & do not wonder why everybody's hearts are breaking. We have wonderful troops, far better fighters than the Hun, but it is known right through the army that our staffs have . . . failed from the beginning.[25]

Yet, the loss of this ground did not seriously damage the Allies' cause and the German targets of strategic significance, the channel ports and the town of Hazebrouck, remained in British hands.

In May 1918 came the third German offensive drive. Codenamed Roland, it struck against the French in the Aisne Valley and at the Chemin des Dames, using forty-one divisions. Two smaller operations followed in Noyon–Montdidier and the Champagne–Marne area but, like the previous offensives, they achieved only limited success. By 17 July 1918 the German offensives in this war had run their course. Ludendorff's hammer blows failed to achieve a single strategic objective. Worse than this, though, was the effect they had on the German Army. They bled it white, resulted in 'almost a million casualties between March and July 1918 [and] led to a vicious spiral of collapse thereafter'.[26] The fighting spirit of those German soldiers who survived these offensives was severely affected. Even a soldier as fanatically dedicated to the cause as Ernst Junger was could admit, in June 1918:

> At such moments there crept over me a mood I had never known before: a certain war-weariness occasioned by the length of time I had been exposed to the war's excitements. Nothing but war and danger; not a night that was not convulsed with shells. Winter came and then summer, and one was always in the war. Tired of it and used to it, one was all the more dispirited and fed up with it just because one was used to it.[27]

Ludendorff's offensives, which had promised so much, finally cost Germany the war.

Some New Zealand units were involved in the fighting during Operation Georgette, though they were not part of the New Zealand Division and were under the command of General Godley in the New Zealand Expeditionary Force. The units used included the 2nd Entrenching Battalion, the Otago Mounted Rifles and the Cyclist Battalion, some artillery units and the New Zealand Tunnellers based at Arras. As Godley explained to Sir James Allen while the offensive was at its height, the BEF had 'had very strenuous times' in the north so that:

> Anything that we could lay our hands on had to be pressed into the fight, among them the 2nd New Zealand Entrenching Battalion made up of reinforcements and remnants of the 4th Brigade. Under command of Major Tonkin . . . they did excellent service, and I sent Malcolm Ross to see the Commander of the Division to which they were attached, and he received from him a most eulogistic account of what they had done.[28]

Though the New Zealanders played a useful role in this offensive, their limited numbers ensured that it remained a minor one. Disaster struck one of the units involved. On 16 April the Germans seized the village of Meteren, surrounding two companies of the 2nd New Zealand Entrenching Battalion. Efforts by a Royal Engineer unit helped one of the companies to escape but the other was captured en masse, all 210 men. It was 'the largest haul of the New Zealanders taken by the Germans during the war'.[29]

On 25 March, in the midst of the great crisis then unfolding in northern France, Field Marshal Sir Douglas Haig received the following telegram from Lloyd George:

> The British Cabinet wishes to express to the Army the thanks of the Nation for its splendid defence. The whole Empire is filled with pride as it watches the heroic resistance offered by its brave troops to overwhelming odds. Knowing their steadfastness and courage whenever the honour of their country depends on their valour, the

Empire awaits with confidence the result of this struggle to defeat
the enemy's last desperate effort to trample down the free nations
of the world. At home we are prepared to do all in our power
to help in the true spirit of comradeship. The men necessary to
replace all casualties and the guns and machine guns required to
make good those lost are either now in France or already on their
way, and still further reinforcements of men and guns are ready to
be thrown into the battle.[30]

Haig, who published the telegram in a special order of the day 'for the
information of all ranks', replied to the Prime Minister the next day:

All ranks of the British Army in France have received with gratitude
the message of confidence which you have sent me on behalf of
the British cabinet. The assurance that no effort will be spared at
home to give us all assistance is of great encouragement to us.[31]

Perhaps spurred on by a guilty conscience, Lloyd George was as
good as his word. During the days of the military crisis in France he
worked tirelessly to redeem the situation (and to deflect criticism from
himself). By 7 April he had managed to persuade the War Office and the
Shipping Controller to send 150,000 men across the Channel, more than
double the normal amount. But a good proportion of these soldiers were
untrained youths: some 50,000 of them were six months or less shy of
their nineteenth birthday. On Wednesday 10 April 1918, a bill passed in
the House of Commons by a majority of 223 votes reflected just how
seriously the military situation was regarded. Under this new legislation
the military age limit was raised to fifty, the government's power to abolish
ordinary exemptions was increased and conscription was extended to
Ireland. The policy of keeping a Home Army for defence against invasion
was abandoned and within a month from 21 March, 355,000 men had
been sent across the Channel to serve in France. In addition to these
measures two divisions and sundry other units were transferred from
Palestine to France. The success of the German offensive brought home

to Lloyd George and his government just how vitally important it was to maintain the BEF on the Western Front. Starving Haig of manpower had proved costly and brought the Allies to the brink of defeat.

Measures were also taken to expedite the transport of American troops to the Western Front. This had been a painfully slow process to date, but in April and May 1918, 120,000 American troops arrived in France, making a total of 240,000 new arrivals. The soldiers were much-needed infantry and machine-gunners. In France a 'big comb-out was commenced' in the BEF.[32] Army Service Corps men were transferred to the infantry and the Royal Engineers who worked on the canal barges suffered a similar fate. The BEF's military prisons were also emptied.

As well as scouring Britain for more men, Lloyd George appealed to the countries of the Empire to do more. This request caused some resentment in New Zealand where the government felt the dominion was doing more than its share in maintaining a division to full establishment in France, along with the non-divisional units there, as well as a mounted rifle brigade in Palestine. As Defence Minister Allen wrote to General Godley in early April:

> I telegraphed you the other day asking if you could supply a rough estimate of casualties. Owing to Lloyd George's appeal for men which I believe to be made more for Australia and Canada than New Zealand, it is possible that our Reserves may be utilised for other purposes than those for which they were devised, namely to reinforce the Division. I have said New Zealand will do its duty if we keep the Division up to its full strength until the war ends.[33]

In another letter written two weeks later Allen admitted, 'You can well imagine we have been much disturbed over the recent developments and the demand for extra reinforcements.'[34] The government sought advice from Britain, who requested that New Zealand create a New Zealand tank battalion and double its number of reinforcements to 1600 per month. The New Zealand government agreed, so long as the shipping was available to take the reinforcements to France. It hoped to despatch around 3000 men by the middle of May 1918 in two reinforcement drafts. As Allen pointed out to Godley, no doubt knowing that he would pass it on to his imperial masters, 'You will realise, therefore, that New Zealand is doing all that she can do to keep the Division up to full strength.'[35] Towards the end of May, as the crisis on the Western Front eased, Allen was in a more relaxed frame of mind when he reported New Zealand's progress to Godley:

> We have been speeding up our Reinforcements and sending away as many men as we can find accommodation for in the available ships. I sincerely hope that they will arrive in time to make up all your casualties and keep the Division up to its full strength. Of course we have had our troubles in this speeding up. Men have been called into Camp earlier than they expected, and some of them resent this. However, the spirit is still sound.[36]

The improvement of the military situation in France and the end of the war curtailed the formation of a New Zealand tank battalion. On 20 July 1918 Haig noted:

> With the failure of his attacks on the 4th and 5th April the enemy's offensive on the Somme battle front ceased for the time being, and conditions rapidly began to approximate to the normal type of trench warfare, broken only by occasional local attacks on either side.[37]

The German attack on 5 April was the last by Germans in this region of the Somme. There were several occasions when a German attack did seem possible, especially on 13 and 17 April, but they proved to be false alarms. For the New Zealanders in the front line the impasse of 'filthy trench warfare' and all its routines returned. The New Zealand Division remained in the front throughout the wet months of April and May. 'The Battalion has been in the line all this week and has had a very rough spin,' wrote Second Lieutenant Roderick Toomath. 'The rain has made the trenches in a terrible condition and we have evacuated many with bad feet.'[38]

Though the Germans were less active during this phase of trench warfare, New Zealand battle casualties from shell-fire numbered about 40 per day.[39] In May, General Godley visited the New Zealand Division on the Somme and found them 'all very flourishing in "Uncle" Harper's Corps, who I think is looking after them well'.[40] But conditions in the trenches remained dreadful and one is left wondering how close Godley went to them before he made his report.

On 24 April there was a significant action south of the New Zealand position. The Germans varied their offensive programme by making a sudden strike at Amiens. In the only tank engagement of the war they managed to capture the key to the city, the town of Villers-Bretonneux. Outside the town thirteen German tanks clashed head on with an equal number of British tanks. The world's first tank battle had opened that morning when a British 'male' tank scored three hits on a German opponent forcing its crew to abandon it. Four British Whippet tanks were put out of action by German tanks later in the day. In an action that has been described as 'one of the finest feats of the war',[41] two Australian brigades and two battalions of the British 8th Division recovered Villers-Bretonneux in a daring moonlight counterattack. Fighting continued into the early hours of the next day as the Australians fought from house to house in the town. On the third anniversary of Anzac Day, the gap created by this surprise attack was closed, so that this offensive, like the last attack here on 4 April, ended in failure. For the Germans, the road to Amiens remained blocked and could not be forced open.

On 21 August 1918, the New Zealand Division, in strength the equivalent of a British Corps of three divisions, advanced from their trenches on the Somme. The New Zealand soldiers never returned to them. The tough Battle of Bapaume was ahead of them, and is featured in the next section of this book. While Bapaume did not fall as easily as expected, 'for the next eleven weeks the New Zealanders were constantly moving forward'.[42] Well trained, equally skilled in open warfare, trench warfare and the set-piece battle, the New Zealand Division was a superb fighting machine. For the remainder of the war, now thankfully only months away, it was used as one of the spearhead divisions of the British

Third Army. Field Marshal Haig visited the New Zealanders during this advance and was impressed with what he saw:

> I spent some time with General Russell and also saw his GSO 1 [the principal staff officer, Henry Maitland Wilson]. The NZ Division has come all the way from Hebuterne [more than 60 miles or 96 kilometres] to the present front on the Selle without a rest. A fine performance.[43]

But 'stopping the storm' on the Somme in March and April of 1918 was also a fine performance, as was recognised at the time. Glowing tributes poured in from generals, politicians and even governments. At the end of the war, General Harper of IV Corps wrote a farewell letter to Russell:

> The [New Zealand] Division joined the IV Corps at a critical time on the 26th March 1918, when it completely checked the enemy's advance at Beaumont-Hamel and Colincamps, and thus closed the gap between the IV and V Corps. By a brilliant stroke it drove enemy from the commanding ground at La Signy Farm and gained observation over the enemy's lines, which greatly assisted in his defeat on the 5th April 1918, when he made his last and final effort to break our front.

Harper went on to say that though the New Zealanders experienced a very tough time while holding their portion of the Somme line — a combination of bad weather and constant harassment by enemy shell-fire and raids — 'During this period I never had the least anxiety about the security of this portion of the front.'[44]

On 9 April 1918, Field Marshal Haig received a telegram from the New Zealand Governor, Lord Liverpool, expressing the nation's 'most intense admiration for the heroism of our soldiers and the utmost confidence in the officers and men of the British Forces, as well as the Forces of our Allies'. New Zealand was 'heart and soul with Britain' and 'nothing will be left undone to support our fighting men and assist in bringing about the deserved victory and permanent peace we all earnestly desire'. Replying the next day, Haig said the message had 'been deeply appreciated'. More than this, though, 'The Empire is proud of the part which New Zealand is playing in this war, and no troops could have fought more gallantly than the New Zealand Division.'[45] There is little reason to question the sincerity of Haig's reply. More than a year after the event the New Zealand Division was still receiving accolades for its performance on the Somme in 1918. In the War Ministry of the Republic of France on 28 November 1919, Major General Sir Andrew Russell's name was recorded in Army Orders with the following explanation:

> Has led to countless victories a splendid Division whose exploits have not been equalled and whose reputation was such that on the arrival of the Division on the Somme Battle Field during the critical days of March, 1918, the departure of the inhabitants was stopped immediately.
>
> The Division covered itself with fresh glory during the battles of the Ancre a la Sambre, at Puisieux au Mont, Bapaume, Crevecoeur, and Le Quesnoy.[46]

It is somewhat ironic that Russell was named by the French, because the only people critical of the New Zealand performance on the Somme were the New Zealand commanders, especially Russell and Godley. Russell, the most outspoken critic, demanded 'something better still . . . I certainly do expect the New Zealand Infantry both in thought and action, to be at least 50 per cent quicker than the new Armies'.[47] At the beginning of April 1918, he told his father and sister in England:

> I don't know that we as a whole have done as well as we might in this first round of the battle. Some troops, of course, fought well — most did — but some want training badly — training and then more training — we all want it. You can practise in war only what you have learnt in peace. It is a grand mistake to think that the battlefield is to be the school room. It is too expensive.[48]

Russell communicated his concerns to General Godley, who duly passed them on to the New Zealand government, writing to the Minister for Defence at the end of April 1918:

> Since I last wrote you will have heard that the New Zealand Division went South, and arrived just in time to help to stem the Boche advance there . . . I hear very good accounts of what they did, and their first attempt, since the landing at Gallipoli, of what was practically open warfare, seems to have been on the whole quite successful, though naturally after all these years of trench warfare, they were not as quick as they should have been, and Russell very rightly has issued criticisms and instructions on the subject.[49]

Lieutenant Colonel S.S. Allen, one of the officers on the receiving end of Russell's criticisms, offered a defence in his short history of the 2nd Auckland Battalion:

> I suppose all the Commanding Officers were like myself, not so well used to acting quickly on our orders as we became later in the year; we had no previous experience of open warfare, and that is probably the reason for much of the delay in attacking which ensued. The 2nd Brigade were moving first, and they seemed the worst offenders.[50]

Lieutenant Colonel Allen's excuses (and his finger pointing) were unnecessary. Godley and Russell were wrong. It is no mean achievement to force march 20 to 30 miles, fight and defeat a skilled, determined enemy for eleven days without respite, in just the clothes you are wearing and in the most appalling weather. The New Zealand soldiers who fought on the Somme in 1918 performed a magnificent feat of arms, perhaps their finest of the war. They also made a crucial difference to the outcome of the battle. Their achievement deserves recognition.

Conclusion

THE DISTINGUISHED BRITISH military historian Professor Richard
Holmes believes that, after so many years, it is possible to make
balanced judgements about the First World War.[1] Such an approach is
especially needed in the case of New Zealand. The First World War is the
bloodiest conflict in which New Zealand has ever been involved. As for
the other nations of the British Empire, the losses left New Zealanders
in 'a profound state of shock that has shaped perceptions of the war
ever since'.[2] Starting with the landing at Gallipoli, those long, usually
inconclusive and costly battles of attrition seemed to have no point.
With no recent experience of total war, and fed a strict diet of imperial
rhetoric about the glories of the Empire, the New Zealanders were soon
disillusioned. The current crop of British generals did not seem to know
how to do their job, which, put simply, was to win on the battlefield.
Worse than this, they seemed to be uncaring, inept and stupid. How
else could they keep making the same terrible mistakes again and again,
resulting in the deaths of millions? And this conflict came to be trumpeted
as the 'war to end all wars'. When, twenty years later, another great
conflict erupted, it made all the deaths and sufferings of the previous
war seem futile. To lose a loved one (and sometimes more than one) was
bad enough. To feel they had died for nothing must have been almost
unbearable. Little wonder the bitterness took root and grew. But in all
this pain and anguish, which even after eighty years is still felt intensely
by the families who lost loved ones, it is easy to lose sight of what the
soldiers from this nation achieved on those distant battlefields and for
what purpose.

Though the First World War is generally accepted as a pivotal event in
New Zealand's history, the New Zealand public has not been well served
in this field by its historians. Even now, the country still does not have
an official history of the conflict. The last detailed account of the war
was Ormond Burton's *The Silent Division*, which appeared nearly seventy
years ago. Few New Zealand academic historians work on this topic,
despite its importance to the development of the nation. As a result, New

Zealand's involvement in the conflict has become, to use the words of Brian Bond, 'a no man's land in the historical landscape'.[3] The lack of a balanced assessment of New Zealand's involvement in the First World War, such as has recently occurred in Britain, Canada and Australia, only adds to the extent of the tragedy for this nation.

New Zealand's involvement in the German spring offensive of 1918 was significant for a number of reasons. In terms of military operations, there were a number of 'firsts' involved. It was the first time large numbers of New Zealand troops were moved by motor transport. It was the first time New Zealand soldiers witnessed the plight of refugees. It was the first and only time New Zealand soldiers were involved in a defensive battle on the Western Front and it was the first time that the New Zealand Division was on the receiving end of a full-scale German attack. In this Second Battle of the Somme, the New Zealanders also experienced what many believe was their heaviest artillery barrage of the war. These are important events in this country's history.

More importantly, though, in March–April 1918 the New Zealand Division played a decisive part in halting the Kaiser's battle, thereby helping prevent Germany from winning the war. As Ernst Junger wrote:

> After forty-four months of hard fighting they [the German soldiers] threw themselves upon the enemy with all the enthusiasm of August 1914. No wonder it needed a world in arms to bring such a storm-flood to a standstill.[4]

In 1918, the New Zealand Division was an important player in this 'world in arms'. The Australians also played a key role in halting the German offensive of March–April 1918, as did many of the British formations in the front line. However, at a time when well-trained, high-quality soldiers were desperately needed, the New Zealand Division, widely acclaimed as one of the best Allied divisions in France, was thrown into the thick of the action in the most dangerous sector of the line. There, between Hébuterne and Beaumont-Hamel, they brought the German advance to a standstill. It was one of the turning points of the battle and a feat of arms that could have been achieved only by the finest troops. As Charles Bean commented, 'no one who came into contact with them [the Australians] or with the New Zealanders in those dark days will deny that there was a special value in their presence.' What impressed the British soldiers and commanders about the Australians and New Zealanders was 'the abounding willingness and virility of the troops themselves, and the calibre of their officers, largely men promoted from the ranks'. Even the Germans who came up against the soldiers of the two dominions 'were aware of a special spirit in all of them'.[5] German intelligence reports confirm that they had considerable respect for the fighting qualities of the Australian and New Zealand formations. A German report captured at Hébuterne had this to say about the New Zealand Division:

> A particularly good assault Division. Its characteristics are a very strongly developed individual self-confidence or enterprise, characteristic of the colonial British, and a specially pronounced hatred of the Germans. The Division prides itself on taking few prisoners. A captured officer taken at the end of April did not hesitate to boast of this while in the prisoner's cage. It is improbable that the New Zealand Division, which is qualitatively and quantitatively much stronger than the [omitted]th Division, should have taken over only the small sector occupied by the latter.[6]

From 26 March to 5 April 1918, and later in the year, these superb soldiers from Australia and New Zealand made their presence felt wherever they were used. In modern military jargon, they had a qualitative edge — the ability to punch far above their weight.

It is a tragedy that New Zealand's role in the German spring offensive is virtually unknown in the country that produced those fine soldiers. It is hardly surprising, however, given the lack of an official history. The British official history after the war devoted the better part of two lengthy volumes to the Second Battle of the Somme. Charles Bean devoted 418 pages, half a volume of an impressive twelve-volume history, to the events of the Michael Offensive. Bean's account was widely read. It first appeared in 1937 and by 1943 was already into its tenth edition. By comparison, the semi-official New Zealand history by Stewart deals with New Zealand's involvement in the events of March–April 1918 in thirty-six pages of dense prose, and the conclusion makes no assessment of the role played by the New Zealand Division.[7] Bean devotes forty pages to the New Zealand contribution, and his assessment is much nearer the mark than Stewart's. It is no wonder that New Zealanders in general know little about the events of March–April 1918.

Most soldiers of the British Empire did not think they were fighting a futile war. The outpourings of novelists in the interwar years should not be taken as typical or as being universally accepted. Captain Cyril Falls was a decorated veteran who served for three years on the Western Front. He later became an outstanding military historian, retiring as the Chichele Professor of the History of War at Oxford University in 1953.[8] He had this to say about the values and achievements of the First World War:

> The flood of antimilitarist literature, for the greater part fiction, which poured from the presses, deriding leadership from top to bottom, treating patriotism as a vice when not as a fraud, as it were bathed in blood and rolled in mud, was astonishing. It was far from being representative but it was assuredly symptomatic of widespread disillusion. Despite many reckless and brutal deeds done in high places, this terrible war of material was for the most part directed by statesmen and conducted by commanders who, for all their faults and errors and despite the trammels of nationalist and racialist bigotry, did not altogether lose their sense of the meaning and value of civilisation, and according to their lights, warred for a future in which civilisation should not cease to flourish.[9]

Cyril Falls had made a similar point much earlier in 1922, in the preface to his first book on the war, *The History of the 36th (Ulster) Division*, the formation in which he had served for much of the war:

The picture now so often painted, representing the war as a single scene in a torture chamber, whence men emerged physical or mental wrecks, may be good anti-militarist propaganda, but it is false, because incomplete. From these experiences many men have emerged happy and strong. Many knew how to snatch some happiness even from their midst. A far greater number can see, in retrospect, that they played a part in one of the most dramatic, as well as one of the most terrible tragedies in history. That stands for something good, amid all its evil, in any man's life.[10]

Falls' opinion was shared by Cecil Malthus, a New Zealand First World War veteran and later Professor of Modern Languages at Canterbury University. Malthus also believed that the conflict had been fought for a just cause. He felt that the war was not 'just a useless, unjustifiable slaughter' but that 'all men of good will [must] be prepared to fight for justice and freedom'. According to Malthus, 'The worst casualty of this unhappy twentieth century has perhaps been the concept of honour and courage.'[11] This is indeed a tragedy. But as the eminent historians Professor Trevor Wilson and Professor Robin Prior wrote in 1995, the survival of liberal values and the system of representative government 'were not light matters, and in 1914 and the ensuing years they seemed worth fighting for'.[12]

The New Zealand Division played its part on the world stage in 'one of the most dramatic, as well as one of the most terrible tragedies in history'. The official historian of the 2nd New Zealand Division's final campaigns in North Africa in 1943 ended his account with these memorable words: 'Not for nothing had these men come ten thousand miles from their homeland in the new world to play their part in restoring a balance in the old.'[13] This line is also appropriate to describe New Zealand's efforts in the war of 1914–18. It was not for nothing that New Zealanders had come to France 'From the Uttermost Ends of the Earth'.[14]

In an earlier volume dealing with his experience on Gallipoli, Malthus had these words of wisdom about the nature of war, 'War is a tragedy, of course, that we must always hope to avoid, but like most tragedies it underlines all that is finest in the human spirit.'[15] It is true that war does bring out the best and the worst in its participants. In March and April 1918, after a long, hard march, New Zealand soldiers met the German advance head on in the valley of the Ancre River and halted it with just the weapons they were carrying. They then stayed in the front line lightly clad, lacking food and water, enduring the most appalling of living conditions while holding their portion of the line. There they resisted the renewed German attempts to break open the British front again as they tried to restore momentum to a failing offensive. During these actions in this Second Battle of the Somme, these fine New Zealand soldiers made a vital and impressive contribution to the outcome of the First World War.

Bloody Bapaume

Introduction

'Dead Lucky' to Survive

IN THE THICK early dawn mist of 21 August 1918, exactly five months to the day since the start of the German spring offensive, the New Zealand Division advanced towards the enemy positions before it. The Division was ready to play its part in the massive Allied offensive that had begun two weeks earlier. One New Zealand infantry battalion recorded the event in its War Diary:

> As we waited ready to move on a misty morning the thunder of many guns broke out in the East and we knew that the battle in which we were destined to play our part had commenced.[1]

In fact, the New Zealand Division would go on to play a key role in the remainder of this offensive, a military action that eventually ended the war. For eleven weeks the New Zealanders constantly moved forward as one of the spearhead divisions of the British Third Army. However, it is the first ten days of its advance that is the subject of this section of the book. The battle fought by the New Zealand Division during this time is the little-known Battle of Bapaume, which lasted from 21 August to 2 September 1918.

It is not surprising this battle is poorly recognised, since even its name is the subject of debate. After the war the British Battles Nomenclature Committee, 'its logic not always clearly comprehensible to veterans', according to Richard Holmes,[2] designated this period of fighting by the Third Army as the Battle of Albert (21–29 August) and the Second Battle of Bapaume (31 August–3 September). However, in his Despatches, Field Marshal Haig called it the Battle of Bapaume (21 August–1 September) and this is the name by which New Zealand veterans know it.[3] For these reasons, New Zealand military historians use the term Battle of Bapaume, although in this use we extend Haig's dates by two days.

Unfortunately, the Battle of Bapaume is virtually ignored in New Zealand's military history; there are several reasons why this is the case. First, it appears that Gallipoli casts a very long shadow over New Zealand's military history of the First World War. As a result, the New Zealand public lacks knowledge about the military experiences of its soldiers on the Western Front and in Sinai–Palestine. Second, in 1918 the New Zealand Division fought as part of the Third Army, then the largest of the five British Armies on the Western Front. As two prominent military historians in the United Kingdom have suggested, study of this army on the Western Front has been much neglected. They note that during the great advance of 1918 the Third Army had 'a key role in the defeat of Germany, a role for which neither [General Sir Julian Byng, General Officer Commanding Third Army] nor his troops have — as yet — received sufficient recognition.'[4] The New Zealand Division, then, is not the only formation to have its role in defeating Germany during the final advance neglected. Third, on 31 August 1918 the 2nd Australian Division carried out a magnificent feat of arms at Mont-St-Quentin, north of the Somme River, and its success caught both sides by surprise. This action, in which seven Australian soldiers won Victoria Crosses, has been described by Fourth Army commander General Sir Henry Rawlinson as 'the finest single feat of the war'.[5] Little wonder that this impressive military action stole the show and overshadowed the achievements of other formations on the Western Front at that time.

However, the Battle of Bapaume deserves to be more widely known. It is the only battle in New Zealand's history in which three of its soldiers were awarded the Victoria Cross for their heroic actions. The Battle of Bapaume was the first time in history that New Zealand soldiers received supplies dropped from the air and it was also the first time that they faced a counterattack by German tanks. More importantly, though, the Battle of Bapaume saw some of the toughest fighting of the war. According to the New Zealand medical historian A.D. Carbery, the Battle of Bapaume was crucial, because it:

was the first great trial of strength of the rallied British Armies and is stated to have been the most anxious, critical and hard fighting battle in the whole war.[6]

Certainly those New Zealand veterans who went through the ordeal of this battle never doubted its significance. Reflecting on the battle some eighty years later Oscar Reston, a runner in the 2nd Canterbury Battalion, recalled:

> We had him on the run. The last heavy go we had was Bapaume and they sent us over with the tanks which were in their infancy stage and the last I saw of the tanks was one stuck in a trench. It couldn't get out. But we had fifty per cent casualties in two hours there at Bapaume. He was just sitting with the machine guns there and we were walking against him and anyone who got through was dead lucky.[7]

Claude Wysocki, a corporal in the 2nd Battalion New Zealand Rifle Brigade (known colloquially as the 2nd Rifles), told a similar story:

> I was there. We went in there with a complete unit of 125 and we came out with less than 50; less than half that number. Bapaume — that was the bloodiest of the lot that one. Bapaume, oh yes that was dirty.[8]

The combat operations of the Battle of Bapaume can be divided into three distinct phases. They were:
- Phase 1 — the advance to the Ancre River, which took place between 21 and 23 August. Only isolated units, primarily from the Rifle Brigade, were involved in this opening phase of the battle. Fighting was sporadic, except around one strongpoint, which changed hands several times.
- Phase 2 — the envelopment of the town of Bapaume and its eventual capture, which occurred between 24 and 29 August. Two-thirds

of the Division were involved in the various assaults on the town. Fighting was heavy — several New Zealand attacks on the town were repulsed and casualties were high.

- Phase 3 — the advance to the line of Riencourt-lès-Bapaume–Bancourt–Frémicourt and the capture of the high ground beyond these villages, which occurred between 29 August and 2 September. During this phase isolated New Zealand units had to face a sizeable German counterattack on 31 August, when they were challenged by infantry supported by tanks.

As this overview shows, Bapaume was a hard fought battle for the New Zealand Division. It was definitely not the walkover many senior officers in the British High Command and even some senior New Zealand officers believed it would be. Nor was the New Zealand Division the well-oiled, well-drilled, perfect fighting formation of which some historians have written.[9] As this section of the book will illustrate, commanders made serious mistakes, orders were not always clear and some units definitely showed signs that they were war weary. These factors combined to make the battle that much harder for the New Zealand soldiers to win.

It was inevitable that such fighting on the Western Front would produce high casualties and it is little wonder that veterans later labelled the battle 'Bloody Bapaume'. However, as Oscar Reston noted, this battle occurred at a time when the Germans were 'on the run' on the Western Front. It was on the portion of the front held by the British Expeditionary Force (BEF) that the German Army, the mightiest military machine the world had seen, was defeated in the First World War and the New Zealand Division was in the thick of the action from 21 August 1918 on. The fighting was tough and costly, but in the end it was decisive. With the ninetieth anniversary of this battle rapidly approaching it is timely to revisit this important battle. Here for the first time is the story of 'Bloody Bapaume', told as much as possible in the words of those who were there.

Chapter 1

The Military Background

F OR THE BRITISH Expeditionary Force (BEF), Bapaume was much more than an important junction town in the Picardy region of the Somme. It was a symbol of their inability to drive back the German forces and progress the war to their own satisfaction. The town had been the main objective of the BEF on 1 July 1916, the opening day of the Somme battle. When that conflict drew to a close five months and hundreds of thousands of casualties later, Bapaume was still some 4 miles behind the German lines. However, in early 1917 this prize fell unexpectedly into the BEF's hands.

In March 1917 the Germans withdrew to new fortified defensive positions which they called the Siegfried Stellung, but which the BEF referred to as the Hindenburg Line. The Germans aimed to shorten their overall frontage, which would not only free up thirteen divisions for service elsewhere, but enable them to meet the Allies on defensive ground of their choosing. As the Germans withdrew to the Hindenburg Line they systematically destroyed buildings, roads, bridges, wells, trees, crops, furniture and anything that could possibly be of use to the Allies. Their activities ruined the lives of the French people amongst whom the German troops had lived for over two years, and the sheer scale and deliberateness of the destruction shocked men who thought they were inured to the horrors of war. Carefully placed booby traps and well-concealed rearguard actions resulted in a number of casualties amongst the British and French who were following the withdrawal.

The Germans were fully conscious of their actions. They named the operation Alberich, after the spiteful dwarf who appears in the classic work of mythology and history *The Nibelungen Saga*. In the middle of one wrecked town, a German soldier left a sign that stated: 'Don't be angry: Only wonder'.[1] Sir Philip Gibbs penned this vivid description of the scorched landscape left to the Allies:

> In the retreat the enemy laid waste to the country behind him . . . It was like wandering through a plague-stricken land abandoned after some fiendish orgy, of men drunk with the spirit of destruction. Every cottage in villages for miles around had been gutted by explosion. Every church in those villages had been blown up. The orchards had been cut down and some of the graves ransacked for their lead. There had been no mercy for historic little towns like Bapaume and Péronne, and in Bapaume the one building that stood when we entered — the square tower of the Town Hall — was hurled up a week later when a slow fuse burnt to its end, and only a hole in the ground shows where it had been.[2]

The Germans did not completely abandon the region, however. In the countryside in front of Bapaume they left behind several rearguards and defended strongpoints. One was at Loupart Wood, which the Germans had riddled with machine-gun nests and deep dugouts. When the BEF arrived here they turned their heavy artillery on the small wood, causing massive devastation. Gibbs, who counted more than seven hundred dead German soldiers in the wood, recalled:

> The place was a shambles of German troops . . . All this garrison . . . [had been] cut to pieces before or after death. Their bodies or their fragments lay in every shape and shapelessness of death, in puddles of broken trenches or on the edge of deep ponds in shell craters.[3]

On 17 March 1917, St Patrick's Day, Australian troops entered Bapaume, having engaged a company of German machine-gunners in a stiff fight. Though he described Bapaume as 'broken and burnt', Gibbs was struck by the significance of the occasion:

> I don't know how much this will mean to people at home, to whom

the town is just a name, familiar only because of its repetition in despatches. To us out here it means enormous things — above all, the completion or result of a great series of battles, in which many of our best gave their lives so that our troops could attain the ridge across which they went today, and hold the town which is the gateway to the plains beyond.[4]

Gibbs did not linger in Bapaume, as it was being heavily shelled by the Germans. His comments on leaving Bapaume are apposite:

I struck across country eastwards to see the promised land, and on the way to the near ridge turned and stared back at Bapaume in the glow of the sunset. Ours at last![5]

Imagine the consternation, then, in the United Kingdom and throughout the BEF when just on a year later Bapaume changed hands for the third time in the war. As covered in the previous section, the Germans launched their spring attack, the Michael Offensive, on 21 March 1918, wiping out all the gains won by the Allies during the battles of Ypres and the Somme. They also reclaimed all the land they had withdrawn from the previous year. It was the darkest of times for the Allies. One young nursing volunteer, Vera Brittain, caught the desperate mood:

I shall never forget the crushing tension of those extreme days. Nothing had ever quite equalled them before — not the Somme, not Arras, not Passchendaele — for into our minds had crept for the first time the secret, incredible fear that we might lose the War . . . One after another, Péronne, Bapaume, Beaumont Hamel were gone, and on March 27th Albert was taken. Even Paris, we learnt, had been shelled by a long-range gun from seventy-five miles away.[6]

The German spring offensive was initially spectacularly successful and shook the Allied military establishment to its core. It was the nearest the

Germans came to victory on the Western Front and as Richard Holmes commented, 'recent research suggests that had Ludendorff clearly identified that the offensive's most valuable objectives were railheads (Amiens in the south and Hazebrouck in the north) the Germans might indeed have broken the Allies on the Western Front'.[7] As it was, the Allies were able to sustain defensive action against the initial (and greatest) attack, and by 5 April 1918 the Allied defensive lines were still intact, albeit a considerable distance further west than they had been before. Subsequent German offensives to the north and south failed to achieve anything like the success obtained on 21 March 1918, and soon petered out. By the middle of July 1918, the German offensives on the Western Front had run their course and the attackers were 'thrown back on the defensive' as the initiative passed back to the Allies.[8] The failure of these offensives cost the German Army more than the initiative, though; they cost it almost a million of its best soldiers, the very backbone of the force.

Just how badly damaged the German Army was as a result of these failed actions was not fully revealed until the start of the August offensive. Then it became obvious to all that 'the morale of the Germans was breaking down rapidly'.[9] The following extracts from a German officer's diary, written in July 1918, reveal the true state of feeling within the force. On 21 July, while his company was facing the New Zealand Division in Rossignol Wood, the officer recorded: 'We have lost our best men and what we have left are such that we cannot rely on them. It makes a man sick to see the good men sinking fast.' Two days later came another bitter complaint: 'Nobody has been up here to look at the situation. The men are done to death. I am relieving them every night to allow them a little sleep.' The German officer was killed the next day.[10]

This is not to imply that the German Army was incapable of further fighting. While large-scale offensive operations were probably beyond it after July 1918, the army was still capable of conducting stubborn defensive operations, which it did until the end of the war. The German Army also modified its tactics to compensate for this loss in quality. It held positions in depth, relying on limited artillery assets and numerous machine-gun nests to wreak damage on the attackers. According to author

John Terraine, the nine actions of the BEF during the last hundred days of the war were

> bitterly contested. If the old steadfastness of the German infantry was now a thing of the past, the fighting spirit of some of their specialised formations remained redoubtable. Machine gunners in particular, and artillery, conducted stubborn rear-guard actions.[11]

However, it was clear that the German Army had suffered a significant decline in quality. If an attack was pressed with vigour and the machine-gun nests subdued, rather than fight it out the German infantry soldiers would follow two negative courses of action. They would either surrender or withdraw to a new defensive position built around more machine-gun posts. Counterattacks, when they came, were usually feeble and much too late. They were definitely not pressed with the determination and skill that German soldiers had shown in 1916 and 1917.

The German cause was not helped by the state of the commander directing its military operations on the Western Front. As John Terraine noted, from mid July 1918 'one side was directed by a man whose nerve and judgement were seriously impaired — Ludendorff — while the other was directed by two men whose confidence was growing day by day, and whose touch was becoming ever more sure — Foch and Haig.'[12]

Ludendorff, out of touch with reality and still confident of success, was unaware of the extent to which his offensives of 1918 had damaged the German Army. On 4 August 1918, he issued the following directive:

> I am under the impression that, in many quarters, the possibility of an enemy offensive is viewed with a certain degree of apprehension. There is nothing to justify this apprehension provided our troops are vigilant and do their duty . . . At the present moment we occupy everywhere positions which have been very strongly fortified, and we have, I am convinced, effected a judicious organisation in depth of the infantry and artillery. Henceforth we can await every hostile attack with the greater confidence. As I have already explained, we

should wish for nothing better than to see the enemy launch an offensive, which can but hasten the disintegration of his forces.[13]

Ludendorff had only a little while longer to wait before his wish was realised.

Compared with the Germans, in July 1918 the Allies were in much better shape. Alarmed by the events of March 1918 the British leaders had steadily reinforced their armies, although many of these new soldiers were barely trained youths of nineteen and twenty. Nonetheless, the BEF had never been stronger in artillery and tanks, and its effective strength was some fifty-two divisions. The movement of troops across the Atlantic had been greatly increased and an American Army was soon to take to the field.[14] In addition, the Allies finally had a Commander-in-Chief in France, Marshal Ferdinand Foch, who was to control the strategic direction of Allied military operations on the Western Front. Foch's role was to coordinate the efforts of all the armies in France to obtain the best results on the battlefield. While Foch lacked the full authority of a Commander-in-Chief equivalent to that given to General Dwight Eisenhower in the Second World War, his role in the forthcoming offensive was pivotal to its success.

On 24 July 1918, Foch called a conference of Allied commanders to plan their offensive operations. Unaware of the declining morale of the German Army, Foch proposed offensives that were both localised and limited in their objectives. He aimed to reduce the salients Ludendorff's recent offensives had created and to free the strategic railways of Paris–Amiens and Paris–Nancy from German interference. As Peter Simkins has commented: 'Foch's plan was, in some ways, surprisingly unambitious for a soldier with his innate attacking spirit.'[15] Yet this planning marked an important transition: the Allies were moving from a period of active defence to one of vigorous offensive action. It was a crucial change.

In mid 1918 the New Zealand Division was the strongest infantry division on the Western Front. There were two reasons for this. First, it had not undergone the restructuring forced on most of the formations of the BEF in February 1918, which reduced the number of infantry battalions in a division from twelve to nine. The armies of the various Dominions could not be forced to make these cuts, although they were encouraged to do so. The Canadian and New Zealand forces kept their divisions at twelve infantry battalions strong for the duration of the war. Second, the New Zealand army had an effective and efficient method of supplying reinforcements to the division in France. This included many trained and experienced soldiers and NCOs from the three entrenching battalions left over when the 4th New Zealand Infantry Brigade had been disbanded in February 1918. Unlike all other divisions in the BEF on the Western Front, the New Zealand Division was nearly always kept at full strength, which contributed significantly to its operational effectiveness. This was acknowledged by the New Zealand Expeditionary Force commander, Lieutenant General Sir Alexander Godley, in a letter to the New Zealand Minster for Defence in early August 1918:

> You will know of course that at present the Division is extremely well off for reinforcements. It has practically had no fighting since Passchendaele last October, and is therefore one of the divisions which is strongest and fittest in every way.[16]

The numerical supremacy of the New Zealand Division is revealed in the numbers within the various divisions after the Battle of Bapaume. In September 1918 most BEF infantry divisions numbered between 7000 and 8000 men; Australian divisions had fewer than this; the Canadians averaged around 10,000. In contrast, the New Zealand Division numbered 12,243 men, with a further 15,000 reinforcements available in the United Kingdom.[17]

The New Zealand Division was in the front line on the Somme from April through to July 1918. It was always active, patrolling no-man's-land at night, raiding the German front-line positions whenever the opportunity presented itself and establishing a dominance over the enemy in its sector of the front. It regularly rotated battalions through the front line with those behind the lines undertaking intensive combined arms training. During this time large numbers of soldiers from the United States of America were attached to the Division so that they could gain knowledge and experience of conditions in the front line. Lieutenant Leslie Averill of 4th Battalion, New Zealand Rifle Brigade (4th Rifles) recalled of these men:

> On one of our periods in the line there were small sections of United States Army troops attached to each platoon so that some experience of trench warfare could be obtained. They were very friendly and efficient soldiers and were on good terms with our own troops. The American troops attached to my platoon were under my command for five days in the front-line trenches and I was very glad to get them all safely out when we were relieved.[18]

Captain Lindsay Inglis of the Otago Machine Gun Company was not so fortunate with his American guests. He wrote to his fiancée:

> We have for some time past been having Americans attached to us all the time for training in the line and very good troops they seem. But it makes one time very full. For a month past I have hardly had a moment to myself between doing my own work and instructing and entertaining these Yanks in addition. One officer we had up for training was killed by a shell . . . We have made a lot of fast friends among them and the diggers and the Yanks are much more friendly than ever the Tommies and the diggers will be. They seem in many ways to be more like ourselves.[19]

These were not just infantry soldiers, either. A company of US soldiers from 2nd Battalion, 305th Regiment was attached to the New Zealand Field Companies of the engineers and on 11 August 1918, an officer and a hundred and fifty men of the United States Army Pioneers were attached to the Maori Pioneer Battalion. The Battalion's history records that the US soldiers were 'newly landed and were very keen' and that they 'got on very well with the Maoris'.[20] These sappers and pioneers arrived at a particularly busy time, as most of August was spent repairing roads or building new ones so that guns and supplies could move forward. (This backbreaking work continued even after the offensive for Bapaume started on 21 August.) At the end of July five officers and a hundred and fourteen other ranks from 313th and 317th Machine Gun Battalions joined the New Zealand Machine Gun Battalion to experience conditions in the front line. They must have been impressed with what they found, as on 4 August the entire US 313th Machine Gun Battalion was attached to this specialist New Zealand battalion.

In July 1918, the New Zealand Division carried out an impressive minor operation that captured Rossiginol Wood. As a result, one of the unit histories commented that the New Zealand infantry were now at their peak and that 'by this time the Divisional infantry had reached such a pitch of confidence and aggressive enthusiasm that there could be but one result to their efforts.'[21] Similarly, many New Zealand accounts quote a German intelligence summary captured in July 1918 that assessed the New Zealand Division as:

> A particularly good assault Division. Its characteristics are a very strongly developed individual self-confidence or enterprise typical of the colonial Englishman, and a specially pronounced hatred of the Germans.[22]

Was the New Zealand Division really that good? Was it really the best infantry division on the Western Front, as some writers have argued?[23] Did it really have 'a staying power to match their tactical standards which their Australian counterparts could not equal and the Canadians could only match'?[24] There is no doubt that in 1918 the New Zealand Division was a battle-hardened, experienced and capable infantry division. The quality of its soldiers and junior officers was probably unsurpassed on the Western Front. It was, though, as the battle for Bapaume would reveal, far from perfect and prior to the start of the offensive some signs of its vulnerability were already apparent.

The first warning sign was the health of Major General Sir Andrew Russell, the Division's commander. Russell, an exceptionally talented commander and a perfectionist, had commanded the Division since its formation in March 1916. In the last year of the war this hard taskmaster was far from well. He had broken his foot in June 1918 after being thrown from a horse and each winter 'suffered from increasingly protracted bouts of sickness.'[25] In fact, Russell was nearing exhaustion and on the verge of a physical collapse. This was certainly the opinion of the NZEF commander, Lieutenant General Sir Alexander Godley. In a letter to Sir James Allen, Godley expressed concern about Russell's health and suggested that he might need to be replaced:

> I am afraid Russell is rather seedy, and cannot walk and I am rather disturbed by it, as it is not right for the Division to go on for so long with him only half fit, and I am inclined to think that the only possible solution might be for him to go to England and command the whole of the N.Z.E.F. from there and let [Major General Sir Edward] Chaytor come to command the Division.[26]

But events in 1918 moved too quickly for the replacement of Russell as divisional commander and Chaytor never got his opportunity. Russell suffered from a breakdown after the war and needed two years of rest and quiet activity before his health fully recovered. In the Battle of Bapaume it could certainly not be stated that Russell was at his best, and this became more and more evident as the conflict unfolded.

The second cause for concern was the high turnover of senior officers within the Division, especially in the last year of the war. This was particularly so prior to the Battle of Bapaume, when most of the senior officers of the Division were newly appointed and fighting their first major action in their new commands. By April 1918 all the original New Zealand brigadiers had gone. Brigadiers C.H.J. Brown and F.E. Johnston had been killed in 1917, while Brigadier William Braithwaite, who many soldiers regarded as the best of the brigade commanders, had been sent back to the United Kingdom after the Passchendaele debacle, exhausted, broken and unfit for active service. Brigadier H.T. 'Bully' Fulton, the last of the original brigade commanders, had been killed in March 1918 when his headquarters received a direct hit from a German heavy gun. Newly appointed in April 1918 were Brigadiers Herbert Hart and R. Young, both of whom had been majors in the Territorial Force before the war, and C.W. Melvill 'who had been a captain in the New Zealand Staff Corps on his first posting to the NZEF in November 1915.'[27] Of the new brigadiers, only Hart had commanded a brigade in a major action before.

The situation was similar at the battalion level. According to Christopher Pugsley, 'The attrition rate for commanding officers was equally high, and it was the generation of subalterns and, in some cases sergeants, of 1914 who were the battalion commanders of 1918.'[28] The battalion commanders of the twelve infantry battalions during the battle for Bapaume and their month of appointment are outlined in the table below.

Unit	Commanding Officer	Date Appointed
1st Auckland	R.C. Allen	February 1917
2nd Auckland	S.S. Allen (until 24 August) W.C. Sinel*	February 1917
1st Wellington	W.F. Narbey* (until 24 August) F.K. Turnbull*	August 1918
2nd Wellington	J.L. Short	January 1918
1st Canterbury	R.A. Row	January 1918
2nd Canterbury	N.R. Wilson*	August 1918
1st Otago	A.B. Charters	March 1916
2nd Otago	W.S. Pennycook (until 24 August) W.G.A. Bishop*	July 1918
1st Rifles	N.F. Shepherd*	23 May 1918
2nd Rifles	J. Murphy*	August 1918
3rd Rifles	P.H. Bell	27 March 1918
4th Rifles	R.StJ. Beere	December 1917

Infantry battalions and their commanding officers during the Battle of Bapaume.
*Temporary appointments[29]

Christopher Pugsley describes these new appointments as a positive development in maintaining the tactical efficiency of the Division.[30] It is true that these appointments were examples of talent rising to the top and all those involved had experience of leading soldiers in the trenches at lower levels of command. However, there is also a negative factor to consider. There is no getting around the fact that commanding an infantry battalion on operations is no easy task and most of these senior officers were new to their current job. In large military organisations such as an infantry battalion or brigade, better performance, more often than not, comes with experience. In August 1918 most of the New Zealand battalion commanders did not have this experience.

The third cause for concern was the large pool of reinforcements absorbed by the Division prior to the Bapaume offensive. The losses incurred during the German Michael Offensive, natural attrition on the Western Front, plus provision for sickness and leave meant that thousands of soldiers were brought in as reinforcements. As mentioned above, the New Zealand Division was fortunate in that during the course of the war it could draw on a pool of well-trained, fit young men. These men, having endured months at sea and the brutal training establishments of Sling Camp in the United Kingdom and Etaples in France, were usually very eager to join the various units of the New Zealand Division. While reinforcements were vital to the lifeblood of any military formation during the First World War, they did bring problems. As Richard Holmes noted: 'Success [on the battlefield] depended very much on the ability of the division's cadre to convert a flood of reinforcements into useful soldiers.'[31] However, until they had participated in their first military action reinforcements were treated as outsiders by existing members of the unit, who held considerable suspicion about their military worth. At the same time, if they were going to survive, reinforcements needed to be shown the way of life at the front by more experienced hands. Yet in 1918 a lot of the old hands were reluctant to do this, as it involved forming a bond and often a friendship with the 'new chums'. New soldiers were the troops most likely to be killed in action and few old hands wanted to go through the pain of losing friends all over again. Often the reinforcements were left to their own devices, which had serious consequences for them and those around them.

Finally, it should not be overlooked that by 1918 many 'old hands' had experienced more than three years of war and were suffering for it. Even the very best soldiers eventually become war weary and their efficiency rapidly declines. These men, if not rested from active military duty, become dangerous to themselves and others nearby. In Ormond Burton's unpublished manuscript there is a hint that in 1918 many of the original Main Body men and Gallipoli veterans were in a poor state. They were burnt out. Burton, a Gallipoli veteran himself, wrote:

> Many of us were now very old soldiers. No man can take it for ever. Keep tension on strongly enough and long enough and almost every man in time will deteriorate. The signs were often very clear — a man would drink more heavily, smoke more heavily. Smoking was a surer indication. A cigarette to steady the nerves, then two, then three, then the chain effect. All the time the nicotine that apparently soothed was steadily undermining the nervous system until another brave man had to toss it in and go back. Dick Travis himself said that he felt the effect of this developing strain. I would say the same. I can look back to the Somme and Messines and feel that not too much was wrong but after that I think mistakes were more common.[32]

While the New Zealand Division of 1918 was battle hardened and experienced, this had come at a price that should not just be measured in the heavy casualties it had suffered along the way. In mid 1918 many of its old soldiers, and the Division as a whole, were paying for their success and fortitude.

Chapter 2

Opening Moves: 8–21 August 1918

EARLY IN JULY 1918 a small military action undertaken by the 4th Australian Division had revealed much about the state of the German Army in France. In addition, it indicated the way that future offensive operations should be carried out. This was the 4 July operation undertaken to recapture the fortified village of Hamel. The Australians, after meticulous planning and taking advantage of all the military assets at their disposal, captured all their set objectives in just over an hour and a half, some three minutes behind schedule. It was an impressive feat of arms and one that attracted considerable attention. At the end of July, the Fourth Army staff, of which the Australian Corps was a part, published a study of the battle and distributed it throughout the British Expeditionary Force (BEF). The reasons given for the Australian success were: the painstaking staff work in planning the operation; the secrecy preceding the attack, which had enabled a tactical surprise to be obtained; the performance of the Australian and US troops involved; and, 'perhaps most importantly', the excellent cooperation achieved between machine-gunners, artillery, tanks, the RAF and infantry.[1] Important lessons were learned (or relearned in some cases) from this attack and in August 1918, General Rawlinson, the Fourth Army commander, was determined to apply these lessons to a much larger offensive than that at Hamel. This offensive — the battle of Amiens — preceded the Battle of Bapaume and would be a turning point on the Western Front. For the first time in the war, all five Australian Divisions would carry out an attack in a single corps. The four divisions of the Canadian Corps would attack on the Australians' right flank and there would be in excess of five hundred tanks in support. The Australian Corps Commander, Lieutenant General Sir John Monash, issued a Special Order, which was read to Australian troops.

The battle 'will be one of the most memorable of the whole war; we shall inflict blows upon the enemy which will make him stagger, which will bring the end appreciably nearer.'[2]

On the eve of the attack, 7 August 1918, C.E. Montague, a gifted author and former lead writer of the *Manchester Guardian*, who had dyed his greying hair black in 1914 so as ensure his enlistment,[3] lay on his back gazing at the stars. After years of war his thoughts were a mixture of optimism and doubt:

> Could it be coming at last, I thought as I went to sleep — the battle unlike other battles? . . . Was it to be only Loos and the Somme and Arras and Flanders and Cambrai all over again?[4]

The next day, 8 August 1918, would provide the answer to Montague's question. In the course of the war, it would be the most critical day of fighting on the Western Front.

Preparations for the attack on 8 August, the opening day of the battle of Amiens, have been described as being 'meticulous and imaginative'.[5] The main thrust of this planning involved the assembly of three key formations which, if detected by the Germans, would have revealed that an attack was imminent. These formations were the Canadian Corps, the Australian Corps and 'the largest number of tanks to be assembled for one battle during the whole war.'[6]

The Canadian Corps, four divisions strong, had not been used since the German spring offensive in March and so was relatively fresh. It was also at full strength. However, before they could participate the Canadians had to be moved from north of the Somme (near Arras), where they formed part of the First Army. Relocating them south to the Fourth Army was 'a strategic problem of the utmost importance' — if the Germans detected the move they would surely realise an attack was planned.[7] In order to get them to the Somme undetected an elaborate plan was hatched that involved the use of dummy radio signals. While the bulk of the Canadian Corps moved south, two of their battalions and some signal units moved north into the Second Army area in Flanders opposite Kemmel Hill, which had been lost on 25 April. Once there the Canadian units started a flow of traffic, aiming to make the enemy believe they were building up for an attack. The deception was only partially successful as the southbound movement of two of the Canadian divisions was detected by the Germans, but they were unable to pinpoint their intended destination. As the Canadian official history recorded: 'If the enemy was not fully deceived, at least he was confused.'[8] The success of the deception is indicated by the fact that at the headquarters of German Army Group, commanded by Prince Rupprecht, they had the Canadians plotted on their situation map on 8 August as still being around Arras.[9] Certainly the Australians were shocked when they learned who their new neighbours were.

The Australians had extended their front southward to screen the arrival of the Canadians, a move that went undetected by the Germans, as did the large concentration of tanks on the Fourth Army Front. There was to be no preliminary artillery barrage for this attack. Instead, the artillery would open fire as the attack commenced and the advancing infantry would be supported by three hundred and forty-two heavy Mark V tanks, seventy-two medium Mark A tanks (the Whippets) and a hundred and twenty supply tanks, in effect armoured freighters, carrying water, food, ammunition and other vital supplies.

There were two reasons for the German failure to detect this massive build-up of force. One was the impressive Allied air cover that prevented German planes carrying out any sort of reconnaisance. Over the Fourth Army front some 800 aircraft of the RAF patrolled ceaselessly, while the French First Army was protected by 1404 aircraft from the French air force.[10] The second reason was the strict security that prevailed on the ground. Throughout the Fourth Army area signs everywhere warned soldiers to 'KEEP YOUR MOUTH SHUT' and the same message was also posted into every soldier's pay book. Conducting reconnaissance over the German lines was severely restricted and no troops or transport were allowed to march towards the front in daylight, all necessary movement being carried out at night. By these means the Fourth Army achieved that most elusive of military goals — an attack that came as a complete surprise to the enemy.

At 3 a.m. on 8 August a thick ground mist began to form in the river valleys of the Somme district. The situation was reminiscent of the German attack on 21 March that year, when mist had concealed the attackers and hampered the defenders. At 4.20 a.m. the British artillery barrage of two thousand guns opened up on the German positions and the tanks and infantry set off. The dominance that the BEF artillery established in this battle was critical to its success. Not only did the artillery fire hundreds of thousands of shells but their accuracy was remarkable. During the course of the battle the BEF gunners, using sound ranging and flash spotting techniques, located all but twenty-six of the five hundred and thirty German guns in the sector. Those located were effectively destroyed with counter-battery fire.[11] With this level of support progress was good and only on the British III Corps sector was the advance held up. By 7 a.m. the Australians were at their first objective and by 10.30 a.m. they were at the second, all their objectives taken, except on the exposed flanks. By 11 a.m. the Canadians were alongside of the Australians, all of their objectives taken except on their exposed right flank. That would be captured by the end of the night. By 1.30 p.m. the main fighting for these two élite corps was over. The British III Corps, however, still had some hard fighting ahead of them to reach their final objective. Most of the Australian casualties had been suffered on their open left flank where III Corps had failed to get forward. In the end, III Corps failed to reach its objective and on 9 August Lieutenant General Monash formed a composite division of Australian and American troops to take over its portion of the front.

For the rest of the units involved, the attack of 8 August was a spectacular success, a complete victory. It has been described as 'a watershed battle, the turning point of the war.'[12] Across a front of 12 miles an advance of some 8 miles had been made, the largest penetration ever in a single day on the Western Front. As well as gaining all its objectives, the Canadian Corps captured 114 officers, 4919 other ranks, 161 guns and a mass of war materiel. Its casualties numbered about 3500. The Australian successes were even more spectacular. They had carried out all their objectives in just half a day's fighting, except on the flanks where neither III Corps nor the Canadians had kept pace with them. They had captured 183 officers, 7742 other ranks and 173 guns. Australian casualties numbered about a thousand.[13] In addition, the French First Army, fighting under command of the BEF, had captured more than 11,000 German prisoners. Field Marshal Haig was surprised but elated by this success. He wrote in his diary that the situation had developed 'more favourably for us than I, optimist though I am, had dared even to hope'.[14]

The Germans were well aware of the extent of their defeat. A German official monograph later recorded:

> As the sun set on the 8th August on the battlefield the greatest
> defeat which the German Army had suffered since the beginning
> of the War was an accomplished fact.[15]

Losses in the German Second Army were estimated at between 650 and 700 officers and 26,000 to 27,000 other ranks, plus 400 guns. Significantly, two-thirds of the casualties were prisoners of war, the first of the mass surrenders experienced by the German Army on the Western Front.

If Haig was elated with this success, Ludendorff was driven to despair. He referred to 8 August 1918 as 'the black day of the German Army in the history of this war.' He later recalled it as 'the worst experience that I had to go through' except for the events of 15 September on the Bulgarian Front.[16] The current situation, he said, was 'a very gloomy one'. The attack had 'completely broken' six or seven divisions that had been battle-worthy. According to Ludendorff:

> The situation was uncommonly serious. If the enemy continued
> to attack with even ordinary vigour, we should no longer be able
> to maintain ourselves west of the Somme.[17]

But in the days that followed Ludendorff was given a brief respite.

The day of 9 August was one of disappointment for the Allies as the offensive followed the same pattern of previous attacks on the Western Front and started to lose momentum. There was an initial break-in, but there was no breakthrough. And 9 August was the critical day. That morning there was a huge gap in front of the Australians and Canadians, and German reserves had not arrived to shore up the defences. The Allies had the chance to strike a decisive blow, but they let it slip through their fingers. The Canadian Corps began their advance late in the morning and did not reach their first objective. The Australians started earlier and ran into heavy German opposition. Australian infantry battalions suffered heavy casualties, their situation made worse by the lack of flank protection, lack of coordination, and poor communications. Dwindling tank support further aggravated matters. Only 145 operational tanks were left from the more than 500 that had been available the previous day. To make matters worse, the Germans were reinforced by seven divisions during the day and had another seven on the way. Ludendorff described the attack on 9 August as being 'fortunately for us, not pressed with sufficient vigour' with its results 'not as bad as expected'.[18] Even so, by the end of the day another 3 miles of ground had been wrenched from the enemy and more than 15,000 prisoners taken. Nonetheless, 9 August was described by Britain's official historian as 'a day of wasted opportunities'[19] and John Terraine summed up the day's progress as 'generally disappointing'.[20] Over the next three days the Allies' disappointment continued to grow.

Fourth Army, by this time supported by only eighty-five serviceable tanks, resumed the advance on 10 August. Results were again 'disappointing', the Canadians making an advance of a little over 2 miles on their front. The German reinforcements that arrived on 9 August were countered on the British front by fourteen additional divisions, and a further ten were deployed on the French front. This left the BEF with only one fresh division available. Above the battlefield, some 480 single-seater fighters, 70 per cent of the RAF fighter strength on the Western Front, provided air cover. Yet it was all too late: German resistance in front of the Fourth Army stiffened. The British official historian is surprisingly critical of the BEF commanders for allowing the offensive to stall. By 10 August:

It was obvious that the offensive was petering out on the whole front, like so many others before it, as the initial success had not been exploited with the necessary rapidity and daring. General Rawlinson pushed the advance with caution from one good line to another, and did not urge infiltration.[21]

Haig recognised that the offensive was stalling and decided it would be better to switch the direction of the attack to the north through the Third Army sector, rather than continuing a frontal assault against strong opposition. To be sure that the enemy opposition was indeed stiffening, Haig visited his forward commanders on the afternoon of 10 August. That he did so is contrary to the view that he was an unthinking buffoon who never ventured near the front lines. Haig called into the Canadian Corps headquarters, where he conferred with its commander, Lieutenant General Sir Arthur Currie, and the Army commander, General Sir Henry Rawlinson. Both were opposed to continuing the advance. Haig went even further forward, to the headquarters of both the Canadian divisions and 32nd Division, which was commanded by Major General T.S. Lambert. Lambert had just returned from visiting his brigades and told Haig that the enemy opposition had definitely stiffened. He also pointed out that any further fighting in this sector would take place in the old Somme battlefields of 1916. These were riddled with old trenches, shell craters and intact barbed wire, and offered a perfect defensive environment for the Germans. Haig needed no further convincing and set off to inform Foch he was going to switch the direction of the attack.

The fourth and last day of the Battle of Amiens took place on 11 August. General Rawlinson ordered the Fourth Army, by then down to just thirty-eight serviceable tanks in support, to press on to the Somme between Ham and Péronne. The ten attacking divisions were very tired and they were up against twelve German divisions, nine of which had come into line since 8 August. Three of these divisions were entirely fresh. Little wonder that limited progress was made. The attacking infantry met heavy opposition and were encouraged not to continue. That evening, Rawlinson, with Haig's support, decided that the Battle of

Amiens should be ended. He had just six serviceable tanks left.

At just over 20,000, British casualties for the four days of battle were not light. German casualties numbered 75,000 killed and wounded, with another 29,873 taken prisoner.[22] However, although Haig had agreed to end the Battle of Amiens, he had no intention of allowing the Germans to recover from this attack. On the same day that he had given approval for the Fourth Army to wind down its operations, Haig had informed the Third Army commander, General Sir Julian Byng, that the torch was about to be passed to his army and that he should prepare for an attack towards Bapaume as soon as his forces were up to strength. He also directed the First Army commander, General Sir Henry Horne, whose army was north of Byng's, to prepare for offensive operations. While this was a sound strategic decision, it brought him into direct conflict with the supreme commander, Marshal Foch, who wanted the Amiens offensive to continue.

The Battle of Amiens had commenced with a dramatic initial advance, but soon followed the pattern of previous encounters. As the attacking soldiers became fatigued and German resistance became stronger and better directed, the momentum of the attack slowed and so it became impossible to exploit any success that was achieved. The Allies had been in this position before; they had learned that it was useless and extremely costly to carry on attacking when the element of surprise was lost and the Germans had committed their reserves to seal any breaches made. Haig knew that this was the time to attack somewhere else, preferably just where the Germans had weakened their defences. He could see a better alternative to a frontal assault and did not hesitate to seize it. Historian Gary Sheffield is adamant that, had Haig continued to bash away at the Germans around Amiens, it would have been 'an effort which would have undoubtedly suffered the fate of all previous attacks'.[23] In a Despatch at the end of the war Haig explained his reasons for switching the direction of the BEF's offensive. They reveal sound tactical judgement:

> The enemy did not seem prepared to meet an attack in this
> direction, and owing to the success of the Fourth Army, he occupied

a salient the left flank of which was already threatened from the south. A further reason for my decision was that the ground north of the Ancre River was not greatly damaged by shellfire, and was therefore suitable for the use of tanks. A successful attack between Albert and Arras in a south-easterly direction would turn the line of the Somme south of Péronne, and gave every promise of producing far-reaching results. It would be a step forward towards the strategic objective St Quentin–Cambrai.[24]

Haig's intentions for the Third Army were confirmed at a conference on 12 August. Byng's army was reinforced by four divisions, two cavalry divisions, several battalions of tanks (numbering around 200 machines) and additional artillery. Byng was ordered to break into the enemy's position on a 4-mile front, some 7 miles south of Arras. Then, if possible, his men were to push southward in the direction of Péronne in order to outflank the enemy opposite the Fourth Army. Third Army's attack was to commence on 20 August, but this was later postponed to 21 August. Three days after Haig issued these instructions he had another meeting, this time with Horne and Byng. BEF intelligence had detected that the Germans were falling back in the centre of the Third Army's front and that there was only one German division in reserve there. Haig therefore directed that the Third Army press on as soon as possible, with Bapaume as its objective. The First Army was also to take offensive action around Aubers Ridge, but the main effort was to be made by the Third Army.

Foch, however, was unhappy at the Amiens offensive being wound down and on 14 August had despatched a telegram to Haig 'in somewhat peremptory terms' demanding that it continue.[25] After the conference with Byng and Horne on 15 August, Haig visited Foch and stood his ground. According to Haig:

I spoke to Foch quite straightly and let him understand that I was responsible to my Government and fellow citizens for the handling of British forces. F's attitude at once changed and he said all he wanted was early information of my intentions so that he might co-ordinate the operations of the other Armies, and that he now thought I was quite correct in my decision not to attack the enemy in his prepared positions.[26]

This exchange does not portray Foch as a strategic genius, as many of his admirers have claimed, nor does it support the theory that the straight-talking Haig was tactically inept. Foch had no choice but to back down. According to John Terraine, this discussion 'set the tone of their relations for the rest of the war'.[27] Haig's armies would play the leading role in the great Allied offensive and at his direction. Foch would be informed and would coordinate the actions of the other armies on the Western Front. That afternoon Foch wrote to Haig stating that he accepted his views and informing him that he was removing the French First Army from his control.

While there were tensions in the Allied camp, things were not much better for the Germans. The attack of 8 August, which Ludendorff described as 'the black day', was in reality a tactical setback only. No strategic objectives had been taken and the attack, like all others before it, soon lost momentum and failed to live up to its initial promise. But the attack of 8 August had produced a crucial strategic outcome. It had revealed to the German commanders the poor condition of their armies and convinced them that they could no longer hope for victory. Ludendorff, the man in effective control of the German armies, was particularly affected by the events of 8 August, and according to Sheffield 'had clearly suffered an enormous psychological shock, perhaps even a nervous breakdown'.[28] Ludendorff later wrote: 'I openly confess, I should not have thought [such behaviour] possible in the German Army; whole bodies of men had surrendered to single troopers or isolated squadrons.' The Allies' success on this day confirmed Ludendorff's worst fears: 'Our war machine was no longer efficient.' In his mind, there was no alternative: 'The war must be ended.' The German Kaiser, too, was deeply affected by the events of 8 August. On 11 August he expressed the view to Ludendorff that, after the failure of their July offensive and the deeds of 8 August, 'he [the Kaiser] knew the war could no longer be won'. A week later, at a meeting of the

German High Command (OHL) and government officials at Spa on 13 and 14 August, a 'very calm' Kaiser instructed the Imperial Chancellor to 'open up peace negotiations, if possible, through the medium of the Queen of the Netherlands'.[29] After 8 August, the question for Germany and its leaders was not whether they should end the war, but how best to do it and how to obtain the most generous surrender terms. As a result of the battle of Amiens and especially the success on the opening day, 'Haig achieved what for early twenty-first century military leaders has become the glittering prize: psychological dominance over the enemy commander.'[30]

However, Haig did not know the full extent of the Allies' advantage as he halted the battle for Amiens and redirected the BEF's main effort to the Bapaume sector, north of the Somme River. Here Third Army would attempt to turn the line of the old Somme defences from the north above Bapaume, so preventing the Germans from destroying the road and rail communications there. The junction town of Bapaume was the key to success in this region. There were important tactical considerations for shifting the main effort to the north. German attention was firmly fixed on the Amiens sector, where they had shifted most of their reserve forces. With careful planning, the Germans could once more be caught off-balance. The terrain around Bapaume was relatively flat and had sustained little shell damage, so it was suitable for tanks. In addition, the Third Army could commence its attack holding the high ground around Bucquoy and Gommecourt. This not only offered good observation over the battlefield, but it also presented the option of a flank attack rather than a direct frontal assault as had been so disastrously attempted in 1916. If the Battle of Bapaume was successful it would set the platform for further attacks north and south of the Somme, and Haig already had set plans in motion to unleash the First Army at Arras to attempt to turn the right flank of the Hindenburg Line. Little wonder that Haig, in his last Despatch of the war, wrote that this attack 'gave every promise of producing far reaching results'.[31] Much, therefore, depended on the outcome of the Battle of Bapaume.

Compared to its campaign in 1916, the BEF had a number of advantages on the Somme in 1918. It held a considerable portion of the high ground, which offered good observation of the land across which it would have to attack. Many German defensive positions in 1918 were poorly sited. In most cases, frontal assaults could be avoided, the enemy lines being taken from the flank in enfilade instead. However, the Somme terrain was still good defensive country, especially for well-sited machine-gun positions, as Ormond Burton described:

> Over the whole area of the Ancre and the Somme the country was much the same. Villages scattered here and there were embowered in groves of trees, while beyond, wide open fields stretched without a vestige of cover for thousands of yards. A succession of chalk ridges, no-where running to any great height, ran like so many waves across the whole battlefield, and in every case formed admirable defensive positions, giving excellent observation and a splendid field of fire on advancing troops.[32]

General Sir Julian Byng's plan for the Third Army involved a series of attacks staged over several days. On 21 August, Third Army would launch a small attack aimed at taking the Albert–Arras railway. The next day would be devoted to preparations for a much larger assault to be made on 23 August, the aim of which was to clear most of the old Somme battlefield. As the Third Army got ready for this attack, the Fourth Army, under Rawlinson, would advance on the right flank to be in line with the Third Army. Then while the Third Army carried out its attack on 23 August, those divisions of the Fourth Army north of the river Somme would also press forward, with the intention of capturing the town of Albert and most of the Ancre Valley. Launching a limited assault followed by a much larger, full-scale attack two days later was an unusual plan and, as will be discussed later, caused considerable consternation for both sides.

For the limited attack on 21 August, the Third Army planned to move on a front of about 9 miles, with its IV and VI Corps in the centre. The New Zealand Division was part of IV Corps. This body alone had some six brigades of heavy artillery (111 guns in total) and fifteen brigades of field artillery to cover its advance. This was formidable artillery support for such limited objectives. The divisions in the IV Corps front were 42nd Division on the right, New Zealand Division in the centre, and 37th Division on the left. Two divisions, 5th Division and 63rd (Royal Naval) Division, were in reserve. The attack was to be made in two stages. On IV Corps' left flank 37th Division was to attack and capture the high ground east of the villages of Bucquoy and Ablainzevelle. This was an advance of just over 1000 yards and would give the attackers observation over Miraumont and the whole Ancre Valley. When this was complete the two reserve divisions (5th and 63rd) plus a battalion of tanks would pass through the 37th Division positions to the second objective, which was the railway line near Miraumont. They were to establish a new line from Irles to Bihucourt beyond the Albert–Arras railway. This was a much longer advance, one that would carry the attacking divisions some 4 miles beyond their start point. In recognition of this an intermediate objective was also given, which was just over halfway to the Irles–Bihucourt line.

Meanwhile, 42nd Division on the right flank and the New Zealand

The general area of the Battle of Bapaume — West

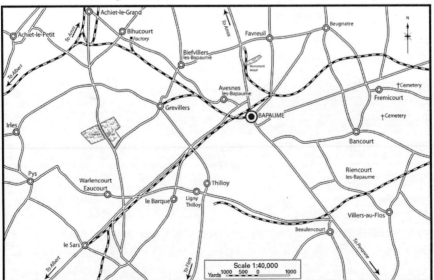

Division in the centre would cooperate by moving forward with 37th Division and supporting it with artillery and machine-gun fire. They were to advance the IV Corps line so that 37th Division would not be left exposed. During the second phase of the attack, when the reserve divisions passed through the new line won by 37th Division, both 42nd and the New Zealand Division were also to advance and conform with the forward movement of the corps. This would cause a problem for the New Zealand Division. This last advance would carry it into a valley east of Puisieux, overlooked on both sides by high ground. The northern slope was to be taken in 5th Division's advance. The southern slope, on which there was a German strongpoint known as the Beauregard Dovecot, was to be taken by 42nd Division in their advance. During the operation the New Zealand front was to be squeezed out by the advance of the two divisions on their flanks and by its general south-eastward movement. This would leave the New Zealand Division with no front at all to cover and no other role to play so General Russell was warned that his division would be used to exploit any success gained in the main attack on 23 August. As events turned out, the New Zealand Division's role in this opening attack was not as limited as had been planned.

The general area of the Battle of Bapaume — East

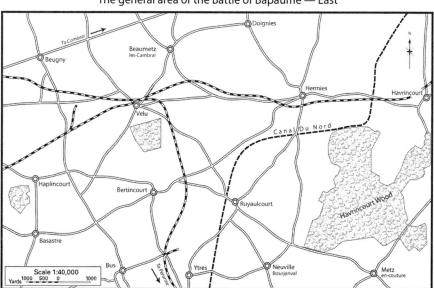

353

With thirteen divisions and 200 tanks, the Third Army was the BEF's strongest field army. It also had a generous supply of artillery, 996 field guns and 482 medium and heavy guns. This, coupled with the ten RAF squadrons allocated to its support, including one designated in support of the Tank Corps for low-flying attacks against the German anti-tank guns, made it a formidable fighting machine.[33] Facing Third Army were eight divisions of the German Seventeenth Army commanded by General Otto von Below, who had a further two divisions in reserve. Of the eight divisions facing Third Army, only one — the 4th Bavarian — was rated as first class.[34]

But the Third Army had an Achilles heel. With the exception of the New Zealand Division, its infantry units were all below strength. Not only were its battalions weak in numbers, but they lacked training in open warfare, and 18–19-year-old boys filled the ranks. In the Third Army alone, 50 per cent of the infantry 'were said to be boys'.[35] The infantry units maintained good discipline, but lacked endurance. On the plus side, these young soldiers recovered quickly from fatigue and were soon ready to fight another day.

Great pains were taken by senior commanders to ensure that the attack of 21 August came as a surprise. However, with the steady build-up of troops, artillery, tanks and supplies behind the lines, experienced soldiers knew a large offensive was only days away. One such New Zealander soldier, Thomas Dale of the 1st Auckland Battalion, recorded in his diary on 14 August: 'Something is going to happen soon. As sure as little apples we shall be in the centre of a big stunt soon.'[36] It was a very accurate prediction.

To further distract the enemy from the main attack, deception operations were carried out. South of the Somme, the Fourth Army gave every appearance of continuing its operations and a feint attack was made by the Tenth French Army on the Aisne, which had the desired effect of draining Ludendorff's dwindling reserves. Artillery support was carefully concealed in woods and villages until the last possible moment, no mean feat given that there was so much of it. No work to improve roads in the area was permitted, no new hospital signs were erected, and infantry movement was kept to a minimum and confined to the hours of darkness. Troops were also forbidden to fire at German reconnaissance planes. By strictly enforcing these measures, all the tell-tale signs that an attack was imminent were eliminated.

The terrain over which the Third Army would attack lay across the watershed between the Somme and Scarpe rivers. While it was relatively flat, it was broken by many cross spurs and valleys. It sloped gently down to the Scarpe. The area had once been covered with villages and small woods, but it had been devastated in the German retirement of March 1917. It lay between the battlefields of the Somme (1916) and Arras (1917). The ground was regarded as very suitable for tanks, a reason that had figured prominently in the planning for the attack. Yet the limitations of even the Mark V and Whippet tanks would be revealed in the days ahead. As the British official historian has commented, tanks and aircraft 'gave valuable assistance, but never brought about decisive results'.[37]

The summer of 1918 was, unlike the previous year, very pleasant and as a result the ground underfoot was firm. Bert Stokes, a New Zealand soldier serving in the New Zealand Field Artillery (NZFA) who had been through the Passchendaele debacle, wrote to his parents describing the weather with a great sense of relief:

> This is glorious Summer, it is simply beautiful weather, almost too hot, but I think we can all stand the heat. We have had quite a long spell of fine weather now, and it is a pleasure to be well enough to enjoy it.

He also noted, though, that 'things have started to get busy in the last two days'.[38]

On 19 August Haig visited Byng at his headquarters, some 23 miles west of Arras. He also visited the Third Army's VI Corps (led by Haldane) and IV Corps (commanded by Harper). Haig was briefed on the plans for the forthcoming attack and was not impressed, recording in his diary:

> He [Byng] explained his plan, which I thought was too limited in

its scope. I told him that his objective was to break the Enemy's front, and gain Bapaume as soon as possible. Now is the time to act with boldness, and in full confidence that, if we only hit the Enemy hard enough, and continue to press him, that he will give way and acknowledge that he is beaten.[39]

Haig felt that an advance of only about 6000 yards in the centre, by his strongest army protected by defensive flanks, with exploitation by infantry advanced guards and tanks, was far too cautious. With the German reserves stretched to breaking point and Third Army's flanks to be secured by an advance of both Fourth and First Armies, it is little wonder that Haig was not impressed with Byng's plan. The events of the following day further confirmed his views. Byng, however, did not alter his plans.

On 20 August the French Tenth Army, under its firebrand general Charles Mangin, attacked with twelve divisions on a 12-mile front near Soissons. Though only two of Mangin's divisions were fresh, the attack was a stunning success. The German defenders were overwhelmed and an advance of 2.5 miles was made. Over 8000 German prisoners were taken. Ludendorff described it as 'another black day with heavy and irreplaceable losses'.[40]

As a result of this French success Foch wrote to Haig, putting further pressure on him to ensure that the Third Army struck a decisive blow. Part of Foch's letter stated:

> The enemy has everywhere been shaken by the blows already dealt him. We must repeat these blows without losing any time . . . I therefore count on the attack of your Third Army, already postponed to the 21st, being launched that day with the utmost violence, carrying forward with it the neighbouring divisions of the First Army and the whole of the Fourth Army. After your brilliant successes of the 8th, 9th and 10th, any timidity on their part would hardly be justified in view of the enemy's situation and the moral ascendancy you have gained over him.[41]

Meanwhile, as the nuances of coalition warfare were being worked out at the higher level, the New Zealand Division prepared to play its part in the limited attack to be launched on 21 August. As the New Zealand Division had only a small part to play, Russell decided to use just one of his infantry brigades, keeping the other two for use after the attack on 23 August. The task for 21 August was given to the 3rd New Zealand (Rifle) Brigade, commanded by Brigadier Herbert Hart. On 18 August the New Zealand Rifle Brigade moved to the front line, where it took over the 2nd Brigade positions. The next day the Rifles extended their front so that by the evening of 20 August this single brigade was holding the whole of the divisional line and was ready to move. The New Zealand sector ran from 1000 yards south of Puisieux to 1000 yards south of Bucquoy. Just two of its battalions, now reduced to 640 rifles by the Left Out of Battle policy, were in the line. The 3rd Rifles were south of Puisieux and the 4th Rifles further north on the Puisieux–Bucquoy road. The 2nd Rifles was in support and the 1st Rifles in reserve. These battalions, too, were reduced to 640 men.[42] During its attack of 21 August the Rifle Brigade would have artillery support from two brigades of New Zealand artillery, plus six medium trench mortars and two machine-gun companies. The third brigade of New Zealand artillery had been placed under command of 37th Division.[43]

Brigadier Hart did not have a lot of time to prepare for this attack. He only learned of the role his brigade would play at a conference at the Divisional Headquarters at midday on 19 August. As his diary recorded:

Spent the remainder of the day in preparing plans and writing orders.

20 August: Conference with all my unit commdrs at 9 AM giving instructions for the attack. Met the G.O.C. [Russell] in conference at 11.30. All the afternoon arranging artillery support, supplies, dumps, signal communications, provision for the wounded, & establishing battle headquarters.[44]

It is a tribute to Hart and his headquarters staff that the preparations were completed in time. The historian of the Division's artillery commented on the haste with which the preparations for the attack were made. According to Byrne, 'a remarkable feature of the opening assault on August 21st was the brevity of the preparations, and the suddenness with which, after their conception, the plans for the attack were put into execution'.[45] Such short notice for an attack meant a period of frantic activity for all those involved.

There was much to prepare for the battle ahead. The Rifle Brigade would have to coordinate its moves with 42nd Division on its right flank and with 37th Division in the north, and then later with the two reserve divisions of IV Corps, once they were committed to the action. It planned its attack in three stages. They were:

- Stage 1: An attack on Puisieux village and an advance to the first objective; the Blue Line, which was about 500 yards east of the village.
- Stage 2: When 5 Division passed through the Blue Line and started its attack on Achiet-le-Petit, the Rifle Brigade would advance about 1000 yards into the triangular valley ahead of it and link its right flank with 42 Division.
- Stage 3: Once 5 Division had captured Achiet-le-Petit and 42 Division had taken the Dovecot strongpoint, the Rifles were to advance a further 1000 yards down the valley north of the Dovecot to clear the ground as far as the Ancre River. If 42 Division had difficulty taking the Beauregard Dovecot (as indeed happened), Rifle Brigade was to offer some assistance in capturing the strongpoint.

Once the first objective was taken and as the front narrowed, only the battalion on the right, the 3rd Rifles, would be needed to carry out Stages 2 and 3. Its maximum advance 'would hardly exceed two and a half miles' and it was not anticipated that the New Zealanders would experience much hard fighting.[46] This initial action was viewed by all as a preliminary operation with strictly limited objectives. As will be seen in the next chapter, the operation did not go entirely to plan and the New Zealanders' role was soon expanded.

Once darkness fell on 20 August the Third Army front was a hive of activity. The 2nd Brigade NZFA recorded in its War Diary:

> Quiet night. Enemy did some intermittent crashing during the small hours of the morning . . . Batteries worked strenuously throughout the night moving up the balance of their weapons. All was reported O.K. by 7 a.m.[47]

On 20 August 1918, a 26-year-old lieutenant of the 2nd Auckland Battalion wrote home to his family in New Zealand. His letter reflected what most of the New Zealand infantry were thinking that night:

> We are still in the same bivvie but there is something doing very soon but I feel quite hopeful that we will come out of it safe and sound. I know that your prayers will go with me and I will do my best to 'carry on' but one can't help wondering what the end will be.[48]

Unfortunately, Douglas Knight, the writer of the letter, would be just one of the many New Zealand casualties in the ten days of hard fighting ahead of the New Zealand Division.

Chapter 3

Attack and Counterattack:
21–23 August 1918

O N 21 AUGUST 1918 THE Third Army opened its multi-stage offensive north of the Somme, with the aim of capturing Albert and most of the Ancre Valley. Five infantry divisions were involved in the initial attack. From right to left they were: the 42nd Division, the New Zealand Division, the 37th Division, the 2nd Division and the Guards Division. Most of these divisions advanced on a single brigade front with a few tanks blundering along behind them. However, Third Army had other resources available, including a further eight divisions, 156 tanks, ten RAF squadrons, and a massive amount of artillery, which had been boosted by transfers from Fourth Army. The IV Corps alone had six brigades of heavy and fifteen brigades of field artillery available to support its efforts. There was a unique aspect to this attack. As the New Zealand artillery historian commented: 'For the first time in the experience of the Division on the Western Front a great attack was to be launched without even the briefest preliminary bombardment.'[1]

One New Zealand gunner marvelled at this new development and at what had been achieved in such a short space of time. He recorded in his memoirs:

> A remarkable feature of the opening assault on August 21st was the brevity of the preparations, and the suddenness with which, after their conception, the plans for attack were put into execution . . . The necessary preparations for attack — the assembly of the infantry, and the pushing forward of the guns — were carried out so silently and unobtrusively as to leave the enemy unaware of the immense storm which was about to burst.[2]

The soldiers of the New Zealand Rifle Brigade were roused at 3 a.m. and given a hot meal and a tot of rum. During the night a dense fog had settled over the area. This was a huge advantage for the attacking troops, as it prevented observation beyond 50 yards and blinded the enemy's aeroplanes. One New Zealand infantry battalion war diary recorded: 'Weather conditions ideal'[3] and a New Zealand soldier noted in his diary: 'I got up to witness the attack but could not see more than a hundred yards as there was a very heavy mist.'[4] Zero hour was set for 4.55 a.m. Right on time the artillery from two brigades opened, firing a standing barrage in front of their trenches for ten minutes. An officer in the 4th Rifles recalled in his memoirs:

> Zero hour was 5 a.m., and we were up and breakfasted before that, so we were all ready when the barrage came down right on the tick of 5. What a wonderful sound. I almost pitied the Germans on the receiving end.[5]

While New Zealand histories of the war have described the New Zealand barrage as being 'very effective' and 'excellent', contemporary records are not so praising.[6] The War Diary of the 2nd Brigade NZFA described the barrage as 'a little ragged', while that of the 2nd Wellington Battalion recorded that 'the noise of our barrage was scarcely audible in the fog'.[7] The War Diary of a Canterbury battalion moving forward in the dark ready to exploit any success recorded that at 4.55 a.m. 'a muffled burst of drumfire from the guns in front announced the beginning of the thrust against the German lines.'[8] Yet another infantry diary complained that 'The barrage on our left flank started two minutes before ZERO.'[9] Therefore, it cannot be said, as one gunner wrote, that: 'The barrage on the 21st completely satisfied the infantry.'[10]

Whatever the state of the barrage, those infantry waiting anxiously behind it knew what it meant. One unit diary eloquently noted: 'we knew that the battle in which we were destined to play our part had commenced.'[11] New Zealander Thomas Dale, of the 1st Auckland Battalion, recorded:

> The guns started at daybreak and almost instantly became a
> continuous rolling drumfire. So it has come at last and we shall be
> in it once more. Our few weeks of quiet time have gone, when are
> we likely to get another?[12]

Dale was not to know when he wrote this entry that the Division's next 'quiet time' would come only when the war was over.

The barrage, a mix of smoke and high-explosive shells, advanced in lifts of 100 yards every four minutes. Five minutes after the barrage opened the lead infantry units left their trenches and crept up to its edge in preparation for the advance. The purpose of this move into no-man's-land was twofold. It would ensure that the infantry advanced on the very heels of the creeping barrage when it lifted and was intended to help the infantry avoid casualties from German artillery fired on their own trenches in retaliation.

In the event there was little opposition initially, as the Germans had thinned out the forward area with their main line of defence being some 3 miles in the rear. The secrecy and planning also meant the attack came as a complete surprise to the enemy forces.

The first objective of the New Zealand Rifle Brigade was the village of Puisieux which it aimed to capture by attacking its northern and southern outskirts. From the outset the infantry attack went well and met little determined opposition. Specially trained sections of the 4th Rifles began to clear the village. Opposition was experienced only on the eastern outskirts of the village, but even this was soon overcome by the gallantry of Corporal N.C. Neilson, who led his Lewis gun section forward to capture two machine-gun positions. In clearing Puisieux, the 4th Rifles captured over a hundred Germans, twelve machine guns and three mortars. Its own casualties were seventeen wounded.[13] Once the village had been captured, the 3rd Rifles were able to pass through it on their way to the Blue Line, which marked the end of Stage 1 of the attack. They were to have a much tougher time reaching their objective.

On the left flank of 3rd Rifles was B Company, which reached the Blue Line with relative ease. Advancing just after Zero Hour it swept through the southern part of Puisieux and progressed to the Blue Line without being checked. There, the men extended the line northwards until they linked up with the 4th Rifles.

On the right flank of 3rd Rifles was C Company, which moved off over open, exposed ground and suffered some casualties from sweeping machine-gun fire coming from a road just short of their objective. The thick fog meant the riflemen could hear the sound of the gunfire but couldn't see where it was coming from. So the leading sections rushed towards the sound of the fire and fell upon four German machine-gun posts, which they quickly subdued. As its advance continued C Company once again came under fire from another gun directly in front. It, too, was overcome. This brought the men to a second road about 100 yards beyond the Blue Line. Once there, although slightly beyond their objective, the soldiers of C Company started to consolidate their position.

Meanwhile the centre company (D Company) met with strong opposition from Germans located in a series of old trenches some 200 yards in front of D Company's objective. Most of the opposition was quickly cleared, but one concealed machine-gun post proved very hard to subdue. It was finally taken in a rush from the flank by two riflemen, C.W. Batty and J. Lowe, who captured the gun and eleven men, including one officer.

During the attack, a 4th Rifles runner had a rather unusual adventure. He was making his way back to the Blue Line, but missed the forward position and blundered into the German lines, where he was disarmed and sent to the rear under armed guard. While he was heading to the rear a British tank appeared, manned by Australians 'who promptly reversed the position'.[14]

The end result of the early morning attack was impressive. All opposition had been overcome and the first objective reached at 6 a.m., in just over an hour of fighting. During this crowded hour Puisieux was taken, the troops were well established on the Blue Line, and nearly a hundred prisoners and several machine guns were captured. The New Zealanders had also patrolled a further 150 yards in front of their newly won positions. Just after 6 a.m. a section of New Zealand machine-gunners reached the forward positions and set up their guns on the Blue Line.

After taking the Blue Line, phase two of the operation began. Troops from the 5th Division passed through the 4th Rifles on their way to Achiet-le-Petit, which they reached at 7.30 a.m. At the same time, A Company of the 3rd Rifles moved through the Blue Line to secure the triangular patch of ground that had been taken in order to provide a link between the 5th and 42nd Divisions. The fog was still lying dense on the ground, restricting visibility and causing considerable confusion. After advancing some 500 yards eastwards and failing to gain touch with its target, the company halted and formed a temporary line. Fighting patrols were sent out and these managed to locate the flank of the 5th Division.

One of those sent to find the 5th Division was Rifleman A. Dalzell. He discovered that the area between his company and the 5th Division was still held by the enemy. Single-handedly Rifleman Dalzell cleared a number of dugouts and captured five prisoners. Then, when he located a machine-gun nest, Dalzell took three men with him to rush it, capturing the gun and killing the crew. One officer, Second Lieutenant R.M. Blackwell, MM, an artillery forward observation officer, took fifteen prisoners. Another forward observation officer, Second Lieutenant W.N. Sievers, with his signaller, captured seven prisoners and passed through a gap in the enemy lines to reach the Beauregard Dovecot. There he spotted a large German force preparing to counterattack, so he brought down artillery fire on them without delay. The German counterattack quickly dispersed.

At 10 a.m. the fog started to lift, which immediately caused problems for the attacking forces. The left platoons of A Company found that they had overrun their objective and were occupying the exposed face of a spur that was in full view of the enemy. There they were swept with vicious machine-gun fire from beyond the Ancre Valley to their left. The platoons obviously could not stay where they were, so they withdrew to conform to the new line established by the 5th Division. At noon these men were joined by two more platoons that had come into position while still maintaining touch with the soldiers in the new front line. The New Zealand line, now about a mile east of Puisieux, was unbroken and all companies started digging in, in preparation for counterattacks.

Even though A Company had retreated from the spur, it was still the most exposed of the New Zealand units. The men of A Company faced south-east, with the outskirts of Miraumont directly to their front and only 1500 yards away. Immediately below them was the bottom of the valley through which a light railway ran westwards to Serre. Beyond the valley the ground sloped up to the Beauregard Dovecot, some 1000 yards away. That afternoon, after digging in was completed, A Company sent out fighting patrols, which worked through to the bottom of the valley and about the slopes on either side. Sending out these patrols helped A Company secure its position by revealing any previously undetected enemy strongpoints and discouraging the Germans from getting too close. The practice was part of New Zealand's doctrine of dominating no-man's-land and maintaining the initiative.

North of the New Zealanders, the 5th Division was having trouble taking its final objective, so some patrols from the rifle battalions were sent to assist. These patrols pushed out to the railway in the Ancre Valley and the ground between it and the New Zealand line was cleared. To the south, on the New Zealand right flank, 42nd Division finally reached its objective and after considerable fighting managed to take the Beauregard Dovecot just after 1.25 p.m. Its progress had been slow during the morning, as the War Diary of the 3rd Rifles reveals: 'The 42nd Division did not make much progress on the right flank and their position was very obscure at times.'[15]

Brigadier Herbert Hart also commented on the slow progress of the 42nd Division. After taking Puisieux, 'which was taken before the Hun was awake', the advance to the Stage 2 objective was:

> much delayed through the slow rate of progress of the neighbouring Divisions, the 42nd was moved slowly forward all day, getting onto our final objective about 3 o'clock. About midday it was expected that other troops would come up & take advantage of the great success obtained, push on towards Bapaume before the Hun recovered, but nothing developed.[16]

IV Corps had made solid if unspectacular progress, having gained just over 3 miles on a 3-mile front and taking over 1400 prisoners. But it had not reached its final objective of the Arras–Albert railway and the Germans still held this with considerable strength. Haig was not pleased with this limited progress. As Cyril Falls wrote of this 21 August attack, the Third Army 'merely ambled forward a couple of miles and halted the next day to bring up guns and shell.'[17] Correlli Barnett, too, has stated that the progress of this attack was 'limited because of the caution and rigidity of the Third Army's plan.'[18] Yet when measured against what had been achieved during the offensives of 1916 and 1917, this was still a considerable amount of ground taken and Byng would not alter his original plan. The next day, 22 August, was earmarked for consolidation and preparation for the big attack planned for the following day.

The New Zealand Rifle Brigade had carried out 'an excellent day's work' and achieved everything asked of it.[19] Its brigadier described the operation as 'a complete surprise to the enemy & a wonderfully successful show.'[20] All objectives had been taken and the forward post of the 3rd Rifles was now 2000 yards east of Puisieux. The Brigade had taken 235 prisoners and thirty machine guns. Private Melville F.S. King witnessed several large groups of German prisoners arriving and was not impressed with them. He recorded in his diary: 'At 10 a.m. the mist lifted and batches of prisoners came down . . . I saw about 500 all told, the majority of them poor looking.'[21]

The Brigade had suffered some sixty casualties. Though the Brigade War Diary described the casualties of this day as 'slight',[22] they were not evenly distributed. A Company of the 3rd Rifles had been heaviest hit. All its officers, with the exception of the acting commander, Lieutenant Russell, were casualties. Included amongst them was Captain R.J.S. Seddon, who had been killed in the shelling just before zero hour that morning. Seddon, a Boer War veteran, was the son of New Zealand Prime Minister Richard 'King Dick' Seddon. In comparison, the 4th Rifles' casualties were seventeen other ranks, all wounded, three of whom remained with the battalion.[23] On learning of the progress of 'the Dinks', as the Rifle Brigade was affectionately known in the New Zealand Division, especially the 'very few casualties to themselves', Thomas Dale recorded in his diary that 'things are moving in a right good manner.'[24] Even Major General Russell was impressed with the Rifle Brigade's progress. He recorded of the day's action: 'Hart's bde carried out our share and did it well — about 220 prisoners, our casualties well under 100 and this is the best feature of the day.'[25] Over the next few days, though, casualties would steadily increase.

The night of 21 August was a quiet one, but the stillness disguised a hive of activity on both sides of the line. A section from the Otago Machine Gun Company moved forward and set up position near the Dovecot amongst the riflemen who were frantically digging defensive positions in preparation for the inevitable German counterattack. Behind them, as soon as darkness fell, guns were moved forward into the Puisieux Valley and new firing positions established. During the night the artillery supply wagons moved bulk quantities of ammunition forward, so that by the morning of 22 August each New Zealand gun in the front line had 450 rounds on hand. Such preparation was not in vain, as on the other side of the line German artillery and infantry prepared to mount a strong counterattack at dawn.

At 5 a.m. on 22 August under cover of a heavy mist the Germans launched their counterattack from Miraumont, with the aim of retaking the Dovecot held by the 42nd Division. The counterattack was made by a fresh German division, the 52nd, and it was supported by accurate counter-battery fire on the New Zealand gun positions. The soldiers of the 42nd Division were soon driven from the Dovecot and the Germans once more occupied it and the nearby trenches. These overlooked the New Zealand positions in the valley, making them vulnerable, and also meant the right flank of the 3rd Rifles was exposed to the enemy. It was a very dangerous situation. As had happened so often in the past, the situation was saved by the quick thinking and courage of a New Zealand non-commissioned officer. Lance Corporal R. Milne saw German soldiers on the skyline trying to outflank the battalion. He rushed to the crest and engaged them with his Lewis gun team at point-blank range, killing twelve Germans, wounding eight, and capturing another five, along with four machine guns. This single action denied the Germans the high ground overlooking the 3rd Rifles and the battalion's exposed flank was refused or bent back and quickly reinforced. As the New Zealand Division's history notes: 'This quick decision and vigorous action saved the commanding positions in our immediate vicinity and freed us from any danger in front.'[26]

Once the German counterattack commenced all the New Zealand guns were soon in action answering SOS calls from the 42nd Division on the right. It was not long before these guns, too, suffered from heavy enemy fire. At one stage, the new line established the day before was so hard pressed that it fell right back to the New Zealand gun positions, one battery being forced to fire on the German infantry over open sights.[27] The War Diary of the 2nd Brigade NZFA recorded: 'A quiet night. At 5 am all Batteries were shelled with 5.9's and 4.2's, also much gas was used causing 5 casualties, 1 killed, 4 wounded.'[28]

An officer in the brigade wrote in his diary that 'the Hun countered and put a considerable strafe on us' and reflected that his battery was 'very lucky though and only two wounded.'[29] The 3rd Brigade of the NZFA supporting the 42nd Division was also having a dangerous time of it. One gunner recorded in his diary:

> At break of day we were heavily shelled and had a rotten time in holes
> we had dug in the ground. No sleep. Later the Hun counterattacked
> three times and each time we were again bombarded with shells
> and gas. Still we all boxed on . . . Our range is only from 1900 to
> 1200 yards so we get a lot of machine-gun bullets.[30]

The infantry positions were also under a heavy artillery barrage. At his battle headquarters near Puisieux, Brigadier Hart's position was deluged with mustard gas shells. As the dugouts being used had no protective gas curtains, the headquarters staff, including Hart, had to stand out in the open for over an hour wearing their box respirators. Hart found the experience a 'great annoyance'.[31]

As had happened the previous day, the mist lifted later in the morning, exposing the attacking side. This time the advancing Germans came into full view of the Otago Machine Gun Company, whose eight guns in excellent firing positions 'opened a deadly fire against them.'[32] The machine-gun fire must have been lethal, as the New Zealand soldiers counted over 400 dead Germans to their front. Another 300 were taken prisoner when they ran into the 5th Division's area in an effort to escape the deadly rain of bullets. 'It was a machine gunners 7th Heaven' wrote Brigadier Hart.[33] The Machine Gun Battalion's War Diary recorded of this action:

> Otago Company carried out this part of the operation and did some very effective shooting. The section under 2/Lieut A.J. Billington was responsible for about 100 casualties amongst a large party of the enemy which approached our lines. The remainder of the party surrendered to the Infantry.[34]

While this counterattack was beaten off, the Germans had succeeded in taking the Beauregard Dovecot and the important trench along the slope eastward to the railway. Though the Allies made several attempts to recapture it throughout the day, it remained in German hands.

The New Zealanders were involved in one of these attempts in the early afternoon. Around 12.30 p.m., following a two-hour bombardment on the Dovecot, three platoons of 3rd Rifle's Support Company advanced from the New Zealand positions in order to assist 42nd Division to capture that troublesome feature. Despite the intense heat — it was the warmest day of the year so far — things initially went well. The New Zealand riflemen established a more advanced position on the lower slopes overlooking the railway and soldiers from 42nd Division reoccupied the Dovecot and its spur. Unfortunately, they were not there long, as the Germans launched a swift counterattack 'and again wrested it from them.'[35]

Behind the scenes, soldiers worked hard to secure any advantage and to support front-line troops. The Maori Pioneers had spent most of their time in August repairing roads or building new ones so that the numerous guns and supplies could move forward. They continued with this backbreaking yet essential task once the offensive started on 21 August, often moving into the danger zone to do so. On 22 August, for example, C Company was despatched to work on the forward part of the Puisieux–Achiet-le-Petit road. As the Battalion's history records, whoever allocated the company this task had been a bit reckless:

> This was rather premature, however, as the Germans were still holding the Irles Ridge, Miraumont, and the slopes east of the Dovecot, and he gave the working parties a hot reception. They were withdrawn immediately, but one man was killed and two were wounded.[36]

In the midst of all this fighting, however, an unusual event occurred immediately behind the front line. The commanders of some New Zealand units were informed that Field Marshal Haig was on his way to inspect the front and that they should arrange an appropriate reception. So these units, the 1st Auckland Battalion amongst them, were ordered to line the road along which any motor vehicle must pass. Sure enough, a large staff car, black and red pennants flying in the breeze, appeared. Thomas Dale was amongst those who witnessed this sight:

> Soon we could see his stiff, thick figure and the well known features looked out upon us from the right hand window of the car. Everyone stood to attention as the car went slowly while Doug saluted soldiers continuously. He never smiled but looked solmn [sic]. Doubtless the responsibility of his great position and the continuous fight, not only with the Germans, but our own politicians, is enough to make any man look grave.[37]

There was also another reason for Haig's stern demeanour. He was not impressed with Third Army's limited progress on 21 August and was annoyed that Byng had insisted on using 22 August to prepare for the large-scale offensive planned for the following day. Haig felt that Third Army was wasting time by such deliberation and missing a golden opportunity to strike a decisive blow. He was particularly annoyed that Third Army had done little on 22 August except repel German counterattacks while

Fourth Army had joined in the offensive and taken Albert. At the very least he had expected Third Army to attempt to take Achiet-le-Grand, one of the objectives of 21 August. On the evening of 21 August, Haig had recorded in his diary:

> About 10.30 pm CGS reported that Byng had decided not to continue the operation against Achiet le Grand tomorrow morning. Troops had suffered much from the heat, and were in disorder. Guns too had to be advanced. I expressed the wish that the attack should be resumed at the earliest possible moment.[38]

Observing the relative inaction on 22 August Haig took decisive action. He sent a strongly worded telegram to his Army commanders in an effort to put some 'ginger' into them.[39] This Directive, in effect a direct order, urged the Army commanders to abandon caution and encouraged them to be aggressive and take risks. It read:

> I request that Army Commanders will, without delay, bring to the notice of all subordinate leaders the changed conditions under which operations are now being carried on, and the consequent necessity for all ranks to act with the utmost boldness and resolution in order to get full advantage from the present favourable situation.
>
> The effect of two very severe defeats, and the continuous attacks to which the enemy has been subjected during the past month, has been to wear out his troops and disorganise his plans . . .
>
> To turn the present situation to account, the most resolute offensive is everywhere desirable. Risks which a month ago would have been criminal to incur, ought now to be incurred as a duty.
>
> It is now no longer necessary to advance in regular lines and step by step. On the contrary, each division should be given a distant objective which must be reached independently of its neighbours, and even if one's flank is thereby exposed for the time being . . .
>
> The situation is most favourable; let each one of us act energetically, and without hesitation push forward to our objective.[40]

Similar appeals had been made before and had produced catastrophic results. Passchendaele in 1917 was a prime example of this. In August 1918, though, the situation was radically altered and Haig was thoroughly justified in making such an appeal. As Gregory Blaxland has noted, in August 1918:

> The enemy's morale was low and his defences were shoddy, and Haig had the guns and the tanks to spread his offensive over a wide frontage, thus enabling him to retain the initiative by making frequent switches of pressure.[41]

The relative inaction of the Third Army on 22 August did produce one positive result, though. It led the German commander of the Seventeenth Army, General Otto von Below, to believe that the attack had been a complete failure and that a counterattack was appropriate and timely. In fact, all the counterattacks made by the Germans on 22 August turned out to be costly failures. Von Below was not the only German commander to be deceived. Ludendorff was also taken in by Byng's staged attack. As the Seventeeth Army fell back on 21 August 'the English attack broke down in front of the new line', he wrote. Neither did he view the German counterattacks of 22 August as complete failures, stating: 'They were successful, but it would have been better not to attempt it.' Overall, Ludendorff appeared to think that the recent 'black days' of the war were on the wane: 'The first two days had gone well for us. I began to hope that here, at last, luck was going to turn.'[42] However, his optimism would evaporate the next day.

Haig's Directive of 22 August produced the desired results and the offensive gathered momentum. General Byng immediately revised his plans for 23 August. With the enemy's position along the Irles–Achiet-le-Grand line described as 'exceedingly strong'[43], taking it in a frontal assault was likely be very costly. Byng, showing how much the BEF had learned since 1916, decided to take a new approach. Instead of using just one corps for the attack, all three would advance along the entire Third Army front in a pincer movement designed to outflank the strongly held Irles–Achiet-le-Grand position. They would be supported by five squadrons of low-flying planes from the RAF. On the right, V Corps was to take Thiepval from the south, VI Corps would take Gommecourt, while IV Corps would advance on Achiet-le-Grand if everything went according to plan. When combined with the efforts of Fourth Army, this made the British offensive front some 35 miles long.

While it had not taken all of its objectives on 21 August, IV Corps was in a good position to play its part in this larger effort on 23 August. Lieutenant General Harper assigned the following roles to the divisions of IV Corps: the 37th Division (which had relieved 63rd Division), in the north, was to capture the village of Bihucourt, while the 5th Division seized Irles. The New Zealand Division and 42nd Division were limited to protecting the right flank of the attack. In support of IV Corps' attack were eleven brigades of field artillery, four brigades of heavy artillery and thirteen tanks. The New Zealand's Division's role in this flank protection was to clear and occupy the branch of the Ancre Valley north of Miraumont. This was an advance of only about 800 yards but would allow them to seize some 1500 yards of the railway line immediately north-east of Miraumont. The New Zealand Division, however, was warned to be ready to exploit any success.

Before this attack could go ahead, the Beauregard Dovecot needed to be taken back from the Germans once more, as it overlooked the assembly position of the divisions making the attack. It also needed to be taken in order to secure IV Corp's flank. The task of its capture fell to the 42nd Division and the New Zealand Rifle Brigade. It involved not only the capture of the Dovecot, but also the ridge to its north-east. Allocated to the attack were four companies of Fusiliers from 42nd Division and two companies of the 1st Rifles. They would have overwhelming artillery support, including the guns from both divisions plus an additional brigade of artillery from the 5th Division.

It was going to be a stiff fight. The 1st Rifles, which had relieved the 3rd Rifles that evening, would have to attack uphill on a front of some 1500 yards. While the advance to the final objective was a short one — only some 800 yards — at the very last minute a change was made.

The Battalion's War Diary recorded: 'At 9 p.m. orders received to extend frontage of attack Northward by about 700 yards.'[44] Despite its lateness this change did not cause the 1st Rifles undue difficulty, a reflection of the high levels of professionalism evident in the New Zealand battalions. Zero hour was set for 2.30 a.m., with the attack to be made in bright moonlight. That evening, expressly forbidden to talk or light cigarettes, the men of the two rifle companies moved quietly to their assembly positions. They reached them in good time and without incident. Then began the nerve-racking wait for zero hour.

Right on 2.30 a.m. a very accurate artillery barrage pushed up the slopes to the Dovecot and down into the valley to the railway beyond. It was joined by a machine-gun barrage firing on the trenches around the Dovecot. The guns of the 5th Division were allocated to the two rifle companies and they 'gave us perfect support throughout'.[45] There was little opposition and it was easily swept aside. The two companies reached their objectives well within the allotted time. The company on the left was just 400 yards short of the railway while that on the right swung back to link up with 42nd Division, which had retaken the Dovecot.

These new positions were much exposed, though, and German machine-gun fire steadily increased throughout the morning. From 9 a.m. parties of German infantry tried to overrun the company on the right flank of this new position. One such attempt was made by a group of Germans advancing under the cover of long grass. One man, Lance Corporal G. Hunter, firing with his rifle from a shell hole in advance of the line checked this attempt, hitting four of the Germans. The remainder took cover and brought forward a machine gun to fire at the troublesome New Zealand soldier. Hunter was wounded three times, yet he held his position and kept up a steady fire on the enemy, an act that undoubtedly stemmed their counterattack. Just beyond the Dovecot, New Zealand engineers uncovered a huge dump of stores, including explosives already prepared for use as road mines and booby traps. The 1st Rifles suffered only light casualties while securing the Dovecot: one officer killed in action, two officers and sixteen other ranks wounded.[46]

With the Dovecot secure, the remainder of the planned attack could be executed. For the New Zealand Division, this meant undertaking a small but 'somewhat peculiar' task.[47] While the 5th Division swept through Achiet-le-Petit and across the slopes to the south, heading for the village of Irles, six platoons from the remaining two companies of the 1st Rifles were to clear the valley immediately to their front in order to protect the rear and right flank of 5th Division during its advance. Once Irles was taken these platoons were to swing more than 90 degrees to the southeast, pivoting on the Dovecot to provide a defensive flank for the new position.

Just before zero hour, set for 11 a.m., Brigadier Hart, who had only learned of his brigade's role in this attack at 5 o'clock that morning, received some information which caused considerable alarm. As his diary records:

> half an hour before Zero got a message that a half company which attacked last night, found this morning they were very forward & near a railway line. This was in an open valley where movement was impossible as the opposite ridge was held by the enemy. Our barrage was opening at 11 o'clock, 300 yards on our side of the half company. Had an awful job to get barrage rearranged and just did it in time.[48]

Hart's decisive and rather desperate action narrowly averted a catastrophe for the New Zealand Division.

The attacked opened promptly at 11 a.m. with an accurate barrage that moved down the railway line, and then lifted left to right at 100 yards every four minutes. The Otago Machine Gun Company in support of 1st Rifles put down a heavy barrage on the furthermost slope of the valley. While machine-gun fire from the Germans was intense, the operation was a complete success and the objectives were taken well within the allocated time. This included the whole of the Ancre Valley north of Miraumont, including the railway. Miraumont village, just 400 yards away, was to be the objective of the following day. During this brief attack the 1st Rifles captured 76 prisoners, seven machine guns and a heavy trench mortar.

Their casualties numbered 51, of which seven had been killed.[49] That evening, in a 'frightfully hurried' relief where information was obtained only with 'great difficulty'[50], 42nd Division took over the New Zealand portion of the line, and the Rifle Brigade moved back to Puisieux where it became the divisional reserve.

The weather on 23 August was very hot, sapping the energy of all the soldiers involved. It was especially harsh on the tank crews, of which 100 were operating with the Third Army. In some cases, crews of the Mark V tanks became unconscious through the heat and fumes. Yet despite this, 23 August was a day of success, with some 8000 prisoners taken. South of the River Somme an advance of 2 miles had been made and more than 2000 prisoners taken. North of the Somme, General Byng was closing in on the town of Bapaume.

Third Army had made the greatest gains. Seven of its divisions attacked an equal number of German divisions facing them and advanced from 2000 to 4000 yards on a front of 11 miles. In doing so, they captured a number of villages and some 5000 prisoners, securing all but one of their objectives. The Germans were driven from the Arras–Albert railway embankment and cutting, which had been their main line of resistance before the Hindenburg position. It was a significant achievement.

As part of Third Army, IV Corps on 23 August 'achieved considerable success.'[51] The Corps had advanced its line an average of 2000 yards. It had captured the strongly defended railway line, which was the German's main line of resistance and which three German divisions had been ordered to hold to the last man. The three defended villages of Irles, Achiet-le-Grand and Bihucourt had been taken, along with more than 5000 prisoners.

German regimental histories speak of a disaster occurring on 23 August 1918. That of 232nd Reserve Infantry Regiment recorded:

> The day was a catastrophe for the regiment. It cost its good old stock. All three battalion staffs, all company commanders, all medical officers, the greater part of the excellent telephone detachment, and more than 600 men: and in the period 8th to 22nd August we had already lost 300 men. Only two officers and 42

other ranks, mostly of the II Battalion, in addition to the regimental staff, escaped.[52]

As the day drew to a close, Third Army was astride the Arras road and menacing the town of Bapaume, which was to become the main objective of the days ahead. At 4 p.m. on 23 August, the New Zealand Division received warning orders to sidestep slightly to the north in order to carry out an attack towards Bapaume the following day. Ahead lay two strongly defended obstacles, barring the way to Bapaume. They were Loupart Wood and the fortified village of Grévillers, both of which had eluded the 5th Division on 23 August. The previous day a prescient Russell had recorded in his diary:

> Minor fighting all day . . . reconnoitred out towards Loupart Wood
> in case we move there. Corps Comdr called in in the afternoon.
> We do not move yet, but are kept in reserve.[53]

The time had arrived for the New Zealand Division to take a leading role in this great offensive.

Chapter 4

The First Attempt on Bapaume:
24 August 1918

BY THE EVENING of 23 August 1918 Bapaume was within reach of the Third Army. South and west of the town, all the ridges bar one had been taken. The uncaptured ridge ran from Loupart Wood to Grévillers and on to Biefvillers-lès-Bapaume (hereafter referred to as Biefvillers) — if it could be taken, then Bapaume would belong to the Allies. As Ormond Burton noted, if these two villages and the wood on this ridge fell to the Allies 'the way was open for a direct encirclement of the town itself'.[1]

The 5th Division, which had failed to take both Loupart Wood and Grévillers on 23 August because of the strong German resistance there, was ordered to form a defensive flank on the right, running from Irles to the wood itself. On the left of this position the 37th Division was charged with capturing Biefvillers, while in the centre the New Zealand Division was to capture Loupart Wood and Grévillers, before pushing on towards Bapaume. While this was happening the 42nd Division was to secure IV Corps' right flank by taking Miraumont and the high ground to its east.

Unfortunately for those making the attack the weather turned sour on this day. While the preceding days had begun with fog and mist, then turned stiflingly hot, on 24 August it was cloudy and cool, with some rain and drizzle. The low cloud was the worst feature of the weather. It seriously hampered the efforts of the RAF to identify enemy artillery and machine-gun positions. The ability to precisely locate enemy points of resistance and pass this information on quickly to artillery units was vital if any advance was to succeed.

The terrain that lay before the Third Army was part of the area between the British front line of 1916 and the Hindenburg Line. There had been no heavy fighting here at all, so the ground was not cut up by shell-fire. There were many hutted camps in the area, which had been used as rest areas by the BEF. When the Germans occupied the area, they turned the huts and camps into strong defensive positions. German soldiers were afforded considerable shelter and concealment amongst the ruins of the villages that had been destroyed by them in March 1917, as they retired to the Hindenburg Line. Shifting soldiers from the ruins of towns, cities or villages is never an easy task and so it would prove on this occasion. Away from the villages, the open country could best be described as rolling hill country. Lieutenant Colonel S.S. Allen left a vivid description of the country over which his battalion attacked on 24 August:

> The ground is fairly elevated, open country, the only enclosures or trees being around the different villages, each of which is hidden away in the grove that surrounds it. There is a succession of low ridges, like waves, from Bucquoy eastward through Bapaume — and to a considerable distance beyond, the ridges running north and south.[2]

The plan for the New Zealand Division on 24 August was to advance in two stages. The first stage involved the advance of the 1st Brigade, supported by two brigades of field artillery and some tanks, to a line 500 yards beyond Loupart Wood and Grévillers, both of which had to be captured. Included in this advance was a quarry on the Baupame–Achiet-le-Grand railway. This movement would secure the right flank of the Division, while the capture of Biefvillers by the 37th Division would secure its left. The total distance of the advance was just over 1500 yards and, if successful, it would leave Third Army in possession of the last ridge before Bapaume.

Once this ridge was taken the second stage of the operation would commence. The New Zealand 2nd Brigade would sweep from this ridge through Bapaume to the high ground east of the town. Bapaume, it was thought, was only lightly held and should fall like a ripe plum into the lap of the New Zealand Division. Unfortunately, things were not going to be that easy.

Recognising that the New Zealanders had the toughest task of the day, IV Corps was generous in allocating the Division additional support. The guns of the 5th Division, the XXVI (Army) Brigade Royal Field Artillery and XC Brigade Royal Garrison Artillery were assigned to the New Zealand Division. In addition, thirteen Mark IV tanks and a company of Whippet tanks were to accompany the New Zealand infantry as it advanced towards its objectives.[3] Most of the tanks were allocated to 2nd Brigade, which would not have the advantage of a creeping barrage in its attempt to snatch Bapaume from the Germans. As it turned out, the 1st Brigade did not have this advantage either.

As night fell on 23 August the men of 1st and 2nd New Zealand Infantry Brigades, who had been nervously waiting for the word to advance since the offensive began, moved forward to assembly points near the new front line. Thomas Dale recorded of this anxious wait:

> We are all impregnated with the desire to move into the stunt despite the fact that many of us know what it is likely to be . . . to move means to go into danger. But there is an urge to be in with the other fellows in the great events which are happening and are going to happen, which is taking full possession of most of us despite every other consideration . . . This hanging around waiting when big events are taking place is the hardest part of a soldier's life.[4]

The front line ran a little east of the Albert–Arras railway, midway between Achiet-le-Petit and Grévillers. The infantry of the 1st Brigade was concentrated near Gommecourt, that of the 2nd Brigade near Bucquoy. They were warned to be ready to move at any moment. Despite the odd gas shell, the night was generally quiet. The infantry soldiers were in the lightest of fighting order, having dumped 'all valises, greatcoats and cooking gear' on the morning of 21 August.[5] At around 10 p.m. on

23 August, rain began falling. Between 11 p.m. and midnight, General Russell, in an advanced HQ between Bucquoy and Achiet-le-Petit, issued his orders for the attack.

In fact, owing to the fluid nature of events, two sets of orders were issued. The first objective was to be the line of Loupart Wood, Grévillers and Biefvillers, but it was uncertain what the New Zealanders' next task would be. Russell therefore outlined two courses of action to his brigadiers. The first and most likely was that 1st Brigade, commanded by Brigadier Melvill, would seize the line of Loupart Wood–Grévillers, an advance of around 1500 yards. Then the 2nd Brigade, commanded by Brigadier Young, would pass through this new line and move on Bapaume, an advance of around 2000 yards. If the 1st Brigade found that Loupart Wood and Grévillers were already taken, then it would push on to Bapaume and try to capture it alone. Each brigade would have heavy and Whippet tanks in support and could call on three artillery brigades should they be needed. Zero hour was set for 4.15 a.m. on 24 August, when an artillery barrage would provide cover for the attack.

The 1st Brigade moved out at 1.30 a.m. on 24 August, skirting along the northern edge of Achiet-le-Grand to its assembly area, which was on a road about half a mile east of the Albert–Arras railway. As no one knew where the front line was at this time, each battalion took the precaution of sending out an advance guard and screens of scouts. The night was overcast with a waning moon, so there was little light and the assembly of the brigade was not detected by the Germans even though it entailed a move of some 3000 yards in the open.

The failure of the Germans to notice the assembling Allied troops is fortunate because, at least for the New Zealand Division, the orders given for the 24 August battle were rushed, chaotic and confused. The brigadiers had received their orders from Russell about midnight on 23 August, so that most units did not get notice until after 2 a.m. on the morning of 24 August, leaving less than two hours to prepare. There was just enough time to issue verbal orders to junior officers; there was no time to put them in writing nor to organise an artillery barrage. A gunner in the 2nd Brigade NZFA recorded of this haste:

The orders for the attack were not issued until 2 a.m. on the 24th and the attack was timed for 4 a.m. It was found that the time available was too brief to enable detailed orders for a barrage to be issued to brigades and thence to batteries. Brigades of artillery were, therefore, attached to the infantry brigades and artillery brigade commanders reported for instructions to the Commander of the infantry brigade to which they were attached. The infantry attack was therefore launched without any organized barrage fire, despite which fact, it made good progress.[6]

However, the lack of an accurate artillery barrage at the start of the attack made it much harder for the infantry units of the 1st Brigade to obtain their objectives. In fact, most New Zealand soldiers had no idea what their objectives were on 24 August or even where the enemy was. As Ormond Burton commented in his history of the Auckland Regiment:

Very few had a clear realisation of just what had to be done, or how it was to be done . . . very quietly the men moved out into the darkness, knowing little save that they must go forward.[7]

Burton was even more critical of the lack of preparations in his unpublished manuscript. He wrote:

Our directions for the attack were vague in the extreme especially by the time they had filtered down to platoon sergeants. We moved off at 4.15 a.m. in the most informal fashion — no artillery support, no knowledge about our flanks, no anything. This did not seem at all right when you had been brought up decently in great shock battles like the Somme, Messines, and Gravenstafel.[8]

Frederick Varnham, the Adjutant of the 1st Wellingtons and a cousin of Douglas Knight, who is quoted elsewhere in this book, made some notes in his pocket diary as the battalion moved forward to Loupart Wood. His words reflect the uncertainty of the situation:

Road congested with troops ahead, tanks and wagons. Our position regarding the attack rather vague. Had Loupart Wood and Grévillers fallen or not? Battalion marched up in columns of route to assembly lines, everything very quiet. By great luck got into position.[9]

One set of orders required the brigade to attack and capture Loupart Wood and the village of Grévillers. Brigadier Melvill directed the 1st Wellington Battalion on the right to take Loupart Wood, while 2nd Auckland on the left was to take Grévillers and the railway on the edge of Biefvillers. In support and covering the junction of the lead battalions was the 2nd Wellington Battalion, while 1st Auckland was designated the brigade reserve. The road running from Achiet-le-Petit to Grévillers was given as the boundary line for the two lead battalions. While both lead battalions were ready by 4 a.m. there was some confusion about whether an artillery barrage would be provided. When none was forthcoming, 2nd Auckland set off at 4.15 a.m., right on time, with 1st Wellington following 45 minutes later. Although the anticipated artillery barrage did not eventuate, the troops were not totally bereft of support. Six large tanks were allocated to assist 1st Wellington Battalion to take Loupart Wood and two to help 2nd Auckland capture Grévillers. Three Whippet tanks were also available for the drive on Grévillers. In addition, a section of machine guns was attached to each battalion, with the remainder of the Machine Gun Battalion providing direct overhead fire.

No reconnaissance had been possible so both lead battalions moved straight towards their objectives. As they did so, heavy rain started falling, which severely limited visibility. The rain gave excellent cover though and the New Zealanders were able to cross the exposed ground under cover of darkness and morning mist. As they moved through the open fields the men could see signs of recent fighting. Thomas Dale of the 1st Auckland Battalion, the brigade reserve, noted:

Once in No-Man's-Land we began to observe the inevitable signs of battle. Sprinkled every here and there were our dead lying in all positions. Soon we began to notice a number of greeny-grey figures mingled with the khaki, in some places where the fighting had been more fierce, these figures lay in twos and threes and sixes.[10]

These 'twos and threes and sixes' were most likely the German machine-gunners who had fought to their last moment. Despite the obvious signs of war, the absence of large numbers of shell holes meant it was hard for men who had been through the Somme and Ypres to realise they were walking over a battlefield.[11]

Both battalion commanders soon realised that they would not be marching on Bapaume and that the line from Loupart Wood to Grévillers to Biefvillers needed to be taken first. Bapaume would have be left to the 2nd Brigade following behind them. With no artillery barrage at zero hour and the blinding rain, it was some time before the Germans realised an attack was in progress. When they did, though, their resistance was fierce.

The 1st Wellington Battalion, commanded by Major W.F. Narbey, had two companies leading the attack. The Taranaki Company was on the left, Wellington West Coast on the right; Hawkes Bay was in support and the Ruahine Company in reserve. The battalion passed through the screen provided by 5th Division on the edge of Loupart Wood and in the rain and darkness reached beyond the first German machine-gun line. Once it was light, though, the job of taking the wood became much tougher. Concealed German machine guns were everywhere and the closely set trees prevented the tanks from entering the wood. Three immediate machine-gun posts were destroyed through the courage and leadership of NCOs and men. Sergeant H.H. Thomason and Corporal J.R. Blake each led a section of bombers against a machine-gun nest, killing the crew and capturing the gun. Sergeant W. Murray and a runner 'put a third out of action, killing the crew of 5'.[12] The advance resumed, but was soon brought to a halt by a new series of machine-gun posts. The machine-gun and rifle fire here was so intense that the two lead companies were held up. Some posts were overcome by NCOs leading small teams forward and dealing with them. However, progress had stalled and the battalion commander had to commit his reserve company. Two tanks did manage to reach the edge of the wood, where they gave the hard-pressed infantry vital support. Sergeant Henry Parmenter of the Divisional Signal Company had set up a communications station close to Loupart Wood and watched the tanks in action:

> We soon established our station and had communication back. Could see the tanks in action. Soon after we arrived a fritz sniper in Loupart Wood had us thinking once or twice. A tank M.G. got him later on in the morning. Fair number of prisoners passed by. Artillery not nearly as severe as we have experienced in other attacks.[13]

With this support, the Wellington West Coast Company, under Lieutenant G.A.A. Barton, was able to get moving again. It pushed on with such vigour that it cleared its section of the wood. Later, an additional company from the 2nd Wellington Battalion was also used. The War Diary of this battalion recorded: 'The enemy machine gun nests proving very troublesome and the wood not negotiable by tanks.'[14]

By 8.30 a.m. Loupart Wood was completely surrounded by the advancing Third Army, but it was not until midday that the wood was completely cleared of Germans. The 1st Wellingtons then established defensive posts on the southern and eastern edges of the wood, with a company in support in the open ground beyond it. According to the New Zealand Division's history, casualties in the 1st Wellington Battalion 'had not so far been severe.'[15] With eighteen killed and forty-six wounded they could not be considered light, either. But for the heavy rain, they would have been much higher. Amongst the three officer casualties was the Commanding Officer, Major Narbey, who had been wounded. The Adjutant, Captain Fredrick Varnham, recorded the day's events in his pocket diary:

> No artillery barrage — strong machine gun fire resistance by enemy — held up — finally wood taken — plenty of prisoners and captured guns. We had 65 casualties. Major Narbey wounded so command of Bn fell to me temporarily.[16]

Clearing this heavily defended wood tree-line by tree-line had been no easy task, as the New Zealand Division's history admits:

> But the fact that they had taken 8 hours to accomplish but a part of their mission, showed clearly the difficulty with which the advance would have to contend in attacking machine gun nests without an artillery barrage.[17]

While 1st Wellington was tied down at Loupart Wood, the 2nd Auckland Battalion was moving towards Grévillers, which was on the reverse side of the ridge. The battalion had not been given much time to organise this attack, Lieutenant Colonel Allen receiving his orders just after midnight. He gathered all his company commanders and the officer commanding the section of Vickers guns attached to the battalion in his dugout, where he explained his plan to them by the weak light of a candle. Allen intended to advance with two companies in the lead. The 15th Company on the right would cover half of the Battalion's front and advance on Grévillers. When it reached the village two platoons would skirt around the northern outskirts, while another did the same around the southern outskirts. These platoons would then link up on the far side of the village. The 3rd Company, which was to immediately follow the 15th, would then move forward and sweep through the village itself. Meanwhile, the 16th Company would cover the left half of the Battalion's front between Grévillers and Biefvillers. It was to advance without stopping to the final objective beyond the village. Allen had the 6th Company in reserve and allocated one of the Vickers guns to cover the left flank, which would probably be unprotected during the advance. The time of the attack was set for 4.15 a.m.

The lack of time, and the conflicting information and confused orders they had received meant that 'in the end we carried out the first alternative after all, with this important difference, that our attack was delivered now without a barrage or any artillery support at all'.[18] Unfortunately for Allen, he had an additional problem. The 2nd Auckland Battalion had reached the start line at 3.30 a.m. and was ready to go, but it was alone.

The 1st Wellington Battalion should have been on the right, but it was not. Some elements of 1st Wellington did arrive on the start line, but the battalion was not ready by zero hour. To further compound matters, the left flank of the 2nd Auckland Battalion was also wide open and the expected tank support had not turned up. Allen had every right to abandon the operation, but decided to go ahead. The battalion moved off in a column at exactly 4.15 a.m., headed for Grévillers and Biefvillers, both of which could be seen against the skyline. Allen described the night as 'curiously still' as his battalion set off.[19]

The nearest Germans were in a machine-gun nest about 300 yards on the left of the battalion's front. The lead company of 2nd Auckland surged forward, but it hit a barbed wire entanglement after only 200 yards. As the soldiers scrambled over it, the noise alerted the Germans in the machine-gun nest and several machine guns opened fire, forcing the platoon on the

The New Zealand attack
24 August 1918

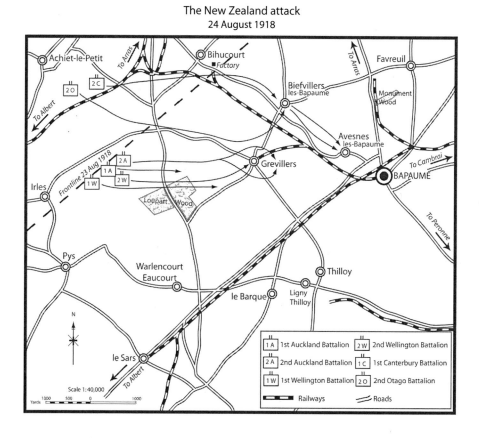

extreme left to take cover. Ormond Burton, a sergeant in the battalion, recalled that the machine guns 'commenced to knock sparks from the strands of wire. Evidently they were trained very accurately on the belt.'[20] The rest of the line continued to advance and surprised some German posts. A section from the supporting company came to the aid of the platoon that was pinned down by the machine-gun fire. It worked around to the rear of the nest, then charged with bayonets fixed. This was enough for the Germans, who 'hastily surrendered.'[21] As a result of this action two 77-mm guns and several machine guns were captured, along with their crews. Only two New Zealand casualties were sustained.

The western outskirts of Grévillers were reached with few casualties. Then the platoons from the lead company swung around on either side of the village, isolating it, and the support company moved up and proceeded to clear the village. A company from the 2nd Wellington Battalion also moved forward and cleared the southern section of the village and the surrounding fields. The War Diary of 2nd Auckland Battalion contains an accurate account of the action:

> The defence consisted of numerous machine gun posts scattered in well concealed positions plus a few light guns and trench mortars . . . The enemy machine gunners showed no liking for a fight at close quarters and surrendered readily. In the village the 3rd Coy found them quite unprepared, and even surprised one party at breakfast. It was on the flanks of the attack that most resistance was met with, much machine gun fire coming from the huts lining the Bihucourt–Biefvillers road.[22]

By 7 a.m. the village was in New Zealand hands, the German garrison there taken by surprise. A German account of the attack on Grévillers recorded of its loss:

> At 6 a.m. the 2nd and 3rd Battalions of 14th Bavarian Infantry Regiment were in position when suddenly, without large artillery preparation, and support from three tanks an English attack

from Grévillers broke loose. Both battalions were weakened by the preceding fights and were not able to withstand the attack. However, before breaking, they took up fire on the whole line and brought the opponent to a halt. The 2nd Machinegun Company [14th Bavarian Infantry Regiment] put a hostile barrage down. Two tanks were forced by our artillery to withdraw.[23]

A soldier in the 2nd Wellington Battalion witnessed the fall of Grévillers. He recorded in his diary:

> At five a.m. we move off together with a . . . of tanks. 'Auckland' is in the first wave and we go in second as supports. We soon come to the top of the first ridge where we get a fine view of the tanks attacking [Grévillers] which is soon captured by the Aucklands who go through the village. We dig in on the near side of the village. Right throughout the stunt we were under heavy machine gun fire but had very few casualties considering.[24]

While the village had fallen easily to the New Zealanders, the rest of the morning's attack did not go quite so well.

As the 15th Company's platoons moved around the edge of Grévillers those south of the village encountered some serious trouble, coming under fire from a high crest to their front and from Loupart Wood to their rear. When dawn broke they also saw a strong German position just 30 yards to their front. The fire from this position forced these platoons to take cover and for a time it seemed as if all further progress was halted. According to Ormond Burton, who was there:

> It was impossible to raise a head while the Huns continued to rattle through belt after belt at such a furious pace. There was nothing to be done but lie still and wait for better times.[25]

Those 'better times' arrived much sooner because of the work of Sergeant Samuel Forsyth, a Gallipoli veteran and an engineer NCO on attachment with 2nd Auckland Battalion. Two British tanks appeared in the distance but made no effort to assist the New Zealanders despite the Kiwis' desperate efforts to attract the attention of the tank crews. Forsyth, who had carried out a reconnaissance of the German positions, ran under fire to the nearest tank and led it forward to assist the beleaguered New Zealanders. While doing so he was wounded in the arm but continued to direct the tanks to a position where they could attack the German machine gun positions. The Germans, aware of the danger, scored a direct hit on the lead tank with an artillery round. Forsyth assisted the crew from the wreck, formed them and several New Zealand soldiers into a section, and led them forward to outflank the German machine guns. The machine-gunners did not stay to face an attack from their flanks, but withdrew, allowing the high ground south of Grévillers to be taken.

Forsyth then helped to organise a new line of resistance on a bare, exposed slope. While doing so he was killed by a German sniper. His heroic actions saw him awarded the Victoria Cross. This was gazetted on 18 October 1918 and his medal presented to his widow Mary by King George V.[26] Ormond Burton knew Samuel Forsyth well and was wounded in the arm by the same sniper that killed his friend. Also decorated for his part in this attack, Burton regarded Forsyth's VC as:

> . . . one of the best of those that went to the New Zealanders. At Grévillers Sam was head and shoulders above us all — a most valorous exhibition of imaginative daring sustained through a long and dangerous advance. Behind it too was a record second to none in the Division. Sam had many days of valour behind him and this was but one of many.[27]

On the left, the 16th Company went over the crest between Grévillers and Biefvillers and was met with heavy fire, especially from the more alert Germans defending Biefvillers. At the same time, several Allied tanks appeared from the direction of Achiet-le-Petit. These opened fire on the attacking forces, most using their machine guns, but one training its six-pounder gun on Lieutenant Colonel Allen's headquarters. The New

Zealanders were caught in crossfire, from the enemy at Biefvillers on the left front and from their own tanks to the right rear. Although no one in the headquarters was hit, as the tanks advanced round Grévillers they fired on the men of 3rd and 15th Companies, causing some casualties. These large tanks were followed by five more of the Whippet variety. Demonstrating considerable courage, Allen and his padre advanced to meet them. As they did so the Whippets trained their machine guns on the two men, but did not fire. Allen went up to the nearest tank and hammered on its metal skin with his pace stick. He then directed the tanks to Biefvillers, where they fired on the enemy and helped suppress some of the German machine-gun fire there. Later, a company from the 2nd Wellington Battalion pushed on to the high ground beyond the road to the north and then, with the assistance of soldiers from two other New Zealand Battalions of the 2nd Brigade, cleared Biefvillers just after 10 a.m. The village was supposed to have been taken by the 37th Division, but the New Zealand battalions were forced to do it in order to secure the 1st Brigade's left flank. Advanced posts were then pushed out for 500 yards east of Grévillers in the direction of Avesnes-lès-Bapaume. The platform had been set for the 2nd Brigade's advance on Bapaume.

The capture of Grévillers was a significant event for the New Zealand Division. There are several reasons for this. First, Lieutenant Colonel Allen believed it was the finest achievement of his battalion during the course of the war. He wrote:

> I consider it to have been the best piece of work the Battalion ever did. An advance of two thousand yards had been made, and a very strong position taken, without any support on either flank or from artillery, the success being solely due to the resolution of all ranks to make good as much ground as possible for the benefit of the troops following us . . . Owing to the light casualties the work done by the Battalion was not much appreciated by some who are prone to judge the difficulties encountered more by the extent of the slaughter than by the success achieved.[28]

Allen was right to be proud of this success. That it was attained at all was primarily due to the surprise attack in darkness, the patchy German defence, and above all, the bold leadership of junior officers and NCOs. The capture of Grévillers 'yielded the first of those hauls of prisoners, guns and war material, which were to characterise the advance of the next three months'.[29] The 2nd Auckland Battalion in this attack captured 386 prisoners, two 77-mm guns, four 8-inch howitzers, six mortars, and thirty-six machine guns. This was a substantial haul for one morning's work. The 8-inch howitzer battery was regarded at the time as 'the most important capture yet made by New Zealand troops'.[30] The battalion won a Victoria Cross in this action, the first of three awarded in this battle.

Although Allen described the casualties as 'light' and Ormond Burton called them 'an astonishingly small cost',[31] 2nd Auckland had suffered significant casualties. These numbered some 113 soldiers (including seven officers), of whom eighteen had been killed in action.[32] Jesse Stayte of the 1st Auckland Battalion noted as he passed through Grévillers that afternoon:

> The place here is strewn with death and war materiel generally. The tanks were used successfully today. I do not know what our casualties were today. Prisoners are coming back freely and very many wounded.[33]

One of the officers injured was Allen himself. He had been 'hit in the face by a nose-cap of a small shell, and became a casualty'.[34] Major McClelland took command of the battalion. That evening, 2nd Auckland Battalion was relieved by the other Auckland battalion in the brigade.

While 1st Brigade was carrying out its attacks on the Loupart Wood and Grévillers objectives, the battalions of 2nd Brigade concentrated near Achiet-le-Petit, ready to play their part. At 8.30 a.m., on learning that the 1st Brigade was having trouble clearing the wood and the two villages, Brigadier Young committed his two leading battalions to the action. They were to protect the exposed flank of the advance by taking Biefvillers and, then, if things went well, push on to Bapaume and capture the town.

The leading troops advanced, with the 2nd Otago Battalion on the right and the 2nd Canterbury on left. They were accompanied by five large tanks and ten Whippets. This force met little opposition until it reached Grévillers and Biefvillers. Then it experienced serious trouble. In front of it, German machine-gun fire from trenches by the Albert road caused heavy casualties and artillery fire damaged most of the tanks.

Upon reaching Grévillers the 2nd Otago Battalion moved into an extended line, with its right flank resting on the northern edge of the village. The line of Biefvillers was gained and 2nd Otago assisted in clearing the enemy from the village. While doing so, the Otago soldiers came under heavy fire from their front and both flanks. The fire, coming from three directions, was intense and it forced the leading soldiers to take cover. As the Battalion's War Diary records: 'Casualties soon became very heavy and the formation disorganized.'[35] The Battalion's reserve company was committed and managed to gain a series of trenches on the eastern side of Grévillers, from where Bapaume could be clearly seen on the next ridge, just a mile away. But the Otago soldiers could not make any further progress. In this brief skirmish the 2nd Otago Battalion suffered over a hundred casualties, eighteen of them being killed in action.

On the left of the 2nd Brigade advance, the 2nd Canterbury Battalion had an easier time, not being exposed to the German fire from the flanks. It assisted with the capture of Biefvillers, linked up with the 37th Division, then the bulk of the Battalion pushed on in the direction of Bapaume, against ever-stiffening machine-gun fire.

As soon as the Canterbury Battalion and their supporting tanks appeared on the ridge south-east of Biefvillers they were fired on by German artillery. The fire was heavy and knocked out the supporting four tanks almost immediately. Biefvillers was soon under artillery fire, too. The advance slowed and the Germans were subjected to accurate counter-battery fire from the New Zealand gunners. However, the enemy defence around Bapaume was 'extremely formidable'.[36] After severe fighting and more heavy casualties some patrols from both leading battalions reached Avesnes-lès-Bapaume, a small hamlet just north-west of Bapaume, and the Bapaume–Albert road to the right of the town. There they captured some 41 prisoners from the 44th Reserve Division, a fresh German division that had just been thrown into the line to defend Bapaume and relieve the shattered remnants of the other defending formations.

The soldiers who reached Avesnes-lès-Bapaume soon found themselves in serious trouble. The divisions flanking them on either side had been left behind, meaning the 2nd New Zealand Brigade was forming a pronounced salient. Highly exposed, the men came under intense fire from three directions.

The situation deteriorated later that morning when both the commanding officer and adjutant of 2nd Otago were killed by snipers while making a personal reconnaissance to check on the situation. It was not a good day for New Zealand commanding officers: Lieutenant Colonel W.S. Pennycook was the third casualty of the morning. Some of the men at the forward posts fell back when their ammunition was exhausted. Those who stayed at Avesnes were captured in an enemy counterattack on Biefvillers made at 1 p.m.

The German counterattack fell on the left flank of the New Zealand position. It was preceded by a process of infiltration, whereby the Germans were able to mass men on this flank. Then came intense machine-gun and rifle fire delivered at close range. According to the historian of the Otago Regiment, this fire 'overwhelmed and practically wiped out the whole of our advanced elements'.[37] As the War Diary of the Divisional Artillery recorded:

> About 1 pm the enemy counterattacked from Bapaume in a north-westerly direction on a front of about 3000 yards compelling us to form up on a line running east of Biefvillers and thence South.[38]

It was fortunate that the Germans did not press home this attack, as it would have caused even greater damage 'but our counter artillery fire, together with Lewis Gun and rifle fire drove him off and our line . . . remained intact.'[39] As it was, Avesnes-lès-Bapaume was abandoned and the New Zealand units dug in where they were: the 2nd Otago Battalion about 400 yards east of Grévillers, the 2nd Canterbury Battalion in front of Biefvillers. The right flank of the new position was secured by the 1st Brigade, but touch was still not made with 37th Division on the left flank. The New Zealanders' first attempt to take Bapaume had failed 'with fairly heavy casualties in spite of the fire from our field Artillery'.[40]

That evening, German aircraft flew over the New Zealanders, circling over the newly established artillery positions and their wagon lines. Within an hour came the cost of this detection, the 2nd Brigade NZFA recording that 'the 2nd Battery and Headquarters were severely shelled with 4.2 gas shells for about half an hour'.[41] The infantry battalions also received their unwanted share of the enemy's attention, the 2nd Otago Battalion recording: 'Enemy continued shelling heavily with H.E. and gas throughout the night.'[42] Its sister battalion witnessed an aerial attack at 5.30 p.m., recording that:

> When the roads were crowded with the incoming Naval Division and the whole reverse slope of the hill was alive with troops and equipment a German aeroplane circus of 13 machines came over. There was great excitement whilst bombs dropped and machine guns rattled.[43]

Luckily this attack caused no casualties in the Otago battalion.

Despite the casualties, 24 August had been 'a very successful day' for the Third Army.[44] Its centre and right wing had advanced on both sides of the Albert–Bapaume road. Thiepval ridge, which had been the scene of a four-month struggle before its capture in 1916, and Pozieres, scene of an Australian bloodbath also in that year, had been captured. The New Zealand Division had reached the outskirts of Bapaume, but was unable to remain there as its flanks were exposed and a strong German counterattack had driven it back. Yet, as the Australian official historian noted, there were signs that the Germans around Bapaume were 'in sore straits'.[45] Both Third and Fourth Armies had, according to the New Zealand history of the campaign, 'made great progress.'[46]

The British official history was less praising of the achievements of Third Army on 24 August, describing IV Corps' efforts as 'disappointing'.[47]

It regarded only the fall of Miraumont as being significant. One reason it gave in mitigation for these small gains was that the eight German divisions originally facing the Third Army on 21 August had been reinforced by a further nine.[48] As a result, German resistance had stiffened and the element of surprise had been lost. Despite this, in the four days of the offensive, IV Corps of Third Army had advanced more than 7 miles. Lieutenant General Harper was happy with this progress and at the end of 24 August he sent a message of thanks to all ranks, congratulating them on their success 'which could have only been attained by great fighting capacity and endurance.'[49]

At the end of 24 August the New Zealand outposts were only 2.5 miles north of the scene of their fighting in 1916. On that day, after heavy fighting, the New Zealand Division had captured three important objectives: Grévillers, Loupart Wood and Biefvillers, as well as nearly 400 prisoners and a mountain of war materiel. However, they had not taken their last and most important objective — the town of Bapaume. Their casualties had been heavy, too. A soldier in 2nd Wellington Battalion, which had followed up behind the 1st Wellington and 2nd Auckland Battalions, noted in his diary that, 'The Division suffered fairly heavy casualties today principally from machine guns.'[50]

And at least one of the battalions involved in the attack was unfit for further action. This was the 2nd Otago Battalion, which had been badly mauled at Grévillers and Avesnes-lès-Bapaume. Its casualties numbered 112, including its commanding officer and adjutant, both of whom had been killed in action. On 25 August the 2nd Otago Battalion did not leave the trenches it had captured. Its War Diary explained why:

> The companies were reorganised and supplies of ammunition and bombs replenished. Most of the men were badly shaken after the attack of the previous day. The enemy continued firing with 'H.E.' and gas so there was little opportunity for rest.[51]

The battalion was relieved that evening and was not used again until 2 September, the very last day of the Battle of Bapaume.

The 2nd Auckland Battalion did not escape lightly, either. Douglas Knight hinted at this in a letter to his parents: 'We have had a lot of wounded especially, but are going strong. War is an awful waste and you have no possible idea of the conditions.'[52]

The conditions he referred to were far from pleasant. The men were in open country, and the rain, muddy trenches and lack of sleep did nothing to improve the lot of the ordinary soldier. An artillery officer recorded in his diary:

> Out of the region of eternal shell holes now. Open position here. The whole N.Z. div has come here where there is a mass of troops. Sleep has been very short since Monday and I am filthy dirty. One wounded. Things pretty rough for the diggers in front here today.[53]

On the afternoon of 24 August Brigadier Hart and General Russell rode forward to check on the progress of the two New Zealand brigades. While doing so they witnessed the wounded being evacuated and the dead being collected for burial. Commenting that the numbers of dead soldiers 'fortunately . . . were not great' Hart recorded: 'The whole scene was very stirring and much less gruesome and awesome than the Somme, Messines or Passchendaele.'[54]

In a similar vein, and often repeated over the next few days, Russell recorded in his diary for 24 August: 'Attacked and carried Grévillers and Biefvillers — light casualties — S.S. Allen wounded.'[55] In fact, casualties had been particularly heavy in three of the lead battalions, all of which had lost their commanding officers. Losses had been particularly high amongst the officers and NCOs, whose vital leadership and experience gave the New Zealand Division its cutting edge. Yet this was only the first day of real fighting for the New Zealand Division in the Battle of Bapaume.

At the end of 24 August the New Zealand line ran east of Grévillers and Biefvillers, with open country in front of it. Ahead, just 1 mile away, the ruins of Bapaume beckoned ominously. For the New Zealand soldiers fighting this battle in the days ahead, this was going to be one of the longest miles they would ever experience.

Chapter 5

Cutting the Crossroads: 25 August 1918

IN THE EVENING of 24 August 1918 General Byng issued his orders to the Third Army for the following day. Well pleased with what had been achieved in the past hours, his orders were for more of the same. He did not dictate how this was to be done, only that the general advance should continue. Edmonds has commented on this rather *laissez faire* approach:

> To a great extent, the operations were treated as being of the character of advanced-guard actions against a somewhat demoralised enemy, who, as in the retreat of March 1917, held on for a time in the hope of inflicting heavy losses before retiring from position to position back to the Hindenburg Line.[1]

Orders issued to IV Corps were more precise. The whole of IV Corps was to conform with the general advance, with the aim of reaching the line from Riencourt-lès-Bapaume to Beugnâtre, which was very near the Hindenburg Line and some 2 miles beyond Bapaume. As a preliminary to reaching this final objective, the 37th Division was to capture the high ground towards Sapignies and, in the process, take over the village of Biefvillers from the New Zealand Division. This would release the New Zealanders and so enable them to make a thrust around the northern and southern edges of Bapaume.

Through the town of Bapaume ran four great highways. To the south-west ran the road to Albert, to the south-east was the road to Péronne, to the east ran the road to Cambrai and to the north was the road to Arras. Cutting these highways would completely isolate Bapaume, something IV Corps planned to do early on 25 August. As part of this manoeuvre, to isolate the town the New Zealand Division was expected to cut the Albert road south of the town and the road to Arras in the north.

The New Zealand Division planned to envelop Bapaume by passing a brigade on either side of the town. The 1st Brigade, based at Grévillers, was to cooperate with the advance of the 63rd Division on the New Zealand Division's right flank. At 5 a.m. the brigade was to move to the south of Bapaume, halting at a line at the northern end of the village of Thilloy. This would place the men well past the Bapaume–Albert road. Meanwhile, the 2nd Brigade was to operate north of Bapaume, capturing Avesnes and the near edge of Monument Wood on the Arras road. On completion, the men were to link up with the 37th Division at Favreuil on the Division's left flank. It was hoped that both New Zealand brigades could reach the line of Riencourt-lès-Bapaume–Bancourt–Beugnâtre. Such a deep objective would mean that Bapaume was virtually surrounded, compelling the Germans to abandon the town and thus avoiding the need for costly street fighting. Both brigades would have tanks in support, plus the backing of three brigades of field artillery.

During the night of 24–25 August German artillery was very active. The New Zealand artillery batteries, in particular, were subjected to a severe gas bombardment. This activity culminated in a heavy barrage along the front at 4 a.m., which drenched the approaches for the attack with gas and high-explosive. The War Diary of the 2nd Brigade NZFA recorded:

> Enemy shelled heavily all night both forward and back areas and put down a very heavy barrage on the front system about 4:00 a. m. The barrage opened up well at 5: a.m . . . [2]

Luckily this barrage caused few casualties.[3] At 5 a.m., under the cover of a heavy fog, the New Zealand infantry swept forward towards its first objectives.

The two battalions of 1st Brigade, the 1st Auckland and 2nd Wellington Battalions, were to brush against Bapaume's southern outskirts, but had been warned 'not to press home their attack against determined opposition'.[4] As the country it was working in was relatively easy and the bulk of the fighting was to be done by the 63rd Division, 1st Brigade had been allocated no artillery support. To its right, the 63rd Division cleared the German line immediately in front of it and captured the village of Le Barque. But the 63rd Division failed to take either Ligny-Thilloy or Thilloy, being unable to make any headway against the fierce machine-gun fire there. The 63rd Division was still some distance from Bapaume. The two North Island battalions managed to seize part of the German line near Grévillers and one battalion, the 2nd Wellington, pushed on to reach the Albert road about 1000 yards north of Thilloy. This was to be the extent of their progress on this day. The two battalions could not get any further, being exposed to the machine-gun posts in Bapaume on their left and checked on their right by an open flank. The infantry of the two battalions spent the rest of the day consolidating their new positions and patrolling forward of them.

Progress of attack
25 August 1918

On the northern side of the town the situation was completely different and as the historian of the New Zealand Division noted: 'a hard day's fighting was to fall to the 2nd Brigade.'[5] The attack on Bapaume was to be renewed with the units of 2nd Brigade that had not been involved in the fighting so far. These were the 1st Canterbury and the 1st Otago Battalions.

After many changes of orders it was finally decided that for 25 August the two battalions would operate side by side, with the 37th Division protecting their left flank. Both battalions assembled under a clear, moonlit sky behind the 2nd Canterbury Battalion on the slopes near Biefvillers. The 1st Canterbury was on the right, closest to Bapaume, with the 1st Otago on its left. The first objective was the line of the Bapaume–Arras road; once that was attained the infantry would advance to a line extending from the village of Favreuil to the Bapaume cemetery, including all of Monument Wood. Ahead of the two attacking battalions the ridge from Biefvillers dropped gently to the hamlet of Avesnes and to the sunken road where the Germans had been in force the previous day. On the far side of this valley the ground rose steeply to a tree-clad embankment and then more gradually to the Arras road. On the Otago sector there was a track from Biefvillers to Favreuil, which cut the road at right angles. At the crossroads there stood an imposing monument, a commemorative pillar to the 1870 Battle of Bapaume.[6] Just south of the monument, and about a mile north of the town, jutted a wide spinney known as Monument Wood. All this was ideal defensive terrain and stiff opposition was expected. The two South Island battalions would have three artillery brigades fired in support of their advance, and further back-up from twenty-three tanks, of which fifteen were Whippets, four were Mark Vs and four Mark IVs. The initial advance, set for 5 a.m., would be supported by a creeping barrage and once again the men were protected by a heavy ground mist.

The two South Island battalions set off on time, using the dense mist and dust raised by the enemy barrage to provide invaluable cover. There was no sign of the tanks, but the creeping barrage 'was of gratifying weight and accuracy.'[7] The German defenders immediately sprang to life and began firing along the fixed lines of their defensive positions.

Despite this stubborn resistance, by 7 a.m. 1st Canterbury had cleared Avesnes and reached its final objective in the broken country beyond the hamlet, capturing the junction of the Albert and Arras roads. Just then the mist lifted quickly, leaving the battalion terribly exposed. Men who had pressed too far forward were captured and the rest of the battalion came under intense machine-gun fire from the northern outskirts of Bapaume. Fortunately there was plenty of good cover and the battalion stayed put and dug in. It established a line of posts on the Bapaume–Arras road, running 200 yards south to the cemetery on the immediate outskirts of the town. The Battalion's War Diary recorded the events of the day:

> At 5.00 a.m. our barrage came down and the Coys moved forward behind it helped by four Mark V and four Mark IV tanks. These unfortunately were a little late in starting, and a very heavy mist increased this disadvantage. The barrage was a good one, but the enemy put up a stubborn resistance. Mist and shell and M.G. fire made the advance difficult. The objective, however, was reached at about 7:00 a.m.[8]

Bapaume was slowly being enveloped. In clearing Avesnes and its outskirts 1st Canterbury took 150 prisoners. Its own losses, according to its War Diary, 'were not heavy' — sixty-six men, of which six were officers. The 1st Canterbury also managed to identify the two divisions opposite it defending Bapaume as the 220th (Prussian) and the 7th (Bavarian) Divisions.[9]

However, it was 1st Otago, under command of Major James Hargest, that would do the bulk of the fighting on 25 August. It moved forward at 2 a.m., assembling in the trenches in front of Biefvillers. The infantry 'hopped the bags' at 5 a.m., with the 8th and 4th Companies leading the assault. The 14th Company was in support and 10th Company in reserve. The move was supported by an effective artillery barrage, as described in the Battalion's War Diary: 'Punctually a first class barrage came down, rested 6 minutes, then advanced at the rate of 100 yds in 3 minutes.'[10]

The infantry advanced on the heels of this creeping barrage, but despite the skill of the gunners, almost immediately it encountered strong German resistance. The dense fog and German gas shells undoubtedly had a dual effect, making it difficult to find the enemy, yet also enabling many of the attackers to reach the German machine-gun positions unobserved. In the Battalion's War Diary it was noted that the mist and gas 'made the keeping of direction very difficult. Heavy M.G. fire was met with and strongpoints could not be located until they were run right into.'[11]

At one location Second Lieutenant Fyfe was challenged by an officer to surrender. Fyfe shot the officer and led his section to capture the German position. However, clearing this first line of enemy strongpoints was taking its toll and a number of platoons lost direction. As a result, when the leading companies of the 1st Otago Battalion topped the crest of the rising ground and gained their first objective, the Bapaume–Arras road, there were several gaps in its line.

The fog lifted as the battalion advanced towards its second objective, exposing the attackers. German machine-gun fire, especially that coming from the road and Monument Wood, was intense and unrelenting. The New Zealand casualties soon started to mount. The Battalion's War Diary recorded:

> It was an anxious time at Headquarters, since the position was very obscure. The leading Coys were not in touch with each other and owing to heavy M.G. fire from both front and flanks could not reach the objective.[12]

Further progress was impossible and the situation was not helped by the arrival of two Mark IV and two Whippet tanks. The New Zealand history explains:

> It was one of those anxious moments which sooner or later befall every battalion in a prolonged experience of war. Nor were prospects improved when the tanks at length arrived and engaged our men with misplaced energy from the rear.[13]

Once the tanks were made aware of their error they engaged the enemy in front of Monument Wood, but were soon knocked out in quick succession. Their support did make a difference, though, and just after 9 a.m. 1st Otago was on the line of its first objective on the Arras road. However, with the barrage lost, further progress was impossible. In front of the battalion was a heap of dead Germans; eighteen machine guns and 150 prisoners had been captured. During the day's fighting, though, the 1st Otago Battalion suffered the largest numbers of casualties yet in this battle. These numbered 220 men, including nine officers.[14] The unit's casualties were especially heavy in the morning, particularly in the 4th Company, on the right, which lost 50 per cent of its attacking force, including the company commander and the company sergeant major.

The 1st Otago Battalion linked up with the 37th Division on the left, which was also held up by the fierce opposition, but there was a big gap on the right where contact with the 1st Canterbury Battalion had not been established. The Otago companies were also widely separated, so the 2nd Canterbury Battalion was moved forward from Biefvillers into close support and a company allocated to 1st Otago to use as an immediate reserve. The three battalions of 2nd Brigade consolidated their new positions and remained in them for the rest of the day. The final New Zealand line was astride the Bapaume–Arras highway just north of Bapaume itself. It was not a good day for armoured support, though. Not only had the New Zealanders come under fire from the tanks during their advance, but once they were established on the road, a British armoured car turned up and fired on them. On learning of its error, it tried to travel along the road into Bapaume, but was soon knocked out by German fire.

In the afternoon the three South Island battalions were subjected to heavy gas shelling and an enemy aircraft dropped some small bombs and then machine-gunned the 1st Otago position about the Arras road. Ground fire was noticeably diminished, though, so during the afternoon small parties from the 1st Otago Battalion were able to penetrate into Monument Wood to a distance of about 200 yards.

With progress momentarily halted, plans were hastily drawn up to renew the attack that evening at 6.30 p.m. Under a heavy artillery barrage the 37th Division on the left was to capture the northern half of Favreuil. In conjunction with this movement, two companies from 1st Otago would advance with their right flank across the road, reaching the cemetery north of Bapaume and linking up with 1st Canterbury. In the centre, all of Monument Wood was to be captured, while the left flank linked with the 37th Division to take the southern half of Favreuil. This included a trench system on the edge of the village. The 2nd Canterbury Battalion would also be used. It was to follow on the heels of the Otago attack, pass through the newly won positions and exploit this success by capturing the high ground north of Bapaume and pushing patrols into the town itself. If the enemy retreated the men were instructed to maintain contact with fighting patrols until the line from Bancourt to Beugnâtre was reached. The attack was to be preceded by a ferocious artillery barrage on Favreuil, the road and Monument Wood.

Meanwhile, the Germans began burning their supply dumps, which was interpreted as a sure sign that they intended to withdraw. This was most likely a deception, though, as the Germans also planned a counterattack using fresh troops of 111th Division, in an effort to regain the ground they had lost at Arras road. This attack was timed to commence just after the New Zealand one. Luckily for the New Zealanders and 37th Division, a British aeroplane detected the German troops massing for the counterattack and struck at them from the air. To add to their woes, the hapless German troops were caught in the open by the barrage that preceded the renewed Allied attack. As the New Zealand history records: 'The bulk of the force was dispersed with serious losses, and the remainder rendered too demoralised either to attack themselves or to resist our onset.'[15]

After this piece of good fortune, the attacking force met little opposition. Monument Wood and the southern portion of Favreuil were easily taken, 'a complete and immediate success' according to the Otago Regiment's history.[16] The 37th Division in the north met tougher resistance, but still managed to clear its portion of the village after dark. On the right, at the cemetery near Bapaume, it was not so easy and strong resistance was encountered. It was so intense, in fact, that a whole company was required to subdue the position, and later, when the Germans counterattacked, soldiers from 2nd Canterbury had to assist this Otago company to repel the attack. All the objectives of the Otago Battalion were taken.

The evening was sultry and heavy; thick smoke hung over Bapaume. At 9 p.m. a violent thunderstorm burst and rain fell for the rest of the night. In the pitch black and driving rain the 2nd Canterbury pushed three companies through the new Otago position. At first the going was easy and a fresh line of outposts was established on the Favreuil road, but when patrols pushed on to the Bapaume–Beugnâtre road, they met stiff opposition. By midnight, though, some of the Canterbury patrols had established a defensive flank on this road, facing south. However, patrols that pushed towards Bapaume encountered fierce resistance. It looked very much as though the Germans intended to stay. Large parties of enemy troops were seen digging trenches and the town bristled with machine-gun posts. It was clear to those on the spot that this objective could not be taken by isolated patrols, which, very prudently, did not try to enter the town. Thus ended the New Zealand Division's second attempt to capture Bapaume.

At Favreuil village and the trenches to its east, the Otago soldiers captured 118 prisoners. One of the prisoners was a regimental commander, and his entire staff was also captured. In addition, much war materiel was captured, including a field gun and forty machine guns. Casualties from this night attack were light, although they included both company commanders who took part.

A German account of the loss of Favreuil is quoted in the British official history:

> On the 25th August the British continued their attacks on both sides of Bapaume with particular determination . . . In vain was the 111th Division brought up on both sides of Favreuil from second line to remedy the damage. In the end, this village also became the prize of a stronger enemy.[17]

Actually, the Germans had two divisions defending Favreuil. It was taken on 25 August by a British brigade of 37th Division and two companies of Otago soldiers.

On 25 August, two corps of the Third Army had achieved 'a considerable advance'. The British official history described this progress as 'remarkable' because Third Army was still using its original thirteen divisions without any reinforcements, while the Germans had reinforced their original eight divisions in line 'by no less than eleven fresh ones.'[18] This was the fifth day of the offensive during which IV Corps advanced well over a mile — in some places it was as much as 3 miles. This was in spite of the fact that two fresh enemy divisions had been put in against them.

The progress of the New Zealand Division on this day had been mixed. The British official history is wrong when it states that: 'Complete success attended the attack of the New Zealanders.'[19] South of Bapaume, the two battalions of the 1st Brigade had taken only part of their first objective and spent most of 25 August carrying out ineffectual fighting patrols. To the north, the 2nd Brigade did better, although the Brigade's War Diary accurately described the attack as 'only partially successful.'[20] However, it had still taken most of its objectives and over 400 prisoners, including a full colonel and his staff. The tally also included three German medical officers, one of whom was a naval officer who had been visiting the front line to gain experience.[21] During the day, 'after a long and bitter fight', the brigade took Avesnes hamlet, and a large section of the Arras road as far north as the monument at the crossroads near Favreuil.[22] That night, a second attack took part of Favreuil and reached the Bapaume–Beugnâtre road. But the ultimate prize of Bapaume again eluded the New Zealanders.

The well-constructed and concealed German defences were primarily responsible for checking the New Zealand Division's progress. The situation wasn't helped by the supporting tanks arriving late and then attacking the New Zealand soldiers. It was not helped, either, by the quality of some of the British troops. Lieutenant L.C.L. Averill of the 4th Rifles, then in reserve behind Biefvillers, left a revealing account of the state of one of the British platoons taking part in this attack. Lieutenant Averill wrote:

I well remember a platoon of one of the English Infantry Regiments continuing the advance near us who, instead of proceeding in the direction of Biefvillers-lès-Bapaume, were moving parallel with our front line. I went out and spoke to a Sergeant of this unit and gave the general direction of the advance for which I was duly thanked. Among other things the Sergeant said 'Unfortunately our officer is drunk, I have never seen him this bad before.' I should think this officer would almost certainly have been killed later in the day as a drunk man is an easy target for a marksman.[23]

One is left to wonder how many of his men suffered from his irresponsibility. One is also left to wonder why the sergeant or another senior NCO did not relieve the officer of command and take over. This most certainly would have happened in a New Zealand (or Australian) platoon.

There is little doubt that it was the 1st Otago Battalion that did the bulk of the fighting in the New Zealand Division on 25 August. Its men alone captured 270 prisoners, one field gun, four trench mortars and over forty machine guns. The next day, Major General Russell visited the headquarters of the 1st Otago Battalion and 'personally offered his congratulations on the success achieved.'[24] There is no question that the battalion deserved this recognition,

Russell's diary entry for 25 August recorded: 'Attacked Favreuil and Carresville — small casualties.'[25] In fact, for one day's fighting the casualties had been heavy, especially in two battalions of the 2nd Brigade. The 1st Canterbury Battalion, whose War Diary records that its casualties 'were not heavy', suffered sixty-six casualties including six officers.[26] The 1st Otago's casualties were far greater, numbering 220 men. Of these, nine were officers.[27] The 2nd Canterbury Battalion, which had been involved primarily in the night attack, suffered 194 casualties, of which twenty-two had been killed. Nine of its casualties were officers.[28]

Some of the supporting units also experienced heavy casualties. The medical history describes those in the 3rd Field Ambulance, which treated some 250 wounded New Zealanders that day, as being particularly heavy.[29] The unit's War Diary describes what happened:

> About 2: p.m. whilst Major Johns . . . was inspecting the forward car collecting post . . . the locality was subjected to a heavy shell fire. Major Johns and 4 Other Ranks KIA.[30]

Private Melville King witnessed what happened, recording in his diary:

> The Medical Corps had a relay post on the opposite side of the road to us at which two motor ambulances were standing. The post suffered badly, several of the men being hit. One of the chaps came into our trench and I bandaged him up, he was hit in the face, and legs two places, and he had the top of his finger taken off. On the commencement of the bombardment the ambulance drivers started their motors and made off in a great hurry and thus saved their cars.

Private King felt that the Allies, the New Zealanders included, were becoming too careless during this advance. He recorded:

> During the day troops by the thousands, transports, guns and limbers etc have been moving about as though there was no war on. I have never seen such movement in daylight before. This no doubt was responsible for the heavy shell fire today.[31]

Major Noel Johns MC, who was killed during this barrage, was a well-known figure in the medical corps and his loss was felt deeply. A stretcher-bearer in the unit wrote home to his parents:

> We learned too, to everybody's deep sorrow, that Major Johns and four men (including Reg Briggs and Len Poole) had been killed by, and some others wounded, all by one big shell.[32]

While the 2nd Brigade remained for two more days in the positions won on 25 August, it played no further part in the battle for the town, primarily because of the heavy losses it had already suffered. The next day the units of the Rifle Brigade moved through the new-won positions to continue the attack. They had a day of hard fighting ahead of them on 26 August. Meanwhile, the units of the 2nd Brigade used the time to collect and bury their dead. The 1st Otago Battalion ended its War Diary for August 1918 on a somber note:

> The majority of the bodies of the men killed in action on 25th were brought together for and buried on the ridge close to the Bapaume Cemetery and the centre of the battlefield of that day. A cross has since been erected over the graves and the names of the NCOs and men who fell inscribed on it.[33]

The New Zealand Division had again tried to capture Bapaume and several hundred more New Zealanders had been killed, captured or wounded as a result. The thick, black smoke that hung over the town on the afternoon of 25 August encouraged many to believe that the Germans were preparing to abandon Bapaume.[34] But this was wishful thinking. As one soldier taking part wrote: Bapaume was 'proving one of the toughest nuts to crack on all of the front.'[35] There were more days of severe fighting ahead for the New Zealanders if the prize of Bapaume was to be theirs.

Chapter 6

The Third Attempt: 26 August 1918

O N 26 AUGUST 1918, THE British Expeditionary Force's First Army joined in the great offensive with the goal of outflanking that portion of the line holding up the left wing of Third Army. With three armies now engaging the enemy, this was 'the greatest battle yet fought by Haig'.[1] Third Army was to continue its advance, its objectives being Flers, Bapaume, Favreuil and Croisilles. The orders given for Third Army that day 'were simple', according to the official historian.[2] The three corps on the right were to keep advancing eastwards; the corps on the left was also to advance, but only if it maintained contact with the First Army. Capturing the central town of Bapaume was the key to this advance and so a third attempt to achieve this was to be made by the Third Army.

The capture of Bapaume, 'the principal object'[3] of the day, was again allocated to IV Corps. On the Corps' right the 63rd Division was to capture or contain Thilloy and then advance on to the road to Péronne. In the centre, the New Zealand Division, positioned well ahead of the flanking formations, was to make a fresh attempt on Bapaume and push on to the high ground east of the town. On the left, the 5th Division was to advance and capture Beugnâtre.

General Russell planned to avoid making a direct attack on Bapaume. Rather, the New Zealand Division would first encircle the town and then, if an attack was needed, approach it from the rear. The 1st Brigade was to continue to encircle the town from the south, while the 3rd (Rifle) Brigade was to take over the attack from the 2nd Brigade in the north. It was to pass through the 2nd Brigade's forward position and envelop the town from this direction. Although there was to be no artillery barrage in support of the initial attack, each battalion had a battery of field artillery allocated to it, as well as a section of machine guns and light trench mortars.

South of Bapaume the 1st Brigade had to conform to the movement of the 63rd Division on Thilloy. The brigade was not to assault Bapaume directly, but once it had reached beyond the town and linked up with the Rifle Brigade, it was to send out fighting patrols to test the town's defences. If these were weak, then both brigades would enter and clear the enemy from Bapaume.

The Rifle Brigade, operating north of Bapaume, had more room to manouevre and therefore had a much greater role to play. It was to advance in cooperation with the 5th Division from the Beugnâtre road, cross the railway and the Cambrai road and seize the high ground towards Bancourt. It would also test the defences of Bapaume from the north. This was an advance of some 1500 yards and on a front of 2500 yards in a south-easterly direction. Such an advance would all but encircle Bapaume and secure a position due east of the town.

To carry out this crucial task the Rifle Brigade would use three battalions in the initial advance, leaving just one in reserve. The 3rd Rifles was placed on the right, the 2nd in centre, with 4th Rifles on the left. The left and centre battalions were to reach the high ground south of Beugnâtre, leaving the capture of the village to the division on their left flank. The battalion on the right (3rd Rifles) had three critical tasks to perform. It was to capture the village of St Aubin immediately south of Favreuil, pass along the northern outskirts of Bapaume and establish a defensive flank around the town's eastern approaches. Finally, it was to reach and cut the road to Cambrai. The start time for the attack was set for 6.30 a.m.

South of Bapaume, the 1st Brigade and the 63rd Division made limited progress. According to the British official historian, this was because both Bapaume and Thilloy 'were still strongly held, and three tired British divisions were attacking nine German, four of which were comparatively, and three quite fresh, but another so battered that it had to be withdrawn during the night of the 26th/27th'.[4] Certainly, the battalions of the 1st Brigade could not get forward owing to the heavy fire coming from Bapaume on its left and the vulnerable open flank on its right. The 1st Brigade accounted for this lack of progress in its War Diary:

'The 63rd Division withdrew slightly and made 2nd Wellington's task still more difficult. Our troops suffered a good number of casualties.'[5]

By mid afternoon of 26 August the commander of 63rd Division had decided against any further attempt on Thilloy and blamed the New Zealanders' inactivity for it. The Division's War Diary recorded:

> Div Comdr spoke to Corps Comdr on telephone. Div Comdr is not in favour of a frontal attack on THILLOY as the troops of N.Z. Div on our left are not going over . . . No frontal attack on THILLOY is to be made. The village is to be contained by infiltration. Attack will not take place today but strong patrols will be sent out.[6]

The 63rd Division did little for the rest of the day, its patrols noting at 10.50 p.m. that 'THILLOY reported still strongly held by the enemy'.[7] At midnight the division received firm orders to capture Thilloy the next day.

Jesse Stayte, of the 1st Auckland Battalion, left a revealing record of the lack of progress on this day and the reasons for it. He wrote:

> We went over the top at 7 am but did not get very far for we were opposed by a great number of machine guns, so we dug a shallow trench and stayed there all day and are also staying here tonight . . . In this trench we found dozens of Fritz rifles leaning against the side and also their packs all ready for moving, and yet all were left behind suggesting a very hasty retreat. We are now alongside Bapaume, our objective. We are under heavy shell fire all day.

In fact, Stayte's platoon remained in the trenches for the next two days.[8]

An event of significance took place south of Bapaume in the afternoon of 26 August. Around noon the 15th Company from the 1st Auckland Battalion was sent to assist the 2nd Wellington Battalion, whose advance was checked. On the way it became involved in a firefight that resulted in the awarding of a Victoria Cross. The battalion's War Diary recorded:

Sergt Judson and four men bombed their way forward 200 yards reaching H31 D 75 capturing 3 M.G. and prisoners. Owing to Division on right returning 2nd Wntn came back to original position and 15 Coy withdrew also to previous positions.[9]

The War Diary entry does not do justice to Judson's actions. No sooner had 15th Company commenced its move forward than it was forced to take cover from the withering machine-gun fire. Sergeant Judson then led a small patrol through the fire and along a sap, where they captured one machine gun and attacked two more machine-gun crews with Mills bombs. The Germans tried to make a hasty withdrawal, but Judson jumped out of the sap and ran fully exposed along its edge to head the fleeing Germans off. He managed to get in front of them, pointed his rifle at the group of twelve Germans and called upon them to surrender. There was a moment's hesitation and then the two German officers ordered their men to fire on Judson, which they did. Judson threw a Mills bomb at the group, waited for it to explode and then leapt into the trench and fought the survivors hand-to-hand. He killed two of the Germans in this struggle; the rest fled, leaving behind their two machine guns. For this remarkable action Judson was recommended for the Victoria Cross, which was duly gazetted on 29 October 1918. That same edition of the *London Gazette* also featured his DCM citation.[10] This was the second Victoria Cross won in this battle. In all previous battles where New Zealand soldiers had won this highest of military honours, only a single award was ever made.

As on the previous day, this was to be a day of very hard fighting for those units operating north of Bapaume. The Rifle Brigade moved forward at 1 a.m. on 26 August, but things went badly even before the attack commenced. All of the battalions experienced heavy shelling and the three battalions in the attack had to fight to reach their start line, which was the sunken Beugnâtre road. It was strongly held by the Germans and presented a formidable obstacle. The shelling caused some casualties, as the diary of Vincent Jervis attests. Jervis, a rifleman in C Company of the 2nd Rifles, was crouching in a sunken road near Biefvillers waiting for zero hour, when:

While waiting in the sunken road I got wounded, a shell landed on the other side about 3 yards away and hit about five of us, one being killed. I did not know at first that I was hit. I got up and ran into a chalk quarry and then noticed that my left wrist and right leg were bleeding. I was uncertain at first whether to go out or not as they did not hurt but after a few minutes my leg began to ache a bit so I decided to go out. It was about 5 am when I was hit and we were to go over the top at 6.30 am . . . After taking what gear I wanted out of the haversack I went for my life out. Fritz was dropping shells around promiscuously and I was ducking and diving continuously.[11]

Second Lieutenant Robert Gilkison, of D Company, 4th Rifles, gave a vivid account of the dreadful conditions facing the riflemen as they moved forward that night:

Next day [25 August] we were just waiting, but at last orders came through, and at about 5.30 p.m. we started to move forward to take up a position between Biefvillers and Grévillers, some miles forward. We were given only a map reference to the place where we were to remain overnight. It started to rain. It got dark. Traffic both ways crowded the narrow roadway. Lost squads of men kept asking the way, the roads became softer and muddier and finally almost liquid. On we went. Derelict vehicles, guns etc. lying about. Only a few shells falling anywhere near us. Somewhere about midnight we found our objective which turned out to be a shallow, wet muddy trench. We were lucky to find an unoccupied hut a few yards away, and although cold and wet, we were soon warm and asleep.

Sleeping in abandoned buildings was a very dangerous practice. They were usually booby-trapped and the German artillery had them registered for their attention. Gilkison was extremely lucky on the morning of 26 August. He records: 'A few minutes after we left the hut, a shell landed on it and blew it to smithereens.'[12]

The rain stopped early that morning and at 6.30 a.m. the attack was launched in good weather. There were no tanks in support, nor had there been time to arrange an artillery barrage. While a battery of field artillery had been allocated to each battalion, it was a poor substitute. The history of the Rifle Brigade noted that as soon as the attack commenced 'the absence of a barrage was felt at all points'.[13] At the first forward movement of the riflemen, German machine-gun fire poured in on the New Zealand soldiers from three sides. Brigadier Hart recorded in his diary:

> The 26th was a very busy day. We had three battalions in line &
> were to feel our way forward constantly. All the morning we were
> establishing ourselves steadily on the Bapaume Beugnâtre road,
> well ahead of units on both flanks. The enemy resisted strongly
> & we suffered much from machine gun fire.[14]

On the left, the 4th Rifles was the battalion operating the furthest distance from Bapaume, but on its open left flank was the heavily fortified village of Beugnâtre. The battalion had been informed that Beugnâtre had been captured by the 5th Division, but soon learned to its cost this was not the case. The 4th Rifles advanced through the wood near Favreuil and reached a section of the sunken road between Beugnâtre and Bapaume. This was its immediate objective, which it captured after a stiff fight. Here, it consolidated. The company on the battalion's extreme left met considerable enemy resistance which it subdued only with the help of the artillery battery attached to the battalion. After half an hour both lead companies were on the Beugnâtre road and a quick German counterattack launched from Beugnâtre village was successfully repelled.

Lieutenant L.C.L. Averill, who would later be awarded a Military Cross for his actions on 26 August, was the officer commanding A Company on the 4th Rifles' left flank. He left a vivid record of what he described as 'An incredible day'. When Averill's company reached the first objective it took cover from both British and German artillery in some huts on the far side of the sunken road. Then Averill experienced a rare opportunity:

From the hut nearest to Beugnâtre I looked through a hole and could see a trench with a number of German soldiers in it, not more than 30–40 yards away. This was a heaven-sent opportunity to do some execution. With my companion's rifle I shot seven of these Germans through the head — I couldn't really miss as they were so close and they could not make out where the firing was coming from. Soon the heads stopped appearing above the trench but one fat German thought he would try to make a dash to the rear and with one leg drawn up was endeavouring to scramble out of the trench just in front our peep hole when a bullet killed him instantly. This made 8 Germans that I killed for certain but later in the day, when the area was cleared, there were 11 dead in that trench and three prisoners. I don't think that any other of our men were firing at this trench and so I think I shot them all. Reading this sounds somewhat callous but war is war and I lost several good friends on that day, including Charles Darling, our Acting Captain.[15]

Only one other officer in Averill's company, Lieutenant Jack Densem, survived this advance. Unfortunately, Densem would be killed later that day when the advance continued. The battalion's commanding officer, Lieutenant Colonel Beere, was also a casualty, being wounded while on his way to attend a brigade conference.

In the brigade's centre, the 2nd Rifles made slightly better progress. It advanced with just one company, D Company, covering its whole front. Two more companies followed in support, B Company on the right and C on the left. A Company was in reserve. The battalion's objective was the line of the Beugnâtre–St Aubin road. Its war diary recorded that 'little or no opposition would be met with except at St Aubin' and therefore 'It had been decided that our advance would take place without tanks or artillery barrage.'[16] The battalion did have the support of two light trench mortars and four Vickers machine guns.

The advancing companies were soon across the Beugnâtre road, but heavy fire from the village prevented further progress. Rifleman Arthur Leslie Ross recorded the action in his diary:

We attacked at six thirty, there was no barrage and no assistance from tanks, we were under heavy machine gun fire, and the high buildings were full of snipers . . . It took two hours to reach our objective, a sunken road. Just before we got there we chased some Fritzies out of huts by throwing Mills bombs through the windows, a quick rush and the road was ours. The road was four feet deep and gave us good cover if we kept down. A third of our men never arrived, casualties had been heavy.[17]

The Battalion's War Diary recorded that 'further progress was impossible, the right flank being absolutely in the air and the machine gun fire from Beugnâtre village was extra severe.'[18] An attempt by Rifleman Ross's officer to get the offensive moving again by attacking a machine-gun post to their front drew a heated protest by his section corporal. The officer insisted that it could be done with six men if they were well spread out and that he would lead them forward. As the section prepared to make the attack the officer was shot dead by a sniper. Ross recorded somewhat laconically: 'The Corporal took over the platoon and needless to say we did not rush the machine gun there had been enough wooden crosses won already.'[19]

The right flank was open and exposed, even though B Company had reached St Aubin village, which it tried to capture. The withering rifle and machine-gun fire from St Aubin and from Beugnâtre forced the attacking soldiers to take cover. The War Diary recorded that the 3rd Rifles:

failed to come up on the right flank leaving this Company completely in the air. Sniping and heavy machine gun fire from the woodstacks and high buildings around St Aubin compelled this Company to dig in and sit tight.[20]

The rest of the 2nd Rifles did likewise south and south-east of St Aubin. 'Thus the advance stopped,' admitted the Battalion's War Diary.[21]

On the brigade's right, the 3rd Rifles made some progress against heavy opposition. As the battalion moved along the northern outskirts of

Bapaume it attracted heavy machine-gun fire. The advancing companies had to deal with some of the isolated machine-gun posts before finally reaching the Beugnâtre road. The company on the left made considerable progress towards St Aubin, clearing the stores dump on the outskirts of the village in a series of hand-to-hand fights. However, machine-gun fire from St Aubin was too strong to enable the village to be taken. The company in the centre was under fire from both Bapaume and St Aubin, but pressed steadily forward to reach a position beyond the Arras road. This short advance contributed significantly to IV Corps' stranglehold on Bapaume, but the battalion was unable to advance any further.

One of the reasons for 3rd Rifles' lack of progress was the tenacity of the German machine-gunners who, more often than not, kept firing their deadly weapons until their positions were overrun. This was certainly the feeling of Allan Watkins from Gisborne, a Gallipoli veteran serving in the New Zealand Field Artillery. Working as a forward observer for the 3rd Brigade of artillery Watkins recorded in his diary on 26 August 1918: 'The boys advanced silently today but are held up by machine guns, hundreds of them.' The next day, with this opposition overcome and the momentum of the attack restored, Watkins recorded:

> We have come to a halt here having got too far ahead of the divisions on our right and left . . . We share great admiration for the way the machine gunners of the enemy stick to their work. Most died at their post.[22]

The Brigade's Narrative of Operations recorded the story of the morning's action:

> Between Bapaume and Favreuil our troops, advancing under heavy machine gun fire from the flanks, reached the line of the Bapaume–Beugnâtre road, our flanks resting about 500 yards from each village. West and Northwest of Bapaume no advance could be made on account of the extremely heavy fire from the town.[23]

Progress in the morning attack
26 August 1918

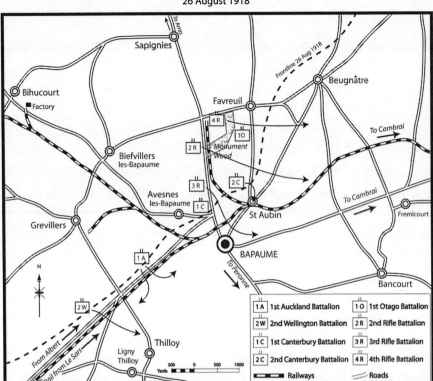

The end result of this dawn attack was disappointing. The first objective was only partially gained and the Germans still held Bapaume, Beugnâtre and St Aubin in considerable force. From these locations they poured a massive amount of machine-gun fire on to the exposed New Zealanders. Shortly before 10 a.m. the New Zealand battalions north and south of Bapaume received the order to sit tight and await further instructions. In fact, by 10 a.m. the advance along the entire IV Corps front was suspended.

Just before midday the Germans launched a quick counterattack from Beugnâtre using two infantry companies, hoping to catch their enemy off guard. The fighting was severe, but the attack 'was completely repulsed by Lewis Gun and Rifle fire, the enemy suffering many casualties'.[24] The 4th Rifles also suffered heavy casualties while repelling this attack, but held their hard-won ground.

With the morning attack clearly stalled, the Rifle Brigade planned another attempt that evening. The attack was to be renewed at 6 p.m., but this time it would be supported by an artillery barrage. Under this protective cover, the 2nd Rifles in the centre was to advance to the original objective on the Cambrai road, some 500 yards east of Bapaume. On the right, the 3rd Rifles would send patrols into the town to test its defences. On the left of the Brigade's line, the 4th Rifles was to swing its right flank forward into a north–south line and provide the link between the 2nd Rifles and the 5th Division, who by this time were expected to have captured Beugnâtre. In an effort to soften the German defenders, that afternoon Bapaume and the high ground to its east were subjected to a heavy artillery barrage.

Preparations for the evening attack were rushed and there was little time to issue detailed instructions. In fact, the orders for the attack only reached the platoon commanders just twenty minutes prior to its commencement. The New Zealand history commented:

> Brief orders were issued, but time did not permit of certain desirable changes in the machine gun positions or of anything but the baldest explanation to the rank and file. Such over-hurried preliminaries do not augur success.[25]

This is an accurate statement, but the situation was actually worse than is recorded in the existing histories. According to Lieutenant Averill, who was commanding a platoon in the 4th Rifles:

> The situation in the 4th Battalion was even more amazing as the orders for the late afternoon advance only reached me 20 to 30 minutes after the barrage which was to help our advance had opened. This was an incredible situation. I never heard the reason for this extraordinary delay in orders reaching us on the left flank company.[26]

For a company to receive its orders only after an attack had started was definitely an 'incredible situation'. It was also dangerous, foolhardy and negligent. Brigadier Hart, on realising the inadequate time given to his company and platoon commanders, did try to have the attack delayed, but he was unsuccessful.[27]

At 6 p.m. the 4th Rifles, with the exception of Averill's company on the left, advanced, keeping touch with the 2nd Rifles in the centre. The 4th Rifles covered some 500 yards, reaching beyond the railway to the high ground east of the Beugnâtre road. The battalion was forced to halt on this high ground. Its outer flank had difficulty maintaining contact with the 5th Division and was under considerable fire. Second Lieutenant Gilkison became another officer casualty that evening. His memoirs explain what happened:

> Just as the 3 Bn started their advance, the German guns opened up on our road, and a few minutes later a shell burst right on the road, a few feet behind me. I was crouched up against the bank, and one fragment penetrated the back of my chest, and another my left thigh. Douglas, the stretcher bearer quickly bandaged me up. I experimented to see if I could walk, but could not, and when the shell fire faded, four members of 16 pl carried me back in a stretcher to the RAP. Here the 4 Bn doctor fixed me up as far as possible, and later I was sent off in a field ambulance.[28]

Though he didn't know it at the time, this was the end of Second Lieutenant Gilkison's war.

Late in the night the 5th Division finally managed to clear Beugnâtre and the 4th Rifles linked up with it to provide a protective flank for the rest of the brigade.

The main role of the attack fell to 2nd Rifles, the centremost of the three battalions to the north of Bapaume. The artillery barrage opened right on time and the riflemen shook themselves out into attacking formations. The 2nd Rifles attacked with two companies forward, but owing to the haste with which the attack had been mounted, 'from the outset there was an inevitable lack of cohesion between the two companies.'[29] At first, things went well. The two companies skirted around St Aubin, crossed the Bancourt trench and pushed on towards the Cambrai road, some 500 yards distant. The railway line, halfway to the objective, was reached with only a handful of casualties. Beyond this line, though, heavy fire was encountered on the right flank from Bapaume and on the left from Beugnâtre, which the 5th Division had not yet captured. The battalion soon lost its supporting artillery barrage, which had lifted too slowly. The casualties started to mount. On the right C Company lost all of its officers, while 50 per cent of those in D Company were hit. The road was reached, but could not be held as it was enfiladed from both flanks. Then German defenders, who had been sheltering in a sunken road leading to a sugar factory, counterattacked and drove a gap between the two rifle companies, which were by then much depleted in strength. The men had little choice but to withdraw back to the railway line near St Aubin.

Evening attack of the Rifle Brigade
26 August 1918

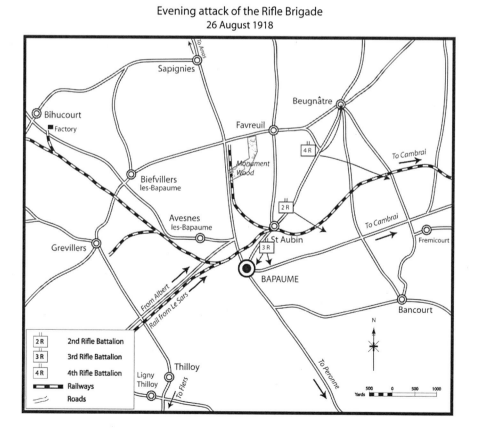

Fortunately, this small village had been cleared and was in New Zealand hands. The battalion's War Diary contains a succinct summary of the evening's action:

> The barrage came down at 6. p.m. and Coys moved off. As the advance progressed, Coys shook themselves into their formations and moved forward in excellent style. Heavy machine gun fire was experienced from the right flank, causing many casualties, C Company losing all their officers. The objective was reached but with a gap between the two Coys. The machine gunning continued and a strong party of Huns came in through the gap, forcing our men to withdraw, the line finally being established 500 yards in advance of the original line where they consolidated.

In this attack, the 2nd Rifles captured one field gun, several machine guns and twenty prisoners.[30] Fortunately for the 2nd Rifles, the rest of the evening was quiet and their consolidation continued without interruption.

Meanwhile, on the right, patrols from the 3rd Rifles pushed their way towards the northern outskirts of Bapaume. They skirted around the north of Bapaume but could not reach the Cambrai road. Steady machine-gun fire coming from a brickyard and the shrine on the road itself prevented these patrols from making any further progress. Both flanks of 3rd Rifles were under fire, so the riflemen from this battalion established a series of posts close to Bapaume's northern outskirts. This ended the New Zealand Division's third attempt to capture the town.

On 26 August New Zealand soldiers in the front line received supplies via aerial drop for the first time. The War Diary of the 1st Otago Battalion recorded the event: 'The feature of the day was the dropping of 5 boxes of SAA [Small Arms Ammunition] by means of parachutes from aeroplanes.'[31]

The technique of aerial supply, which would become such an important feature of the Second World War, had been pioneered by the Australian Corps, who first trialled it during the battle of Hamel on 4 July 1918.[32]

When the New Zealanders were supplied by this innovative technique, they were greatly impressed.

The advance of the New Zealand Division on 26 August amounted to about 1000 yards on a 2500-yard front. This was to the north of Bapaume; the ground taken south of the town amounted to little more than a few hundred yards. At the end of the day the Beugnâtre road was behind the Division and the Rifle Brigade was well to the east of Bapaume. There is no doubt, though, that the progress of the New Zealanders on 26 August had been limited and was well short of the intended objectives set the previous evening. General Russell's notes in his diary for this day demonstrate his isolation from the battlefield: 'Attacked North East of Bapaume this afternoon and got all objectives — advance however small, but will help in ringing Bapaume.'[33]

Bapaume, in fact, had been enveloped from the north and was directly menaced from this direction. Clearly the German defenders could not remain in the town for much longer. In fact, that night the German General Headquarters gave the order for a general retirement, which included abandoning Bapaume and falling back to a line 15 to 20 miles in front of the Hindenburg Line.[34]

For a day's fighting that achieved only limited objectives, losses in the New Zealand Division had been heavy. Particularly hard hit were the battalions of the Rifle Brigade, which had suffered more than 300 casualties.[35] Over half of these were in one battalion, the 2nd Rifles, which had been in the centre of the battle line. It had incurred 178 casualties this day, including twelve officers. Forty-two of these soldiers had been killed in action and another three later died from their wounds.[36] On the morning of the offensive, the 2nd Rifles had a complement of 537 men.[37] Only two-thirds of these remained to fight another day.

L.B. Quartermain of 3rd New Zealand Field Ambulance worked as a stretcher-bearer for the wounded on 26 August. In one of his letters he gave some indication of the conditions facing the New Zealand soldiers.

> . . . we had a busy 24 hours from then. We had a long carry (a mile
> or two) and used wheeled stretchers over the tracks and woods —

all littered with German helmets and other gear. In the night it came on to rain, and the thick dust turned into mud! Traffic was thick and congested and the going was very hard indeed. We all got soaked to the skin — I could feel it trickling down all over me and my boots were squelching — and we had no chance of a rest, dry or change.[38]

The British historian, reflecting on the day's limited progress, noted that 'it became very obvious that the divisions were tiring'.[39] This was certainly the case for the New Zealanders in the front line. Allan Watkins, who was with the 3rd Brigade NZFA recorded in his diary the previous day that he was 'very tired. Have never been more so.'[40] Douglas Knight, of the 2nd Auckland Battalion, must have been incredibly tired at this time, too. He wrote to his parents on 27 August that he 'slept under a bit of board in a hole, sitting on my tin hat. Slept like a top too.'[41] Yet there was little sleep to be had for those in the front line around Bapaume. Thomas Dale, of the 1st Auckland Battalion, recorded the reason for this:

> Making ourselves as comfortable as possible under the circumstances we turned in to get as much sleep as possible but what most of us expected happened. The old Hun had either seen us or had marked this bit of a place for a few shells. Over they came bursting amongst men and horses, but the horses suffered the worst. It was not a nice sensation lying in a bit of a bivvie with only a piece of old canvas between you and a whizz bang.[42]

There was nothing the New Zealand soldiers could do but endure these conditions and fight on. As one perceptive writer noted, the German defenders' 'desperate resistance seemed to increase rather than diminish as the days dragged on.'[43] The battle of Bapaume was far from over.

Chapter 7

The Battle for the Town: 27–29 August 1918

O N THE MORNING of 27 August 1918 IV Corps had three divisions in line, with a further two held in reserve. One of the divisions — the 63rd — was located south of Bapaume and it was on this body of men that the advance of IV Corps rested. If 63rd Division could capture Thilloy, the left flank would be secure, so protecting the remainder of IV Corps from attack. The New Zealand Division was in the centre of the Corps, and closing in on Bapaume from the north and the south. To its north was the 5th Division, which had taken the village of Beugnâtre the previous night. Third Army and IV Corps had received orders to continue the advance made the day before. This meant the New Zealand Division was to continue its envelopment of Bapaume while the 5th Division moved with them on the left. A direct assault on the town was to be avoided, given the strength of the German defences there. It was hoped that enveloping the town would make a direct attack unnecessary. If the German defenders could not be shifted, then such an assault would have to be considered. However, it could only be carried out after considerable planning, something that would use up valuable time.

The immediate progress of the battle of Bapaume rested on the 63rd Division and its attempts to take Thilloy. This village was attacked by the 190th Brigade of the 63rd Division at 11 a.m. after an hour's heavy bombardment. Some patrols from New Zealand Division assisted in this attack, but despite the reinforcements it made no progress at all. Another attempt on Thilloy was made at 6 p.m. after the village had been shelled by the Corps' heavy artillery and the Division's field artillery. The results, however, were similar to the morning's effort. The Division's War Diary recorded the fate of this night attack:

6.00 p.m.

190 Brigade advanced to the attack. Enemy put down smoke barrage.

6.43 p.m.

Our Infantry have been seen entering THILLOY & prisoners are coming back.

7.20 p.m.

Our right has been held up & position on the left is obscure. Infantry were again forced to withdraw from the village.

8.20 p.m.

GOC 188 Brigade states attack failed on account machine gun fire from flanks. Position as before attack.[1]

At the end of the day the 190th Brigade dug in only some 300 yards ahead of its starting point. During the night the 63rd Division was relieved by the 42nd Division. As the British official historian noted, IV Corps on 27 August had 'made no progress whatever'.[2] This was primarily because Thilloy, like Bapaume, was still strongly held by its German defenders, who showed no signs of leaving. In an effort to persuade them to do so and in preparation for an assault on Bapaume, should that become necessary, the town and surrounding roads were heavily bombarded. The artillery firing on Bapaume ranged from heavy and medium guns to the mortars of the New Zealand Division. The War Diary of the Divisional Artillery recorded that at 10.45 p.m. 'Heavy Artillery asked to commence bombarding BAPAUME and its eastern exits, our 4.5-inch howitzers cooperating continuing through the night.'[3]

During the day, while the Rifle Brigade followed a policy of 'consolidation and sitting tight',[4] New Zealand patrols south of the town tested the German defences at Bapaume. They found them little changed from the previous day. One battalion's War Diary recorded the typical result: 'Patrol endeavoured to enter Bapaume, but was met by heavy M.G.

fire and suffered three casualties. Patrol then withdrew.'⁵

Henry Parmenter, of the Divisional Signal Company, recorded in his diary:

> Usual activity on this sector today, our troops are gradually surrounding the town. Our artillery is very active. Enemy aeroplanes have been fairly active of late. Dozens of our planes are up in the air all day long.⁶

Thomas Dale, of the 1st Auckland Battalion, also commented on the day in his diary:

> Most of this day was passed in standing to, ready to move at a moment's notice but we did not move. We heard all sorts of rumours, some that the enemy were evacuating Bapaume but it does not seem to be correct. Indeed he seems to be holding us up here. We heard one lot went over at 11 a.m. but could not get any reliable information. The guns snarl and bark occasionally but there has been nothing of a barrage nature during the day. This spot, in which we find ourselves, is anything but pleasant, we are on pins and needles wondering when the next shells are coming over. Fritz has his Jaeger troops in front of Bapaume, or rather in it. They are stiff with machine guns and are holding it well.⁷

That evening, when Dale was having dinner some 50 yards from the front line, more German shells were fired at his battalion. He wrote:

> this sort of thing is most nerve trying. It's bad enough when you have a good, deep trench to protect you but this, out-in-the-open stunt is past a joke. I suppose we shall get a good bit of this sort of thing now.⁸

During the night the 1st Brigade took over the front of the Rifle Brigade as far as the cemetery on the Arras road. This meant that Bapaume was effectively enveloped from the south and it left the Rifle Brigade free to confine its operations to north of the town.

With the Germans still entrenched in Bapaume and showing no signs of leaving, General Russell made plans for a direct assault on the town. He recorded in his diary:

> No great advance made yesterday evening so made a new plan which I submitted to Corps Comdr. & after lunch to brigadiers, who quite rightly want assurance as to advance on the left, which is imperative — this I got from Corps Comdr later, and hope that by waiting 24 hours all will go well.[9]

The main role in this attack was allocated to the 1st Wellington Battalion. Frederick Varnham recorded in his diary:

> Major Turnbull called to a Brigade Conference. This Battalion is to attack the town of Bapaume the day after tomorrow. We spend the evening studying with maps & aeroplane photographs the ways & means.[10]

Bapaume had taken a pounding from Allied artillery all day and into the night and there was a feeling that this bombardment might encourage the Germans to leave the town during the hours of darkness. IV Corps was ready to take any advantage that developed. General Russell, who had promised a flag bearing the word 'Bapaume' to the battalion that captured the town, made sure that several of his battalions were ready to move at a moment's notice. However, the German defenders remained in Bapaume that night, their resistance as fierce as ever.

It was evident, though, that despite the lack of progress made by IV Corps on this day, the Germans could not remain in Bapaume much longer. The town had been effectively enveloped by the New Zealand Division, and the First Army, fighting further north on the Scarpe, had made considerable progress. The Germans planned to hold the town just long enough to cover a retirement to the Hindenburg Line, and the time for them to leave the IV Corps' front was rapidly approaching.

Wednesday 28 August was a dull day with light showers, but the weather cleared in the evening, leaving a fine night. During the day there was relatively little activity across the IV Corps' front. As the British official historian noted, for Third Army 'the 28th was a day of comparative quiet and only small advances were made.'[11] This was particularly so on the New Zealand Division's front, where German artillery and machine-gun fire remained constant during the day. The infantry units stayed where they were during the day, 'completing arrangements for the attack, making reconnaissances etc'.[12]

That day Douglas Knight took the opportunity to write two letters to his parents. The first, to his father, described the day's events:

> Things are moving along slowly here & we are doing very well considering, but have not yet beaten old Fritz, but hope very soon to give him good cause for thinking so.[13]

The next letter, his last, described how he and his friends had escaped a close call the previous evening:

> Our 'bivvie' is just on top of the ground & near a road. It has had some narrow shaves & a tank nearly walked over it. They are great affairs and move quietly, not much more noise than a motor lorry.

Douglas' letter also contained some bad news. A close friend of the Knight family, Roy McDowell, had been killed. It deeply affected the young officer:

> Bad luck seems to follow everyone these days, but let us hope there is a change for the better soon. We have done very well here all along the line & let us hope, are very much nearer the victory we desire.

He ended his letter on a most poignant note: 'afterwards, God willing,

431

may we be able to build up again a prosperous home & a happy one.'[14] Three days later, he was dead. He was the third son his parents lost to the war, killed in action. It is unlikely that his last hope for the Knight family was ever fulfilled.

New Zealand artillery continued to rain down on Bapaume during the day of 28 August, as Jesse Stayte recorded in his diary:

> Our big guns are pounding Bapaume heavily today and our 18 pounder Batteries are very close up now. We expect Bapaume to fall to us tomorrow as we have it almost surrounded, but Fritz is fighting very hard for it now.[15]

There was no let-up for the German defenders at nightfall either. Twice during the night the New Zealand guns concentrated all their strength in a hurricane barrage, which started on the western outskirts and then rolled across the town. The War Diary of the artillery recorded that at 9.30 p.m.: 'Barrage fired commencing West of BAPAUME and lifting by 100 yards until it reached a line about 100 yards EAST of the town. This was repeated at 4.45 a.m.'[16]

New Zealand infantry patrols were sent out and some managed to reach the rest billets at Frémicourt on the high ground east of Bapaume. Everywhere the New Zealand infantry probed they found the Germans alert and active. As the historian of the Rifle Brigade noted: 'The enemy was found to be everywhere alert, and not a few casualties were sustained during the progress of this reconnaissance work.'[17]

The 1st Auckland Battalion, to which Thomas Dale belonged, took part in these night patrols. Dale wrote:

> Patrols are pushing out all the time. Old Fritz does not tell us what he is holding or where he is. We have to find out, & the only way to do this is to advance patrols until we come up with him then the heads decide what is to be done. Almost before they reach a decision Fritz has retired or altered his position in some way. Sometimes he catches us where we don't expect it. In sunken roads

& such places. These roads are sometimes like deep trenches only wider of course and the consequences if Fritz can enfilade them with mg fire, which he always does, they prove a death trap from which there is no shelter whatever. Again we snuggled as close to the earth as possible hoping that old Fritz would be kind to us & keep his shells and bombs to himself. And he did.[18]

At 6 p.m. that evening Lieutenant General Harper visited Russell's headquarters and 'propounded a scheme to rush Bapaume' the next day.[19] However, as a result of the way events unfolded that night, such a quick attack and the direct assault being planned by the two New Zealand brigades in line would prove to be unnecessary.

While the New Zealand artillery fire on Bapaume was ferocious on the night of 28 August, German retaliation was noticeably much weaker than previous nights. Private Lewis Nairn, of the 2nd Wellington Battalion, was in a trench near Irles, which had 'machine guns left by Fritz and dozens of dead' close by. He had witnessed twenty horses killed by German artillery during the day, and his diary recorded that evening: 'Fritz shelling off and on all night. Sleeping in trench.'[20]

In the early hours of 29 August German machine-gun fire and flares coming from Bapaume gradually slackened until at last firing ceased altogether. 'A strange silence fell upon Bapaume',[21] the New Zealand medical historian noted. East of the town, the glare of burning supply dumps was a sure sign that the Germans were leaving. The New Zealand infantry moved cautiously towards Bapaume to investigate.

On the night of 28–29 August the Germans facing the Third Army carried out a major withdrawal. South of the Somme River they withdrew as much as 4 miles to the river's far bank. North of the river the average distance of the withdrawal was much shorter — about 4000 yards. Even this short distance meant abandoning the key defensive positions of Ligny, Thilloy and Bapaume, and a new line was formed in the villages immediately before the ridgeline about 1.5 miles east of Bapaume. On the morning of 29 August both V and IV Corps of Third Army were able to advance from 2000 to 4000 yards before they struck any serious opposition. This was a considerable relief, as the Germans' 'superior numbers had delayed the IV Corps for four days.'[22] Yet while their initial progress on the morning of 29 August was good, IV Corps soon learned that the Germans were as capable as ever of holding up their eastward advance.

The German withdrawal left Bapaume unusually silent and empty. New Zealand infantry brigades at once sent out fighting patrols towards the town. Brigadier Hart recorded in his diary:

> An air of quietness prevailed at dawn & shortly afterwards reports came in that our patrols were entering Bapaume unopposed. The Hun had withdrawn, owing to our encircling tactics, while he still had time to do so.[23]

The New Zealand patrols entered Bapaume just after dawn on 29 August 1918. The first arrivals were fighting patrols from A Company of the 3rd Rifles, headed by Captain H.C. Meikle, MC. At 8.30 a.m. they entered Bapaume by the Arras road and worked their way eastward through the northern half of the town. They found no Germans there. The War Diary of the 2nd Rifles Battalion recorded:

> About 9.30 a.m. a report came through that the enemy had withdrawn from the southern side of BAPAUME. Our three line Coys each sent out patrols and found he was evacuating our part of the front. Each Coy moved forward in sections while the 3rd Battalion on our right, moved through the edge of Bapaume.

There was no opposition to this advance, but A Company of the 2nd Battalion 'was just in time to see the last of the enemy disappear over the ridge making for BANCOURT.'[24]

Shortly after the 3rd Rifles reached Bapaume, patrols from the 1st Auckland Battalion swept through the southern portion of the town, which was also empty. These patrols reached a factory 1000 yards beyond the Albert road. The Battalion's War Diary recorded:

At 6:00 a.m. 6th Company advised that enemy were suspected of evacuating and orders immediately issued for Patrols to push forward. At 8:30 a.m. our 3rd Company reported they had gone forward 1000 yds had reached H 32 8.5. Battn on left having reported they were moving through Bapaume.[25]

The order was given for the New Zealand artillery to cease firing while the 1st Wellington Battalion passed through the town and set off in pursuit of the German rearguards. An officer of the battalion wrote of the great haste to get forward and of the 'perks' of doing so:

Patrols and aeroplanes report enemy evacuated Bapaume. A great bustle. Battalion immediately advanced protected by scouts on Bapaume, entered and passed through same and established ourselves on the outskirts and in touch with the enemy . . . Boys obtaining plenty of souvenirs.[26]

At least one New Zealand soldier experienced a sense of history that morning. Sergeant Henry Parmenter of the Divisional Signal Company recorded in his diary:

Enemy shelling a little last night . . . Our troops found that Fritz evacuated Bapaume during the night. Our men went forward several thousand yards before getting in touch with the enemy again. In 1917 the Australians were the first troops to pass through the town when Fritz evacuated and this year our boys were the first to enter the battle scarred town.[27]

However, there was no time to savour the victory. That morning the two infantry brigades received a scribbled message from Divisional Headquarters written by Lieutenant H.M. Wilson, later to become a British Field Marshal:

Indications point to enemy withdrawal south of BAPAUME and

435

patrols have reached H 32. RUGO and PUHE [the codenames for each infantry brigade] will keep touch with the enemy and be prepared to follow him up with advance guards directed towards BANCOURT FRÉMICOURT and high ground east of it.[28]

The brigades did not need much prompting. Brigadier Hart recorded in his diary that:

Immediately the whole Army got a bustle on and there was great excitement. Our front troops pushed onward pressing the Hun rearguard which made a stand one-and-a-half miles East of the town. Battn, Brigade and Divisional Hdqrs all commenced moving forward, also artillery, Engineers & every branch of the service. For a while there was much activity, but by two o'clock we had pinned down the Hun positions everywhere.[29]

At least one German was not impressed with the occupation of Bapaume and the pursuit that followed.

6 a.m. [29 August] An enormous fire is directed on the length of the old vacated positions and on Bapaume. The opponent, who finds courage where he can use his machines [that is mortars and machine guns and artillery] notices the departure [from Bapaume]. At around 11.30 a.m., the first hostile patrol dares to venture forwards to Bapaume. From noon on, the hostile fire falls on Frémicourt and the positions at Bancourt and Riencourt. Under this protection the opponent, from 1.30 p.m., forges ahead first individually, and then in groups. From 4.00 p.m., the opponent is on the ridge between the Cambrai–Bapaume national highway and the Bancourt–Bapaume road with stand-alone posts and machine gun nests.[30]

In the centre of the Rifle Brigade's line the 2nd Rifles advanced and reached the Cambrai road a mile east of the town without a shot being fired at them. There the riflemen saw the last of the enemy rearguard disappear over the ridge towards Bancourt. The 2nd Rifles then swung back to its right to link up with the 3rd Rifles. Much equipment, including six howitzers and many machine guns, was captured by both battalions. Few prisoners were taken, though. On the left, meanwhile, the 4th Battalion was not able to advance as the Germans were still holding the railway sidings opposite the town. Two Whippet tanks attempted to crash through this position, but brought down upon them every German artillery piece in the neighbourhood. They were cut down before they had gone 200 yards.

By 2 p.m. the Rifle Brigade had established a new line some 1500 yards east of Bapaume and Beugnâtre and was only the same distance from the villages of Bancourt and Frémicourt. At the time, Frémicourt was heavily defended, but the Germans appeared to be retiring from Bancourt. The three battalions had suffered few casualties during this advance and the battalion commanders were anxious to push on and capture Bancourt village. However, they were not permitted to do so until the flanking units had caught up with them. The Rifle Brigade's historian implied that this decision was a mistake. He wrote:

> This was unfortunate, for presently the enemy troops began to filter back again, and there was to be some stiff fighting before the village, a veritable strong-point elaborately entrenched and wired, finally passed into our hands.[31]

In hindsight, though, it appears that waiting for flanking support was the best choice. Heavy machine-gun fire poured in from east of Favreuil and from Frémicourt. The fire from Frémicourt was particularly deadly as it swept down the Cambrai road in enfilade fire.

The 1st Brigade, approaching from south of Bapaume, advanced over a mile to reach a sugar factory on the Cambrai road to the north-west of Bancourt. No further progress was possible that day as the Germans to their front put up strong resistance, with heavy machine-gun and artillery fire. The brigadier called the advance to a halt, as recorded by the New Zealand historian:

The advance was temporarily discontinued, the troops took breath, and arrangements were made to press the pursuit together with the rest of the Army at dawn on the morrow (30 August).[32]

Thomas Dale of the 1st Auckland Battalion realised why 'old Fritz' had been 'so kind' to his battalion in keeping 'his shells and bombs to himself' on the night of 28 August. Bapaume had been evacuated the next morning, the Rifle Brigade had set off in pursuit and at 2 p.m. his battalion did likewise:

> The battalion moved off and pushed to the right of the town until they came near Bancourt when their scouts reported the enemy in strength and holding the village, so we simply settle down in front of him until things can be arranged for a general advance once more.[33]

It had certainly been an eventful day for the New Zealanders.

On 29 August General Russell moved his headquarters forward to dugouts in front of Bucquoy. Surprisingly, his diary entry for the day makes no mention of the fall of Bapaume. It did mention his ill health, though:

> Very bad cold — fortunately only in the head. Corps comdr came up at 10.30 — conferred till nearly 1. p.m. after which Wilson and I rode up to see brigadiers and on to Sapienies [Sapignies].[34]

That night Russell issued orders for the advance to continue on 30 August. Brigadier Hart recorded in his diary:

> At 8 p.m. I got orders to attack at dawn and worked until midnight making arrangements for artillery support, cooperation with flanking units, preparing dispositions and issuing orders.[35]

The 1st and 3rd Brigades were to push on to Riencourt-lès-Bapaume and Bancourt on a line due east from Bapaume. They were to push as far as Haplincourt if possible, which entailed an advance of about 3 miles. As events were to prove, this was an overly optimistic order.

During the night the New Zealand Engineers, a section from the 3rd Field Company and 500 men from the reserve brigade, laboured hard to dig a line of trenches in front of Bancourt. This was to provide vital cover for the New Zealand infantry in case of counterattack. It was tough, dangerous work, with the men exposed to heavy gas shelling and rifle fire. The Engineers stuck tenaciously to the job and completed the task by daylight. In the end, though, the New Zealand infantry did not use the trenches. The history of the Engineers records this wasted effort in a philosophical light: 'Similar unavoidable sacrifices of time and labour were of constant occurrence all through these days of rapid movement.'[36]

As well as digging trenches, the Engineers also built and maintained roads, water supplies, and communications. The War Diary of the 2nd Field Company recorded:

> Work was commenced on excavating posts and clearing out old trenches . . . but owing to the capture of BAPAUME this work was discontinued and the sections concentrated on road repairs. Grévillers–Bapaume and Biefvillers–Bapaume roads were patrolled and repaired and rendered suitable for two-way motor traffic.[37]

In the task of road building and repair the Engineers were assisted by the New Zealand Pioneers Battalion. When Bapaume fell on the night of 28 August, A and B Companies of the Maori Pioneer Battalion repaired the roads right up to Bapaume and also attended to the Bapaume–Albert road. On 30 August, C Company repaired the road to Cambrai to 1000 yards beyond Bapaume. James McWhirter was in the process of delivering a message to his battalion headquarters on 29 August when he came across a party of New Zealand Pioneers repairing a road. He recorded the event in his diary:

> Just this side of Puisieux the Pioneers, I mean our pioneers, the diggers were fast getting a road through. There is very little

our division does without the Maoris getting here up with the infantry — the best pioneers in the Army.

While he had considerable respect for the Maori Pioneers he was reluctant to leave his bicycle with them, even though he was unable to ride it any further. His diary explains why:

The New Zealand pioneers are a body of men I would trust with my life, but not with anything, they loved salvage, so I humped the old bike, I carried the beastly old thing for fully half a mile.[38]

There was another vital and dangerous task that fell to the Engineers — the dismantling of the numerous booby traps left behind by the Germans. The 2nd Field Company recorded in its War Diary the day after the fall of Bapaume: 'Work was continued on patrolling and examining roads for "Booby Traps" and repairing them where necessary fit for two-way motor traffic.'[39] The Engineers' history records:

Apart from the extensive and well-organised general schemes of destruction carried out on roads, railways and bridges, with which as a definite factor in war, no one can have any reasonable complaint, the retreating Germans appeared to have spent an enormous amount of time and ingenuity on all kinds of petty traps and devices of a malignant nature.[40]

The booby traps were everywhere. They included trip wires attached to explosives along pathways and behind doors. Books, mirrors and military souvenirs were all booby-trapped. Some were quite callous. A German Aid Dressing Station (ADS) full of wounded men might contain a dead body whose removal would set off an explosive charge.[41] All German dugouts were dangerous. If the entrance step did not have a pressure explosive device on it, then 'the furniture was almost certain to be well equipped with explosive.'[42] Delayed-action mines were yet another headache for the hard-pressed Engineers.

Private Monty Ingram had been wounded at Passchendaele and was serving in an Entrenching Battalion in August 1918. He was a keen observer of conditions on the Western Front and recorded in his diary in early September:

> Old Jerry is an extremely wily and dirty old dog! He is leaving behind all sorts of death traps for our especial quick destruction. They are cunningly contrived and one has to be extremely careful in touching the most ordinary-looking objects. The dug-outs also merit close inspection before one sleeps in one. A party of men may put in the night in a nice, deep dug-out, to all intents snug and safe, only to awaken in the morning very badly gassed from a hidden leaking gas shell; purposely hidden and left behind for the purpose by the retreating Hun. Even a clock would, as likely as not, explode in one's hand upon lifting. Any object we consider in the slightest degree suspicious, we leave alone. It is the duty of the Engineers to find these traps, and you can bet your life we leave them to it.[43]

These booby traps caused many casualties amongst the souvenir-hungry New Zealanders and the Engineers who had the task of removing them. Monty Ingram witnessed two New Zealand Engineers killed just 200 yards from him when they inspected a lidded box. It was booby-trapped and the two Engineers 'were blown to fragments as they raised the lid.'[44]

Another couple of examples are worth noting. One house in a recently captured village had a grandfather clock that had been rigged so that the running down of the weight completed an electrical circuit that set off an explosion large enough to destroy the whole building. In addition: 'Bathing places were fully provided with pointed stakes and barbed wire arranged below the water level.'[45] Rifleman Ross had seen first-hand the tragic effect of these booby traps. He recorded that his company had occupied a captured German trench on 22 August:

> Here I seen a booby trap and it worked. The Germans had left a small heap of wood to use in the bottom of the trench and was

441

out ready for a fire. A new man in the platoon set fire to it and sat down to warm his feet. It was foggy and cold. All of a sudden this fire blew up and the explosion blew the two legs off this man. I am sure he did not know his legs were gone. Some one gave him a cigarette and lit it for him . . . Poor devil, he just bled to death, in three minutes he was dead.[46]

It was just one of the Engineers' roles to detect and demolish these devices. Another was to establish safe water sources with easy access. This was not easy, as the Germans had destroyed wells and pumping equipment or had contaminated water supplies in the region. No water in the area could be used until it had been tested and the Engineers had given it the all clear. All of these tasks kept the New Zealand Engineers extremely busy during any advance.

The New Zealanders who entered Bapaume on the morning of 29 August or who saw the town in the days that followed were shocked at the level of destruction that had been inflicted on it. The town for which the New Zealanders had been fighting for the past five days and which they had finally captured on their fourth attempt had been reduced to 'one mass of ruins.'[47] The historian of the Otago battalions recorded a vivid picture of the state of Bapaume in August 1918:

Bapaume had fallen, and was occupied by the New Zealand Division. Battered and crumbling from the repeated blows of two Armies, its streets choked with debris and enemy dead lying in its main thoroughfares, this once prosperous town presented a grim and pathetic spectacle of almost entire destruction.[48]

'Bapaume is nothing but a few acres of bricks,' Jesse Stayte recorded in his diary.[49] Allan Watkins, a gunner in the 12th Battery of the 3rd Brigade NZFA walked through Bapaume on the afternoon of 29 August. He noted: 'There is not a building that isn't badly knocked about.'[50] James McWhirter believed that Bapaume was 'in much the same condition as Ypres was 6 months ago,'[51] while L.B. Quartermain wrote in a letter home on 1 September that he was in 'one of the few rooms left in this poor old battered town'.[52]

So, on 29 August 1918 Bapaume finally fell into the hands of 'the superb New Zealand Division.'[53] *The Times* newspaper stated that capturing Bapaume was 'an honour . . . they [the New Zealand Division] had well earned'.[54] Now that the Allies held capture of the ruins of Bapaume, the Battle of Albert was officially over. However, there were still three more days of hard fighting for IV Corps and the New Zealand Division before the Battle of Bapaume was finally complete.

Chapter 8

The Battle for the Surrounds:
30 August–2 September 1918

W ITH THE FALL of Bapaume on 29 August 1918 the British Expeditionary Force's main effort switched to the First Army's front. GHQ
orders stated that the Third Army should cooperate by maintaining pressure
on the Germans 'with the object of holding the enemy on their front.'[1] In
addition, the Third Army was to try to advance with the First Army in order
to protect that army's right flank. However, Byng issued more aggressive
orders to the Third Army before those of GHQ arrived. He directed that IV
and V Corps were to press the enemy's rearguards vigorously in an easterly
direction to a line just short of the Canal du Nord.

For IV Corps, two sets of objectives were issued. If German resistance
was light, then the Corps would aim to attain the line stretching from
Ytres to Bertincourt to Vélu, an advance of just over 4 miles. If heavy
opposition was encountered, as indeed happened, then the men would
aim for much shorter primary objectives. To the south, the 42nd Division
was to capture Riencourt-lès-Bapaume, while the New Zealand Division
in the centre seized the two villages of Bancourt and Frémicourt. To the
north, and protecting IV Corps' left flank, the 5th Division was to take
the village of Beugny.

Although the Germans had withdrawn from Bapaume, they had
not gone far. They held strong defensive positions on high ground to
Bapaume's east, including several fortified villages and the strongly wired
Beugny trench system. The history of the 2nd Auckland Battalion has a
description of the terrain facing the New Zealanders:

> The country consists of a succession of low, grassy undulations
> running north and south. Bancourt is in the bottom of one such

hollow, with a well-defined ridge to the east of it running from Riencourt northwards. Where the road to Bertincourt crosses this ridge there were a number of iron huts on both sides of the road.[2]

General Russell issued his orders to the New Zealand Division's brigadiers on the night of 29 August. The 1st Brigade, on the right, was to take Bancourt, while the Rifle Brigade, operating on the left, was to capture Frémicourt. Once the villages had been taken both brigades were to advance to and capture Bancourt Ridge, a line some 800 yards east of both villages. Once on Bancourt Ridge the 1st Brigade was to link with the 42nd Division on its right and with the Rifle Brigade on its left, thus securing this vital patch of high ground. In support of the two infantry brigades would be a harassing machine-gun barrage, directed at the trenches in front of the villages, and an artillery creeping barrage. One of those responsible for this machine-gun support was Captain Lindsay Inglis, who had rejoined the Machine Gun Battalion on 27 August after leave in the United Kingdom. Inglis' Company, the Otago Machine Gun Company, was at the time attached to the New Zealand Rifle Brigade. Inglis recalled that on the evening of 29 August he and others were informed by Brigadier Hart at an Orders Group that the Rifle Brigade would be attacking at 5 a.m. the next morning 'and half our night was occupied with preparations for supporting this move.'[3] The War Diary of the 2nd Brigade NZFA recorded: 'At 3 a.m. orders were received for creeping barrage to take place at 5. a. m. under which our infantry were to advance and take FREMECOURT [sic], BANCOURT.'[4] Each infantry brigade also had some artillery batteries placed directly under its command.

In the north, in front of the village of Frémicourt, the Rifle Brigade's front of 1000 yards could be covered by a single battalion. This task was allocated to the 1st Rifles commanded by Lieutenant Colonel W.S. Austin. At the time, the 1st Rifles was in reserve, waiting behind Monument Wood near Favreuil, so had a march of 2 miles to reach its start line, which was about 1500 yards due west of Frémicourt. It moved off at 3 a.m. on the morning of 30 August. A Company was placed on the right astride the Cambrai road, while D Company was on the left. C Company was in support immediately behind the two lead companies and B Company was in reserve.

At 5 o'clock that morning the attack started with the artillery and machine-gun barrage. After six minutes the barrage advanced due east by lifts of 100 yards every three minutes. The attacking infantry set off behind it, following as closely as safety would permit. As the New Zealand history of the division noted: 'From the outset it was clear that the operation was to be no "walk-over".'[5] On the Cambrai road, just west of Frémicourt, there was an old British camp that had been used as rest billets by the Germans. The camp was heavily fortified and contained several machine-gun nests. From here, the enemy began firing at the 1st Rifles' screen. Both A and D Company met heavy machine-gun opposition from the huts just beyond the line of the first barrage. However, an outflanking manoeuvre meant the line of infantry was able to keep pace with the barrage. The trench behind the billets was cleared at bayonet point, enabling the men to reach the outskirts of Frémicourt.

In accordance with instructions and doctrine of the time the two leading companies skirted around either side of the village, leaving the support company to mop up any resistance within the town. A Company, moving around the southern edge of the village, made good progress, clearing some isolated buildings and a trench system running south of the village 'without serious difficulty'.[6] The men then pressed on to the slope and rushed up it to secure the top. They encountered some opposition in the sunken road marking the left flank and from a dugout position halfway up the slope, but these attacks were easily subdued. However, when the riflemen crested the rise they struck serious trouble. Both flanks were exposed and the heavy enfilade fire coming in from the right, where the 1st Brigade should have been, took a heavy toll.

On the left, D Company had a much tougher time getting around Frémicourt. In the north-west corner of the village outskirts was a large, camouflaged strongpoint containing three machine guns. This needed to be disabled before D Company could progress safely. The riflemen kept as close to the barrage as possible and then the leading sections rushed the strongpoint and took it without sustaining a casualty. In the process, though,

D Company lost touch with the 5th Division, which had been drawn away to the north. To compensate for this, D Company extended its line considerably to the left in a vain effort to maintain contact. This brought it up against several enemy posts at a large railway dump. By the time the men had cleared this resistance (taking fifty prisoners in the process), the barrage had moved on. The last stage was particularly tough going, as the outer flank faced another well-defended obstacle — a railway cutting. The fighting was intense and made more difficult by the lack of troops on the flank. Fortunately, a tank arrived and helped the riflemen capture the cutting. Another fifty prisoners were taken here and by 8 a.m. the left flank of D company had reached its objective, the right flank having attained its position somewhat earlier.

Meanwhile, C Company, in support, approached Frémicourt and once the barrage had stopped sent three platoons into the north section of the village, and one into the south. These riflemen soon dealt with the German garrison there and by 6.30 a.m. had cleared Frémicourt. The company took 117 prisoners, including seven officers. Of these, five officers and seventy-six soldiers had been taken by Corporal E. Sheldrake and five men.[7] C Company then passed through the village and dug in astride the highway and abreast of the cemetery.

Although both leading companies were on the ridge, their flanks were 'in the air'. Some 300 yards behind the right flank of A Company the 1st Brigade's extreme left was digging in on a subsidiary spur. On the left flank, D Company still had not linked up with the 5th Division, despite having extended some 300 yards into the neighbouring division's area. The reserve company sent a platoon of men to assist D Company. This platoon was fired on by some British tanks, who mistook it for Prussian infantry. Once the situation had been cleared up the New Zealanders used the tanks to help remove some machine-gun nests that had been bypassed during the advance to Frémicourt. The Brigade recorded in its Narrative of Operations that the 1st Rifles took:

> Frémicourt and the ridge east of it by 6.30 a.m. Touch was lost with
> the Units on both flanks and later it was ascertained that neither
> the Right nor the Left Brigade had gained the ridge.[8]

The 1st Rifles had gained its objectives, but its hold on the ridge was 'an exceedingly perilous one.'[9] Sustained heavy fire from three directions and an enemy counterattack at 12.50 p.m. forced the 1st Rifles to withdraw to a trench 300 yards from the crest. There it linked up with the 1st Brigade and the 5th Division. In total the 1st Rifles had advanced the line some 2200 yards, capturing 402 prisoners, including a battalion commanding officer and his staff.[10] 'Casualties while on the ridge had been severe', admitted the Battalion's Narrative of Operations.[11] Its losses were twenty killed, 106 wounded and seventeen missing.[12] One of its companies ended up being commanded by a second lieutenant, since it had lost all its officers, while Sergeant R.J. Sinclair had to take command of his platoon, which numbered just eight survivors out of an initial fifty-five. The situation was precarious, so three platoons of the reserve company were moved forward to reinforce the exposed left flank, and a company from 2nd Rifles was placed in reserve. At nightfall some Vickers machine guns were also placed on the exposed flank to cover the road from Beugny.

An intense firefight had also occurred to the south of the 1st Rifles. The 1st Brigade, attacking on a wider front, had allocated two battalions to secure its objectives. The 1st Wellington Battalion was on the left and formed the link with the 1st Rifles on the ridge beyond Frémicourt. The 2nd Auckland was on the right and had been allocated the task of capturing and clearing Bancourt village. Once again the men had little time to prepare for the attack, the orders having only arrived two hours before zero hour, 5 a.m. As soon as the New Zealand artillery barrage started, the Germans responded by laying down their own heavy barrage in front of Bancourt, which caused considerable problems. The Wellington companies sustained a number of casualties from this artillery fire while they were assembling for the assault.

Nonetheless, the infantry soldiers of 1st Wellington, with two tanks in support, advanced right on time behind the barrage, as did the Rifle Battalion on their left. However, the 2nd Auckland Battalion did not move at all. This meant that the Wellington Battalion was advancing with an open flank, a dangerous position to be in. The Battalion's history records the event with typical understatement: 'The operation became thus a rather difficult one for 1st Wellington.'[13] However, the men still made good progress and with the assistance of two tanks, which were 'handled by their commanders with great skill and courage' the battalion was soon beyond Bancourt village and heading for the ridge.[14] When the men of 1st Wellington pushed on to the ridge, they met heavy opposition. From their open flank on the right the Germans poured in a massive concentration of machine-gun fire. It was intense and it soon became obvious that the exposed soldiers could not remain in position. The Battalion withdrew to a small spur about half a mile in front of Bancourt but some 300 yards short of the ridge. There they dug in. Yet even there the Battalion was in an exposed position. Its War Diary recorded:

> During the day our line, being on the rear slope and subject to enemy observation was swept by machine gun fire as well as shelling, and was also subjected to several half-hearted counter-attacks.

Its casualties at the end of the day numbered twelve killed in action and another thirty-seven wounded.[15]

Yet while these casualties were bad, they were even worse for the 2nd Auckland Battalion. Just before the fixed hour of attack, the 42nd Division informed Major W.C. Sinel, who was commanding the 2nd Auckland Battalion, that it would not be ready in time. The Battalion's War Diary recorded the effect of this unwelcome news:

> On getting in touch with the 42nd Division, who were to secure our right flank by accounting for Riencourt, we were informed that as orders had not reached them until 4.30 they could not be ready to advance until 6. am. We therefore had no option but to wait until they were ready, meanwhile the Battalions on our left moved forward under our barrage, in reply to which the enemy put down a defensive barrage.[16]

Major Sinel postponed the start of the attack, and, as the Battalion's history bluntly stated: 'The result was bad.'[17] When the German artillery responded to the opening of the attack it fell squarely on the 2nd Auckland Battalion, which was assembled and ready to go. Worst affected was the battalion headquarters. The Regimental Medical Officer (RMO) and most of his orderlies became casualties. The Battalion's padre, the Reverend C.J.H. Dobson, took over as the RMO and organised a regimental aid post (RAP) to take care of the wounded.

When 2nd Auckland did move off with the 42nd Division at 6 a.m. it was broad daylight and the support of the creeping barrage was lost to them. Worse still, by then the Germans knew what was coming. As the 2nd Auckland history records: 'the Hun was, of course, fully alive to the attack, and it [2nd Auckland] suffered heavily from machine gun fire'.[18] The left company of 2nd Auckland, 6th Company, still managed to clear Bancourt by 8 a.m. and link up with the 1st Wellingtons. Two companies from the 2nd Rifles assisted the 6th Company in the difficult task of clearing the village, capturing thirty-four prisoners in the process. The rest of 2nd Auckland, consisting of the 3rd Company on the right and the 15th Company on the left, pushed on beyond the village and reached the ridge. However, they were not able to secure its top. Progress beyond the village had been difficult as the Germans held the ridge in force, the 42nd Division had been unable to take Riencourt, which exposed the right flank of 2nd Auckland, and the New Zealand soldiers were attacking up an open slope devoid of cover. The Battalion's War Diary recorded the result:

> The advance went forward quickly and steadily at first, but before very long the right found the unchecked machine gun fire from the two woods behind Riencourt very troublesome, and artillery fire on this point . . . was asked for, no effective reply resulted and for the next two days our right flank was very much harassed by machine gun fire.[19]

As the history of the Auckland Regiment records:

> On the open slope, bare of all cover, men went down in scores. Soon all was confusion . . . It was impossible to get further

forward, but what ground had been gained was resolutely held against counterattacks that continued to develop throughout the day.[20]

While they could not reach the final objective, the Aucklanders managed to form a defensive flank well up on the ridge. There they awaited the pending fall of Riencourt. However, 2nd Auckland's hold on the ridge was tenuous. German snipers and machine-gunners poured in a massive volume of fire from huts on the Haplincourt road and from Riencourt itself. Mortars, too, were used against the New Zealand soldiers, as were several anti-tank guns. It was clear that the 2nd Auckland Battalion could not remain on the ridge's exposed face, so it withdrew to the foot of the ridge.

It had been a strenuous day for 2nd Auckland and its casualties had been heavy. They numbered eighteen men killed and a further 120 wounded.[21] In fact, the battalion had so many wounded that 'soon it was found that the supply of bearers, having regard for the length of the carry (over 2 miles) was insufficient'. In response the battalion shifted its RAP closer to the battlefield and was provided with two light ambulances and twenty extra stretcher-bearers from the brigade headquarters. Even then, as the War Diary noted: 'some of the wounded had unfortunately to be out a long time before they could be carried in'.[22]

Bad news certainly travelled fast in the New Zealand Division. Thomas Dale, a runner in the 1st Auckland Battalion, recorded in his diary on Friday 30 August:

> I heard that the 2nd Auck had gone over early this morning and things were not working out too good . . . We are held up in front of Bancourt and the 2nd Auck attacked this village with the 42nd division on the right attacking Reincourt [sic], and the 1st Well to the left attacking Frémicourt. We heard later that 2nd Auck took Bancourt but lost a lot of men with machine gun fire.[23]

Unlike much news received behind the lines, this report was accurate.

The New Zealand Attack
30 August 1918

The general advance by the three New Zealand battalions on 30 August amounted to 1.25 miles. Parties of enemy were seen digging in east of Bancourt and were shelled by the New Zealand artillery. From noon large parties of Germans were seen streaming back towards Villers-au-Flos. However, the Germans held the ridge directly in front of the New Zealanders and they showed little signs of leaving. Allan Watkins, operating as a forward observer for the artillery, described the day as 'a properly messed up affair.' He recorded the day's progress and dangers:

> We have advanced another 2000 yards but Fritz's artillery was never stronger and he pasted us all day — casualties in the N.Z. Divn tallied up today — I thought my number was up several times.[24]

At the end of the day the New Zealanders were occupying a pronounced salient, a dangerous position to be in. Lindsay Inglis recalled:

> . . . but once more there was what we had almost come to regard as inevitable — a salient of our own caused by the failure of the divisions on both flanks to make equal progress. To make matters worse these divisions gave exaggerated reports of their progress, which gave our own divisional headquarters, deceived by this information, a false idea that immediate further progress could be made.[25]

However, no further progress would be possible until the New Zealand Division's flanks were secure. This would occur only when Riencourt was taken by the 42nd Division and the 5th Division cleared Beugny.

During the night of 30–31 August, the New Zealand artillery maintained a constant harassing barrage on the German positions on Bancourt Ridge. The three battalions in line sent out fighting patrols that night too, but these achieved little other than confirming that the Germans still occupied the ridge. Of greater significance was that the 42nd Division launched two attacks on Riencourt that night, one at 7 p.m. and another at 9.30. The second venture was successful and Riencourt was captured. This was welcome news, as it meant the New Zealanders' right flank was secure. However, dawn of 31 August brought a most unwelcome development for the New Zealand battalions entrenched beneath Bancourt Ridge. At about 4.30 a.m. the Germans launched a very heavy barrage aimed right at the heart of the New Zealand Division. It lasted just over half an hour and was followed by an advance of three or four German A7 V *Sturmpanzerwagen*. It was the first time New Zealand soldiers had been attacked by tanks, and close behind them were large parties of German infantry.

The New Zealanders sent up SOS rocket signals but these were obscured by poor light and all three battalions were forced to withdraw about 200 yards. The artillery batteries attached to the battalions held their ground, though, and kept up a withering fire on the advancing Germans, on occasions firing over open sights. Finally, the signal rockets were observed by the artillery brigades, who joined in the fight. Their effort, combined with the intense rifle and machine-gun fire of the New Zealand infantry, soon drove the attackers away.

The German tanks were accounted for, too, although the New Zealanders could claim only partial credit for this. The tanks rumbled up towards Frémicourt, but, under heavy fire from the New Zealand infantry and artillery, they did not try to enter the village. As the tanks moved back towards their own lines the German infantry mistook them for British ones and peppered them with armour-piercing ammunition. In their panicked efforts to escape from this deadly fire two of the tanks ran down a bank, where the unstable machines floundered. Both had to be abandoned and they fell into the New Zealand Division's hands two days later. Brigadier Hart inspected both tanks and was not impressed with them:

> They are about the same size as ours, but not so good. They couldn't climb mounds or trenches nearly as well as ours & are more like huge iron boxes, the caterpillar drive is low and covered in.[26]

The War Diary of the 2nd Auckland Battalion recorded the morning's action and claimed one of the tanks for the New Zealanders:

> At 4.40 am a very heavy enemy bombardment of the whole sector began & lasted for nearly two hours. At 6.20 am 6th Coy reported having seen a German tank behind our front line on the left, & our troops retiring; the Field Artillery dealt with the tank which was put out of action.[27]

However, the German attack was not over. Later that morning it was found that two parties of German infantry, each about 50 strong, had skirted around the open left flank of the 1st Rifles and were operating at the rear of the New Zealand front. One of these groups was captured thanks to the leadership and skill of Sergeant A.J. Cunningham of the 1st Rifles' B Company, who discovered the German party while conducting a reconnaissance. He then borrowed a section from a neighbouring platoon and attacked the Germans. The Rifle Brigade history comments that: 'so skilfully did he [Sergeant Cunningham] handle his men that within a few minutes the little operation was over and 46 prisoners were on their way to the rear.'[28] The second party of Germans reached the northern edge of Frémicourt near a position held by a Vickers machine-gun section and a platoon of B Company. The Germans were called upon to surrender, but made no response. Machine guns and rifle fire then raked the enemy in deadly fashion. Only four Germans survived to be taken prisoner.[29]

By 10 a.m. the ground that had been lost was retaken, and a little more added. Units from the 1st Brigade were moved forward to plug the gaps in the line. Later that morning, a similar attack was made in the centre of the 5th Division's position, but it too was repulsed.

A German account of the counterattack gives the following reason for its failure:

On the 31 August the 23rd Infantry Division 16th Bavarian Infantry Division and 4th Bavarian Infantry Division attacked with our own tanks, and our battalions, particularly 2nd Battalion, 14th Bavarian Infantry Regiment, were involved. The attack ran without result, however, because of insufficient preparation.[30]

To outsiders, though, it appeared the counterattack failed because it was weak and not pushed with sufficient vigour.

New Zealander Jesse Stayte summed up the Allies' feelings when he wrote that 'Fritz counterattacked this morning and gained nothing'.[31] However, during the counterattack an incident occurred that showed even an experienced formation like the New Zealand Division could still have problems. Lindsay Inglis was forward observing Lieutenant Arthur Billington's machine-gun section that morning. Suddenly up to thirty figures appeared in the mist in front of their guns. Inglis later recalled the event:

Were they Germans infiltrating? Anyway, it was not safe to fire on them till we made certain. They turned out to be twenty or thirty raw reinforcements who had joined one of the Rifle Brigade battalions after dark on the previous evening & who had quietly slipped away with the 'wind up' and straggled to the rear. There was not a single old soldier among them and, all animated by the same notion, they had left various posts while the attention of the old hands was otherwise engaged. Rounded up and cursed, they came shamefacedly but willingly enough back to their posts. They would never do it again. After this they would be soldiers . . . This was the one occasion in which I ever saw New Zealand stragglers![32]

Battlefield straggling was a serious problem during the First World War and the individuals that Inglis saw were very fortunate on two counts. First, they narrowly escaped being shot by their own machine-gunners and second, they were not charged with deserting their posts in the presence of the enemy. This was a serious crime that could attract the death penalty in the BEF. That such an event occurred indicates that even a division with the reputation of the New Zealand Division was not immune to problems of morale, leadership and discipline.

After weathering the German counterattack, the New Zealanders concentrated their efforts on holding the ground they had won and preparing to recover the heights of the ridge lost on the previous day. It was a hard time for all the New Zealand battalions holding the front line, with near continuous fighting throughout the day. As expected, casualty figures steadily mounted. The 2nd Auckland Battalion suffered another thirty-five casualties, while the 1st Wellington Battalion had forty-three.[33] Unfortunately, both these battalions would suffer more casualties the following day. Even units behind the line suffered casualties, as Bapaume and its environs were heavily shelled throughout the day, the Germans making liberal use of phosgene and mustard gas shells.

By the end of August it was clear that a planned set-piece attack was needed to eject the Germans from Bancourt Ridge. Assuming the enemy was well prepared for an attack, then it would be necessary to launch a full-scale artillery barrage prior to the infantry going in. This was confirmed that evening when New Zealand patrols reported that the Germans were still well entrenched on the heights. The War Diary of the 1st Rifles recorded that: 'During the night patrols ascertained that the Ridge was strongly held by the enemy and it was decided to await the barrage before attempting to secure it.'[34]

The attack, set for 4:55 a.m. the next morning, aimed to seize the entire ridge line. With Riencourt in Allied hands, the task was expected to be easier than the attempt of the previous day. Three divisions would be used: the 42nd Division on the right, the New Zealand Division in the centre, and the 5th Division on the left. In the centre of the line the New Zealand attack would be made by the two brigades then in line — the Rifle Brigade on the left and the 1st Brigade on the right. Both brigades would have considerable artillery support throughout the attack, which would be provided by seven brigades of field artillery.[35] As events were to prove, it would be sorely needed.

Precisely at 4.55 a.m. the artillery barrage came down on the German positions on Bancourt Ridge. A New Zealand gunner recorded the event:

> The attack was taken up with vigour on the 1st September, when the Division attacked under cover of a barrage at 4.55 a.m. and advanced the line to the high ground east of Bancourt and Frémicourt.[36]

In the northern sector of the New Zealand position — with C Company on the right and B Company on the left — the 1st Rifles moved through the outpost line and advanced on to the ridge. Machine-gun fire from both flanks was heavy, but the riflemen pushed on. The leading platoons were on the crest by 5:30 a.m., securing all of their objectives and projecting well beyond the final objective in the centre of the advance. They took seventy prisoners from the 23rd Saxon Division and a large amount of war materiel. Contact was soon established with the 1st Brigade on the right, but not with the 5th Division on the left. The Battalion's War Diary explains why:

All the objectives were reported taken by 5.30 a.m. Liaison was quickly established with 1st Brigade on Right, but the Right Company of the Brigade on the left did not arrive in time to participate in the attack. Eventually they moved forward as far as possible in daylight, and, under cover of darkness, advanced and occupied the gap.[37]

The 5th Division had been unable to advance at zero hour, which meant that for most of 1 September the 1st Rifles had to contend with an open flank. Despite the late start, the 5th Division pushed forward as far as possible during the day and 'under cover of darkness, dribbled its troops up into line'.[38] The 1st Rifles casualties during the day numbered eighty-four, most being lightly wounded. Only nine of its soldiers had been killed in this attack, but the commanding officer, Lieutenant Colonel Austin, DSO, was one of the wounded. He had been hit by a shell splinter just after 7.30 a.m.[39]

Meanwhile, the 1st Brigade, facing the 44th (Reserve) Division, 'were not able to gain their objective with the same uneventful smoothness'[40] nor with the relatively small number of casualties. In close touch with the 1st Rifles on its left, the 1st Wellington Battalion attacked with three of its rifle companies in line. Two met serious opposition on the ridge that morning. Frederick Varnham recorded in his pocket diary: 'Heavy machine fire . . . enemy thrown back finally and objectives gained.'[41] The Battalion's War Diary has a similar comment:

This operation was carried out quite successfully, all Coys being on their objective well up, to time, but on account of machine gun fire patrols could not push as far forward as was hoped.[42]

It was during the 1st Wellington's attack on Bancourt Ridge that the New Zealanders were awarded the third Victoria Cross of the Battle of Bapaume. Never before or since have New Zealand soldiers won three Victoria Crosses in the one battle. In this instance, the recipient was John Gildroy Grant, a builder and contractor from Hawera, who had joined the New Zealand Expeditionary Force in June 1915. On 1 September Sergeant Grant was in command of a platoon, usually the job of a commissioned officer, and for the previous two days had 'displayed coolness, determination and valour of the highest order.'[43] When the Wellington infantry reached the top of the ridge they came under heavy fire from five machine-gun posts, but they pushed on and reached to within 20 yards of the guns, where they were forced to take cover. It was at this critical time that Sergeant Grant and Lance Corporal C.T. Hill crawled towards the guns, leapt up in front of the machine-gun fire in the centre post and attacked the position. The German machine-gunners fled, so Grant turned his attention to the post on the left, which he also subdued. At point-blank range Grant rushed forward and cleared three machine-gun posts inspiring the men of his platoon to do likewise. The German resistance then died away. It was an impressive feat and, as the history of the division comments:

> No one but the panic-stricken Germans at the gun could tell how the fire missed him. He leapt into the post, demoralising the gunners. His men were close on his heels.[44]

Lance Corporal Hill received the DCM for his actions during this foray, and Grant received the VC, which was gazetted on 26 November 1918.

At the south of the attacking line, on the right flank, the three companies from the 2nd Auckland Battalion had a much tougher time:

> At 5 a.m. the barrage opened and 3rd, 6th and 16th Coys moved forward to take the high ground immediately in front of us. At 5.50 a.m. 16th Coy reported that they were on top of the ridge . . . and digging in there. 10 minutes later word was received from 6th Coy that they had gained their objective, with few casualties but that they were getting machine gun fire from both flanks.[45]

A German counterattack at 6.30 a.m. was driven off by artillery support, but the situation on the ridge remained precarious. Heavy machine-gun fire coming from the huts on the road to Haplincourt inflicted a considerable number of casualties. Only when a British tank attacked the huts was 2nd Auckland able to surge forward and capture its objective. When the tank left, though, German snipers and machine-gun teams occupied the huts once more and kept 2nd Auckland under fire. The battalion also took heavy mortar fire from a sunken road and anti-tank gun fire from the village of Villers-au-Flos. The relentless nature of the various attacks meant 'that movement of any kind was hazardous and consolidation an impossibility'.[46] Casualties steadily mounted, so much so that 2nd Auckland could not remain on the objective. As the division's history noted:

> Movement and consolidation became alike impossible, and after suffering severely the survivors, too weak to attack the enemy, even if attack were feasible, were forced to withdraw behind the crest.[47]

It was the second time that the 2nd Auckland Battalion had failed to take its portion of Bancourt Ridge. Its War Diary candidly admitted that 'the men were feeling the effects of recent heavy fighting'.[48] A company from the 2nd Wellington Battalion was made available to help the Aucklanders, but it was too late to renew the attack.

During the attack the 2nd Auckland Battalion had captured 150 prisoners and fifty-one machine guns. However, the cost was high: thirty-four men killed, 104 wounded, and one soldier captured.[49] Amongst those killed were three officers, including the young Lieutenant Douglas Knight, who 'was fighting bravely when he was killed by Machine Gun fire'.[50] Amidst the loss, men took small victories where they could. Private Leonard Grey of the 6th Hauraki Company had taken his best friend to the RAP in Bapaume on the afternoon of 1 September, pleased that he 'had 5 Fritzies to carry him down'. In his diary, Grey recorded the high cost of the three days' fighting around Bancourt: 'We found the rest of the Coy only about 50 out of a 120 strong. There was only 5 out of my platoon of 30.'[51]

Private William Malcolm of 2nd Auckland Battalion had taken a bullet just below his lower lip on 1 September while digging in on Bancourt Ridge. He wrote to his parents two days later:

I have been over the top four or five times now and I consider that is any amount for a while. Most of the boys got a bit of a crack all but young Lu. Our Platoon was eight strong when I left and we were going over then.[52]

The 2nd Brigade, commanded by Brigadier R. Young, relieved the three New Zealand front-line battalions that night and made preparations to renew the attack the next day. Behind the 2nd Brigade the New Zealand artillery moved forward to new positions, ready to provide the necessary fire support. For the men who had survived the fight for the villages and high ground east of Bapaume, life was again worth living. In his diary, Jesse Stayte recorded the effects of the last two weeks:

Some of the New Zealand Companies have been badly cut up last night, notably 2nd Auckland and 1st Wellington. There is a rumour to the effect that we may be relieved tonight. We are all very rough, no shave or wash for a fortnight and are all very lousy.[53]

It was more than a rumour and the exhausted, grateful survivors of the three battalions made their way back towards Bapaume. The 2nd Auckland Battalion, which had suffered most heavily in this three-day ordeal, recorded:

Cookers came forward and all ranks appreciated hot meals and a comparative rest after the strain of the last three days. Greatcoats were sent up and the men soon made themselves comfortable. Burial and salvage parties made a systematic clean up of the area but otherwise no work was done. Parties of men were sent daily to the Baths at Bapaume.[54]

The orders that had been issued to IV Corps for 2 September stated that the 5th Division should aim to capture Beugny and Delsaux Farm and the low ridge beyond them, while the 42nd Division should attempt to capture Villers-au-Flos. Between these two divisions was the New Zealand Division, and it was expected to conform to the advance of both flanks and seek any opportunities for exploitation. However, the immediate task facing the New Zealand Division was the capture of the portion of Bancourt Ridge still held by the Germans. This would prove to be no easy task.

It took the 2nd Brigade three separate attacking moves before it was able to capture the last section of Bancourt Ridge on 2 September. The first was at 5.15 a.m., when the 2nd Otago and 1st Canterbury Battalions advanced on to the ridge behind a creeping barrage provided by three brigades of field artillery. The two infantry battalions were soon halted by machine-gun fire from a well-defended trench and a derelict tank. One of the supporting artillery brigades recorded of this attack:

> Barrage opened up well. The Bosche replied about 5 minutes later with a fairly heavy barrage. Reports came through about 7.30 a. m. that our Infantry had been held up with heavy M.G. fire from huts in cross roads.[55]

The attack was renewed at 1 p.m. behind a heavy artillery barrage that targeted the crossroads. Initial resistance, especially around the huts and crossroads, was heavy but they were taken after a stiff fight. Many Germans were killed during this intense fighting and over a hundred prisoners, eighteen machine guns and one anti-tank gun were captured.[56]

The third attack was made at 6 p.m. in order to clear the Germans from a sunken road. Again, a heavy barrage was fired on the position and this time enemy resistance just melted away. The Germans began surrendering in droves, having reached the limits of their endurance. The 2nd Otago Battalion alone took 200 prisoners, one enemy tank and sixty machine guns. Its own casualties were 'fairly heavy'.[57]

The following day Lindsay Inglis was able to view the huts on Bancourt Ridge that

> had seen severe fighting the previous day. The enemy had grouped here what appeared to us enough machine guns to stop the British Army, but he had sited them too much in a line without provision

for mutual support and had not protected their flanks properly by intelligent digging or the distribution of the guns. The result was that our infantry had worked around their flanks and slaughtered them, judging from the number of field grey dead, to a man. To ensure that the neighborhood would remain habitable, we spent some hours hauling the bodies to a trench which we filled in on top of them.[58]

Although the bodies of the dead were removed, other evidence of the devastation remained. Private Monty Ingram was with a New Zealand Entrenching Battalion when it moved forward about a mile on 4 September. Ingram took a keen interest in his surroundings, part of the New Zealand obsession of looking for souvenirs. He noted:

Many German dead lying about and the ground is littered with the ransacked equipment and clothing of the dead. Two wrecked German tanks lie close to our bivvy here. They are clumsy, unwieldy looking affairs. I searched them for anything in the nature of a souvenir, but found nothing worth taking except a combination spoon and fork which had belonged to one of the late crew.[59]

After clearing Bancourt Ridge the 2nd Brigade moved forward to link up with the divisions on its flanks, all of which had taken their objectives.

The victory of the IV Corps was not the only Allied success at the time. Elsewhere, the Australians had seen victory at Mont-St-Quentin near Péronne and the Canadian Corps had broken the Germans between Drocourt and Quéant. As a result of these achievements by the BEF the Germans carried out another general retirement on the night of 2–3 September. This night was exceptionally dark, so it was not until dawn that the British armies realised that the Germans had gone. IV Corps of the Third Army had intended to do no more on 3 September than to capture Beugny, which the 5th Division had surrounded on three sides.

When the attack was launched at 5:20 a.m. it found that the village was empty. Its War Diary recorded the non-event:

> At 5.20 a.m. the Division attacked in accordance with instructions but during the night the enemy had withdrawn and consequently touch with the enemy was temporarily lost . . . In the meantime strong patrols were pushed forward to get in touch with the enemy.[60]

At 7.30 a.m. patrols from the 2nd New Zealand Infantry Brigade and the 127th Brigade of 42nd Division reported that both Haplincourt and Barastre were also empty. A New Zealand War Diary recorded that morning: 'A quiet night. At 7 a.m. the Infantry reported that their patrols were through HAPLINCOURT and had still not got touch with the Boche and were still going forward.'[61] While it meant another shift in location for the artillery batteries, it was still very welcome news.

At 8.30 a.m. General Harper issued an order for the line of Ytres–Bertincourt–Vélu to be reached and the entire Third Army surged forward. Brigadier Hart recorded in his diary:

> It was a strange sight to see Infantry, gunners with guns from 18 pdrs to 15 inch, tanks, Whippets, supply wagons all moving forward. Even the balloons still flying high, moved forward a corresponding distance.[62]

As it turned out progress was better than General Harper expected. The 2nd New Zealand Brigade pressed on through Haplincourt and Bertincourt to reach Ruyaulcourt, where some fighting took place. The Germans retreated still further east, finally stopping on the high ground on the edge of Gouzeaucourt Wood, Trescault and Havrincourt villages, just 3 miles from the Hindenburg Line defences. This was a retreat of 8 miles. Once again the New Zealand Division outpaced the flanking divisions. That evening it linked up with the 5th Division on its left, but the 42nd Division did not advance beyond Ytres, leaving the New Zealand Division once more with an open flank.

That afternoon the BEF's GHQ issued the following order:

> The successful operations carried out by the British Armies since the 8th August have forced the enemy to withdraw practically along the whole British Front. The principle on which Army commanders will now operate will be to press the enemy with advanced guards with the object of driving the enemy's rear guards and outposts and ascertaining his dispositions.
>
> No deliberate operation on a large scale will be undertaken for the present. Troops will as far as possible, be rested, our resources conserved, and our communications improved with a view to the resumption of a vigorous offensive in the near future, in conjunction with an operation to be carried out on a large scale by our Allies.
>
> In accordance with the above, Army commanders will draw as many divisions as possible into reserve for rest and training.[63]

This order did not prevent further soft advances, but it put an end to large-scale, organised attacks. It also closed the second period of the 'Advance to Victory', which had begun on 21 August with Third Army joining in the offensive started by Fourth Army on 8 August. In this second stage of the offensive, Third and Fourth Armies, comprising twenty-three divisions, had, in ten days' fighting, driven thirty-five German divisions from one side of the old Somme battlefield to the other. The offensive had also turned the line of the Somme River, as had been intended, and forced the Germans back on the Hindenburg Line defences. In doing so the BEF had taken 34,000 prisoners and some 270 guns.[64] At the end of this series of attacks the New Zealand front line was over 20 miles east of Hébuterne, from where it had commenced the offensive. Although the war would still go on for the New Zealand Division, which would be at the forefront of Third Army's advance in a few days' time, the battle of Bapaume — 'Bloody Bapaume' — was finally over.

Chapter 9

'Bloody Bapaume':
Retrospective

NEARLY ALL ACCOUNTS of the Battle of Bapaume acknowledge that it was a hard-fought action, with casualties on both sides being very heavy. In early September 1918 a wounded New Zealand soldier wrote home to his sister attesting to the efficiency of both the German machine guns and anti-tank guns. In his letter, Private William Malcolm of the 2nd Auckland Battalion recorded:

> The machine guns are Fritz's best weapon. It is just about impossible to get past them. He holds his line with them. His anti-tank guns are deadly both for tank and infantry. He keeps them well up, too.[1]

A young rifleman, who had been 'smacked by a shell just outside Bapaume', admitted quite candidly to his mother: 'We had a pretty awful time by Bapaume and our casualties were heavy — the price of glory.'[2] Ormond Burton was just one of the many injured during this period of fighting. When he returned to the 2nd Auckland Battalion after being wounded at Grévillers he saw more evidence of the losses faced by the Allies:

> Back again with the Battalion I found that they had fought again at Bancourt and that between this and Grévillers the casualties had been very heavy. The Company had many new officers and many new faces in the ranks.[3]

Even a commander as remote from the action as Ludendorff wrote that, in the last week of August 1918, 'the English, who had but few fresh reserves at their disposal, gained ground towards Bapaume after very severe fighting.'[4]

Victor Rayner, who had captured a German soldier 'just as frightened as I was' at Bapaume, was later involved in burying the dead. Seventy years later he said that he wasn't concerned for his own mortality initially, even while interring his comrades:

> That didn't disturb me much . . . When you are young, it never occurred to me, so I must have been happy go lucky. But when there was only two of us left of our lot, I began to think: This is not too good.[5]

Victor Rayner survived the war physically unscathed, unlike most members of his infantry section. In his mind, he survived because: 'I was no hero. I think why I am here today was when things got too hot I got around to the nearest shell hole and got in.'[6] It was a simple but effective survival strategy and Victor Rayner was not the only soldier who used it.

Obtaining accurate casualty figures for a battle is a notoriously difficult task for a historian, as they vary so greatly amongst sources. The history of the New Zealand Division in France has a pronounced tendency to underestimate New Zealand casualty figures. Acknowledging that the casualty figures for the Battle of Bapaume had not been light, it gave the following figures for this battle:

For IV Corps: over 600 officers and nearly 11,000 men

In the New Zealand Division:
    1st Brigade: 120 killed, 536 wounded
    2nd Brigade: 157 killed, 678 wounded
    3rd (Rifle) Brigade: 134 killed, 634 wounded

In addition; 24 men were taken prisoner.[7]

The New Zealand medical history, which is usually a more reliable source of casualty figures, recorded exactly the same number for New Zealand casualties between 21 and 31 August 1918.[8]

Both sets of figures are inaccurate and far too low. Stewart, the Division's historian, has not calculated the casualties for those vital supporting elements that fought in this battle, some of whom became casualties. This especially applies to the artillery brigades that supported the New Zealanders throughout the battle, as well as the various medical units, Engineers, the Machine Gun Battalion, the Pioneer Battalion, the trench mortar batteries, transport drivers and so on. Carbery, the medical historian, who admits his figure is an estimate only, stops at 31 August, thereby omitting the two days of fighting needed to finally capture Bancourt Ridge. The 2nd Auckland Battalion alone suffered 139 casualties on Bancourt Ridge on 1 September, and the 1st Rifles eighty-four.[9]

Those figures that can be obtained from primary records reveal further problems with the numbers quoted above and it appears that Stewart, too, ended the casualty count on 31 August 1918. Casualty figures for the 2nd New Zealand Infantry Brigade for the month of August were 157 killed in action, 673 wounded and fourteen missing, making a combined total of 844.[10] Those in the 3rd New Zealand (Rifle) Brigade numbered 128 killed in action, 533 wounded and forty missing, making a total of 701.[11] Although these figures are for the entire month, during this period the pattern of engagement by the forces mentioned would have meant that nearly all casualties would have occurred after 21 August.

A recently constructed database has painstakingly recorded the number of New Zealand soldiers who died while serving in the NZEF. Between 21 August and 3 September 1918, those killed in action or who died from their wounds and who were serving in units at the Battle of Bapaume number 821.[12] This is double the number of deaths recorded by both Carbery and Stewart. The New Zealand casualty returns for August and early September list the figures as significantly more than 2000, as featured in the table on the next page.

NZEF Wounded 21 August–15 September 1918

Unit/Formation	Number Wounded
NZ Machine Gun Corps	58
NZ Field Artillery	196
NZ Engineers	20
Auckland Infantry Regiment	343
Wellington Infantry Regiment	346
Canterbury Infantry Regiment	334
Otago Infantry Regiment	403
NZ Rifle Brigade	625
Army Service Corps	4
NZ Medical Corps	24
NZ Maori Contingent	20
Total wounded	2,373[13]

The wounded have been included up to 15 September, as a random check showed that it took an average of ten days (and sometimes longer) for a casualty to be recorded as reported. It is also clear that some names have been missed altogether. Captain R.J.S. Seddon, killed in action on 21 August, is one who is missing from this list. In addition, the New Zealand Division did not see major action again until 9 September, when it fought at Trescault Ridge. Given the time it took to report casualties, it is unlikely many of those injured in this later battle would be included in the above figures.

This makes the Battle of Bapaume one of the most costly encounters of the New Zealand Division on the Western Front. It was recognised as such by the New Zealand soldiers who took part. One of those wounded on Bancourt Ridge wrote from his hospital bed at the No. 2 General Hospital, Walton-on-Thames:

> I think there are more 31st [Reinforcements] boys here than in
> France and a good many of the later reinforcements have been

smacked up. The losses for the Division must be as it suffered at Passcendale [sic].[14]

While the casualty figures for Passchendaele, which was just two days of fighting, were in fact much higher, it is significant to note that more New Zealand soldiers were killed and wounded in the Battle of Bapaume than in the Battle of Crete in the next war.[15]

A disturbing feature of the casualties suffered during the battle was the large number of officers involved. This was not something confined to the New Zealand Division, either. Casualty rates, especially for junior officers, were high across the entire BEF. This fact struck Lawrence 'Curly' Blyth when he was promoted to Second Lieutenant in the Diamond Dinks, the 1st Battalion of the Rifle Brigade (whose black colour patch was in the shape of a diamond). Many years later, Curly recalled that:

> On the back pages of the *London Times* they had a casualty list and they stretched column, column, column, after column. And they were headed 'Second Lieutenant Unless Otherwise Stated'. There would be only a few majors or colonels, but the life of a 2nd Lieutenant was put down at seven days and you'd read this thing, all those names that were there and they were 2nd Lieutenants unless otherwise stated.[16]

Second Lieutenant Leslie Averill won a Military Cross for his 'exceptional gallantry and fine leadership' during the 4th Rifles' attack at Frémicourt on 26 August. When the Rifle Brigade was relieved the next day, Averill visited the 2nd Rifles to catch up with an old friend, Paul Clark, also a second lieutenant. He later wrote:

> For some reason it had never entered my head that he would have been killed, but when I enquired from his Company N.C.O.s they could only tell me that such was the case; in fact all the officers in his Company had been killed. Needless to say I was very sad indeed because we had been closely associated for nearly eleven years.[17]

Paul Clark was one of thirteen officers lost to the 2nd Rifles in August. The battalion recorded in its War Diary: 'Our casualties in officers were extremely heavy and the loss of so many sterling officers is severely felt.'[18] This emotion was common across the New Zealand Division, which could ill afford to lose the courage, leadership and experience of these junior officers.

After the Battle of Bapaume Averill was sent to a 'soft job' as an officer in the Divisional Traffic Control Branch. This posting probably saved his life, as he later acknowledged:

> Although I didn't want to go I am quite sure that this decision saved my life as the survival rate of subalterns in the front line was very short, particularly in offensive warfare such as we were engaged in.[19]

Given Averill's magnificent performance at the battle of Le Quesnoy at the end of the war, where he was the first man to scale the ramparts of the walled city, there is little reason to doubt his assessment.

The extent of the casualties from the Battle of Bapaume is reflected in the activity at the two major New Zealand hospitals in the United Kingdom. On 5 September the No. 1 New Zealand General Hospital at Brockenhurst recorded in its War Diary:

> We have today 1501 patients in hospital. 800 fresh cases have been admitted during the last 8 days. This constitutes a record beating the two previous occasions in June 1917 when we had 1130 patients and in Oct 1917 after Passchendaele when we showed 1280 as our total.[20]

This record would be broken continuously throughout September as the great offensive rolled on, with the New Zealand Division playing a lead role in it. The New Zealand hospitals were to experience their busiest two months of the war. The reason for this was simple. As one New Zealand soldier commented seventy years later: 'We had more battles in

1918 than we had in the whole war.'[21] The period from August through to September 1918 was one of the most costly of the war for the BEF, and the New Zealand Division was part of this experience. On 23 September the War Diary recorded that '1615 patients were in hospital', a number which fell to 1592 at the end of the month.[22]

Similarly, the No. 2 New Zealand General Hospital at Walton-on-Thames experienced an influx of patients from 27 August on, when it received its first convoy of wounded from the recent fighting in France. On 3 September its War Diary noted: 'The hospital is now beginning to fill up rapidly. All available canvas has been equipped in readiness for further admissions.'[23]

And the admissions kept coming. On 23 September the hospital had 1647 patients, 'the largest number of patients that have ever been in Hospital at one time since the opening of the institution.' At the end of the month the number of patients was 1690, 'again having exceeded any previous number.'[24] The large number of patients placed an enormous strain on both hospitals. As the War Diary of the No. 2 Hospital noted on 23 September: 'The number of operations is at present very heavy, the theatre being constantly in use with 3 tables going at the same time.'[25]

There was, however, a positive aspect to this influx of patients. On 9 September the No. 2 General Hospital noted:

> The cases arriving from France are coming in very well looked after, very few requiring any dressing on the night of arrival. The wounds are for the most part, clean and dressed recently. A large number of Machine Gun Bullet wounds are noted.

The Hospital repeated this observation on 23 September, when its record for patient numbers was first broken:

> The cases continue to be well cared for, the difference is very marked between the condition of the patients arriving from the present offensive, and those received in previous operations.[26]

After three years of costly offensives on the Western Front, the BEF had at last perfected the necessary treatment and methods for transporting wounded soldiers to the United Kingdom. This was fortunate, for the system would be severely tested in the last months of 1918.

However, despite all the evidence to the contrary, the GOC of the New Zealand Division, Major General Andrew Russell, did not recognise the Battle of Bapaume as the tough, bloody struggle it was. Whenever Russell mentioned the casualties incurred during this battle it was with the adjective 'light' or 'small'.[27] In the two days after the fall of Bapaume, Russell wrote revealing letters to his sisters in the United Kingdom. The first, to 'Dear Milly', recorded his impression of the battlefield:

> Yesterday we got thro' Bapaume without casualties, as during the night the enemy evacuated save for a few M.G. So far the defence is mainly M.G. with an occasional counterattack. Consequently but few prisoners comparatively, nor do I see many dead about.[28]

One wonders from this letter how far Russell went forward after the capitulation of Bapaume. All New Zealand accounts of the town after its fall comment on the great destruction caused and the large number of dead Germans lying in the streets.

The second letter was written the following day. It read in part:

> I write to supplement the War correspondent's accounts of our doings. And they are good enough to warm one's heart — *envers mes braves*. I make plans, lead a life of inglorious and comparative safety — while they do the trick. Bapaume was not a hard nut. We bombarded it thoroughly, the Bosche walked out of it one end, and we walked into it at the other. As a matter of fact, I should say the laugh was on his side, as he slipped out under our noses, and if we lost no men, neither did he. Such is not always the case, and we have caught prisoners, more of his men than our casualties. In fact his divisions opposite us are melting fast, and fresh ones thrown in on top of disorganized units is not economical.[29]

This letter reveals how detached Russell had become from his command during the battle. All accounts of those at the sharp end reveal what a tough struggle it was to win Bapaume and the high casualty rate proves that it was no walkover. James McWhirter was right when he wrote that:

> Bapaume was proving one of the toughest nuts to crack on all of the front. In a commanding position and admirably suited for defence, with its dug-outs and cellars it enables him [the enemy] to make a stubborn resistance. Every place is covered with machine guns which spit furiously at advancing troops. He is employing his best troops in its defence and his advance and his advance positions [are] defended by infantry and machine guns.[30]

Nor did the New Zealanders simply pound the town with artillery and walk in as the Germans left. They made three attempts on the town before finally enveloping it from the north and south and forcing the Germans to retire. They lost many good soldiers trying to win the town and when the Germans left Bapaume they did not go far. There were still four more days of heavy fighting for the New Zealanders, during which the Germans clung tenaciously to the outlying villages and high ground east of the town.

Russell's comments in the letter of 31 August cannot be dismissed as sugar-coating the battle for home consumption. When writing to his family he was always quite candid about New Zealand losses and mistakes. These two letters depict a commander who has lost touch with the reality of the situation because he has become too remote from the action. During this battle, Russell became almost the stereotypical 'Chateau' general.

It should be noted, though, that in the closing months of the war Russell was a sick man and definitely not at his best. He had a foot injury and a bad cold and his diary entry on 7 September confirmed that the latter was taking its toll: 'Not feeling at all up to the mark — the result of this cold which somehow never leaves me.'[31]

It was fortunate that Russell had trained the New Zealand Division to such a high standard, that he had turned it into a learning organisation and that he had picked talented men to command the various brigades. This was his lasting legacy to the Division. Both he and the New Zealand Division were fortunate, too, in the calibre of the brigadiers, who were more than capable of running the show. One cannot help feeling, however, that it would have been better for both Russell and the New Zealand Division had he been replaced prior to the commencement of this great offensive.

It is surprising that a battle of the scale, intensity and significance of Bapaume is so little known in New Zealand. Three factors have contributed to this. First, recent histories of the New Zealanders on the Western Front have either mentioned the battle in passing or ignored it altogether. Christopher Pugsley, in his impressive and influential *On the Fringe of Hell*, falls into the latter category, while the authoritative *Oxford Companion to New Zealand Military History* allocates the battle some ten half-lines with a grand total of eighty-two words.[32] This compares with two pages (134 half-lines) covering the 1916 Battle of the Somme, forty-seven half-lines for Messines and La Basseville, and another two full pages for the Third Ypres / Passchendaele conflict.[33] The battle fares a little better in more recent publications on the New Zealanders in France, but unfortunately all too often authors accept without question Russell's view that 'the New Zealand troops found it was . . . not a hard nut'.[34]

Second, New Zealand newspapers reporting the battle gave the overwhelming impression that it had been a cakewalk, with light casualties and inevitable victory. Typical of this is the report written by Mr Gordon Gilmour, the Australian Press Association correspondent, and carried by a number of the daily newspapers:

BAPAUME ALREADY VISIBLE FROM NEW FRONT

Australian and N.Z.   (Received 1.30 pm)   LONDON, Aug 22
Mr Gordon Gilmour, Australian correspondent, states: With splendid vigour the New Zealanders participated in the general British attack at daylight on August 21 east of Hébuterne and Gommecourt, where for the past four months they have been in

close touch with the uneasy enemy. It is impossible to learn the actual results on the battlefield, but the New Zealand commander states that by evening they had gained all their objectives. Two of the units engaged sustained very light casualties, eight occurring in one and 30 in the other. They captured over 200 Germans before the evening. The conditions were ideal for the thrust, which was designed to accelerate the enemy's retreat. An officer who was well forward reported early in the day that the advance might continue probably for some miles.

During early morning the ground was covered with mist, which was only dispersed by the sun after the operation was completed. The New Zealanders jumped off from the ruins of Puisieux, which patrols had penetrated during the past few days. The Germans offered little resistance. They could not see the attackers until the latter were within a few yards. I walked a considerable distance during the heat of the day towards Achiet-le-Petit, where English troops were strongly consolidated. I saw only one New Zealander who had been killed by shell-fire. I spoke to an officer from Nelson, whose men were digging a strong post. He explained the ease with which the advance was made.

Large batches of prisoners are constantly marching back. The total will be many hundreds. The New Zealanders are thrilled by the prospect of getting ahead of the old Somme country. To-day Loupart Wood appears outlined in the foreground, and it is possible to see Bapaume on the horizon, where probably the Germans are already establishing their main line of defence. There is every indication that the enemy, consequent on the allied gigantic offensive spreading, is taking the precaution to reach a defensive line without disaster. The New Zealanders are almost within sight of Flers.

Although to-day the New Zealanders took a comparatively small share in the main battle, their entire units are ready for any offensive.[35]

Two days later it was more of the same:

REMARKABLE REPUTATION FURTHER ENHANCED

Australian and N.Z. (Received 5.5 p.m.) LONDON, Aug. 24
Correspondents describe a feat by the New Zealanders in trapping a
German force attempting to counter-attack. Apparently they made
no attempt to stop the enemy until he had gone too far to withdraw.
Then suddenly all the machine-guns put down an impassable
barrier in the German rear, and moved it slowly forward. When
the Germans realised their position, those who had not been killed
or wounded ran forward and surrendered. Nearly 300 unwounded
prisoners were taken.

Mr H.W. Nevinson writes: Thursday's attack was carried out by
part of Sir Julian Byng's Third Army in the northern sector, and part
of Sir Henry Rawlinson's Fourth Army in the southern. It is now
permitted to mention that the New Zealanders held a distinguished
place in the Third Army and the Australians in the Fourth. Both,
during these last two or three days, have maintained their remarkable
reputation for qualities which count in war. There is hardly anything
to choose between them. At the same time we must not forget the
silent stolid battalions of the old British counties. Australian staff
officers repeatedly praised a brigade of a certain British division.
They kept saying that the brigade did extraordinarily well. Praise
from such a quarter is weighty and valuable.[36]

The misreporting continued throughout the Battle of Bapaume. On
26 August came the news of the capture of Loupart Wood, Grévillers
and Biefvillers. According to the report in the *Dominion*, it had been easy
going:

BRILLIANT ATTACK BY NEW ZEALANDERS

Probably the best budget of news since Foch's great offensive
began appears in the war despatches to-day. Along the whole front
from the Somme to the Aisne the Allies have been scoring heavily.

The British total of prisoners from August 15 to date is 14,000 and many guns; the French have captured several thousands, but they have not attempted to count them. Both Australia and New Zealand figure prominently, the Australians at Bray-sur-Somme, and the New Zealanders before Bapaume. The New Zealanders, attacking with irresistible dash, swept through Loupart, taking 400 prisoners, and, pressing forward, captured Grévillers and Biefvillers, and reached Avesnes-lès-Bapaume. 'Nothing stops all ranks from pressing forward,' says Sir Douglas Haig. The French patrols have crossed the Ailette, and one unconfirmed statement states that they are now at the famous Chemin-des-Dames ridge. The enemy's losses have been appalling, while on our side our casualties in killed and wounded have been less than the number of prisoners captured by us.[37]

So distorted was this reporting in the New Zealand newspapers that several reported the capture of Bapaume two days before it actually happened. 'BRITISH IN BAPAUME', 'BAPAUME ONCE MORE IN OUR HANDS', 'HOW THE NEW ZEALANDERS FOUGHT' announced the headlines of the *Dominion* on Tuesday 27 August. 'BRITISH ARMIES STILL ADVANCING', 'CAPTURE OF BAPAUME' proclaimed those of the *Otago Daily Times* on the same day.[38] No one seemed to notice when almost the exact same headlines appeared four days later. This time, though, they were accurate. Those of the *Dominion* announced: 'NEW ZEALANDERS TAKE BAPAUME' and 'SPLENDID PROGRESS MADE'. Such inaccurate and misleading reporting made the battle appear a relatively easy affair with a foregone conclusion. It is little wonder that anyone away from the front lines took much notice of the Battle of Bapaume.

The third reason for the comparative anonymity of this battle is that on 31 August 1918 an event occurred that pushed the New Zealand capture of Bapaume into the shade. This was the taking of Mont-St-Quentin, just outside Péronne, by two weak battalions of the 5th Brigade, 2nd Australian Division. As the Australian official historian wrote, the capture of Mont-St-Quentin and later the town of Péronne 'is held by many Australian soldiers to be the most brilliant achievement of the A.I.F.' General Monash certainly regarded it as such, while the Fourth Army commander, General Rawlinson, 'more than once referred to the operation as the finest single feat of the war'.[39]

Mont-St-Quentin is a hill some 140 feet high, a mile north of Péronne. During the First World War it dominated the Somme approaches to the north and the south. So important was it that the Germans had dug in a formidable force on the feature to defend it. Despite these fortifications the hill was taken in a surprise attack by two Australian battalions who could muster only 550 rifles between them. A further 200 infantrymen from other battalions were allocated in support. But 'this absurdly small force of infantry', to use the words of John Terraine,[40] had massive artillery support. Some five brigades of field artillery and four brigades of heavy artillery provided 'a great bombardment'.[41] This overwhelming fire support, combined with the aggression and skill of the Australian diggers, resulted in Mont-St-Quentin being taken from the demoralised German defenders. The Australians captured more than 700 prisoners in this attack and then held the Mont against five successive German counterattacks delivered by elements of five German divisions, including the élite Prussian guard. Péronne was captured the next day. As Bean so rightly states in his history: 'An astonishing feat had been achieved.'[42] Both Haig and Rawlinson were incredulous when they heard the news and Haig took some convincing that Mont-St-Quentin had indeed been captured.

A monument to the 2nd Australian Division commemorates this amazing feat of arms, and according to Martin and Mary Middlebrook, it 'is one of the most striking memorials in France'.[43] The original monument — of an Australian digger bayoneting a sprawled Imperial eagle — was destroyed by the Germans in 1940, so the Australian government replaced it with a digger standing legs astride, gazing in the direction of the attack.[44] It is highly appropriate that this is such a striking monument, as there is little doubt that at the end of August 1918 the Australians stole the show with this surprise attack. It tended to push other significant achievements — like the capture of Bapaume — into the background.

The New Zealand Division experienced several setbacks before achieving success in the Battle of Bapaume. It had to adapt quickly to a new type of warfare as battles were being fought less from static trenches and more through rapid movement. For the New Zealanders the start of this change occurred during the Battle of Bapaume and, as the history of the Division noted, it involved 'certain novel and at the outset some bewildering features'.[45]

One of the characteristics of rapid-movement warfare was the need for speed of action and fast decision-making in order to gain surprise and exploit success. At the same time, however, it was necessary to keep officers and men informed of changes to plans, something that was often difficult in practice. One of the biggest gripes of the New Zealand soldiers at this time was the lack of information being passed on to them. The War Diary of the 2nd Rifles made a typical complaint:

> Our main difficulties were the lack of time & opportunity to give orders & reconnoitre the country. Many N.C.O.s & nearly all the men were at one time or another sent off to do their work without having the task properly explained to them. We thus lost one of our most valuable assets — the intelligence of the 'digger'.[46]

The 3rd New Zealand Rifle Brigade issued a set of lessons learned from recent operations that mirrored earlier German stormtroop tactics. This was then disseminated throughout the division. It urged the bypassing of pockets of resistance, explained how best to cope with machine-gun nests and stressed the advantages of the night attack:

> In recent fighting it was found that a Battalion could operate successfully on a frontage of 1000 yards. Fewer troops, skilfully led, greatly reduced the casualties. Enemy Machine Guns were skilfully sited. If the enemy rearguard is very weak in Machine Guns, Patrols using concealed approach were able to stalk & outflank enemy Machine Guns. Where the rearguard is strong in Machine Guns it is a very lengthy process, and very costly to advance otherwise than with a barrage. Our most successful operations against

positions held with Machine Guns were carried out before dawn or by moonlight. In these cases our casualties were negligible . . . The enemy offers no resistance when his flanks have been turned or if taken in rear.

. . . Too much regard was often paid to enemy points of resistance. The advance should be continued, where possible, by 'shying off' pockets of the enemy, the ultimate surrender of which can be obtained by supporting troops. The advantage of pushing forward at every point where progress can be made cannot be emphasised too much . . . Machine Guns used well forward with the attacking troops did excellent work. They got good targets & repelled counterattacks, causing heavy casualties.

General

During the recent operations it was often felt that a bolder policy was possible, & deeper advances could have been made. Formations should allow of better exploitation of success to enable the capture of the enemy's guns, equipment, stores & personnel.

H Stewart Commander 3 NZ (Rifle) Brigade
9/9/18 [47]

Also part of this lesson package was some practical advice prepared by the 4th Rifles. Four points were particularly stressed:

1. On reaching an objective men must not begin to collect souvenirs or to make 'bivvies'. The first thing is to make fire step accommodation; to make enough, not only for themselves, but for reinforcements who may be sent up.
2. The enemy never waits for a bayonet charge.
3. Now that we have so many Lewis Guns an attack across the open resolves into a business of working Lewis Guns up by stages. When they get near the enemy's position & round his flanks he will probably give in.
4. Aeroplanes can do good work dropping boxes of S.A.A. [48]

The first point is particularly apt and had been learned on the Somme in 1916. When an enemy trench or firing position was captured, the fire step that enabled soldiers to fire from the position had to be reversed so that the soldiers could fire in the direction of the enemy. This meant shifting a large amount of dirt from one side of the trench to the other. It was laborious, often backbreaking work, but it needed to be completed as soon as possible and before the enemy launched a counterattack.

The close-quarter fighting in open country led to a change in artillery doctrine at the end of September 1918. A note issued by the General Staff and circulated throughout the New Zealand Division stressed the crucial need for artillery support to always be available to the lead infantry units:

> It is of vital importance that the advance of the leading infantry should be closely supported by field guns. What is required is the immediate application of accurate artillery fire at the point of resistance combined with successful manoeuvre by the infantry at points where the enemy is giving way. This demands close liaison between infantry & artillery commanders & good observation . . . The battalion commander must keep the arty informed of the situation of his leading troops by any means at his disposal. The artillery commander should not be dependent on what he can find out for himself, though he should take every step to keep in touch with the situation. It is the essence of liaison that its maintenance is the duty of both parties concerned.[49]

To enable close and more effective cooperation with the infantry, artillery units in direct support of an operation would be formed into a single group and the group commander would be attached to the headquarters of the infantry brigade then in line. Those not part of this group were to remain under the direct control of the Divisional Artillery Headquarters. It had been the artillery units, under direct control of local infantry commanders, that had been primarily responsible for foiling the German counterattack of 31 August. This was an important change and the history of the divisional artillery notes that it:

. . . was regarded as one of the most effective means of providing for that close co-operation between the two arms which the rapidity and sweeping character of the advance, with its ever changing situations, made desirable.[50]

These examples of the forces learning from the experiences and sharing that knowledge with others are testament to the culture created by Russell. As a result, the New Zealand Division quickly adapted to the changing conditions on the Western Front.

During the battles of August 1918 the Third and Fourth Armies, comprising twenty-three divisions of the BEF, attacked and drove thirty-five German divisions from one side of the Somme battlefield to the other. In doing so they turned the line of the River Somme and inflicted a severe tactical defeat on the German Army. German losses included some 34,000 prisoners and 270 guns. In the Third Army, IV Corps' share was nearly 8000 of these prisoners. The New Zealand Division, which after 24 August had been one of the spearhead divisions of IV Corps and would remain so until the end of the war, captured 1650 of these 8000, including forty-seven officers.[51] While the New Zealanders had not always taken their objectives in this offensive, they had been one of the most consistent and reliable divisions in the Third Army. The New Zealand Division had often outpaced the formations on both its flanks during the Battle of Bapaume, a feature that would continue for the rest of the war. There is some truth to the complaint made by Geoffrey Potts of the Wellington Regiment, when he wrote to his wife Florence that:

> Our boys are getting a pretty bad time around Bapaume now. I saw a chap from Brockenhurst today & he said they are getting around 60 cot cases in per day & a 100 today & are expecting a lot more. I suppose Walton is getting the same, if there are as many cot cases as that, there must be a devil of a lot of slightly wounded. From all accounts they are in the hottest part of the line. They always put the Australians & ourselves in hot corners, because it is a fact they can't trust the Tommies. The Scotties are alright. Old Fritz is

getting a bad time now anyhow, I hope it will last, for every one prisoner taken, you can reckon on 3 being killed.[52]

The New Zealand Division experienced serious problems during the Battle of Bapaume, including the high turnover of people in key leadership roles and the inexperience of many of its soldiers. Despite this, Chris Pugsley is right when he states that in 1918 the Division had a 'quantitative and qualitative superiority' and 'was acknowledged as one of the finest fighting divisions in France.'[53] Other divisions, lacking the quantitative advantage of the New Zealand Division, for example the Australians at Mont-St-Quentin, were equally good. Despite Geoffrey Potts' assertion of it as a 'fact', there is no evidence that all English divisions were untrustworthy.

It was noticeable, too, that after the Battle of Bapaume most New Zealand soldiers were confident of victory. This was certainly not the case before the battle commenced. Bill Batchelor, a Lewis gunner with the Rifle Brigade, fought at Bapaume. Unfortunately, he was wounded shortly after that by a New Zealand artillery shell at the Canal du Nord. He noted the difference in the New Zealanders: 'After Bapaume you knew you were going to win. Morale sort of picked up.'[54] At the beginning of September Major Lindsay Inglis wrote to his fiancée in New Zealand that the German prisoners he had spoken to

all seem resigned to the fact that the Hun has lost the war, but then they are bound to have rather a distorted view of things judging only from their own recent experiences as they do. We all feel too as if we were at last really permanently gaining the upper hand, though of course the old Hun may have quite a lot of sting left in him yet.[55]

The German prisoners turned out to have a more accurate view of the war than Inglis, in this case.

The victory attained in August 1918 was tactical gain rather than strategic except in one important sense.[56] As the British official historian commented, as a result of the battles of Amiens and Bapaume, 'the Germans from O.H.L. to the soldier in the ranks had lost faith in final victory.'[57] This was a critical outcome. In support of this statement, Edmonds quotes the Bavarian Official History, which records that in August 1918:

> the German front ached and groaned in every joint under the increasing blows delivered with ever fresh and increasing force. Heavy losses in men, horses and material had been suffered and the expenditure of man-power had reached terrifying proportions. The German divisions just melted away . . . The rations remained meagre and unvaried. In these circumstances, the troops deteriorated both spiritually and physically. For the most part they were worn out [literally burnt-out cinders].[58]

Both Edmonds and John Terraine have rightly commented that, for the Germans, it wasn't just 8 August 1918 that was a black day, it was the entire month.[59]

The sorry condition of the German Army quickly became obvious to the New Zealand soldiers. The War Diary of the Machine Gun Battalion recorded in its summary for August that:

> During his retirement the enemy has suffered heavy losses in prisoners, casualties & in war material. Over 1500 prisoners have been captured by the Division & abundant evidence exists of his casualties . . . The eagerness with which his men surrender & the half hearted stand they make in face of our attacks have hastened our progress & caused disorder in the enemy ranks. Intelligence reports show that the unusual disorder exists amongst units hastily brought from various sectors to stem the advance.[60]

Curly Blyth, Second Lieutenant in the 'Diamond Dinks', used a sporting analogy to describe the state of the German Army after August 1918. He noted that after Bapaume:

it was obvious that the Germans were only playing sort of like football in injury time. The time was running out for them, our offensive had under Foch, you know he was Commander-in-Chief, had really taken on & the Germans were in no shape at all.[61]

As the New Zealand history records, the Battle of Bapaume 'had been no facile triumph.'[62] It was part of the larger BEF offensive, but was a vital component of it. For that offensive to succeed the Germans needed to be ejected from their defensive positions all along the BEF's front line. Each of these enemy sites had been carefully chosen as a rearguard and had been well prepared so that it offered maximum advantage to the defender. Realising that their troops were deteriorating in quality, the Germans made especially good use of machine guns and artillery support. The defenders were resolute and knew that they were fighting for time. Each village and any commanding ground prepared as centres of resistance 'were in themselves formidable'.[63] Overcoming these positions was never going to be easy, but it had to be done. In the Battle of Bapaume the New Zealand Division 'had experienced its share of checks and disappointments but these were outweighed by its repeated successes.'[64] It is a tribute to both the quality of the Division and the adaptability and endurance of the New Zealand soldier on the Western Front that these checks and disappointments never affected their determination to overcome the most stubborn of opposition. This determination led to eventual victory and another battle honour for the New Zealand Division. But the 'price of glory', to use the words of one who was there, had been very high. More than 800 New Zealanders would not be returning home and thousands more would carry the scars of war for the rest of their lives. Both the achievement and price of the Battle of Bapaume should never be forgotten.

Conclusions: A Significant Milestone

T HE OFFENSIVE THAT opened against the German armies on 8 August 1918 ended a hundred days later when a new German government formally requested an end to hostilities. It made this request because the offensive, the culmination of four years of effort on the Western Front, had decisively defeated the armies of Imperial Germany. Reduced to just four effective divisions at the beginning of November 1918,[1] the German Army would soon be incapable of any significant resistance if the fighting on the Western Front was not stopped.

The British Expeditionary Force played a key role in this defeat. From the start of the offensive on 8 August to the Armistice on 11 November, the British Expeditionary Force (BEF) had been relentless in its attacks against the German armies. It was joined in this by the armies of France and the USA in the south, and the Belgian Army in the north. However, it was the BEF that took the lead, consistently applying the pressure that finally brought the German military to its knees. Within the BEF the ten Dominion divisions were allocated leading roles in this offensive.

The Third Army was the largest BEF army on the Western Front, and the New Zealand Division was used to spearhead its attacks from 24 August 1918 until the end of the war. This was a crucial role and it is almost unique in New Zealand's history. The country's major military formation was part of the Allies' main effort in the decisive theatre of war and it played a crucial role in the defeat of Germany, which at the time was rightly recognised as the greatest threat to the possibility of a peaceful world. For one of the few times in its history New Zealand was at the forefront of world events, events that shaped the rest of the twentieth century. Many historians now recognise what Hew Strachan, the Chichele Professor of the History of War at Oxford University, so eloquently expressed in his last two sentences of a 2004 publication: 'In short it [the First World War] shaped not just Europe but the world in the twentieth century. It was emphatically not a war without meaning or purpose.'[2]

What is often forgotten, though, is just how costly obtaining victory on the Western Front was. The BEF experienced its greatest losses in the last four months of 1918, when it was winning the war. Martin and Mary Middlebrook have commented on the BEF's casualties for August–September 1918: 'it is not generally known that this was one of the costliest periods of the war for the British Army'.[3] In fact, the BEF suffered more than 100,000 casualties in the opening month of the offensive.[4] This was one of the most costly periods for the New Zealand Division, too. Being at the forefront of world affairs came at a very heavy price.

Part of the reason for these large casualty figures is the horrific nature of the fighting on the Western Front. The wise and experienced military commander Major General Howard Kippenberger survived the killing fields of the Somme in 1916 as a boy soldier, although he was seriously wounded soon after. He rose to senior command appointments in the Second World War. Kippenberger had seen enough of war to know its true nature. He once advised Kenneth Sandford, who was then seeking to write the story of Charles Upham, VC and Bar, that: 'My own feeling is that it would be extremely difficult to "write up" an infantryman. Infantry fighting is a hard, brutal business.'[5]

This was certainly the case for soldiers fighting on the Western Front. In 2006 Canadian historian Tim Cook remarked:

> More than nine million soldiers were killed during the Great War. They were not all victims of artillery, which blasted soldiers from miles away. Death also resulted from shooting men through the head as they crouched to defecate, tossing grenades into dugouts full of scared soldiers, mercilessly machine-gunning to death attackers that milled like sheep in uncut barbed wire, and although far less frequently, running a soldier through with cold steel. The infantry were there to win control of No Man's Land and, at some point to break through the enemy trenches to end the stalemate. While some frontsoldaten [front line soldiers] realized the futility of fighting to the last man or the absurdity of waiting to become a statistic in the daily wastage of the trenches, most realized that victory could only be won by killing the enemy.[6]

The world the infantry and other *frontsoldaten* knew was certainly a savage and brutal one, and it consumed many of those who lived in it.

In the last months of the war the New Zealand Division was in the thick of this harsh and merciless world. What is remarkable is that the Division could function so well within it. Despite problems of command, the loss of so many of its experienced junior leaders and the large number of raw reinforcements the New Zealand Division was forced to absorb, it never lost its qualitative edge on the Western Front battlefields. Although the Division did not always obtain the objectives allocated to it, it continued to perform consistently well and never stopped trying, as its attempts on Bapaume showed. During the Battle of Bapaume the New Zealand Division often had to contend with an open flank, and sometimes two open flanks, as a result of outpacing other divisions of IV Corps. It would continue to do this for the rest of the war, demonstrating, according to Christopher Pugsley, 'its superiority over both retreating Germans and neighboring British divisions'.[7]

What is noticeable about the New Zealand Division during the Bapaume battle is the high level of skill it had attained. Despite the occasional lack of firm direction and insufficient time to make the necessary arrangements, junior leaders and soldiers could act with the courage and determination necessary to secure their allocated objectives. This occurred at Grévillers and Loupart Wood on 24 August and again on 26 August, when one company of the Rifle Brigade actually received its orders after the attack had commenced. It still moved forward to secure its objectives.

It is worth commenting on the importance of courage here. Most New Zealand soldiers would deny they were heroes, but the ability to function effectively on the Western Front demanded a special type of courage. Most men who fought there were determined to perform well, never to let their mates down and to preserve a sense of their self worth by seeing a difficult job through to the end. These values meant that on many occasions individuals performed outstanding feats of courage when things went wrong on the battlefield. They could be ordinary privates, like Rifleman Dalzell, whose exploits were described in Chapter 3. More often than not, though, they were non-commissioned officers, like the three men who won the Victoria Cross for their heroism during this battle. They could also be officers, like Second Lieutenant Averill, although the sad fact is that many of these courageous junior officers became casualties during the battle while just doing their jobs. This courage deserves recognition. It is something vital to hold on to as part of New Zealand's military heritage.

Though the struggle to capture the town of Bapaume is a relatively unknown battle in New Zealand's military history, it does not deserve this obscurity. It was one of the most costly and hard-fought battles undertaken by the New Zealand Division on the Western Front. More than 800 New Zealanders lie buried in military cemeteries near Bapaume and more than 2000 New Zealanders were wounded in the savage fighting around the town. The battle was also notable for a number of significant military 'firsts'. It was the first time the New Zealand Division carried out an attack in France without a preliminary artillery barrage. It was the first time New Zealand troops were supplied from the air. It was the first time that the New Zealand Division attacked with a large number of tanks in support, although this proved to be rather a mixed blessing at times. The German counterattack on 31 August was the first time the New Zealanders had been on the receiving end of a tank attack. The Battle of Bapaume is also the only time in New Zealand's military history that three Victoria Crosses have been awarded during the one military action.

These military firsts, the human cost and the fact that more than 10,000 New Zealand soldiers fought in the Battle of Bapaume, make this an encounter to remember. There is little doubt that the Battle of Bapaume was a significant milestone in the New Zealand Division's long, dark journey across the Western Front.

Endnotes

Abbreviations

ANZ   Archives New Zealand, Wellington

ATL   ATL

KMARL Kippenberger Military Archive and
       Research Library, Army Museum, Waiouru

Massacre at Passchendaele

Introduction

1 J. Laffin, *Guide to Australian Battlefields of the Western Front 1916–1918*, Sydney, 1992, p. 51.

2 Sir Philip Gibbs, *The Realities of War*, quoted in J. Terraine, *The Road to Passchendaele*, London, 1977, p. xix.

3 J. Terraine, *The Western Front 1914–18*, London, 1964, p. 153.

4 Diary of W.K. Wilson, Accession No. 9402314, KMARL.

5 Quoted in D. Winter, *Haig's Command. A Reassessment*, London, 1991, pp. 108–9.

6 Nicholas Boyack, *Behind the Lines. The Lives of New Zealand Soldiers in the First World War*, Wellington, 1989, p. 78.

7 Jay Winter and Blaine Baggett, *1914–18. The Great War and the Shaping of the 20th Century*, London, 1996, p. 195.

1 The Military Background

1 P. Fussell, *The Great War and Modern Memory*, London, 1975, p. 36.

2 Major General J.F.C. Fuller, Introduction, in Leon Wolff, *In Flanders Fields. The 1917 Campaign*, London, 1958, p. xi.

3 Trevor Wilson, *The Myriad Faces of War*, Cambridge, 1986, p. 458.

4 Quoted in General Sir Charles Harington, *Plumer of Messines*, London, 1935, p. 109.

5 George A.B. Dewar and J.H. Boraston, *Sir Douglas Haig's Command December 19, 1915, to November 11, 1918*, London, 1922, p. 340.

6 Dewar and Boraston, p. 340.

7 W.S. Churchill, *The World Crisis 1916–1918 Part II*, London, 1927, p. 331.

8 Linus T.J. Ryan, 'A Brief Record of My Three Years in Khaki', p. 128, unpublished manuscript, property of Smyth family, Hamilton.

9 Fussell, p. 49.

10 D. Winter, *Haig's Command*, London, 1991, p. 168.

11 Colonel Repington, quoted in J. Terraine, *The Road to Passchendaele*, p. 61.

12 Marshal von Hindenburg, *Out of My Life*, London, 1920, pp. 288–9.

13 For an account of this learning process see P. Griffith, *Battle Tactics of the Western Front. The British Army's Art of Attack 1916–18*, London, 1994.

14 Haig's Diary, 10 May 1917, Terraine Papers, quoted in Terraine, *Road to Passchendaele*, p. 91.

15 Wilson, p. 468.

16 Dewar and Boraston, p. 359.

17 Haig's Diary, 2 August 1917, Terraine Papers, quoted in Terraine, *Road to Passchendaele*, p. 217.

18 General Ludendorff, *My War Memories 1914–1918* Vol II, London, 1920, p. 480.

19 C. Falls, *The First World War*, London, 1960, p. 283.

20 Wilson, p. 462.

21 Ludendorff, p. 489.

22 Harington, p. 87.

23 Harington, p. 88.

24 Wilson, p. 474.

25 Ludendorff, p. 488.

26 Terraine, *The Western Front*, p. 172.

27 Ludendorff, p. 488.

28 Ludendorff, p. 288.

29 Record of Conference held at Second Army HQ, CASSEL at 11 am 2 October 1917, OAD 645, WA 11 / 4 Box 3, Item 14 Future Operations of Second Army, ANZ.

30 Birdwood to Allen, 28 September 1917, Papers of Sir James Allen, J Box 9a Correspondence with Mr Massey, Birdwood and Russell, ANZ.

31 Fussell, p. 12.

32 Major General J.F.C. Fuller, Introduction, in Leon Wolff, *In Flanders Fields. The 1917 Campaign*, London, 1958, p. xiii.

33 Ludendorff, p. 476.

34 Birdwood to James Allen, 28 September 1917, Allen Papers, File 9a Correspondence with Mr Massey, Birdwood and Russell, ANZ.

35 C. Pugsley, 'The New Zealand Division at Passchendaele', p. 274, in Liddle, Peter H. (ed.) *Passchendaele in Perspective. The Third Battle of Ypres*, London, 1997.

36 Ludendorff, p. 488.

2 Success

1 Linus T.J. Ryan, 'A Brief Record of my Three Years in Khaki', pp. 118–19.

2 Diary of Gunner Bert Stokes, 8601028 KMARL.

3 A.E. Byrne, *Official History of the Otago Regiment, N.Z.E.F. in the Great War 1914–1918*, Second Edition, Dunedin, n.d., p. 202.

4 Diary of Brigadier Sir Herbert Hart, 28 September 1917, KMARL.

5 Linus T.J. Ryan, p. 35.

6 Leonard Hart to Mother, Father and Connie, letter, 19 October 1917, MS Papers 2157, ATL.

7 A. Stratton, 'Recollections of the First World War 1916–18 in France after Gallipoli', MS Papers 3823, ATL.

8 C.H. Weston, *Three Years With the New Zealanders*, London, n.d., p. 227.

9 George McLaren, letter to Tina, 28 September 1917, Letters to family, MS Papers 6535-4, ATL.

10 War Diary General Staff of II Anzac Corps, WA 11/1 War Diary General Staff 2nd A & NZ Army Corps 1-7-17 – 31-12-17, ANZ.

11 Diary of Brigadier Sir Herbert Hart, KMARL.

12 WA 50/1 War Diary HQ NZ Divisional Artillery October 1917, ANZ.

13 J.H. Luxford, *With the Machine Gunners in France and Palestine*, Auckland, n.d., pp. 86–8, 88–9.

14 War Diary of 2nd Auckland Bn, WA 72/1, ANZ.

15 General Sir Andrew Russell, diary, 2 October 1917, The Russell Saga, Vol III World War I 1915–1919, ATL.

16 Edward Wright, 'The Smashing Victory of Broodseinde', in H.W. Wilson (ed.), *The Great War*, Part 182, Week ending February 9, 1918, London, p. 514.

17 Weston, p. 221.

18 Luxford, p. 88.

19 A.D. Carbery, *The New Zealand Medical Service in the Great War 1914–18*, Auckland, 1924, p. 332.

20 Report on Operations Carried Out by 1st NZ Infantry Brigade 30 Sept–6 Oct, ANZ.

21 War Diary 1st Auckland Battalion, WA 71/1, ANZ.

22 Henry Ashton (Harry) Highet, oral testimony, OH AB 478, Oral History Centre, ATL.

23 Burton, *Auckland Regiment*, p. 173.

24 Report on Operations Carried Out by 1st NZ Infantry Brigade 30 Sept–6 October 1917, ANZ.

25 Linus T.J. Ryan, p. 134.

26 Diary of Pte R. Hamley, 3 October 1917, KMARL.

27 Diary of Brigadier Sir Herbert Hart, KMARL.

28 O.E. Burton, *The Silent Division. New Zealanders at the Front: 1914–1919*, Sydney, 1935, p. 240.

29 Stewart Callaghan, letter to Tot and Willie, 9 October 1917, MS Papers 5004, ATL.

30 Gordon Kirkpatrick Neill, oral testimony, OH AB 503-1, Oral History Centre, ATL.

31 Capt F.S. Varnham, Folder 2, Diary Entry 4 Oct 1917, MS Papers 4303, ATL.

32 W.H. Cunningham, C.A.L. Treadwell, J. S. Hanna, *The Wellington Regiment N.Z.E.F. 1914–1919*, Wellington, 1928, p. 217.

33 Sidney George Stanfield, oral testimony, OH AB 516/1, Oral History Centre, ATL.

34 Weston, p. 228.

35 War Diary of 2nd Auckland Bn 1–5 Oct 1917, WA 72/1, ANZ.

36 War Diary General Staff of II Anzac Corps, WA 11/1 War Diary General Staff 2nd A & NZ Army Corps 1-7-17–31-12-17, ANZ.

37 Malcolm Beaven to Mother and Father, letter, 7 October 1917, MB 195, Box 83, MacMillan Brown Library, Canterbury University.

38 See Diary of Capt E.H. Northcroft, 3 Battery, NZFA, 9300 995 KMARL.

39 Luxford, p. 88.

40 Report on Operations Carried Out by 1st NZ Infantry Brigade 30 Sept–6 Oct 1917, ANZ.

41 Narrative of Events For Operations Undertaken on October 4th 1917, BM 455 8 Oct 1917, Hart Papers, KMARL.

42 H. Stewart, *The New Zealand Division 1916–1919*, Auckland, 1921, p. 271.

43 Walter Curruthers to family, letter, 9 Oct 1917, MS Papers 4107, ATL.

44 Diary of Gunner Bert Stokes, 8601028 KMARL.

45 Narrative by G.H. Gavin, 3 Jan 1918, WA 10/3 Box 1 ZMR 1/1/3 Chaplain' Reports, ANZ.

46 Weston, p. 234.

47 Weston, p. 235.

48 Linus T.J. Ryan, p. 138.

49 Linus T.J. Ryan, p. 138.

50 German Official Account, quoted in Terraine, *The Road to Passchendaele*, p. 281.

51 From the history of the 92nd Regiment, 20th Division, quoted in N. Cave, *Ypres. Passchendaele. The Fight for the Village*, London, 1997, p. 99.

52 C.E.W. Bean, *The Official History of Australia in the War of 1914–1918. Volume IV The AIF in France: 1917*, Sydney, Angus and Robertson, 1933, p. 875.

53 Wolff, p. 194.

54 Diary of W.K. Wilson, 9402314 KMARL.

55 Godley to Allen, letter, 7 October 1917, WA 252/4 Letters of Colonel Sir James Allen and General Sir Alexander Godley Jan–Dec 1917, ANZ.

56 Monash to Rosenhain, quoted in G. Serle, *John Monash. A Biography*, Melbourne, 1982, p. 296.

57 Diary of H.S. Muschamp, 4 October 1917, 1991.2219 KMARL.

58 Diary of Gunner Bert Stokes, written November 1917, 8601028 KMARL.

59 Diary of Cpl H. Green, 4 October 1917, KMARL.

60 Leonard Hart to Mother, Father and Connie, letter, 19 October 1917, MS Papers 2157, ATL.

61 Terraine, *The Western Front*, p. 173.

62 General Sir Andrew Russell, diary, 4 October 1917, The Russell Saga, Vol III World War I 1914–1919, ATL.

63 Russell to Allen, 4 October 1917, Papers of Sir James Allen, Box 9a Correspondence with Mr Massey, Birdwood and Russell, ANZ.

64 Diary of Brigadier Sir Herbert Hart, KMARL.

65 Peter Howden to Mrs Rhoda Howden, letter, 6 October 1917, Folder 4, MS Papers 1504, P. Howden, ATL.

66 *Dominion*, 6 and 8 October 1917.

67 *Press*, 5 and 8 October 1917.

68 *Dominion*, 8 October 1917.

69 Malcolm Beaven to Mother and Father, letter, 7 October 1917, MB 195, Box 83, MacMillan Brown Library, Canterbury University.

70 Peter Howden to Mrs Rhoda Howden, letter, 6 October 1917, Folder 4, MS Papers 1504, P. Howden, ATL.

71 *New Zealand Herald*, 8 October 1917.

3 Prelude to Disaster

1 Lieut K.E. Luke to his family, letter, 7 October 1917, MS Papers 6027, ATL.

2 J.E. Edmonds, *Military Operations in France and Belgium 1917 Volume II*, London, 1948, p. 327.

3 Charles to Alice Ivory, letter, 14 October 1917, Ivory, Alice Maud, ARC 1991.54 Canterbury Museum.

4 HQ NZ Div Engineers War Diary Oct 1917, 6 October 1917, WA 60/1, ANZ.

5 War Diary NZ Pioneer Battalion Oct 1917, WA 97/1, ANZ.

6 War Diary NZ Pioneer Battalion Oct 1917, WA 97/1, ANZ.

7 Captain S.D. Rogers to Harold Rogers, letter, 30 September 1917, MS Papers 5553 Letters to Stanley Dick Rogers. (The date indicates when the letter was started and it covers the whole month of October 1917.) ATL.

8 Captain S.D. Rogers to Harold Rogers, letter, 30 September 1917, MS Papers 5553 Letters to Stanley Dick Rogers, ATL.

9 Ernest Henry Looms, diary, 6 October 1917, 1998.222, KMARL.

10 Malcolm Beaven to Mother and Father, letter, 7 October 1917, MB 195, Box 83, MacMillan Brown Library, Canterbury University.

11 Bean, p. 881.

12 Harington, p. 111.

13 Haig Diary, quoted in Terraine, *The Road to Passchendaele*, p. 287.

14 Bean, p. 883.

15 Bean, p. 884.

16 Wilson, p. 479.

17 Lieut C.F. Sharland, 8 October 1917, quoted in Wilson, p. 479.

18 Quoted in Wolff, p. 208.

19 Edmonds, *1917 Vol. II*, p. 331.

20 Captain S.D. Rogers to Harold Rogers, letter, 30 September 1917, MS Papers 5553 Letters of Stanley Dick Rogers, ATL.

21 Linus T.J. Ryan, p. 143.

22 William Roy Robson, Diary Entries from 11 Oct 1917, MS Papers 3834, ATL.

23 Bean, p. 901.

24 General Sir Andrew Russell, diary, 9 October 1917, The Russell Saga, Vol III World War I 1914–1919, ATL.

25 Quoted in Wolff, p. 226.

26 Quoted in Wolff, p. 226.

27 Edmonds, *1917 Vol. II*, p. 342.

4 Disaster

1 Diary of Harold Sinclair Muschamp, 11 Oct 1917, 1991.2219 KMARL.

2 Diary of Cpl Edward Duthie, 10 Oct 1917, 9402342 KMARL.

3 Vincent Jervis, Diary 10 October 1917, MS Papers 2241, ATL.

4 Luxford, p. 100.

5 Peter Howden to Rhoda Howden, letter, 14 October 1917, MS Papers 1504, P. Howden, ATL.

6 Percy Williams, *A New Zealanders's Diary. Gallipoli and France 1915–1917*, Christchurch, 1998, p. 265.

7 Mr Bright Williams, ex 3rd Bn, NZRB, interview, Havelock North, 27 March 1998.

8 Haig's Diary, Terraine papers, quoted in Terraine, *The Road to Passchendaele*, pp. 297–8.

9 Dewar and Boraston, p. 379.

10 Remarks Capt L. J. Taylor (OC, B Coy 3 Bn), WA 20/5 Item 36 Passchendaele Offensive, ANZ.

11 Quoted in Stewart, p. 292.

12 Luxford, p. 92.

13 Luxford, p. 93.

14 General Sir Andrew Russell, diary, 11 October 1917, The Russell Saga, Vol III World War I 1914–1919, ATL.

15 Robert Vincent Closey, oral testimony, OH0006/11 Tape 4, Oral History Centre, ATL.

16 Experiences of Gunner Alfred Thomas Stratton, 35467 KMARL.

17 Diary of Brigadier Sir Herbert Hart, 12 Oct 1917, KMARL.

18 Captain S.D. Rogers to Harold Rogers, letter, 30 September 1917, MS Papers 5553 Letters of Stanley Dick Rogers, ATL.

19 Edmonds, *1917 Vol. II*, p. 328.

20 Bean, p. 907–8.

21 Malcolm Beaven to Mother and Father, letter, 4 November 1917, MB 195, Box 83, MacMillan Brown Library, Canterbury University.

22 A.E. Byrne, p. 213.

23 Percy Williams, p. 265.

24 Patrol under Sgt Mjr R.C. Travis, Intelligence Reports 8:05 pm, 11 Oct 1917, WA 76/1 War Diary HQ 2nd NZIB, ANZ.

25 A.E. Byrne, p. 211.

26 Quoted in R. Prior and T. Wilson, *Passchendaele. The Untold Story*, London, 1996, p. 57.

27 W.S. Austin, *The Official History of the New Zealand Rifle Brigade*, Wellington, 1924, p. 229.

28 Austin, p. 230.

29 A.E. Byrne, p. 210.

30 Mr Bright Williams, interview.

31 Report on Operations 11–14 October 1917, (Written by CO Lt Col Owen Mead), War Diary 2 Cant Bn, WA 78/1 ANZ.

32 Leonard Hart to Mother, Father and Connie, letter, 19 October 1917, MS Papers 2157, ATL.

33 James Harold Vincent Martin, oral testimony, OH AB 496, Oral History Centre, ATL.

34 A.E. Byrne, p. 215.

35 D. Ferguson, *The History of the Canterbury Regiment, N.Z.E.F. 1914–1919*, Auckland, 1921, p. 197.

36 NZ Div Narrative of operations for Passchendaele Attack Oct 12 1917, GOC NZ Div 3 Nov 1917, WA 20/3 Box 12, Item 151/42 Operations Somme/Ypres October 1917–February 1918 General Reports, ANZ.

37 Stewart, p. 282.

38 Quoted in O. Burton, *The Silent Division. New Zealanders at the Front: 1914–1919*, Sydney, 1935, p. 246.

39 Mr Bright Williams, interview.

40 Austin, p. 238.

41 Stewart, p. 285.

42 Leonard M. Hart to Mother, Father and Connie, letter, 19 October 1917, Folder 2, MS Papers 2157, Leonard M. Hart, ATL. This letter, one of the best primary sources on the attack of 12 October, is some 42 pages long as Leonard Hart unburdens himself to his family. In order to avoid the Army censors the letter was posted from the United Kingdom.

43 Private Ernest H. Langford, Diary entry 12 Oct 1917, MS Papers 2242, ATL.

44 Gerald Craig Beattie, oral testimony, MSC 2540, Oral History Centre, ATL.

45 James Frederick Blakemore, oral testimony, OH AB 453, Oral History Centre, ATL.

46 Diary of N.C. Rowe, 12 Oct 1917, 9301005 KMARL.

47 Henry Ashton (Harry) Highet to The Senior Officer, 1st Canterbury Regiment, letter, n.d., in oral testimony, OH AB 478, Oral History Centre, ATL.

48 Percy Williams, p. 266.

49 Percy Williams, pp. 266–7.

50 Charlie Lawrence, oral testimony, OH AB 489, Oral History Centre, ATL.

51 Leonard Leary Reminiscences, MS Papers 4022, ATL.

52 Ferguson, p. 198.

53 David Albert Grant to Leslie, letter, 36 October 1917, MS Papers 542, ATL.

54 Vincent Jervis, Diary 12 October 1917, MS Papers 2241, ATL.

55 Vincent Jervis, Diary 12 October 1917, MS Papers 2241, ATL.

56 Leslie Frederick Harris, oral testimony, OH AB 476, Oral History Centre, ATL.

57 Vincent Jervis, Diary 12 October 1917, MS Papers 2241, ATL.

58 Diary of Cpl Harold Green, 12 Oct 1917, 18926 KMARL.

59 Mr Bright Williams, interview.

60 Report of 2nd Lt M.G. Luxford, Int Off, 3rd Bn, 3 NZRB 17/10/17, WA 20/5 Item 36 Passchendaele Offensive, ANZ.

61 George Brunton, oral testimony, MSC 2579, Oral History Centre, ATL.

62 Diary of Cpl Edward Duthie, 12 Oct 1917, 9402342 KMARL.

63 Cpl A.D. (Decie) Bridge, letter to wife, 19 October 1917, MS Papers 4689, Folder 3, Bridge File, ATL.

64 Mr Bright Williams, interview.

65 Serle, p. 298.

66 Carbery, p. 348.

67 Percy Williams, p. 268.

68 Figures for the KIA and DOW are from New Zealand and World War One, Roll of Honour, 1917. http://freepages. genealogy.rootsweb.com. New Zealand historians owe Christine Clement of Te Puke an enormous debt of gratitude for compiling this database. These figures have also been confirmed by Andrew Macdonald's research.

69 J. Philips, N. Boyack and E.P. Malone, The Great Adventure, Wellington, 1988, p. 3.

70 Report on Operations 10–20 October 1917, WA 76/1 War Diary HQ 2nd NZIB, ANZ.

71 Report on Operations 11–14 October 1917, (Written by CO Lt Col Owen Mead), WA 78/1 War Diary 2 Cant Bn, ANZ.

72 A.E. Byrne, p. 220.

73 Major Richardson's Papers, WA 250/8, ANZ.

74 Report on Operations 10–20 October 1917, War Diary HQ 2nd NZIB, WA 76/1, ANZ.

75 Austin, p. 244.

76 General Sir Andrew Russell, diary, 12 October 1917, The Russell Saga, Vol III World War I 1914–1919, ATL.

77 Henry Ashton (Harry) Highet to The Senior Officer, 1st Canterbury Regiment, letter, n.d., in oral testimony, OH AB 478, Oral History Centre, ATL.

78 Translation of Captured Message from 29 Infantry Regiment (2nd Battalion) on 12 October 1917, Current Papers Lt Cory Wright, Intelligence Enemy Back Lines Disposition of Troops, WA 21/2 Box 1 Item 4, ANZ.

79 Prior to the German attack in the Battle of the Metz on 9 June 1918, for example, German POWs indicated to the French that an attack was imminent while a German deserter revealed the exact date and time of the planned attack. See J. H. Johnson, 1918. The Unexpected Victory, London, 1997, p. 77.

80 Report on Operations 10–20 October 1917, War Diary HQ 2nd NZIB, WA 76/1, ANZ.

81 II Anzac Intelligence Summary to 8 pm 13 October 1917, Passchendaele Offensive, WA 20/5 Item 36, ANZ.

82 Edward Wright, 'The Conquest of Poelcapelle and the Reverse of Passchendaele', in H.W. Wilson (ed.), The Great War, Part 183, Week ending February 16, 1918, London, p. 537.

83 New Zealand Herald, 16 October 1917.

84 Leslie Frederick Harris, oral testimony, OH AB 476, Oral History Centre, ATL.

85 Godley to Allen, Letter, 16 Oct 1917, WA 252/4 Letters of Colonel Sir James Allen and General Sir Alexander Godley Jan–Dec 1917, ANZ.

86 See Christopher Pugsley, Te Hokowhitu a Tu. The Maori Pioneer Battalion in the First World War, Auckland, 1995.

87 Quoted in Pugsley, Maori Pioneer Battalion, p. 67.

88 General Sir Andrew Russell, diary, 14 October 1917, The Russell Saga, Vol III World War I 1914–1919, ATL.

89 Vincent Jervis, Diary 14 October 1917, MS Papers 2241, ATL.

90 George Brunton, oral testimony, MSC 2579, Oral History Centre, ATL.

91 Linus T.J. Ryan, p. 144.

92 J.H. Luxford, p. 99.

93 Gordon Kirkpatrick Neill, oral testimony, OH AB 503-1, Oral History Centre, ATL.

94 Gordon Kirkpatrick Neill, oral testimony, OH AB 503-1, Oral History Centre, ATL.

95 Sidney George Stanfield, oral testimony, OH AB 516/1, Oral History Centre, ATL.

96 A.E. Byrne, p. 224.

97 A. Stratton, 'Recollections', MS Papers 3823, ATL.

98 Sidney George Stanfield, oral testimony, OH AB 516/1, Oral History Centre, ATL.

99 Linus T.J. Ryan, p. 152.

100 Sister A.E. Shadforth, quoted in Jan Bassett, *Guns and Brooches. Australian Army Nursing from the Boer War to the Gulf War*, Melbourne, 1992, p. 65.

101 Private Ernest H. Langford, Diary entry 12 Oct 1917, MS Papers 2242, ATL.

102 General Sir Andrew Russell, diary, 16 October 1917, The Russell Saga, Vol III World War I 1914–1919, ATL.

103 General Sir Andrew Russell, diary, 9 November 1917, The Russell Saga, Vol III World War I 1914–1919, ATL.

104 Russell to Allen, 7 November 1917, Papers of Sir James Allen, Allen, J Box 9a Correspondence with Mr Massey, Birdwood and Russell, ANZ.

105 Allen to Russell, 29 January 1918, Papers of Sir James Allen, Allen, J Box 9a Correspondence with Mr Massey, Birdwood and Russell, ANZ.

106 Russell to Allen, 3 April 1918, Papers of Sir James Allen, Allen, J Box 9a Correspondence with Mr Massey, Birdwood and Russell, ANZ.

107 A.E. Byrne, p. 228.

108 Wilson Diary, 14 Oct 1917, 9402314 KMARL.

109 Godley to Allen, letter, 16 Oct 1917, Letters of Colonel Sir James Allen and General Sir Alexander Godley Jan–Dec 1917, WA 252/4, ANZ.

110 Godley to Wigram, letter, 14 Oct 1917, Godley Papers, WA 252/14 (Micro Z 5083), ANZ.

111 Wigram to Godley, letter, 16 Oct 1917, Godley Papers, WA 252/14 (Micro Z 5083), ANZ.

112 Godley to Allen, letter, 16 Oct 1917, Letters of Colonel Sir James Allen and General Sir Alexander Godley Jan–Dec 1917, WA 252/4, ANZ.

113 Captain S.D. Rogers to Harold Rogers, letter, 30 September 1917, MS Papers 5553 Letters of Stanley Dick Rogers, ATL.

114 NZ Div Narrative of operations for Passchendaele Attack Oct 12 1917, GOC NZ Div 3 Nov 1917, Operations Somme/ Ypres October 1917–February 1918 General Reports, WA 20/3 Box 12, Item 151/42, ANZ.

115 2nd Lt M.G. Laxford, Intelligence Officer 3rd Bn 3 NZRB 17/10/17 Passchendaele Offensive 12 October 1916 [sic], ANZ.

116 Diary of Brigadier Sir Herbert Hart, 12 Oct 1917, KMARL.

117 Report on Operations Carried out by 3rd NZ (Rifle) Brigade 9 October–14 October 1917, ANZ.

118 Linus T.J. Ryan, p. 143.

119 Bean, p. 921.

120 Prior and Wilson, p. 169.

121 Edward Wright, 'The Conquest of Poelcapelle and the Reverse of Passchendaele', in H.W. Wilson (ed.), *The Great War*, Part 183, Week ending February 16, 1918, London, p. 538.

122 *Dominion*, 15 October 1917.

123 *Dominion*, 16 October 1917.

124 *New Zealand Herald*, 15 October 1917.

125 Wilson Diary, 15 Oct 1917, 9402314 KMARL.

5 The Legacy of Passchendaele

1 Haig Diary, 13 October 1917, quoted in Terraine, *The Road to Passchendaele*, pp. 301–2.

2 Bean, p. 376.

3 Ludendorff, p. 491.

4 Ludendorff, p. 512.

5 Ludendorff, p. 497.

6 Sir Philip Gibbs, quoted in Terraine, *The Road to Passchendaele*, p. 341.

7 Malcolm Beaven to Mother and Father, letter, 4 November 1917, MB 195, Box 83, MacMillan Brown Library, Canterbury University.

8 Wolff, p. 2.

9 L.M. Inglis, letter 26 October 1917, Folder 5 MS Papers 421, Inglis Papers, ATL.

10 George McLaren, letters to Tina, 1 November 1917 and 20 December 1917, MS Papers 6536-1, ATL.

11 Edmonds, *1917 Vol. II*, p. 330.

12 Burton, *The Auckland Regiment*, p. 180.

13 Stewart, p. 290.

14 R.W. Toomath, Diary, 13 Oct 1917, MS Papers 2301, ATL.

15 Comments by Lt Gen Freyberg, VC, Second Libyan Campaign 1941, Vol 1, Correspondence Libya, WA II Series 11 No. 5, ANZ.

16 Bert Stokes, letter to Mum and Dad, 6 November 1917, MS Papers 4683, Folder 7, ATL.

17 Diary of J.C. Heseltine, 4 November 1917, MSX Papers 4338, ATL.

18 Recollections of General Russell's Aide (Colonel G.F. Gambrill), MS Papers 1619, Folder 215, ATL.

19 Sidney George Stanfield, oral testimony, OH AB 516/1, Oral History Centre, ATL.

20 Luxford, p. 95.

21 General Sir Andrew Russell, diary, 9 November 1917, The Russell Saga, Vol III World War I 1914–1919, ATL.

22 Burton, *Silent Division*, p. 253.

23 F.J. (Gwynne) Potts, letter to Queenie, 24 October 1917, MS Papers 4302, Folder 4, ATL.

24 Report of No. 1 NZ General Hospital Brockenhurst, England, WA 4/1 Item 1, New Zealand Hospitals 1914–18, ANZ.

25 Boyack, p. 78.

26 J.F.C. Fuller, *The Decisive Battles of the Western World and their influence upon history*, Volume III, London, 1956, p. 272.

27 Boyack, p. 79.

28 Haig Diary, 13 October 1917, quoted in Terraine, *The Road to Passchendaele*, pp. 302–3.

29 Charlie Lawrence, oral testimony, OH AB 489, Oral History Centre, ATL.

30 Gerald Craig Beattie, oral testimony, MSC 2540, Oral History Centre, ATL.

31 General Sir Andrew Russell, diary, 5 October 1917, The Russell Saga, Vol III World War I 1914–1919, ATL.

32 Recollections of General Russell's Aide (Colonel G.F. Gambrill), MS Papers 1619, Folder 215, ATL.

33 Harington, p. 130.

34 Fred Majdalany, *Cassino. Portrait of a Battle*, London, 1957, p. 193.

35 Major General Russell to James Allen (NZ Minister of Defence), 7 November 1917, Allen Papers, ANZ.

36 Gunner Thomas Ward, Diary, 1997.1829, KMARL.

37 Leonard Hart to Mother, Father and Connie, letter, 19 October 1917, MS Papers 2157, ATL.

38 Gunner A. Stratton, 'Recollections', MS Papers 3823, ATL.

39 Leonard Hart, letter, 19 Oct 1917, MS Papers 2157, ATL.

40 Leonard Leary Reminiscences, MS Papers 4022, ATL.

41 Gordon Kirkpatrick Neill, oral testimony, OH AB 503-1, Oral History Centre, ATL.

42 Sir Edward Beddinton-Behrens, *Daily Telegraph*, 7 July 1967, quoted in Terraine, *Road to Passchendaele*, p. xx.

43 Mr Bright Williams, interview.

44 Robert Vincent Closey, oral testimony, OH0006/11 Tape 4, Oral History Centre, ATL.

45 Russell to Allen, 7 November 1917, Papers of Sir James Allen, Allen, J., Box 9a Correspondence with Mr Massey, Birdwood and Russell, ANZ.

46 *New Zealand Parliamentary Debates*, Vol. 181, October 11 to November 1, 1917, Wellington, 1917, p. 742.

47 Jay Winter and Blaine Baggett, *1914–18 The Great War and the Shaping of the 20th Century*, London, 1996, p. 15.

48 W.C. Smith to Mrs C.M. Smith, letter, 23 September 1917, MS Papers 2352 W.C. Smith, ATL.

49 Mrs N. Knight, letter to Georgie, n.d., MS Papers 5548 File 10, ATL.

50 Mrs N. Knight, letter to My Dear Boy, n.d., MS Papers 5548 File 10, ATL.

51 F.W. Hamill to Mrs N. Knight, letter, 31 October 1917, MS Papers 5548 File 11, ATL.

52 Stuart Varnhauss to Mrs N. Knight, letter, 15 October 1917, MS Papers 5548 File 11, ATL.

53 Lt Col G.S. Smith to Mrs N. Knight, letter, 18 October 1917, MS Papers 5548 File 11, ATL.

54 Copy of Lt Col G.S. Smith's letter to Mrs N. Knight, 18 October 1917, MS Papers 5548 File 11, ATL.

55 Brigadier W.G. Braithwaite to Mrs N. Knight, letter, 4 November 1917, MS Papers 5548 File 11, ATL.

56 Nancy Croad, *My Dear Home: The letters of three Knight brothers who gave their lives during World War I*, Auckland, 1995, p. 5.

57 Narrative by G.H. Gavin, 3 Jan 1918, WA 10/3 Box 1 ZMR 1/1/3 Chaplain's Reports, ANZ.

58 Quoted in M. King, *New Zealanders at War*, Auckland, 1981, p. 167.

59 Sir Ernest Scott, *The Official History of Australia in the War of 1914–1918, Volume XI, Australia During the War*, Sydney, 1936, p. 864.

60 Weston, p. 233.

61 Stanley Frederick Herbert, oral testimony, OH AB 482, Oral History Centre, ATL.

62 'They did the hard yards — yard by sodden yard', Jeremy Rees, *Central Leader*, date unknown.

63 Robin Hyde, *Nor the Years Condemn*, New Women's Press Edition, 1986, p. 118.

64 John Mulgan, *Report on Experience*, Auckland, 1947, p. 33.

65 A.J.P. Taylor, *The First World War. An Illustrated History*, Harmondsworth, 1966, p. 140.

66 Sidney George Stanfield, oral testimony, OH AB 516/1, Oral History Centre, ATL.

67 Oliver Duff, *New Zealand Now*, Wellington, 1941, p. 108.

68 Name withheld by request, interview, 20 April 1999.

69 Scott, p. viii.

70 Stanley Frederick Herbert, oral testimony, OH AB 482, Oral History Centre, ATL.

71 James Harold Vincent Martin, oral testimony, OH AB 496, Oral History Centre, ATL.

72 J.A. Lee, *Civilian into Soldier*, London, 1963, p. 44.

73 Fussell, p. 87.

74 Charlie Lawrence, oral testimony, OH AB 489, Oral History Centre, ATL.

75 Mr Bright Williams, interview.

76 Bert Stokes, letter to Mum and Dad, 14 October 1917, MS Papers 4683, Folder 6, ATL.

77 J. Phillips, *A Man's Country? The image of the Pakeha male — a history*, Auckland, 1987, p. 212.

78 From work undertaken by Dr James Conner. See also D. Grossman, *On Killing: The psychological cost of learning to kill in war and society*, Boston, 1995.

79 Michael King, *New Zealanders at War*, Auckland, 1981, p. 1.

80 Scott, p. 858.

Conclusion

1 Major R.E. Beebe, 'Course at the Army War College, Command, Problem No. 1 — The Principles of War', US Army War College Curriculum Archives 227-53, US Army Military History Institute, Carlisle, Pennsylvania.

2 Harington, p. 112.

3 Gordon Kirkpatrick Neill, oral testimony, OH AB 503-1, Oral History Centre, ATL.

4 Ludendorff, p. 492.

5 Gordon R. Sullivan and Michael V. Harper, *Hope is Not a Method*, New York, 1996, p. 229.

6 Sidney George Stanfield, oral testimony, OH AB 516/1, Oral History Centre, ATL.

7 J. Keegan, *The First World War*, London, 1998, p. 262.

8 'They did the hard yards — yard by sodden yard', Jeremy Rees, *Central Leader*, date unknown.

Spring Offensive

Introduction

1 Ernst Junger, *The Storm of Steel. From the Diary of a German Storm-troop Officer on the Western Front*, London, 2000, pp. 253–4.

2 Gary Sheffield, *Forgotten Victory. The First World War: Myths and Realities*, London, 2001, p. 189.

3 Gerhard Loose, *Ernst Junger*, New York, 1974, p. 22. The decoration was instituted by Frederick the Great of Prussia, who preferred the French language to German.

4 Junger, p. 250.

5 Lieutenant E.C. Allfree, quoted in J.H. Johnson, *1918. The Unexpected Victory*, London, 1997, p. 27.

6 Sheffield, p. 60.

7 A.D. Carbery, *The New Zealand Medical Service in the Great War 1914–1918*, Auckland, 1924, p. 383.

8 *Ibid.*

1 Storm Clouds

1 Quoted in John Terraine, *To Win a War. 1918 The Year of Victory*, London, 2000, p. 27.

2 Cyril Falls, *The Great War*, New York, 1959, p. 255.

3 Terraine, *To Win a War*, p. 37.

4 John Coates, *An Atlas of Australia's Wars*, Melbourne, 2001, p. 72.

5 Quoted in Anthony Farrar-Hockley, *Goughie. The Life of General Sir Hubert Gough CGB, GCMG, KCVO*, London, 1975, p. 243.

6 He had once addressed a victorious army cross-country team: 'I congratulate you on your running. I hope you will run as well in the presence of the enemy.' Haig remained unaware of his *faux pas*. (Used as the frontispiece for William Moore's *See How They Ran*, Sphere Books, London, 1975.)

7 Farrar-Hockley, p. 243.

8 Farrar-Hockley, p. 242.

9 Sir James Edmonds, *History of the Great War. Military Operations in France and Belgium 1918 Volume I*, London, 1935, p. 53.

10 Terraine, *To Win a War*, p. 49.

11 William Moore, *See How They Ran. The British Retreat of 1918*, London, 1975, p. 41.

12 Jeffrey Grey, *A Military History of Australia*, Melbourne, 1999, pp. 108–9.

13 G.D. Sheffield, 'The Indispensable Factor: The Performance of British Troops in 1918', in Peter Dennis and Jeffrey Grey (eds), *1918. Defining Victory*, Canberra, 1999, p. 77.

14 Figures are from Edmonds, *1918 Vol. I*, p. 24.

15 General Sir Hubert Gough, *Soldiering On*, London, 1954, p. 146.

16 Edmonds, *1918 Vol. I*, p. vii.

17 W.S. Austin, *The Official History of the New Zealand Rifle Brigade*, Wellington, 1924, p. 271.

18 Winston Churchill, *The World Crisis 1914–1918 Part II*, London, 1927, p. 385.

19 C.E.W. Bean, *Official History of Australia in the War of 1914–18. Vol. V. The A.I.F. in France: December 1917–May 1918*, Sydney, 1943, p. 671.

20 John Mosier, *The Myth of the Great War. A New Military History of World War I*, New York, 2001, pp. 312–14.

21 Falls, p. 259.

22 Falls, p. 180.

23 Churchill, p. 405.

24 General Ludendorff, *My War Memories 1914–18, Volume II*, London, 1919, p. 542.

25 Terraine, *To Win a War*, p. 35.

26 Ludendorff, p. 537.

27 *Ibid.*, p. 542.

28 *Ibid.*, p. 585.

29 Terraine, *To Win a War*, p. 35.

30 Ludendorff, p. 542.

31 There is remarkable agreement on these figures among the sources. Stewart, Edmonds, Churchill, Bean and Terraine agree that the Germans began the offensive with 192 infantry divisions and over 6000 artillery pieces.

32 Terraine, *To Win a War*, p. 37.

33 Barrie Pitt, 'Germany: 1918. New strategy, new tactics', in *History of the First World War*, Volume 6, Number 14, London, 1971, p. 2616.

34 Ludendorff, p. 590.

35 Pitt, p. 2616.

36 For most of the war the German front was organised into three army groups under the command of a royal prince. This was a Prussian, and later German, tradition. In 1918 the Army Group commanders were the Bavarian Crown Prince (Rupprecht), the German Crown Prince Wilhelm and Duke Albrecht of Wurttemberg. Later three Army Groups proved insufficient so another smaller one was created under General von Gallwitz.

37 Notes on the Offensive Battle, GHQ 25-1-18, WA 20/3 Box 2, Translation of German Documents 1/29/261, ANZ.

38 *Ibid.*

39 John Buchan, *Nelson's History of the War. Volume XXII The Darkest Hour*, London, n.d., p. 17.

40 Terraine, *To Win a War*, p. 38.

41 Farrar-Hockley, p. 250.

42 Edmonds, *1918 Vol. I*, p. 118.

43 Bean, *Official History. Vol V*, p. 105.

44 Buchan, p. 19.

45 Notes on the Offensive Battle, GHQ 25-1-18. WA 20/3 ANZ.

46 *Ibid.*

47 Ludendorff, p. 573.

48 Junger, p. 240.

49 *Ibid.*, p. 240.

50 *Ibid.*, p. 244.

51 Terraine, *To Win a War*, p. 39.

52 Ludendorff, p. 543.

53 *Ibid.*, pp. 587–8.

54 Sheffield, p. 61.

55 Quoted in Buchan, p. 12. Italics original.

56 Edmonds, *1918 Vol. I*, p. 71.

57 Ludendorff, p. 594.

58 Edmonds, *1918 Vol. I*, p. 39.

59 Falls, p. 332.

60 Gregory Blaxland, *Amiens: 1918*, London, 1981, p. 23.

61 Mosier, pp. 314–15.

62 Gough, p. 151.

63 Austin, p. 272.

64 Moore, p. 42.

65 Farrar-Hockley, p. 265.

66 Colonel H. Stewart, *The New Zealand Division 1916–1919*, Auckland, 1921, p. 335.

67 Major W.E. Grey, quoted in Blaxland, pp. 33–4.

2 A Brief Interlude

1 Oscar Glen Reston, interview, 21 October 1989, OH Int 006/69, Oral History Centre, ATL. All interviews in this section of the book attributed to the ATL were conducted by Jane Tolerton and Nicholas Boyack.

2 *Ibid.*

3 Thomas Eltringham, interview, 2 October 1988, OH Int 0006/29, ATL.

4 James McWhirter, Diary of the Great War (Written about 1920.), MSX 4915, ATL.

5 A.E. Byrne, *Official History of the Otago Regiment, N.Z.E.F. in the Great War 1914–1918*, Dunedin, 1921, p. 270.

6 Reston interview, ATL.

7 McWhirter diary, ATL.

8 O.E. Burton, *The Silent Division. New Zealanders at the Front: 1914–1919*, Sydney, 1935, p. 263.

9 War Diary, 2nd NZ Infantry Brigade, March 1918, WA76/1, ANZ.

10 Ezekiel Mawhinny, letter to Bill and Laura, 10 March 1918, MS Papers 1687 Mawhinny Family, ATL.

11 War Diary, 2nd NZ Infantry Brigade, 12–21 March 1918, WA76/1, ANZ.

12 War Diary, 2nd Battalion Otago Regiment, 2nd NZ Infantry Brigade, March 1918, WA80/1, ANZ.

13 Extracts from the Diary of Sir Andrew Russell, The Russell Family Saga, Vol III, MS Papers QMS0822, ATL.

14 Stewart, p. 338.

15 War Diary, 2nd NZ Infantry Brigade 23 March 1918, WA76/1, ANZ.

16 Russell diary, ATL.

17 See for example Chris Pugsley, 'Russell of the New Zealand Division' in *New Zealand Strategic Management*, Autumn 1995.

18 Reston interview, ATL.

19 Burton, *Silent Division*, p. 253.

20 Russell diary, 4 March 1918, ATL.

21 Burton, *Silent Division*, p. 264.

22 Edward Stuart Bibby, interview, 19 May 1988, OH Int 0006/09, Oral History Centre, ATL.

23 Russell diary, 22 March 1918, ATL.

24 Bean, *Official History. Vol. V*, p. 116.

3 The Storm Breaks

1 Diary of an Officer of the 119 Infantry Regiment (26 Division), 18 March 1918, WA 20/3 Box 2, Translation of German Documents (1/29/261), ANZ.

2 Loose, p. 23.

3 Moore, p. 59. Junger, p. 250, states that the message 'was greeted with enthusiasm'.

4 Ludendorff, p. 596.

5 *Otago Daily Times*, 20 March 1918.

6 Barrie Pitt, 'The Ludendorff Offensive Phase 1', in *History of the First War*, Volume 6, Number 15, London, 1971, p. 2638.

7 Jonathan B.A. Bailey, 'The First World War and the birth of Modern Warfare', in M. Knox and W. Murray (eds), *The Dynamics of Military Revolution 1300–2050*, Cambridge, Cambridge Press, 2001, p. 144.

8 Churchill, p. 411.

9 Moore, p. 64.

10 Gough, p. 153.

11 Junger, p. 251.

12 War Diary 51 (Highland) Division, 21 March 1918, WA241/21, ANZ.

13 Farrar-Hockley, p. 276.

14 Blaxland, p. 112.

15 Pitt, p. 2639.

16 *Ibid.*, p. 2639–43.

17 Ludendorff, p. 598.

18 Diary of an Officer of the 119 Infantry Regiment (26 Division), WA20/3, ANZ.

19 Quoted in Moore, p. 73.

20 Moore, p. 90.

21 Churchill, p. 417.

22 Blaxland, p. 63.

23 Gough, p. 160.

24 Quoted in Blaxland, p. 68.

25 Buchan, p. 40.

26 Edmonds, *1918 Vol. I*, p. 399.

27 Edmonds, *1918 Vol. I*, p. 400.

28 Moore, p. 152.

29 Edmonds, *1918 Vol. I*, p. 489.

30 Quoted in Blaxland, p. 70.

31 Quoted in Farrar-Hockley, p. 294.

32 Blaxland, p. 69.

33 *Otago Daily Times*, 25 March 1918.

34 Ludendorff, p. 604.

35 Brigadier General Sir Herbert Hart KBE, CB, CMG, DSO, diary entry, 29 March 1918, MS 0552 (Micro), ATL.

36 Churchill, p. 43.

37 Bean, *Official History. Vol. V*, p. 243.

38 Quoted in Moore, p. 137.

39 Bean, *Official History. Vol. V*, p. 256.

40 *Ibid*. This is from *La Crise du Commandement Unique*, p.154. As Bean explains: 'The narrative as often happens, wrongly includes the New Zealand Division as "Australian". The word should be "Anzac".'

41 Blaxland, p. 71.

42 Falls, p. 335.

43 Quoted in Farrar-Hockley, p. 302.

44 *Ibid*.

45 J.H. Johnson, *1918. The Unexpected Victory*, London, 1997, p. 46.

46 Quoted in Farrar-Hockley, p. 306.

47 Carbery, p. 386.

48 Sir James E. Edmonds, *History of the Great War. Military Operations France and Belgium 1918 Volume II*, London, 1937, p. 1.

49 *New Zealand Herald*, 25 March 1918.

50 *New Zealand Herald*, 26 March 1918.

51 *Dominion*, 27 March 1918.

52 *Press*, 25 March 1918.

53 *New Zealand Herald*, 30 March 1918.

54 Ministerial Statement, House of Representatives, 15 April 1918, New Zealand Parliamentary Debates, 182nd Volume.

4 A Hurried Journey

1 John Gordon Harcourt, diary entry, 23 March 1918, MS Papers 6293, ATL.

2 *Ibid*.

3 Kenneth Luke, letter to My Dear People, March/April 1918, Letters of Kenneth Ewart Luke, MS Papers 6027, ATL.

4 War Diary, 3rd Battalion New Zealand Rifle Brigade, March 1918, WA 84/1, ANZ.

5 War Diary, NZ (Maori) Pioneer Battalion, 21–25 March 1918, WA97/1, ANZ.

6 *Ibid*., 23 and 24 March 1918, ANZ.

7 Diary of Bombardier N. Bailey, SAA Section, NZFA, 1999–1010, KMARL.

8 Russell diary, 24 March 1918, ATL.

9 *Ibid*., 25 March 1918.

10 Ira Robinson, letter to Lizzie, 12 April 1918, in Chrissie Ward (ed.), *Dear Lizzie*, Auckland, 2000, p. 87.

11 Captain George Albert Tuck, diary entry, 25 March 1918, MS Papers 2164-2166 (Micro 0052), ATL.

12 Lieutenant Colonel S.S. Allen, *2/ Auckland, 1918*, Auckland, Whitcombe & Tombs Ltd, 1920, p. 25.

13 War Diary, 2nd Battalion Otago Regiment, 2nd NZ Infantry Brigade, 25 March 1918, WA80/1, ANZ.

14 William Murray Morris, interview, 4 July 1989, OH Int 006/58, Oral History Centre, ATL.

15 Burton, *Silent Division*, p. 267.

16 Jesse Williams Stayte, Rough Notes from my Diary, 26 March 1918, MS Papers 7198, ATL.

17 William Douglas Knight, letter to Mother and Father, Easter Sunday, 1918, MS Papers 5548-08, ATL.

18 Corporal Gerald Beattie, diary entry, 25 March 1918, MS Papers 3908 Folder 3, Diary of Gerald Craig Beattie, ATL.

19 From N.M. Ingram, 'Anzac Diary, A Nonentity in Khaki', p. 91, quoted in Christopher Pugsley, *On the Fringe of Hell*, Auckland, 1991, p. 269.

20 John Coleman, letter to My Dear Mary, 29 April 1918, quoted in Glyn Harper (ed.), *Letters from the Battlefield*, Auckland, 2001, p. 137.

21 War Diary, 2nd Auckland Battalion, WA 72/1, ANZ.

22 Bernard Victor Cottrell, letter to Dad, 10 April 1918, MS Papers 1389, Papers of Bernard Cottrell, ATL.

23 Charlie Lawrence, interview, 9 October 1989, OH Int 0006/47, Oral History Centre, ATL.

24 Sergeant Leonard William Hutchinson, diary entry, 2000-64, KMARL.

25 Claude Sheenan Wysocki, interviews, 19 October and 22 October 1988, OH AB 526, Oral History Centre, ATL.

26 John Ralph Bartle, letter to Nita, 27 June 1918, MS Papers 1630, ATL.

27 Vincent Jervis, diary entries for 24 and 27 March 1918, MS Papers 2241, ATL.

28 *Ibid.*, 13 and 17 April 1918.

29 William Jamieson, interview, 3 July 1989, OH Int 0006/43, Oral History Centre, ATL.

30 Beattie diary, 29 March 1918, ATL.

31 Bean, *Official History. Vol. V*, p. 236.

32 John Coleman, letter to My Dear Mary, 29 April 1918, quoted in Harper (ed.), p. 137.

33 Kenneth Luke letters, ATL.

34 Harold Sinclair Muschamp, diary entry, 25 March 1918, 1991.2219 KMARL.

35 Beattie diary, 26 March 1918, ATL.

36 Ronald Watson, letter 'In the Field', Monday April 1st. 1918, *Letters from a Padre. A Record of the War Service of Ronald S. Watson MC, ED, MA*, p. 27.

37 Cecil Jepson, 1918 Pocket Diary, Tuesday 26 March 1918, MS Papers 1480 Cecil John Jepson, ATL.

38 Burton, *Silent Division*, p. 266.

39 Ira Robinson, letter to Lizzie, 12 April 1918, Ward (ed.), p. 89.

40 McWhirter diary, ATL.

41 See for example, William Donovan Joynt, *Saving the Channel Ports*, Melbourne, 1975.

42 Bean, *Official History. Vol. V*, p. 120.

43 C.E.W. Bean, *Anzac to Amiens*, Melbourne, 1993, p. 415.

44 Alfred Stratten, manuscript, 'First World War 1916–1918 In France After Gallipoli', MS Papers 3283 Stratton Alfred Thomas, ATL.

45 Bernard Cottrell, letter to Dad, 10 April 1918, ATL.

46 *Otago Daily Times*, 4 April 1918.

47 Reported in *New Zealand Herald*, 1 April 1918.

48 Bean, *Official History. Vol. V*, p. 118.

49 *The Fortieth* by F.C. Green, p. 113, quoted in Bean, *Official History. Vol. V*, p. 145.

50 Kenneth Luke letters, ATL.

51 Moore, p. 157.

52 2nd NZ Infantry Brigade Order No. 132 – 26 March 1918, War Diary 2nd NZ Infantry Brigade, WA76/1, ANZ.

53 Extract of Appendix 1, War Diary. 3rd Battalion New Zealand Rifle Brigade, WA 84/1, ANZ.

54 A.E. Byrne, p. 278.

55 O.E. Burton, *The Auckland Regiment*, Auckland, 1922, p. 197.

56 Quoted in Pugsley, 'Russell of the New Zealand Division', p. 48.

5 Into the Storm

1 Stewart, p. 343.

2 Frederick Avery, interview, 23 November 1989, OH Int 0006/02, Oral History Centre, ATL.

3 A.E. Byrne, p. 279.

4 Harcourt diary, ATL.

5 *Ibid.*

6 Morris interview, ATL.

7 War Diary, 2nd Battalion Canterbury Regiment, 26 March 1918, WA78/1, ANZ.

8 War Diary, 1st Battalion Canterbury Regiment., 2nd NZ Infantry Brigade, 26 March 1918, WA77/1, ANZ.

9 War Diary, 2nd NZ Infantry Brigade, 26 March 1918, WA76/1, ANZ.

10 *Ibid.*

11 Harcourt diary, ATL.

12 Stayte diary, ATL.

13 Eltringham interview, ATL.

14 Burton, *The Auckland Regiment*, p. 199.

15 War Diary, 1st Auckland Battalion, 26 March 1918, WA71/1, ANZ.

16 Burton, *The Auckland Regiment*, p. 199.

17 War Diary 2nd Battalion Auckland Regiment, 26 March 1918, WA72/1, ANZ.

18 Eltringham interview, ATL.

19 Bean, *Official History. Vol. V*, p. 126.

20 Diary of Private Ernest John Painter, 8 Southland Company, 2 Otago Battalion, 2000-654, KMARL.

21 Edmonds, *1918 Vol. I*, p. 534.

22 Edmonds, *1918 Vol. II*, p. 9.

23 John Douglas Coleman, letter to My dear Mary, 29 April 1918, in Harper (ed.), p. 138.

24 Bean, *Official History. Vol. V*, pp. 269–70.

25 Stewart, p. 349.

6 Stopping the Storm

1 Austin, p. 286.

2 Bernard Cottrell, letter, Dear Mother & Father, 2 April, Papers of Bernard Cottrell, ATL.

3 Bean, *Official History. Vol. V*, p. 129.

4 *Ibid.*

5 Burton, *The Silent Division*, p. 270.

6 *Ibid.*

7 Burton, *The Auckland Regiment*, p. 201.

8 McWhirter diary, ATL.

9 Reston interview, ATL.

10 Morris interview, ATL.

11 Edmonds, *1918 Vol. II*, p. 35.

12 Tuck diary, 27 March 1918, ATL.

13 Burton, *The Auckland Regiment*, p. 203.

14 War Diary, NZ Machine Gun Battalion, 27 March 1918, WA98/1, ANZ.

15 *Ibid.*

16 J.H. Luxford, *With the Machine Gunners in France and Palestine*, Auckland, 1923, p. 118.

17 War Diary, NZ Machine Gun Battalion, 27 March 1918, WA98/1, ANZ.

18 Luxford, p. 118.

19 Tuck diary, 27 March 1918, ATL.

20 War Diary, 2nd Battalion Auckland Regiment, 27 March 1918, WA72/1, ANZ.

21 Harry Highet, interview, 8 June 1988, OH Int 0006/36, Oral History Centre, ATL.

22 James Frederick Blakemore, interview, 5 August 1988, OH 0006/11, Oral History Centre, ATL.

23 Harcourt diary, 27 March 1918, ATL.

24 Stayte diary, 27–28 March 1918, ATL.

25 Carbery, p. 389.

26 War Diary, 1st NZ Infantry Brigade, 27 March 1918, WA 70/1, ANZ.

27 Roderick William Toomath, diary, MS Papers 2301, ATL.

28 Bibby interview, ATL.

29 William Horne Milne, diary entries March 1918, MS Papers 1879, ATL.

30 William Bertrand, interview, 3 November 1989, OH Int 0006/06, Oral History Centre, ATL.

31 War Diary, 3 NZ Field Artillery, 27 March 1918, WA53/1, ANZ.

32 J.R. Byrne, *New Zealand Artillery in the Field 1914–18*, Auckland, 1922, p. 222.

33 Stewart, p. 356.

34 Russell diary, ATL.

35 Edmonds, *1918 Vol. II*, p. 41.

36 Moore, p. 160.

37 Edmonds, *1918 Vol. II*, p. 40.

38 Bean, *Official History. Vol. V*, pp. 286–7; Edmonds, *1918 Vol. II*, p. 41.

7 Holding the Storm

1 Falls, p. 336.

2 *Ibid.*

3 Edmonds, *1918 Vol. II*, p. 53; Bean, *Official History. Vol. V*, p. 288; Blaxland, p. 84. Blaxland's figures for the number of German formations used are nine fresh divisions with a further two in support.

4 Churchill, p. 419.

5 Edmonds, *1918 Vol. II*, p. 53.

6 Edmonds, *1918 Vol. II*, p. 56.

7 War Diary, 3 NZ Field Artillery, January – December 1918, WA53/1, ANZ.

8 J.R. Byrne, p. 223.

9 War Diary, 2nd New Zealand Infantry Brigade, 28 March 1918, WA76/1, ANZ.

10 War Diary, New Zealand Machine Gun Battalion, 28 March 1918.

11 War Diary, 2nd Auckland Battalion, WA72/1, ANZ.

12 War Diary, 1st Canterbury Battalion, WA77/1, ANZ.

13 Leslie Frederick Hearns, interview, 7 August 1988, OH Int0006/34, Oral History Centre, ATL.

14 Austin, p. 299.

15 Russell diary, ATL.

16 Godley, letter to Sir James Allen, 22 April 1918 WA 252/5, ANZ.

17 James Cowan, 'Te Hokowhitu a Tu': The Maoris in the Great War, Auckland, 1926. p. 136.

18 Edmonds, 1918 Vol. II, p. 58.

19 Quoted in Stewart, p. 357.

20 Diary of an Officer of the 119 Infantry Regiment (26 Division), ANZ.

21 A.E. Byrne. p. 282.

22 Bernard Cottrell, letter to Dear Mother & Father, 2 April 1918, Papers of Bernard Cottrell, ATL.

23 Bibby interview, ATL.

24 War Diary, 3 New Zealand Field Artillery, 29 March 1918, WA53/1, ANZ.

25 Bailey diary, 29 March 1918, KMARL.

26 William Roy Robson, diary entries, MSX 3484, ATL.

27 John Coleman, letter to Mary, 29 April 1918, in Harper (ed.), p. 138.

28 Harold Sinclair Muschamp, diary entry, 1991.2219 KMARL.

29 Allen, p. 44.

30 Burton, The Auckland Regiment, p. 204.

31 Stewart, p. 363.

32 Allen, p. 44.

33 Ibid., p. 45.

34 Stewart, p. 365.

35 Allen, p. 46.

36 War Diary, 2nd Auckland Battalion, WA72/1, ANZ.

37 Stewart, p. 366.

38 Ibid., p. 367.

39 Report on Line Captured by 1st NZ Infantry Brigade on 30 March 1918 by Brigade Major, dated 31 March 1918, WA 70/1, ANZ.

40 John Coleman, letter to Mary, 29 April 1918, in Harper (ed.), p. 138.

41 Ira Robinson, letter to Lizzie, 12 April 1918, in Ward (ed.), p. 90.

42 Tuck diary, 9.50 p.m. 30 March 1918, ATL.

43 Stewart, pp. 363, 366.

44 Private William Malcolm, letter to 'Poor Dad and You', 18 April 1918, 1991-2782 KMARL.

45 Private William Malcolm, letter to Mum, 12 June 1918, in Harper (ed.), p. 145.

46 Burton, The Auckland Regiment, p. 206.

47 Stewart, p. 367.

48 Bean, Official History. Vol. V, p. 141.

49 Edmonds, 1918 Vol. II, p. 96.

8 A Lull

1 War Diary, 2nd NZ Infantry Brigade, 1 and 2 April 1918, WA76/1, ANZ.

2 War Diary, 1st Battalion Otago Regiment, 2nd NZ Infantry Brigade April 1918, WA 79/1, ANZ.

3 War Diary of 2nd Battalion Otago Infantry Regiment, 2nd NZ Infantry Brigade, April 1918, WA80/1, ANZ.

4 Roderick William Toomath , diary entries 1–4 April 1918, MS Papers 2301, ATL.

5 Report of Conference held at Souastre 2 April 1918, Notes of Conferences, WA 20/3 Box 8, ANZ.

6 Moore, p. 160.

7 War Diary, 1st Otago Battalion, 1 April 1918, WA79/1, ANZ.

8 Stayte diary, ATL.

9 Burton, The Auckland Regiment, p. 206.

10 Tuck diary, ATL.

11 War Diary, 1st Battalion New Zealand Rifle Brigade, April 1918, WA 82/1, ANZ.

12 War Diary, NZ (Maori) Pioneer Battalion, April 1918, WA 97/1, ANZ.

13 Stayte diary, ATL.

14 War Diary of 2nd Battalion Otago Regiment, 2nd NZ Infantry Brigade, March 1918, WA 80/1, ANZ.

15 War Diary, 2nd Battalion Canterbury Regiment, 2nd NZ Infantry Brigade, 3 April 1918, WA 78/1, ANZ.

16 War Diary, 2nd Battalion Wellington Regiment, 1st NZ Infantry Brigade, 1 April 1918, WA 74/1, ANZ.

17 Bert Stokes, letter to My Dearest Mum & Dad , 7 April 1918, MS Papers 4683 Folder 9, ATL.

18 War Diary, 2nd New Zealand Infantry Brigade, 31 March 1918, WA76/1, ANZ.

19 Quoted in Nigel M. Watson (ed.), *Letters from a Padre. A Record of the War Service of Ronald S. Watson, MC, ED, MA, 1891–1959*, Melbourne, 1970, p. 27.

20 Lindsay Merrit Inglis, letter to Dearest Old Lady, 31 March 1918, MS Papers 0421, ATL.

21 Bernard Cottrell, letter to Dad, 10 April 1918, Papers of Bernard Cottrell, ATL.

22 Painter diary, KMARL.

23 Arthur Leslie Ross, diary extracts, 2000-589, KMARL.

24 Lieutenant Marcus Smith, letter to Mrs Georgina A. Smith, 17 March 1918, 2003-69, KMARL.

25 Smith, letter to Mrs Georgina A. Smith, 30 March 1918, KMARL.

26 Bean, *Amiens*, p. 423.

27 Bean, *Official History. Vol. V*, p. 344.

9 Weathering the Storm

1 Moore, p. 195.

2 Austin, p. 306.

3 Bean, *Official History. Vol. V*, p. 414.

4 Stewart, p. 369; A.E. Byrne, p. 285; Luxford, p. 124.

5 J.R. Byrne, p. 225.

6 War Diary, 3 NZ Field Artillery, WA 53/1, ANZ.

7 J.R. Byrne, p. 225.

8 McWhirter diary, 5 March 1918 [McWhirter has confused the month here], ATL.

9 Tuck diary, ATL.

10 War Diary, 2nd Canterbury Battalion, 2nd NZ Infantry Brigade, WA78/1, ANZ.

11 War Diary, 2nd Auckland Battalion, ANZ.

12 War Diary, 1st Canterbury Battalion, 2nd NZ Infantry Brigade, WA77/1, ANZ.

13 Harcourt diary entry, ATL.

14 Bibby interview, ATL.

15 War Diary, 2nd NZ Infantry Brigade, 5 April 1918.

16 Narrative of Operations at Colincamps on 5th April 1918, War Diary 1 Battalion, New Zealand Rifle Brigade, WA82/1, ANZ.

17 War Diary, 4th Battalion New Zealand Rifle Brigade, 5 April 1918, WA85/1, ANZ.

18 Austin, p. 304.

19 War Diary, 3 New Zealand Rifle Brigade, WA81/1, ANZ.

20 Austin, p. 305.

21 War Diary, 4th Battalion New Zealand Rifle Brigade, 5 April 1918, WA85/1, ANZ.

22 Quoted in Bean, *Official History. Vol. V*, p. 416.

23 War Diary, 1st Canterbury Battalion, 2nd NZ Infantry Brigade, 5 April 1918, WA77/1, ANZ.

24 Harcourt diary, ATL.

25 Edmonds, *1918 Vol. II*, p. 135.

26 Ferguson, p. 234.

27 War Diary, 1st Canterbury Battalion, 2nd NZ Infantry Brigade, 5 April 1918, WA77/1, ANZ.

28 Harcourt diary, ATL.

29 War Diary, 2nd Otago Battalion, WA80/1, ANZ.

30 War Diary, 2nd NZ Field Ambulance, 5 April 1918, WA 120/1 ANZ.

31 War Diary, 1st NZ Field Ambulance, WA119/1, ANZ.

32 Bailey diary, 5 April 1918, KMARL.

33 Luxford, p.124.

34 War Diary, NZ Machine Gun Battalion, 5 April 1918, WA98/1, ANZ.

35 Major Lindsay Inglis, letter to 'Dearest Old Pal' 7 April 1918, MS Papers 0421, ATL.

36 GHQ Summary 8-4-18, quoted in War Diary, NZ Machine Gun Battalion, 5 April, 1918, WA98/1, ANZ.

37 *Ibid*. This extract is also quoted in Stewart, p. 370 and Luxford, pp. 125–6.

38 Harcourt diary, ATL.

39 Austin, p. 305.

40 Ludendorff, p. 600.

41 Edmonds, *1918 Vol. II*, p. 136.

10 Damage Assessment

1 Mosier, p. 318; Sheffield, p. 195; Blaxland, p. 107.

2 Ludendorff, p. 602. One of the casualties was Ludendorff's stepson, a pilot killed on 23 March. Ludendorff had 'the sad task' of identifying the body. Like many other parents, Ludendorff could write, with some bitterness, 'The war has spared me nothing.'

3 Moore, p. 197.

4 Blaxland, p. 107.

5 Mosier, p. 318.

6 Stewart, p. 372.

7 Allen, letter to Godley, 2 April 1918, Letters to Colonel Sir James Allen Jan 1918–1920, Godley Correspondence, WA252/5, ANZ.

8 Ian McGibbon (ed.), *The Oxford Companion to New Zealand Military History*, Auckland, 2000, p. 606.

9 Stewart, p. 372.

10 Carbery, p. 538.

11 A.E. Byrne, p. 288.

12 From *New Zealand Expeditionary Force, Book XII List of Casualties and a Summary of Casualties in order of Units, Reported from 15th February to 14th May, 1918*, Wellington, Government Printer, 1918.

13 Falls, p. 337.

14 Bean, *Official History. Vol. V*, p. 665.

15 Buchan, p. 71.

16 Wigram, letter to Godley, 11 May 1918, WA252/14 Colonel Clive Wigram, ANZ.

17 Ludendorff, p. 600.

18 Churchill, p. 421.

19 Sheffield, p. 196.

20 War Diary, 1st Canterbury Battalion, 6 April 1918, WA77/1, ANZ.

21 George Albert Tuck, letter To My Dear Father and Mother, 22 April 1918, MS Papers MS2164-2166 Tuck (Micro 0052), ATL.

22 George Albert Tuck, letter To My Dear Father and Mother, 14 April 1918, ATL.

23 Carbery, p. 395.

24 Austin, p. 309.

25 Lieutenant Marcus Smith, letter to Mrs Georgina A. Smith, 18 April 1918, KMARL.

26 Bailey, in Knox and Murray, p. 145.

27 Junger, pp. 285–6.

28 Godley, letter to Allen, 22 April 1918, ANZ, WA252/5, ANZ.

29 Moore, p. 228.

30 Telegram, To F-M Sir Douglas Haig from the PM, 25-3-18, WA 1/5 NZEF Routine Orders and Special Orders Vol. 2 Field Marshal Sir Douglas Haig, ANZ.

31 Telegram, To PM from F-M Sir Douglas Haig, 26-3-18, WA1/5, ANZ.

32 Moore, p. 241.

33 Allen, letter to Godley, 11 April 1918, WA252/5, ANZ.

34 Allen, letter to Godley, 26 April 1918, WA252/5, ANZ.

35 *Ibid*.

36 Allen, letter to Godley, 21 May 1918, WA252/5, ANZ.

37 Quoted in Ferguson, p. 235.

38 Toomath, Memorandum, 7 April 1918, ATL.

39 Carbery, p. 395.

40 Godley, letter to Lord Liverpool, 27 May 1918, WA252/8, His Excellency the Earl of Liverpool Oct 1914 – Oct 1918, Godley Papers and Correspondence, ANZ.

41 Moore, p. 236.

42 Burton, *Silent Division*, p. 298.

43 Haig's Diary, 12 October 1918, quoted in Pugsley, *Fringe of Hell*, p. 277.

44 Quoted in Russell diary, ATL.

45 Telegrams, To Field Marshal Sir Douglas Haig from the Governor of New Zealand and Haig's reply, 9 April 1918 and 10 April 1918, WA 1/5, ANZ.

46 A copy of this order is on Russell's Personal File, Personnel Archives, Wellington. It also appears in Ferguson, pp. 235–6.

47 Quoted in Pugsley, 'Russell of the New Zealand Division', p. 49.

48 Russell, letter to My dear Milly & Gwen, 4 April 1918, MS QMS0822, ATL.

49 Godley, letter to Allen, 22 April 1918, WA252/5, ANZ.

50 Allen, p. 32.

Conclusion

1 Richard Holmes, *The Western Front*, London, 1999, pp. 14–16.

2 Sheffield, p. xii.

3 Brian Bond (ed.), *The First World War and British Military History*, Oxford, 1991, p. 1.

4 Junger, p. 242.

5 Bean, *Official History. Vol. V*, pp. 674, 675.

6 Quoted in Stewart, pp. 617–18. Stewart points out in a footnote that 'Undue importance must not be attached to this remark', that is, to the officer's claim that the New Zealand Division took few German prisoners.

7 Stewart, pp. 372–3. This volume, like the others in the series, was a sponsored project of the New Zealand Army.

8 Hew Strachan, 'The Real War': Liddell Hart, Cruttwell and Falls', in Bond (ed.), *The First World War and British Military History*, pp. 61–2. Cyril Falls was twice mentioned in despatches and awarded the Croix de Guerre.

9 Falls, p. 421.

10 Quoted in Strachan, 'The Real War', in Bond (ed.), *The First World War and British Military History*, 62–3.

11 Cecil Malthus, *Armentieres and the Somme*, Auckland, 2002, pp. 14, 15.

12 Robin Prior and Trevor Wilson, 'Was Britain's sacrifice necessary?', in Craig Wilcox (ed.), *The Great War. Gains and Losses – ANZAC and Empire*, Canberra, 1995, p. 170.

13 W. Stevens, *Official History of New Zealand in the Second World War 1939–45. Bardia to Enfidaville*, Wellington, 1962, p. 383.

14 This inscription is prominent on three of New Zealand's battlefield memorials in France. See Ian McGibbon, *New Zealand Battlefields and Memorials of the Western Front*, Auckland, 2001, pp. 6–7.

15 Cecil Malthus, *ANZAC. A Retrospect*, Auckland, 2002, p. 100.

Bloody Bapaume

Introduction

1 War Diary, 1st Otago Battalion, 5 a.m. 21 August 1918, WA 79/1, ANZ.

2 Richard Holmes, *Tommy. The British Soldier on the Western Front 1914–1918*, London, Harper Perennial, 2005, p. 44.

3 J.H. Boraston, *Sir Douglas Haig's Despatches*, London, J.M. Dent and Sons Ltd, 1920, pp. 264–5.

4 Gary Sheffield and John Bourne (eds), *Douglas Haig. War Diaries and Letters 1914–1918*, London, Weidenfeld and Nicholson, 2005, p. 498.

5 C.E.W. Bean, *The Official History of Australia in the War of 1914–1918 Volume VI The Australian Imperial Force in France During the Allied Offensive, 1918*, St Lucia, Brisbane, University of Queensland Press in association with The Australian War Memorial, 1983, p. 873. One of the Victoria Cross winners was the New Zealand born Corporal Lawrence Weathers of the 43 Battalion AIF.

6 A.D. Carbery, *The New Zealand Medical Service in the Great War 1914–1918*, Auckland, Whitcombe & Tombs, 1924, p. 407.

7 Oscar Glen Reston, interview, recorded 21 October 1989, OH Int 0006/69 Oral History Centre, ATL.

8 Claude Wysocki, interview, recorded 19 and 22 October 1988, OH 0006/84, ATL.

9 See, for example, Christopher Pugsley, *The Anzac Experience. New Zealand, Australia and Empire in the First World War*, Auckland, Reed Publishing, 2004, pp. 286–99.

1 The Military Background

1 Richard Holmes, *Tommy. The British Soldier on the Western Front 1914–1918*, London, Harper Perennial, 2005, p. 51. The sign is now in a museum in Péronne, just one of many towns systematically destroyed during Operation *Alberich*.

2 Sir Philip Gibbs, *From Bapaume to Passchendaele 1917*, London, William Heinemann, 1918, pp. 3–4.

3 Gibbs, p. 43.

4 Gibbs, pp. 52, 49.

5 Gibbs, p. 55.

6 Vera Brittain, *Testament of Youth. An Autobiographical Study of the Years 1900–1925*, London, Victor Gollancz Ltd, 1933, p. 411.

7 Holmes, *Tommy*, p. 68.

8 H. Stewart, *The New Zealand Division 1916–1919. A Popular History Based on Official Records*, Auckland, Whitcombe and Tombs, 1921, p. 415.

9 O.E. Burton, *The Auckland Regiment, N.Z.E.F. 1914–18*, Auckland, Whitcombe and Tombes, 1922, p. 239.

10 Extracts from a German Diary of an Officer of 9th Company, 73rd Fusiliers Regiment, WA 76/4 Box 6 Item 30 German Diary and Translations, ANZ.

11 John Terraine, *The Great War 1914–18*, London, Arrow Books Ltd, 1967, p. 225.

12 John Terraine, *To Win a War. 1918 the Year of Victory*, London, Cassell & Co., 2000, p. 103.

13 Quoted in Brigadier-General Sir James Edmonds, *History of the Great War. Military Operations France and Belgium 1918 Volume IV 8th August-26 September. The Franco-British Offensive*, London, HMSO, 1947, p. 38. All references to Edmonds in the Bloody Bapaume section of the book are from this volume of the British Official History.

14 This was the newly formed American First Army which attacked the St Mihiel salient on 12 September. By the end of the war the United States had 42 divisions in France.

15 Peter Simkins, *World War 1. The Western Front*, Godalming, Surrey, Colour Library Books, 1992, p. 209.

16 Godley, letter to Sir James Allen, 9 August 1918, Ministerial Files 2M1/15 Correspondence with General Godley Part 6, PERS Vol. 1 Papers of Sir James Allen 1912–19, ANZ.

17 Pugsley, *The Anzac Experience*, pp. 291, 279.

18 L.C.L. Averill, 'First Generation New Zealander', p. 45, unpublished manuscript, copy in author's possession.

19 Lindsay Inglis, letter to Dearest, 18 August 1918, MS Papers 421 Major General L.M. Inglis, Folder 8 Letters to his Fiancée, 14–29 August 1918, ATL.

20 James Cowan, *Te Hokowhitu a Tu. The Maoris in the Great War*, Auckland, Whitcombe and Tombes, 1926, p. 143.

21 From Officers and NCOs, *Official History of the New Zealand Engineers during the Great War 1914–1919*, Wanganui, Evans, Cobb and Sharpe, n.d, pp. 196–7.

22 Lieutenant-Colonel W.S. Austin, *The New Zealand Rifle Brigade*, Wellington, L.T.Watkins Ltd, 1924, p. 338, Colonel H. Stewart, *The New Zealand Division 1916–1919*, Auckland, Whitcombe and Tombs Ltd, 1921, pp. 617–18.

23 See, for example, Chapter 16 of Christopher Pugsley's *On the Fringe of Hell. New Zealanders and Military Discipline in the First World War*, Auckland, Hodder and Stoughton, 1991. The chapter is headed '1918: the best in the world.' See also the conclusion in Matthew Wright's *Western Front. The New Zealand Division in the First World War 1916–18*, Auckland, Reed Publishing, 2005.

24 Pugsley, *The Anzac Experience*, p. 299.

25 Pugsley, *The Anzac Experience*, p. 280.

26 Godley, letter to Sir James Allen, 9 August 1918, Ministerial Files 2M1/15 Correspondence with General Godley Part 6, PERS Vol. 1 Papers of Sir James Allen 1912–19, ANZ.

27 Pugsley, *The Anzac Experience*, p. 281.

28 Pugsley, *The Anzac Experience*, p. 281.

29 These officers still held the rank of Major and were temporary appointments. Shepherd, who commanded 1st Rifles until 30 August, was filling in for Lieutenant Colonel W.S. Austin, then commanding the Brigade awaiting the arrival of Brigadier Hart. Nareby was commanding 1st Wellington while Lieutenant Colonel H. Holderness was sick. Wilson had command of 2nd Canterbury while Lieutenant Colonel H. Stewart was on leave. Murphy commanded 2nd Rifles in place of Lieutenant Colonel L.H. Jardine, who was also on leave. Sinel and Turnbull took over command of their battalions on the same day when their respective Commanding Officers were wounded, while Bishop took over when his CO was killed in action.

30 Pugsley, *The Anzac Experience*, p. 281.

31 Holmes, *Tommy*, p. 181.

32 O.E. Burton, 'A Rich Old Man', p. 192, MS Papers 0144, ATL. Dick Travis was a legendary figure in the NZEF and won the Victoria Cross shortly before he was killed in July 1918. This manuscript is one of the most revealing ever written by a veteran of the First World War.

2 Opening Moves

1 Gary Sheffield, *Forgotten Victory. The First World War: Myths and Realities*, London, Headline Book publishing, 2001, p. 197. About 1000 US soldiers then attached to the Australians had participated in this attack, much to the annoyance of the US commander General John Pershing.

2 John Toland, *No Man's Land. The Story of 1918*, London, Methuen Paperbacks Ltd, 1982, p. 356.

3 Richard Holmes, *Tommy. The British Soldier on the Western Front 1914–1918*, London, Harper Perennial, 2005, p. 277.

4 Toland, p. 359.

5 John Terraine, *The Great War 1914–18*, London, Arrow Books Ltd, 1967, p. 220.

6 John Terraine, *To Win a War. 1918 the Year of Victory*, London, Cassell & Co., 2000, pp. 106–7.

7 Edmonds, *1918 Volume IV*, p. 20.

8 Terraine, *To Win a* War, p. 107.

9 S.F. Wise, 'The Black Day of the German Army: Australians and Canadians at Amiens, August 1918' in Peter Dennis and Jeffrey Grey, *1918. Defining Victory*, Canberra, Army History Unit, 1999, pp. 23–4.

10 Terraine, *To Win a* War, p. 108.

11 Sheffield, p. 201.

12 Sheffield, p. 198.

13 Edmonds, *1918 Volume IV*, p. 58.

14 Gary Sheffield and John Bourne (eds), *Douglas Haig. War Diaries and Letters 1914–1918*, London, Weidenfeld & Nicholson, 2005, p. 440.

15 Quoted in Edmonds, *1918 Volume IV*, p. 88.

16 General Ludendorff, *My War Memories 1914–1918 Volume II*, London, Hutchinson & Co, 1919, p. 679,

17 Ludendorff, pp. 680, 681–2.

18 Ludendorff, p. 682.

19 Edmonds, *1918 Volume IV*, p. 93.

20 Terraine, *To Win a War*, p. 115.

21 Edmonds, *1918 Volume IV*, p. 132.

22 Edmonds, *1918 Volume IV*, p. 155.

23 Sheffield, p. 203.

24 Haig's Final Despatch of 21 December 1918, Boraston (ed.), p. 264.

25 Edmonds, *1918 Volume IV*, p. 119.

26 Haig's Diary, Thursday 15 August, Sheffield and Bourne (eds), p. 446.

27 Terraine, *To Win a War*, p. 120.

28 Sheffield, p. 200.

29 Ludendorff, pp. 683, 684, 685, 687.

30 Sheffield, p. 200.

31 J.H. Boraston (ed.), p. 264. Note that all of these tactical reasons are mentioned in Haig's last Despatch.

32 O.E. Burton, *The Auckland Regiment, N.Z.E.F. 1914–18*, Auckland, Whitcombe and Tombes, 1922, pp. 238–9.

33 Edmonds, *1918 Volume IV*, p. 180.

34 Edmonds, *1918 Volume IV*, p. 181.

35 Edmonds, *1918 Volume IV*, p. 181.

36 Thomas Dale, diary entry 14 August 1918, Diary 1918 Vol. V, MS Papers MSX 7716 Dale Family Papers, ATL.

37 Edmonds, *1918 Volume IV*, p. 184.

38 Bert Stokes, letter to My Dearest Mum and Dad, 12 August 1918, MS Papers 4683 Folder 10, ATL.

39 Haig's Diary, Monday 19 August 1918, in Sheffield and Bourne (eds), p. 447.

40 Ludendorff, p. 691

41 Edmonds, *1918 Volume IV*, p. 173, also quoted in Terraine, *To Win a War*, p. 125, albeit with a slightly different translation.

42 Stewart, p. 419. It was now policy to leave about 10 per cent of a battalion's strength out of the battle (LOB) so that if the worst happened, the battalion could be rebuilt with these remnants.

43 This was the NZ 3rd Brigade. 1st and 2nd Brigades NZFA were to cover the New Zealand front. War Diary of HQ Divisional Artillery, 18–19 August 1918, WA 50/1, ANZ.

44 Diary of Brigadier General Sir Herbert Hart KBE, CB, CMG, DSO, 19 and 20 August 1918, Micro MS 552, ATL.

45 J.R. Byrne, *New Zealand Artillery in the Field 1914–18*, Auckland, Whitcombe and Tombs Ltd, 1922, p. 253.

46 Carbery, p. 408.

47 War Diary 2nd Brigade NZFA, 20 August 1918, WA 52/1, ANZ.

48 Douglas Knight, letter to Dear Mother and Everyone, 19 August 1918, MS Papers 5548-11 Knight Family, ATL.

3 Attack and Counterattack

1 J.R. Byrne, *New Zealand Artillery in the Field 1914–18*, Auckland, Whitcombe and Tombs Ltd, 1922, p. 253.

2 Memoirs: New Zealand, Gallipoli, Western Front, Accession Number 1999.720, KMARL. The memoirs are of a gunner in the 2nd Battery, 2nd Brigade NZFA.

3 War Diary, 2nd Wellington Battalion, 21 August 1918, WA 74/1, ANZ.

4 Diary of Melville F.S. King, 21 August 1918, Accession Number 2000.267, KMARL.

5 Memoirs of Second Lieutenant Robert Gilkison, D Company, 4th Battalion, NZRB, Accession Number 1996.489, KMARL.

6 J.R. Byrne, p. 253. Austin, p. 345.

7 War Diary, 2nd Brigade NZFA, 21 August 1918, WA 52/1, War Diary 2nd Wellington Battalion, 21 August 1918, WA 74/1, ANZ.

8 War Diary, 1st Canterbury Battalion, 21 August 1918, WA 77/1, ANZ.

9 War Diary, 2nd Rifles Battalion, 21 August 1918, WA 83/1, ANZ.

10 Memoirs: New Zealand, Gallipoli, Western Front, Accession Number 1999.720, KMARL.

11 War Diary, 1st Otago Battalion, 21 August 1918, WA 79/1, ANZ.

12 Thomas Dale, diary entry Wednesday 21 August 1918, Diary 1918 Vol. V, MS Papers MSX 7716 Dale Family Papers, ATL.

13 War Diary, 4th Battalion NZRB, 21 August 1918, WA 85/1, ANZ.

14 Austin, p. 347.

15 War Diary, 3rd Battalion, NZRB, 21 August 1918, WA 84/1, ANZ.

16 Diary of Brigadier Sir Herbert Hart, 21 August 1918, Micro MS 552, ATL.

17 Cyril Falls, *The Great War*, New York, G.P. Putmans, 1959, p. 378.

18 Correlli Barnett, *The Great War*, London, BBC Worldwide, 2003, p. 198.

19 Austin, p. 350.

20 Diary of Brigadier Sir Herbert Hart, 21 August 1918, Micro MS 552, ATL.

21 Diary of Melville F.S. King, 21 August 1918, Accession Number 2000.267, KMARL.

22 War Diary, Headquarters NZRB, 21 August 1918, WA 81/1, ANZ.

23 War Diary, 4th Battalion NZRB, 21 August 1918, WA 85/1, ANZ.

24 Diary of Thomas Dale, Wednesday 21 August 1918, Diary 1918 Vol. V, MS Papers MSX 7716 Dale Family Papers, ATL.

25 Diary of Major General Andrew Russell, 21 August 1918, qMS 0822 The Russell Saga Vol. III World War 1 1914–1919, ATL.

26 Stewart, p. 423.

27 Gunners who were firing 'over open sights' did not have to worry about finding the range of their guns, since the enemy was so close that the guns could simply be fired to the front.

28 War Diary, 2nd Bde NZFA, 22 August 1918, WA52/1, ANZ.

29 Diary of Lieutenant James Hutchinson, 5 Battery, 2nd NZFA, 22 August 1918, MS Papers 4172 Sir James Douglas Hutchinson, ATL.

30 Diary of Allan Watkins, 12 Battery, 3 Bde NZFA, 21–22 August 1918, MS Papers 2354-2358, Diaries of Allan Watkins 1880-1981, ATL.

31 Hart Diary, 22 August 1918, Micro MS 552, ATL.

32 J.H. Luxford, *With the Machine Gunners in France and Palestine*, Auckland, Whitcombe and Tombs, 1923, p. 136.

33 Hart Diary, 22 August 1918, Micro MS 552, ATL.

34 War Diary NZ Machine Battalion, 22 August 1918, WA 98/1, ANZ.

35 Stewart, p. 424.

36 Cowan, p. 144.

37 Dale Diary, Wednesday 21 August 1918, Diary 1918 Vol. V, MS Papers MSX 7716 Dale Family Papers, ATL.

38 Sheffield and Bourne (eds), p. 448.

39 Edmonds, *1918 Volume IV*, p. 207.

40 Terraine, *To Win a War*, p. 126, This order (OAD 911) is also summarised in Sheffield and Bourne (eds), p. 448.

41 Gregory Blaxland, *Amiens: 1918*, London, W.H. Allen & Co. Ltd, 1981, p. 205.

42 Ludendorff, p. 692.

43 Edmonds, *1918 Volume IV*, p. 220.

44 War Diary, 1st Battalion NZRB, 22 August 1918, WA 82/1, ANZ.

45 Austin, p. 353.

46 War Diary, 1st Battalion NZRB, 22 August 1918, WA 82/1, ANZ.

47 Austin, p. 354.

48 Hart Diary, 23 August 1918, Micro MS 552, ATL.

49 Austin, p. 355.

50 Hart Diary, 23 August 1918, Micro MS 552, ATL.

51 Edmonds, *1918 Volume IV*, p. 232.

52 Quoted in J.H. Johnson, *1918. The Unexpected Victory*, London, Arms and Armour Press, 1997, p. 119.

53 Russell Diary, 22 August 1918, qMS 0822 The Russell Saga Vol. III World War 1 1914–1919, ATL.

4 The First Attempt on Bapaume

1 Burton, *The Auckland Regiment*, p. 230.

2 Lieutenant-Colonel S.S. Allen, *2/Auckland, 1918*, Auckland, Whitcome and Tombs Limited, 1920, p. 93.

3 Edmonds, *1918 Volume IV*, p. 251.

4 Thomas Dale, diary entry, Friday 23 August 1918, MSX 7716, ATL.

5 War Diary, 2nd Auckland Battalion, 21 August 1918, WA 72/1, ANZ.

6 Memoirs: New Zealand, Gallipoli, Western Front, Accession Number 1999.720, KMARL.

7 Burton, *Auckland Regiment*, p. 232.

8 Burton, 'A Rich Old Man', p. 195, MS Papers 0144, ATL.

9 Frederick Stuart Varnham, dairy entry, 23 March 1918, MSX 3314 and MS Papers 4303-2, ATL.

10 Thomas Dale, diary entry, Saturday 24 August 1918, MSX 7716, ATL.

11 Burton, *Auckland Regiment*, p. 231.

12 Stewart, p. 429.

13 Henry Parmenter, diary entry 24 August 1918, MS 1760 Henry Edley Parmenter Diary 1916-1919, ATL.

14 War Diary, 2 Battalion Wellington Regiment, 24 August 1918, WA 74/1, ANZ.

15 Stewart, p. 430.

16 Frederick Stuart Varnham, diary entry, 24 March 1918, MSX 3314 and MS Papers 4303-2, ATL.

17 Stewart, p. 430.

18 Allen, p. 97.

19 Allen, p. 98.

20 Burton, 'A Rich Old Man', p. 195, MS Papers 0144 ATL.

21 Stewart, p. 430.

22 War Diary, 2nd Bn Auckland Regiment, 24 August 1918, WA 72/1, ANZ.

23 Officers of the Regiment, *Das K.B. 14. Infanterie-Regiment Hartmann*, Munchen, 1931, p. 311. I am grateful to Andrew Macdonald for providing translated accounts of these German histories.

24 Diary of W.H. English, 2nd Wellington Battalion, 24 August 1918, Accession number 2006.1061, KMARL.

25 Burton, *Auckland Regiment*, p. 234.

26 The VC was subsequently sold to a Melbourne dealer on 26 January 1982 for $20,900. At the time this was the second highest price ever paid for a VC. 'New Zealand Victoria Cross brings $20,000 plus', undated newspaper clipping, MSZ 0933 Scrapbook Relating to NZ VC Winners, ATL.

27 Ormond Burton, 'A Rich Old Man', p. 198, MS Papers 0144, ATL.

28 Allen, p. 106.

29 Stewart, p. 432.

30 Burton, *Auckland Regiment*, p. 233.

31 Burton, *Auckland Regiment*, p. 235.

32 War Diary, 2nd Bn Auckland Regiment, 24 August 1918, WA 72/1, ANZ.

33 William Jesse Stayte, 'Rough Notes from my Diary', Sunday 24 August 1918, MS Papers 7198, ATL.

34 Allen, p. 105.

35 War Diary, 2nd Otago Battalion, 24 August 1918, WA 80/1, ANZ.

36 Stewart, p. 434.

37 Byrne, p. 332.

38 War Diary, HQ Divisional Artillery, 24 August 1918, WA 50/1, ANZ.

39 War Diary, HQ 2nd NZ Infantry Brigade, 24 August 1918, WA 76/1, ANZ.

40 War Diary, HQ 2nd NZ Infantry Brigade, 24 August 1918, WA 76/1, ANZ.

41 War Diary, 2nd Bde NZFA, 6 p.m., 24 August 1918, WA 52/1, ANZ.

42 War Diary, 2nd Otago Battalion, 24 August 1918, WA 80/1, ANZ.

43 War Diary, 1st Otago Battalion, 24 August 1918, WA 79/1, ANZ.

44 Johnson, p. 119.

45 Bean, *Volume VI*, p. 764.

46 Stewart, p. 436.

47 Edmonds, *1918 Volume IV*, p. 254.

48 Edmonds, *1918 Volume IV*, p. 262.

49 Stewart, p. 436.

50 Diary of Melville F.S. King, 24 August 1918, Accession Number 2000.267, KMARL.

51 War Diary, 2nd Otago Battalion, 25 August 1918, WA 80/1, ANZ.

52 Douglas Knight, letter to Mother and Dad, 27 August 1918, MS Papers 5548-09, ATL.

53 James Hutchinson, diary entry, 24 August 1918, MS 4172, ATL.

54 Hart diary, 24 August 1918, Micro MS 552, ATL.

55 Russell diary, 24 August 1918, qMS 0822, ATL.

5 Cutting the Crossroads

1 Edmonds, *1918 Volume IV*, p. 266.

2 War Diary, 2nd Bde NZFA, 25 August 1918, WA 52/1, ANZ.

3 Stewart, p. 438.

4 Stewart, p. 437.

5 Stewart, p. 438.

6 The memorial commemorates the battle for Bapaume that was fought on 3 January 1871. Although inconclusive, the important battle of the Franco-Prussia War was claimed as a victory by both sides. In reality it was a strategic victory for the Prussians.

7 Stewart, p. 438.

8 War Diary, 1st Canterbury Battalion, 25 August 1918, WA 77/1, ANZ.

9 War Diary, 1st Canterbury Battalion, 25 August 1918, WA 77/1, ANZ.

10 War Diary, 1 Otago Battalion, 25 August 1918, WA 79/1, ANZ.

11 War Diary, 1 Otago Battalion, 25 August 1918, WA 79/1, ANZ.

12 War Diary, 1 Otago Battalion, 25 August 1918, WA 79/1, ANZ.

13 Stewart, p. 439.

14 War Diary, 1 Otago Battalion, 25 August 1918, WA 79/1, ANZ.

15 Stewart, p. 440.

16 Byrne, *Otago Regiment*, p. 336.

17 Edmonds, *1918 Volume IV*, p. 279.

18 Edmonds, *1918 Volume IV*, p. 278.

19 Edmonds, *1918 Volume IV*, p. 272.

20 War Diary, HQ 2nd NZ Inf Bde, 25 August 1918, WA 76/1, ANZ.

21 War Diary, Assistant Director Medical Services (ADMS) NZ Division, 25 August 1918, WA 26/1, ANZ.

22 Austin, p. 358.

23 L.C.L. Averill, 'First Generation New Zealander', p. 47, unpublished manuscript, copy in author's possession.

24 Byrne, *Otago Regiment*, p. 337.

25 Russell diary, 25 August 1918, qMS 0822 The Russell Saga Vol. III, ATL.

26 War Diary, 1st Canterbury Battalion, 25 August 1918, WA 77/1, ANZ.

27 War Diary, 1st Otago Battalion, 25 August 1918, WA 79/1, ANZ.

28 War Diary, 2nd Canterbury Battalion, 25 August 1918, WA 78/1, ANZ.

29 Carbery, p. 412.

30 War Diary, 3rd NZ Field Ambulance, 25 August 1918, WA 121/1, ANZ.

31 Diary of Melville F.S. King, 25 August 1918, Accession Number 2000.267, KMARL.

32 L.B. Quartermain, letter to Dear Dad and Mum, 26 August 1918, Folder 15 L.B. Quartermain, MS Papers 1807, ATL.

33 War Diary, 1st Otago Battalion, 31 August 1918, WA 79/1, ANZ.

34 Officers and NCOs, *Engineers History*, p. 203.

35 James McWhirter, Diary of 1914–1818 War, MS Papers MSX 4915, ATL.

6 The Third Attempt

1 Carbery, p. 413.

2 Edmonds, *1918 Volume IV*, p. 298.

3 Edmonds, *1918 Volume IV*, p. 301.

4 Edmonds, *1918 Volume IV*, p. 301.

5 War Diary, 1st NZ Inf Bde, 26 August 1918, WA 70/1, ANZ.

6 War Diary, 63 (RN) Division, 2.40 p.m. 26 August 1918, WA 241/25, ANZ.

7 War Diary, 63 (RN) Division, 2.40 p.m. 26 August 1918, WA 241/25, ANZ.

8 William Jesse Stayte, Rough Notes from my Diary, MS Papers 7198, ATL.

9 War Diary, 1st Bn Auck Regiment, 26 August 1918, WA 71/1, ANZ.

10 New Zealand Army Information Sheet, ABFK W4312, Box 2, Victoria Cross — R.S. Judson, ANZ.

11 Vincent Jervis, diary entry, Monday 26 August 1918, MS Papers 2241, ATL.

12 Memoirs of Second Lieutenant Robert Gilkison, D Company, 4th Battalion, NZRB, Accession Number 1996.489, KMARL.

13 Austin, p. 360.

14 Hart diary, 26 August 1918, Micro MS 552, ATL.

15 L.C.L. Averill, 'First Generation New Zealander', pp. 48–9, unpublished manuscript, copy in author's possession.

16 War Diary, 2nd Bn NZRB, 26 August 1918, WA 83/1, ANZ.

17 Diary of Arthur Leslie Ross, 2nd Battalion NZRB, Accession number 2000.589, KMARL. It is likely that this diary was rewritten after the war.

18 War Diary, 2nd Bn NZRB, 26 August 1918, WA 83/1, ANZ.

19 Diary of Arthur Leslie Ross, 2nd Battalion NZRB, Accession number 2000.589, KMARL.

20 War Diary, 2nd Bn NZRB, 26 August 1918, WA 83/1, ANZ.

21 War Diary, 2nd Bn NZRB, 26 August 1918, WA 83/1, ANZ.

22 Diaries of Allan Watkins, MS 2354-2358, ATL.

23 Narrative of Operations, 3rd NZ (Rifle) Brigade, 26 August 1918, WA 83/3 Box 6 Item 41, ANZ.

24 Narrative of Operations, 3rd NZ (Rifle) Brigade, 26 August 1918, WA 83/3 Box 6 Item 41, ANZ.

25 Stewart, p. 445.

26 L.C.L. Averill, 'First Generation New Zealander', p. 49, unpublished manuscript, copy in author's possession. Emphasis in the original.

27 War Diary, 2nd Bn NZRB, 26 August 1918, WA 83/1, ANZ.

28 Memoirs of Second Lieutenant Robert Gilkison, D Company, 4th Battalion, NZRB, Accession Number 1996.489, KMARL.

29 Stewart, p. 445.

30 War Diary, 2nd Bn NZRB, 26 August 1918, WA 83/1, ANZ.

31 War Diary, 1st Otago, 26 August 1918, WA 79/1, ANZ.

32 C.E.W. Bean, *Anzac to Amiens*, Melbourne, Penguin Books, 1993, p. 462. According to Bean the technique was the invention of the Australian pilot Captain L.J. Wackett.

33 Russell diary, 26 August 1918, The Russell Saga Vol. III, qMS 0822, ATL.

34 Edmonds, *1918 Volume IV*, p. 314.

35 War Diary, HQ NZRB, 28 August 1918, WA 81/1, ANZ.

36 War Diary, 2nd Bn NZRB, 26 August 1918, WA 83/1, ANZ.

37 War Diary, HQ NZRB, 4 August 1918, WA 81/1, ANZ.

38 L.B. Quartermain, letter to Dear Mum and Dad, 26 August 1918, MS papers 1807, Folder 15, ATL.

39 Edmonds, *1918 Volume IV*, p. 323.

40 Allan Watkins, diary entry, 25 August 1918, MS 2354-2348, ATL.

41 Douglas Knight, letter to Mother and Dad, 27 August 1918, MS papers 5548-11, ATL.

42 Thomas Dale, diary entry, Monday 26 August 1918, Diary 1918 Vol. V, MS Papers MSX 7716, ATL.

43 Carbery, p. 413.

7 The Battle for the Town

1 War Diary, 63 (RN) Division, 27 August 1918, WA241/25, ANZ.

2 Edmonds, *1918 Volume IV*, p. 324.

3 War Diary, HQ Div Arty NZ Div, 27 Aug 1918, WA50/1, ANZ.

4 War Diary, 2Bn NZRB, 27 August 1918, WA 83/1, ANZ.

5 War Diary, 1 Cant Bn, 27 August 1918, WA77/1, ANZ

6 Henry Edley Parmenter, diary entry 27 August 1918, MS1760, ATL.

7 Thomas Dale, diary entry, 27 August 1918, MSX-7717 Dale Family Papers, ATL.

8 Thomas Dale, diary entry, 27 August 1918, MSX-7717 Dale Family Papers, ATL.

9 Russell diary, 27 August 1918, qMS 0822 The Russell Saga Vol. III, ATL.

10 Frederick Stuart Varnham, diary entry, 27 August 1918, MSX 3314, ATL.

11 Edmonds, *1918 Volume IV*, p. 334.

12 Hart diary, 28 August 1918, Micro MS 552, ATL.

13 Douglas Knight, Letter to Dear Dad, 28 Aug 1918, Ms Papers 5548-11, ATL.

14 Douglas Knight, letter to Dear Mother & Dad, 'Somme' France 28 Aug 1918, MS Papers 5548-09 Knight Family, ATL.

15 William Jesse Stayte, Rough Notes from my Diary, 28 August 1918, MS Papers 7198, ATL.

16 War Diary, HQ Div Artillery, 28 August 1918, WA50/1, ANZ.

17 Austin, p. 365.

18 Diary of Thomas Dale, 28 August 1918, MSX-7717 Dale Family papers, ATL.

19 Russell's diary, 28 August 1918, qMS 0822 The Russell Saga Vol. III, ATL.

20 Diary of Lewis G. Nairn, 2nd Wellington Battalion, 28 August 1918, 2006.1062, KMARL.

21 Carbery, p. 414.

22 Edmonds, *1918 Volume IV*, p. 344.

23 Hart diary, 29 August 1918, Micro MS 552, ATL.

24 War Diary, 2nd Bn NZRB, 29 August 1918, WA 83/1, ANZ.

25 War Diary, 1st Bn Auckland Regiment, 29 August 1918, WA 71/1, ANZ.

26 Frederick Stuart Varnham, diary entry, 29 August 1918, MSX 3314, ATL.

27 Henry Edley Pamenter, diary entry, 29 August 1918, MS 1760, Diary 1916–19, ATL.

28 Field Notebook Message, Lieutenant Colonel H.M.Wilson, 29 August 1918, WA 50/2 New Zealand Division Orders and Instructions, ANZ.

29 Hart diary, 29 August 1918, Micro MS 552, ATL.

30 Julius Ritter von Bram, *Das KB Reserve-Infanterie-Regiment Nr. 21*, Munchen, 1923, p. 107. Note that German clocks were one ahead of GMT, which accounts in part for the discrepancies in the timings given here.

31 Austin, p. 366.

32 Stewart, p. 449.

33 Thomas Dale, diary entry, 29 August 1918, MSX-7717 Dale Family Papers, ATL.

34 Russell diary, 29 August 1918, qMS 0822 The Russell Saga Vol. III, ATL.

35 Hart diary, 29 August 1918, Micro MS 552, ATL.

36 Officers and NCOs, *Official History of the New Zealand Engineers during the Great War 1914–1919*, Wanganui, Evans, Cobb and Sharp, n.d., p. 204.

37 War Diary, 2nd Field Company, 29 August 1918, WA 62/1, ANZ.

38 James McWhirter, diary entry, 29 August 1918, MS Papers MSX 4915 James McWhirter, ATL.

39 War Diary, 2nd Field Company, 30 August 1918, WA 62/1, ANZ.

40 Officers and NCOs, p. 204.

41 Officers and NCOs, p. 205.

42 Officers and NCOs, p. 205.

43 Monty Ingram, *In Flanders Fields. The World War One Diary of Private Monty Ingram*, Auckland, David Ling Publishers, 2006, pp. 123–4.

44 Ingram, p. 124.

45 Officers and NCOs, p. 205.

46 Diary of Arthur Leslie Ross, 22 August 1918, 2nd Battalion NZRB, Accession number 2000.589, KMARL.

47 Henry Edley Pamenter, diary entry, 3 September 1918, MS 1760, Diary 1916–19, ATL.

48 Byrne, p. 338.

49 William Jesse Stayte, Rough Notes from my Diary, 30 August 1918, MS Papers 7198, ATL.

50 Allan Watkins, diary entry, 29 August 1918, MS2354-2358, ATL.

51 James McWhirter, diary entry, 29 August 1918, MS Papers MSX 4915 James McWhirter, ATL.

52 L.B. Quartermain, letter to Dear Mum and Dad, 1 September 1918, MS papers 1807, Folder 15, ATL.

53 Barnett, p. 198.

54 Quoted in Terraine, *To Win a War*, p. 128.

8 The Battle for the Surrounds

1 Edmonds, *1918 Volume IV*, p. 355.

2 Allen, p. 109.

3 Lindsay Inglis, 29 August 1918, Inglis Manuscript, MSY 5456, ATL.

4 War Diary, 2nd Bde NZFA, 30 August 1918, WA 52/1, ANZ.

5 Stewart, p. 450.

6 Austin, p. 367.

7 Narrative of Operations of 1st Bn, NZRB at Frémicourt 29 August–1 September 1918, WA 82/1, ANZ.

8 3rd NZ Rifle Brigade, Narrative of Operations from 21 to 31 August 1918, WA 81/3 Item 41, ANZ.

9 Austin, p. 370.

10 3rd NZ Rifle Brigade, Narrative of Operations from 21 to 31 August 1918, WA 81/3 Item 41, ANZ.

11 Narrative of Operations of 1st Bn, NZRB at Frémicourt 29 August–1 September 1918, WA 82/1, ANZ.

12 War Diary, 1st Bn NZRB, 30 August 1918, WA 82/1, ANZ.

13 W.H. Cunningham, C.A.L. Treadwell and J.S. Hanna, *The Wellington Regiment N.Z.E.F. 1914–1919*, Wellington, Ferguson and Osborn Ltd, 1923, pp. 281–2.

14 Cunningham, Treadwell and Hanna, pp. 282.

15 War Diary, 1st Wellington Battalion, 30 August 1918, WA 73/1, ANZ.

16 War Diary, 2nd Battalion Auckland Regiment, 30 August 1918, WA 72/1, ANZ.

17 Allen, p. 110.

18 Allen, p. 110.

19 War Diary, 2nd Battalion Auckland Regiment, 30 August 1918, WA 72/1, ANZ.

20 Burton, *The Auckland Regiment*, p. 240.

21 War Diary, 2nd Battalion Auckland Regiment, 30 August 1918, WA 72/1, ANZ.

22 War Diary, 2nd Battalion Auckland Regiment, 30 August 1918, WA 72/1, ANZ.

23 Thomas Dale, diary entry, Friday 30 August 1918, Diary 1918 Vol. V, MS Papers MSX 7716, ATL.

24 Allan Watkins, diary entry, 30 August 1918, MS2354-2358, ATL.

25 Lindsay Inglis, 30 August 1918, Inglis Manuscript, MSY 5456, ATL.

26 Hart diary, 31 August 1918, Micro MS 552, ATL.

27 War Diary, 2nd Battalion Auckland Regiment, 31 August 1918, WA 72/1, ANZ.

28 Austin, p. 371.

29 War Diary, 1st Bn NZRB, 31 August 1918, WA 82/1, ANZ.

30 Officers of the Regiment, *Das K.B. 14. Infanterie-Regiment Hartmann*, Muenchen, 1931, p. 314.

31 William Jesse Stayte, Rough Notes from my Diary, 31 August 1918, MS Papers 7198, ATL.

32 Lindsay Inglis, 30 August 1918, Inglis Manuscript, MSY 5456, ATL.

33 War Diary, 2nd Battalion Auckland Regiment, 31 August 1918, WA 72/1, War Diary, 1st Wellington Battalion, 30 August 1918, WA 73/1, ANZ.

34 War Diary, 1st Bn NZRB, 31 August 1918, WA 82/1, ANZ.

35 Edmonds, *1918 Volume IV*, p. 382.

36 Memoirs: New Zealand, Gallipoli, Western Front, Accession Number 1999.720, KMARL.

37 War Diary, 1st Bn NZRB, 1 September 1918, WA 82/1, ANZ.

38 Stewart, p. 456.

39 War Diary, 1st Bn NZRB, 1 September 1918, WA 82/1, ANZ.

40 Stewart, p. 546.

41 Frederick Stuart Varnham, diary entry, 1 September 1918, MSX 3314, ATL.

42 War Diary, 1st Wellington Battalion, 1 September 1918, WA 73/1, ANZ.

43 Stewart, p. 546.

44 Stewart, p. 456.

45 War Diary, 2nd Battalion Auckland Regiment, 1 September 1918, WA 72/1, ANZ.

46 War Diary, 2nd Battalion Auckland Regiment, 1 September 1918, WA 72/1, ANZ.

47 Stewart, p. 457.

48 War Diary, 2nd Battalion Auckland Regiment, 1 September 1918, WA 72/1, ANZ.

49 War Diary, 2nd Battalion Auckland Regiment, 1 September 1918, WA 72/1, ANZ.

50 Captain E.G. Moncrief, letter to Mrs Knight, 8 September 1918, MS Papers 5548-11, Knight Family, Letters of Sympathy, ATL.

51 Diary of 31992 Leonard Grey, 2nd Auckland Battalion, 2nd September 1918, Accession Number 1991.2742, KMARL.

52 William Malcolm, letter to Dear Mum, 3 September 1918, Accession Number 1991.2782, KMARL.

53 William Jesse Stayte, Rough Notes from my Diary, 31 August 1918, MS Papers 7198, ATL.

54 War Diary, 2nd Battalion Auckland Regiment, 2 September 1918, WA 72/1, ANZ.

55 War Diary, 2nd NZ Bde, NZFA, 2 September 1918, WA 52/1, ANZ.

56 War Diary, 2nd NZ Bde, NZFA, 2 September 1918, WA 52/1, ANZ.

57 A.E. Byrne, p. 340.

58 Lindsay Inglis, 3 September 1918, Inglis Manuscript, MSY 5456, ATL.

59 Ingram, p. 122.

60 War Diary, 5 Division, 3 September 1918, WA 241/6, ANZ.

61 War Diary, 2nd NZ Bde, NZFA, 3 September 1918, WA 52/1, ANZ.

62 Hart diary, 3 September 1918, Micro MS 552, ATL.

63 Edmonds, *1918 Volume IV*, p. 421

64 Edmonds, *1918 Volume IV*, p. 422.

9 'Bloody Bapaume'

1 William Malcolm, letter to Dear Sis, 7 September 1918, Accession Number 1991.2782, Letters of Private William Malcolm, KMARL.

2 Alexander Hutton, letter to Dear Mother, 8 September 1918, Letters to Hutton Family from Alexander Louis Hutton, MS Papers 3906, ATL.

3 Burton, *A Rich Old Man*, p. 199, MS Papers 0144, ATL.

4 Ludendorff, p. 692.

5 Victor Rayner, interview, 21 October 1988, OH Int 0006/67, ATL.

6 Victor Rayner, interview, 21 October 1988, OH Int 0006/67, ATL.

7 Stewart, p. 458.

8 Carbery, p. 418.

9 War Diary, 2nd Bn Auckland Regiment, 1 September 1918, WA 72/1, ANZ.

10 War Diary, Headquarters 2nd NZ Inf Bde, 31 August 1918, WA76/1, ANZ.

11 War Diary, Headquarters NZRB, Appendix W, August 1918, WA 81/1, ANZ. Note that the casualty list of the 1st New Zealand Infantry Brigade for August 1918 has not been found.

12 New Zealand and World War One, Roll of Honour, June–September 1918, pp. 37–113. http://freepages .genealogy. rootsweb.com. New Zealand historians owe Christine Clement of Te Puke an enormous debt of gratitude for compiling this database.

13 From NZEF List of Casualties and a Summary of Casualties in Order of Units, Book IV, Reported from 15 August 1918 to 6 January 1919, Wellington, Marcus F. Marks, 1919.

14 William Malcolm, letter to Dear Boys, 15 September 1918, Accession Number 1991.2782, KMARL.

15 The figures for Crete are 671 killed and 967 wounded. There were, of course, more New Zealanders captured on Crete, some 2180 becoming prisoners of war. Figures are from Ian McGibbon (ed.), *The Oxford Companion to New Zealand Military History*, Auckland, Oxford University Press, 2000, p. 128.

16 Lawrence Morris Blyth, MM, ED, JP, interview, 28 September and 20 October 1988, OH Int 0006/12, ATL.

17 L.C.L. Averill, 'First Generation New Zealander', p. 51, unpublished manuscript, copy in author's possession.

18 War Diary, 2nd Bn NZRB, 31 August 1918, WA 83/1, ANZ.

19 L.C.L. Averill, 'First Generation New Zealander', pp. 51–2, unpublished manuscript, copy in author's possession.

20 War Diary, No.1 New Zealand General Hospital, 5 September 1918, WA 140/1, ANZ.

21 William (Bill) Batchelor, Interview, Recorded 12 May 1988, OH AB 445, ATL.

22 War Diary, No.1 New Zealand General Hospital, 23 and 30 September 1918, WA 140/1, ANZ.

23 War Diary, No.2 New Zealand General Hospital, 3 September 1918, WA 141/1, ANZ.

24 War Diary, No.2 New Zealand General Hospital, 23 and 30 September 1918, WA 141/1, ANZ.

25 War Diary, No.2 New Zealand General Hospital, 23 September 1918, WA 141/1, ANZ.

26 War Diary, No.2 New Zealand General Hospital, 9 and 23 September 1918, WA 141/1, ANZ.

27 Russell diary, 21, 24, and 25 August 1918, The Russell Saga Vol. III, qMS 0822, ATL.

28 Russell, letter to Dear Milly, 30 August 1918, Part 5, The Russell Saga Vol. III, qMS 0822, ATL.

29 Russell, letter to Dear Gwen, 31 August 1918, Part 5, The Russell Saga Vol. III, qMS 0822, ATL.

30 James McWhirter, Diary of 1914–1818 War, MS Papers MSX 4915, ATL.

31 Russell diary, 7 September 1918, The Russell Saga Vol. III, qMS 0822, ATL.

32 Christopher Pusgley, *On the Fringe of Hell. New Zealanders and Military Discipline in the First World War*, Auckland, Hodder and Stoughton, 1991; Ian McGibbon (ed.), *The Oxford Companion to New Zealand Military History*, Auckland, Oxford University Press, 2000, pp. 607–8.

33 McGibbon (ed.), pp. 601–2, p. 603, pp. 604–5.

34 Matthew Wright, *Western Front. The New Zealand Division in the First World War 1916–18*, Auckland, Reed Publishing, 2005, pp. 145–7 and p. 147.

35 *The Dominion*, Saturday 24 August 1918, *New Zealand Herald*, Saturday 24 August 1918.

36 *New Zealand Herald*, Monday 26 August 1918.

37 *The Dominion*, Monday, 26 August 1918.

38 *The Dominion* and *The Otago Daily Times*, 27 August 1918.

39 Bean, *Volume VI*, p. 873.

40 Terraine, *To Win a War*, p. 128.

41 Bean, *Vol. VI*, p. 810.

42 Bean, *Vol. VI*, p. 815.

43 Martin and Mary Middlebrook, *The Somme Battlefields*, Viking Press, London, 1991, p. 268.

44 M. and M. Middlebrook, p. 268.

45 Stewart, p. 459.

46 War Diary, 2 Bn NZRB, 31 August 1918, WA 83/1, ANZ.

47 3rd NZ Rifle Bde HQ to HQ NZ Div, 19 September 1918, WA 81/3 Box 3 Item 16, Notes on Recent Fighting and Lessons Learnt, ANZ

48 4Bn NZRB, Tactical Lessons Learnt or Relearnt since 21 August, 16 September 1918, WA81/3 Box 3 Item 16 Notes on Recent Fighting & Lessons Learnt, ANZ.

49 Notes on Recent Fighting No. 21, Issued by the General Staff 25 September 1918, WA81/3 Box 3 Item 16 Notes on Recent Fighting & Lessons Learnt, ANZ.

50 J.R. Byrne, New Zealand Artillery in the Field 1914–18, Auckland, Whitcombe and Tombs Ltd, 1922, p. 261.

51 Stewart, p. 459.

52 Geoffrey Potts, Letter My Dearest Old Love, 29 August 1918, Papers relating to Geoffrey Potts & Llewelyn Fitzmaurice, MS Papers 4302 Florence Julia Potts (Nixon), ATL.

53 Pugsley, On the Fringe of Hell, p. 277.

54 William (Bill) Batchelor, Interview, Recorded 12 May 1988, OH AB 445, ATL.

55 L.M. Inglis, Letter to Dear Old Chap, 2 September 1918, MS Papers 421 Major Gen L.M. Inglis Folder 9, Letters to Fiancée 1/9/18–16/1/19, ATL.

56 In the military sense, tactics may be regarded as the art of winning battles, while strategy is the art of winning wars. Strategic victories are much more important than tactical ones, since they will contribute materially to the winning of the war. Tactical victories, while important, do not necessarily lead to strategic victories.

57 Edmonds, 1918 Volume IV, p. 510.

58 Edmonds, 1918 Volume IV, p. 423.

59 Edmonds, 1918 Volume IV, p. 422, Terraine, To Win a War, p. 130.

60 War Diary, NZ Mg Bn 31 August 1918, WA 98/1, ANZ.

61 Lieutenant Colonel Lawrence Morris Blyth MM, ED, JP, interviews, 28 September and 20 October 1988, OH Int 0006/12, ATL.

62 Stewart, p. 458.

63 Stewart, p. 458.

64 Stewart, p. 459.

Conclusions

1 Jonathon B.A. Bailey, 'The First World War and the birth of modern warfare, in M. Knox and E. Murray (eds), The Dynamics of Military Revolution 1300 2050, London, Cambridge Press, 2002, p. 145.

2 Hew Strachan, The First World War, New York, Viking Penguin, 2004, p. 340.

3 Middlebrook, p. 252.

4 Terraine, To Win a War, p. 130.

5 Howard Kippenberger, letter to Kenneth Sandford, 22 July 1955, IA 77/30 K.L. Sandford Publication of book on Captain C.H. Upham, VC and Bar, ANZ.

6 Tim Cook, 'The Politics of Surrender: Canadian Soldiers and the Killing of Prisoners in the Great War', The Journal of Military History, vol. 70, no. 3, July 2006, pp. 664.

7 Pugsley, On the Fringe of Hell, p. 281.

Appendix 1

Structure of the New Zealand Division

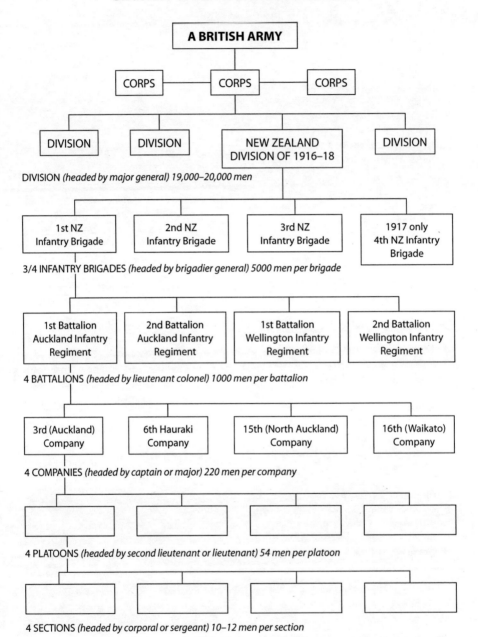

A BRITISH ARMY

CORPS — CORPS — CORPS

DIVISION   DIVISION   NEW ZEALAND DIVISION OF 1916–18   DIVISION

DIVISION *(headed by major general) 19,000–20,000 men*

1st NZ Infantry Brigade   2nd NZ Infantry Brigade   3rd NZ Infantry Brigade   1917 only 4th NZ Infantry Brigade

3/4 INFANTRY BRIGADES *(headed by brigadier general) 5000 men per brigade*

1st Battalion Auckland Infantry Regiment   2nd Battalion Auckland Infantry Regiment   1st Battalion Wellington Infantry Regiment   2nd Battalion Wellington Infantry Regiment

4 BATTALIONS *(headed by lieutenant colonel) 1000 men per battalion*

3rd (Auckland) Company   6th Hauraki Company   15th (North Auckland) Company   16th (Waikato) Company

4 COMPANIES *(headed by captain or major) 220 men per company*

4 PLATOONS *(headed by second lieutenant or lieutenant) 54 men per platoon*

4 SECTIONS *(headed by corporal or sergeant) 10–12 men per section*

The Infantry Units of the New Zealand Division:
An Explanatory Note

When the New Zealand Expeditionary Force (NZEF) left New Zealand in October 1914 the infantry units consisted of the Auckland, Wellington, Canterbury and Otago battalions. The four military districts into which the dominion was then divided had each provided a battalion. In 1916, with the decision to expand New Zealand's commitment to a full division for service in France, the original battalions were split into two and four new battalions were formed carrying the designation 2nd in front of their name (2nd Auckland Battalion or 2nd Otago Battalion, for example). The numbers in all the battalions were brought up to full establishment by the arrival of reinforcements.

The third brigade needed to complete a division was formed in New Zealand and called the 3rd New Zealand Rifle Brigade. Its battalions were numbered one to four. As this was the last brigade formed, the soldiers were said to be 'fair dinkum' about their motives for enlisting so they became known as 'the Dinks'. As the brigade's honorary colonel was the Governor, Lord Liverpool, the Rifle Brigade was also designated The Earl of Liverpool's Own.

Initially all of the battalions designated '2nd' were placed in the 2nd Brigade, which seemed to be a logical solution. In January 1917, however, the 1st and 2nd Brigades were reorganised so that all the North Island units were placed in the 1st Brigade and all those from the South Island in the 2nd Brigade. From most accounts, this reorganisation was not very popular, partly because the South Island lacked the numbers to sustain a full brigade and many North Island soldiers found themselves serving in units from Otago and Canterbury. Later in the year, surplus reinforcements from New Zealand enabled the establishment of a fourth infantry brigade consisting of the 3rd Auckland, Wellington, Canterbury and Otago Battalions. The Fourth New Zealand Infantry Brigade fought at Passchendaele on 4 October 1917, its only action of the war. The brigade was disbanded on 7 February 1918.

Appendix 2

Battle Order of the British Third Army

This appendix lists all the divisions that were part of the British Third Army (under the control of General Sir Julian Byng) during the Second Battle of the Somme. It details when additional divisions were added to the Army in order to boost its flagging numbers. The New Zealand Division joined the Third Army on 25 March 1918 and remained with it for the duration of the war.

Front: 28 miles. *Divisions:* 14. *Guns:* 1120 including 461 heavies

XVII Corps (Lieutenant General Charles Fergusson)
15th (Scottish) Division, 4th Division

VI Corps (Lieutenant General Sir J. Haldane)
3rd Division, 34th Division, 59th (2nd North Midland) Division

IV Corps (Lieutenant General Sir George Harper)
6th Division, 51st (Highland) Division

V Corps (Lieutenant General Sir E. Fanshawe)
47th (2nd London) Division, 63rd (Royal Naval) Division, 17th (Northern) Division

All the above divisions were in the line on 21 March.

Reserves under Byng's command:
Guards Division, near Arras; 25th Division at Bapaume; 19th and 2nd Divisions behind IV and V Corps

Reserves under the command of GHQ and placed behind Third Army:
40th Division in old Somme battle area and the 41st Division some 20 miles behind the line

Additional reserves committed to aid Third Army during March:
31st Division (from evening March 22); 42nd Division (24 March); 12th Division, 62nd Division (25 March); New Zealand Division and 4th Australian Division (25–26 March); 3rd Australian Division (27 March)

French reserves sent to the aid of the Fifth Army during the crisis:
125th Division (22 March); 9th, 10th and 1st Dismounted Cavalry (23 March); 55th Division (24 March); 1st, 56th and 35th Divisions (25 March); elements of two divisions (26 March)

The 22nd and 62nd French cavalry divisions also came into action in the area around March 24.

(From William Moore, *See How They Ran. The British Retreat of 1918*, p. 280)

Appendix 3

Order of Battle, Third Army, August 1918

The brigades making up the division are the numbers in the brackets.

Third Army (General the Honourable Sir Julian Byng)

IV Corps (Lieutenant-General Sir G.M. Harper)
    37th Division (63, 111, 112 Brigades)
    42nd Division (125, 126, 127 Brigades)
    62nd Division (185, 186, 187 Brigades)
    63rd Division (188, 189, 190 Brigades) to XVII Corps from 31 August
    New Zealand Division (1, 2, 3rd (Rifle) NZ Brigades)
    5th Division (13, 15, 95 Brigades) from XI Corps 13 August

V Corps (Lieutenant-General C.D. Shute)
    21st Division (62, 64, 110 Brigades)
    38th Division (113, 114, 115 Brigades)
    17th Division (50, 51, 52 Brigades) from Australian Corps 20 August
    33rd Division (19, 98, 100 Brigades) from II Corps 18 August

VI Corps (Lieutenant-General J. Haldane)
    Guards Division (1, 2, 3 Guards)
    2nd Division (5, 6, 99 Brigades)
    3rd Division (8, 9, 76 Brigades) from XIII Corps 13 August
    59th Division (176, 177, 178 Brigades) to XI Corps 26-28 August
    52nd Division (155, 156, 157 Brigades) from XVII Corps on 22 August, back to XVII
        Corps on 25 August
    56th Division (167, 168, 169 Brigades) from old XXII Corps
    57th Division (170, 171, 172 Brigades) from XVII Corps on 22 August, back to XVII
        on 25 August

XVII Corps (Lieutenant-General Sir Charles Ferguson Bt)
    (From the First Army 23 August)
    51st Division (152, 153, 154th Brigades) from old XXII Corps
    52nd Division (155, 156, 157 Brigades) from VI Corps
    56th Division (167, 168, 169 Brigades) from old XXII Corps
    57th Division (170, 171, 172 Brigades) from VI Corps
    63rd Division (188, 189, 190 Brigades) from IV Corps from 31 August

(From Brigadier Sir James E. Edmonds, *History of the Great War. Military Operations France and Belgium, 1918 Volume IV*, p. 522)

Bibliography

Primary sources

Three centres of research provided the bulk of the primary source material. They were the Alexander Turnbull Library, Archives New Zealand, both in Wellington, and the Kippenberger Military Archive and Research Library at Waiouru. Of these, working in the Alexander Turnbull Library proved to be the most fruitful. The Manuscript and Archives Collection alone had more than 250 separate records of the New Zealand Division in France in 1918. The Turnbull's Oral History Centre also provided much useful material.

Other primary sources consulted included:

Glyn Harper (ed.), *Letters from the Battlefield. New Zealand Soldiers Write Home 1914–18*, Auckland, HarperCollins, 2001.

List of Casualties and a Summary of Casualties in Order of Units Reported from 15 August to 14 November, 1917, Wellington, Marcus F. Marks, Government Printer, 1917.

List of Casualties and a Summary of Casualties in Order of Units Reported from 15 February to 14 May, 1918, Wellington, Marcus F. Marks, Government Printer, 1918.

List of Casualties and a Summary of Casualties in Order of Units Reported from August 1918 to 6 January, 1919, Wellington, Marcus F. Marks, Government Printer, 1919.

New Zealand at the Front 1918, London, Cassell and Company Limited, 1918.

Gary Sheffield and John Bourne (eds), *Douglas Haig. War Diaries and Letters 1914–1918*, London, Weidenfeld and Nicholson, 2005.

Chrissie Ward (ed.), *Dear Lizzie. A Kiwi Soldier Writes from the Battlefields of World War One*, Auckland, HarperCollins, 2000.

Nigel M. Watson (ed.), *Letters from a Padre. A Record of the War Service of Ronald S. Watson MC, ED, MA, 1891–1959*, Melbourne, 1970.

Unpublished manuscripts

L.C.L. Averill, 'First Generation New Zealander'.

Stewart Collis and Graham Langton (eds), 'Les Collis First World War Diaries', Palmerston North, 1999.

Linus T.J. Ryan, 'A Brief Record of My Three Years in Khaki', p. 128, unpublished manuscript, property of Smyth family, Hamilton.

Secondary sources

Books

Lieutenant-Colonel S.S. Allen, *2/Auckland, 1918*, Auckland, Whitcombe and Tombs Limited, 1920.

Lieutenant-Colonel W.S. Austin, *The Official History of the New Zealand Rifle Brigade*, Wellington, L.T. Watkins Ltd, 1924.

Correlli Barnett, *The Great War*, London, BBC Worldwide, 2003.

Jan Bassett, *Guns and Brooches. Australian Army Nursing from the Boer War to the Gulf War*, Melbourne, Oxford University Press, 1992.

C.E.W. Bean, *The Official History of Australia in the War of 1914–1918. Volume IV The AIF in France: 1917*, Angus and Robertson, Sydney, 1933.

C.E.W. Bean, *The Official History of Australia in the War of 1914–1918. Volume V The Australian Imperial Force in France during the Main German Offensive, 1918*, Sydney, Angus and Robertson, 1943.

C.E.W. Bean, *The Official History of Australia in the War of 1914–1918. Volume VI The Australian Imperial Force in France during the Allied Offensive, 1918*, St Lucia, Brisbane, University of Queensland Press in association with The Australian War Memorial, 1983.

C.E.W. Bean, *Anzac to Amiens*, Melbourne, Penguin Books, 1993.

Gregory Blaxland, *Amiens: 1918*, London, W.H. Allen & Co. Ltd, 1981.

Brian Bond (ed.), *The First World War and British Military History*, Oxford, Clarendon Press, 1991.

Brian Bond and Nigel Cave (eds), *Haig. A Reappraisal 70 Years On*, Barnsley, Leo Cooper, 1999.

J.H. Boraston, *Sir Douglas Haig's Despatches*, London, J.M. Dent and Sons Ltd, 1920.

N. Boyack, *Behind the Lines. The Lives of New Zealand Soldiers in the First World War*, Allen & Unwin and Port Nicholson Press, Wellington, 1989.

Vera Brittain, *Testament of Youth. An Autobiographical Study of the Years 1900–1925*, London, Victor Gollancz Ltd, 1933.

Malcolm Brown, *The Imperial War Museum Book of the First World War*, London, Sidgwick and Jackson, 1991.

John Buchan, *Nelson's History of the War. Volume XXII The Darkest Hour*, London, Thomas Nelson and Sons, n.d.

John Buchan, *Nelson's History of the War. Volume XXIII The Dawn*, London, Thomas Nelson and Sons, n.d.

O.E. Burton, *The Auckland Regiment, N.Z.E.F. 1914–1918*, Auckland, Whitcombe and Tombs, 1922.

O.E. Burton, *The Silent Division. New Zealanders at the Front: 1914–1919*, Sydney, Angus and Robertson, 1935.

A.E. Byrne, *Official History of the Otago Regiment, N.Z.E.F. in the Great War 1914–1918*, Dunedin, J. Wilkie and Co, 1921.

J.R. Byrne, *New Zealand Artillery in the Field 1914–18*, Auckland, Whitcombe and Tombs Ltd, 1922.

A.D. Carberry, *The New Zealand Medical Service in the Great War 1914–1918*, Auckland, Whitcombe & Tombs Ltd, 1924.

Nigel Cave, *Ypres. Passchendaele. The Fight for the Village*, Leo Cooper, London, 1997.

G. Chapman, *Vain Glory*, Cassell and Company, London, 1937.

Winston S. Churchill, *The World Crisis 1914–1918 Part II*, London, Thornton Butterworth Limited, 1927.

John Coates, *An Atlas of Australia's Wars*, Melbourne, Oxford University Press, 2001.

James Cowan, *'Te Hokowhitu a Tu'. The Maoris in the Great War*, Auckland, Whitcombe and Tombs, 1926.

Nancy Croad, *My Dear Home: The letters of three Knight brothers who gave their lives during World War I*, Auckland, Nancy Croad, 1995.

W.H. Cunningham, C.A.L. Treadwell and J.S. Hanna, *The Wellington Regiment N.Z.E.F. 1914–1919*, Wellington, Ferguson and Osborn Ltd, 1923.

Peter Dennis and Jeffrey Grey (eds), *1918. Defining Victory*, Canberra, The Army History Unit, 1999.

George A.B. Dewar and J.H. Boraston, *Sir Douglas Haig's Command December 19, 1915, to November 11, 1918*, London, 1922.

Oliver Duff, *New Zealand Now*, Wellington, Department of Internal Affairs, 1941.

Brigadier Sir James E. Edmonds, *History of the Great War. Military Operations France and Belgium, 1917 Volume II 7th June–10th November. Messines and Third Ypres (Passchendaele)*, HMSO, London, 1948.

Brigadier Sir James E. Edmonds, *History of the Great War. Military Operations France and Belgium, 1918 Volume I*, London, Macmillan and Co., 1935.

Brigadier Sir James E. Edmonds, *History of the Great War. Military Operations France and Belgium, 1918 Volume II*, London, Macmillan and Co., 1937.

Brigadier Sir James E. Edmonds, *History of the Great War. Military Operations France and Belgium, 1918 Volume IV, 8th August–26th September. The Franco-British Offensive*, London, HMSO, 1947.

John Ellis and Michael Cox, *The World War I Databook*, London, Arum Press, 1993.

Cyril Falls, *The Great War*, New York, G.P. Putmans, 1959.

Anthony Farrar-Hockley, *Goughie. The Life of General Sir Hubert Gough CGB, GCMG, KCVO*, London, MacGibbon, 1975.

David Ferguson, *The History of the Canterbury Regiment, N.Z.E.F. 1914–1919*, Auckland, Whitcombe and Tombs, 1921.

J.F.C. Fuller, *The Decisive Battles of the Western World and Their Influence upon History*, Volume III, London, Eyre & Spottiswoode Publishers, 1956.

P. Fussell, *The Great War and Modern Memory*, London, Oxford University Press, 1975.

Sir Philip Gibbs, *From Bapaume to Passchendaele 1917*, London, William Heinemann, 1918.

General Sir Hubert Gough, *Soldiering On*, London, Arthur Barker Ltd, 1954.

Jeffrey Grey, *A Military History of Australia*, Melbourne, Cambridge University Press, 1999.

P. Griffith, *Battle Tactics of the Western Front. The British Army's Art of Attack 1916–18*, London, Yale University Press, 1994.

D. Grossman, *On Killing: The psychological cost of learning to kill in war and society*, Boston, Little Brown and Company, 1995.

General Sir Charles Harington, *Plumer of Messines*, London, John Murray, 1935.

Richard Holmes, *The Western Front*, London, BBC Worldwide Ltd, 1999.

Richard Holmes, *Tommy. The British Soldier on the Western Front 1914–1918*, London, Harper Perennial, 2005.

Robin Hyde, *Nor the Years Condemn*, New Women's Press Edition, 1986.

Monty Ingram, *In Flanders Fields. The First World War Diary of Private Monty Ingram*, Auckland, David Ling Publishing, 2006.

J.H. Johnson, *1918. The Unexpected Victory*, London, Arms and Armour Press, 1997.

William Donovan Joynt, *Saving the Channel Ports*, Melbourne, Wren Publishing, 1975.

Ernst Junger, *The Storm of Steel. From the Diary of a German Storm-Troop Officer on the Western Front*, London, Chatto & Windus, 1929.

John Keegan, *The First World War*, London, Hutchinson, 1998.

Michael King, *New Zealanders at War*, Auckland, Heinemann Publishers, 1981.

M. Knox and W. Murray (eds), *The Dynamics of Military Revolution 1300–2050*, Cambridge, Cambridge Press, 2001.

John Laffin, *Guide to Australian Battlefields of the Western Front 1916–1918*, Sydney, Kangaroo Press and the Australian War Memorial, 1992.

J.A. Lee, *Civilian into Soldier*, London, T. Werner Lawrie, 1963.

Peter H. Liddle (ed.), *Passchendaele in Perspective. The Third Battle of Ypres*, Leo Cooper, London, 1997.

David Lloyd George, *War Memoirs of David Lloyd George Volume II*, London, Odhams Press Limited, 1936.

Gerhard Loose, *Ernst Junger*, New York, Twayne Publishers, 1974.

General Ludendorff, *My War Memories 1914–1918 Volume II*, London, Hutchinson & Co, 1919.

J.H. Luxford, *With the Machine Gunners in France and Palestine*, Auckland, Whitcombe and Tombs Ltd, 1923.

C. McCarthy, *The Third Ypres Passchendaele. The Day-by-Day Account*, Arms & Armour Press, London, 1995.

Andrew Macdonald, *On My Way to the Somme. New Zealanders and the bloody offensive of 1916*, Auckland, HarperCollins, 2005.

L. Macdonald, *They Called it Passchendaele*, Penguin Books, London, 1993.

Ian McGibbon (ed.), *The Oxford Companion to New Zealand Military History*, Auckland, Oxford University Press, 2000.

Ian McGibbon, *New Zealand Battlefields and Memorials of the Western Front*, Auckland, Oxford University Press, 2001.

Fred Majdalany, *Cassino. Portrait of a Battle*, London, Longmans, Green and Co., 1957.

Cecil Malthus, *ANZAC. A Retrospect*, Auckland, Reed Publishing, 2002.

Cecil Malthus, *Armentieres and the Somme*, Auckland, Reed Publishing, 2002.

Martin and Mary Middlebrook, *The Somme Battlefields. A Comprehensive Guide from Crecy to the Two World Wars*, London, Viking, 1991.

William Moore, *See How They Ran. The British Retreat of 1918*, London, Sphere Books, 1975.

John Mosier, *The Myth of the Great War. A New Military History of World War I*, New York, HarperCollins Publishers, 2001.

John Mulgan, *Report on Experience*, Auckland, Blackwood and Janet Paul Limited, 1947.

Officers and NCOs, *Official History of the New Zealand Engineers during the Great War 1914-1919*, Wanganui, Evans, Cobb and Sharpe, n.d.

Officers of the Regiment, *Das K.B. 14. Infanterie-Regiment Hartmann*, Munchen, 1931.

Albert Palazzo, *Seeking Victory on the Western Front. The British Army & Chemical Warfare in World War I*, Lincoln, University of Nebraska Press, 2000.

J. Philips, N. Boyack and E.P. Malone, *The Great Adventure*, Wellington, Allen & Unwin, 1988.

J. Phillips, *A Man's Country? The image of the Pakeha male — a history*, Auckland, Penguin Books, 1987.

R. Prior and T. Wilson, *Passchendaele. The Untold Story*, London, Yale University Press, 1996.

Christopher Pugsley, *Te Hokowhitu a Tu. The Maori Pioneer Battalion in the First World War*, Auckland, Reed Publishing, 2006.

Christopher Pugsley, *The Anzac Experience. New Zealand, Australia and Empire in the First World War*, Auckland, Reed Publishing, 2004.

Christopher Pugsley, *On the Fringe of Hell. New Zealanders and Military Discipline in the First World War*, Auckland, Hodder & Stoughton, Auckland, 1991.

Sir Ernest Scott, *The Official History of Australia in the War of 1914–1918, Volume XI, Australia During the War*, Sydney, Angus and Robertson, 1936.

Geoffrey Serle, *John Monash. A Biography*, Melbourne, Melbourne University Press, 1982.

Gary Sheffield, *Forgotten Victory. The First World War: Myths and Realities*, London, Headline Book Publishing, 2001.

Peter Simkins, *World War 1. The Western Front*, Godalming, Surrey, Colour Library Books, 1992,.

W. Stevens, *Official History of New Zealand in the Second World War 1939–45. Bardia to Enfidaville*, Wellington, War History Branch, Department of Internal Affairs, 1962.

H. Stewart, *The New Zealand Division 1916–1919*, Auckland, Whitcombe and Tombs Ltd, 1921.

Hew Strachan, *The First World War*, New York, Viking Penguin, 2004.

Hew Strachan (ed.), *The Oxford Illustrated History of the First World War*, Oxford, Oxford University Press, 1998.

Gordon R. Sullivan and Michael V. Harper, *Hope is Not a Method*, New York, Random House, 1996.

A.J.P. Taylor, *The First World War. An Illustrated History*, Harmondsworth, Penguin Books, 1966.

John Terraine, *The Western Front 1914–18*, Arrow Books, London, 1964.

John Terraine, *The Great War 1914–18*, London, Arrow Books, 1967.

John Terraine, *The Road to Passchendaele*, Leo Cooper, London, 1977.

John Terraine, *To Win a War. 1918 The Year of Victory*, London, Cassell & Co, 2000.

John Toland, *No Man's Land. The Story of 1918*, London, Methuen Paperbacks, 1980.

Tim Travers, *The Killing Ground. The British Army, the Western Front and the Emergence of Modern Warfare, 1900–1918*, Allen & Unwin, London, 1987.

Julius Ritter von Bram, *Das KB Reserve-Infanterie-Regiment Nr. 21*, Munchen, 1923.

Marshal von Hindenburg, *Out of My Life*, London, Cassell, 1920.

C.H. Weston, *Three Years With the New Zealanders*, London, Skeffington & Son, n.d.

Craig Wilcox (ed.), *The Great War. Gains and Losses — ANZAC and Empire*, Canberra, The Australian National University and The Australian War Memorial, 1995.

Percy Williams, *A New Zealanders's Diary. Gallipoli and France 1915–1917*, Christchurch, 1998.

Trevor Wilson, *The Myriad Faces of War*, Cambridge, Polity Press, 1986.

D. Winter, *Haig's Command. A Reassessment*, Viking, London, 1991.

Jay Winter and Blaine Baggett, *1914–1918. The Great War and the Shaping of the 20th Century*, London, BBC Books, 1996.

L. Wolff, *In Flanders Fields. The 1917 Campaign*, Longman, Green and Co., London, 1958.

Matthew Wright, *Western Front. The New Zealand Division in the First World War 1916–18*, Auckland, Reed Publishing, 2005.

Articles

Tim Cook, 'The Politics of Surrender: Canadian Soldiers and the Killing of Prisoners in the Great War', *The Journal of Military History*, vol. 70, no. 3, July 2006, pp. 637–65.

H. Essame, 'The Breaking of the Hindenburg Line', *History of the First War*, vol. 7, no. 10, London, 1971, pp. 2945–57.

James McRandle and James Quirk, 'The Blood Test Revisited: A New Look at German Casualty Counts in World War I', *The Journal of Military History*, vol. 70, no. 3, July 2006, pp. 667–701.

Barrie Pitt, 'Germany: 1918. New strategy, new tactics', *History of the First World War*, vol. 6, no. 14, London, 1971, p. 2616.

Barrie Pitt, 'The Ludendorff Offensive Phase 1', *History of the First War*, vol. 6, no. 15, London, 1971, p. 2638.

Christopher Pugsley, 'Russell of the New Zealand Division', *New Zealand Strategic Management*, Autumn 1995, pp. 47–50.

Christopher Pugsley, 'Russell. Commander of Genius', *New Zealand Defence Quarterly*, no. 23, Summer 1998, pp. 25–29.

H.W. Wilson (ed.), *The Great War*, Part 182, Week ending February 9, 1918, London.

H.W. Wilson (ed.), *The Great War*, Part 183, Week ending February 16, 1918, London.

Peter Young, 'August 8, 1918. Germany's Black Day', *History of the First World War*, vol. 7, no. 9, 1971, pp. 2917–27.

Index